D1279484

CURRENT TRENDS IN
THEORETICAL
COMPUTER SCIENCE

The Challenge of the New Century

FORMAL MODELS AND SEMANTICS   VOL.2

CURRENT TRENDS IN
THEORETICAL
COMPUTER SCIENCE

The Challenge of the New Century

FORMAL MODELS AND SEMANTICS   VOL. 2

editors

G PĂUN
Romanian Academy, Romania &
Rovira I Virgili University, Spain

G ROZENBERG
University of Leiden, The Netherlands &
University of Colorado, USA

A SALOMAA
Turku Centre for Computer Science, Finland

World Scientific

NEW JERSEY • LONDON • SINGAPORE • SHANGHAI • HONG KONG • TAIPEI • CHENNAI

Published by

World Scientific Publishing Co. Pte. Ltd.

5 Toh Tuck Link, Singapore 596224

USA office: Suite 202, 1060 Main Street, River Edge, NJ 07661

UK office: 57 Shelton Street, Covent Garden, London WC2H 9HE

British Library Cataloguing-in-Publication Data
A catalogue record for this book is available from the British Library.

*QA76
.C878
2004
vol.2*

055286615

ISBN 981-238-783-8 (Set)
ISBN 981-238-965-2 (Vol. 2)

Printed in Singapore by World Scientific Printers (S) Pte Ltd

PREFACE

This book continues the tradition of two previous books *Current Trends in Theoretical Computer Science*, published by World Scientific Publishing Company in 1993 and 2001. We have been very impressed and encouraged by the exceptionally good reception of the two previous books. The positive comments received show that books of this nature are really needed.

The book is based on columns and tutorials published in the *Bulletin of the European Association for Theoretical Computer Science (EATCS)* in the period 2000-2003. The columnists selected themselves the material they wanted to be included in the book, and the authors were asked to update their contributions. Special effort has been given to presentation – most articles are reader-friendly and do not presuppose much knowledge of the area in question. We believe that the book will constitute suitable supplementary reading material for various courses in computer science. Indeed, the book highlights some key issues and challenges in theoretical computer science, as they seem to us now at the beginning of the new millennium. A glance through the subsequent table of contents should show that many of the most active current research lines in theoretical computer science are represented. Both survey articles and papers dealing with specific problems are included.

In addition to the chapters covered in the two previous books, the current one has two new chapters, "Algorithmics" and "Distributed Computing", that include selected contributions from the corresponding two new columns of the *EATCS Bulletin* (i.e., columns initiated in the period 2000–2003).

As a matter of fact, with the two new chapters the ammount of material to be covered became much too big for a single book, and therefore the chapters were divided into two volumes: "Algorithms and Complexity" and "Formal Models and Semantics". This is by now a traditional division of theoretical computer science (used, e.g., by the "Handbook of Theoretical Computer Science" and by ICALP – the major general conference devoted to theoretical computer science).

The first volume, "Algorithms and Complexity", includes the following chapters: "Algorithmics", "Complexity", "Distributed Computing", and "Natural Computing", while the current second volume, "Formal Models and Semantics", consists of the following chapters: "Formal Specification", "Logic in Computer Science", "Concurrency", and "Formal Language Theory".

The editors are obliged to the columnists of the Bulletin, as well as to their many guest authors, for their timely assistance in producing this volume. We are also indebted to Dr. Lu Jitan from World Scientific Publishing Company for his encouragement and cooperation.

October, 2003

Gheorghe Păun
Grzegorz Rozenberg
Arto Salomaa

CONTENTS

Preface v

CHAPTER 1 1
FORMAL SPECIFICATION
by H. Ehrig and guest authors

Introductory Remarks 3
The Role of Mathematics and Formal Specification
    Techniques in Software System Development
    (by H. Ehrig and G. Schröter) 5
Failure-Divergence Semantics as a Formal Basis
    for an Object-Oriented Integrated Formal Method
    (by C. Fischer and H. Wehrheim) 15
Bigraphs Meet Double Pushouts (by H. Ehrig) 27
A New Experience with Graph Transformation
    (by A. Qemali) 41
Meta-Modelling and Graph Transformation for
    the Simulation of Systems (by J. de Lara) 47
Net Transformations for Petri Net Technology
    (by M. Urbášek) 63
On the Relevance of High-Level Net Processes (by H. Ehrig) 89

CHAPTER 2 95
LOGIC IN COMPUTER SCIENCE
by Y. Gurevich and guest authors

Introductory Remarks 97
A New Zero-One Law and Strong Extension Axioms
    (by A. Blass and Y. Gurevich) 99
Tree-Decompositions and the Model-Checking Problem
    (by J. Flum) 119
Is Randomness "Native" to Computer Science?
    (by M. Ferbus-Zanda and S. Grigorieff) 141
How to Find a Coin: Propositional Program Logics
    Made Easy (by N.V. Shilov and K. Yi) 181

Algorithms vs. Machines (by A. Blass and Y. Gurevich) 215
Pairwise Testing (by A. Blass and Y. Gurevich) 237
Newman's Lemma – A Case Study in Proof Automation
    and Geometric Logic (by M. Bezem and T. Coquand) 267
Algorithms: A Quest for Absolute Definitions
    (by A. Blass and Y. Gurevich) 283

CHAPTER 3 313
CONCURRENCY
by M. Nielsen and guest authors

Introductory Remarks 315
Some of My Favourite Results in Classic Process
    Algebra (by L. Aceto) 317
Roadmap of Infinite Results (by J. Srba) 337
Construction and Verification of Concurrent Performance and
    Reliability Models (by H. Hermanns) 351
Does Combining Nondeterminism and Probability Make Sense?
    (by P. Panangaden) 377
The Algebraic Structure of Petri Nets (by V. Sassone) 385

CHAPTER 4 411
FORMAL LANGUAGE THEORY
by A. Salomaa and guest authors

Introductory Remarks 413
Combinatorics on Words — A Tutorial
    (by J. Berstel and J. Karhumäki) 415
Two Problems on Commutation of Languages
    (by J. Karhumäki and I. Petre) 477
Counting (Scattered) Subwords (by A. Salomaa) 495
Post Correspondence Problem – Recent Results
    (by V. Halava and T. Harju) 511
The DF0L Language Equivalence Problem
    (by J. Honkala) 533
An Overview of Conjunctive Grammars
    (by A. Okhotin) 545

State Complexity of Finite and Infinite Regular Languages
(by S. Yu) 567

GSMs and Contexts
(by C. Martín-Vide and A. Mateescu) 581

The Depth of Functional Compositions (by A. Salomaa) 589

Language Generating by Means of Membrane Systems
(by C. Martín-Vide and Gh. Păun) 599

Membrane Computing: New Results, New Problems
(by C. Martín-Vide, A. Păun, and Gh. Păun) 613

About the Editors 625

CONTENTS OF VOLUME 1

Preface v

CHAPTER 1 1
ALGORITHMICS
by J. Díaz and guest authors

Introductory Remarks 3
H-Coloring of Graphs (by J. Díaz) 5
Open Problems in the Theory of Scheduling
    (by G.J. Woeginger) 19
Analysis of Algorithms (AofA). Part I: 1993 – 1998
    ("Dagstuhl Period") (by W. Szpankowski) 39
Analysis of Algorithms (AofA). Part II: 1998 – 2000
    ("Princeton–Barcelona–Gdańsk")
    (by M. Drmota and W. Szpankowski) 63
Algorithm Engineering
    (by C. Demetrescu, I. Finocchi, and G.F. Italiano) 83
PRIMES $\in$ P (Without Assumptions) (by J. Díaz) 105
Selfish Task Allocation (by E. Koutsoupias) 111

CHAPTER 2 121
COMPUTATIONAL COMPLEXITY
by L. Fortnow and guest authors

Introductory Remarks 123
A Physics-Free Introduction to the Quantum Computation
    Model (by S.A. Fenner) 125
The Division Breakthroughs (by E. Allender) 147
Derandomization: A Brief Overview (by V. Kabanets) 165
Recent Developments in Explicit Constructions of Extractors
    (by R. Shaltiel) 189
The Art of Uninformed Decisions: A Primer to Property
    Testing (by E. Fischer) 229
Time-Space Lower Bounds for NP-Complete Problems
    (by D. van Melkebeek) 265

CHAPTER 3 293
DISTRIBUTED COMPUTING
by M. Mavronicolas and guest authors

Introductory Remarks 295
A Combinatorial Characterization of Properties Preserved by
    Antitokens (by C. Busch, N. Demetriou, M. Herlihy,
    and M. Mavronicolas) 297
Distributed Computation Meets Design Theory:
    Local Scheduling for Disconnected Cooperation
    (by A. Russell and A. Shvartsman) 315
Distributed Communication Algorithms
    for Ad-hoc Mobile Networks
    (by I. Chatzigiannakis, S. Nikoletseas, and P. Spirakis) 337
Selfish Routing in Non-Cooperative Networks: A Survey
    (by R. Feldman, M. Gairing, T. Lücking,
    B. Monien, and M. Rode) 373
Distributed Algorithmic Mechanism Design:
    Recent Results and Future Directions
    (by J. Feigenbaum and S. Shenker) 403
Stability in Routing: Networks and Protocols
    (by M. Mavronicolas) 435

CHAPTER 4 451
NATURAL COMPUTING
by G. Rozenberg and guest authors

Introductory Remarks 453
Quantum Computation Explained to My Mother
    (by P. Arrighi) 455
Universality and Quantum Computing
    (by M. Hirvensalo) 469
Some Open Problems Related to Quantum Computing
    (by M. Hirvensalo) 477
Aqueous Computing: Writing Into Fluid Memory
    (by T. Head and S. Gal) 493
Biomolecular Computing *in silico* (by M.H. Garzon) 505
Gene Assembly in Ciliates. Part I: Molecular Operations
    (by T. Harju, I. Petre, and G. Rozenberg) 527

Gene Assembly in Ciliates. Part II: Formal Frameworks
    (by T. Harju, I. Petre, and G. Rozenberg) 543
A Grand Challenge for Computing: Towards Full Reactive
    Modeling of a Multi-Cellular Animal
    (by D. Harel) 559
Evolutionary Computation: A Guided Tour
    (by Th. Bäck) 569
Artificial Chemistries (by P. Speroni di Fenizio) 613
Neural Computing (by H.T. Siegelmann) 633

About the Editors 661

1
FORMAL SPECIFICATION

Hartmut EHRIG

CONTENTS

Introductory Remarks
The Role of Mathematics and Formal Specification
       Techniques in Software System Development
       (by H. Ehrig and G. Schröter)
Failure-Divergence Semantics as a Formal Basis
       for an Object-Oriented Integrated Formal Method
       (by C. Fischer and H. Wehrheim)
Bigraphs Meet Double Pushouts (by H. Ehrig)
A New Experience with Graph Transformation
       (by A. Qemali)
Meta-Modelling and Graph Transformation for the Simulation
       of Systems (by J. de Lara)
Net Transformations for Petri Net Technology
       (by M. Urbášek)
On the Relevance of High-Level Net Processes (by H. Ehrig)

Hartmut Ehrig

Technical University of Berlin
Computer Science Department
Sekr. FR 6-1, Franklinstrasse 28729
D-10587 Berlin, Germany
E-mail: ehrig@cs.tu-berlin.de

INTRODUCTORY REMARKS

Specification and modelling techniques for software systems are highly important in the software development process. In this chapter we consider formal specification techniques, which means that they have a well-defined mathematical syntax and semantics.

In the first contribution we discuss the role of mathematics and formal specification techniques in software development. An object-oriented integrated formal method based on CSP and Object-Z is proposed in the second contribution; a large variety of process calculi have been modelled by Milner and others in the concept of bigraphs and transitions of graphs which are compared with the algebraic double pushout approach of graph transformations in the contribution "Bigraphs Meet Double Pushouts". The role of graph transformation for modelling web applications and simulation of systems is discussed in subsequent contributions. Finally, the last two contributions are concerning Petri nets. The role of net transformations for Petri net technology is discussed in the first, and an extension of the concept of process from low-level to high-level Petri nets is presented in the second contribution.

Last but not least, I would like to thank to all authors and coauthors for their contributions which have been selected for this chapter of the Formal Specification Column in the *EATCS Bulletin*. Indeed, some of the material here appears in an updated version compared with the original in the *Bulletin*.

Hartmut Ehrig

THE ROLE OF MATHEMATICS AND FORMAL SPECIFICATION TECHNIQUES IN SOFTWARE SYSTEM DEVELOPMENT

HARTMUT EHRIG, GUNNAR SCHRÖTER

Technical University of Berlin
Computer Science Department
Sekr. FR 6-1, Franklinstrasse 28729
D-10587 Berlin, Germany
E-mail: `ehrig@cs.tu-berlin.de`

The aim of this note is to give a short overwiev on the role of mathematics and formal specification techiques for software system development. In order to address not primarily experts in formal specification techniques, but even more a general theoretical computer science and sofware engineering audience, we first discuss the role of formal specification techniques for software system development and give an overview of corresponding formal specification techniques on a non technical level. In the second part we summarize the main areas of mathematics which are important in order to formulate these techniques and to build up a corresponding mathematical theory.

1 Introduction

Mathematics and electrical engineering are the classical roots of computer science.

Numerical mathematics has played the major role in the early phases of computer science and software system development in order to implement numerical methods for the solution of large systems of differential equations in physics and other areas of natural science. Numerical mathematics is still of central importance for this kind of numerical software systems. Due to a significant extension of the application areas of computer science other branches of mathematics become more and more important for computer science and the general area of software system development today and in the future.

In addition to the central role of mathematics in the application areas of computer science, mathematics has an increasing importance for software system development independent of the application area.

Today computers and software systems have entered almost any branch of science, engineering, economics and even daily life. Unfortunately most of the software systems which are dominant on the market today are not based on mathematical techniques and are not fully reliable such that crashes of software systems are usually considered as an unavoidable fact of life. In

5

the late 60'ies a first software crisis was recognized by people in academics leading to the new discipline of Software Engineering and the new concept of abstract data types. In the 70'ies and 80'ies mathematical foundations for abstract data types and communicating processes have been developed which have been integrated into formal techniques for software system development. Unfortunately, these mathematical techniques were not mature enough to be used in practical software development. Most people – at least in the U.S. – learned about the existence of a practical software crisis after the event that AT & T's long distance switching systems were shut down in January 1990 due to a software 'bug'. In the last decade it became clear that at least for safety critical software systems it is necessary to use formal specification and verification techniques based on mathematical techniques in algebra and logics.

Typical examples for successful use of formal specification techniques are the use of statecharts for automotive systems, like a cruise control system developed in the ESPRESS project including the Technical University of Berlin and the DaimlerChrysler Company in Germany, and the use of Petri nets for European Train Control (ETCS) in a joint project of Technical University of Braunschweig and the German Rail Company (Deutsche Bahn AG). Based on well-known mathematical techniques in algebra, logic and category theory new formal techniques have been developed to define the semantics of formal specification techniques, consistency of horizontal structuring and vertical refinement in the software development process, and verification of software design versus formal requirements of software systems. For many of these new techniques exist tools to support the specification process and automatic (or interactive) verification. Since these tools become more and more powerful and fast, the practical importance of these formal techniques is permanently increasing.

In section 2 we discuss the role of formal – in contrast to informal and semi-formal – specification techniques for software system development, before giving an overview of the large variety of formal specification techniques in section 3. The role of mathematics for formal specification techniques and software system development is discussed in section 4 leading to a matrix showing which areas of mathematics are relevant for which aspects of formal specification techniques. In the conlusion (section 5) we point out the main importance of algebra, logic and category theory for this purpose.

A more detailed version of this note is given in our paper [5]. For interesting examples of applications of mathematics and formal specification techniques for software system development in the areas of transportation, healthcare, financial services, fishery industry, and the market we refer to [1].

2   Role of Formal Specification Techniques

It is common sense to use all kinds of diagrammatic and textual notations in the specification phases of software development. Roughly, we can distinguish between informal, semi-formal and formal notations and techniques.

A formal notation is required to have a formal syntax and semantics, semi-formal notation has a formal syntax, but usually no formal semantics, while an informal notation has an intuitive syntax and semantics, where both are not formalized. Formal syntax and semantics in this context means that they are based on one or a combination of mathematical theories, like set theory, logic, algebra or category theory.

The advantage of informal notations is its high flexibility and easy comprehensibility at least on an intuitive level of understanding.

The main disadvantage is the lack of precision and ambiguity of interpretation, which especially does not allow automatic interpretation or automatic code generation. A semi-formal notation has higher precision and less ambiguity, which allows automatic treatment on the syntactical but not on the semantical level. The main aspects are summarized in figure 1:

	Informal	Semi-formal	Formal
Syntax	intuitive	formal	formal
Semantics	intuitive	intuitive	formal
Comprehensibility	easy	good	more difficult
Ambiguity	very high	high	low
Precision	low	higher	high

Figure 1. Classification of Specification Techniques

It is well-known that the specification phases within the software development process become more and more important. Usually, the starting point is a problem description in natural language, followed by a requirements analysis leading to a requirements specification and via some transformation steps to a design specification, which is the basis for coding. Traditionally, all these specification phases and documents are presented using an informal or semi-formal notation. The main advantages to use formal rather than informal or semi-formal techniques for software specification are the following:

1. Mathematical Precision: As pointed out already, the main disadvantage of traditional techniques is the lack of precision and the ambiguity of interpretation. A formal technique with mathematical syntax and semantics leads to mathematical precise specification documents with a well-defined mathematical semantics. Of course, it is important that the software engineer is able to understand and handle the formal technique in an appropriate way, which can be supported by suitable structuring and visualization techniques.

2. Formal Analysis: Mathematical precision and semantical foundation are the basis for the formal analysis of the specification, especially concerning safety and liveness properties. Moreover, the formal specification can be used for test case generation and tests not only on the program, but already on the specification level of the system. This is an important issue for system validation.

3. Executability: Since traditional specifications usually are not able to be executed, an early prototype has to be provided in addition to the specification. The new perspective of formal techniques is to come up with executable specifications which can be used already as an early prototype of the corresponding systems. Of course, not every formal specification in executable. But in several cases it is possible to obtain an executable version via suitable transformations.

4. Automatic Code Generation: In traditional software, the development specification and code generation are different phases, where code generation cannot be done automatically due to the lack of precision of the specification. Since formal specifications are formal documents with well-defined semantics there is a good chance for automatic code generation by means of a compiler from the formal specification to a suitable programming language.

5. Verification: In traditional software development, the verification is often not possible in a rigorous mathematical way, although it is important especially for safety critical systems. In fact, a rigorous mathematical verification of document A against document B requires to have a formal semantics of both documents, but unfortunately most system implementation languages usually don't have a formal semantics. The new perspective is to verify the design specification against the requirement specification, provided that both are formal specifications.

6. Consistency: Structuring and refinement in traditional software development are important techniques to master large systems, but it is often not clear in which way they are compatible with each other. Hence there is a high risk of inconsistencies in the software development process. For most of the formal specification techniques there are already concepts for structuring and refinement and it is possible to analyse in a mathematical way under which conditions structuring and refinement are compatible such that inconsistencies can be avoided.

7. Parameterization: Generic software development is an important issue for reusability not only on the implementation but also on the specification level. In order to provide generic specifications we need a concept of parameterized specifications with formal parameters and instantiation of formal by actual parameters. Such a formal parameterization concept is available for most formal specification techniques and it is the basis for reusability of specifications with well-defined semantical compatibility between formal parameterized and actualized specifications.

8. Reusability of Design: Another important aspect concerning reusability is to reuse formal design instead of code. Especially, changes should be done on the specification level where usually the main part of the specification can be reused such that also formal analysis can be reused to a large extend.

All the aspects mentioned above allow to master more complex systems using formal instead of traditional specification techniques. This is especially important for complex communication based and embedded systems, where mastering means to have the full control of the system behavior.

3 Overview of Formal Specification Techniques

In order to obtain a first rough classification of specification formalisms we distinguish between basic formalisms, concerning mainly one view of a system, and integrated formalisms, taking care of different views and aspects. In this section we consider as basic views the data type and process view as well as time constraints and give a short overview of corresponding basic and some examples of integrated specification formalisms within the framework of formal specification techniques.

Let us point out that even basic specification formalisms can be used in different styles for the specification of different views of a system. However, most of them are especially useful for one particular view, which will be considered in our following classification.

Further details, examples and references can be found in [4].

3.1 Data Type View and Formalisms

The following specification formalisms are especially useful to specify data types and hence the functional view of a system. We distinguish the following classes of data type specification formalisms:

- **Algebraic/axiomatic approaches**
  including especially all kinds of algebraic and logic specification for-

malisms, where the axioms are ranging from classical equations, via conditional equations and Universal Horn to first and higher order logical formulas.

- **State/model-oriented approaches**
  including techniques like VDM, Z, B and abstract state machines, formerly called evolving algebras.

- **Class-oriented approaches**
  are closely related to object-oriented modeling techniques, where class diagrams in the sense of the universal modeling language UML have become a quasi-standard already.

3.2 Process View and Formalisms

The process view of a system is concerned with the dynamic behavior of the system, especially with the process or activities of a system which realize the different scenarios. We distinguish the following classes of process specification formalisms:[a]

- **Petri net approaches**
  including classical low level approaches, where we have no distinguished data elements, but only black tokens, up to high level approaches, with colored tokens representing different data elements from a given data type or domain.

- **Process algebraic approaches**
  including Hoare's CSP, Milner's CCS, Π-calculus and algebraic approaches to process algebras and all kinds of variants.

- **Automata/statechart-oriented approaches**
  including all kinds of automata, statecharts, transition systems and event structures.

- **Graph transformation approaches**
  including all kinds of approaches, where system states are modeled by graphs and state transformations by graph transformations. Here the notation of graphs is considered in a broad sence including also diagrams and other visual sentences.

---

[a] In each of these classes there are low level variants, where data types are only supported in a weak way by fixed data domains or alphabets, and also high level variants which are defined by integration with some data type specification technique. In the following we only consider the low level variants, which are the basic formalisms.

3.3 Time Aspects

Time aspects of a system are important already on the level of the specification. We consider the following classes of time formalisms:

- **Discrete, Continuous and Stochastic Time**
  Several process formalisms have been extended by suitable annotations concerning time, which can be given explicitly (discrete and continuous time) or by a probability distribution (stochastic time). Discrete and continuous time are important to model and analyse explicit time constraint of system processes while stochastic time is especially useful for performance analysis of the system.

- **Timing Diagrams**
  or interaction diagrams have been developed in order to model the time dependencies for the exchange of messages between different objects or components of a system.

- **Temporal Logic**
  can be used, to express and satisfy safety or liveness properties of a system.

3.4 Integration of Formal Specification Techniques

In subsections 3.1 – 3.3 above we have considered basic specification formalisms for data type, process and time aspects of systems respectively. In most practical applications it is necessary to combine or integrate these basic techniques in order to handle combination and integration of different aspects. Typical examples are LOTOS, an integration of algebraic specification and CCS, attributed graph transformation and algebraic high-level nets, an integration of algebraic specification with graph transformation and Petri nets respectively, and μSZ, an integration of Z and statecharts.

4 Role of Mathematics for Formal Specification Techniques and Software System Development

In section 2 we have pointed out the role of formal specification techniques in software system development and we have given an overview of formal specification techniques in section 3. It remains to analyse the role of mathematics in the area of formal specification techniques which is an important indication for the role of mathematics in software system development.

As pointed out already in section 2, syntax and semantics of a formal specification technique are based on mathematical theories. Moreover, mathematics is necessary in order to express and verify formal properties and to formulate horizontal structuring, refinement, as well as compatibility and compositionality of structuring and refinement with behavioral semantics.

4.1 Mathematics for Syntactical Presentation

The syntactical presentation of all formal specification techniques is given by terms and/or expressions over some algebraic or logic signature or by a suitable diagrammatic or graphical notation. The underlying mathematics is formal grammar and language theory, algebra and logic, graph and category theory.

4.2 Mathematics for Semantical Meaning

The semantical meaning of a formal specification is usually given by a semantical mapping from the syntactical presentation to a semantical domain (denotational and/or algebraic semantics) or by rules how to transform the syntactical presentation step by step (operational semantics) leading to a labeled transition system, a transition or derivation category, an algebraic domain or an event structure.

The underlying mathematics for semantical domains and mappings is set theory, partially ordered sets, algebra or category theory. In the case of operational semantics we need formal rewriting systems based on formal language and automata theory, logic, graph and category theory. Labeled transition systems and categories, domains and event structures are based on set and category theory, algebra and partially ordered sets.

4.3 Mathematics for Formal Properties and Verification

Formal properties and verification for data type formalisms are based on different kinds of classical logic ranging from equational logic to first and even higher order predicate logic, while process and time formalisms are based on several other kinds of automata, categories and logic, like ω-automata, cartesian closed categories, modal and temporal logic, and also graph and probability theory in the case of Petri nets and graph grammars.

4.4 Mathematics for Structuring and Refinement

Structuring and refinement techniques for most of the formal specification techniques discussed above are formulated using set theoretical, algebraic, automata and graph theoretical notations and results. For compatibility and

	Syntax	Semantics	Verification	Struct. & Ref.
Set Theory	+	+		+
Partial Orders	+	+		
Algebra	++	++	+	++
Logic	+	+	++	+
Graph Theory	+	+	+	+
Category Theory	++	+	+	++
Probability Theory			++	
Automata Theory		++	+	+
Formal Languages	++	+		

Figure 2. Role of mathematics for formal specification techniques

compositionality in addition also techniques from logic, like compositional proof techniques, are important.

4.5 Summary

The role of different mathematical theories for formal specification techniques is summarized in figure 2, where significance is marked by + and high significance by ++.

Since formal specification techniques are most important for the software system development (see section 2), figure 2 shows also the role of different mathematical theories in this important area of computer science.

If we consider software systems for specific application domains, then of course also the mathematics for the application domain is relevant for software system development. In this broader sense, almost all branches of mathematics are relevant for software system development in general.

In spite of the relevance of mathematics, it is not at all common practice up to now to use the corresponding mathematical techniques in commercial and industrial software development. However at least for safety critical systems this situation has already changed.

5 Conclusion

In the early phases of computer science and software system development only numerical mathematics has played a mayor role for the the development of software, because it was mainly numerical software. For application software in all kinds of application domains the specific mathematics for the application domain is of course relevant for the corresponding application software. This includes almost all branches of mathematics.

In this paper we have discussed in more detail the role of mathematics and formal specification techniques in software development. This concerns the way in which mathematics can support the software development process. In sections 2 – 4 we have shown the role of formal specification techniques and the corresponding mathematical theories for this task.

Unfortunately, software system development in general, and especially commercial and industrial software development, is not based on formal specification techniques. However, the practical software crisis in the 90'ies has convinced leading people in the scientific and political communities that at least for safety critical software systems it is necessary to use formal specification and verification techniques. These techniques are based on mathematics, especially on specific areas of algebra, logic and category theory, where an introduction can be found in the textbooks [2,6,3].

References

1. Bjørner, D.: Informatics: A Truly Interdisciplinary Science – Computing Science and Mathematics, *Abstracts of the International Colloquium on Numerical Analysis and Computer Science with Applications*, Plovdiv 2000, to appear in *International Journal of Applied Mathematics*.
2. Ehrig, H., Mahr, B.: *Fundamentals of Algebraic Specification 1. Equations and Initial Semanticas.* EATCS Monographs on Theoretical Computer Science, Vol. 6, Springer-Verlag, 1985.
3. Ehrig, H., Mahr, B., Cornelius, F., Grosse-Rohde, M., Zeitz, P.: *Mathematisch-strukturelle Grundlagen der Informatik*, Springer-Verlag, 1999.
4. Ehrig, H., Orejas, F., Padberg, J.: From Basic Views and Aspects to Integration of Specification Formalisms. *Bulletin of the EATCS*, No. 69, 1999.
5. Ehrig, H., Schröter, G.: The Relevance of Mathematics in Software System Development, *Abstracts of the International Colloquium on Numerical Analysis and Computer Science with Applications*, Plovdiv 2000, to appear in *International Journal of Applied Mathematics*.
6. Manna, Z., Pnueli, A.: *The Temporal Logic of Reactive and Concurrent Systems, Specification.* Springer-Verlag, 1992.

FAILURE-DIVERGENCE SEMANTICS AS A FORMAL BASIS FOR AN OBJECT-ORIENTED INTEGRATED FORMAL METHOD

CLEMENS FISCHER

BTC Business Technology Consulting AG
Escherweg 3, 26121 Oldenburg, Germany
E-mail: `clemens.fischer@btc-ag.com`

HEIKE WEHRHEIM

Universität Oldenburg
Department Informatik
Postfach 2503, 26111 Oldenburg, Germany
E-mail: `wehrheim@informatik.uni-oldenburg.de`

The integration of several different modelling techniques into a single formal method has turned out to be advantageous in the formal design of software systems. Giving a semantics to an *integrated* formal method is currently a very active area of research. In this paper we discuss the advantages of a failure-divergence semantics for data and process integrating formal methods, in particular for those with a concept of inheritance. The discussion proceeds along the lines of the formal method CSP-OZ, a combination of CSP and Object-Z, developed in Oldenburg.

1 Introduction

Recently, there is an emerging interest in *integrated* specification methods combining different formalisms into one. The advantage of integrating several formal methods is that it allows for more convenient specifications, choosing the most suitable technique for every aspect of the system. The most prominent representative for an integrated (although not completely formal) method is certainly the Unified Modelling Language UML [21,2] which combines standard object-oriented class diagrams with a number of diagrams for describing the dynamic behaviour of systems. On the side of formal methods, combinations of process algebras with Z [26,23,14], B [4], abstract data types [1] or functional languages [15] or combinations of Z with statecharts [16] can be found as examples for the integration of different formalisms.

While most of these works are concerned with defining an appropriate common semantics for integrations, a different line of research is pursued by those studying the general nature of such integrations [7,17]. In this paper we will neither propose an abstract integration paradigm or metamodel nor define a semantics for an integrated specification formalisms. Instead we discuss the advantages of one particular semantic model which is used for giving a semantics to the object-oriented integrated formal method CSP-OZ [8,10]. CSP-OZ is a formal specification language which combines the state-based method Object-Z [6,24], an object-oriented extension of Z, with the process algebra CSP [22]. The semantic basis for this combination is the failure-divergence model of CSP. In this paper, we explain the design choices made when giving a failure-divergence semantics to CSP-OZ, and discuss the main advantages of this particular semantics.

CSP-OZ is only one of a number of combinations of Z with a process algebra. For a comparison of the different approaches, see [9]; another conceptually different integration of Z and CSP with a failure-divergence semantics is [25].

2   CSP-OZ

CSP-OZ is an object-oriented formal method which integrates Object-Z with the process algebra CSP. Object-Z or in general Z is a *state-oriented* method and thus good at describing data types and operations. Z is currently being standardised by the ISO [30] and has been successfully applied in a number of industrial case studies. A large range of tools (for instance editors, parsers and theorem provers) support the writing of Z specifications. The process algebra CSP on the other hand is mainly concerned with the description of the *dynamic behaviour* of distributed communicating systems. For CSP, a commercial model checker (FDR) can be used to perform correctness checks. CSP-OZ has been used in a number of case studies from the area of telecommunication systems, production automatisation and satellite technology [3,27,20].

The basic idea behind the integration of the two formalisms is to identify every Object-Z class with a CSP process. For this, every class specification of Object-Z is equipped with a *communication interface* and a *behaviour description* in the style of CSP. Then, while the Object-Z part defines the attributes and methods of a class (possibly with a guard and an effect predicate for every method), the CSP part fixes the possible orderings of method execution. A method invocation is thus identified with a CSP communication event.

A CSP-OZ specification typically consists of a number of Z type definitions and CSP-OZ classes (possibly using inheritance as a structuring concept) together with a description of the architecture of the system, consisting of an instantiation of classes into objects and their composition via CSP operators.

CSP-OZ fits perfectly into the integration paradigm proposed in [7], which consists of four hierarchically organised layers: in CSP-OZ layer 1 (describing data types) contains all Z axiomatic descriptions, data type definitions etc.; layer 2 (data states and transformations) contains pure Object-Z class descriptions, defining the state schema (attributes) of classes and the method schemas; layer 3 (processes) is captured by the CSP behaviour definitions within a class and layer 4 (architecture) is the final instantiation of classes into objects and their composition via CSP operators, most often parallel composition and hiding. The semantics of layer 1 is the standard Z semantics, the semantics of layer 2 lifts this basis to the failure-divergence model, and the upper level semantics are obtained by applying standard CSP theory.

2.1 Example

We explain this concept with the example of a vending machine.

Layer 1. The data types of the vending machine are given as Z types.

$$[MONEY]$$
$$DRINK ::= TEA \mid COFFEE$$

A drink can either be tea or coffee; *MONEY* is an uninterpreted basic type. We assume the existence of two functions and the relation $\leq$ on *MONEY*.

$$price : DRINK \rightarrow MONEY$$
$$diff : MONEY \times MONEY \rightarrow MONEY$$
$$\leq : MONEY \leftrightarrow MONEY$$

The function *price* gives the prices of a drink; *diff* computes the difference between two amounts of money.

Layer 2. For the second layer, we use the Object-Z class *VM-Data* (see Figure 1).

It comprises five state variables (attributes): *store*, a store for drinks; *s-money*, a store for money; *inserted*, an intermediate store for the inserted money; *drink*, for the chosen drink; and the boolean flag *ok*, to check whether enough money has been inserted.

Four operation schemas define the transformations on this state space (the methods of the class): *choose* stores a chosen drink in the variable *drink*. The so called delta-list $\Delta(drink)$ specifies that *choose* can only change the variable *drink*. The schema *choose* has two parts: The declaration part above the line specifies the delta list and the parameter $d?$ of the operation. The predicate part below the line is a predicate describing the state transformation. The final value of *drink* is there written as *drink'*. The operation *pay* stores the inserted money; *change* calculates the change according to the chosen drink. If not enough money was inserted, *ok* is set to *false*. Finally, the operation

```
┌─ VM-Data ──────────────────────────────────────────────────┐
│ ┌──────────────────────────┐  ┌─ serve ──────────────────┐ │
│ │ store : DRINK ⇸ ℕ        │  │ Δ(ok, store)             │ │
│ │ s-money, inserted : MONEY│  │ d! : DRINK               │ │
│ │ drink : DRINK            │  ├──────────────────────────┤ │
│ │ ok : 𝔹                   │  │ d! = drink ∧ ok = true   │ │
│ └──────────────────────────┘  │ store'(d!) = store(d!) − 1│ │
│                                │ {d!} ⩤ store' = {d!} ⩤ store│ │
│                                │ ok' = false              │ │
│                                └──────────────────────────┘ │
│                                                              │
│ ┌─ choose ─────────────────┐  ┌─ pay ────────────────────┐ │
│ │ Δ(drink)                 │  │ Δ(s-money)               │ │
│ │ d? : DRINK               │  │ m? : MONEY               │ │
│ ├──────────────────────────┤  ├──────────────────────────┤ │
│ │ drink' = d?              │  │ s-money' = m?            │ │
│ └──────────────────────────┘  └──────────────────────────┘ │
│                                                              │
│ ┌─ change ─────────────────────────────────────────────┐   │
│ │ Δ(ok)                                                 │   │
│ │ m! : MONEY                                            │   │
│ ├───────────────────────────────────────────────────────┤   │
│ │ price(drink) ≤ s-money ⇒                              │   │
│ │     (m! = diff(s-money, price(drink)) ∧ ok' = true)   │   │
│ │ price(drink) > s-money ⇒                              │   │
│ │     (m! = s-money ∧ ok' = false)                      │   │
│ └───────────────────────────────────────────────────────┘   │
└──────────────────────────────────────────────────────────────┘
```

Figure 1. Layer 2: The Object-Z Class *VM-Data*

serve offers the chosen drink and decreases the value of the corresponding store.

Layer 3. For the third layer, we use a so called CSP-OZ class (see Figure 2). It is an Object-Z class enriched with an interface and a CSP process.

The interface is a list of typed channels. The CSP process restricts the behaviour of the class: First a drink must be chosen, then money has to be inserted, the change is given back and finally the drink is served. Because we have specified the possibility of inserting not enough money, serving the drink can be skipped ($\square$ denotes the choice operator). However, this is not controlled by the CSP part, rather we use Z schemas for this purpose, since this part depends on certain attribute values.

VM-Contrl

  chan *choose* $[\,d? : DRINK\,]$
  chan *serve* $[\,d! : DRINK\,]$
  chan *pay* $[\,m? : MONEY\,]$
  chan *change* $[\,m! : MONEY\,]$

  main $\overset{c}{=}$ *choose* $\rightarrow$ *pay* $\rightarrow$ *change* $\rightarrow$
        $((serve \rightarrow \text{main})\ \Box\ \text{main})$

  inherit *VM-Data*

Init
$ok = false$

enable_*choose*
$d? : DRINK$
$ok = false$ $store(d?) > 0$

enable_*serve*
$ok = true$

  effect_*choose* $\widehat{=}$ *choose*   effect_*change* $\widehat{=}$ *change*
  effect_*pay* $\widehat{=}$ *pay*   effect_*serve* $\widehat{=}$ *serve*

Figure 2. Layer 3: The CSP-OZ Class *VM-Contrl*

The class *VM-Contrl* is a specialisation of the *VM-Data*, inheriting all its attributes and methods. That makes all items declared in *VM-Data* available for *VM-Contrl*.

To link Z operation schemas to behaviour, special keywords are used: **enable** specifies the guard of an operation, **effect** specifies the corresponding state transition. Thus a drink can only be chosen when it is stored and a drink is only served if the customer has paid enough money. The effect of all operations is mapped directly to the corresponding Object-Z operations. The schema **Init** specifies the allowed initial states.

In this example we have a very strict separation of data and behaviour aspects: the Object-Z class specifies the effect of operations on the data and the CSP-OZ class specifies all aspects relevant to the ordering of operation execution. This separation may also be weakened: the specification of data can be put directly into the CSP-OZ class, completely omitting an Object-Z

20

class specification. For larger systems, it may however be useful to adhere to a strict separation in order to enhance modularity of the specification.

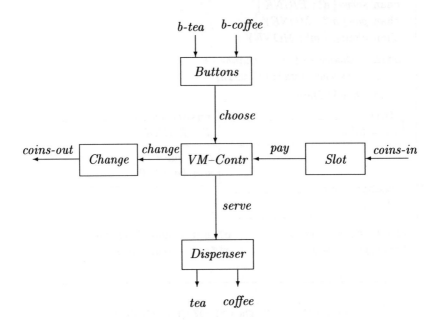

Figure 3. Layer 4: Architecture of the Vending Machine

Layer 4. In layer 4 we combine CSP-OZ classes by standard CSP operators. An overview of the system is given in Fig. 3. There, the class *VM-Contrl* communicates with four other classes which we have not explicitly given here: *Buttons* controls the two buttons to choose a drink, *Dispenser* controls the process of making coffee or tea, *Slot* stores inserted coins, and *Change* hands out the change.

The diagram in Figure 3 corresponds to the following CSP process:

$$VendingMachine \,\hat{=}\, ((Buttons ||| Dispenser ||| Change ||| Slot)$$
$$\underset{\{|choose,serve,change,pay|\}}{||} VM\text{-}Contrl)$$
$$\backslash\{|choose, serve, change, pay|\}$$

where ||| denotes interleaving, || parallel composition synchronising on the set
A

of events A, $\backslash A$ hides the events from A and $\{|choose, serve, change, pay|\}$ is the set of events corresponding to the channels *choose*, *serve*, *change* and *pay*.

2.2 Semantics

CSP-OZ possesses a uniform formal semantics on the basis of CSP's failure-divergence model. A failure-divergence model records the possible execution traces of a system, the sets of events which may be refused after a particular trace and the points of divergence, i.e., execution of an infinite number of internal events (livelock). The semantics of a CSP-OZ class specification is derived in two steps:

- the Z part of the class is given a failure-divergence semantics (via a translation into CSP) and

- the semantics of the Z part is combined with the (standard) semantics of the CSP part via the CSP parallel composition operator.

The CSP-OZ semantics is built on the Z semantics as defined in the current committee draft of the ISO [30]. Types, expressions and schemas are interpreted according to this semantics. Every Object-Z class is then viewed as a process where the class' methods play the role of communication events. The following four points explain the main considerations underlying the semantics of Object-Z classes:

- every method whose guard evaluates to true in the current state can be executed,

- the values for input parameters are fixed by the environment communicating with the object (*external* choice over all possible values for input parameters),

- the values for output parameters and next state are internally chosen from the set of possible values according to the effect schema of the method (*internal* choice),

- an invocation of a method, whose guard evaluates to true but whose precondition of the effect predicate is not fulfilled leads to divergence.

This semantics supports a blocking as well as a non-blocking view of methods: guards can be used to block the execution of methods, in particular, states of the object, the execution of non-blocked methods whose effect predicates can however not be fulfilled leads to divergence (every behaviour possible after invocation of method). The non-blocking view has its origin in Z, where undefinedness is usually interpreted as 'all possible values'. The blocking view is typically encountered in the design of distributed communicating systems, for which CSP can be used as a modelling language.

The reference model of [17] for integrated formalisms proposes to use abstract transition systems as the semantical basis for layer 2 specifications. Although this is also possible for CSP-OZ [10] (the transition system can then be the basis for deriving failures and divergences), we will directly discuss the failure-divergence semantics here. The choice for a failure-divergence semantics has several advantages.

▶ The failure-divergence model is the basis for defining three different *implementation* relations for CSP: trace refinement, stable failures refinement and failure-divergence refinement. These relations compare an implementation towards a given specification according to the dynamic behaviour they exhibit (*process refinement*), requiring that the implementation exhibits only a subset of the traces/failures/divergences of the specification. Having given a failure-divergence semantics to CSP-OZ, all these implementation relations are applicable to CSP-OZ specifications.

▶ All process refinement relations are *monotone* wrt. the operators on the architectural level (layer 4), which is clearly a prerequisite for a good implementation relation. By monotonicity we mean that the process refinement relations are preserved under all CSP operators: if *op* is a (binary) CSP operator (for instance, parallel composition) and $\sqsubseteq$ is one of the refinement relations then we have:

$$P \sqsubseteq P', Q \sqsubseteq Q' \rightarrow P \; op \; Q \sqsubseteq P' \; op \; Q'.$$

This is a standard result for CSP.

▶ Not only CSP but also Z comes with a specific refinement concept. The standard refinement concept for state-oriented formalisms is *data refinement*, used for instance for Z or VDM specifications. Data refinement is concerned with the change of data structures on different abstraction levels. An initial specification often uses different data structures than the final implementation which in its choice of data structures has to be oriented towards efficiency. Data refinement rules are used to show the correctness of the implementation with respect to the specification.

Since we have a clear separation of the Z- and CSP-part within a CSP-OZ class, the concept of data refinement can also be applied to CSP-OZ classes, i.e., it can be determined whether a class is a data refinement of another class. It is hence most important that this layer 2 (data) refinement concept neatly fits to the layer 3 (process) refinement concept. The relationship between data refinement and failures refinement has been intensively studied, and the duality of data and process refinement has been shown in [18,5]: given a failure-divergence semantics for a state-oriented formalism, data refinement induces process refinement. In [11] these results have been extended to CSP-OZ with its specific combination of blocking and non-blocking views of method invocation.

▶ CSP-OZ is an object-oriented formal method. Specifications define a number of *classes* which may be instantiated into objects and afterwards combined. Classes may *inherit* attributes, methods or behaviour of superclasses. Semantically inheritance is interpreted as the *conjunction* of the Z-part and the *parallel composition* of the CSP-part of a class. As usual, inheritance in CSP-OZ is primarily a concept for re-use of already written specification code. However, closely connected with inheritance is the question of *subtyping*: when is a subclass a proper subtype of its superclass? Subtypes always have to fulfil the principle of *type substitutability*: an exchange of a superclass by a subclass should be transparent to clients. In the context of process-oriented formalisms, subtyping is not so much concerned with types in the usual sense but with the *behaviour* associated with a class. A replacement of a superclass by one of its subclasses is only possible if the subclass closely resembles the behaviour of the superclass.

One candidate for such a *behavioural subtyping* relation obviously seems to be failure-divergence refinement. Failure-divergence refinement is however not able to capture the issue of extension of functionality (i.e., addition of new methods to the subclass) which arises when using inheritance. Nevertheless failure-divergence semantics can be the basis for defining a number of behavioural subtyping relations, varying in the degree in which they fulfil the principle of type substitutability [13,29]. The principle idea is to use various kinds of restriction and hiding operators of process algebras (applied to the methods added in the subclass) when comparing superclasses with subclasses. In [13] the adequateness of such behavioural subtyping relations has been shown by giving testing characterisations for the relations. In [28] it has furthermore been shown that, analogous to the relationship between state-based and behaviour-oriented refinement, there is also a close correspondence between behavioural subtyping and state-based subtyping definitions [19].

▶ Because the semantic model for CSP-OZ equals that of CSP, we are able to use all *tool-support* available for CSP. This concerns the use of the CSP modelchecker FDR: in [12] a translation from CSP-OZ to the input language of FDR is given which is consistent with the failure-divergence semantics of

CSP-OZ. This translation allows to use FDR both for refinement and for subtyping checks.

Summarising, failure-divergence semantics provides a clear basis for formal methods integrating state and process based languages. The refinement concepts of the different layers fit well together and the composition operators of the architectural level preserve the refinement relations. Moreover, a failure-divergence model can also be used for defining behavioural subtyping relations; a failure-divergence semantics for an object-oriented formal method thus additionally gives us the possibility of determining subtype relationships among classes.

References

1. T. Bolognesi and E. Brinksma, Introduction to the ISO Specification Language LOTOS. *Computer Networks and ISDN Systems*, 14: 25–59, 1987.
2. G. Booch, J. Rumbaugh and I. Jacobson, *The Unified Modeling Language user guide*. Addison Wesley, 1999.
3. J. Bredereke, Maintaining Telephone Switching Software Requirements. *IEEE Communications Magazine*, 40(11): 104–109, 2002.
4. M. Butler, csp2B: A Practical Approach to Combining CSP and B. In J. Wing, J. Woodcock and J. Davies, Eds., *FM'99: Formal Methods*, number 1708 in *Lecture Notes in Computer Science*, pages 490–508, Springer, 1999.
5. W.-P. de Roever and K. Engelhardt, *Data-Refinement: Model Oriented Proof Methods and their Comparison*. Cambridge University Press, 1998.
6. R. Duke, G. Rose and G. Smith, Object-Z: A Specification Language Advocated for the Description of Standards. *Computer Standards and Interfaces*, 17: 511–533, 1995.
7. H. Ehrig, J. Padberg and F. Orejas, From Basic Views and Aspects to Integration of Specification Formalisms, *Bulletin of the EATCS*, 69: 8–108, 1999.
8. C. Fischer, CSP-OZ: A Combination of Object-Z and CSP. In H. Bowman and J. Derrick, Eds., *Formal Methods for Open Object-Based Distributed Systems (FMOODS '97)*, vol. 2, pages 432–438, Chapman & Hall, 1997.
9. C. Fischer, How to Combine Z with a Process Algebra. In J. Bowen, A. Fett and M. Hinchey, Eds., *ZUM'98 The Z Formal Specification Notation*, volume 1493 in *Lecture Notes in Computer Science*, pages 5–23, Springer, 1998.

10. C. Fischer, *Combination and Implementation of Processes and Data: from CSP-OZ to Java*. PhD Thesis, University of Oldenburg, 2000.
11. C. Fischer and S. Hallerstede, *Data-Refinement* in CSP-OZ. Technical Report TRCF-97-3, University of Oldenburg, 1997.
12. C. Fischer and H. Wehrheim, Model-Checking CSP-OZ Specifications with FDR. In K. Araki, A. Galloway and K. Taguchi, Eds., B*Proceedings of the 1st International Conference on Integrated Formal Methods (IFM)*, pages 315–334, Springer, 1999.
13. C. Fischer and H. Wehrheim, Behavioural Subtyping Relations for Object-Oriented Formalisms. In T. Rus, Ed., *AMAST 2000: International Conference on Algebraic Methodology And Software Technology*, number 1816 in *Lecture Notes in Computer Science*, pages 469–483, Springer, 2000.
14. A.J. Galloway and W. Stoddart, An Operational Semantics for ZCCS. In M. Hinchey and Shaoying Liu, Eds., *Int. Conf. of Formal Engineering Methods (ICFEM)*, IEEE, 1997.
15. T. Gehrke and M. Huhn, ProFun – a Language for Executable Specifications, in H. Kuchen and S.D. Swierstra, Eds., *Proceedings of the 8th International Symposium on Programming Languages: Implementations, Logics and Programs (PLILP '96)*, vol. 1140 of *Lecture Notes in Computer Science*, pages 304–318, Springer, 1996.
16. W. Grieskamp, M. Heisel and H. Dörr, Specifying Embedded Systems with Statecharts and Z: An Agenda for Cyclic Software Components. In E. Astesiano, Ed., *Proc. of the 1st Intl. Conf. on Fundemantal Approaches to Software Engineering – FASE'98*, volume 1382 of *Lecture Notes in Computer Science*, pages 88–106, Springer, 1998.
17. M. Große-Rhode, On a Reference Model for the Formalization and Integration of Software Specification Languages, *Bulletin of the EATCS*, 68: 81–89, 1999.
18. He Jifeng, Process Refinement. In J. McDermid, Ed., *The Theory and Practice of Refinement*, Butterworths, 1989.
19. B. Liskov and J. Wing, A Behavioural Notion of Subtyping. *ACM Transactions on Programming Languages and Systems*, 16(6): 1811–1841, 1994.
20. A. Mota and A. Sampaio, Model-Checking CSP-Z: Strategy, Tool Support and Industrial Application. *Science of Computer Programming*, 40: 59-96, 2001.
21. Object Management Group, *OMG Unified Modeling Language Specification*. June 1999, version 1.3.
22. A.W. Roscoe, *The Theory and Practice of Concurrency*. Prentice-Hall, 1997.

23. G. Smith, A Semantic Integration of Object-Z and CSP for the Specification of Concurrent Systems. In J. Fitzgerald, C. B. Jones and P. Lucas, Eds., B*Proceedings of FME 1997*, volume 1313 in *Lecture Notes in Computer Science*, pages 62–81, Springer, 1997.
24. G. Smith, *The Object-Z Specification Language*. Kluwer Academic Publisher, 2000.
25. G. Smith and J. Derrick, Refinement and Verification of Concurrent Systems Specified in Object-Z and CSP. In M. Hinchey and Shaoying Liu, Eds., *Int. Conf. of Formal Engineering Methods (ICFEM)*, pages 293–302, IEEE, 1997.
26. K. Taguchi and K. Araki, Specifying Concurrent Systems by Z + CCS, *International Symposium on Future Software Technology (ISFST)*, pages 101–108, 1997.
27. H. Wehrheim, Specification of an Automatic Manufacturing System – A Case Study in Using Integrated Formal Methods. In T. Maibaum, Ed., *FASE 2000: Fundamental Aspects of Software Engineering*, Springer, 2000.
28. H. Wehrheim, Relating State-Based and Behaviour-Oriented Subtyping. *Nordic Journal of Computing*, 9(4): 405–435, 2002.
29. H. Wehrheim, Behavioral Subtyping Relations for Active Objects. *Formal Methods in System Design*, 23: 143–170, 2003.
30. Z Notation, Final Committee Draft, CD 13568.2, ISO Panel JTC1/SC22/WG19 (Rapporteur Group for Z), August 1999. See `www.comlab.ox.ac.uk/oucl/groups/zstandards/` for the current status of the Z standardisation.

BIGRAPHS MEET DOUBLE PUSHOUTS

HARTMUT EHRIG

Technical University of Berlin
Computer Science Department
Sekr. FR 6-1, Franklinstrasse 28729
D-10587 Berlin, Germany
E-mail: `ehrig@cs.tu-berlin.de`

1 Preface

The intention of this contribution is to discuss the relationship between Bigraphical reactive systems [10] and the Double Pushout Approach for Graph Transformation Systens [4,11] on a conceptual level. For this purpose we give a short introduction to the main concepts of both approaches, especially to bigraphs and double pushout transformations. The relationship between both approaches has been established concerning the following aspects:

- Presentation and Composition of Graphs,
- Categorical Frameworks and Transfer of Concepts,
- Rewrite Relations an Transformations.

Especially we point out which concepts correspond to each other and which of them have no counterpart in the other one. In some cases we are able to provide missing counterparts. Concerning the presentation of both approaches we abstract from some details, which are not essential for the comparison within the scope of this paper. On the other hand, we hope that our presentation is detailed enough for the bigraph and the double pushout community to achieve at least an intuitive understanding of each other. This should allow to present a more formal relationship between the two approaches in forthcoming papers. In this sense we are confident that bigraphs and double pushouts are on the way to meet each other.

Acknowledgments

This report is based on detailed discussions between Robin Milner and myself on the occasion of my one-week visit to Cambridge, in the end of May 2002. I am very grateful to Robin that he explained me his approach to bigraphical reactive systems very carefully. On the other hand, I am glad that he was patient to listen to my presentation of the double pushout approach to graph transformation. Although the approaches are quite different, we were able to establish some new links which are presented in this paper. Once again, I would like to thank Robin for his great hospitality during my visit, concerning not only scientific but also personal communication.

2 Bigraphs versus Double Pushouts

The notion of bigraphs has been proposed by Milner [10] at CONCUR 2001 as the basis for a model of mobile interaction based on joint work with Leifer [9] at CONCUR 2001 and several other papers on action calculi in the last decade. A bigraph consists of a "topograph" and a "monograph" representing locality and connectivity of reactive systems respectively. Bigraphs are equipped with reaction rules to form bigraphical reactive systems, which include versions of the $\pi - calculus$ and the ambient calculus. A more abstract categorical version of the bigraphical approach are "Reactive Systems", which allow to study reaction and transition relations with bisimilarity using variants of pushouts, called reactive and idem pushouts. On the other hand, the double pushout approach, in short, the DPO approach, for graph transformation has been proposed by Ehrig, Pfender and Schneider in [7] as a general model for graph rewriting and transformation.

The first intention was to generalize Chomsky grammars and term rewriting systems from strings resp. trees to general graphs. A first introduction to this approach has been given at the First International Workshop on Graph Grammar with Applications in Computer Science and Biology (see [4]). Meanwhile the DPO-approach has been studied and further developed by a growing community leading to a well-developed graphical modeling technique with concurrent semantics and various applications in Computer Science and related areas [11,2,5]. This approach is called DPO-approach, because a direct transformation $G \Longrightarrow H$ via p from graph G to graph H via a production p consists of two pushouts (1) and (2) in the category **Graphs** of graphs and graph morphisms

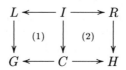

The upper row of the double pushout represents the production $p = (L \leftarrow I \to R)$, where I is the interface between the left hand side L and the right

hand side R of the production. The graph C represents the context graph, such that the gluing of L with C via I (resp. R with C via I) leads to the graph G (resp. H) (see subsection 5.2 for more details). This approach has been generalized from **Graphs** to other categories, where the objects can be considered as "high-level structures", leading to the concept of "high- level replacement systems" in [3].

3 Presentation and Composition of Graphs

In this section we discuss in more detail in which way graphs and composition of graphs are modeled in the bigraphical approach in contrast to the DPO approach. We show that graphs are presented as morphisms in the first and as objects in the second approach. Composition of graphs is modeled by composition of morphisms in the first approach in contrast to gluing constructions defined by pushouts in the second one. Finally we discuss the relationship between composition and gluing of graphs in both approaches.

3.1 Bigraphs in the Bigraphical Approach

Similar to the idea of Lawiere categories, where terms are presented as morphisms, also bigraphs are presented as morphisms between suitable interfaces. The essential idea of a bigraph is to comprise two different aspects of the state of a reactive system. The locality is presented by a hierarchical structure on the set of nodes, while the connectivity structure is presented by connections between distinguished ports of the nodes. In order to be able to study these two different aspects separately, both structures are presented as separate graphs, called "topograph" an "monograph" respectively, which, however, share the same set of nodes. The hierarchical structure of a topograph is presented by a forest of trees. The connectivity structure of a monograph, on the other hand, is presented by an equivalence relation on the ports of the nodes and the interfaces, where each equivalence class of ports can be represented by a hyperedge connecting all the ports in this equivalent class. In what follows, we give a more detailed presentation of topographs, monographs and bigraphs, respectively.

A topograph $G_T = (V, ctrl, prt) : m \to n$ consists of a set V of nodes, finite numbers m and n, called inner and outer width, a control function $ctrl : V \to K$ (where K is a given signature with arity $ar : K \to N$), and an acyclic parent function $prt : m - V \to V + n$ (where $+$ is disjoint union and m, n are now considered as sets $m = 0, ..., m - 1$ and $n = 0, ..., n - 1$). In other words, G^T is a forest of n trees with roots $0, ..., n - 1$ and m sites

$0, ..., m-1$. The sites are those leaves of the trees where other trees may be matched. This allows to define a composition $H^T \circ G^T : m \to l$ of topographs $G_T : m \to n$ and $H_T : n \to l$ leading to a precategory **TOP** of topographs. In fact, the composition is only defined if the node sets of G^T and H^T are disjoint, because this approach uses explicit names for nodes to handle sharing of nodes. This means that **TOP** becomes a precategory, where – in contrast to categories – composition of morphisms is defined only partially. Fortunately, the categorical constructions needed in the bigraphical approach are well-defined already in precategories.

A monograph $G_M = (V, ctrl, \equiv) : X \to Y$ shares the same set of nodes V and control function $ctrl$ with G^T. Moreover, X and Y are finite sets called conames and names of G^M, and $\equiv$ is an equivalence relation upon the set $X + P + Y$ of parts. Here the set P of inner ports in the disjoint union of node arities, i.e., $P = \sum_{v \in V} ar(ctrl(v))$. The composition $H^M \circ G^M : X \to Z$ of monographs $G_M : X \to Y$ and $H^M : Y \to Z$ is again only defined if the node sets of G_M and H_M are disjoint. The equivalence relation of $H^M \circ G^M$ is generated by the union of those from G_M and H^M, where elements from Y are deleted. This leads to a precategory **Mog** of monographs and – combining topo- and monographs – to a precategory **Big** of bigraphs $G = (V, ctrl, G_T, G_M) : I \to J$. Here $I = \langle m, X \rangle$ and $J = \langle n, Y \rangle$ are called inner and outer interfaces of G. This means that the bigraphical approach graphs (i.e., topographs, monographs and bigraphs) are morphisms in the corresponding precategories, whereas the interfaces (resp. width, names and conames) are objects.

3.2 Graphs in the DPO Approach

In the DPO framework for graph transformation we have – in contrast to the bigraphical framework – general graphs $G = (E, V, s, t)$ with sets E and V of edges resp. vertices and functions $s : E \to V, t : E \to V$, called source and target, respectively. More precisely, the DPO framework has been formulated in [7,4] for labeled graphs, where edges and vertices are labeled using label alphabets. Meanwhile the DPO approach has been extended to several other variants of graphs. For graphs $G_1 = (E_1, V_1, s_1, t_1)$ and $G_2 = (E_2, V_2, s_2, t_2)$, a graph morphism $f = (f_E, f_V) : G_1 \to G_2$ consists of functions $f_E : E_1 \to E_2$ and $f_V : V_1 \to V_2$, s.t. $f_V \circ s_1 = s_2 \circ f_E$ and $f_V \circ t_1 = t_2 \circ f_E$. This means that graphs and graph morphisms can be considered as algebras and homomorphisms in the sense of algebraic specifications [6] leading to the category **Graphs**.

In contrast to the bigraphical framework, graphs are objects in the DPO framework and graph morphisms are morphisms in **Graphs**. Interfaces are also graphs, i.e., edges are allowed in interfaces, and hence also objects. The gluing of two graphs G_1 and G_2 with interface I and embeddings $f_1 : I \to G_1$, $f_2 : I \to G_2$ given by graph morphisms is defined by the pushout object G with graph morphisms $g_1 : G_1 \to G$ and $g_2 : G_2 \to G$, s.t. we obtain the following pushout (PO) in the category **Graphs**:

$$
\begin{array}{ccc}
I & \xrightarrow{\;f_1\;} & G_1 \\
{\scriptstyle f_2}\downarrow & (PO) & \downarrow{\scriptstyle g_1} \\
G_2 & \xrightarrow{\;g_1\;} & G
\end{array}
$$

4 Categorical Frameworks and Transfer of Concepts

In this section we compare the categorical constructions used in the bigraphical and the DPO approach for graph transformation, respectively. As pointed out already in section 2, both approaches have been generalized to abstract categorical frameworks, which, however, are only roughly sketched in this section. The main aim of this section is to show that the constructions of slice, coslice and cospan categories are useful for the transfer of concepts and hence for the comparison of the two abstract frameworks.

4.1 Categorical Frameworks for the Two Approaches

In the previous section we have seen already that we need precategories **Top**, **Mog**, **Big** in the bigraphical approach in contrast to the use of categories of graphs in the DPO-approach. The fact that we have a precategory instead of a category, however, is not at all essential. It is more essential that graphs are presented by morphisms in the bigraphical approach in contrast to the representation by objects in the DPO-approach. This different point of view remains valid in the corresponding abstract frameworks.

The abstract framework for the bigraphical approach will be called reactive approach in the following, because it is based on a categorical framework, called wide reactive systems in [10]. It is based on a suitable precategory with relative pushouts which are used to define the transition relation in this framework, see subsection 5.4 below. In fact, pushouts are not required in the reactive approach, because in general they do not exist in the precategories of the bigraphical approach.

The abstract framework for the DPO graph transformation approach will be called DPO-approach in the following, because it is based on general categories with pushouts in order to construct DPO transformations of general objects, see subsection 5.2 below. This general DPO approach was introduced in [3], where the corresponding abstract transformation systems are called high-level replacement systems. For the comparative study in this paper it is not essential to give a more detailed presentation of these two abstract frameworks, except for the formulation of rewrite relations and transformations in each of these frameworks which will be presented in section 5.

In order to relate corresponding concepts in both abstract frameworks we review in the following some general constructions in category theory and discuss in which sense they are useful for the transfer of concepts.

4.2   Cospan Category and Transfer of Concepts

The category **Cospan(C)** over a category **C** has as objects the objects of **C** and a morphism $G : I \to J$ in **Cospan(C)** is a conspan $I \to G \leftarrow J$ of morphisms in **C**. The composition $H \circ G : I \to K$ of morphisms $G : I \to J$ and $H : J \to K$ in **Cospan(C)** – represented by cospans $I \to G \leftarrow J$ and $J \to H \leftarrow K$ in **C**, respectively – is represented by the cospan $I \to H \circ J \leftarrow K$ constructed by a pushout in **C** in the following diagram:

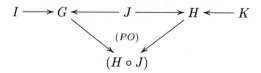

For a graph G with interfaces I and J, the graph with interfaces can be considered as a cospan $I \to G \leftarrow J$ and hence as a morphism in **Cospan(Graphs)**. This idea has been used already by Gaducci and Heckel [8] in an inductive view of DPO graph transformations. Moreover it has been used by Sobocinsky [12] as abstraction of graphs and bigraphs in the bigraphical approach. More precisely, Sobocinsky has presented a general construction of relative pushouts in **Cospan(C)** provided that **C** is a suitable category with pushouts.

For our comparison of abstract approaches the following observation is essential.

If the objects in a category **C** represent our graphs of interest, like in the DPO approach, then in **Cospan(C)** the morphisms represent the corresponding graphs. like in the reactive approach. Moreover, the cospan category is useful for the transfer of concepts in the following sense.

We formulate a concept of the reactive approach in a category

Cospan(C) over **C** and interpret this construction in the category **C**. As a result we obtain a corresponding concept in the DPO approach. This will be shown in subsections 5.3 and 5.5 below.

4.3 Coslice and Slice Categories with Transfer of Concepts

The category **Coslice(C)** over a category **C** has as objects coslices, which are morphisms in **C** of the form $a : \varepsilon \to I$, in short (I, a), where ε is a fixed object in **C**. A morphism $D : (I, a) \to (J, b)$ in **Coslice(C)** is a morphism $D : I \to J$ in **C** with $D \circ a = b$.

Dually to **Coslice(C)** the category **Slice(C)** over **C** has as objects slices $a : I \to \varepsilon$ with fixed object ε, and morphisms in **Slice(C)** from $a : I \to \varepsilon$ to $b : J \to \varepsilon$ are morphisms $D : I \to J$ in **C** with $b \circ D = a$. The composition of morphisms in **Slice(C)** and **Coslice(C)** are defined by composition in **Slice(C)**.

The slice and the coslice construction and category have been considered by Cattani, Leifer and Milner already in [1] in connection with the bigraphical approach. For our comparison of approaches the following is essential.

If the morphisms in a category **C** represent our graphs of interest, like in the reactive approach, then in **Slice(C)** and **Coslice(C)** the objects represent the corresponding graphs, like in the DPO approach.

Dually to the transfer of concepts from the reactive approach to the DPO-approach using the cospan category we might expect a transfer in the opposite direction using the slice of the coslice category. Unfortunately, this seems to be difficult or not possible at all. But both categories are of interest for the transfer of concepts within the reactive approach.

In fact, the slice category allows to transfer coproducts and pushouts into slice sums and relative pushouts, respectively, as introduced in [1]. In more detail, a coproduct resp. pushout in **Slice(C)** corresponds exactly to a slice sum resp. relative pushout in **C**. This corresponcende allows to conclude directly that slice sums resp. relative pushouts have the same nice properties (e.g., composition and decomposition) like coproducts and pushouts.

The coslice category on the other hand allows to transfer coproducts and slice sums into pushouts and relative pushouts respectively. This means that a coproduct resp. slice sum in **Coslice(C)** corresponds exactly to a pushout resp. relative pushout in **C**. Hence, in order to study existence and construction of pushouts or relative pushouts in a category **C** like **Top**, **Mog** or **Big**, it is equivalent to study coproducts or slice sums in **Coslice(C)** or any suitable category **C'** which is isomorphic or equivalent to **Coslice(C)**. In [1] a category **C** of action graphs, which is in some sense a predecessor of **Top**,

Mog and **Big** has been studied concerning pushouts and relative pushouts. According to the transfer of concepts discussed above a suitable category **C'** of embeddings has been constructed and shown to be isomorphic to **Coslice(C)**. Now coproducts and slice sums have been studied in **C'** leading to pushouts and relative pushouts in **C** via the isomorphism **C'** $\cong$ **Coslice(C)**.

5 Rewrite Relations and Transformations

In this section we introduce the rewrite relations and transformations in both abstract approaches in more detail and compare them with each other. First we discuss the reaction relation and corresponding reaction steps in the reactive approach, where DPO transformations are the counterpart in the DPO approach. Then we introduce the main concept of the reactive approach, called transition relation, and a corresponding notion of transition steps. The essential idea of the transition relation is the possibility to borrow a context from the environment in order to be able to perform a transition step. Such a concept is not known in the DPO approach up to now, but a corresponding new concept is defined in this section as the counterpart for transition steps in the reactive approach.

5.1 Reaction Relation and Step

In the reactive approach a rewrite rule is called reaction rule and consists essentially of a pair (r, r') of morphisms $r, r' : \varepsilon \to I$ in **A**, where ε is a fixed object in **A** and generalizing $(0, \emptyset)$ in **Big**. Morphisms $a : \varepsilon \to I$ in **A** are called agents and general morphisms $D : I \to J$ are called contexts in **A**. A reaction relation between agents $a, a' : \varepsilon \to J$ is defined, written

$$a \to a',$$

if there exists a reaction rule r, r' and a context D such that $a = D \circ r$ and $a' = D \circ r'$ in **A** are defined as shown in the following commutative diagram:

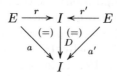

Note that the wide reactive approach only defines a relation $a \to a'$ between agents, not showing the rule (r, r') and the context D. Making both of them explicit, we call

$a \to a'$ via (r, r') and D.

A reaction step with rule (r, r') and context D, if we have $a = D \circ r$ and $a' = D \circ r'$ in **A** as above.

5.2   DPO Transformation

A rewrite rule in the DPO approach is a rule or production $p = (L \leftarrow I \to R)$ as discussed in section 2. A context for p in this framework is an object C together with a morphism $i : I \to C$. An application of rule p to this context leads to a (direct) transformation

$$G \Longrightarrow H \text{ via } p \text{ with context } i : I \to C,$$

where G and H are constructed as pushouts (1) resp. (2) in the following diagram

$$
\begin{array}{ccccc}
L & \longleftarrow & I & \longrightarrow & R \\
{\scriptstyle m}\downarrow & (1) & \downarrow & (2) & \downarrow{\scriptstyle n} \\
G & \longleftarrow & C & \longrightarrow & H
\end{array}
$$

In practical examples for the DPO-approach, however, we do not apply in general a rule p to a context C via i, but we apply p to an object G via a match morphism $m : L \to G$. The match morphism determines where L, the redex of the rule, occurs in G. In fact, there may be several different match morphisms or none at all. An essential step in order to apply p at m is now to find an object C and morphisms $i : I \to C$ and $C \to G$ such that (1) becomes a pushout complement construction. In the category **Graphs** – and similarly in other categories – the match m has to satisfy a suitable gluing condition in order to be able to construct the pushout complement C. Otherwise the rule r is not applicable at m. If $I \to L$ is injective, then the pushout complement construction is unique up to isomorphism. In the graph case this first step corresponds to removing from G all items of the graph L (more precisely, $m(L)$) which are not in the interface I (more precisely, not in the image of I in G). The result is the context graph C sucht that the gluing of L and C via I leads to the graph G, i.e., (1) becomes a pushout in **Graphs**. In a second step we construct the gluing of R and C via I leading to the graph H via pushout (2).

5.3   Relationship between Reaction Steps and DPO Transformations

Applying a rule p to an object G via match $m : L \to G$ in the DPO approach, it corresponds in the reactive approach to the situation that we have given a reaction rule (r, r') and an agent $a : \varepsilon \to J$. In the first step we would have to check the existence and to give a construction of a context $D : I \to J$ such that $D \circ r = a$, and in the second step we can construct the agent a' by the composition $a' = D \circ r'$.

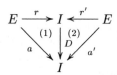

Now let us show how we can use the cospan idea to construct from a reaction step in the wide reactive approach, given by triangles (1) and (2) above, a corresponding DPO transformation $a \Longrightarrow a'$ via (p, D), where p is constructed from the reaction rule (r, r'). For this purpose we assume that the triangles (1) and (2) are given in a cospan category **Cospan(C)** over **C**, i.e., we have cospans $\varepsilon \to r \leftarrow I$, $\varepsilon \to r' \leftarrow I$ and $I \to D \leftarrow J$ leading to cospans $\varepsilon \to a \leftarrow J$ and $\varepsilon \to a' \leftarrow J$ by composition in **Cospan(C)**. Since composition in **Cospan(C)** is defined via pushouts in **C**, we obtain the following diagram, where (3) and (4) is a double pushout in **C** leading to the DPO transformation $a \Longrightarrow a'$ via (p, D).

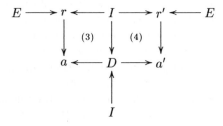

5.4   Transition Relation and Step

In order to be able to model all kinds of transitions in the $\pi - calculus$ and in the ambient calculus it is not sufficient to consider in the reactive approach reaction relations as introduced above. In fact, we need a more general rewrite relation, called transition relation in [10]. The idea is that we may have to borrow a context F in order to be able to apply a reaction rule $(r : \varepsilon \to I, r' : \varepsilon \to I)$ to an agent $a : \varepsilon \to J$. The problem is how to construct an additional context F in some minimal way, such that the following diagram (1) commutes:

$$E \xrightarrow{\ a\ } J$$

with r (1) f and $I \xrightarrow{\ D\ } K$

The required minimality would be satisfied if (1) would be a pushout in the category **CATA**. However – as discussed above – we cannot assume to have pushouts in **CATA**.

For this reason, the reactive approach requires a slightly weaker version of a pushout, called relative pushout (see subsection 4.3). Roughly speaking, a relative pushout is a pushout for the pair (r, a) with respect to a given upperbound. Diagram (1) is called idem pushout, if it is a relative pushout w.r.t. the upper bound (D, F). Fortunately, the categories **Top**, **Mog** and **Big** have relative pushouts and hence idem pushouts such that they can be required in the framework of reactive systems.

The essential idea of the transition relation in [10] is the following.

The triple (a, F, a') with agents $a : \varepsilon \to J$, $a' : \varepsilon \to K$ and context $F : J \to K$ is a transition, written

$$a \xrightarrow{\ F\ } a',$$

if there exists a reaction rule (r, r') with agents $r : \varepsilon \to I, r' : \varepsilon \to I$ and a context $D : I \to K$ such that diagram (1) above is an idem pushout and $a' = D \circ r'$. Similar to subsection 5.1, we will call in this case

$$a \xRightarrow{\ F\ } a' \text{ via } (r, r') \text{ and } (D, F)$$

a transition step, where the rule and the contexts are shown explicitly.

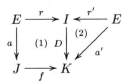

The main aim of the abstract framework of wide reactive systems in [10] is to define wide bisimilarity for agents $a, b : \varepsilon \to J$ w.r.t. the transition relation sketched above and to show that wide bisimilarity is a congruence. This allows to conclude by instantiation a corresponding result in the bigraphical framework, which can be applied to suitable versions of the $\pi - calculus$ and the ambient calculus.

5.5 DPO-Transformations with Partial Match and Borrowed Context

In subsection 5.3 we have shown that DPO-transformations are the counterpart of reaction steps. Up to now, however, there is no DPO counterpart for transition steps discussed in subsection 5.4. According to the idea of the transition relation we will construct such a counterpart, called DPO transformation with partial match and borrowed context. In contrast to the DPO approach, we assume now that we only have a partial match of the redex L of our rule $p = (L \leftarrow I \rightarrow R)$ in G. This means that we have a partial match morphism $m' : L \dashrightarrow G$, represented by a span

$$L \leftarrow^i D \rightarrow^m G$$

of total morphisms, where D corresponds to the domain of the partial morphism m' and $i : D \rightarrow L$ to the inclusion of D into L. According to a well-known construction in **Graphs**, we assume to have in our general DPO-framework a boundary construction for $i : D \rightarrow L$, i.e., a minimal interface B with morphism $b : B \rightarrow D$ such that the pair (b, i) has a pushout complement F in diagram (1) below. In a second step, we construct the pushout $\overline{G}$ in (2) with morphisms $\overline{m} : L \rightarrow \overline{G}$ and $g : G \rightarrow \overline{G}$, where $\overline{G}$ is the minimal extension of G such that we obtain a total match $\overline{m} : L \rightarrow \overline{G}$. In steps (3) and (4) we construct a standard DPO transformation from $\overline{G}$ to H via p as discussed in subsection 5.2. The following diagram

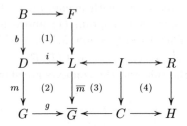

consisting of 4 pushouts (1) – (4) is called DPO-transformation from G to H with rule p, partial match $m' = (i, m)$ and borrowed context F, written

$G \xRightarrow{F} H$ via (p, m').

Note that according to the composite pushout (1) + (2), $\overline{G}$ is the gluing of G and F via B. This means that F is the minimal context, which has to be borrowed and glued to G, such that the partial match m' can be extended to a total match $\overline{m} : L \rightarrow \overline{G}$.

The relationship between reaction steps and DPO-transformations in subsection 5.3 can now be extended to a relationship between transition steps in subsection 5.4 and DPO transformations with partial match and borrowed context. In fact, diagram (1) in subsection 5.4 in **Cospan(C)** interpreted in **C** leads to the two pushout diagrams (1) + (2) and (3) above, while the triangle (2) in subsection 5.4 leads to pushout (4) above. Moreover, the minimality of diagram (1) in subsection 5.4 expressed by the idem pushout property corresponds to the fact that for given $i : D \to L$ the boundary B and the borrowed context F are minimal such that L is the gluing of D and F via B in (1) above.

6 Conclusion

In this contribution we have discussed the relationship between bigraphs, bigraphical and reactive systems, on one hand, and graphs, DPO graph transformation and DPO transformations in general categrries, on the other hand. The correspondence beween the first and the second approach has been established using the cospan construction and the corresponding category **Cospan(C)** over (C). We have shown via this correspondence that a DPO transformation is the counterpart of a reaction step (relation) and the new concept of a DPO transformation with partial match and borrowed context is the counterpart of a transition step (relation) in the reactive systems approach. In addition to the cospan construction for the category **Cospan(C)**, also the slice and the coslice constructions for the categories **Slice(C)** resp. **Coslice(C)** allow to define an interesting transfer of concepts. This has already been observed in [1] but deserves a more detailed study in forthcoming papers. Moreover, it remains open to transfer the main bisimilarity result in the first approach into the DPO framework. Vice versa, it might be interesting to transfer constructions like parallel, concurrent and amalgamated rules and corresponding transformations from the DPO approach to reactive systems.

References

1. G.L. Cattani, J. J. Leifer, and R. Milner. *Contexts and Embeddings for Closed Shallow Action Graphs.* Technical Report 496, Univ. Cambridge, 2000.
2. H. Ehrig, G. Engels, H.-J. Kreowski, and G. Rozenberg. *Handbook of Graph Grammars and Computing by Graph Transformation, Volume 2: Applications, Languages and Tools.* World Scientific, 1999.
3. H. Ehrig, A. Habel, H.-J. Kreowski, and F. Parisi-Presicce. From Graph Grammars to High Level Replacement Systems. In *4th Int. Workshop on Graph Grammars and their Application to Computer Science, LNCS*

532, pages 269–291. Springer-Verlag, 1991.

4. H. Ehrig. Introduction to the Algebraic Theory of Graph Grammars (A Survey). In *Graph Grammars and their Application to Computer Science and Biology.* Springer-Verlag, LNCS 73, 1979.

5. H. Ehrig, H.-J. Kreowski, U. Montanari, and G. Rozenberg, editors. *Handbook of Graph Grammars and Computing by Graph Transformation, Volume 3: Concurrency, Parallelism, and Distribution.* World Scientific, 1999.

6. H. Ehrig and B. Mahr. *Fundamentals of Algebraic Specification 1: Equations and Initial Semantics*, volume 6 of *EATCS Monographs on Theoretical Computer Science.* Springer-Verlag, Berlin, 1985.

7. H. Ehrig, M. Pfender, and H.J. Schneider. Graph Grammars: An Algebraic Approach. In *14th Annual IEEE Symposium on Switching and Automata Theory*, pages 167–180. IEEE, 1973.

8. F. Gaducci and R. Heckel. An Inductive View of Graph Transformations. In *Proc. CTCS'99*, 1999.

9. J. J. Leifer and R. Milner. Deriving Bisimulation Congruences for Reactive Systems. In *Proc. CONCUR 2000*, pages 243–258, 2000.

10. R. Milner. Bigraphical Reactive Systems. In *Proc. CONCUR 2001*, volume 2154 of *Lecture Notes in Computer Science*, pages 16–35. Springer, Sept. 2001. Long version appeared as manuscript.

11. G. Rozenberg, editor. *Handbook of Graph Grammars and Computing by Graph Transformations, Volume 1: Foundations.* World Scientific, 1997.

12. P. Sobocinski. Relative Pushouts in Graphical Reactive Systems, February 2002. Unpublished manuscript.

A NEW EXPERIENCE WITH GRAPH TRANSFORMATION

ANILDA QEMALI

Department of Computer Science
Technische Universität Berlin, Germany
E-mail: aqemali@cs.tu-berlin.de

The following contribution is not so much technical paper in the usual sense, but more an experience report by a young scientist in a changing evironment. In fact, she was growing up and studied computer science in Albania, a country which had been isolated until 1990. In the following she is going to report about her experience with computer science, especially Web application in Tirana on one hand, and her new experience with formal methods especially graph tranformation in Berlin on the other hand.

1 Computer Science and Technology in Albania

Albania has been an isolated country for nearly 50 years. In 1990 a new democratic system was settled similar to other East European countries. This new economic and social development of Albania had effected also the university structure, especially computer science which is a part of the Natural Science Faculty of Tirana University. computer science was introduced for the first time to Albanian students in 1985. A lot of new subjects were possible to be studied now, especially mathematical topics, programming language and classical theoretical computer science like automata, formal languages etc. With the changes in Albanians life, new requirements from students came out, such that in 1991 and the following years the program's structure was updated. The majority of new subjects had to do with new programming languages, operating systems and algorithm theory, but there was still a total lack of formal methods.

Meanwhile the technology had been developed very quickly. According to the needs of industry in Albania, the conditions for new companies and programming teams to be build up were very good. By now many software developing companies have nearly 10 years of experience. In Tirana, the capital of the country, several new companies were founded, in particular a small company, called GSG (Global Systems Group). Its main area is internet solution, providing web based applications for Albanian and foreign clients. The most important projects of this company are design for British and American clients. This development causes new main problems in Albania. On one hand, the technology is growing fast and with good results, but, on the other hand, the science is not able to change its own state in order to be able to solve new practical problems in connection with the evolving technology. Presently there are no courses to teach students new theoretical subjects in computer science and no support to build up new research groups to solve these problems and to support the needs concerning research and development of computer science in Albania.

2 From Web Application in Tirana to Graph Transformation in Berlin

After finishing the hight school in Albania, I began my studies in computer science, in Tirana in 1996. My generation was know as a "new computer science" generation in the university because that year the number of persons that could attend the course was much larger than in the previous year. Most of the subjects that I had to study in the first two years were purely mathematical and purely practical, but nothing to bridge the gap between mathematics and practice. In January 1998 I had the chance to work as a part-time student for LCDC (Lincoln Curriculum Development Center). LCDC was a team of 5 persons (3 students and 2 graduated) that was built and supported by the Abraham Lincoln Foundation in Tirana. On one hand, the aim of this team, and that of the American foundation, was to provide and help high school education in the computer area with online tutorials and interactive learning. On the other hand, the computer science students in the LCDC team gained working experience in programming and new computer technologies. It was a very good time for me, working hard and at the same time learning a lot concerning web-programming. Since we were the first web-programming team in Albania, we were supported by LCDC to have also short-time training out of Albania.

In this way I had a unique chance to leave my country in order to explore what happened out of Albania in computer science and to attend ICALP'99 in Prague. In fact, the ICALP organizers offered to me free registration, because I was the first participant from Albania in the history of this conference. The theoretical contents of all the papers presented in ICALP were very new things to me and most of them I could not understand at all. But talking with very friendly people doing research in different areas gave me the good impression and feeling that some of these topics would be important for me to go further in computer science. I had a new point of view of computer science and I began to read more about it. That was the reason that I went to Geneva for the following conference ICALP'01 where I talked about my situation and further plans to study abroad with Hartmut Ehrig. Back in Albania, I left LCDC (now called LDIT) to work for the company GSG mentioned above.

Meanwhile, I was a member of EATCS and I received the *EATCS Bulletin* and kept contact by exchanging e-mails with some of the ICALP's participants. That helped me to know more about the last updated news from theoretical computer science. It was not easy for me to understand all what I was reading, but sometimes it helped me to understand practical problems in programming applications. Just in the middle of the summer of 2001, I had my final exams for the diploma, then I got an offer by Hartmut Ehrig to work as an assistant in one of the DFG projects in Berlin.

After solving several problems concerning the scientific equivalence of my degree and my visa for Germany, I left GSG in Tirana in October 2001 and began to work in a DFG-project of the TFS-researcher group in Berlin. According to the tradition of this group I was introduced to algebraic specification, graph transformation and Petri nets. Although almost everything was new to me, what I was going to learn in the first months I am still convinced that it will be important for me. On the other hand, I do not regret about what I have done in Tirana, and I see a good chance to combine it with my new experience in Berlin. Talking with my colleagues and reading papers I got the impression that I can model web-applications with formal specification techniques which I have learned in Berlin. So, still these days I am working to know more about graph transformation in order to use them for modeling web application and to solve in this way some of the problems from my own experience concerning web application in Tirana. This new experience for me with graph transformation is the subject of the next section.

3   Towards Formal Methods Modeling of Web Applications with Graph Transformation

In wjat follows we discuss two examples how graph transformation can be used to describe and model web applications. Graph transformation is a rule based approach to change the structure of graphs, which has been developed during the last thirty years, and has now a sound theoretical background, and several practical applications [4].

The architecture of most web applications is not much different from dynamic Web sites, but we admit that they are much more complex. The design of web applications includes capturing and organizing the structure of a domain making it clear and accessible to the user. In addition, multimedia aspects of web systems raise a lot of new difficulties. Web application design is a difficult process that can be considered more as an art than a science. Modeling and intensive testing with users is even more difficult in web application development than it is with common software systems.

Let us consider a first example: Lukas Faulstich has shown in [3] how a graph transformation based view mechanisms in his HyperView model can be used to build a virtual web site on the top of a graph database. Figures 1 shows the layered architecture of this HyperView system. Each layer contains graphs that are views of the graphs at the underlying layer. These graphs are modeled as a cluster within a large global graph. The HTML layer consists of graphs of HTML pages loaded from the underlying web sites. Relevant data from these pages are extracted and used to build the graphs at the ACR (Abstract Context Representation) layer. Data from several ACR graphs are combined in the Database Layer into a single integrated database graph. Finally the User Interface Layer provides a view on the database graph in form of a dynamically generated web-site.

In HyperView, queries are essentially graphs containing variables and boolean constrains over the variables. Views are defined by sets of graph-transformation rules. The activation of a rule causes the left hand side (LHS) of a rule to be posed as a query against the layer beneath. For more details on the formal framework, see [2]. Let us now have a closer look at the HTML

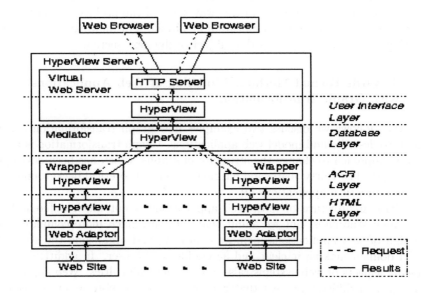

Figure 1. Conceptual Architecture of HyperView

code generation. The parts of the HTML cluster called page(P) in Figure 2 are generated by requesting the html edge emanating from node P:page. The rule implementing this edge will typically generate all fixed parts of the HTML graph such as the 'html', 'head', 'title', 'body' tags and other. This may include values of attributes of database nodes associated with page(P). In Figure 2 a simple example of such a rule is shown together with the resulting HTML code. The LHS of the rule is depicted as a subgraph of the RHS. The graph elements added by the rule are indicated by the edge *html* and the cluster *page(P)*. Variables such as *P* and *Name* are capitalized. Graph clusters are indicated by rounded boxes.

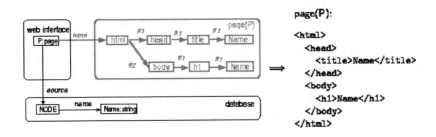

Figure 2. A simple example of generating HTML code

This example can be summarized as follows: The infrastructure for the web interface in the HyperView system enables the building of HyperView based virtual web-sites on the top of a graph database. We are dealing with a mechanism for the generation of HTML code and a method for designing appropriate graph-transformation rules that can be triggered by this mechanism. For futher information see [2].

Another example, with a different point of view of using graph transformation for web applications is presented by G. Busatto and Jan't Hoen, in their paper *Graph-Grammar Approach to the Specification of Hypermedia Application Dynamics*, see [1]. They consider graph and (rule-based) graph transformation as a conceptual model of hyperweb transformation. Hyperwebs can be seen as graphs: they are networks of documents (pages) with links between them and the graph transformation provides an intuitive way of specifying operations on these documents.

This choice has two motivations. Firstly, a hyperweb is essentially a graph, so that graph grammars are a candidate for specifying hyperweb transformations. Secondly, graph-grammars rules can be visually represented, and allow the specification of complex graph transformation in an intuitive way. These aspects fit well with the character of the hypermedia data models.

In addition, we would like to describe an approach which we still are working with. One of the challenges faced by web developers is how to create a coherent application out of a series of independent web pages. This problem is a particular concern in web development because HTTP as underlying protocol is stateless. Each browser request to a Web server is independent, and the server retains no memory of a browser past requests. To overcome this limitation, application developers require a technique to provide consistent user sessions on the web. Before implementing a web application, developers have to decide which session data is to store. We provide a modelling approach for powerful and flexible web session management, based on UML. We propose the definition of a session model which contains version management issues and thus, supports guided user input. The validation of a session model concerning consistency issues is possible, due to the formal basis of our approach using graph transformations.

The two short examples explained in this section together with the last approach, which is still not a complete one, are intended to motivate our claim that is worthwhile to model web applications by graphs and rules-based graph transformations.

References

1. G. Busatto and P. Hoen. A graph-grammar approach to the specification of hypermedia application dynamics. 2000.
2. L. Faulstich. *The HyperView Approach to the Integration of Semistructure Data*. PhD thesis, Freie Universtitaet Berlin, 1999.
3. L. Faulstich. Building virtual web site based on graph transformation. 2000.
4. G. Rozenberg, editor. *Handbook of Graph Grammars and Computing by Graph Transformations, Volume 1: Foundations*. World Scientific, 1997.

META-MODELLING AND GRAPH TRANSFORMATION FOR THE SIMULATION OF SYSTEMS

JUAN DE LARA

Escuela Politécnica Superior, Dep. Informática
Universidad Autónoma de Madrid
Ctra. Colmenar km. 15, Campus Cantoblanco
28049 Madrid, Spain
E-mail: Juan.Lara@ii.uam.es

Complex (physical and software) systems have components with different nature that may have to be described using different formalisms. For the simulation or analysis of properties of the whole system, our approach is to transform each component into a common formalism with appropriate analysis or simulation methods. This approach is realized by building meta-models of the different formalisms and expressing their translation using attributed graph transformation. Other model manipulations such as simulation and optimization can also be expressed with graph transformation.

1 Introduction

Complex systems are characterized by interconnected components which may have either continuous or discrete behaviour. Hybrid systems contain both classes of components. There are several approaches to deal with the modelling, analysis and simulation of these systems. For example, one may try to use a formalism general enough to express the behaviour of all the components of the system. In the most general case, finding such formalism is difficult, and usually engineers prefer to use more specific formalisms, well-known in the simulation community and adapted to the special characteristics of the component.

In other approaches, the user models each component of the system using the most appropriate formalism. The *co-simulation* approach provides each system component with a simulator. All of them have to synchronize by means of events at the trajectory (simulation data) level. Note how with this approach it is no longer possible to answer questions in a symbolic way about the behaviour of the whole system. The *multi-formalism* approach identifies a single formalism into which each component is symbolically transformed [15]. In this approach we can verify properties of the whole system if we choose for the transformation a formalism with appropriate analysis methods. The Formalism Transformation Graph (FTG) shown in Figure 1 (adapted from [14]) can help in identifying a common, appropriate formal-

47

ism to transform each component. The FTG depicts a small part of the "formalism space", in which formalisms are shown as nodes in the graph. Formalisms are divided in continuous (to the left) and discrete (to the right) depending on how the state variables change with time. In the continuous part, there is a distinction between causal and non-causal formalism. Among the non-causal formalisms, the graph depicts Partial Differential Equations (PDE) and Differential-Algebraic Equations (DAE). In the discrete part the four classical *discrete-event world views* [7] have been represented, together with different types of Petri-Nets (black and white and High-Level), automata and the DEVS [16] (Discrete EVent System specification) formalism.

The solid arrows between them denote a homomorphic relationship *"can be mapped onto"*, using symbolic transformations between formalisms. These transformations may lead to a loss of information. For example, when transforming from Petri-Nets to Automata (that is, when calculating the *coverability graph* [11]), the information about the exact number of tokens at each state (marking) may be lost if the net is unbounded. Nonetheless, by performing the transformation we are able to solve questions that were harder or impossible to answer in the source formalism. The vertical (dashed) arrows denote the existence of a simulator for the formalism. This indeed can be seen as a special case of transformation into the *"execution traces"* formalism. The dotted loop-arrows denote the existence of optimization transformations (to reduce complexity, improve performance, etc.) for the formalism.

Multi-Paradigm Modelling [15] combines multi-formalism, meta-modelling, and multiple levels of abstraction for the modelling, analysis and simulation of complex systems. Meta-modelling is a means to formally describe the syntax of the different formalisms in the FTG and drastically reduces the necessary effort to create the modelling tools. Meta-modelling tools are able to generate modelling environments from the description of a formalism, usually performed using graphical, high-level formalisms. In this work, we propose to model transformation, simulation and optimization arrows in the FTG as graph grammars [12], as meta-models can be represented as attributed, typed graphs and thus its manipulation can be naturally, graphically and formally expressed using attributed graph transformation.

The rest of this column is organized as follows: section 2 explains the basic concepts of meta-modelling. Section 3 discusses the use of graph grammars for model manipulations in our context, especially model transformation. Section 4 shows the implementation of these concepts in the AToM^3 tool [4]. Section 5 discusses the related work and finally, section 6 presents the conclusions and future work.

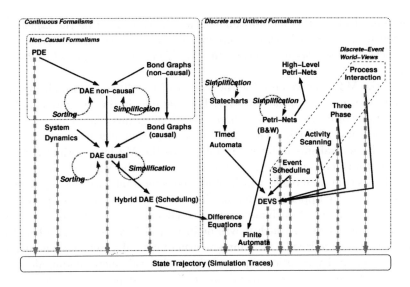

Figure 1. Formalism Transformation Graph (adapted from [14]).

2 Meta-Modelling

Meta-modelling allows describing the formalisms themselves using a (possibly graphical) high-level notation that we call a *meta-formalism*. These are formalisms expressive enough to describe other formalisms' syntax. A formalism is defined by a meta-model, while a meta-formalism is described by a meta-metamodel.

Most modelling environments (see for example the UML specification [9]) are organized in four meta-modelling layers. The highest layer (M4) contains the description of different meta-formalisms, used for specifying formalisms at the M3 layer. At the M4 level we must have at least a means to specify entities (*MetaClasses*), data (*MetaAttributes*), operations (*MetaOperations*) and relationships (*MetaRelationships*). These concepts are organized in the description of the different meta-formalisms. For example, in the UML meta-architecture, these elements are organized as the MOF (Meta Object Facility [9]) meta-metamodel, which is very similar to a core subset of UML class diagrams. This meta-metamodel is used to describe the UML syntax (the UML meta-model) at the M3 level. In the AToM^3 tool, we also have the possibility of using a meta-formalism with the form of Entity-Relationship diagrams. In fact, this meta-formalism was used to describe the other meta-formalism (similar to *UML class diagrams*), as in AToM³ *MetaClasses* can be instances of *MetaClasses* and the same for *MetaAttributes* and *MetaRelationships*.

In the M3 layer we describe the syntax of the different formalisms, using the meta-formalisms in the M4 layer. For example, in this layer we could have descriptions of Petri-Nets, the different UML diagrams, Differential Algebraic Equations and so forth. The different models that can be described using one of the formalisms in layer M3 belong to the M2 layer. Finally, the M1 layer contains data resulting from the execution of the M2 layer. Note how all meta-levels contain models, which should be consistent with the description of the model at the upper layer and are instances of these. The exception is the highest layer, in which each meta-formalism definition must be consistent with the meta-formalism in which it was defined (possibly itself). In AToM³ this circularity was realized by first implementing by hand a meta-metamodel with the form of Entity-Relationship, and then using this meta-metamodel to describe the Entity-Relationship and *core UML class diagrams* meta-formalisms, to bootstrap the tool.

A meta-modelling environment is able to generate a modelling tool for a formalism given the description of its meta-model. For the generation of such a tool, not only one must include in the meta-model information about the entities and their relationships (abstract syntax), but also about the visualization of the different elements (concrete syntax). It may be possible to have a "one to many" mapping from abstract to concrete syntax. Note how textual languages are a special case in which the concrete syntax is textual.

Additionally, for expressing certain syntactical aspects of the formalism to be described, constraint languages are normally used. For example, when describing the formalism *"Deterministic Finite Automata"* one would like to specify that all arrows departing from the same state must have different labels. This cannot be expressed using the Entity-Relationship or UML meta-formalisms alone. The UML uses the OCL (Object Constraint Language) for this purpose.

As an example, Figure 2 shows a meta-model of a discrete event notation in the *process-interaction* style [7]. It specifies that a model is composed of a number of *machines* interconnected via *queues* in which *pieces* can be stored. These are produced by *generators* at certain rates (a random number in the range [IAT-Desp, IAT+Desp]). A global *timer* controls the current simulation time and the final time. There is also a *future event list*, which stores the scheduled events (either a *piece* generation or the end of the processing of a *machine*). Events are linked to the elements in the model that produced

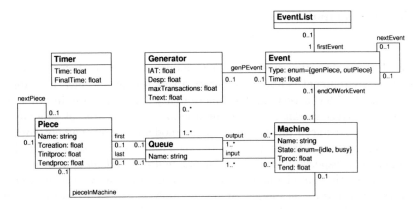

Figure 2. A meta-model of a discrete-event formalism (*process-interaction style*).

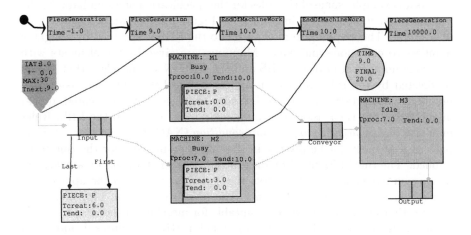

Figure 3. A model showing a *machine configuration*, instance of the meta-model in Figure 2.

them (either *generators* or *machines*). Figure 3 shows a model, instance of the previous meta-model, once the meta-model is assigned a concrete syntax. The model shows two *busy* machines; both of them have scheduled events at time 10 that signals the end of processing of the *pieces*. Note also how the next *piece* generation is imminent, as the *generator* has scheduled a *"piece generation"* event for the current simulation time.

3 Model Manipulations

With the information given by a meta-model as described before, a meta-modelling environment is able to generate a tool for the specified formalism. Usually this tool has a very limited functionality, basically verifying that the models are correct instances of the meta-model. In the area of simulation, we need more advanced functionality in the modelling tools, namely, simulation, optimization and transformation between different formalisms. This last manipulation is especially important for our *multi-formalism* approach.

To express these model manipulation in a uniform way we use attributed graph transformation, as models at all meta-levels can be expressed as attributed, typed graphs [12]. Expressing computations in the form of graph grammars has the advantage of being a natural, high-level, visual and formal notation.

As an example, some of the rules for the specification of a simulator for the *process-interaction* notation introduced in Figure 2 are shown in Figures 4, 5, 6, 7 and 8. The mapping from the LHS to the RHS is specified by assigning numbers to each node and edge. Mappings are given by the elements with the same number in both the LHS and the RHS. Nodes or edges that should be deleted by the rule application appear in the LHS, but their associated number is not present in the RHS. Nodes or edges that are created appear in the RHS, but their associated numbers do not appear in the LHS. Rules may also have a *negative application condition* (NAC) that specifies a certain pattern that must not be present in the matching in order for the rule to be applied. The rule in Figure 4 models the generation of a *piece* by a *generator* into a non-empty *queue*. Note how the *generator* points to the appropriate *generation event* in the *event queue*. The "⟨ANY⟩" label in LHS attributes denotes that any attribute value is suitable for matching (otherwise a specific value has to be given). The "⟨COPY⟩" label in RHS attributes denotes that the attribute value is not modified by the rule execution. An application condition states that the generation time (*Tnext* attribute) of the *generator* must be the same as the simulation time (*Time* attribute of the *timer* entity). In the *"condition"* section we use the notation $N(x)$ to refer to the node in the host graph with which node with label x made a match. In the RHS, the *Tnext* attribute of the *generator* is updated appropriately with the time of the next *piece* generation, and the *generation event* is consumed. The scheduling of a new *generation event* is modelled in the rule shown in Figure 8.

Rule in Figure 5 models the consumption of a *piece* by an *idle* machine. Note how in this case, the *piece* is consumed as soon as the *machine* is *idle*

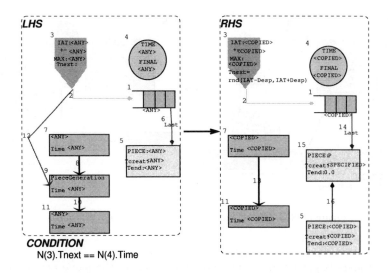

Figure 4. Rule for the production of *pieces* by *generators*.

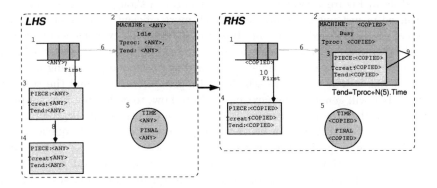

Figure 5. Rule for the consumption of *pieces* by *machines*.

and there is a *piece* in an input *queue*. The time of the end of processing is stored in attribute *Tend* of *machine*, the scheduling of an *"end of processing" event* is modelled in another rule (not shown in this column, but similar to the one in Figure 8).

Rule in Figure 6 models the end of processing of a *piece* by a *machine*. Note how the corresponding event is deleted from the queue of pending events,

54

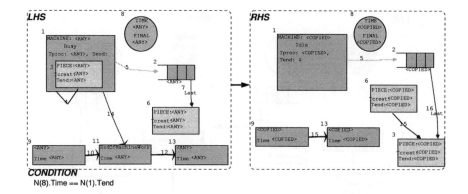

Figure 6. Rule for the end of processing of *pieces* by *machines*.

and the *piece* is placed in the last position of one of the *queues* connected to
the *machine*. The condition for this rule to be applied is that the simulation
time should be equal to the time of the end of processing by the *machine*.

Rule in Figure 7 models the time advance. Although the time could be
advanced in just one time unit, it is much more efficient to advance it to the
time of the next scheduled event. In our case, there are two classes of events:
"end of processing" and *"generation of piece"*. The former are scheduled
by *machines*, to signal the time at which they finish the processing of their
current piece. The latter are scheduled by *generators*, to signal the time at
which they will generate the next piece. Note how, to make the rules simpler,
we assume that the *event queue* has two special events, at the beginning and
at the end of the *queue*. In order to keep them always in the queue, their
schedule time is special: they are scheduled to occur at a negative time, and
after the simulation end time. This is the reason why the simulation time
advances to the time of the second event in the queue. Note how several rules
can be applied before the rule for time advancing is applied. This models the
fact that for simulation purposes, the actions modelled by rules in Figures 4-6
take no time.

Rule in Figure 8 models the scheduling of a new event for the generation
of a *piece*. In order for this rule to be executed the event must have not been
scheduled before (this is modelled with the negative application condition –
NAC –). As the event queue is a list ordered by scheduled time, the LHS
selects the events in the queue that precede and follow the event that is
going to be scheduled. An additional applicability condition ensures that the
scheduling of a new event is only possible if the event occurs before the end of

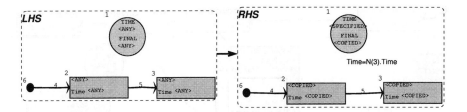

Figure 7. Rule for advancing the simulation time.

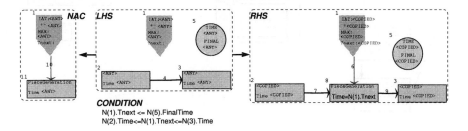

CONDITION
N(1).Tnext <= N(5).FinalTime
N(2).Time<=N(1).Tnext<=N(3).Time

Figure 8. Rule for scheduling the generation of a new *piece*.

the simulation. If the rule gets applied, a reference is created to the *generator* that created the event. This reference is used in the rule in Figure 4 to execute the event.

Only some rules of the graph grammar are shown, but other similar rules to the previous ones are needed. A rule similar to the one in Figure 8 is needed to create events produced by the end of processing of *machines*. Two additional rules similar to the ones in Figures 4 and 6 are needed to model the special cases of empty *queues*. Finally another rule similar to the rule in Figure 5 is needed to model the case in which the *queue* becomes empty after the rule application.

Figure 9 shows the result of the application of the rule shown in Figure 4 to the model shown in Figure 3. Note how, as the generation of a *piece* was imminent, the rule could be applied, and as a result of this, the *"piece generation"* event was removed from the list, a new *piece* was generated and the *Tnext* attribute of the *generator* was updated with the time of the next *piece generation* (12 as the *generator* was configured with an interarrival time of 3). The repeated application of the rules in the grammar results in the simulation of the model.

Coding the simulator in a textual language can be more efficient, but

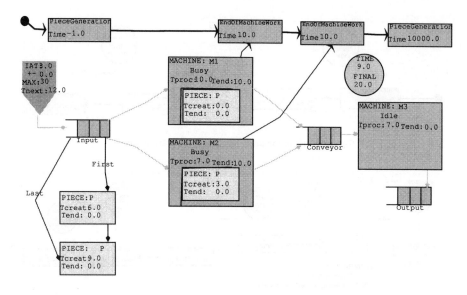

Figure 9. Result of the application of the rule in Figure 4 to the model in Figure 3.

for our purposes, graph grammars have a number of advantages over using a textual programming language (besides the ones expressed before). Graph grammars should be considered as a notation for high-level modelling (in opposite to programming). Thus, a simulator expressed with graph grammars may be viewed as a reference (and executable) specification from which more efficient simulators can be derived. The theoretical foundations of graph transformation may help demonstrating properties of the simulator. They also have advantages from the point of view of education [3]. Modelling a simulator with graph grammars is natural and intuitive, and one gets insight in the process one is modelling. Additionally, some tools (such as AToM[3]) are able to animate and execute step by step the graph grammars. In this case, the simulation can be visually traced without having to code complex graphical routines. On the other hand, one could use a textual language to express computations on models, but in this case, the user has to know the textual language syntax and some of the internal details of the tool, such as the way in which models are stored in memory, how nodes are connected and so on.

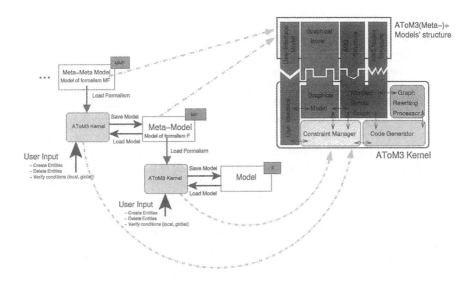

Figure 10. AToM^3's architecture.

4 Realization in the AToM^3 Tool

These concepts have been implemented in the AToM^3 tool [4], whose architecture is shown in Figure 10. The main idea of the tool is *"everything is a model"* as most of its components were described under some formalism, and can be modified by the user. This includes the user interface, the type system, a part of the graphical editor, etc.

In Figure 10 models (at any meta-level) are represented as white boxes, having on their upper-right corner an indication of the (meta-)formalism they were specified with. The AToM^3 Kernel is responsible for loading, saving, creating and manipulating models, as well as for generating code for the defined formalisms (the code structure is shown in the upper-right corner in the figure, labelled as *"AToM^3 (Meta-)Models' structure"*). Part of this code-generation task is performed using a graph grammar. The generated code must be loaded on top of the Kernel to allow the user building models in the defined formalism. One of the components of the generated files is a model of a part of the AToM^3 user interface. This user interface model follows the *"Buttons"* formalism, and has its own meta-model. Initially, this model represents the necessary buttons to create the entities defined in the formalism's meta-model, but can be modified to include, for example, buttons to execute graph grammars on the current model.

Entity-Relationship and UML class diagrams (with constraints) are available at the meta-meta-level to define other formalisms and meta-formalisms. Constraints can be specified as Python expressions, and the designer decides when (pre- or post- and on which event) the condition must be evaluated. Events can be related to *abstract syntax* (such as editing an attribute or connecting two entities) as well as to *concrete syntax* (such as dragging, dropping or moving.) The *Constraint Manager* checks at run-time whether the constraints associated with the events are satisfied or not. In the latter case, the event is not performed (or its effects are undone, if it was a post-condition).

In AToM^3, computations can be expressed either directly in Python, or as graph grammars. These are modelled graphically, and the graph grammar engine can be configured to work either in the *Single Pushout* or *Double Pushout* approaches [12]. To control the graph grammar execution, rules are assigned priorities (partial order), in such a way that the rules with the highest priority are checked first; if none of them makes a match, then the control is passed to the set of rules in the next priority order. When a rule is executed, the control goes back to the set of rules with the highest priority. The execution ends when no rule could be applied in the set of lowest priority rules. In the example of the previous section, we have assigned the highest priority (1) to the rules modelling *event scheduling* (like the one shown in Figure 8). Rules for the generation of *pieces* (like the one shown in Figure 4) have received priority 2. Rules modelling the end of processing of *pieces* by machines (like the one shown in Figure 6) have received priority 3. Finally, the rule for advancing time (see Figure 7) has the lowest priority.

The AToM^3 graph rewriting engine can be configured to allow (in the matching process) either an exact type matching between the nodes of the LHS and the nodes in the host graph or a subtype matching. In the latter case AToM^3 checks at run-time whether the node (or the connection) in the host graph has at least the same set of attributes as the node in the LHS, that is, if the node in the host graph is a subtype of the node in the LHS. We do not need to express the subtyping relationship in the meta-models (in fact, if the Entity-Relationship meta-formalism is used, we cannot include inheritance relationships in the meta-models), but this relationship is found at run-time. This idea is useful as one can write general graph grammars and reuse them for many formalisms, in unexpected situations. For example, one could adapt the formalism defined in the previous section introducing different kinds of *Pieces* and *Machines* with extra attributes. This could be done by subclassifying the *Piece* and *Machine* classes in the meta-model of Figure 2. In spite of the modifications performed to the meta-model, the graph grammar for simulation would still be valid. The newly created elements have the same subset of attributes as the ones that appear in the graph grammar rules and these could make a match with the new kinds of *Pieces* and *Machines*.

Finally, with respect to the execution mode, graph grammar rules can be applied *step-by-step*, *animated* or in *continuous* mode. In the first mode, the rewriting engine waits for the user to press a button after each rule application. The second mode makes use of the *delay* attribute of rules to produce an animation of the graph grammar execution. This attribute can be changed by the rules. Finally, in the third mode, only the initial and the final graphs are shown.

5 Related Work

There are similar tools in the graph grammars community. For example, GenGed [2] allows defining visual notations and manipulate them by means of graph grammars (the graph rewriting engine is based on AGG [1]). Whereas the visual language parsing in the GenGed approach is based on graph grammars, in AToM^3 we rely on constraints checking to verify that the model is correct. The mapping from abstract to concrete syntax is very limited in AToM^3, as there is a "one to one" relationship between graphical icons and entities.

On the contrary, this mapping is more flexible in GenGed, which in addition uses a constraint language for the concrete syntax layout. In AToM^3 this layout should be coded as Python expressions. This is lower-lever, but usually more efficient. In AToM^3, one can define formalisms as well as meta-formalisms. There is no structural difference between the generated editors (which could be used to generate other ones), and the editor which generated them. One of the main differences of the approach taken in AToM^3 with other similar tools is the concept that (almost) everything in AToM^3 has been defined by a model (under the rules of some formalism) and thus the user can change it.

In the simulation community, the approach of [10] is somehow similar to the one presented in this work. They have implemented several editors for continuous (sequential function charts) and discrete formalisms (Statecharts) using the meta-modelling tool DoME [5]. The user builds his composite models with these editors, and they are subsequently translated into the object oriented simulation language MODELICA [6]. In DoME, model manipulations should be expressed either in the Lisp-like language Alter or in Smalltalk; in our approach they can be visually specified graphically by means of graph grammars (combined with Python if desired).

6 Conclusions

This column has presented a multi-paradigm approach for the modelling of complex systems. In this approach, the different formalisms to be used are meta-modelled. Model manipulations are formally expressed by attributed graph transformation. Typical manipulations include simulation, transformation between formalisms and optimization. These concepts have been implemented in the AToM^3 tool, which is able to automatically generate modelling environments from the meta-model information. These environments can be given additional functionality by graphically defining manipulations (simulation, optimization, transformation into other formalism) using graph grammars.

It is worth exploring the applicability of additional graph transformation concepts in the area of simulation, such as amalgamation, parallel and distributed graph grammars [13]. For example, parallel graph grammars can be useful to describe simulators for formalisms in which parallel, synchronized actions should occur. A typical case is the Petri-Net formalism [11], in which the firing of a transition means consuming tokens in the set of incoming places and producing tokens in the set of outgoing places. Note how the variable number of places in both sets makes difficult expressing such a (parallel) action with regular graph transformation rules. In addition, analysis techniques for graph transformation could be used for demonstrating properties of the transformations. For example, critical pair analysis [8] can be used to prove confluence of the grammars for formalism transformation.

Acknowledgments

I would like to aknowledge the SEGRAVIS network and the Spanish Ministry of Science and Technology (MCYT) (project number TIC2002-01948) for supporting this work, and the Theoretical Computer Science/Formal Specification group at TU Berlin for their useful comments and discussions.

References

1. AGG home page: http://tfs.cs.tu-berlin.de/agg/

2. Bardohl, R., Ermel, C., Weinhold, I., AGG and GenGED: Graph Transformation-Based Specification and Analysis Techniques for Visual Languages. In *Proc. GraBaTs 2002, Electronic Notes in Theoretical Computer Science*, 72, 2 (2002).

3. de Lara, J., Educational Simulation by means of Meta-Modelling and Graph Grammars (in Spanish). *Revista de Enseñanza y Tecnología*, 23 (2002), 5–17. (See http://chico.inf-cr.uclm.es:8080/adie/revista/r23/23art1.pdf)

4. de Lara, J., Vangheluwe, H., AToM^3: A Tool for Multi-Formalism Modelling and Meta-Modelling. In *European Conferences on Theory And Practice of Software Engineering* ETAPS02, Fundamental Approaches to Software Engineering (FASE). LNCS 2306, 2002, 174–188. Springer-Verlag. See also the AToM^3 home page: http://atom3.cs.mcgill.ca.

5. DOME guide. http://www.htc.honeywell.com/dome/, Honeywell Technology Center. Honeywell, 2000, version 5.3.

6. Elmqvist, H. and Mattson, S.E., An Introduction to the Physical Modeling Language Modelica, *Proceedings 9th European Simulation Sympossium* ESS97, SCS Int., Erlangen, 1997, 110–114. See also http://www.Dynasim.se/Modelica/index.html.

7. Fishman, G.S., *Discrete Event Simulation. Modeling, Programming and Analysis.* Springer Series in Operations Research, 2001.

8. Heckel, R., Küster, J. M., and Taentzer, G., Confluence of Typed Attributed Graph Transformation Systems. In *Proceedings of Applied Graph Transformation* AGT'2002. Grenoble, 2002.

9. OMG Home Page: http://www.omg.org/UML.

10. Pereira Remelhe, M., Engel, S., Otter, M., Derarade, A., Mosterman, P., An Environment for Integrated Modelling of Systems with Complex Continuous and Discrete Dynamics. In *Lecture Notes in Control and Information Systems*, 279, 2002, 83–105.

11. Peterson, J.L., *Petri Net Theory and the Modeling of Systems.* Prentice-Hall, INC., Englewood Cliffs, N.J., 1981.

12. Rozenberg, G., ed., *Handbook of Graph Grammars and Computing by Graph Transformation.* World Scientific. Volume 1, 1997.

13. Taentzer, G., *Parallel and Distributed Graph Transformation. Formal Description and Application to Communication-Based Systems.* PhD. Dissertation, Shaker Verlag, 1996..

14. Vangheluwe, H., DEVS as a common denominator for multi-formalism hybrid systems modelling. *IEEE Symposium on Computer-Aided Control System Design*, IEEE Computer Society Press, 2000, 129–134.

15. Vangheluwe, H., de Lara, J., Mosterman, P., An Introduction to Multi-

Paradigm Modelling and Simulation. *Proc. AIS2002*, SCS International, 2002, 9–20.

16. Zeigler, B., Praehofer, H. and Kim, T.G., *Theory of Modelling and Simulation: Integrating Discrete Event and Continuous Complex Dynamic Systems*. Academic Press, second edition, 2000.

NET TRANSFORMATIONS FOR PETRI NET TECHNOLOGY

MILAN URBÁŠEK

Metada s.r.o., Brno, Czech Republic
E-mail: `milan.urbasek@metada.com`

Petri net transformations are used as powerful techniques for manipulation of system models based on Petri nets. They allow arbitrary modification of a given net. Two kinds of transformations are distinguished, namely net model and net class transformations. Both kinds of transformations are formaly defined and a lot of important results are available, e.g., compatibility of transformations with each other, compatibility with horizontal structuring, preservation of structural and system properties. Net transformations provide a framework for modelling of Petri net based systems for several classes of Petri nets. This paper presents the main ideas of net transformations as developed at the Technical University Berlin. There are motivation, role, informal description, formal background, and examples of Petri net transformations presented in this paper.

1 Introduction

The application-oriented presentation of Petri nets has been developed during several years in the Petri net research group at the Technical University and Humbold University Berlin. The definition of different Petri net techniques has been one of the main research areas in this project (see papers in proceedings [30] and [31]). The main concept focuses on Petri nets as a specification technique, hence, it means more than mere Petri net based model. It comprises, e.g., structuring and refinement of nets, tool support, exchange formats, or process model and exemplary methodology, so that adequate and scalable use of nets is provided for specific application domains. Net transformations are very important for manipulation with Petri nets in specific Petri net techniques for their formal background and applicability. We distinguish between net model and net class transformations.

The idea of net model transformations follows the development in the area of graph transformations and its application to Petri nets as described in [8]. This idea was formally extended by the so-called Q-theory in order to handle net model transformations preserving certain system properties in [20] and in [21]. Preservation of certain system properties like safety properties, deadlock freedom, liveness, etc. is of great importance for net system designers as these transformations make the verification of properties of the final model easier.

Net class transformations describe a change of the underlying Petri net class. They add or remove certain aspects of a net like marking, time features, etc., while preserving relations between nets represented by morphisms. They are based on the approach presented in [12,13].

The brief summary of latest results in the area of net transformations was presented in [29]. This topic is elaborated in [28] in detail.

Next, we describe net transformations from an informal point of view. We will give a motivation for research on net transformations and show the role of net transformations in the above mentioned Petri net technology, called »Petri Net Baukasten«.

2 The Notion of Petri Net Technology

Within the last four decades of research on Petri nets numerous Petri net notions and methods as well as tools and tool environments have evolved. These have been successfully employed in various application areas, such as automatic production, control systems, workflow management, etc. In such large scale of applications, different Petri net variants, called Petri net classes, can be employed. A Petri net class represents a Petri net variant including a set of techniques based on that variant like structuring, analysis, and verification techniques. To identify adequate Petri net classes and methods for the use of Petri nets within the system development process in a specific application domain is still a difficult task. Hence, there was a strong need for a structured approach to various Petri net techniques comprising methodological procedures, tool support, and formal techniques. A structured presentation of various methods and techniques is called a technology. The strong motivation for such a technology derives from the rich and diverse Petri net theory and its various applications [24,15,25].

In this paper we refer to a technology, called »Petri Net Baukasten«, which has been previously presented in [30,6]. The »Petri Net Baukasten« has been developed within the joint research project "DFG-Forschergruppe PETRINETZ-TECHNOLOGIE", involving H. Weber (Coordinator), H. Ehrig (Technische Universität Berlin) and W. Reisig (Humboldt Universität zu Berlin), supported by the German Research Council (DFG).

The »Petri Net Baukasten« provides a classification of Petri nets and corresponding notions, which is independent of their use in applications, their formalizations, and tool support. The semi-formal classification is given by class diagrams that describe Petri net class and its notions. It is represented using UML and constitutes the base of the »Petri Net Baukasten«.

The »Petri Net Baukasten« enables more straightforward understanding of Petri net classes and the development of Petri net tools, to aid in the application of Petri net classes, and to provide a unified representation of the formal definitions of Petri net classes. The »Petri Net Baukasten« includes a classification concept for Petri nets that serves these purposes.

These representations of Petri net notions are given in specific views. They concern the use of the Petri net notions within a certain application domain, their formalization in the theory of Petri nets, and their implementation as Petri net tools. These views are called Application Developer View, Expert View, and Tool Developer View, respectively. These techniques allow visualization, formal description, early evaluation, and verification of models based on nets.

Generally, we consider a Petri net technology to be a Petri net based manner of accomplishing the task of system development using methods for employing Petri net techniques. A method deals with principles of employing Petri net techniques in applications.

3 Motivation and Requirements for Net Transformations

For the development of concurrent and distributed systems Petri nets [23] are a well-known specification technique. They are successfully employed in many different application areas like workflow management, traffic control, automated production etc. (see, e.g., [5,14,15]). Their intuitive graphic representation on the one hand and the good mathematical foundation on the other hand are the main reasons for employing them in modeling, verification, and simulation of systems. Therefore, numerous variants have been proposed for specific purposes and application areas, each supplied with their own theoretical foundation.

These variants differ in their complexity and expressivity, as well as in the available operations like structuring, analysis, and verification techniques.

3.1 Motivation for Net Transformations

A design of Petri net based models employs a methodology how and in which order the Petri nets are to be used.

The common approach of the Petri net based process models is to start with a simple model which is gradually enhanced. The final model usually comprises causalities among the system's actions as well as the functionality of the entire system. This includes data, time aspects, exception handling, business rules, etc. Thus, although significantly differing in paradigms, enhancement is of central importance. We make the enhancement explicit leading to the concept of transformation.

Petri net based models in literature, see, e.g., [19,16,4,17,18,2,3], propose enhancing a simple start model in order to proceed from analysis to design phase. The enhancement of models is given mainly on an informal level in these papers. Enhancement comprises addition of new aspects like data and time as well as addition of details like exception handling and business rules. The enhancement leads to different Petri nets for different phases in the development process. With respect to the used Petri net formalisms there are two opposed paradigms: [19,16,18,2,3] basically use one rich high-level Petri net formalism throughout the whole development process. This has the advantage of an integrated presentation of all aspects and details of a system. However, due to the complexity of the employed Petri net formalism there are few, if any, structuring, analysis, or verification techniques. Moreover, the constructed Petri nets are complex and therefore difficult to understand. In contrast, [4,17] propose varying Petri net formalism according to the development phase. The used Petri net formalism comprises only those aspects which are relevant in a given development phase. The advantage is that Petri net models are simpler and generally there are more analysis, verification, and structuring techniques available, see [6,10].

According to these paradigms, the enhancement of Petri net models differs: it means some modification of Petri nets (first paradigm) or it additionally comprises a change of the Petri net formalism (second paradigm).

In order to cover enhancement of Petri nets within both basic paradigms, we now introduce our concept of transformations. We distinguish transformations of Petri nets on two different levels: on the level of the Petri net formalism and on the level of the Petri net. These transformations can be combined in order to enhance both the formalism and the Petri net model.

Net class transformation The Petri net formalism determines the aspects that are modeled in a corresponding Petri net. In order to enhance a model by additional aspects like data, time, or roles, the Petri net formalism has to cover a new aspect. In other words, the new aspect has to be integrated into the Petri net formalism. The addition of new aspects is realized by *net class transformation*, which changes the underlying Petri net formalism. This change comprises enrichment of or abstraction from certain aspects of the system.

Net model transformation In contrast, enhancing a model by additional details operates on one level of abstraction. Addition of details like exception handling, refining the description of the model, etc. means specifying or changing a Petri net model, not the underlying formalism. This kind of transformation is called *net model transformation*. An important special case is a change of a single aspects, e.g., data.

Combined transformation In order to enhance a model by an aspect, e.g., data, we have to perform both transformations. By net class transformation we change the net formalism resulting in formalism, which comprises data. Subsequently, we specify the actual data by net model transformation. The net model transformation yields then data of a specific system. For an example, see Section 6.

Summarizing, net transformation is given as a net class transformation, or a net model transformation, or their combination. Apparently, this concept of transformation covers enhancement of Petri net based models described in literature, as presented above. In the first paradigm only net model transformation is used, whereas the second paradigm employs both net class and net model transformation.

3.2 Formal Foundation of Net Transformations

The formal foundation of net model and net class transformations is different for each kind of transformation because they operate on different abstraction levels. The underlying theories are category theory, see, e.g., [1], for net class transformation and the theory of high-level replacement systems, see, e.g., [9,8], for net model transformation.

Net class transformation Technically, net class transformation is achieved by a functor between the appropriate categories of Petri nets. Functors are known from category theory as some kind of mapping between categories. Intuitively, a functor is a mapping which assigns a Petri net of the new formalism to each Petri net of the old formalism and which is compatible with relations between Petri nets given by morphisms.

Net model transformation To realize model transformation we employ the concept of rules and applications of rules. This approach has been originally introduced for graphs in [7] and generalized to all kind of structures — including Petri nets — in high-level replacement systems [9,8]. Conceptually, rules are given by $r : L \implies R$ with two nets L and R, called left-hand side and right-hand side of the rule, respectively. Application of a rule to a Petri net informally means replacing the left-hand side of the rule by the right-hand side. This notion comprises any kind of changes of the model including the replacement of the whole system.

Combined Transformation A combined transformation is given by an arbitrary sequence of net class and net model transformations. The results

68

of one (net class or net model) transformation is transformed further by a subsequent transformation.

3.3 Requirements for Net Transformations

Obviously, when proceeding from one model to a more specific model we suppose there exists a relation between the two models. As the second model is based on the first one, they both have "something" in common. Depending on the development step, this similarity may refer to, e.g., the flow structure, the number of transitions or places, or other structural properties. Also preservation of behavioral properties like liveness, deadlock freedom, or safety properties are important during the development of the system. In order to ensure preservation of these properties by net transformations, both net class transformations and net model transformations have to be classified according to the preservation of these properties. This leads to the first requirement given on transformations:

1. Classification of net transformations w. r. t. preservation of system and/or structural properties.

For large systems, adequate structuring techniques for composing subsystems and decomposing are indispensable. For transformation of subsystems and composition of transformed models, structuring is needed to be compatible with net transformations. Hence, the next requirement:

2. Compatibility of structuring and net transformations.

In Petri net based process models several models of the system are achieved on different levels of abstraction. Of course, all of these models should be consistent to each other, meaning that each model is a proper enhancement of the start model. Or, vice versa, each model is a proper abstraction of the final model. With respect to net transformations this means that each modification on one level of abstraction should be reflected in the other ones. This leads to the following requirement for net transformations:

3. Compatibility of net model transformation with net class transformation.

In the system development the integration of various models into one model is of major importance. With respect to Petri net based system development this means that several Petri net models of different abstraction levels are integrated into one. This fact yields the next requirement:

4. Integration of Petri net models of different abstraction levels.

The semantics of net classes is of importance. Net class transformations should address the question of semantics, too. Generally, it is hard to to develop net class transformations with respect to semantics. But the semantics must not be neglected. It is an important feature of a Petri net based model. In practice it is sufficient that semantics of net classes is defined independently of net class transformations of syntactical descriptions. The defined semantics has to be compositional, i.e., compatible with structuring techniques. Therefore, the last requirement is

5. Definition of compositional semantics of net classes.

The first four requirements were already published in [13] in a slightly different form.

4 The Role of Net Transformations in the Petri Net Technology

The Petri net technology mentioned in Section 1 is considered as a unified presentation of theory, applications, and tools of Petri nets. In this section we will describe the role of net transformations within the Petri net technology as used in the »Petri Net Baukasten«.

Petri net transformations (or succinctly net transformations) are used to perform modifications of a net. They are formalized on a rigorous mathematical foundation, see [20] and [12,13]. For a systematic study two levels of transformations, called *net model transformations* and *net class transformations*, are distinguished, as discussed in the foregoing section. The purpose of the formal transformations is twofold:

- On the one hand, net class transformations extend the theory of a given net class in the following sense. Petri net operations in the target net class are made available also for the source net class by transforming the net class, performing the operation, and subsequently interpreting back the result of the operation in the source net class.

- On the other hand, both kinds of transformations together allow arbitrary modifications of a (start) net. Therefore, they are suitable to support stepwise enhancement of nets in the context of system development. In this sense, they yield a formal support of the models based on nets.

The net transformations are essential for realizing a stepwise system development within the given process models. These process models present a methodology in the way Petri nets are to be used in the different steps during the development of models based on nets. They typically start with an abstract model of the system which is refined in further development steps. Refinement here means integration of system aspects like time, reactiveness, roles, data, etc. as well as modification of these aspects for incorporating exception handling, etc.

The main idea of stepwise development of systems is to offer a number of net transformation techniques to an application developer. These techniques describe how to change a net model in order to obtain another more elaborated, refined and expressive net model.

The sequence of net transformations provides a transformation from the initial net G to the final net H:

$$G = G_0 \overset{p_1}{\Longrightarrow} G_1 \overset{p_2}{\Longrightarrow} \ldots \overset{p_n}{\Longrightarrow} G_n = H.$$

Each step $G_i \overset{p_{i+1}}{\Longrightarrow} G_{i+1}$ denotes a single net class or net model transformation. The transformation process is either rule-based (net model transformation) or based on functors (net class transformation).

The preservation of suitable system or structural properties during the transformation process is of interest in most applications, since the final model may become very large and hence difficult to check for certain properties. It is of great importance for the application developer to check only the initial – usually quite small system – directly and to apply property preserving net transformations. For this reason structure and property preserving transformations are supported by net transformations and other net techniques, especially by rule-based refinement, horizontal structuring techniques (union and fusion), property preserving net model transformations, and formal transformations of net classes.

5 Informal Description of Net Transformations

In this section we describe informally the ideas used in the theory of net transformations. The explanatory example is presented in Section 6 afterwards. Formal definitions of net transformations are given in [20] and [12,13] in detail.

The net model transformations are defined as rule-based. Each net model transformation represents a specific application of a given rule on a transformed net. Net class transformations are defined as functors.

Generally, rules and net model transformations of Petri nets are given by the instantiation of high-level replacement systems. These can be con-

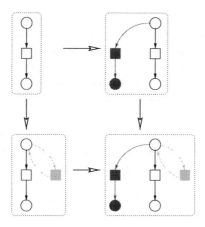

Figure 1. An example of a pushout

sidered as a general description of replacement systems, where the left-hand side of the rule is replaced by the right-hand side. Rules and transformations fully capture the replacement and thus can define any kind of system development or modification. High-level replacement systems have been introduced in [9] as a categorical generalization of graph transformations. The application of high-level replacement systems to different domains as place/transition nets, algebraic specification [8], etc. requires a suitable category. High-level replacement systems are formulated for an arbitrary category **NET** with a distinguished class $\mathcal{M}$ of morphisms called $\mathcal{M}$-morphisms. Here we give the corresponding notions of replacement systems in terms of Petri nets and not on the abstract level as in [21].

We now explain the used notions rather informally to show that the complex category theory behind them can be omitted in applications. The most important notion from category theory used almost throughout the whole theory of high-level replacement systems is the notion of a pushout. In the next paragraph we describe the pushout construction. For illustration, see also Figure 1. Next we briefly address other necessary notions, as rules, net model and net class transformations, property preserving rules, structuring techniques and proof rules.

Pushouts of Petri nets. A pushout is a categorical construction that requires a commutative square and has some universal properties. Informally, a pushout can be characterized as the "largest" object, that yields a commutative square for two given morphisms without "new" nodes. A pushout of two Petri nets can be considered as a union of nets with respect to a common interface.

That is, for objects and injective morphisms as on the top and left of Figure 1 we glue the nets together as illustrated in the same figure and we achieve right and bottom morphisms with the common object. For other net classes the construction of pushouts has to take additional components like, e.g., the data, arc inscription, transition guards, etc. into account. Basically the construction of these components is analogous to the presented construction of the net structure.

Rules. A rule $r = (L \xleftarrow{l} K \xrightarrow{r} R)$ consists of the Petri nets L, K and R, called left-hand side, interface, right-hand side, respectively, and two $\mathcal{M}$-morphisms $K \xrightarrow{l} L$ and $K \xrightarrow{r} R$.

Net model transformations. Given a rule $r = (L \xleftarrow{k_1} K \xrightarrow{k_2} R)$, a direct net model transformation $N_1 \xRightarrow{r} N_2$, from N_1 to N_2 is given by the following two pushout diagrams **(1)** and **(2)**. The morphisms $L \longrightarrow N_1$ and $R \longrightarrow N_2$ are called occurrences. The net C is called pushout complement.

$$
\begin{array}{ccccc}
L & \xleftarrow{k_1} & K & \xrightarrow{k_2} & R \\
\downarrow & \text{(1)} & \downarrow & \text{(2)} & \downarrow \\
N_1 & \longleftarrow & C & \longrightarrow & N_2
\end{array}
$$

Informally, a rule $r = (L \xleftarrow{l} K \xrightarrow{r} R)$ is given by three nets L, K, and R. Moreover, K is a subnet of both L and R expressed by the morphisms l and r. Application of a rule to the net N_1 is a net model transformation of N_1. The net model transformation means replacing a subnet specified by the left-hand side of the rule with the net specified by the right-hand side. More precisely, we first identify the subnet L in N_1. Then we delete those parts of the subnet L which are not subnets of the interface net K. This results in an intermediate net C, where in a further step we add the difference of R and K to the preserved subnet C to obtain the transformed net N_2. In case the left-hand side is empty, we simply add the right-hand side to the first net.

(Horizontal) Structuring. There are two abstract structuring constructions in the theory of high-level replacement systems, namely union and fusion. Generally, they combine two subnets or two different nets into one. The union of two Petri nets is given with respect to a defined subnet. Union is defined as the pushout of two nets and is given by a span of morphisms. The resulting net preserves the common subnet, i.e., the source of both morphisms and keeps the rest of the two nets distinct, e.g., see Figure 1. The fusion is the gluing of two subnets within one Petri net.

Refinement. Based on the notion of rules and transformations, the general theory of high-level replacement systems has been enriched by the $\mathcal{Q}$-theory in order to formulate abstraction/refinement morphisms of structures. These morphisms are more suitable for the stepwise development of systems. The main idea is to add an abstraction/refinement morphism to a rule going from left-hand side of a rule to the right-hand side or vice versa (see the drawing in the paragraph *Property preserving net model transformations*). The main advantage of this approach is the fact that the additional abstraction/refinement morphisms can be defined as preserving or reflecting certain properties. This means that certain important system properties may be preserved by transformations as defined below. The general theory of rules and net model transformations with additional refinement morphisms has been introduced in [20] in the general framework of high-level replacement systems.

System properties. Petri nets are an adequate specification technique for behavioral aspects of systems. So, the desired properties of the system to be specified usually concern the behavior of the model. These properties can be expressed in various ways, e.g., in terms of Petri nets (as liveness, boundedness etc.), in terms of logic (e.g., temporal logic, logic of actions etc.) in terms of relation to other models (e.g., bisimulation, correctness, etc.) and so on. Up to now we have focused on liveness of Petri nets and on safety properties in the sense of temporal logic. Liveness of nets means that no deadlock and even livelock of a net can occur, i.e., there always exists a firing sequence which enables any chosen transition from any reachable marking. A safety property is expressed by a logic formula stating facts about markings of a net. A formula is given in terms of numbers of tokens on places. For a place/transition net the static formula $2\mathbf{d} \wedge 3\mathbf{a}$ is true for a marking m where at least 2 tokens are present on the place $\mathbf{d}$ and at least 3 tokens on the place $\mathbf{a}$. The always operator $\square$ in a safety property $\square(2\mathbf{d} \wedge 3\mathbf{a})$ requires that the static formula $(2\mathbf{d} \wedge 3\mathbf{a})$ is true for all reachable markings from m.

Q-Rules. A pair (r, q) is a property preserving rule if $r = (L \xleftarrow{l} K \xrightarrow{r} R)$ is a rule with morphisms $l, r \in \mathcal{M}$ and with
 – either a property preserving morphism $q : L \dashrightarrow R$ s.t. $q \circ l = r$,
 – or a property respecting morphism $q : R \dashrightarrow L$ s.t. $q \circ r = l$.

According to the notion of property preserving morphisms and rules, we can now define property preserving transformations. The general idea is that the application of a property preserving rule leads to a net transformation that also preserves this property.

Property preserving net model transformations. Consider a property preserving rule $(r = (L \leftarrow K \rightarrow R), q)$ with $q : L \rightarrow R$ being a property preserving morphism ($q : R \rightarrow L$ being property respecting, respectively). Then the

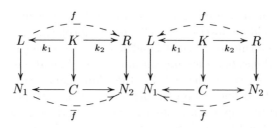

direct net model transformation $N_1 \overset{(r,q)}{\Longrightarrow} N_2$ is a property preserving transformation[a] with a property preserving (respecting, respectively) morphism $\overline{q} : N_1 \; - - - \rightarrow \; N_2$ ($\overline{q} : N_2 \; - - - \rightarrow \; N_1$, respectively). The graphical representation of such net model transformations is depicted above. Preservation of certain system properties during transformation saves the time necessary to verify the modified net.

Net class transformations. Net class transformations are based on the notion of a functor. Informally, the net class transformations assign to each net of a specified source net class an appropriate net of the target net class. The net class transformations preserve the relations between nets, which are represented by morphisms. Net class transformation can be applied to all nets of the source class. So, it is possible to say that the source net class is transformed to the target net class. The net class transformations are depicted in a usual functorial notation, i.e., $F : \mathbf{NC_1} \rightarrow \mathbf{NC_2}$ stands for the transformation from the net class $\mathbf{NC_1}$ to the net class $\mathbf{NC_2}$. The net class transformations are developed to be compatible with other techniques as horizontal structuring and net model transformations. This is important for transferring the results (as stepwise development) achieved within one net class to another net class.

6 Explanatory Example

In this section an explanatory example is shown, which presents the application of net transformations on a simple system. We will show the use of net model transformations first, followed by the discussion of property preservation. We will conclude the example by showing the use of net class transformations.

To illustrate the net transformations, a simple communication based system is constructed as interconnection of three components: a buffer with two

---

[a]Provided the morphisms satisfy certain assumptions.

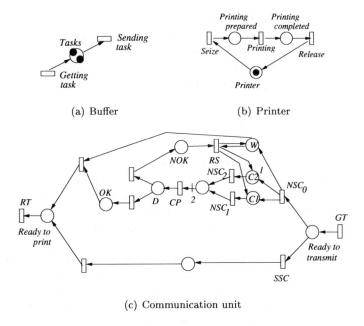

(a) Buffer   (b) Printer

(c) Communication unit

Figure 2. Components of the system

tasks, a printer, and a communication unit (network) between buffer and printer. The communication unit consists of a secure and a non-secure channel. All components are depicted in Figure 2. The buffer and the printer are modeled using elementary nets, the communication unit by a place/transition net (arc weights are used).

The behavior of the printer and the buffer are obvious from the figure. The communication unit serves a secure or a non-secure communication from the buffer to the printer.

This unit receives a task which has to be sent over the transition (**GT**). It can send the message forward through a secure channel (**SSC**) or via a non-secure one (**NSC$_0$, NSC$_1$, NSC$_2$**). On the non-secure channel the message may become corrupted. Therefore, when a non-secure channel is used, two copies (**C1, C2**) of the message are to be sent and a transmission subunit waits (**W**) for an acknowledgment. A receiving subunit in the other end receives both copies and compares them (**CP**). (We assume that a message cannot be lost during the transfer.) If both copies are the same, the **OK** acknowledgment is sent back to the transmission subunit and the communication will end. If the copies differ, then **NOK** acknowledgment is sent back to the transmission subunit and the transmission subunit resends (**RS**) the message again (in two copies). The two possible results of the comparison are modeled by a nondeterministic choice (conflict) in place **D**. The communication ends when a successful transfer is performed (**RT**).

6.1   Net Model Transformations

The net model transformations are used in the development process to build up the whole system from its components.

Thus, the three components of the system shown in Figure 2 are interconnected by the application of the rules shown in Figure 3. In a first step we apply the buffer-printer rule in Figure 3(a) to the buffer and printer components in Figure 2. The corresponding net model transformation is shown in Figure 3(a).

The rule buffer-printer is shown in the top row of Figure 3(a). It consists of a left-hand side net L, a right-hand side net R, and an interface net I. The transformation from net N_1 to net N_2 via this rule is constructed in two steps. In the first step we apply L to N_1 and remove all items of L in N_1 which do not belong to the interface I. It leads to the intermediate net N_0. In the second step we glue together nets N_0 and R via the interface I leading to the net N_2. It is important to note that also N_1 can be considered as a result of a gluing construction, namely the gluing of N_0 and L along I such that the transformation in Figure 3(a) consists of two gluing constructions shown in diagrams (1) and (2), respectively, according to the general construction of net model transformations (see [20]).

In a similar way we can apply the two other rules in Figures 3(b),(c) to the net N_2 combined with the communication unit net in Figure 2 leading to the net in Figure 4.

Finally, we can apply the rule in Figure 5 modeling the mutual exclusion between the secure and the non-secure channel leading to the final model in Figure 6.

One wants to show suitable safety properties for the final model in Figure 6 from corresponding properties of the basic components in Figure 2 and the fact that the net model transformations from the basic components to the final model in Figure 6 considered above are safety properties preserving.

In our example the system has the safety property

$$\Box((\mathbf{NOK} \vee \mathbf{OK}) \implies \mathbf{W})$$

for the communication unit in Figure 2(c). This property expresses a fact that,

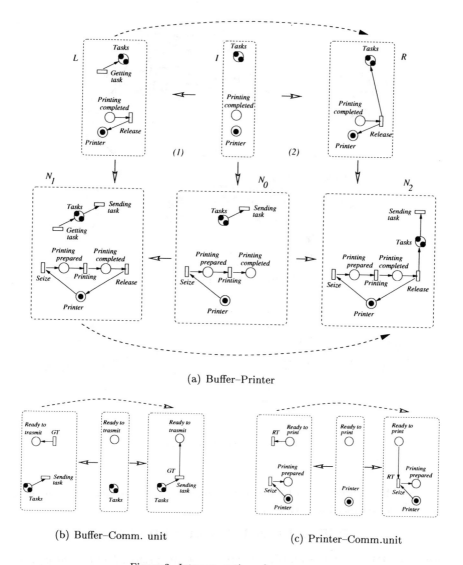

(a) Buffer–Printer

(b) Buffer–Comm. unit

(c) Printer–Comm.unit

Figure 3. Interconnection of components

independently of the result **NOK** or **OK** of the comparison of the two copies **C1** and **C2** modeled by nondeterministic choice in place **C**, the transmission subunit waits for acknowledgment in place **W**.

78

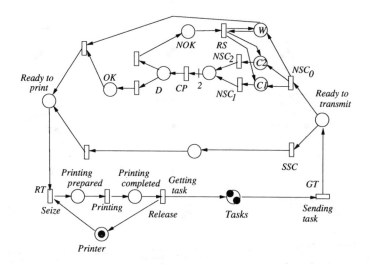

Figure 4. Simple tasks' model

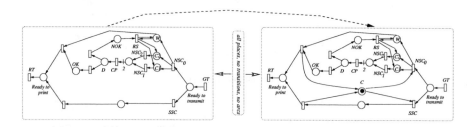

Figure 5. Modeling exclusivity

For the printer net in Figure 2 we have the safety property that at most one job is processed at a time, i.e.,

$$\Box((\mathbf{P} \text{ xor } \mathbf{PP} \text{ xor } \mathbf{PC}) \wedge \neg(\mathbf{P} \wedge \mathbf{PP} \wedge \mathbf{PC})),$$

where **P**, **PP** and **PC** stand for *Printer*, *Printing prepared* and *Printing completed*, respectively and xor for exclusive or operator.

Surely, we would like to keep these safety properties valid during net model transformation. There are two classes of rules available for the application developer which preserve safety properties for P/T Petri nets, namely transition gluing and place preserving rules, see [22].

The main result concerning safety property preserving net model trans-

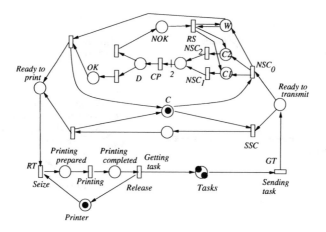

Figure 6. Final model

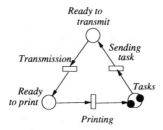

Figure 7. Simple model of printing tasks

formations depicted in [22] states that for each net model transformation sequence $N_1 \Longrightarrow^* N_2$ via safety property preserving rules, where N_1 satisfies a safety property $\Box\varphi$, we can conclude that net N_2 satisfies a corresponding translated safety property $\mathcal{T}(\Box\varphi)$. In our small case study the rules shown in Figure 3 are *transition gluing* rules and the rule in Figure 5 is *place preserving*. This implies that the two safety properties for the communication unit and the printer considered above are also true in the final model in Figure 6. Let us recall that a net is called live if for each reachable marking m and each transition t there is some other marking m' reachable from m such that t is enabled under m'. We want to show via liveness preserving net model transformations that the final model in Figure 6 is live (see the main results concerning liveness preserving transformations in [11,27]). For this purpose we consider the simple model of printing tasks in Figure 7, where it is easy to

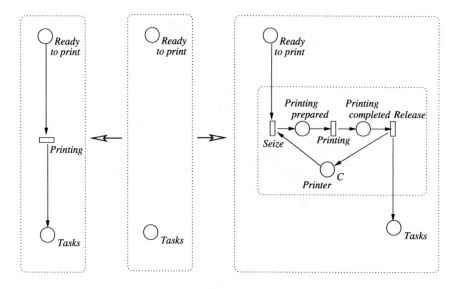

(a) Printing-refinement

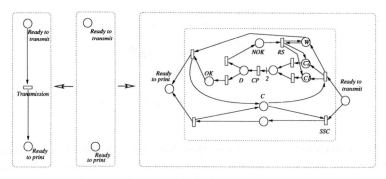

(b) Transmission-refinement

Figure 8. Liveness preserving transition refinement

check directly that this net is live. The printing-refinement and transmission-refinement rules in Figure 8 are liveness preserving rules and can be applied to the net in Figure 7 leading to the final model in Figure 6. Since the net in Figure 7 is live and the rules liveness preserving, the final model is live as well.

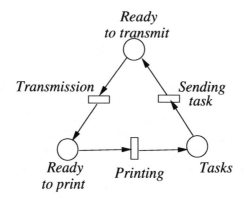

Figure 9. Simple elementary net EN_1

6.2 Net Class Transformations

Net class transformations can be used to begin the modeling in an abstract class with simple nets and to switch to a more expressive class in later development steps. Moreover, it is important for the development process, that net class transformations are compatible with net model transformations and with the horizontal structuring techniques union and fusion.

In the following we present a development process to derive an algebraic high-level net AHL_4 in Figure 11, via the place/transition net PT_3 in Figure 6 (without marking) from the simple elementary net EN_1 in Figure 9 using net model transformations from the previous section and net class transformations $Weight$: $\mathbf{EN} \to \mathbf{PT}$ and $Data$: $\mathbf{PT} \to \mathbf{AHL}$ as shown in Figure 12. In this section we only consider nets without an initial marking. The initial marking is dealt similarly. We can start the modeling of our example with the elementary net EN_1 in Figure 9. Then we can use an elementary net version $printref_{EN}$ of the printing-refinement as in Figure 8(a) to elaborate the modeling of the printer. This results is the elementary net EN_2 in Figure 10.

Elementary nets are similar to place/transition nets but do not involve arc weights in the description of the net. To use the transmission-refinement $transref_{PT}$ as well, we need to transform the model to the class of place/transition nets, because the refinement adds an arc with weight 2. The net class transformation $Weight$ assigns the weight 1 to each arc leading to place/transition nets $PT_1 = Weight(EN_1)$ and $PT_2 = Weight(EN_2)$ and a net model transformation $printref_{PT}$ between them. After the application of the transmission-refinement $transref_{PT}$ we get the same model PT_3 as in

82

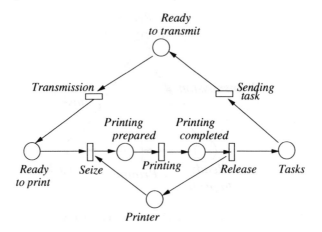

Figure 10. Refinement of the printer EN_1

Figure 6 without marking.

In order to be able to distinguish between different tasks, we first transform our model to the class of algebraic high level nets. We obtain algebraic high level nets $AHL_1 = Data(PT_1)$, $AHL_2 = Data(PT_2)$ and $AHL_3 = Data(PT_3)$, where the net class transformation $Data\colon \textbf{PT} \rightarrow \textbf{AHL}$ adds a trivial data type specification and algebra (see [12,26]). The model transformations $printref_{PT}$ and $transref_{PT}$ can be transformed as well yielding transformations $printref_{AHL}$ and $transref_{AHL}$ in Figure 12.

Then we can further refine the net AHL_3 by an AHL net model transformation $specref_{AHL}$, which changes the arc inscriptions of AHL_3 to the ones of AHL_4 given in Figure 11 and adds the following specification with a suitable algebra (for the algebra see [28]).

In the net AHL_4 we are able to model the comparison of the two tasks sent through the insecure channel by inscribing the transition CP with the equation

$$r = \text{if } equ(t', t'') \text{ then } ok(t') \text{ else } nok.$$

For simplicity we assume that our non-secure channel either transmits the duplicated task in a correct way (ok-case, $t' = t'' = t$) or t' and t'' are modifications of t with $t' \neq t''$ (nok-case). In the second case the transmission is repeated with the old value t of the task.

The whole development process is depicted in Figure 12, where horizontal steps are net model transformations and vertical steps are net class transfor-

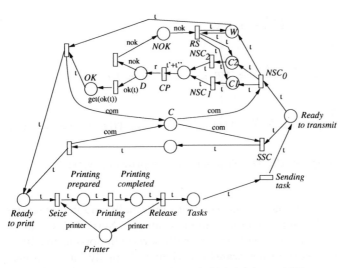

Figure 11. Final algebraic high level net AHL_4

BOOL+

sorts:	Printer, Task, Comm, Result
opns:	printer: $\rightarrow$ Printer
	com: $\rightarrow$ Comm
	$task_1$:$\rightarrow$ Task
	$task_2$:$\rightarrow$ Task
	equ: Task Task $\rightarrow$ Bool
	ok: Task $\rightarrow$ Result
	nok: $\rightarrow$ Result
	get: Result $\rightarrow$ Task
vars:	t: Task, r: Result
eqns:	get(ok(t))=t
	equ(t,t)=true
	equ(t,t$'$)=false $\forall t' \neq$ t

mations. The used net class transformations are elaborated formally in [12], [26], and [28].

7 Conclusion

We conclude with several remarks to the area of net transformations.

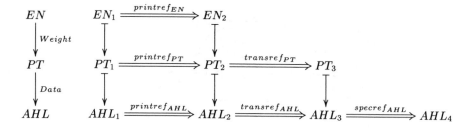

Figure 12. Development of the printing system

We have described net transformations informally and demonstrated the applicability of this approach on a simple example. Nevertheless, the theory of net transformations is a wide theory with several important results.

The formal theory of net transformations is formally based on category theory. It presents net transformations either as rule-based modification of nets (net model transformations) or as functors between categories of nets (net class transformations). This theory offers many important results for Petri net experts, e.g., several compatibility results, preservation of structural and system's properties.

The complexity of the theory can be kept hidden in applications. The concept of transformations can be turn to algorithms easily. With tool support the user-driven application of net transformations would supply a methodology for modeling Petri net based systems by net transformations. Thus, net transformations are of interest for system designers as well.

There are several open questions in this area. The most important task is the development of a Petri net tool supporting the given transformations fully.

References

1. J. Adamek, H. Herrlich, and G. Strecker. *Abstract and Concrete Categories.* Series in Pure and Applied Mathematics. John Wiley and Sons, 1990.
2. A. Borusan. A Petri Net Based Modelling Technology for Manufacturing System Engineering. In *Proceedings Cars And FOF'93 International Conference on CAD, CAM, Robotics and Factories of the Future*, pages 41–50, New Jersey, USA, 1993.
3. A. Borusan. Modelling and Design of Complex Systems with Petri Nets.

In E. Schnieder, editor, *Entwurf komplexer Automatisierungssysteme*, pages 237–247. TU Brauschweig, June 1995.

4. K.R. Damavandi. Eine Methodenkette zur integrierten Software-Entwicklung: Von der Problemstellung zum Programmsystem mit Petrinetze. Technical Report N91–15769, Technische Universität Berlin, Fachbereich 20, Informatik — Washington, DC, USA: National Aeronautics and Space Administration (/3/XAD, ETN–91–98497), 1990. Dissertation.

5. W. Deiters and V. Gruhn. Software Process Model Analysis Based on FUNSOFT Nets. *Mathematical Modelling and Simulation*, 8, May 1991.

6. DFG-Forschergruppe PETRI NET TECHNOLOGY. Initial realization of the »Petri Net Baukasten«. Informatik-Berichte 129, Humboldt-Universität zu Berlin, October 1999.

7. H. Ehrig. Introduction to the Algebraic Theory of Graph Grammars. In V. Claus, H. Ehrig, and G. Rozenberg, editors, *1st Graph Grammar Workshop, Lecture Notes in Computer Science 73*, pages 1–69. Springer Verlag, 1979.

8. H. Ehrig, M. Gajewsky, and F. Parisi-Presicce. *High-Level Replacement Systems with Applications to Algebraic Specifications and Petri Nets*, chapter 6, pages 341–400. Number 3: Concurrency, Parallelism, and Distribution in Handbook of Graph Grammars and Computing by Graph Transformations. World Scientific, 1999.

9. H. Ehrig, A. Habel, H.-J. Kreowski, and F. Parisi-Presicce. From Graph Grammars to High Level Replacement Systems. In *4th Int. Workshop on Graph Grammars and their Application to Computer Science, LNCS 532*, pages 269–291. Springer Verlag, 1991.

10. M. Gajewsky. The Expert View of the Petri Net Baukasten. [30], pages 243–265.

11. M. Gajewsky, J. Padberg, and M. Urbášek. Rule-Based Refinement for Place/Transition Systems: Preserving Liveness-Properties. Technical Report 2001-8, Technical University of Berlin, 2001.

12. M. Gajewsky and F. Parisi-Presicce. Formal Transformations of Petri Nets. Technical Report 2000-12, Technical University Berlin, 2000.

13. M. Gajewsky and F. Parisi-Presicce. On Compatibility of Model and Class Transformations. In M. Cerioli and G. Reggio, editors, *15th International Workshop on Algebraic Development Techniques and General Workshop of the CoFI WG*, volume 2267 of *Lecture Notes in Computer Science*, pages 109–27. Springer Verlag, 2001.

14. A. Janhsen, K. Lemmer, B. Ptok, and E. Schnieder. Formal Specifications of the European Train Control System. In *IFAC Transportation*

    Systems, 8th Symposium on Transportation Systems, 1997.

15. K. Jensen. *Coloured Petri Nets - Basic Concepts, Analysis Methods and Practical Use*, volume 3: Practical Use. Springer Verlag, EATCS Monographs in Theoretical Computer Science edition, 1997.

16. S. Lembke. Anwendungsentwicklung in der LION-Entwicklungsumgebung (LEU). In H. Ehrig, W. Reisig, and H. Weber, editors, *Kick-Off-Workshop der DFG-Forschergruppe Petrinetz-Technologie*, number 73 in Informatik-Berichte der Humboldt-Universität zu Berlin, pages 72–81, July 1996.

17. A. Martens. Software-Engineering von Workflow-Applikationen mit Petrinetzen. Diplomarbeit, Humboldt-Universität zu Berlin, Institut für Informatik, 1997.

18. S. Müller. *Ablaufmodellierung als Analyse-, Entwurfs- und Realisierungsmethodik im Softwareentwicklungsprozeß*. Reihe Wirtschaftsinformatik, Band 15. Verlag Josef Eul, Bergisch Gladbach, Köln, 1995.

19. A. Oberweis. *Modellierung und Ausführung von Workflows mit Petri-Netzen*. Teubner-Reihe Wirtschaftsinformatik. B.G. Teubner Verlagsgesellschaft, Stuttgart Leipzig, 1996.

20. J. Padberg. *Abstract Petri Nets: A Uniform Approach and Rule-Based Refinement*. PhD thesis, Technical University Berlin, 1996. Shaker Verlag.

21. J. Padberg. Categorical Approach to Horizontal Structuring and Refinement of High-Level Replacement Systems. *Applied Categorical Structures*, 7(4):371–403, December 1999.

22. J. Padberg, M. Gajewsky, and C. Ermel. Rule-Based Refinement of High-Level Nets Preserving Safety Properties. In E. Astesiano, editor, *Fundamental Approaches to Software Engineering*, pages 221–238. Springer Verlag, Lecture Notes in Computer Science 1382, 1998.

23. C.A. Petri. *Kommunikation mit Automaten*. PhD thesis, Schriften des Institutes für Instrumentelle Mathematik, Bonn, 1962.

24. W. Reisig. *Petri Nets*, volume 4 of *EATCS Monographs on Theoretical Computer Science*. Springer Verlag, 1985.

25. E. Schnieder, editor. *Methoden der Automatisierung: Beschreibungsmittel, Modellkonzepte und Werkzeuge für Automatisierungssysteme*. Studium Technik. Vieweg, 1999.

26. R. Tavakoli. Transformation of Open and Algebraic High-Level Petri Net Classes. Technical Report 2002-24, Technical University of Berlin, 2002.

27. M. Urbášek. New Safety Property and Liveness Preserving Morphisms of P/T Systems. Technical Report 2002-14, Technical University Berlin, 2002.

28. M. Urbášek. *Categorical Net Transformations for Petri Net Technology.* PhD thesis, Technical University Berlin, to appear in 2003.
29. M. Urbášek. Modeling Petri Net Based Systems by Net Transformations: New Developments. In R. Bardohl and H. Ehrig, editors, *Electronic Notes in Theoretical Computer Science*, Vol. 82, No. 7, Elsevier, 2003.
30. H. Weber, H. Ehrig, and W. Reisig, editors. *Int. Colloquium on Petri Net Technologies for Modelling Communication Based Systems, Part II: The »Petri Net Baukasten«.* Fraunhofer Gesellschaft ISST, October 1999.
31. H. Weber, H. Ehrig, and W. Reisig, editors. *2nd Int. Colloquium on Petri Net Technologies for Modelling Communication Based Systems*, Berlin, Germany, Sept. 2001. Researcher Group Petri Net Technology, Fraunhofer Gesellschaft ISST.

ON THE RELEVANCE OF HIGH-LEVEL NET PROCESSES

HARTMUT EHRIG

Technical University of Berlin
Computer Science Department
Sekr. FR 6-1, Franklinstrasse 28729
D-10587 Berlin, Germany
E-mail: `ehrig@cs.tu-berlin.de`

1 General Motivation

The notion of nondeterministic and deterministic processes based on occurrence nets is an essential concept to capture the non-sequential truly concurrent behavior of Petri nets. This concept is well-known for elementary nets and safe place-transition nets and has been generalized to other low-level net classes. Let us call a net class low-level if the firing is based on black tokens only, while a high-level net class has colored tokens which are defined as data elements of a suitable data type. The concept of high-level nets is certainly very useful to model more complex communication based systems, because it allows to use an adequate balance between data type and net features. This avoids to represent even basic data types by nets as it is necessary in the case of low-level nets. For high-level nets, however, the standard technique to define processes is to consider them as processes of the low-level net $Flat(N)$ which is obtained from N via the well-known flattening construction. This low-level notion of processes for high-level nets, however, is not really adequate, because the high-level structure using data types is completely lost. For this reason we have introduced in our paper [1] a new notion of high-level net processes for high-level nets which captures the high-level structure. The key notion is a high-level occurrence net K, which generalizes the well-known notion of occurrence nets from low-level to high-level nets.

It is important to note that the flattening of high-level occurrence nets and processes in general does not lead to low-level occurrence nets and processes. This effect is due to so called "assignment conflicts" which can occur in high-level occurrence nets. This means that different assignments for the same transitions may lead to forward or backward conflicts in the flattening. In [1] we have given a syntactical characterization of such assignment conflicts. In fact, it would be possible to restrict the notion of high-level processes to those where the corresponding high-level occurrence net has no assignment conflicts. Another important difference between low-level and high-level occurrence nets and processes is the fact that there is a unique choice for the initial marking of a low-level occurrence net: this is the marking of all input places with one black token each.

In the high-level case it does not make any sense to consider only one initial marking of the input places, but a set of initial markings. This corresponds to a set of possible input data for a procedure in a high-level programming language. Similar to a procedure which in general leads only to a partial function, we cannot expect that a high-level process terminates for all initial markings. Even in the case of a finite high-level occurrence net we may have deadlocks, i.e., we may have a firing sequence which cannot be extended to a complete firing sequence. Here we call a firing sequence of an occurrence net complete if each transition is fired exactly once.

Of course, it is an interesting problem to analyse under which conditions there is a complete firing sequence $s : init \xrightarrow{*} \bullet$ for a given initial marking. Similarly, it is interesting to know under which conditions we have deadlock-freeness and uniqueness of the final marking on the output places.

In the case of low-level occurrence nets all of these problems have an easy solution. In the next section we summarize these results and give an outline of how to solve these and related problems in the high-level case. A more detailed presentation will be given in our technical report [2].

In the low-level case the notion of processes has been extended already from Petri nets to graph transformation system [3]. Hence our notion of high-level net processes is also relevant in view of graph transformations in the high-level case, i.e., attributed graph transformation systems.

2 From Low-Level to High-Level Net Processes

For low-level Petri nets the notion of nondeterministic and deterministic processes is an essential concept to capture their non-sequential truly concurrent behavior. Especially in the case of elementary net systems and safe place/transition nets this has been worked out in a fully satisfactory way by Rozenberg, Winskel, Nielsen, Goltz, Reisig, Degano, Meseguer, Montanari and other authors [4,5,6,7,8,9,10,11] leading to different notions of deterministic and nondeterministic processes and to a truly concurrent semantics of Petri nets in terms of prime algebraic domains and event structures.

For finite (deterministic) low-level processes the following behavior is well-known or at least folklore. Given the initial marking consisting of all input places of an occurrence net, there is at least one *complete firing sequence*, where each transition fires exactly once and the final marking consists exactly of all output places. Moreover, the occurrence net is concurrently enabled.

This means that for each total order of the transitions which is compatible with the causal order of the occurrence net, there is exactly one such complete firing sequence. In addition, also each place of the occurrence net is visited by each complete firing sequence exactly once and each incomplete firing sequence can be extended to a complete firing sequence (deadlock-freeness). Similar properties are valid for infinite occurrence nets and processes, provided that the set of transitions is countably infinite. Of course, such infinite complete firing sequence do not have a final marking which is equal to all output places, but the output places are approximated by the infinite sequence of markings.

The main challenge is now to find out which properties for the behavior of low-level occurrence nets are still valid in the high-level case, or can be obtained under suitable additional assumptions.

In our paper [1] we have defined high-level processes (AHL-processes) for algebraic high-level nets (AHL-nets) and the flattening of AHL-nets as well as AHL-processes already. We have pointed out that due to so called "assignment conflicts" the flattening of an AHL-process is in general not a low-level process.

Moreover, there is no canonical initial marking for AHL-occurrence nets, because in general there are different meaningful markings of the input places. For this reason we study marked AHL-occurrence nets $(K, INIT)$, where K is an AHL-occurrence net and $INIT$ is a set of markings of the input places of K. We say that K is *enabled* for $init \in INIT$ if there is a complete firing sequence $s : init \xrightarrow{*} \bullet$, where completeness means that each transition in K is fired exactly once. In fact, it is an important problem to analyse under which conditions K is enabled for some $init \in INIT$, similar to the problem whether a procedure is well-defined for given input data.

We were able to show in [2] that K is enabled for $init \in INIT$ if and only if there is an *instantiation* L of $(K, init)$. An *instantiation* L of $(K, init)$ is a low-level occurrence net $L \subseteq Flat(K)$ where the net structures of L and K are equal and $init$ is the set of all input places of L. In general, there may be none, one or several instantiations L for $(K, init)$, but we are able to give sufficient conditions for existence and uniqueness.

The next interesting question is which properties for the behavior of low-level occurrence nets are still valid in the high-level case, provided that $(K, init)$ is at least enabled. In fact, we are able to show in this case that $(K, init)$ is concurrently enabled, each complete firing sequence $s : init \xrightarrow{*} \bullet$ visits each place and each transition of K exactly once, and terminates for finite K with a final marking on the output places of K, while for countably infinite K the final marking of the output places is approximated. But in general the final marking is not uniquely defined for each $init \in INIT$ and we may have deadlocks. These problems, however, can be avoided if the AHL-occurrence net K has *functional assignments*, i.e., even for different consistent assignments of the variables for a transition the data on the output places of the transition are functional dependent on the data of the input places. Moreover, we can ensure that $(K, init)$ is enabled and deadlock-free if K has *full assignments*, i.e., for each choice of data on the input places of a transition there is at least one consistent assignment matching this choice of data.

Finally let us analyse the relationship between the flattening $Flat(K)$ of an AHL-occurrence net and all the instantiations L of $(K, init)$ for $init \in INIT$. In general, $Flat(K)$ may contain places and transitions which do not belong to an instantiation. But if $(K, INIT)$ is *flat-reachable*, i.e., each item of $Flat(K)$ is visited by at least one complete firing sequence $s : init \xrightarrow{*} \bullet$ with $init \in INIT$, then $Flat(K)$ can be represented by the union of all instantiations of $(K, INIT)$ and vice versa. In general, however, different instantiations are not disjoint, but overlap with each other. In spite of this, we are able to characterize under which conditions $Flat(K)$ can be represented as disjoint union of all instantiations of $(K, INIT)$, where for each $init \in INIT$ there is a unique instantiation $L(init)$ for $(K, init)$ in [2]. We show that these conditions are satisfied for the AHL-occurrence net of a high-level process for the dining philosophers. On the other hand, there are also meaningful cases of high-level processes, where the corresponding AHL-occurrence net K has assignment conflicts and $Flat(K)$ is not the union of all instantiations of $(K, INIT)$. Finally let us point out that several possible extensions of high-level processes are discussed in section 4 of our paper [1].

References

1. H. Ehrig, K. Hoffmann, J. Padberg, P. Baldan, and R. Heckel. High-Level Net Processes. In W. Brauer, H. Ehrig, J. Karhumäki, and A. Salomaa, editors, *Formal and Natural Computing*, LNCS 2300, pages 191–219. Springer, 2002.
2. H. Ehrig. *Behaviour and Instantiation of High-Level Net Processes. Full Technical Version*. Technical Report 2003-01, Technical University of Berlin, 2003. To appear.
3. A. Corradini, U. Montanari, and F. Rossi. Graph Processes. Special Issue of *Fundamenta Informaticae*, 26(3,4):241–266, 1996.
4. M. Nielsen, G. Plotkin, and G. Winskel. Petri Nets, Event Structures and Domains, Part 1. *Theoretical Computer Science*, 13:85–108, 1981.
5. U. Goltz and W. Reisig. The Non-Sequential Behaviour of Petri Nets. *Information and Computation*, volume 57, pages 125–147. Academic

Press, 1983.

6. G. Rozenberg. Behaviour of Elementary Net Systems. In W. Brauer, W. Reisig, and G. Rozenberg, editors, *Advances in Petri Nets 1986*, pages 60–94. Springer Verlag Berlin, LNCS 254, 1987.

7. G. Winskel. Petri Nets, Algebras, Morphisms, and Compositionality. *Information and Computation*, 72:197–238, 1987.

8. G. Winskel. Event Structures. In W. Brauer, W. Reisig, and G. Rozenberg, editors, *Petri Nets: Applications and Relationships to Other Models of Concurrency*, pages 324 – 392. Springer, LNCS 255, 1988.

9. P. Degano, J. Meseguer, and U. Montanari. Axiomatizing Net Computations and Processes. In *Proc. of LICS'89*, pages 175–185, 1989.

10. J. Engelfriet. Branching Processes of Petri Nets. *Acta Informatica*, 28:575–591, 1991.

11. J. Meseguer, U. Montanari, and V. Sassone. On the Semantics of Place/Transition Petri Nets. *Mathematical Structures in Computer Science*, 7:359–397, 1997.

2
LOGIC IN COMPUTER SCIENCE
Yuri GUREVICH

CONTENTS

Introductory Remarks
A New Zero-One Law and Strong Extension Axioms
    (by A. Blass and Y. Gurevich)
Tree-Decompositions and the Model-Checking Problem
    (by J. Flum)
Is Randomness "Native" to Computer Science?
    (by M. Ferbus-Zanda and S. Grigorieff)
How to Find a Coin: Propositional Program Logics Made Easy
    (by N.V. Shilov and K. Yi)
Algorithms vs. Machines (by A. Blass and Y. Gurevich)
Pairwise Testing (by A. Blass and Y. Gurevich)
Newman's Lemma – A Case Study in Proof Automation
    and Geometric Logic (by M. Bezem and T. Coquand)
Algorithms: A Quest for Absolute Definitions
    (by A. Blass and Y. Gurevich)

Yuri Gurevich

Microsoft Research
One Microsoft Way
Redmond, WA 98052, USA
E-mail: gurevich@microsoft.com

INTRODUCTORY REMARKS

Mathematical logic emerged in the early part of the 20th century as an effective tool for dealing with foundational problems in mathematics. I studied logic in the 1960s. By that time, the foundational problems of mathematics had been more or less settled. This is not to say that logic had become boring. Set theory was undergoing rapid changes as a result of the recent discovery of the forcing method. In general, logic was growing into a respected mathematical discipline. Still, I was envious of those who lived in the right time to work on the foundational problems.

In the early 1980s, I moved to computer science. It dawned on me that computer science was full of open foundational problems and that logic was more relevant than ever. What is an algorithm? Which computations are feasible? Since databases should be independent of their implementations, what is the right notion of a database? What does concurrent computation really mean? What is the right notion of a software specification? And so on and so forth. I was surprised to see the gap between the logic literature and the logic needs of the computer industry. For example, the industry used hastily designed many-valued logics for commercial logic-circuit simulators. A good logician could come up with cleaner logics for the same purposes, with better algebraic properties which would simplify various computations. However, the experts in many-valued logics, known to me, had never heard about commercial logic-circuit simulators.

In the meantime, some major successes have been achieved. Model checking is one of the success stories. Still, most of the foundational problems of computer science are still wide open, and the gap still exists. I see the Logic in Computer Science column as a natural place to address the foundational problems and to bridge the gap. However, one never knows what logic advances will play an important role in future. Besides, logic is such fun. So, this column is open to all areas of logic in computer science, without any exception whatsoever.

This chapter is composed of articles published in the column on Logic in Computer Science in *The Bulletin of the European Association for Theoretical Computer Science* from October 2000 through October 2003. The articles appear in the order of their publication dates.

I am thankful to past contributors of the column, and new contributors are most welcome.

Yuri Gurevich

A NEW ZERO-ONE LAW AND STRONG EXTENSION AXIOMS

ANDREAS BLASS

Mathematics, University of Michigan
Ann Arbor, MI 48109-1109, USA

YURI GUREVICH

Microsoft Research
One Microsoft Way
Redmond, WA 98052, USA
E-mail: `gurevich@microsoft.com`

One of the previous articles in this column was devoted to the zero-one laws for a number of logics playing prominent role in finite model theory: first-order logic FO, the extension FO+LFP of first-order logic with the least fixed-point operator, and the infinitary logic $L^\omega_{\infty,\omega}$. Recently Shelah proved a new, powerful, and surprising zero-one law. His proof uses so-called strong extension axioms. Here we formulate Shelah's zero-one law and prove a few facts about these axioms. In the process we give a simple proof for a "large deviation" inequality à la Chernoff.

1 Shelah's Zero-One Law

Quisani: What are you doing, guys?

Author: We[a] are proving a zero-one law which is due to Shelah.

Q: Didn't Shelah prove the law?

A: Oh yes, he proved it all right, and even wrote it down [14].

Q: So what is the problem? Can't you read his proof?

A: Reading Shelah's proofs may be research in its own right. His great mathematical talent is not matched by his talent of exposition.

Q: I suspect that you don't limit yourself to reproving Shelah's theorem.

A: We have proved some related results [1].

Q: Tell me about this zero-one law which is exciting enough to divert your attention from abstract state machines.

---

[a]The record of the conversation was simplified by blending the two authors into one who prefers "we" to "I".

99

A: Actually the law is related to ASMs. It is about the BGS model of computation [3] which is based on ASMs. The model was defined with the intention of modeling computation with arbitrary finite relational structures as inputs, with essentially arbitrary data types, with parallelism, but without arbitrary choices.

Q: What arbitrary choices?

A: Here's an example of what we mean. Recall the Bipartite Matching Problem: Given a relation A between some number of boys and the same number of girls, find a subset of A that constitutes a one-to-one correspondence between the boys and the girls. The problem is solvable in polynomial time in the usual computation models where the input bipartite graph is given by means of some presentation such as the adjacency matrix; see for example the book [9]. Having such a presentation, the algorithm may start with the first boy. A BGS algorithm may be unable do that. The reason is that, contrary to the usual computation models, the bipartite graph may be given directly and not via some representation. In particular there may be no notion of "first." And there may be no way to choose an arbitrary boy.

Q: With parallelism, the lack of a choice mechanism makes no difference. An algorithm can produce all possible linear orderings of its input. If the input has size n, you have $n!$ independent subcomputations, each using one of the orderings to make whatever choices are needed. I guess the output is supposed to depend only on the isomorphism type of the input. So all these computations produce the same output.

A: That's right, if you have unlimited resources. We require the total computation time (summed over all parallel subprocesses) to be polynomially bounded. So there isn't time to construct all the linear orderings. The inability to make arbitrary choices really matters. According to [3], choiceless polynomial time, ČPTime, the complexity class defined by BGS programs subject to a polynomial time bound, does not contain the Bipartite Matching Problem. In fact, ČPTime does not contain even the parity problem: Given a set, determine whether its cardinality is even. The proofs build on symmetry considerations, i.e., on automorphisms of the input structure.

Subsequently, Shelah [14] proved a zero-one law for ČPTime properties of graphs and similar structures. Notice a crucial difference from the earlier results in [3]: Almost all finite graphs have no non-trivial automorphisms, so symmetry considerations cannot be applied to them. Shelah's proof therefore depends on a more subtle concept of partial symmetry.

Q: We spoke once about zero-one laws [10]. I remember that one distinguishes, at least in principle, between labeled and unlabeled structures. In the case of labeled structures, one assumes that the base set of an n-element structure is the set $\{1, 2, \ldots, n\}$. The labels $1, \ldots, n$ help us in counting but they do not belong to the vocabulary of the structure. More importantly, a zero-one law requires a probability distribution on structures.

A: For simplicity, let us restrict our attention to labeled structures and the uniform probability distribution. Define the *probability* of a class (assumed closed under graph isomorphisms) of n-vertex graphs by considering all graphs with vertex set $\{1, 2, \ldots, n\}$ to be equally probable. This probability measure can also be defined by saying that, for each potential edge, i.e., each set of two distinct vertices, we flip a fair coin to decide whether to include the edge in our graph. It is presumed that the coin flips are independent.

The *asymptotic probability* of a class of graphs is defined as the limit, as $n \to \infty$, of the probability of its intersection with the class of n-vertex graphs with vertex set $\{1, 2, \ldots, n\}$. We sometimes refer to the probability of a property of graphs, meaning the probability of the class of graphs that have that property. In general, a zero-one law says that definable classes have asymptotic probability 0 or 1, but, as we shall see, some care is needed in formulating the zero-one law for $\tilde{C}$PTime.

Q: Explain $\tilde{C}$PTime.

A: To this end, we need to describe the BGS model of computation [3]. It is a version of the abstract state machine (ASM) paradigm [11]. The input to a computation is an arbitrary finite relational structure. For simplicity, let us restrict attention to the case when the input is an undirected, loopless graph $\langle V, A \rangle$ where V is the set of vertices and A is the adjacency relation. A state of the computation is a structure whose base set is the set $\mathrm{HF}(V)$ which consists of the set V together with all hereditarily finite sets over it. $\mathrm{HF}(V)$ is the smallest set containing all vertices in V (which are assumed to be atoms, not sets) and all finite subsets of itself. In other words, it is the union of the sets $\mathcal{P}_n(V)$ defined inductively by

$$\mathcal{P}_0(V) = V,$$
$$\mathcal{P}_{n+1}(V) = V \cup \mathcal{P}_{\mathrm{fin}}(\mathcal{P}_n(V)),$$

where $\mathcal{P}_{\mathrm{fin}}(X)$ means the set of all finite subsets of X.

The structure has the adjacency relation A, some set-theoretical apparatus (for example the membership relation $\in$), and some dynamic functions. The computation proceeds in stages, always modifying the dynamic functions in accordance with the program of the computation. The dynamic functions are initially constant with value $\emptyset$ and they change at only finitely many arguments at each step. So, although HF(V) is infinite, only a finite part of it is involved in the computation at any stage. The computation ends when and if a specific dynamic 0-ary function Halt acquires the value $\mathtt{true} = \{0\}$, and the result of the computation is then the value of another dynamic 0-ary function Output.

Q: Why $\mathtt{true} = \{0\}$?

A: We have adopted the convention that the truth values are identified with the first two von Neumann ordinals, $\mathtt{false} = 0 = \emptyset$ and $\mathtt{true} = 1 = \{0\}$. Recall that the finite von Neumann ordinals represent the natural numbers by identifying n with the set $\{0, 1, \ldots, n-1\}$.

This model was used to define choiceless polynomial time $\tilde{C}$PTime by requiring a computation to take only polynomially many (relative to the size of the input structure $\langle V, A \rangle$) steps and to have only polynomially many active elements.

Q: Which elements are active?

A: Roughly speaking, an element of HF(V) is active if it participates in the updating of some dynamic function at some stage.

Further, Output was restricted to have Boolean values, so the result of a computation could only be true, or false, or undecided.

Q: I guess the "undecided" situation arises if the computation exhausts the allowed number of steps or the allowed number of active elements without Halt becoming $\mathtt{true}$.

A: Precisely. We shall use the phrase *polynomial time BGS program* to refer to a BGS program, with Boolean Output, together with polynomial bounds on the number of steps and the number of active elements.

Two classes $\mathcal{K}_0$ and $\mathcal{K}_1$ of graphs are $\tilde{C}$PTime-*separable* if there is a polynomial time BGS program Π such that, for all input structures from $\mathcal{K}_0$ (resp. $\mathcal{K}_1$), Π halts with output $\mathtt{false}$ (resp. $\mathtt{true}$) without exceeding the polynomial bounds. It doesn't matter what Π does when the input is in neither $\mathcal{K}_0$ nor $\mathcal{K}_1$.

Theorem 1.1 (Shelah's Zero-One Law) *If $\mathcal{K}_0$ and $\mathcal{K}_1$ are $\tilde{C}$PTime-separable classes of undirected graphs, then at least one of $\mathcal{K}_0$ and $\mathcal{K}_1$ has asymptotic probability zero.*

An equivalent formulation of this is that, for any given polynomial time BGS program, either almost all graphs produce output true or undecided or else almost all graphs produce output false or undecided.

Q: Is it true that either almost all graphs produce true, or almost all produce false, or almost all produce undecided?

A: No, we can give you a counterexample, but this would require a more thorough review of the definition of BGS programs.

The theorem was, however, strengthened considerably in another direction in [14]. It turns out that the number of steps in a halting computation is almost independent of the input.

Theorem 1.2 *Let a BGS program* Π *with Boolean output and a polynomial bound for the number of active elements be given. There exist a number* m, *an output value* v, *and a class* C *of undirected graphs, such that* C *has asymptotic probability one and such that, for each* $\langle V, A \rangle \in C$, *either*

- Π *on input* $\langle V, A \rangle$ *halts after exactly* m *steps with output value* v *and without exceeding the given bound on active elements, or*

- Π *on input* $\langle V, A \rangle$ *either never halts or exceeds the bound on active elements.*

The proof of the theorem gives a somewhat more precise result. If there is even one input $\langle V, A \rangle \in C$ for which Π eventually halts, say at step m, without exceeding the bound on active elements, then in the second alternative in the theorem the computation will exceed the bound on active elements at or before step m.

Notice that this theorem does not assume a polynomial bound on the number of steps. It is part of the conclusion that the number of steps is not only polynomially bounded but constant as long as the input is in C and the number of active elements obeys its bound.

Intuitively, bounding the number of active elements, without bounding the number of computation steps, amounts to a restriction on space, rather than time. Thus, Theorem 1.2 can be viewed as a zero-one law for choiceless polynomial space computation.

Q: Is the BGS logic more powerful than the extension FO+LFP of first-order logic with the least fixed-point operator?

A: Yes, every property definable in FO+LFP is $\tilde{C}$PTime, and there are $\tilde{C}$PTime properties that are not definable in FO+LFP. The BGS logic is quite expressive [4].

Q: In the case of FO+LFP, the almost sure theory, that is the set of sentences with asymptotic probability 1, is decidable. What about the almost sure theory of the BGS logic?

A: It is undecidable.

Proposition 1.3 *The class of almost surely accepting polynomially bounded BGS programs and the class of almost surely rejecting polynomially bounded BGS programs are recursively inseparable.*

The proof is easy. We can sketch it for you. Consider Turing machines with two halting states h_1 and h_2. For $i = 1, 2$, let H_i be the collection of Turing machines that eventually halt in state h_i if started on the empty input tape. It is well-known that H_1 and H_2 are recursively inseparable. Associate to each Turing machine T a polynomial time BGS program as follows. The program Π ignores its input graph and simulates T on empty input tape (working exclusively with pure sets). Π outputs `true` (resp. `false`) if T halts in state h_1 (resp. h_2). The polynomial bounds on steps and active elements are both twice the number of atoms. Then if $T \in H_1$ (resp. $T \in H_2$) our polynomial time BGS program will accept (resp. reject) all sufficiently large inputs.

Q: A question about the class $\mathcal{C}$ in Theorem 1.2. Do you just prove the existence of it?

A: The class $\mathcal{C}$ has a fairly simple description. It consists of the graphs that satisfy the so-called strong extension axioms for up to some number n of variables. The parameter n can be easily computed when the program Π and the polynomial bound on the number of active elements are specified.

2 Strong Extension Axioms

Q: What are strong extension axioms?

A: Do you remember the ordinary extension axioms?

Q: It would be good to review them. I remember though that the extension axioms played a key role in the zero-one law for first-order logic, that they explained the mystery of that law.

A: The ordinary extension axioms (for graphs) assert the existence of vertices in any possible "configuration" relative to finitely many given vertices; strong extension axioms assert not only existence but plentitude.

More precisely, a k-parameter *type* is a formula $\tau(y, x_1, \ldots, x_k)$ of the form

$$\bigwedge_{1 \leq i \leq k} (y \neq x_i \wedge \pm(yAx_i)).$$

Here $\pm$ before a formula means that the formula may or may not be negated. So τ specifies the adjacency and non-adjacency relationships between y and the k parameters x_i; in addition, it says that y is distinct from the x_i's (which is redundant when yAx_i is not negated, since the adjacency relation A is irreflexive). The *extension axiom* $EA(\tau)$ associated to a type τ is

$$\forall x_1, \ldots, x_k \left(\left(\bigwedge_{1 \leq i < j \leq k} x_i \neq x_j \right) \rightarrow \exists y \, \tau(y, x_1, \ldots, x_k) \right).$$

For a fixed k, there are 2^k of these extension axioms, because of the k choices for the $\pm$ signs in τ. We write EA_k for their conjunction together with the statement that there are at least k vertices (so that the $EA(\tau)$'s aren't vacuous). Thus, EA_k says that there exist at least k vertices and that every possible configuration for a vertex y, relative to k distinct, given vertices, is realized at least once.

We say that a graph satisfies the *strong extension axiom* $SEA(\tau)$ if, for every k distinct vertices $x_1, \ldots, x_k$, there are at least $\frac{1}{2}n/2^k$ vertices y satisfying $\tau(y, x_1, \ldots, x_k)$. Unlike the extension axioms, strong extension axioms are not first-order formulas. We write SEA_k for the conjunction of all 2^k of the strong extension axioms $SEA(\tau)$ as τ ranges over all the k-parameter types, together with the statement that there are at least k vertices. Thus, SEA_k says that there exist at least k vertices and that each possible configuration of y relative to k distinct x_i's is realized not just once (as EA_k says) but fairly often, $\frac{1}{2}n/2^k$ times.

Q: I remember seeing somewhere a stronger version of extension axioms.

A: Phokion Kolaitis and Moshe Vardi introduced a version of strong extension axioms with $\sqrt{n}$ instead of $\frac{1}{2}n/2^k$. They proved that their extension axioms were almost surely true and then used the axioms to derive a zero-one law for a fragment of second-order logic [12].

Q: Where did that number $\frac{1}{2}n/2^k$ come from?

A: Consider any particular k-parameter type with fixed values for the k parameters, say $\tau(y, a_1, \ldots, a_k)$. On the average, how many vertices would you expect to realize this type?

Q: Well, since τ says that y is distinct from all the a_i, there are $n - k$ vertices that could conceivably realize τ, and each of them has probability $1/2^k$ of realizing τ. So the expected number of realizers is $(n - k)/2^k$.

A: Right. Since k is fixed and we are interested in asymptotics for large n, this expected number is very nearly $n/2^k$.

Q: And the strong extension axiom says that the type has at least half the expected number of realizers. That sounds plausible, but why "half"?

A: It doesn't matter. We could use any constant strictly smaller than 1, and $\frac{1}{2}$ is the simplest choice. The analogous axiom with a constant α in place of $\frac{1}{2}$ will be denoted by SEA_k^α.

Q: I said the strong extension axiom sounds plausible, but now I think that it is definitely true.

A: You are right.

Proposition 2.1 *For each k, the asymptotic probability of SEA_k is 1.*

Q: I see how to prove it, using the central limit theorem. Here's the idea. First, I can ignore the distinction between $n - k$ and n as you suggested, because it can be compensated for by slightly increasing the $\frac{1}{2}$. So let me pretend there are n rather than $n - k$ vertices that could conceivably realize $\tau(y, a_1, \ldots, a_k)$. The number of these vertices that actually realize it is a Bernoulli random variable X with mean $n/2^k$ and standard deviation proportional to $\sqrt{n}$. I don't remember the constant of proportionality, but I don't think it'll matter. So for $\tau(y, a_1, \ldots, a_k)$ to be realized fewer than the desired number of times would mean that X differs from its mean by an amount linear in n, and that's more than some constant times $\sqrt{n}$ standard deviations. That probability can be estimated, for large n, by the central limit theorem, and it decreases exponentially (or at least like $\exp(-\sqrt{n})$ — again I don't remember exactly but it won't matter). Now there are only polynomially many (at most n^k) choices for $a_1, \ldots, a_k$, so the probability that *some* choice of the a_i's has fewer than the desired number of y's realizing τ still approaches zero.

A: This sounds good, but unfortunately the central limit theorem doesn't quite provide the information you need.

Q: What's the problem?

A: Well, the central limit theorem says that, as n approaches infinity, the probability that a Bernoulli random variable is more than β standard deviations below its mean approaches

$$\frac{1}{\sqrt{2\pi}} \int_{-\infty}^{-\beta} \exp\left(-\frac{1}{2}t^2\right) dt.$$

But it says this for each fixed β, not for a β that depends on n. And you needed a β proportional to $\sqrt{n}$.

Q: I guess you're right. So is there a better version of the central limit theorem that salvages the argument?

A: Actually, there's an extensive theory of so-called large deviations, designed to handle just this sort of thing. To establish that the strong extension axioms have asymptotic probability one, we need only a little bit of that theory — a version of Chernoff's inequality [7].

Lemma 2.2 *Fix numbers β, r in the open interval $(0,1)$. There is a constant c, also in $(0,1)$, such that the following is true for every positive integer m. Let X be the number of successes in m independent trials, each trial having probability r of success. Then $Prob\,[X \leq \beta mr] \leq c^m$.*

That is, the probability that the number of successes (X) is smaller than the expected number (mr) by at least the (fixed) factor β decreases exponentially as a function of the number m of trials. The proof of this proposition depends on a "large deviation" inequality of the sort given in Chernoff's paper [7] and Loève's book [13, Section 18]. The references we have found prove stronger results than we need and therefore give more complicated proofs than we need. But here is a simple proof of an inequality strong enough for our purposes.

Proof We begin with the well-known observation that, if Z is a non-negative random variable and q is a positive real number, then

$$\text{Prob}\,[Z \geq q] \leq \frac{E(Z)}{q},$$

where E means "expectation." Indeed,

$$
\begin{aligned}
E(Z) &= E(Z|Z \geq q)\text{Prob}\,[Z \geq q] + E(Z|Z < q)\text{Prob}\,[Z < q] \\
&\geq E(Z|Z \geq q)\text{Prob}\,[Z \geq q] \\
&\geq q \cdot \text{Prob}\,[Z \geq q].
\end{aligned}
$$

We apply this with $Z = \exp[t(mr - X)]$, where t is a positive parameter to be chosen later. Thus, we have

$$
\begin{aligned}
\text{Prob}\,[X \leq \beta mr] &= \text{Prob}\,[Z \geq \exp[t(mr - \beta mr)]] \\
&= \text{Prob}\,[Z \geq \exp[tmr(1 - \beta)]] \\
&\leq \frac{E(Z)}{\exp[tmr(1 - \beta)]}.
\end{aligned}
$$

We continue by computing $E(Z)$. The random variable $mr - X$ can be viewed as the sum, over all m trials, of $r - S$, where S is 1 if the trial is a success and 0 if not. Thus, Z is the product over all trials of $\exp[t(r - S)]$. But the trials are independent, so the expectation of this product is the product of the individual expectations. For each individual trial, we have

$$E(\exp[t(r-S)]) = r \cdot \exp[t(r-1)] + (1-r) \cdot \exp[t(r-0)]$$
$$= \exp[tr](r\exp[-t] + 1 - r).$$

Therefore,

$$E(Z) = \exp[tmr](r\exp[-t] + 1 - r)^m.$$

Substituting this into the inequality for $\text{Prob}\,[X \le \beta mr]$, we find

$$\text{Prob}\,[X \le \beta mr] \le \left(\frac{\exp[tr](r\exp[-t] + 1 - r)}{\exp[tr(1-\beta)]} \right)^m$$
$$= [\exp[t\beta r] \cdot (r\exp[-t] + 1 - r)]^m.$$

So the lemma will be proved if we can find a positive t for which the value of

$$f(t) = \exp[t\beta r] \cdot (r\exp[-t] + 1 - r)$$

is in the open interval $(0,1)$, for then this value can serve as the required c. Notice that $f(0) = 1$ and that

$$f'(t) = \beta r \exp[t\beta r] \cdot (r\exp[-t] + 1 - r) + \exp[t\beta r] \cdot (-r)\exp[-t].$$

Thus, $f'(0) = \beta r - r < 0$ (because $\beta < 1$ and $r > 0$). Therefore, any sufficiently small positive t will give $0 < f(t) < 1$ as required. $\square$

Q: The best, i.e., smallest value of c obtainable by the preceding argument is the minimum value of $f(t)$.

A: Right. A routine calculation, setting $f'(t) = 0$, shows that this minimum is

$$\left(\frac{1-r}{1-\beta r} \right)^{1-\beta r} \cdot \left(\frac{1}{\beta} \right)^{\beta r}.$$

Notice that this is the weighted geometric mean of two quantities whose correspondingly weighted arithmetic mean is

$$\left(\frac{1-r}{1-\beta r} \right) \cdot (1 - \beta r) + \left(\frac{1}{\beta} \right) \cdot (\beta r) = 1.$$

Since the two quantities are not equal to 1 (as $\beta < 1$), the arithmetic-geometric mean inequality shows again that the optimal c is smaller than 1.

Q: Now prove the proposition.

A: All right.

Proof of Proposition 2.1   We shall show that, for each fixed k-parameter type τ, the probability that SEA(τ) fails, in a random graph on vertex set $\{1, 2, \ldots, n\}$, approaches 0 as $n \to \infty$. Then, as SEA$_k$ is the conjunction of a fixed number 2^k (independent of n) of SEA(τ)'s, its probability of failure also approaches 0, as required.

So we concentrate henceforth on a single τ. Temporarily, also concentrate on k specific, distinct vertices $a_1, \ldots, a_k \in \{1, 2, \ldots, n\}$. Let X be the number of vertices b satisfying $\tau(b, a_1, \ldots, a_k)$. In a random graph, each of the $n - k$ vertices other than $a_1, \ldots, a_k$ has probability $1/2^k$ of satisfying τ, and these $n - k$ trials are independent. So, applying the lemma with $m = n - k$, with $r = 1/2^k$, and with some β in the interval $(\frac{1}{2}, 1)$, and noting that, as $\beta > \frac{1}{2}$, we have $\beta \cdot (n - k) \geq \frac{1}{2}n$ for large n, we obtain some $c \in (0, 1)$ such that

$$\text{Prob}\left[X < \frac{1}{2}n/2^k\right] \leq \text{Prob}\left[X < \beta(n - k)/2^k\right]$$
$$\leq c^{n-k}.$$

This bounds the probability that our specific choice of $a_1, \ldots, a_k$ is a counterexample to SEA(τ).

Now un-fix $a_1, \ldots, a_k$. Since the number of choices for this k-tuple is $\leq n^k$, the probability that at least one choice gives a counterexample, i.e., the probability that SEA(τ) fails, is at most

$$n^k c^{n-k}.$$

Since $0 < c < 1$, this bound approaches 0 as $n \to \infty$. $\square$

The same proof can be used to show that, for each k and each $\alpha \in (0, 1)$, the axiom SEA$_k^\alpha$ has asymptotic probability 1.

3   Inadequacy of Extension Axioms

Q: You needed strong extension axioms to define the class $\mathcal{C}$ in Theorem 1.2. Might the ordinary extension axioms suffice to define $\mathcal{C}$? Maybe the use of strong extension axioms is just an artifact of the proof.

A: Ordinary extension axioms are too weak to support the zero-one law for $\tilde{\mathrm{C}}$PTime. We will show you a particular polynomial-time BGS program that separates structures satisfying arbitrarily many extension axioms. So strong extension axioms are really needed for the $\tilde{\mathrm{C}}$PTime zero-one law.

Though our general policy has been, for expository purposes, to concentrate on algorithms whose inputs are graphs, this program will use as input a graph together with a single distinguished vertex, i.e., a rooted graph. That is, we add a constant symbol d to the vocabulary $\{A\}$ of graphs. We expect that a similar example could be given without introducing the constant symbol.

Notice that the zero-one laws for the logics that you mentioned above, e.g. FO+LFP, continue to hold and to follow from the extension axioms, in the presence of a distinguished vertex.

Q: They fail when there are two distinguished vertices, because these two are adjacent with probability $\frac{1}{2}$.

A: Right. But one distinguished vertex is benign. Instead of a distinguished vertex, we could add a unary relation R to the vocabulary and modify the extension axioms to specify, in addition to adjacency information, whether y should satisfy R. In that version of the construction, R would play the role played in our proof by the set of neighbors of d.

Proposition 3.1 *There is a polynomial time BGS program Π such that, for any given k, there are two rooted graphs, both satisfying EA_k, such that Π produces output* true *on one of them and* false *on the other.*

Proof We begin by exhibiting the BGS program Π; the polynomial bounds on the number of steps and the number of active elements will be n and $2n+3$, respectively. The program Π computes the parity of the maximum size of a clique containing the distinguished vertex d. It does this by building up the collection of all i-element subsets of $\{x : xAd\}$ for $i = 0, 1, \ldots$, checking at each step whether any cliques remain. One essential ingredient of the proof will be that d has so few neighbors in our graphs that the time used by this computation is polynomial relative to the sizes of these graphs.

Π uses four dynamic 0-ary function symbols: Halt, Output, Mode, and C. Recall that in the initial state of a computation these have the value $\emptyset = $ false $= 0$. The program Π is

```
do in parallel
   if Mode = 0 then
      do in parallel
         C := {∅}, Mode := 1
      enddo
   endif
   if Mode = 1 then
      do in parallel
         C := {x ∪ {y} : x ∈ C, y ∈ Atoms : yAd ∧ y ∉ x},
```

```
        Output := ¬Output, Mode := 2
      enddo
    endif
    if Mode = 2 then
      if (∃x ∈ C)(∀u, v ∈ x) uAv
      then Mode := 1
      else Halt := true
      endif
    endif
enddo.
```

After the first part of Π, with Mode = 0, has been executed, C is initialized to $\{\emptyset\}$, the family of 0-element subsets of the set R of neighbors of d. After i executions of the part with Mode = 1, C has become the family of i-element subsets of R. The part with Mode = 2 checks whether there are any cliques in C. If so, we return to Mode 1 to enlarge the sets in C; if not, then the common size i of the sets in C is one more than the maximum size of a clique included in R. Since Output reverses its truth value at each Mode 1 step and since it is initially **false**, we see that, the final value of Output is **true** if and only if the maximum clique size in R is even, if and only if the maximum size of a clique containing d is odd.

Let us estimate the number of steps and the number of active elements in a computation of our program. Writing n for the number of vertices in the input graph, r for the number of neighbors of d, and s for the maximum size of a clique among these neighbors, we find that the Mode 0 part of Π is executed once and the Mode 1 and Mode 2 parts are executed $s + 1$ times each. So the whole computation takes $2s + 3$ steps.

According to the definition in [3], the truth values, the atoms and the set of atoms, altogether $n + 3$ entities, are active already in the initial state. The elements that the computation activates are the number 2 (which is one of the values of Mode), the subsets of R of cardinality at most $s + 1$ and the $s + 2$ values taken by C. For non-trivial values of r and s, the number of activated elements is easily seen to be majorized by $(r + 1)^{s+1}$.

Q: But 0 is also among the subsets of R and $1 = \{0\}$ is also among the values of C.

A: So we have a slight overcount of activated elements. In any case, the total number of active elements in this computation is at most $n + 3 + (r + 1)^{s+1}$. We shall design our graphs to have quite small r and s (relative to n), so that $n + 3 + (r + 1)^{s+1}$ is below the bound $2n + 3$ that we imposed on the number of active elements, and $2s + 3$ is below the bound n on the number of steps.

The graphs required in the proposition will be described in three steps. First, we give a general description depending on two parameters: the (large) number n of vertices and the (much smaller but still rather large) number r of neighbors of d. Second, leaving n arbitrary (but large), we prescribe two values for r, to produce the two graphs we want. Finally, we fix n so large that these graphs have all the required properties. Actually, the description in the first step involves randomization, and rather than fixing n in the last step we simply show that, for all sufficiently large n, the graphs have the required properties with high probability. This clearly suffices for the existence claim in the proposition.

Given n and r, we build a (random) graph $G(n, r)$ as follows. The vertex set consists of the distinguished vertex d and $n - 1$ others which we denote by $1, 2, \ldots, n - 1$.

Q: This introduces an ambiguity, since these vertices are atoms in $HF(I)$ and the same symbols denote natural numbers (finite von Neumann ordinals) which are sets.

A: Fortunately, the ambiguity never leads to a confusion. Let's proceed. d is adjacent to the vertices $1, 2, \ldots, r$ and no others. The rest of the adjacency relation is chosen at random; flip independent, fair coins for all potential edges to decide whether to include them in the graph. This completes the description of $G(n, r)$. Notice that the subgraph induced by the set $R = \{1, 2, \ldots, r\}$ of neighbors of d is a random graph (in the usual sense) on r vertices.

The next part of the proof, choosing r as a function of n, is the most delicate. We need r small enough so that Π stays within the bound on active elements, but if we take r too small then $G(n, r)$ will violate the extension axioms. We need the following result from [6, Section XI.1].

Lemma 3.2 *There is a function ρ from natural numbers to natural numbers with the following two properties. First,*

$$C_1 s 2^{s/2} \leq \rho(s) \leq C_2 s 2^{s/2}$$

for certain positive constants C_1 and C_2. Second, if $p(s)$ denotes the probability that a random graph on $\rho(s)$ vertices has maximum clique size exactly s, then $p(s) \to 1$ as $s \to \infty$.

Actually, Bollobás proves a far more precise result. The constants in the lemma can be taken to be any constants satisfying $C_1 < 1/(e\sqrt{2}) < C_2$ provided s is sufficiently large. All we shall need, however, is the lemma as stated.

Using this lemma, we associate to each (large) n two values of r as follows. Let s and s' be the two largest integers below $3 \log \log n$.

Q: What is the base of logarithm?

A: We use log to mean base 2 logarithm and ln to mean base e logarithm.

Let $r = \rho(s)$, $r' = \rho(s')$, $G = G(n,r)$, and $G' = G(n,r')$. According to the lemma, when n is large enough there is a very high probability that, among the neighbors of d, the largest clique in G has size s and similarly for G' and s'. In particular, since s and s' are consecutive integers, the program Π will (unless it runs out of time) produce output `true` for one of G and G' and `false` for the other.

We next address the question whether Π with these inputs G and G' succeeds in carrying out its computation within the bounds on the number of steps (n) and active elements $(2n + 3)$. We already computed the number of steps and an upper bound for the number of active elements. In the present context, these are, with high probability for large n,

$$2s + 3 < 3 \log \log n + 3 < n$$

and

$$n + 3 + (r + 1)^{s+1} < n + 3 + \left(C_3 s 2^{s/2} \right)^{s+1}$$

for G (where C_3 is slightly larger than C_2 to compensate for changing from $r + 1$ to r), and similarly for G' with s' and r' in place of s and r. So the bound on steps is satisfied with high probability for sufficiently large n. As for the bound on active elements, we must show that

$$\left(C_3 s 2^{s/2} \right)^{s+1} \leq n.$$

To this end, we first compute that, since $s < 3 \log \log n$,

$$C_3 s 2^{s/2} < C_3 \cdot 3 \log \log n \cdot (\log n)^{3/2} < (\log n)^2$$

for large n. The desired inequality follows because the logarithm of its left side is at most

$$(s + 1) \log \left((\log n)^2 \right) < (3 \log \log n + 1) \cdot 2 \log \log n < \log n.$$

To complete the proof of the proposition, we must still verify that (with high probability, when n is large) G and G' satisfy EA_k. We give the argument for G; it applies equally well to G'. Recall that G was defined as $G(n,r)$ with n sufficiently large and $r = \rho(s) \geq C_1 s 2^{s/2}$, where s is one of the largest two integers below $3 \log \log n$. In particular, $s > 2 \log \log n$ (for large n), and so

$$r \geq C_1 \cdot 2 \log \log n \cdot \log n = \gamma(n) \log n,$$

where all we need to know about $\gamma(n) = C_1 \cdot 2 \log \log n$ is that it tends to infinity with n. We can therefore complete the proof by showing that, for each fixed k-parameter type τ, the probability that $G(n, r)$ satisfies $\mathrm{EA}(\tau)$ is close to 1 when n is large and $r \geq \gamma(n) \log n$.

Fix, therefore, an arbitrary k-parameter type τ, and temporarily fix values $a_1, \ldots, a_k$ for its parameters. There are three cases to consider, according to whether d is among the parameters and, if it is, whether τ says y should be adjacent or non-adjacent to d. Since d has so few neighbors (only r, compared with approximately $n/2$ for other vertices), the probability that $\tau(y, a_1, \ldots, a_k)$ holds is smallest in the case where some a_i is d and τ says y is adjacent to d. We calculate this case first and then indicate the changes for the other cases.

So suppose τ says y must be adjacent to d. Then the only candidates for values of y satisfying τ are the r neighbors $1, 2, \ldots, r$ of d. For any one of these neighbors b, distinct from the other parameters, the probability that it satisfies τ, i.e., that it satisfies $k - 1$ additional adjacency or non-adjacency requirements each of which has probability $\frac{1}{2}$, is $1/2^{k-1}$. Since these probabilities are independent for different b's and since there are at least $r - k + 1$ available b's (the r neighbors of d minus at most $k - 1$ that are among the other parameters),

$$\text{Prob [no } b \text{ satisfies } \tau(y, a_1, \ldots, a_k)] \leq \left(1 - \frac{1}{2^{k-1}}\right)^{r-k+1}$$
$$\leq e^{-(r-k+1)/2^{k-1}},$$

where we used the fact that $1 - t \leq e^{-t}$.

In the case where d is one of the parameters but τ says that y is not adjacent to d, the computation works the same way but with $n - r - k$ in place of $r - k + 1$. In the case where d is not one of the parameters, the result is again similar but with $(n - k)/2$ in place of $r - k + 1$. In either of these cases, $r - k + 1$ has been replaced with something larger (when n is large), so the upper bound for the probability of failure is even smaller than in the first case. Summarizing, we have, for every choice of k distinct parameters, an upper bound of $e^{-(r-k+1)/2^{k-1}}$ for the probability that τ has no solution. Therefore, the probability that $\mathrm{EA}(\tau)$ fails is at most

$$\binom{n}{k} e^{-(r-k+1)/2^{k-1}} \leq n^k e^{-(r-k+1)/2^{k-1}}.$$

To estimate this, we consider its natural logarithm, which is at most

$$k \ln n - \frac{r - k + 1}{2^{k-1}} \leq -\frac{\gamma(n) \log n}{2^{k-1}} + k \ln n + \text{constant}.$$

Since $\gamma(n) \to \infty$ as $n \to \infty$, the right side of this formula tends to $-\infty$. So our upper bound for the probability that $EA(\tau)$ fails tends to 0 as $n \to \infty$. $\square$

It should perhaps be pointed out explicitly that the graphs constructed in the preceding proof violate SEA_1, for the number of neighbors of the special vertex d is far smaller than the $n/4$ that SEA_1 would require.

4 Rigidity and Hamiltonicity

Q: From the conversation [10] I remember that almost all finite graphs are rigid[b] but rigidity does not follow from the ordinary extension axioms. Does it follow from strong extension axioms?

A: No dice.

Proposition 4.1 *For any k, there exists a non-rigid graph satisfying SEA_k.*

Proof We use the same randomizing construction as in [5]. Let l be a large natural number, and let $G(l)$ have the integers from $-l$ through l as vertices. We require that, if a is adjacent to b, then $-a$ is adjacent to $-b$; this ensures that $G(l)$ is not rigid, for $a \mapsto -a$ is a non-trivial automorphism. Except for this symmetry requirement, $G(l)$ is random. That is, for each pair of corresponding potential edges $\{a, b\}$ and $\{-a, -b\}$, we decide whether to include both or neither in $G(l)$ by flipping a fair coin. We shall show that, for any fixed k, the probability that the graph $G(l)$ satisfies SEA_k tends to infinity with l.

Q: The pair of potential edges $\{a, b\}$ and $\{-a, -b\}$ is a single potential edge if $a = -b$, but I guess this does not change anything.

A: Right. As usual, it suffices to check the asymptotic probability for $SEA(\tau)$ for every single k-parameter type τ. So let τ be given, and temporarily fix values $a_1, \ldots, a_k$ for the parameters. Let b range over positive vertices different from all the $\pm a_i$'s. For each such b, the probability that it satisfies τ with our fixed parameters is $1/2^k$, and for different b's these probabilities are independent. By Lemma 2.2, for any $\beta \in (0, 1)$, the probability that fewer than $\beta \cdot \frac{l-k}{2} \cdot 2^{-k}$ of these b's satisfy τ decreases exponentially with l. Of course the same goes for negative b's. Therefore, the same goes for the probability that fewer than $\beta \cdot (l - k) \cdot 2^{-k}$ vertices altogether satisfy τ.

Q: Why do you consider positive and negative b's separately?

---

[b]A graph is *rigid* if its only automorphism is the identity.

A: Because their behavior is not independent as required for application of Lemma 2.2.

Taking β slightly larger than $\frac{1}{2}$, to get $\beta \cdot (l - k) > \frac{1}{2} \cdot l$ for large l, we find that the probability that our fixed $a_1, \ldots, a_k$ constitute a counterexample to SEA(τ) decreases exponentially with l.

Now un-fix the parameters a_i. Notice that the number of choices of the parameters is bounded by a polynomial in l, namely $(2l + 1)^k$. Therefore, the probability that SEA(τ) fails is small for large l. $\qquad\square$

We remark that the proof shows that even the axioms SEA_k^α for arbitrary $\alpha \in (0, 1)$ do not imply rigidity.

Q: What about hamiltonicity? From the sane conversation [10] I remember that almost all finite graphs are hamiltonian[c] but hamiltonicity does not follow from the ordinary extension axioms. Does it follow from strong extension axioms?

A: In the case of hamiltonicity, we have only a partial answer.

Proposition 4.2 *For any k and any $\alpha \in (0, \frac{1}{2})$, there is a graph that satisfies SEA_k^α but is not hamiltonian.*

Proof We simplify a randomizing construction from [5]. Let l be a large natural number, and let $G(l)$ be the graph produced as follows. The vertices are the natural numbers from 0 to $2l$; we call the first l of these vertices *friendly* and the remaining $l + 1$ *unfriendly*. No two unfriendly vertices will be adjacent. For each potential edge subject to this constraint, i.e., for each two vertices of which at least one is friendly, flip a fair coin to decide whether to include that edge in $G(l)$.

No matter what happens in the randomization, this graph cannot be hamiltonian. Indeed, in any cycle, at most half the vertices can be unfriendly, since unfriendly vertices are not adjacent. But in the whole graph, more than half of the vertices are unfriendly.

To complete the proof, we show that, with high probability for large l, $G(l)$ satisfies SEA_k^α. As usual, it suffices to show, for each fixed k-parameter type τ and each choice of values $a_1, \ldots, a_n$, that the probability that fewer than $\alpha \cdot (2l + 1) \cdot 2^{-k}$ vertices b satisfy τ (with the chosen parameters) decreases exponentially as a function of l. So let τ and the parameters be fixed, and let b range over friendly vertices distinct from all the parameters. So there are at least $l - k$ values for b, and each satisfies τ with probability 2^{-k}, these events being independent for different b's. We apply Lemma 2.2 with $\beta > 2\alpha$ to this situation. Since $\alpha < \frac{1}{2}$, we can find such a $\beta < 1$, so Lemma 2.2 is applicable.

---

[c]A graph is *hamiltonian* if it includes a cycle containing all its vertices.

It gives us exponentially decreasing probability for the event that fewer than $\beta \cdot (l - k) \cdot 2^{-k}$ friendly vertices satisfy τ with the chosen parameters. But since $\beta > 2\alpha$, we have $\beta \cdot (l - k) > \alpha \cdot (2l + 1)$ once l is large enough. Thus, we also have exponentially decreasing probability for the event that fewer than $\alpha \cdot (2l + 1)$ vertices satisfy τ with the chosen parameters. □

We do not know whether the preceding proposition can be extended to $\alpha \geq \frac{1}{2}$. Its proof made crucial use of the assumption that $\alpha < \frac{1}{2}$. The non-hamiltonicity of the graph depended on the presence of an independent set containing more than half the vertices (the unfriendly ones), and no such set can exist when $\alpha > \frac{1}{2}$. More precisely, we have the following proposition, which prevents any construction like the preceding one from working when $\alpha > \frac{1}{2}$. (The specific randomizing construction in the preceding proof doesn't work for $\alpha = \frac{1}{2}$ either.)

Proposition 4.3 *Let $\alpha > \frac{1}{2}$. There exists a number k (depending on α) such that, for every sufficiently large n and every n-vertex graph satisfying SEA_k^α, no independent set contains more than half of the vertices.*

Proof Given α, choose k so large that

$$\left(1 - \frac{1}{2^k}\right)\alpha > \frac{1}{2},$$

and let n be much larger yet. Consider an n-vertex graph satisfying SEA_k^α, and suppose it had an independent set U of cardinality at least $n/2$. Fix k distinct elements $a_1, \ldots, a_k \in U$, and consider the axioms $SEA(\tau)$ applied to these k parameters, where τ ranges over all k-parameter types *except* the one that says y is adjacent to none of the parameters. Thus, we are considering $2^k - 1$ types, and each can be satisfied only by elements outside U. Thus, these types altogether have at most $n/2$ elements satisfying them. But, by SEA_k^α, each of them is realized by at least $\alpha \cdot n \cdot 2^{-k}$ vertices, so altogether they are realized by at least $\alpha \cdot n \cdot 2^{-k} \cdot (2^k - 1)$ vertices. But this number exceeds $n/2$ by our choice of k. □

Q: I guess you told me all that you know about strong extension axioms.

A: Actually, [1] has a little bit more information. By the way, most of Shelah's proof (of his zero-one law for $\tilde{\mathrm{C}}$PTime) uses ordinary extension axioms. Only one combinatorial lemma requires strong extension axioms. But it looks like you had enough strong extension axioms.

Q: Indeed enough, for today anyway.

Acknowledgments. The first author was partially supported by a grant from Microsoft Research.

References

1. A. Blass and Y. Gurevich, *Strong extension axioms and Shelah's zero-one law for choiceless polynomial time*, in preparation. See an abridged version, named *Choiceless Polynomial Time Computation and the Zero-One Law*, in *Computer Science Logic 2000*, editors P. Clote and H. Schwichtenberg, Springer Lecture Notes in Computer Science 1862 (2000) 18–40.

2. A. Blass, Y. Gurevich, and D. Kozen, A zero-one law for logic with a fixed-point operator, *Information and Control*, 67 (1985) 70–90.

3. A. Blass, Y. Gurevich, and S. Shelah, Choiceless polynomial time, *Ann. Pure Applied Logic*, 100 (1999) 141–187.

4. A. Blass, Y. Gurevich and J. Van den Bussche, Abstract state machines and computationally complete query languages, in *Abstract State Machines: Theory and Applications*, editors Y. Gurevich et al., Springer Lecture Notes in Computer Science 1912, 2000.

5. A. Blass and F. Harary, Properties of almost all graphs and complexes, *J. Graph Theory*, 3 (1979), 225–240.

6. B. Bollobás, *Random Graphs*, Academic Press, 1985.

7. H. Chernoff, A measure of asymptotic efficiency for tests of a hypothesis based on the sum of observations, *Ann. Math. Statist.* 23 (1952), 493–507.

8. H.-D. Ebbinghaus and J. Flum, *Finite Model Theory*, Springer-Verlag, 1995.

9. S. Even, *Graph Algorithms*, Computer Science Press, 1979.

10. Y. Gurevich, Zero-one laws, Bulletin of the EATCS, 46 (Feb. 1992), 90–106. [Reprinted in G. Rozenberg and A. Salomaa, editors, *Current Trends in Theoretical Computer Science*, World Scientific, 1993, 293–309.]

11. Y. Gurevich, Evolving algebras 1993: Lipari guide, in *pecification and Validation Methods*, ed. E. Börger, Oxford University Press (1995) pp. 9–36. See also the *May 1997 draft of the ASM guide*, Tech. Report CSE-TR-336-97, EECS Dept., Univ. of Michigan, 1997. Found at http : //www.eecs.umich.edu/gasm/.

12. P. Kolaitis and M. Vardi, 0–1 laws and decision problems for fragments of second-order logic, *Information and Computation*, 87 (1990) 302–339.

13. M. Loève, *Probability Theory*, Van Nostrand 1955.

14. S. Shelah, Choiceless polynomial time logic: inability to express [paper number 634], in *Computer Science Logic 2000*, editors P. Clote and H. Schwichtenberg, Springer Lecture Notes in Computer Science 1862 (2000) 72–125.

TREE-DECOMPOSITIONS AND THE MODEL-CHECKING PROBLEM

JÖRG FLUM

Albert-Ludwigs-Universität Freiburg
79104 Freiburg, Germany
E-mail: `flum@ruf.uni-freiburg.de`

1   Introduction

The notion of tree-decomposition (as the related one of tree-width) is of great importance in the theory of graphs. It has been introduced by Robertson and Seymour [27] (and, independently, by Halin [23]) who used it systematically in their analysis of graphs. Tree-decompositions have turned out to be a valuable tool in various areas of logic and computer science (in fact, Ajtai and Gurevich reinvented this notion in [1]). In logic, the concept of tree-decomposition has been used most systematically for the model-checking problem. This problem is one of the main issues of descriptive complexity; it analyzes the complexity of problems of the form:

Decide if a given structure is a model of a given sentence (of a fixed logic).

The model-checking problem arises very naturally in various areas of computer science. Let us see two examples.

In the *computer-aided verification* area the basic problem is the model-checking problem: does a given program (the "structure") satisfy a desired property (the "sentence") expressed in some specification language (the "logic"). And in *database theory*, (relational) databases are viewed as structures and (Boolean) queries to the databases as sentences; thus, the query evaluation problem is the model-checking problem for the corresponding query language (the "logic"). We mostly deal with logics relevant for this second area and do not consider logics like modal and temporal logics relevant for computer-aided verification.

Already in 1973, Stockmeyer [29] showed that the model-checking problem for first-order logic is PSPACE-complete. Since then, various results handling this high worst-case complexity have been obtained. Let us briefly recall two of the pioneering results due to Yannakakis and Courcelle, respectively (later we give precise statements and explain the notions):

- The model-checking problem for acyclic conjunctive sentences can be solved in polynomial time.

- For every sentence of monadic second-order logic, the model-checking problem on a class of structures of bounded tree-width can be solved in linear time.

The concept of acyclic conjunctive sentences appearing in Yannakakis' theorem is defined via the notion of tree-decomposition; Courcelle restricts the admitted sructures to a class of structures of bounded tree-width. Thus, in both cases, the concept of tree-decomposition yields the frame that allows one to formulate and prove the corresponding result. Of course, it is conceivable that there is a more far-reaching concept than that of tree-decomposition and that the theorems above can be extended to this broader framework. However, results obtained quite recently show that sometimes the concept of tree-decomposition allows the separation of "manageable" instances of the model-checking problem from "unmanageable" ones. Therefore, these recent results suggest that the concept of tree-decomposition really is an essential concept for descriptive complexity, and thus for logic in computer science.

The purpose of this article is to survey some of the results on model-checking based on the notion of tree-decomposition. Various papers surveying the graph-theoretic, algorithmic, or logical relevance of this concept already exist. We just mention two, which appeared in this Bulletin: [3,8].[a]

2 Preliminaries

A *vocabulary* τ is a finite set of relation symbols. A τ-*structure* $\mathcal{A}$ consists of a non-empty set A, called the *universe* of $\mathcal{A}$, and a relation $R^{\mathcal{A}} \subseteq A^r$ for each r-ary relation symbol $R \in \tau$. We only consider finite structures. If $\mathcal{A}$ is a structure and $B \subseteq A$ non-empty, then $\langle B \rangle^{\mathcal{A}}$ denotes the substructure induced by $\mathcal{A}$ on B. We denote by STR the class of all structures.

We consider *graphs* as $\{E\}$-structures $\mathcal{G} = (G, E^{\mathcal{G}})$, where $E^{\mathcal{G}}$ is an irreflexive and symmetric binary relation. A *directed graph* is an $\{E\}$-structure $\mathcal{G} = (G, E^{\mathcal{G}})$ where $E^{\mathcal{G}} \subseteq G \times G$ is arbitrary. Then, its *underlying graph* $\mathcal{G}^u$ is given by $\mathcal{G}^u := (G, \{(a,b) \mid a \neq b, (E^{\mathcal{G}}ab$ or $E^{\mathcal{G}}ba)\})$.

We assume that the reader is familiar with first-order logic and monadic second-order logic. FO and MSO denote the class of first-order formulas and the class of monadic second-order formulas, respectively.

---

[a]I thank Joe Flenner for some helpful comments.

We use lowercase letters $x, y, \ldots$ to denote first-order variables and uppercase letters $X, Y, \ldots$ to denote monadic second-order variables. The set of free variables of a formula φ is denoted by free(φ). We write $\varphi(X_1, \ldots, X_l, x_1, \ldots, x_m)$ to indicate that free(φ) $= \{X_1, \ldots, X_l, x_1, \ldots, x_m\}$. However, if we just write φ this does not mean that φ is a sentence, i.e., that free(φ) $= \emptyset$.

We often denote tuples $(a_1, \ldots, a_k)$ of elements of a set A by $\bar{a}$, and we write $\bar{a} \in A$ instead of $\bar{a} \in A^k$. Similarly, we denote tuples $(B_1, \ldots, B_k)$ of subsets of A by $\bar{B}$ and write $\bar{B} \subseteq A$ instead of $\bar{B} \in (\mathrm{Pow}(A))^k$. We denote tuples of variables by $\bar{x}$ or $\bar{X}$.

For a structure $\mathcal{A}$ and a formula $\varphi(X_1, \ldots, X_l, x_1, \ldots, x_m)$ we let

$$\varphi(\mathcal{A}) := \big\{(B_1, \ldots, B_l, a_1, \ldots, a_m) \mid \bar{B} \subseteq A,\ \bar{a} \in A,\ \text{and}\ \mathcal{A} \models \varphi(\bar{B}, \bar{a})\big\}$$

be the set of assignments satisfying φ in $\mathcal{A}$.

The *size* $\|\mathcal{A}\|$ of a structure $\mathcal{A}$ and the size $\|\varphi\|$ of a formula φ are the lengths of a reasonable encoding of $\mathcal{A}$ and of φ, respectively.

Let C be a class of structures and L a logic. By MC(C, L) we denote the *model-checking problem for structures in* C *and sentences in* L:

Input:	Structure $\mathcal{A} \in$ C, sentence φ in L.
Problem:	Is $\mathcal{A}$ a model of φ?

MC(C, L) $\in$ COMPL, where COMPL is a complexity class, means that there is an algorithm in COMPL solving MC(C, L) (its complexity being measured as a function of both the size of the input structure and the size of the input sentence (*combined complexity*)).

D-MC(C, L) $\in$ COMPL means that the *database complexity* of the model-checking problem for C and L is in COMPL, that is, that

for all sentences $\varphi \in$ L there is an algorithm in COMPL solving the problem

Input:	Struture $\mathcal{A} \in$ C.
Problem:	Is $\mathcal{A}$ a model of φ?

(i.e., for every sentence in L there is a corresponding algorithm whose complexity is measured as a function of the size of the input structure).

3 Trees

A *tree* $\mathcal{T}$ is a connected acyclic graph. Often we tacitly fix an (arbitrary) *root* $r^{\mathcal{T}} \in T$ in a tree $\mathcal{T}$. Then we have a natural partial order $\leq^{\mathcal{T}}$ on T, which is

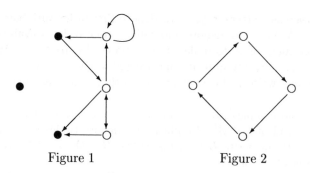

Figure 1   Figure 2

defined by

$$t \leq^{\mathcal{T}} u \iff t \text{ appears on the (unique) path from } r^{\mathcal{T}} \text{ to } u.$$

We say that u is a *child* of t or t is the *parent* of u if $(t, u) \in E^{\mathcal{T}}$ and $t <^{\mathcal{T}} u$. For every $t \in T$ we let $\mathcal{T}_t := \langle \{u \mid t \leq^{\mathcal{T}} u\} \rangle^{\mathcal{T}}$ be the subtree rooted at t. A tree $\mathcal{T}$ is *binary* if every vertex has either 0 or 2 children. A *directed tree* is a directed graph whose underlying graph is a tree.

Our starting point is the observation that some hard problems for graphs are easy for trees. For example, Hamiltonicity is an NP-complete problem for graphs, but a tree has no Hamiltonian cycle, since it has no cycle at all. Similarly, 3-colorability is an NP-complete for graphs, but every tree is 3-colorable (even 2-colorable, just alternate colors from level to level).

We present a further example: A set K of vertices in a directed graph $\mathcal{G}$ is a *kernel* if

$$\forall x, y \in K : \text{ not } E^G xy \text{ and } \forall x \in (G \setminus K) \exists y \in K : E^G xy.$$

The directed graph in Figure 1 has a unique kernel consisting of the marked points. One easily verifies that the directed graph in Figure 2 has two kernels. The problem to decide whether a given directed graph has a kernel is NP-complete (cf. [6]). The situation is different for directed trees: we present an algorithm that works in linear time. Its underlying idea will then be generalized in order to prove some further theorems.

Let $\mathcal{T} = (T, E^{\mathcal{T}})$ be a directed tree and $\mathcal{T}^u$ its underlying tree. For $a \in T$ let $\mathcal{T}_a = (T_a, E_a)$ be the directed tree induced by $\mathcal{T}$ on $T_a := \{b \mid a \leq^{\mathcal{T}^u} b\}$ (i.e. induced by $\mathcal{T}$ on the universe of the subtree of $\mathcal{T}^u$ rooted at a). If a is distinct from the root, let parent(a) denote the parent of a in $\mathcal{T}^u$.

Essentially, the algorithm proceeds as follows: From the leaves to the root, it checks, for every node a, whether there is a kernel of $\mathcal{T}_a$ containing a and whether there is a kernel of $\mathcal{T}_a$ not containing a.

More precisely, we associate with every vertex $a \in T$ a pair $(k_a, n_a) \in \{0,1\} \times \{0,1,2\}$ where

$$k_a := \begin{cases} 1 & \text{if there is a kernel of } \mathcal{T}_a \text{ containing } a; \\ 0 & \text{otherwise;} \end{cases}$$

and

$$n_a := \begin{cases} 1 & \text{if there is a kernel of } \mathcal{T}_a \text{ not containing } a; \\ 2 & \text{if there is no kernel of } \mathcal{T}_a \text{ not containing } a, \\ & \text{but } E^T a\,\text{parent}(a) \text{ and there is a kernel of} \\ & (T_a \cup \{\text{parent}(a)\}, E_a \cup \{(a, \text{parent}(a))\}) \text{ not containing } a; \\ 0 & \text{otherwise.} \end{cases}$$

These pairs of numbers can easily be computed from the leaves to the root: If a is a leaf then

$$k_a = \begin{cases} 1 & \text{if not } E^T aa \\ 0 & \text{otherwise,} \end{cases} \quad \text{and} \quad n_a = \begin{cases} 2 & \text{if } E^T a\,\text{parent}(a) \\ 0 & \text{otherwise.} \end{cases}$$

If a is not a leaf, then

$k_a = 1$ iff not $E^T aa$ and for all children b of a (in $\mathcal{T}^u$): $n_b \neq 0$;

$n_a = 1$ iff for all children b of a ($k_b + n_b > 0$ and ($n_b = 2$ implies $k_b = 1$))

and there is a child b of a s.t. ($E^T ab$ and $k_b = 1$);

$n_a = 2$ iff for all children b of a ($k_b + n_b > 0$ and ($n_b = 2$ implies $k_b = 1$)),

there is no child b of a s.t. ($E^T ab$, and $k_b = 1$), and $E^T a\,\text{parent}(a)$

(cf. Figure 3 and Figure 4). Now, the directed tree $\mathcal{T}$ has a kernel just in case $n_r + k_r > 0$ holds for the root r. In the positive case one can construct a kernel by traversing the tree again, now from the root to the leaves; altogether, the algorithm needs a time linear in the size of $\mathcal{T}$ to decide if $\mathcal{T}$ has a kernel and if so, to construct one.

Not every NP-complete problem for graphs has a feasible algorithm on trees, one of the best-known examples being the band-width optimization problem, which remains NP-complete for the class of trees [25]. It asks for the least k such that there is an ordering of the vertices such that in this ordering at most k elements are between the ends of any edge.

While the formulation of the band-width problem involves the existence of a binary relation (the ordering), the existence of a 3-coloring and the existence of a kernel can be expressed in monadic second-order logic MSO – the latter, for instance, by

$$\exists X (\forall x \forall y ((Xx \wedge Xy) \to \neg Exy) \wedge \forall x (\neg Xx \to \exists y (Xy \wedge Exy))).$$

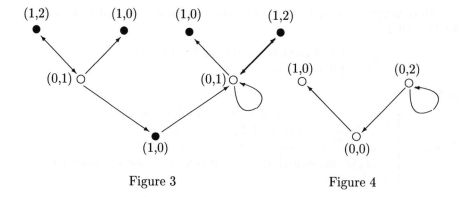

Figure 3   Figure 4

We denote by TREE the class of all trees. The positive results for trees mentioned above are special instances of the following theorem:

Theorem 3.1 ([30]) D-MC(TREE, MSO) ∈ LINTIME, *that is, for every sentence φ of* MSO *there is an algorithm that given a tree $\mathcal{T}$, checks if $\mathcal{T} \models \varphi$ in time $O(\|\mathcal{T}\|)$.*[b]

Theorem 3.1 can be generalized from trees to tree-like structures. In section 5 we will sketch a proof of this generalization. In the main step of the original proof of Theorem 3.1, it was shown that the classes of trees axiomatizable in MSO are just those acceptable by a (deterministic) tree-automaton.

Tree-decompositions yield the right concept of tree-like structures. We recall the definition in the next section.

4 Tree-Decompositions

Let $\mathcal{A}$ be a structure of vocabulary τ. $(\mathcal{T}, (X_t)_{t \in T})$ is a *tree-decomposition* of $\mathcal{A}$ (or, $(\mathcal{T}, (X_t)_{t \in T})$ is a decomposition of $\mathcal{A}$ along the tree $\mathcal{T}$), if

- $\mathcal{T}$ is a tree;

- For $a \in A$ the set $\{t \mid a \in X_t\}$ is non-empty and connected (in $\mathcal{T}$);

- For every $R \in \tau$ and every $\bar{a}$ with $R^{\mathcal{A}}\bar{a}$ there is $t \in T$ such that $\bar{a} \in X_t$.

The set X_t is called the *block* at t. The *width* of $(\mathcal{T}, (X_t)_{t \in T})$ is $\max\{|X_t| \mid t \in T\} - 1$.

---

[b]The result remains true for the class of labelled trees which "contains" the directed trees.

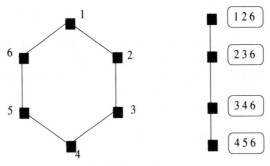

Figure 5

The *tree-width* tw($\mathcal{A}$) of $\mathcal{A}$ is the minimal width over all possible tree-decompositions of $\mathcal{A}$. If C is a class of structures, then tw(C) := max{tw($\mathcal{A}$) | $\mathcal{A} \in$ C}. And C is of *bounded tree-width*, if tw(C) $< \infty$. For $w \geq 1$, let STR$_w$ denote the class of structures of tree-width $\leq w$.

The tree-width of a graph $\mathcal{G}$ is a parameter that measures how close to a tree $\mathcal{G}$ is. Trees and forests have tree-width ≤ 1, cycles tree-width 2 (cf. Figure 5) and a clique of k vertices has tree-width $k - 1$; thus, a clique has maximal tree-width, since tw($\mathcal{A}$) $\leq |A| - 1$ for every structure $\mathcal{A}$.

The *graph* $\mathcal{G}(\mathcal{A})$ of a structure $\mathcal{A}$ of vocabulary τ is the graph with universe A in which two elements $a \neq b$ are adjacent if there is an $R \in \tau$ and a tuple $\bar{a} \in R^{\mathcal{A}}$ such that both a and b occur in the tuple $\bar{a}$. One can verify that the tree-decompositions of $\mathcal{G}(\mathcal{A})$ are precisely the tree-decompositions of $\mathcal{A}$ and thus, tw($\mathcal{G}(\mathcal{A})$) = tw($\mathcal{A}$). So, in many contexts, it would be possible to restrict our attention to graphs, but we do this only if the formulations for graphs are more natural.

We mentioned in the introduction that the notion of tree-decomposition had been reinvented in logic and called *nostrum* by Ajtai and Gurevich (cf. [1], 8.1 and 8.2). Before turning to the model-checking problem, we just want to state the main property of tree-decompositions proved and applied in [1].

Let $(\mathcal{T}, (X_t)_{t \in T})$ be a tree-decomposition of $\mathcal{A}$. For $t \in T$ and t_1, t_2 in distinct connected components of $\mathcal{T} \setminus t$, we have:

$(*) \qquad \forall a \in (X_{t_1} \setminus X_t) \, \forall b \in (X_{t_2} \setminus X_t) \, \forall R \in \tau : \text{ not } R^{\mathcal{A}} \ldots a \ldots b \ldots$

i.e., the distance of $a \in (X_{t_1} \setminus X_t)$ and $b \in (X_{t_2} \setminus X_t)$ in the graph $\mathcal{G}(\mathcal{A})$ is at least two. Recall that a subset X of $\mathcal{A}$ is *d-scattered*, if the distance in $\mathcal{G}(\mathcal{A})$ between any two elements of X exceeds d. Thus, $\{a, b\}$ above is 1-scattered. The following lemma essentially says that sufficiently large structures of tree-width $< w$ have reasonably big d-scattered subsets, if you remove up to w appropriate elements:

Lemma 4.1 ([1]) *There is a function f such that for all $m, d, w \geq 1$ and all structures $\mathcal{A}$ of tree-width $< w$ with $|A| \geq f(m, d, w)$ there exists $S \subseteq A$, $|S| \leq w$, such that in $\langle A \setminus S \rangle^{\mathcal{A}}$ there is a d-scattered subset of cardinality m.*

Ajtai and Gurevich used this property of tree-decompositions to prove the main result of their paper, namely:

Every DATALOG query expressible in first-order logic is bounded.

5 The Model-Checking Problem for Tree-Like Structures

In the Introduction we already mentioned our belief that the model-checking problem is the area of logic where the notion of tree-decomposition has been used most systematically. In this section and in section 6 we will present and discuss some of the results obtained.

5.1 Monadic Second-Order Logic

By the following theorem, 3-colorability and the existence of a kernel can be checked quickly for classes of graphs of bounded tree-width.

Theorem 5.1 ([9]) *Let C be a class of structures of bounded tree-width. Then, D-MC(C, MSO) $\in$ LINTIME.*

We sketch a proof (cf. [21]). It builds on an idea already present in our treatment of the kernel problem for directed trees. This idea will be further generalized later. Moreover, it uses the following result showing that tree-decompositions can be computed quickly:

Theorem 5.2 ([4]) *There is an algorithm that, given a structure $\mathcal{A}$ and $w \geq 1$, computes a tree-decomposition of $\mathcal{A}$ of width at most w if $\mathrm{tw}(\mathcal{A}) \leq w$, or rejects if $\mathrm{tw}(\mathcal{A}) > w$. The algorithm needs time $O(2^{c \cdot w^3} \cdot \|\mathcal{A}\|)$.*

We come to the proof of Theorem 5.1: Fix an MSO-sentence φ, say of quantifier rank q. Set $w := \mathrm{tw}(C)$. Let $\mathcal{A}$ be a structure in C. First, using the previous result, the desired algorithm computes a tree-decomposition $(\mathcal{T}, (X_t)_{t \in T})$ of tree-width $\leq w$. W.l.o.g. we assume that $\mathcal{T}$ is a binary tree.

For $t \in T$ let $Y_t := \bigcup_{s \geq t} X_s$. Define the sequence $\bar{a}^t := a_1 \ldots a_{w+1}$ such that $X_t = \{a_1, \ldots, a_{w+1}\}$. The q-type of $\bar{a}^t$ is the set of formulas of MSO of quantifier rank $\leq q$ satisfied by $\bar{a}^t$ in $\langle Y_t \rangle^{\mathcal{A}}$. (As already mentioned, the algorithm proceeds as the corresponding one for the kernel problem for directed trees: for $t \in T$, the role of the tree rooted at t is now taken over by Y_t, the role of t by $\bar{a}^t$ and the role of (k_t, n_t) by the q-type of $\bar{a}^t$.)

Using a tool of model theory, the Ehrenfeucht-Fraïssé games for MSO (e.g., cf. [12]), one can show that, for $t \in T$ with children u, v, the q-type of $\bar{a}^t$ only depends on the following data:

- the isomorphism type of the substructure induced by $\bar{a}^t$;

- the q-types of $\bar{a}^u$ and $\bar{a}^v$;

- the "intersection" of $\bar{a}^t$ and $\bar{a}^u$, and of $\bar{a}^t$ and $\bar{a}^v$.

The function giving these dependencies (for the fixed q) can be computed in advance. From the leaves to the root the algorithm we aim at calculates the q-type of any t.[c] From the q-type of the root it gets the information whether $\mathcal{A} \models \varphi$. Thus, the algorithm passes the tree once and performs at any node a bounded number of steps; altogether, the number of steps is $O(\|\mathcal{A}\|)$. $\square$

For graphs of bounded tree-width one can also exhibit a concrete kernel (if there is at least one) in linear time:

Theorem 5.3 ([13]) *Let* C *be a class of bounded tree-width and* $\varphi(\bar{Y}, \bar{x})$ *an* MSO-*formula. There is an algorithm that, given* $\mathcal{A} \in$ C, *decides whether* $\varphi(\mathcal{A}) \neq \emptyset$ *and, in the positive case, computes* $B_1, \ldots, B_l \subseteq A$ *and* $a_1, \ldots, a_m \in A$ *such that*

$$\mathcal{A} \models \varphi(B_1, \ldots, B_l, a_1, \ldots, a_m)$$

in time $O(\|\mathcal{A}\|)$.

This result has recently been applied (cf. [20]) to show that, for every $k \geq 0$, there is a quadratic time algorithm deciding whether a given graph has crossing number at most k and, in the positive case, to compute a drawing of the graph in the plane with at most k crossings.

We already mentioned that the class of trees axiomatizable in MSO are just those accepted by so-called deterministic tree-automata. Using these deterministic automata one can extend the previous results and get fast algorithms computing, on classes of bounded tree-width, all satisfying assignments (i.e., solving the so-called *evaluation problem*):

Theorem 5.4 ([13]) *Let* C *be a class of structures of bounded tree-width and* $\varphi(\bar{Y}, \bar{x})$ *an* MSO-*formula. There is an algorithm solving*

Input:	*Structure* $\mathcal{A} \in$ C.
Problem:	*Compute* $\varphi(\mathcal{A})$.

---

[c]Simple techniques from logic show that there is a finite set $\Phi(q, w)$ of MSO-formulas $\varphi(x_1, \ldots, x_{w+1})$ of quantifier rank $\leq q$ such that every MSO-formula $\psi(x_1, \ldots, x_{w+1})$ of quantifier rank $\leq q$ is equivalent to one in $\Phi(q, w)$; thus, we can assume that the q-types are finite objects.

in time $O(\|\mathcal{A}\| + \|\varphi(\mathcal{A})\|)$.

Example 5.5 *Let* $w \geq 1$. *There is an algorithm that, given a graph* $\mathcal{G}$ *with* $\mathrm{tw}(\mathcal{G}) \leq w$, *lists all kernels of* $\mathcal{G}$ *in time* $O(|\mathcal{G}| + \sum_{K \text{ kernel in } \mathcal{G}} |K|)$.

We fix $w \geq 1$ and consider $\mathrm{MC}(\mathrm{STR}_w, \mathrm{MSO})$ (recall that STR_w denotes the class of structures of tree-width $\leq w$) . This problem – as most combined complexity model-checking problems – has a high complexity. In fact, an analysis of the proof of Courcelles's Theorem 5.1 given above reveals that $\mathcal{A} \models \varphi$ can be decided in time $\leq f(\|\varphi\|) \cdot \|\mathcal{A}\|$, where f is some (fast-growing) function that bounds the number of steps needed to calculate the dependencies of the q-types, where q is the quantifier rank of φ; note that φ now is part of the input and thus, these dependencies cannot be computed in advance. Therefore, the main factor contributing to the high complexity of $\mathrm{MC}(\mathrm{STR}_w, \mathrm{MSO})$ is the sentence φ. In database theory, (relational) databases are viewed as structures and queries to the databases as formulas. Queries are often short, mostly much shorter than the size of the databases. The so-called *parameterized complexity* tries to take care of this difference (cf. [11]). We denote by $\mathrm{P\text{-}MC}(\mathrm{C}, \mathrm{L})$ the parameterized complexity of the model-checking problem for C and L, and define the parameterized complexity classes FPT and FPLIN just for the model-checking problem:

$\mathrm{P\text{-}MC}(\mathrm{C}, \mathrm{L}) \in \mathrm{FPT}$ – read: the model-checking for C and L is *fixed-parameter tractable* – if there is a computable function $f : \mathrm{L} \to \mathbb{N}$, a constant c, and an algorithm solving

Input:	Structure $\mathcal{A} \in \mathrm{C}$, sentence φ in L.
Problem:	$\mathcal{A} \models \varphi$?

in time $\leq f(\varphi) \cdot \|\mathcal{A}\|^c$ (note that the constant c does not depend on φ).

We write $\mathrm{P\text{-}MC}(\mathrm{C}, \mathrm{L}) \in \mathrm{FPLIN}$, if c can be chosen to be 1.

Clearly,

$$\mathrm{MC}(\mathrm{C}, \mathrm{L}) \in \mathrm{PTIME} \text{ implies } \mathrm{P\text{-}MC}(\mathrm{C}, \mathrm{L}) \in \mathrm{FPT};$$
$$\mathrm{P\text{-}MC}(\mathrm{C}, \mathrm{L}) \in \mathrm{FPT} \text{ implies } \mathrm{D\text{-}MC}(\mathrm{C}, \mathrm{L}) \in \mathrm{PTIME};$$

thus, the fixed-parameter tractability of the model-checking problem is a notion lying between the feasibility of the "database model-checking problem" and the feasibility of the "combined model-checking problem".

As remarked above:

Corollary 5.6 *Let* C *be a class of bounded tree-width. Then,* $\mathrm{P\text{-}MC}(\mathrm{C}, \mathrm{MSO})$ $\in \mathrm{FPLIN}$.

For classes of graphs closed under minors[d] the corollary is optimal, as shown by:

Theorem 5.7 ([21]) *Assume* P $\neq$ NP. *Let* C *be a class of graphs closed under minors. Then, the following are equivalent:*

(i) P-MC(C, MSO) $\in$ FPLIN.

(ii) P-MC(C, MSO) $\in$ FPT.

(iii) tw(C) $< \infty$.

In view of Corollary 5.6 it suffices to show the implication (ii) $\Rightarrow$ (iii). Hence, let C be a class of graphs closed under minors and assume, by contradiction, that tw(C) $= \infty$. Then, by the Excluded Grid Theorem ([28]), C contains all planar graphs. But 3-colorability is NPTIME-complete on the class of planar graphs, contradicting (ii). $\qquad\square$

Thus, for monadic-second order logic, the notion of tree-width allows to characterize the fixed-parameter tractable instances of the model-checking problem.

5.2 First-Order Logic

For first-order logic we obtain a generalization of Courcelle's Theorem by applying Gaifman's Theorem [16]. Essentially, Gaifman's Theorem states that every first-order sentence only claims the existence of a certain number of pairwise disjoint balls whose centers satisfy some first-order property in (the substructure generated by) the balls. Therefore, for first-order sentences, we are not forced to require that the whole structure has bounded tree-width, but that the balls do. More precisely:

The *local tree-width* of $\mathcal{A}$ is the function ltw($\mathcal{A}$) : $\mathbb{N} \to \mathbb{N}$ defined by

$$\mathrm{ltw}^{\mathcal{A}}(r) := \max\{\mathrm{tw}(\langle B_r(a)\rangle^{\mathcal{A}}) \mid a \in A\},$$

where $B_r(a)$ denotes the ball of radius r around a in the graph $\mathcal{G}(\mathcal{A})$ of $\mathcal{A}$. A class C of structures has *bounded local tree-width*, if there is a function $f : \mathbb{N} \to \mathbb{N}$ such that

$$\text{for all } \mathcal{A} \in C \text{ and all } r \geq 1 : \mathrm{ltw}^{\mathcal{A}}(r) \leq f(r).$$

As already indicated one gets:

Theorem 5.8 ([15]) *Let* C *be a class of structures of bounded local tree-width. Then,* P-MC(C, FO) $\in$ FPT.

---

[d]A graph $\mathcal{H}$ is a *minor* of a graph $\mathcal{G}$, if $\mathcal{H}$ can be obtained from a subgraph of $\mathcal{G}$ by contracting edges.

Of course, every class of structures of bounded tree-width is of bounded local tree-width. Further examples of classes of bounded local tree-width are the class of graphs of bounded valence or the class of planar graphs.

We sketch the idea leading to a further generalization for first-order logic. For this purpose, we again look at the proof of Courcelle's Theorem: there, we essentially need that the first-order q-types of the blocks are computable quickly; so, at this stage, blocks of bounded local tree-width would suffice. Moreover, we do not need that the the sizes of the blocks X_t are bounded, but that the sizes of the intersections $X_t \cap X_s$ with $t, s \in T$, $t \neq s$, are bounded. A decomposition theorem of Grohe [19] based on deep graph theoretic results due to Robertson and Seymour says: If C is a class of graphs such that there is a graph that is not a minor of any graph in C, then we get such tree-decompositions for the members in C (compare [19] for the precise statement).

Theorem 5.9 ([14]) *Let C be a class of graphs such there exists a graph that is not a minor of a graph in C. Then* P-MC(C, FO) $\in$ FPT.

In parameterized complexity theory the class FPT plays the role that PTIME does in classical complexity theory, and the role of NPTIME is taken over by a class denoted by $W[1]$. As with PTIME $\neq$ NPTIME the status of FPT $\neq$ $W[1]$ is not known; but FPT $\neq$ $W[1]$ would imply PTIME $\neq$ NPTIME.

As for MSO, also for FO we have a characterization of the classes with fixed-parameter tractable model-checking problem.

Theorem 5.10 ([21]) *Assume* FPT $\neq$ $W[1]$. *Let* C *be a class of graphs closed under minors. Then,*

P-MC(C, FO) $\in$ FPT *iff* C *is not the class of all graphs.*

6 The Model-Checking Problem for Tree-Like Sentences

Stockmeyer [29] showed that the satisfiability problem for quantified Boolean formulas is PSPACE-complete, thus:

Theorem 6.1 MC(STR, FO) *is* PSPACE-*complete.*

To get feasible instances of the model-checking problem, so far we restricted the class of structures (to classes of bounded tree-width) but considered the class of all sentences of a given logic. Now we shall restrict the class of sentences.

A *literal* is an atomic or a negated atomic formula. A first-order formula is *existential* if it is built from literals with the connectives $\wedge, \vee$ and with the existential quantifier. Every existential formula is equivalent to a Σ_1-*formula*, i.e., to a formula of the form $\exists x_1 \ldots \exists x_k \psi$ with quantifier-free ψ.

And every Σ_1-formula is equivalent to a disjunction of conjunctive formulas, where a *conjunctive formula* (or, *conjunctive query*) is a formula of the form $\exists y_1 \ldots \exists y_m (\lambda_1 \wedge \ldots \wedge \lambda_l)$ with literals λ_i. Denote by Σ_1 and CONJ the class of Σ_1-formulas and the class of conjunctive formulas, respectively.

In a certain sense, CONJ is the most simple "classical" subclass of FO containing sentences. Nevertheless, concerning the model-checking problem for CONJ, the results are disappointing. Since $\exists x_1 \ldots \exists x_k \bigwedge_{1 \leq i < j \leq k} E x_i x_j$ is a conjunctive sentence expressing that there is a clique of size k, one gets:

Theorem 6.2 ([5]) MC(STR, CONJ) *is* NPTIME-*complete.*

Theorem 6.3 ([10]) *If* FPT $\neq W[1]$, *then* P-MC(STR, CONJ) $\in W[1] \setminus$ FPT (*in fact,* P-MC(STR, CONJ) *is* $W[1]$-*complete under parameterized reductions*).

Let us have a look at the canonical algorithm deciding whether a first-order sentence φ holds in $\mathcal{A}$: Starting with the atomic subformulas of φ this algorithm inductively computes the set $\psi(\mathcal{A})$ for every subformula $\psi(\bar{x})$ of φ, therefore the algorithm can take up to $O(\|\varphi\| \cdot |A|^{|\mathrm{var}(\varphi)|})$ number of steps. This motivates the following restriction: We consider the *finite variable fragments* FO^s of FO. For $s \geq 1$ denote by FO^s the class of formulas of FO that contain at most s variables; define CONJ^s, Σ^s, ... similarly.

For a class C of structures and a set L of first-order formulas we denote by EVAL(C, L) the *evaluation problem* for C and L:

Input:	Structure $\mathcal{A} \in$ C; formula φ in L.
Problem:	Compute $\varphi(\mathcal{A})$.

The canonical algorithm mentioned above shows:

Theorem 6.4 ([31]) *For every* $s \geq 1$, EVAL(STR, FO^s) $\in$ PTIME *and thus,* MC(STR, FO^s) $\in$ PTIME.

6.1 Formulas of Bounded Tree-Width

What does FO^s have to do with tree-decompositions, the theme of our article? We explain the relationship and derive further results.

For a first-order formula φ let at(φ) be the set of atomic subformulas of φ, and let free(φ) and var(φ) be the set of free and the set of all variables of φ, respectively.

The *graph* $\mathcal{G}(\varphi)$ of φ has vertex set $G(\varphi) := \mathrm{var}(\varphi)$ and edge set

$$E^{\mathcal{G}(\varphi)} := \{(x, y) \mid x \neq y,\ x, y \in \mathrm{var}(\alpha) \text{ for some } \alpha \in \mathrm{at}(\varphi)\}$$
$$\cup \{(x, y) \mid x \neq y,\ x, y \in \mathrm{free}(\varphi)\},$$

i.e., $E^{\mathcal{G}(\varphi)}$ takes care of the "input relations" (the atomic relations) and the "output relation" $\varphi(\_)$. By definition, the *tree-width* of φ is the tree-width of the graph $\mathcal{G}(\varphi)$.

For example, in graphs the sentence $\varphi := \exists x_1 \ldots \exists x_k \bigwedge_{1 \leq i < j \leq k} E x_i x_j$ expresses that there is a clique of size k and $\mathcal{G}(\varphi) = \mathcal{K}_k$ is the k-clique with vertex set $\{x_1, \ldots, x_k\}$. Similarly, $\varphi := \exists x_1 \ldots \exists x_k (\bigwedge_{1 \leq i < k} E x_i x_{i+1} \wedge E x_k x_1)$ expresses that there is a cycle of size k and $\mathcal{G}(\varphi) = \mathcal{C}_k$ is such a cycle.

If L is a fragment of FO and C a class of graphs, we denote by L(C) the set of L-formulas φ with $\mathcal{G}(\varphi) \in$ C. Thus, for $w \geq 1$, L(STR$_w$) denotes the set of L-formulas of tree-width $\leq w$.

We state a first relationship between the finite variable fragments and the fragments of bounded tree-width. Note that FO$^{w+1} \subseteq$ FO(STR$_w$). In fact, for $\varphi \in$ FO^{w+1} with var$(\varphi) = \{x_1, \ldots, x_{w+1}\}$ we have the tree-decomposition consisting of the single block $\{x_1, \ldots, x_{w+1}\}$. Moreover:

Proposition 6.5 ([24,14]) *Let $w \geq 1$. There is a linear time algorithm that, applied to a formula in* CONJ(STR$_w$), *yields an equivalent existential formula in* FO^{w+1}.

We sketch a proof: Let $\varphi(\bar{x}) = \exists y_1 \ldots \exists y_m (\lambda_1 \wedge \ldots \wedge \lambda_l)$ be of tree-width $\leq w$. We compute a tree-decomposition $(\mathcal{T}, (X_t)_{t \in T})$ of $\mathcal{G}(\varphi)$ of tree-width $\leq w$ (cf. 5.2). Since the variables in $\bar{x}$ form a clique in $\mathcal{G}(\varphi)$ there must be a single block containing all these variables; we choose a corresponding node of the tree as root $r^{\mathcal{T}}$. For $t \in T$ let λ_t be the conjunction of the literals λ_i such that var$(\lambda_i) \subseteq X_t$. By induction from the leaves to the root $r^{\mathcal{T}}$ we define, for $t \in T$ with children $t_1, \ldots, t_n$ and parent s, the formula φ_t by

$$\varphi_t := \exists y_1 \ldots \exists y_k (\lambda_t \wedge \varphi_{t_1} \wedge \ldots \wedge \varphi_{t_n}),$$

where $X_t \setminus X_s = \{y_1, \ldots, y_k\}$ (and $X_{(r^{\mathcal{T}})} \setminus \{\bar{x}\} = \{y_1, \ldots, y_k\}$). Then, φ and $\varphi_{(r^{\mathcal{T}})}$ are equivalent; since every subformula of $\varphi_{(r^{\mathcal{T}})}$ has at most $w + 1$ free variables, $\varphi_{(r^{\mathcal{T}})}$ (and hence, φ) is equivalent to a formula in FO^{w+1}. □

Proposition 6.5 and Theorem 6.4 yield:

Corollary 6.6 ([7]) *Let $w \geq 1$. Then,* EVAL(STR, CONJ(STR$_w$)) $\in$ PTIME *and thus,* MC(STR, CONJ(STR$_w$)) $\in$ PTIME.

For later purposes we sketch a direct proof of the last claim of the Corollary, namely of MC(STR, CONJ(STR$_w$)) $\in$ PTIME. Let $\varphi = \exists y_1 \ldots \exists y_m (\lambda_1 \wedge \ldots \wedge \lambda_l) \in$ CONJ(STR$_w$) be a sentence. Let $(\mathcal{T}, (X_t)_{t \in T})$ and λ_t be as in the preceding proof.

Assume given a structure $\mathcal{A}$. From the leaves to the root $r^{\mathcal{T}}$ we compute, for every node t with children $t_1, \ldots, t_n$, the set Γ_t of assignments $\gamma : X_t \to A$ that satisfy λ_t in $\mathcal{A}$ and that, for $i = 1, \ldots, n$, are compatible with at least one $\gamma' \in \Gamma_{t_i}$ (γ and γ' are *compatible* if they agree on $X_t \cap X_{t_i}$). One can verify that $\mathcal{A} \models \varphi$ iff $\Gamma_{(r^\tau)} \neq \emptyset$. As $|\Gamma_t| \leq |A|^{w+1}$ we obtain the claim. $\quad\square$

Since a Σ_1-sentence can effectively be transformed into a disjunction of conjunctive formulas[e], we get:

Corollary 6.7 ([14]) *Let* $w \geq 1$. *Then,* P-MC(STR, Σ_1(STR$_w$)) $\in$ FPT.

Quite recently it has been shown that for conjunctive formulas these results are the best possible ones. Again the notion of tree-decomposition allows to characterize the feasible instances of the model-checking problem.

Theorem 6.8 ([22]) *Let* C *be a class of graphs. Then*

1. *Assume* PTIME $\neq$ NPTIME. *If* C *is closed under minors, then*

$$\text{MC(STR, CONJ(C))} \in \text{PTIME} \;\; \textit{iff}\, \text{tw}(\text{C}) < \infty.$$

2. *Assume* FPT $\neq W[1]$. *Then,*

$$\text{P-MC(STR, CONJ(C))} \in \text{FPT} \;\, \textit{iff}\, \text{tw}(\text{C}) < \infty.$$

We give an application of 6.7. Let $\mathcal{A}$ be a τ-structure, $|A| = n$, and $A = \{a_1, \ldots, a_n\}$. Set

$$\varphi_{\mathcal{A}} := \exists x_1 \ldots \exists x_n \bigwedge_{R \in \tau,\, (a_{i_1}, \ldots, a_{i_m}) \in R^{\mathcal{A}}} R x_{i_1} \ldots x_{i_m}.$$

Then, for every τ-structure $\mathcal{B}$,

$$\mathcal{B} \models \varphi_{\mathcal{A}} \text{ iff there is a homomorphism from } \mathcal{A} \text{ into } \mathcal{B}.$$

Since $\mathcal{G}(\mathcal{A}) \cong \mathcal{G}(\varphi_{\mathcal{A}})$ we have by 6.6:

Corollary 6.9 ([26]) *Let* $w \geq 1$. *There is a* PTIME-*algorithm solving*

Input:	*Structure* $\mathcal{A}$ *of tree-width* $\leq w$; *structure* $\mathcal{B}$.
Problem:	*Is there a homomorphism from* $\mathcal{A}$ *into* $\mathcal{B}$?

Recalling that the cycles $\mathcal{C}_k$ have tree-width 2, we see that there is a PTIME-algorithm that, for every cycle $\mathcal{C}_k$ and every graph $\mathcal{G}$, decides whether $\mathcal{G}$ contains a homomorphic image of $\mathcal{C}_k$. But what if we want to know whether $\mathcal{G}$ contains a k-cycle? The following proposition shows to what extend we can generalize the results from homomorphisms to embeddings (= injective homomorphisms). A sentence expressing the existence of an embedding of $\mathcal{A}$ is

$$\psi_{\mathcal{A}} := \exists x_1 \ldots \exists x_n (\bigwedge_{1 \leq i < j \leq n} \neg x_i = x_j \wedge \bigwedge_{R \in \tau,\, (a_{i_1}, \ldots, a_{i_m}) \in R^{\mathcal{A}}} R x_{i_1} \ldots x_{i_m}).$$

---

[e]It is unlikely that such a transformation can be done in polynomial time.

For a first-order formula φ let $\varphi^{\neq}$ be the formula obtained from φ by deleting all subformulas $x = y$ which occur negatively (i.e., in the scope of an odd number of negation symbols) in φ. Thus, $\psi_{\mathcal{A}}^{\neq} = \varphi_{\mathcal{A}}$. Moreover, let $\Sigma_1^{\neq}(\text{STR}_w)$ be the class of Σ_1-formulas φ such that $\varphi^{\neq}$ has tree-width $\leq w$. Clearly, $\Sigma_1(\text{STR}_w) \subseteq \Sigma_1^{\neq}(\text{STR}_w)$. The following extension of 6.7 holds:

Proposition 6.10 ([14]) *Let* $w \geq 1$. *Then,* P-MC(STR, $\Sigma_1^{\neq}(\text{STR}_w)$) $\in$ FPT.

The previous results cannot be extended literally to the class of all existential first-order formulas: For every $k \geq 3$ the existential sentence

$$\varphi_k := \exists x_1 \ldots \exists x_k \bigwedge_{1 \leq i < j \leq k} \exists y \exists z (y = x_i \wedge z = x_j \wedge Eyz)$$

saying that a graph contains a k-clique has tree-width 2. It is well-known that no FO^s contains all the φ_k's and that there is no PTIME-algorithm checking, for all graphs $\mathcal{G}$ and all $k \geq 1$, whether $\mathcal{G}$ satisfies φ_k (unless PTIME=NPTIME).

To generalize our results for conjunctive formulas we proceed as follows. First note that a conjunctive formula

$$\varphi(\bar{x}) = \exists y_1 \ldots \exists y_m (\lambda_1 \wedge \ldots \wedge \lambda_l)$$

corresponds to the non-recursive datalog rule

$$Q\bar{x} \leftarrow \lambda_1, \ldots, \lambda_l$$

where Q is a new relation symbol. The rule is *non-recursive*, since Q – the *head symbol* – does not occur in the body of the rule. Conversely, a non-recursive datalog rule

$$Q\bar{x} \leftarrow \lambda_1, \ldots, \lambda_l,$$

where we always tacitly assume that $\{\bar{x}\} \subseteq \text{var}(\lambda_1 \wedge \ldots \wedge \lambda_l)$, is equivalent to the conjunctive formula $\varphi(\bar{x}) := \exists y_1 \ldots \exists y_m (\lambda_1 \wedge \ldots \wedge \lambda_l)$ with $\{\bar{y}\} = \text{var}(\lambda_1 \wedge \ldots \wedge \lambda_l) \setminus \{\bar{x}\}$. A *non-recursive datalog program* is a set of non-recursive datalog rules:

$$Q\bar{x} \leftarrow \lambda_{11}, \ldots, \lambda_{1l_1}$$
$$\vdots$$
$$Q\bar{x} \leftarrow \lambda_{s1}, \ldots, \lambda_{sl_s}.$$

Q is its *head symbol*.

While conjunctive formulas correspond to datalog rules, first-order formulas correspond to NRSD-programs, i.e., to *non-recursive stratified datalog programs*. A NRSD-program Π is a sequence $\Pi := (\Pi_1, \ldots, \Pi_d)$ of non-recursive datalog programs Π_i with the property that for $1 \le i < j \le d$ the head symbol of Π_j does not occur in Π_i. The Π_i's are called the *strata*. The value $\Pi(\mathcal{A})$ of Π in the structure $\mathcal{A}$ is the value of the head symbol of Π_d obtained by evaluating first Π_1, then $\Pi_2,\ldots$, and finally Π_d (e.g., cf. [12] for details). It is well-known that:

Proposition 6.11 *First-order logic and* NRSD-*programs have the same expressive power.*

For example, the sentence $\forall x \exists y(Exy \vee \neg Py)$ is equivalent to the program

$$Q_1 x \leftarrow Exy$$
$$Q_1 x \leftarrow \neg Py, x = x$$
$$\ldots\ldots\ldots\ldots\ldots$$
$$Q_2 x \leftarrow \neg Q_1 x$$
$$\ldots\ldots\ldots\ldots\ldots$$
$$Q_3 \leftarrow Q_2 x$$
$$\ldots\ldots\ldots\ldots\ldots$$
$$Q_4 \leftarrow \neg Q_3.$$

By definition, a datalog rule has *tree-width* $\le w$ if the corresponding conjunctive formula does. And a NRSD-program has *tree-width* $\le w$ if every rule does. Denote by NRSD(w) the set of NRSD programs of tree-width $\le w$. By using 6.6 one gets:

Corollary 6.12 ([13]) *Let* $w \ge 1$. *Then,* EVAL(STR, NRSD(w)) $\in$ PTIME.

We mentioned that NRSD has the same expressive power as FO. But what fragment of FO corresponds to NRSD(w)?

Theorem 6.13 ([13]) *Let* $w \ge 1$. *For every first-order formula* φ *we have*

$$\varphi \underset{\sim}{\in} \text{NRSD}(w) \text{ iff } \varphi \underset{\sim}{\in} \text{FO}^{w+1}$$

($\varphi \underset{\sim}{\in} L$ *means that* φ *is equivalent to a formula or program in* L). *More precisely: There is a linear time algorithm associating with every formula in* FO^{w+1} *an equivalent program in* NRSD(w). *And there is an algorithm associating with every* NRSD(w)-*program an equivalent* FO^{w+1}-*formula.*

Using the first algorithm we see that the previous corollary implies Theorem 6.4. By contrast, the canonical algorithm translating NRSD-programs into first-order formulas is not a linear time algorithm: NRSD-programs allow more succinct representations than formulas, since a single stratum can take care of a subformula occurring several times in a given formula.

So far the evaluation methods used the fact that, in a structure $\mathcal{A}$, a conjunctive formula φ of tree-width $\le w$ can be evaluated along a corresponding tree-decomposition $(\mathcal{T}, (X_t)_{t \in T})$ of $\mathcal{G}(\varphi)$: at any node t we evaluate the literals of φ whose variables are in X_t; this can be done in time $O(\|\mathcal{A}\|^{w+1})$.

6.2 Acyclic formulas

We turn to Yannakakis' approach: He considered conjunctive formulas φ whose graphs $\mathcal{G}(\varphi)$ have tree-decompositions $(\mathcal{T}, (X_t)_{t \in T})$, where each node $t \in T$ is "guarded" by a positive atomic subformula $R\bar{x}$, i.e., $X_t = \{\bar{x}\}$. Then, when evaluating φ, at the node t one can restrict to the tuples in $R^{\mathcal{A}}$. This yields a fast algorithm. Let us give precise definitions and results.

A conjunctive formula $\varphi = \exists y_1 \ldots \exists y_m (\lambda_1 \wedge \ldots \wedge \lambda_l)$ is *acyclic* if there is a tree-decomposition $(\mathcal{T}, (X_t)_{t \in T})$ of $\mathcal{G}(\varphi)$ such that for every $t \in T$ there is a positive λ_i s.t. $X_t = \mathrm{var}(\lambda_i)$. Then, λ_i is called a *guard* at t.

For example, for $n \geq 3$, the sentence $\varphi := \exists x_1 \ldots \exists x_n \bigwedge_{1 \leq i < n} E x_i x_{i+1} \wedge E x_n x_1$ is not acyclic, since every tree-decomposition of φ has at least one node with ≥ 3 variables. However, $\exists x_1 \ldots \exists x_n \bigwedge_{1 \leq i < n} E x_i x_{i+1}$ is acyclic.

We denote by ACYCLIC the class of acyclic conjunctive formulas. Yannakakis' result reads as follows:

Theorem 6.14 (([32]) EVAL(STR, ACYCLIC) $\in$ PTIME *and therefore,* MC(STR, ACYCLIC) $\in$ PTIME.

Again, we can generalize this result via datalog. We call a datalog rule *acyclic*, if the corresponding conjunctive formula is acyclic. An NRSD-program is *acyclic*, if every rule is acyclic and, moreover, has a tree-decomposition whose guards can be chosen among the literals containing no head symbols of previous strata. Denote by ACY-NRSD the class of acyclic NRSD-programs.

Then, in a straightforward manner one obtains the following generalization of Yannakakis' result:

Theorem 6.15 ([13]) EVAL(STR, ACY-NRSD) $\in$ PTIME *and therefore,* MC(STR, ACY-NRSD) $\in$ PTIME.

Again we ask: What fragment of first-order logic corresponds to the class of acyclic NRSD-programs? It turns out that this is just the guarded fragment, which has recently been studied intensively ([2,17]). We recall its definition: The set GF of formulas of the *guarded fragment* is obtained by closing the set of atomic first-order formulas under the connectives $\wedge$, $\vee$, and $\neg$ and under the rule

If φ is a GF-formula, α is atomic, and free$(\varphi) \subseteq \mathrm{var}(\alpha)$ then, for every tuple $\bar{y}$ of variables, $\exists \bar{y}(\alpha \wedge \varphi)$ is a GF-formula.

As indicated above we have:

Theorem 6.16 ([13]) *For every first-order sentence φ we have*

$$\varphi \underset{\sim}{\in} \text{ACY-NRSD } \textit{iff } \varphi \underset{\sim}{\in} \text{GF}.$$

Moreover, there is a quadratic time algorithm that associates with every GF-sentence an equivalent ACY-NRSD-program. Hence:

Theorem 6.17 ([17]) $\text{MC}(\text{STR}, \text{GF}) \in \text{PTIME}$.

Gottlob, Leone, and Scarcello [18] introduce the notion of bounded hypertree-width, a further generalization of (positive) acyclic conjunctive formulas; in fact, acyclic conjunctive queries are conjunctive queries of hypertree-width one. They show that the model-checking problem for most classes of tree-like conjunctive queries considered so far is in the parallel complexity class LOGCFL and actually is complete for this class.

References

1. M. Ajtai and Y. Gurevich. Datalog vs. first-order logic. *Journal of Computer and System Sciences*, 49:562–588, 1994.
2. H. Andréka, J. van Benthem, and I. Németi. Modal languages and bounded fragments of first-order logic, 1996. ILLC Research Report ML-96-03, University of Amsterdam.
3. H.L. Bodlaender. Some classes of graphs with bounded treewidth. *Bulletin of the EATCS*, 36:116–126, 1988.
4. H.L. Bodlaender. A linear-time algorithm for finding tree-decompositions of small treewidth. *SIAM Journal on Computing*, 25:1305–1317, 1996.
5. A.K. Chandra and P.M. Merlin. Optimal implementation of conjunctive queries in relational data bases. In *Proceedings of the 9th ACM Symposium on Theory of Computing*, pages 77–90, 1977.
6. V. Chvátal On the computational complexity of finding a kernel. *Centre des Recherches Mathématiques, Université de Montréal*, Report No. CRM–300, 1973.
7. Ch. Chekuri and A. Rajaraman. Conjunctive query containment revisited. In Ph. Kolaitis and F. Afrati, editors, *Proceedings of the 5th International Conference on Database Theory*, volume 1186 of *Lecture Notes in Computer Science*, pages 56–70. Springer-Verlag, 1997.
8. B. Courcelle. Graphs and monadic second-order logic, some open problems. *Bulletin of the EATCS*, 49:110–124, 1993.
9. B. Courcelle. Graph rewriting: An algebraic and logic approach. In J. van Leeuwen, editor, *Handbook of Theoretical Computer Science*, volume 2, pages 194–242. Elsevier Science Publishers, 1990.

138

10. R.G. Downey and M.R. Fellows. Fixed-parameter tractability and completeness II. *Theoretical Computer Science*, 141:109–131, 1995.
11. R.G. Downey and M.R. Fellows. *Parameterized Complexity*. Springer-Verlag, 1999.
12. H.-D. Ebbinghaus and J. Flum. *Finite Model Theory*. Springer-Verlag, 1995.
13. J. Flum, M. Frick and M. Grohe. Query evaluation via tree-decompositions. In J. van den Busche and V. Vianu, editors, *Proceedings of the 8th International Conference on Database Theory*, Lecture Notes in Computer Science, Springer-Verlag, 2001. To appear.
14. J. Flum and M. Grohe. Fixed-parameter tractability and logic. To appear in *SIAM Journal of Computing*.
15. M. Frick and M. Grohe. Deciding first-order properties of locally tree-decomposable graphs. In *Proceedings of the 26th International Colloquium on Automata, Languages and Programming*, Lecture Notes in Computer Science 1644. Springer-Verlag, 1999.
16. H. Gaifman. On local and non-local properties.. In *Proceedings of the Herbrand Symposium, Logic Colloquium' 81*, 105–135, North Holland,1982.
17. G. Gottlob, E. Grädel, and H. Veith. Datalog lite: Temporal versus deductive reasoning in verification. Technical Report DBAI-TR-98-22, Technische Universität Wien, 1998.
18. G. Gottlob, N. Leone, and F. Scarcello. Hypertree decompositions and tractable queries. In *Proceedings of the 18th ACM Symposium on Principles of Database Systems*, 21–32, 1999.
19. M. Grohe. Local tree-width, excluded minors, and approximation algorithms. Submitted.
20. M. Grohe. Computing crossing numbers in quadratic time. In preparation.
21. M. Grohe. Descriptive and parameterized complexity. In *Computer Science Logic 1999*, Lecture Notes in Computer Science 1683, Springer-Verlag, 1999.
22. M. Grohe, T. Schwentick, and L. Segoufin. When is the evaluation of conjunctive queries tractable? Submitted.
23. R. Halin. *S*-functions for graphs. *Journal of Geometry*, 8:171–186, 1976.
24. Ph.G. Kolaitis and M.Y. Vardi. Conjunctive-query containment and constraint satisfaction. In *Proceedings of the 17th ACM Symposium on Principles of Database Systems*, pages 205–213, 1998.
25. C.H. Papadimitriou. *Computational Complexity*. Addison-Wesley, 1994.
26. J. Plehn and B. Voigt. Finding minimally weighted subgraphs. In

R. Möhring, editor, *Graph-Theoretic Concepts in Computer Science, WG '90*, volume 484 of *Lecture Notes in Computer Science*, pages 18–29. Springer-Verlag, 1990.

27. N. Robertson and P.D. Seymour. Algorithmic aspects of tree-width. *Journal of Algorithms*, 7:309–322, 1986.

28. N. Robertson and P.D. Seymour. Graph minors V. excluding a planar graph. *Journal of Combinatorial Theory, Series B*, 41:92–114, 1986.

29. L.J. Stockmeyer. *The Complexity of Decision Problems in Automata Theory*. PhD thesis, Department of Electrical Engineering, MIT, 1974.

30. J.W. Thatcher and J.B. Wright. Generalized finite automata theory with an application to a decision problem of second-order arithmetic.. *Mathematical Systems Theory*, 2:57–81, 1968.

31. M. Y. Vardi. On the complexity of bounded-variable queries. In *Proceedings of the 14th ACM Symposium on Principles of Database Systems*, pages 266–276, 1995.

32. M. Yannakakis. Algorithms for acyclic database schemes. In *7th International Conference on Very Large Data Bases*, pages 82–94, 1981.

IS RANDOMNESS "NATIVE" TO COMPUTER SCIENCE?

MARIE FERBUS-ZANDA
Université Paris 7
2, pl. Jussieu 75251 Paris Cedex 05, France
E-mail: `ferbus@logique.jussieu.fr`

SERGE GRIGORIEFF
LIAFA, Université Paris 7
2, pl. Jussieu 75251 Paris Cedex 05, France
E-mail: `seg@liafa.jussieu.fr`

1 Kolmogorov Complexity

1.1 Randomness and Probability Theory

Quisani: Hello, can I talk with you?

Authors: Some more wisdom may come out from a discussion.

Q: I just found a surprising assertion on Leonid Levin's home page:

> *While fundamental in many areas of Science, randomness is really "native" to Computer Science.*

Common sense would rather consider randomness as intrinsically relevant to probability theory!

A: Levin also adds: *"The computational nature of randomness was clarified by Kolmogorov."*
   The point is that, from its very origin to modern axiomatization around 1933 [20] by Andrei Nikolaievitch Kolmogorov (1903–1987), probability theory carries a paradoxical result: *if we toss an unbiaised coin 100 times then 100 heads are just as probable as any other outcome!*
   As Peter Gács pleasingly remarks ([16], p. 3), this convinces us only that the axioms of probability theory, as developped in [20], do not solve all mysteries that they are sometimes supposed to.
   In fact, since Laplace, much work has been devoted to get *a mathematical theory of random objects*, notably by Richard von Mises (1883–1953) (cf. §8.2). But none was satisfactory up to the 60's when such a theory emerged on the basis of computability.

As it sometimes occurs, the theory was discovered by several authors independently.[a] In the USA, Ray J. Solomonoff (b. 1926), 1964 [40] (a paper submitted in 1962) and Gregory J. Chaitin (b. 1947), 1966 [7], 1969 [8] (both papers submitted in 1965). In Russia, Kolmogorov, 1965 [22], with premisses announced in 1963 [21].

Q: Same phenomenon as for hyperbolic geometry with Gauss, Lobatchevski and Bolyai. I recently read a citation from Bolyai's father: "When the time is ripe for certain things, these things appear in different places in the manner of violets coming to light in early spring".

A: Mathematics and poetry... Well, pioneered by Kolmogorov, Martin-Löf, Levin, Gács, Schnorr (in Europe) and Chaitin, Solovay (in America), the theory developped very fruitfully and is now named *Kolmogorov complexity* or *Algorithmic Information theory*.

Q: So, Kolmogorov founded probability theory twice! In the 30's and then in the 60's.

A: Hum... In the 30's Kolmogorov axiomatized probability theory on the basis of measure theory, i.e. integration theory on abstract spaces. In the 60's, Kolmogorov (and also Solomonoff and Chaitin independently) founded a mathematical theory of *randomness*. That it could be a new basis for probability theory is not clear.

Q: What? Randomness would not be *the* natural basis for probability theory?

A: Random numbers are useful in different kinds of applications: simulations of natural phenomena, sampling for testing "typical case", getting good source of data for algorithms, ... (cf. Donald Knuth, [19], chapter 3).

However, the notion of random object as a mathematical notion is presently ignored in lectures about probability theory. Be it for the foundations or for the development of probability theory, such a notion is neither introduced nor used. That's the way it is... There is a notion of random variable, but it has really nothing to do with random objects. Formally, they are just functions over some probability space. The name "random variable" is a mere vocable to convey the underlying *non formalized* intuition of randomness.

Q: That's right. I attended several courses on probability theory. Never heard anything precise about random objects. And, now that you tell me, I realize that there was something strange for me with random variables.

---

[a]For a detailed analysis of *who did what, and when*, see [29] p.89–92.

So, finally, our concrete experience of chance and randomness on which we build so much intuition is simply removed from the formalization of probability theory.

Hum... Somehow, it's as if the theory of computability and programming were omitting the notion of program, real programs.

By the way, isn' it the case? In recursion theory, programs are reduced to mere integers: Gödel numbers!

A: Sure, recursion theory illuminates but does not exhaust the subject of programming.

As concerns a new foundation of probability theory, it's already quite remarkable that Kolmogorov has looked at his own work on the subject with such a distance. So much as to come to a new theory: the mathematization of randomness. However, it seems (to us) that Kolmogorov has been ambiguous on the question of a new foundation. Indeed, in his first paper on the subject (1965, [22], p. 7), Kolmogorov briefly evoked that possibility:

> ... to consider the use of the [Algorithmic Information theory] constructions in providing a new basis for probability theory.

However, later (1983, [24], p. 35–36), he separated both topics

> "there is no need whatsoever to change the established construction of the mathematical probability theory on the basis of the general theory of measure. I am not inclined to attribute the significance of necessary foundations of probability theory to the investigations [about Kolmogorov complexity] that I am now going to survey. But they are most interesting in themselves.

though stressing the role of his new theory of random objects for *mathematics as a whole* ([24], p. 39):

> The concepts of information theory as applied to infinite sequences give rise to very interesting investigations, which, without being indispensable as a basis of probability theory, can acquire a certain value in the investigation of the algorithmic side of mathematics as a whole."

Q: All this is really exciting. Please, tell me about this approach to randomness.

1.2 Intuition of Finite Random Strings and Berry's Paradox

A: OK. We shall first consider finite strings.

If you don't mind, we can start with an approach which actually fails but conveys the basic intuitive idea of randomness. Well, just for a while, let's say that a finite string u is random if there is no shorter way to describe u but give the successive symbols which constitute u. Saying it otherwise, the shortest description of u is u itself, i.e., the very writing of the string u.

Q: Something to do with intensionality and extensionality?

A: You are completely right. Our tentative definition declares a finite string to be random just in case it does not carry *any* intensionality. So that there is no description of u but the extensional one, which is u itself.

Q: But the notion of description is somewhat vague. Is it possible to be more precise about "description" and intensionality?

A: Diverse partial formalizations are possible. For instance within any particular logical first-order structure. But they are quite far from exhausting the intuitive notion of definability. In fact, the untamed intuitive notion leads to paradoxes, much as the intuition of truth.

Q: I presume you mean the liar paradox as concerns truth. As for definability, it should be Berry's paradox about
"the smallest integer not definable in less than eleven words"
and this integer is indeed defined by this very sentence containing only 10 words.

A: Yes, these ones precisely. By the way, this last paradox was first mentioned by Bertrand Russell, 1908 ([36], p.222 or 150) who credited G.G. Berry, an Oxford librarian, for the suggestion.

1.3 Kolmogorov Complexity

Q: And how can one get around such problems?

A: What Solomonoff, Kolmogorov and Chaitin did is a very ingenious move: *instead of looking for a general notion of definability, they restricted it to computability*. Of course, computability is a priori as much a vague and intuitive notion as is definability. But, as you know, since the thirties, there is a mathematization of the notion of computability.

Q: Thanks to Kurt, Alan and Alonzo.[b]

A: Hum...Well, with such a move, general definitions of a string u are replaced by programs which compute u.

---

[b]Kurt Gödel (1906–1978), Alan Mathison Turing (1912–1954), Alonzo Church (1903–1995).

Q: Problem: we have to admit Church's thesis.

A: OK. In fact, even if Church's thesis were to break down, the theory of recursive functions would still remain as elegant a theory as you learned from Yuri and other people. It would just be a formalization of a proper part of computability, as is the theory of primitive recursive functions or elementary functions. As concerns Kolmogorov theory, it would still hold and surely get extension to such a new context.

Q: But where do the programs come from? Are you considering Turing machines or some programming language?

A: Any partial recursive function $A : \{0,1\}^* \to \{0,1\}^*$ is considered as a programming language. The domain of A is seen as a family of programs, the value $A(p)$ — if there is any — is the output of program p. As a whole, A can be seen both as a language to write programs and as the associated operational semantics.

Now, Kolmogorov complexity relative to A is the function $K_A : \{0,1\}^* \to \mathbb{N}$ which maps a string x to the length of shortest programs which output x:

Definition 1. $K_A(x) = \min\{|p| \; : \; A(p) = x\}$.

(Convention: $\min(\emptyset) = +\infty$, so that $K_A(x) = +\infty$ if x is outside the range of A.)

Q: This definition reminds me of a discussion I had with Yuri some years ago ([18] p.76–78). Yuri explained me things about Levin complexity. I remember it involved time.

A: Yes. Levin complexity is a very clever variant of K which adds to the length of the program the log of the computation time to get the output. It's a much finer notion. We shall not consider it for our discussion about randomness. You'll find some developments in [29] §7.5.

Q: There are programs and outputs. Where are the inputs?

A: We can do without inputs. It's true that functions with no argument are not considered in mathematics, but in computer science, they are. In fact, since von Neumann, we all know that there can be as much tradeof as desired between input and program. This is indeed the basic idea for universal machines and computers.

Nevertheless, Kolmogorov [22] points a natural role for inputs when considering *conditional Kolmogorov complexity* in a sense very much alike that of conditional probabilities.

To that purpose, consider a partial recursive function $B : \{0,1\}^* \times \{0,1\}^* \to \{0,1\}^*$. A pair (p,y) in the domain of B is interpreted as a program

p together with an input y. And $B(p, y)$ is the output of program p on input y. Kolmogorov [22] defines the conditional complexity relative to B as the function $K_B(\ |\ ) : \{0,1\}^* \times \{0,1\}^* \to \mathbf{N}$ which maps strings x, y to the length of shortest programs which output x on input y:

Definition 2. $K_B(x \mid y) = \min\{|p| \ : \ B(p, y) = x\}$.

1.4   Why Binary?

Q: Programs and outputs should be binary strings?

A: This is merely a reasonable restriction.

Let's first consider the outputs. In Kolmogorov approach, outputs are the finite objects for which a notion of randomness is looked for. Dealing with effectiveness, representation of objects does matter. Whence strings and not abstract integers. Binary strings constitute a simple convenient choice.

As for programs, binary strings surely have some flavor of machine level programming. But this has nothing to do with the present choice. In fact, binary strings just allow for a fairness condition. The reason is that Kolmogorov complexity deals with lengths of programs. Squaring or cubing the alphabet divides all lengthes by 2 or 3 as we see when going from binary to octal or hexadecimal. So that binary representation of programs is merely a way to get an absolute measure of length. If we were to consider programs p written in some finite alphabet Σ, we would have to replace the length $|p|$ by the product $|p| \log(card(\Sigma))$ where $card(\Sigma)$ is the number of symbols in Σ. This is an important point when comparing Kolmogorov complexities associated to diverse programming languages, cf. 3.4.

2   How Complex is Kolmogorov Complexity?

Q: Well, let me tell you some points I see about K_A.

The domain of K_A appears to be the range of A. So that K_A is total in case A is onto.

Since there are finitely many programs p with length $\leq n$, there can be only finitely many x's such that $K_A(x) \leq n$. So that, $\lim_{|x| \to +\infty} K_A(x) = +\infty$.

Also, in the definition of $K_A(x)$, there are 2 points:
1) find some program which outputs x,
2) make sure that all programs with shorter length either do not halt or have output different from x.

Point 2 does not match with definitions of partial recursive functions!

2.1 Approximation from Above

A: Right. In general, K_A *is not* partial recursive.

Q: So, no way to compute K_A.

A: Definitely not, in general. However, K_A can be approximated from above:

Proposition 3. K_A *is the limit of a recursive decreasing sequence of functions.*

Moreover, we can take such a sequence of functions with finite domains.

To see this, fix an algorithm $\mathcal{A}$ for A and denote A_t the partial function obtained by applying up to t steps of algorithm $\mathcal{A}$ for the sole programs with length $\leq t$. It is clear that $(t, p) \mapsto A_t(p)$ has recursive graph. Also,
$$K_{A_t}(x) = \min\{|p| \ : \ p \in \{0, 1\}^{\leq t} \text{ and } A_t(p) = x\}$$
so that $(t, x) \mapsto K_{A_t}(x)$ has recursive graph too.

To conclude, just observe that $(t, x) \ \mapsto \ K_{A_t}(x)$ is decreasing in t (with the obvious convention that $undefined = +\infty$) and that $K_A(x) = \lim_{t \to \infty} K_{A_t}(x)$.

The same is true for conditional Kolmogorov complexity $K_B(\ | \ )$.

Q: If K_A is not recursive, there should be no recursive modulus of convergence for this approximation sequence. So what can it be good for?

A: In general, if a function $f : \{0, 1\}^* \to \mathbf{N}$ can be approximated from above by a recursive sequence of functions $(f_t)_{t \in \mathbf{N}}$ then $X_n^f = \{x : f(x) \leq n\}$ is recursively enumerable (in fact, both properties are equivalent). Which is a very useful property of f. Indeed, such arguments are used in the proof of some hard theorems in the subject of Kolmogorov complexity.

Q: Could you give me the flavor of what it can be useful for?

A: Suppose you know that X_n^f is finite (which is indeed the case for $f = K_A$) and has exactly m elements then you can explicitly get X_n^f.

Q: Explicitly get a finite set? What do you mean?

A: What we mean is that there is a recursive function which associates to any m, n a code (in whatever modelisation of computability) for a partial recursive function which has range X_n^f in case m is equal to the number of elements in X_n^f. This is not trivial. We do this thanks to the f_t's.

Indeed, compute the $f_t(x)$'s for all t's and all x's until you get m different strings $x_1, \ldots, x_m$ such that $f_{t_1}(x_1), \ldots, f_{t_m}(x_m)$ are defined and $\leq n$ for some $t_1, \ldots, t_m$.

That you will get such $x_1, \ldots, x_m$ is insured by the fact that X_n^f has at least m elements and that $f(x) = \min\{f_t(x) \ : \ t\}$ for all x.

Since $f \leq f_t$, surely these x_i's are in X_n^f. Moreover, they indeed constitute the whole of X_n^f since X_n^f has exactly m elements.

2.2 Dovetailing

Q: You run infinitely many computations, some of which never halt. How do you manage them?

A: This is called *dovetailing*. You organize these computations (which are infinitely many, some lasting forever) as follows:
— Do up to 1 computation step of $f_t(x)$ for $0 \leq t \leq 1$ and $0 \leq |x| \leq 1$,
— Do up to 2 computation steps of $f_t(x)$ for $0 \leq t \leq 2$ and $0 \leq |x| \leq 2$,
— Do up to 3 computation steps of $f_t(x)$ for $0 \leq t \leq 3$ and $0 \leq |x| \leq 3$,
...

Q: Somehow looks like Cantor's enumeration of $\mathbf{N}^2$ as the sequence
$$(0,0) \quad (0,1)\ (1,0) \quad (0,2)\ (1,1)\ (2,0) \quad (0,3)\ (1,2)\ (2,1)\ (3,0)\ldots$$

A: This is really the same idea. Here, it would rather be an enumeration à la Cantor of $\mathbf{N}^3$. When dealing with a multi-indexed family of computations $(\varphi_t(\vec{x}))_{\vec{t}}$, you can imagine computation steps as tuples of integers $(i, \vec{t}, \vec{x})$ where i denotes the rank of some computation step of $f_{\vec{t}}(\vec{x})$ (here, these tuples are triples). Dovetailing is just a way of enumerating all points in a discrete multidimensional space $\mathbf{N}^k$ via some zigzagging à la Cantor.

Q: Well, Cantor wandering along a broken line which fills the discrete plane here becomes a way to sequentialize parallel computations.

2.3 Undecidability

Q: Let's go back to K_A. If A is onto then K_A is total. So that if A is also recursive then K_A should be recursive too. In fact, to get $K_A(x)$ just compute all $A(p)$'s, for increasing $|p|$'s until some has value x: this will happen since A is onto.

You said K_A is in general undecidable. Is this undecidability related to the fact that A be partial recursive and not recursive?

A: No. It's possible that K_A be quite trivial with A as complex as you want. Let $f : \{0,1\}^* \to \mathbf{N}$ be any partial recursive function. Set $A(0x) = x$ and $A(1^{1+f(x)}0x) = x$. Then, A is as complex as f though K_A is trivial since $K_A(x) = |x| + 1$, as is easy to check.

Q: Is it hard to prove that some K_A is indeed not computable?

A: Not that much. And this is where Berry's paradox comes back. For $A : \{0,1\}^* \to \{0,1\}^*$ we shall consider an adequate version of $PASCAL$ programming language.[c]

First, we start with a version of $PASCAL$ admitting arbitrary large integers and strings: no bound like $maxint = 2^{15} - 1$ or $maxlongint = 2^{31} - 1$. In this version we should have $maxint = +\infty$. This can obviously be done via an implementation using pointers rather than fixed size arrays.

Q: This is actually done in some languages like LISP or ML. Static bounds for programs and data are today no more justified, at least in such a drastic way as we see in programming languages like $PASCAL$. Only the physical limitations inherent to the machine should remain.

A: Sure. $PASCAL$ programs may ask for inputs and may write non binary outputs. So, suppress the $read$ routine of $PASCAL$: now programs will not ask for any input, though procedures will still have inputs. Also, constrain the $write$ routine to output solely binary strings. In this way — which can be made quite effective —, we obtain $PASCAL^0$.

Now, $PASCAL^0$ programs are not written in binary: most of the 128 ASCII symbols are used. So, let $PASCAL^{bin}$ be obtained by replacing each symbol used in $PASCAL^0$ by its associated (7 digits) binary code.

Thus, to each piece of $PASCAL^0$ source code π, we associate a binary string π^{bin} which is 7 times longer and is a piece of $PASCAL^{bin}$ source code with the very same behaviour as π.

Finally, we get our partial recursive function $A : \{0,1\}^* \to \{0,1\}^*$ which we shall rather call $U^{PASCAL^{bin}}$ to enhance its significance. $U^{PASCAL^{bin}}(p)$ is defined only if p is of the form $p = \pi^{bin}$ where π is a $PASCAL^0$ program (which is easy to check). And in that case we set $U^{PASCAL^{bin}}(p)$ to be the output of π (if there is any).

One more thing. Consider the length-lexicographic or hierarchical order on binary strings: $u <_{hier} v$ if and only if $|u| < |v|$ or $|u| = |v|$ and u is lexicographically before v.

Now, look, we come to the core of the argument. The key idea is to introduce the function $T : \mathbf{N} \to \{\mathbf{0},\mathbf{1}\}^*$ defined by

$$T(i) = \text{the } <_{hier} \text{ smallest } x \text{ such that } K_{U^{PASCAL^{bin}}}(x) > i.$$

As you see, this function is nothing but an implementation of the very statement in Berry's paradox modified according to Kolmogorov's move from definability to computability.

---

[c]Such a $PASCAL$ context for the argument of the proof (rather than the usual recursion theoretic one) is taken from the introduction of Machtey & Young's book [32].

Clearly, by very definition, we have

$$K_{UPASCAL^{bin}}(T(i)) > i \tag{1}$$

Suppose, by way of contradiction, that $K_{UPASCAL^{bin}}$ is computable. Then so is T. So, there is a $PASCAL^0$ procedure π which asks for an integer type input i and outputs $T(i)$ written in binary.

Using this procedure π, it is easy to get for each $i \in \mathbf{N}$ a $PASCAL^0$ program π_i which outputs $T(i)$ written in binary: just call procedure π on input i. Writing down the binary representation of i in program π_i requires $1 + \lfloor \log(i) \rfloor$ digits, so that the length of π_i is $\lfloor \log(i) \rfloor + |\pi| + c$ where c is some constant.

Translating π_i into $PASCAL^{bin}$, we get π_i^{bin} with length $7(\lfloor \log(i) \rfloor + |\pi| + c)$ which outputs $T(i)$ written in binary. Thus,

$$K_{UPASCAL^{bin}}(T(i)) \leq 7(\lfloor \log(i) \rfloor + |\pi| + c). \tag{2}$$

Equations (1), (2) lead to $i < 7\log(i) + 7|\pi| + 7c$ which is a contradiction for i large enough since $\lim_{i \to +\infty} \frac{\log(i)}{i} = 0$.

2.4   No Non Trivial Recursive Lower Bound

Q: Quite nice an argument.

A: Can get much more out of it:
Theorem 4. *1) No restriction of $K_{UPASCAL^{bin}}$ to an infinite recursive set is computable.*
2) Worse, if $X \subseteq \{0,1\}^*$ is recursive and $f : X \to \mathbf{N}$ is a recursive function and $f(x) \leq K_{UPASCAL^{bin}}(x)$ for all $x \in X$ then f is bounded!
    To prove this, just change the above definition of $T : \mathbf{N} \to \{0,1\}^*$ as follows:

$$T(i) = \text{ the } <_{hier} \text{ smallest } x \in X \text{ such that } f(x) > i$$

Clearly, by very definition, we have $f(T(i)) > i$. Since $T(i) \in X$ and $f(x) \leq K_{UPASCAL^{bin}}$ for $x \in X$, this implies equation (1) above. Also, f being computable, so is T, and the above argument leads to the very same equation (2) above. Now, as already seen, equations (1), (2) lead to a contradiction.

Let's reformulate this result in terms of the greatest monotonous (with respect to $\leq_{hier}$) lower bound of $K_{UPASCAL^{bin}}$ which is

$$m(x) = \min_{y \geq_{hier} x} K_{UPASCAL^{bin}}(y)$$

This function m is monotonous and tends to $+\infty$ but it does so incredibly slowly: *on any recursive set it can not grow as fast as any unbounded recursive function.*

3 Optimal Kolmogorov Complexity

3.1 Universality

Q: This function $U^{PASCAL^{bin}}$ seems to be a universal partial recursive function in the sense of recursion theory, as is stressed by the letter U.

A: Right. Let's explicit the universality property via a quick redo of the above §2.3. Let $A : \{0,1\}^* \to \{0,1\}^*$ be partial recursive. Using a $PASCAL^0$ procedure π_A computing A, to each $p \in \{0,1\}^*$ we associate a $PASCAL^0$ program $\pi_{A,p}$ which outputs $A(p)$ and has length $|p| + |\pi_A| + c$ where c is some constant. Translating $\pi_{A,p}$ into $PASCAL^{bin}$, we get $\pi_{A,p}^{bin}$ which is 7 times longer.

Thus, to each partial recursive function A we can associate a recursive function $\theta_A : p \mapsto \pi_{A,p}^{bin}$ such that $A = U^{PASCAL^{bin}} \circ \theta$. This is the universality property. Moreover,

$$|\theta_A(p)| = 7|p| + d \text{ for some constant } d \text{ depending on } A. \tag{3}$$

Q: What about the multiplicative constant 7?

A: Of course, it is contingent to the way we transformed $PASCAL^0$ programs into binary strings. The factor 7 comes from the binarization of the non binary string $\pi_{A,p}$. But, $\pi_{A,p}$ is a mixing of π_A and p and p is already binary. So that it is not very reasonnable to binarize p through the replacement of its digits by the 7 digits long ASCII binary codes for $0, 1$. A better way to mix π_A and p into a binary string will allow to get rid of the constant 7 in equation (3).

3.2 Coding Pairs of Strings

A: First, we need a trick to encode two binary strings u, v as a binary string w. The word *encoding* here means a recursive injective function $\{0,1\}^* \times \{0,1\}^* \to \{0,1\}^*$. Observe that concatenation does not work: if $w = uv$ then we don't know which prefix of w is u. A new symbol 2 inserted as a marker allows for an encoding: from $w = u2v$ we can indeed recover u, v. However, w is no more a *binary* string.

A simple solution uses this last idea together with a padding function applied to u which allows 1 to become an end-marker. Let $pad(u)$ be obtained by inserting a new zero in front of every symbol in u. For instance, $pad(01011) = 0001000101$. Now, a simple encoding w of strings u, v is the concatenation $w = pad(u)1v$. In fact, the very definition of pad insures that the end of the prefix $pad(u)$ in w is marked by the first occurrence of 1 at an odd position (obvious convention: first symbol has position 1). Thus, from w

we get $pad(u)$ — hence u — and v in a very simple way: a finite automaton can do the job! Observe that

$$|pad(u)1v| = 2|u| + |v| + 1 \tag{4}$$

Q: Is the constant 2 the best one can do?

A: No, one can iterate the trick. Instead of padding u, one can pad the string $\overline{|u|}$ which is the binary representation of the length of u. Look at the string $w = pad(\overline{|u|})1uv$. The first occurrence of 1 at an odd position tells you which prefix of w is $pad(\overline{|u|})$ and which suffix is uv. From the prefix $pad(\overline{|u|})$, you get $\overline{|u|}$, hence $|u|$. From $|u|$ and the suffix uv, you get u and v. Nice trick, isn't it? And since $|\overline{|u|}| = 1 + \lfloor\log(|u|)\rfloor$, we get

$$|pad(\overline{|u|})1uv| = |u| + |v| + 2\lfloor\log(|u|)\rfloor + 3 \tag{5}$$

Q: Exciting! One could altogether pad the length of the length.

A: Sure. $pad(\overline{\overline{|u|}})1\overline{|u|}uv$ is indeed an encoding of u, v. The first occurrence of 1 at an odd position tells you which prefix of w is $pad(\overline{\overline{|u|}})$ and which suffix is $\overline{|u|}uv$. From the prefix $pad(\overline{\overline{|u|}})$, you get $\overline{\overline{|u|}}$ hence $|\overline{|u|}|$. Now, from $|\overline{|u|}|$ and the suffix $\overline{|u|}uv$ you get $\overline{|u|}$ — hence $|u|$ — and uv. From $|u|$ and uv, you get u and v. Also, a simple computation leads to

$$|pad(\overline{\overline{|u|}})1\overline{|u|}uv| = |u| + |v| + \lfloor\log(|u|)\rfloor + 2\lfloor\log(1 + \lfloor\log(|u|)\rfloor)\rfloor + 3 \tag{6}$$

Q: How far can we go that way?

A: Up to $\log^*$. This function is defined as follows. Observe that for $t > 0$ the sequence

$$t, \ \log(t), \ \log(\log(t)), \ \log(\log(\log(t))), \ldots$$

is defined and strictly decreasing up to the point some term becomes ≤ 0. The number of iterations to get this point is, by definition, $\log^*(t)$.

Though $\log^*$ is monotonous and tends to $+\infty$, it does so extremely slowly: the smallest x such that $\log^*(x) = n$ is $2^{2^{\cdot^{\cdot^{2}}}}$, a tower of iterated exponentiations with $n - 1$ times 2.

Q: Nevertheless, $\log^*$ is not slower than the greatest monotonous lower bound of $U^{PASCAL^{bin}}$ ...

A: Right. But, let's leave such refinements (cf. [29] p.79–80) and go back to the universality of $U^{PASCAL^{bin}}$.

3.3   Universality Which Does Not Increase Length

A: Let's focus on the universal character of $U^{PASCAL^{bin}}$ and how to get rid of the multiplicative factor 7 encountered in the previous universality character (§3.1).

Partial recursive functions $A : \{0,1\}^* \to \{0,1\}^*$ correspond to $Pascal^0$ procedures π_A with exactly one parameter in $\{0,1\}^*$ (recall we did constrain the *write* routine so that any output must be a binary string).

$U^{PASCAL^{bin}}$ emulates A on p via the $Pascal^0$ program $\pi_{A,p}$ and its binary associate $\pi_{A,p}^{bin}$ in $Pascal^{bin}$.

Now, we change the syntax of $U^{PASCAL^{bin}}$ to get the partial recursive function $U : \{0,1\}^* \to \{0,1\}^*$ defined as follows:

i) The domain of U is included in the family of binary strings $pad(\pi^{bin})1p$ where π is the binary associate in $Pascal^{bin}$ of some $Pascal^0$ procedure having exactly one parameter lying in $\{0,1\}^*$, and p is some binary string.

ii) $U(pad(\pi^{bin})1p)$ is the output of procedure π on p if it does halt (this makes sense because from $pad(\pi^{bin})1p$ we unambiguously get π^{bin} and p).

Observe that in the encoding $pad(\pi^{bin})1p$ procedure π has been binarized but p has been kept untouched.

Clearly, U behaves exactly as $U^{PASCAL^{bin}}$ does. The only difference is the way syntax conveys the operational semantics. In particular, U is universal: to each partial recursive function $A : \{0,1\}^* \to \{0,1\}^*$ is associated a recursive function $\lambda_A : p \mapsto pad(\pi_A^{bin})1p$ such that

$$A = U \circ \lambda_A \quad \text{and} \quad |\lambda_A(p)| = |p| + d \quad \text{for some constant } d \qquad (7)$$

(namely, $d = 2|\pi_A^{bin}| + 1 = 14|\pi_A| + 1$). We shall say that such an U has the property of *universality with no increase of length but for an additve constant*.

Q: That constant d in equation (7) is somehow a trace of an A-compiler written in the programming language U.

A: Exactly.

3.4   The Invariance Theorem

A: Now, comes the fundamental result of the theory. We shall state it uniquely for Kolmogorov complexity but it also holds for conditional Kolmogorov complexity.

First, a useful notation. For $f, g : \{0,1\}^* \to \mathbf{N}$, let's write $f \leq g + O(1)$ (resp. $f = g + O(1)$) to mean that there exists a constant c such that $\forall x \ f(x) \leq g(x) + c$ (resp. $\forall x \ |f(x) - g(x)| \leq c$) , i.e., f is smaller than (resp. equal to) g up to an additive constant c.

Now, we have:

$$K_U(x) = \min\{|q| \ : \ U(q) = x\} \qquad \text{(definition of } K_U)$$
$$\leq \min\{|\lambda_A(p)| \ : \ U(\lambda_A(p)) = x\}$$
$$= \min\{|\lambda_A(p)| \ : \ A(p)) = x\} \qquad \text{(equation (7))}$$
$$= \min\{|p| + d \ : \ A(p) = x\} \qquad \text{(again equation (7))}$$
$$= K_A(x) + d \qquad \text{(definition of } K_A)$$

This can be expressed as the following theorem independently obtained by Kolmogorov (1965 [22] p.5), Chaitin (1969 [8] §9-11, submitted 1965) and Solomonoff (1964 [40] p.12, who gives the proof as an informal argument).

Theorem 5 (Invariance theorem). $K_U \leq K_A + O(1)$ *for any partial recursive* $A : \{0,1\}^* \to \{0,1\}^*$. *In other words, up to an additive constant,* K_U *is the smallest one among the* K_A*'s.*

As a corollary, we see that if U and V both have the property of universality with no increase of length then $K_U = K_V + O(1)$. Whence the following definition.

Definition 6 (Kolmogorov complexity). Kolmogorov complexity $K :$ $\{0,1\}^* \to \mathbf{N}$ is any fixed such function K_U.

The invariance theorem means that, up to an additive constant, there is an intrinsic notion of Kolmogorov complexity and we can speak of *the* Kolmogorov complexity of a binary string.

Q: Which is an integer defined up to a constant... Somewhat funny.

A: You witty! Statements that only make sense in the limit occur everywhere in mathematical contexts.

Q: Do not mind, I was joking.

A: In fact, Kolmogorov argued as follows about the constant, [22] p. 6:

> Of course, one can avoid the indeterminacies associated with the [above] constants, by considering particular [... functions U], but it is doubtful that this can be done without explicit arbitrariness. One must, however, suppose that the different "reasonable" [above universal functions] will lead to "complexity estimates" that will converge on hundreds of bits instead of tens of thousands. Hence, such quantities as the "complexity" of the text of "War and Peace" can be assumed to be defined with what amounts to uniqueness.

3.5 Non Determinism

Q: Our problematic is about randomness. Chance, randomness, arbitrariness, unreasonned choice, non determinism... Why not add randomness to programs by making them non deterministic with several possible outputs?

A: Caution: if a single program can output every string, then Kolmogorov complexity collapses. In order to get a non trivial theory, you need to restrict non determinism. There is a lot of reasonable ways to do so. It happens that all lead to something which is essentially usual Kolmogorov complexity up to some change of scale ([39], [17]). Same with the prefix Kolmogorov complexity which we shall discuss later.

4 Algorithmic Information theory

4.1 Zip/Unzip

Q: A moment ago, you said the subject was also named Algorithmic Information theory. Why?

A: Well, you can look at $K(x)$ as a measure of the information contents that x conveys. The notion can also be vividly described using our everyday use of compression/decompression software (cf. Alexander Shen's lecture [38]). First, notice the following simple fact:

Proposition 7. $K(x) \leq |x| + O(1)$.

Indeed, let $A(x) = x$. Then $K_A(x) = |x|$ and the above inequality is a mere application of the Invariance Theorem.

Looking at the string x as a file, any program p such that $U(p) = x$ can be seen as a *compressed file* for x (especially in case the right member in Proposition 7) is indeed $< |x| \ldots$).

So, U appears as a *decompression algorithm* which maps the compressed file p onto the original file x. In this way, $K(x)$ measures the length of the shortest compressed files for x.

What does compression? It eliminates redundancies, explicits regularities to shorten the file. Thus, maximum compression reduces the file to the core of its information contents which is therefore measured by $K(x)$.

4.2 Some Relations in Algorithmic Information Theory

Q: OK. And what does Algorithmic Information theory look like?

A: First, a simple fact.
Proposition 8. Let $f : \{0,1\}^* \to \{0,1\}^*$ be partial recursive.
1) $K(f(x)) \leq K(x) + O(1)$.
2) If f is also injective, then $K(f(x)) = K(x) + O(1)$.

Indeed, denote U some fixed universal function such that $K = K_U$.

To get a program which outputs $f(x)$, we just encode a program π computing f together with a program p outputting x.

Formally, let $A : \{0,1\}^* \to \{0,1\}^*$ be such that $A(pad(\pi)1z)$ is the output of π on input $U(z)$ for all $z \in \{0,1\}^*$. Clearly, $A(pad(\pi)1p) = f(x)$ so that $K_A(f(x)) \leq 2|\pi| + |p| + 1$. Taking p such that $K(x) = |p|$, we get $K_A(f(x)) \leq K(x) + 2|\pi| + 1$.

The Invariance Theorem ensures that $K(f(x)) \leq K_A(f(x)) + O(1)$, whence point 1 of the Proposition.

In case f is injective, it has a partial recursive inverse g with domain the range of f. Applying point 1 to f and g we get point 2.

Q: Conditional complexity should give some nice relations as is the case with conditional probability.

A: Yes, there are relations which have some probability theory flavor. However, there are often logarithmic extra terms which come from the encoding of pairs of strings. For instance, an easy relation:

$$K(x) \leq K(x \mid y) + K(y) + 2\log(\min(K(x \mid y), K(y))) + O(1) \qquad (8)$$

The idea to get this relation is as follows. Suppose you have a program p (with no parameter) which outputs y and a program q (with one parameter) which on input y outputs x, then you can mix them to get a (no parameter) program which outputs x.

Formally, suppose that p, q are optimal, i.e. $K(y) = |p|$ and $K(x \mid y) = |q|$. Let $A_1, A_2 : \{0,1\}^* \to \{0,1\}^*$ be such that
$$A_1(pad(|z|)1zw) = A_2(pad(|w|)1zw) = V(w, U(z)),$$
where V denotes some fixed universal function such that $K(\ |\ ) = K_V(\ |\ )$. It is clear that $A_1(pad(|p|)1pq) = A_2(pad(|q|)1pq) = x$, so that
$$K_{A_1}(x) \leq |p| + |q| + 2\log(|p|) + O(1),$$
$$K_{A_2}(x) \leq |p| + |q| + 2\log(|q|) + O(1),$$
whence, p, q being optimal programs,
$$K_{A_1}(x) \leq K(y) + K(x \mid y) + 2\log(K(y)) + O(1,)$$
$$K_{A_2}(x) \leq K(y) + K(x \mid y) + 2\log(K(x \mid y)) + O(1).$$
Applying the Invariance Theorem, we get (8).

4.3 Kolmogorov Complexity of Pairs

Q: What about pairs of strings in the vein of the probability of a pair of events?

A: First, we have to define the Kolmogorov complexity of pairs of strings. The key fact is as follows:

Proposition 9. *If* $f, g : \{0,1\}^* \times \{0,1\}^* \to \{0,1\}^*$ *are encodings of pairs of strings (i.e., recursive injections), then* $K(f(x,y)) = K(g(x,y)) + O(1)$.

As we always argue up to an additive constant, this leads to:

Definition 10. The Kolmogorov complexity of pairs is $K(x,y) = K(f(x,y))$ where f is any fixed encoding.

To prove Proposition 9, observe that $f \circ g^{-1}$ is a partial recursive injection such that $f = (f \circ g^{-1}) \circ g$. Then, apply Proposition 8 with argument $g(x,y)$ and function $f \circ g^{-1}$.

4.4 Symmetry of Information

A: Relation (8) can be easily improved to

$$K(x,y) \leq K(x \mid y) + K(y) + 2\log(\min(K(x \mid y), K(y))) + O(1). \qquad (9)$$

The same proof works. Just observe that from both programs $pad(|p|)1pq$ and $pad(|q|)1pq$ one gets q hence also y.

Now, (9) can be considerably improved:

Theorem 11. $|K(x,y) - K(x \mid y) - K(y)| = O(\log(K(x,y)))$.

This is a hard result, independently obtained by Kolmogorov and Levin around 1967 ([23], [48] p.117). We better skip the proof (you can get it in [38] p. 6–7 or [29] Thm 2.8.2 p. 182–183).

Q: I don't really see the meaning of that theorem.

A: Let's restate it in another form.

Definition 12. $I(x : y) = K(y) - K(y \mid x)$ is called the algorithmic information about y contained in x.

This notion is quite intuitive: you take the difference between the whole information contents of y and that when x is known for free.

Contrarily to what was expected in analogy with Shannon's classical information theory, this is not a symmetric function However, up to a logarithmic term, it is symmetric:

Corollary 13. $|I(x : y) - I(y : x)| = O(log(K(x,y)))$

For a proof, just apply Theorem 11 with $K(x,y)$ and $K(y,x)$ and observe that $K(x,y) = K(y,x) + O(1)$ (use Proposition 9).

5 Kolmogorov Complexity and Logic

5.1 What to Do with Paradoxes

Q: Somehow, Solomonoff, Kolmogorov and Chaitin have built up a theory from a paradox.

A: Right. In fact, there seems to be two mathematical ways towards paradoxes. The most natural one is to get rid of them by building secured and delimited mathematical frameworks which will leave them all out (at least, we hope so...). Historically, this was the way followed in all sciences. A second way, which came up in the 20th century, somehow integrates paradoxes into scientific theories via some clever and sound (!) use of the ideas they convey. Kolmogorov complexity is such a remarkable integration of Berry's paradox into mathematics.

Q: As Gödel did with the liar paradox which is underlying his incompleteness theorems. Can we compare these paradoxes?

A: Hard question. The liar paradox is about truth while Berry's is about definability. Viewed in computational terms, truth and definability somehow correspond to denotational and operational semantics.

This leads to expect connections between incompleteness theorems à la Gödel and Kolmogorov investigations.

5.2 Chaitin Incompleteness Results

Q: So, incompleteness theorems can be obtained from Kolmogorov theory?

A: Yes. Gregory Chaitin, 1971 [9], pointed and popularized a simple but clever and spectacular application of Kolmogorov complexity (this original paper by Chaitin did not consider K but the number of states of Turing machines, which is much similar).

Let T be a recursive theory containing Peano arithmetic such that all axioms of T are true statements.

Theorem 14. *There exists a constant c such that if T proves $K(x) \geq n$, then $n \leq c$.*

The proof is by way of contradiction and is a redo of the undecidability of $K_{U_{PASCAL^{bin}}}$. Suppose that T can prove statements $K(x) \geq n$ for arbitrarily large n's. Consider a recursive enumeration of all theorems of T and let $f : \mathbf{N} \to \mathbf{N}$ be such that $f(n)$ is the first string x such that $K(x) \geq n$ appears as a theorem of T. Our hypothesis ensures that f is total, hence a recursive function. By very definition,

$$K(\overline{f(n)} \geq n. \tag{10}$$

Also, applying Propositions 8 and 7 we get

$$K(\overline{f(n)}) \leq K(\overline{n}) + O(1) \leq \log(n) + O(1), \tag{11}$$

whence $n \leq \log(n) + O(1)$, which is a contradiction if n is large enough.

Q: Quite nice. But this does not give any explicit statement. How to compute the constant c ? How to get any explicit x's such that $K(x) > c$?

A: Right. Hum... you could also see this as a particularly strong form of incompleteness: you have a very simple infinite family of statements, only finitely many can be proved but you don't know which ones.

5.3 Logical Complexity of K

A: By the way, there is a point we should mention as concerns the logical complexity of Kolmogorov complexity.

Since K is total and not recursive, its graph can not be recursively enumerable (r.e.). However, the graph of any K_A (hence that of K) is always of the form $R \cap S$ where R is r.e. and S is co-r.e. (i.e., the complement of an r.e. relation).

We can see this as follows. Fix an algorithm P for A and denote A^t the partial function obtained by applying up to t computation steps of this algorithm. Then
$$K_A(x) \leq n \Leftrightarrow \exists t \, (\exists p \in \{0,1\}^{\leq n} \, A^t(p) = x)$$
The relation within parentheses is recursive in t, n, x, so that $K_A(x) \leq n$ is r.e. in n, x.

Replacing n by $n - 1$ and going to negations, we see that $K_A(x) \geq n$ is co-r.e. Since $K_A(x) = n \Leftrightarrow (K_A(x) \leq n) \wedge (K_A(x) \geq n)$, we conclude that $K_A(x) = n$ is the intersection of an r.e. and a co-r.e relations.

In terms of Post's hierarchy, the graph of K_A is $\Sigma_1^0 \wedge \Pi_1^0$, hence Δ_2^0. The same with $K_B(\mid)$.

Q: Would you remind me about Post's hierarchy?

A: Emil Post introduced families of relations $R(x_1 \ldots x_m)$ on strings and/or integers. Let's look at the first two levels:

Σ_1^0 and Π_1^0 are the respective families of r.e. and co-r.e. relations,

Σ_2^0 is the family of projections of Π_1^0 relations,

Π_2^0 consist of complements of Σ_2^0 relations.

Notations Σ_i^0 and Π_i^0 come from the following logical characterizations:

$R(\vec{x})$ is Σ_1^0 if $R(\vec{x}) \Leftrightarrow \exists t_1 \ldots \exists t_k \, T(\vec{t}, \vec{x})$ with T recursive.

$R(\vec{x})$ is Σ_2^0 if $R(\vec{x}) \Leftrightarrow \exists \vec{t} \, \forall \vec{u} \, T(\vec{t}, \vec{u}, \vec{x})$ with T recursive.

Π_1^0 and Π_2^0 are defined similarly with quantifications $\forall$ and $\forall \exists$.

Each of these families is closed under union and intersection. But not under complementation since Σ_i^0 and Π_i^0 are so exchanged.

A last notation: Δ_i^0 denotes $\Sigma_i^0 \cap \Pi_i^0$. In particular, Δ_1^0 means r.e. and co-r.e. hence recursive.

As for inclusion, Δ_2^0 strictly contains the Boolean closure of Σ_1^0, in particular it contains $\Sigma_1^0 \cup \Pi_1^0$. This is why the term hierarchy is used.

Also, we see that K_A is quite low as a Δ_2^0 relation since $\Sigma_1^0 \wedge \Pi_1^0$ is the very first level of the Boolean closure of Σ_1^0.

6 Random Finite Strings and Their Applications

6.1 Random Versus How Much Random

Q: Let's go back to the question: "what is a random string?"

A: This is the interesting question, but this will not be the one we shall answer. We shall modestly consider the question: "To what extent is x random?"

We know that $K(x) \leq |x| + O(1)$. It is tempting to declare a string x random if $K(x) \geq |x| - O(1)$. But what does it really mean? The $O(1)$ hides a constant. Let's explicit it.

Definition 15. A string is called c-incompressible (where $c \geq 0$ is any constant) if $K(x) \geq |x| - c$. Other strings are called c-compressible. 0-incompressible strings are also called incompressible.

Q: Are there many c-incompressible strings?

A: Kolmogorov noticed that they are quite numerous.

Theorem 16. *For each n the proportion of c-incompressible among strings with length n is $> 1 - 2^{-c}$.*

For instance, if $c = 4$ then, for any length n, more than 90% of strings are 4-incompressible. With $c = 7$ and $c = 10$ we go to more than 99% and 99.9%.

The proof is a simple counting argument. There are $1 + 2 + 2^2 + \cdots + 2^{n-c-1} = 2^{n-c} - 1$ programs with length $< n - c$. Every string with length n which is c-compressible is necessarily the output of such a program (but some of these programs may not halt or may output a string with length $\neq n$). Thus, there are at most $2^{n-c} - 1$ c-compressible strings with length n, hence at least $2^n - (2^{n-c} - 1) = 2^n - 2^{n-c} + 1$ c-incompressible strings with length n. Whence the proportion stated in the theorem.

Q: Are c-incompressible strings really random?

A: Yes. Martin-Löf, 1965 [33], formalized the notion of statistical test and proved that incompressible strings pass all these tests (cf. §8.3).

6.2 Applications of Random Finite Strings in Computer Science

Q: And what is the use of incompressible strings in computer science?

A: Roughly speaking, incompressible strings are strings without any form of local or global regularity. Consideration of such objects may help almost anytime one has to show something is complex, for instance a lower bound for worst or average case time/space complexity. The accompanying key tool is Proposition 8.

And, indeed, incompressible strings have been successfully used in such contexts. An impressive compilation of such applications can be found in Ming Li and Paul Vitanyi's book ([29], chapter 6), running through nearly 100 pages!

Q: Could you give an example?

A: Sure. The very first such application is quite representative. It is due to Wolfgang Paul, 1979 [35] and gives a quadratic lower bound on the computation time of any one-tape Turing machine $\mathcal{M}$ which recognizes palindromes.

Up to a linear waste of time, one can suppose that $\mathcal{M}$ always halts on its first cell.

Let n be even and $xx^R = x_1 x_2 \ldots x_{n-1} x_n x_n x_{n-1} \ldots x_2 x_1$ be a palindrome written on the input tape of the Turing machine $\mathcal{M}$.

For each $i < n$ let CS_i be the crossing sequence associated to cell i, i.e., the list of successive states of $\mathcal{M}$ when its head visits cell i.

Key fact: *string $x_1 x_2 \ldots x_i$ is uniquely determined by CS_i.*

I.e., $x_1 x_2 \ldots x_i$ is the sole string y such that — relative to an $\mathcal{M}$-computation on some palindrome with prefix y —, the crossing sequence on cell $|y|$ is CS_i.

This can be seen as follows. Suppose $y \neq x_1 x_2 \ldots x_i$ leads to the same crossing sequence CS_i on cell $|y|$ for an $\mathcal{M}$-computation on some palindrome $yzz^R y^R$. Run $\mathcal{M}$ on input $y x_{i+1} \ldots x_n x^R$. Consider the behaviour of $\mathcal{M}$ while the head is on the left part y. This behaviour is exactly the same as that for the run on input $yzz^R y^R$ because the sole useful information for $\mathcal{M}$ while scanning y comes from the crossing sequence at cell $|y|$. In particular, $\mathcal{M}$ – which halts on cell 1 — accepts this input $y x_{i+1} \ldots x_n x^R$. But this is not a palindrome! Contradiction.

Observe that the way $x_1 x_2 \ldots x_i$ is uniquely determined by CS_i is quite complex. But we don't care about that. It will just charge the $O(1)$ constant in (12).

Using Proposition 8 with the binary string associated to CS_i which is c times longer (where $c = \lceil |Q| \rceil$, $|Q|$ being the number of states), we see that

$$K(x_1 x_2 \ldots x_i) \leq c|T_i| + O(1). \tag{12}$$

If $i \geq \frac{n}{2}$ then $x_1 x_2 \ldots x_{\frac{n}{2}}$ is uniquely determined by the pair $(x_1 x_2 \ldots x_i, \frac{n}{2})$.

162

Hence also by the pair $(CS_i, \frac{n}{2})$. Since the binary representation of $\frac{n}{2}$ uses $\leq \log(n)$ bits, this pair can be encoded with $2c|CS_i| + \log(n) + 1$ bits. Thus,

$$K(x_1 x_2 \ldots x_{\frac{n}{2}}) \leq 2c|CS_i| + \log(n) + O(1). \tag{13}$$

Now, let's sum equations (13) for $i = \frac{n}{2}, \ldots, n$. Observe that the sum of the lengthes of the crossing sequences $CS_{\frac{n}{2}}, \ldots, CS_n$ is at most the number T of computation steps. Therefore, this summation leads to

$$\frac{n}{2} K(x_1 x_2 \ldots x_{\frac{n}{2}}) \leq 2cT + \frac{n}{2} \log(n) + O(\frac{n}{2}). \tag{14}$$

Now, consider as x a string such that $x_1 x_2 \ldots x_{\frac{n}{2}}$ is incompressible, i.e. $K(x_1 x_2 \ldots x_{\frac{n}{2}}) \geq \frac{n}{2}$. Equation (14) leads to

$$(\frac{n}{2})^2 \leq 2cT + \frac{n}{2} \log(n) + O(\frac{n}{2}) \tag{15}$$

whence $T \geq O(n^2)$. Since the input xx^R has length $2n$, this proves the quadratic lower bound. QED

7 Prefix Complexity

7.1 Self Delimiting Programs

Q: I heard about prefix complexity. What is it?

A: Prefix complexity is a very interesting variant of Kolmogorov complexity which was introduced around 1973 by Levin [27] and, independently, by Chaitin [10].

The basic idea is taken from some programming languages which have an explicit delimiter to mark the end of a program. For instance, $PASCAL$ uses "*end.*". Thus, no program can be a proper prefix of another program.

Q: This is not true with $PROLOG$ programs: you can always add a new clause.

A: To execute a $PROLOG$ program, you have to write down a query. And the end of a query is marked by a full stop. So, it's also true for $PROLOG$.

Q: OK. However, it's not true for C programs nor $LISP$ programs.

A: Hum... You are right.

7.2 Chaitin-Levin Prefix Complexity

A: Let's say that a set X of strings is prefix-free if no string in X is a proper prefix of another string in X. A programming language $A : \{0,1\}^* \to \{0,1\}^*$ is prefix if its domain is a prefix-free set.

Q: The programming language $U^{PASCAL^{bin}}$ you introduced a moment ago is prefix, as is $PASCAL$. So, what's new?

A: Sure, $U^{PASCAL^{bin}}$ is prefix. But, caution, to get universality which does not increase length, we defined a syntactic variant U of $U^{PASCAL^{bin}}$ (cf. 3.3) which is no more prefix as you can check.

Now, Kolmogorov Invariance Theorem from §3.4 goes through with prefix programming languages, leading to the prefix variant H of K.

Theorem 17 (Invariance theorem). *There exists a prefix partial recursive function* $U^{prefix} : \{0,1\}^* \to \{0,1\}^*$. *such that* $K_{U^{prefix}} \leq K_A + O(1)$ *for any prefix partial recursive function* $A : \{0,1\}^* \to \{0,1\}^*$. *In other words, up to an additive constant,* $K_{U^{prefix}}$ *is the smallest one among the* K_A's.

Definition 18 (Prefix Kolmogorov complexity). Prefix Kolmogorov complexity $H : \{0,1\}^* \to \mathbf{N}$ is any fixed such function $K_{U^{prefix}}$.

7.3 Comparing K and H

Q: How does H compare to K ?

A: A simple relation is as follows:

Proposition 19. $K(x) - O(1) \leq H(x) \leq K(x) + 2\log(K(x)) + O(1)$. *Idem with* $K(\mid)$ *and* $H(\mid)$.

The first inequality is a mere application of the Invariance Theorem for K (since U^{prefix} is a programming language). To get the second one, we consider a programming language U such that $K = K_U$ and construct a prefix programming language U' as follows: the domain of U' is the set of strings of the form $pad(|p|)1p$ and $U'(pad(|p|)1p) = U(p)$. By very construction, the domain of U' is prefix-free. Also, $K_{U'}(x) = K_U(x) + 2\log(K_U(x)) + 1$. An application of the Invariance Theorem for H gives the second inequality of the Proposition.

This inequality can be improved. A better encoding leads to
$$H(x) \leq K(x) + \log(K(x)) + 2\log\log(K(x)) + O(1).$$

Sharper relations have been proved by Solovay, 1975 (unpublished [42], cf. also [29] p. 211):

Proposition 20. $H(x) = K(x) + K(K(x)) + O(K(K(K(x)))),$
$$K(x) = H(x) - H(H(x)) - O(H(H(H(x)))).$$

7.4 How Big is H ?

Q: How big is H ?

A: K and H behave in similar ways. Nevertheless, there are some differences. Essentially a logarithmic term.

Proposition 21. $H(x) \leq |x| + 2\log(|x|) + O(1)$

To prove it, apply the H Invariance Theorem to the prefix function
$$A(pad(|x|)1x) = x.$$
Of course, it can be improved to
$$H(x) \leq |x| + \log(|x|) + 2\log\log(|x|) + O(1)$$

Q: How big can be $H(x) - |x|$?

A: Well, to get a non trivial question, we have to fix the length of the x's. The answer is not a simple function of $|x|$ as expected, it does use H itself:
$$\max_{|x|=n}(H(x) - |x|) = H(|x|) + O(1).$$

Q: How big can be $H(x) - K(x)$?

A: It can be quite large:
$$K(x) \leq |x| - \log(|x|) \leq |x| \leq H(x)$$
happens for arbitrarily large x's ([29] Lemma 3.5.1 p. 208).

7.5 Convergence of Series

Q: What's so really special with this prefix condition?

A: The possibility to use Kraft's inequality. This inequality tells you that if Z is a prefix-free set of strings then $\Sigma_{p \in Z} 2^{-|p|} \leq 1$.

Kraft's inequality is not hard to prove. Denote I_u the set of infinite strings which admit u as prefix. Observe that:

1) $2^{-|p|}$ is the probabilty of I_u.
2) If u, v are prefix incomparable then I_u and I_v are disjoint.
3) Since Z is prefix, the I_u's, $u \in Z$ are pairwise disjoint and their union has probabilty $\Sigma_{p \in Z} 2^{-|p|} < 1$.

The $K_A(x)$'s are lengthes of distinct programs in a prefix set (namely, the domain of A). So, Kraft's inequality implies
$$\Sigma_{x \in \{0,1\}^*} 2^{-K_A(x)} < 1.$$

In fact, H satisfies the following property, proved by Levin [28] (which can be seen as another version of the Invariance Theorem for H):

Theorem 22. *Up to a multiplicative factor, 2^{-H} is maximum among functions $F : \{0,1\}^* \to \mathbf{R}$ such that $\Sigma_{x \in \{0,1\}^*} F(x) < +\infty$ and which are approx-*

imable from below (in a sense dual to that in §2.1, i.e.. the set of pairs (x, q) such that q is rational and $q < F(x)$ is r.e.).

8   Random Infinite Sequences

8.1   Top-Down Approach to Randomness of Infinite Sequences

Q: So, we now come to random infinite sequences.

A: It happens that there are two equivalent ways to get a mathematical notion of random sequences. We shall first consider the most natural one, which is a sort of "top-down approach".

Probability laws tell you that with probability one such and such things happen, i.e., that some particular set of sequences has probability one. A natural approach leads to consider as random those sequences which satisfy all such laws, i.e., belong to the associated sets (which have probability one).

An easy way to realize this would be to declare a sequence to be random just in case it belongs to all sets (of sequences) having probability one or, equivalently, to no set having probability zero. Said otherwise, the family of random sequences would be the intersection of all sets having probability one, i.e., the complement of the union of all sets having probability zero.

Unfortunately, this family is empty! In fact, let r be any sequence: the singleton set $\{r\}$ has probability zero and contains r.

In order to maintain the idea, we have to consider a not too big family of sets with probability one.

Q: A countable family.

A: Right. The intersection of a countable family of set with probability one will have probability one. So that the set of random sequences will have probability one, which is rather an expected property.

8.2   Frequency Tests and von Mises Random Sequences

A: This top-down approach was pionneered by Richard von Mises in 1919 ([46], [47]) who insisted on frequency statistical tests. He declared an infinite binary sequence $a_0 a_1 a_2 \ldots$ to be random (he used the term *Kollektiv*) if the frequence of 1's is "everywhere" fairly distributed in the following sense:

i) Let S_n be the number of 1's among the first n terms of the sequence. Then $\lim_{n \to \infty} \frac{S_n}{n} = \frac{1}{2}$.

ii) The same is true for every subsequence $a_{n_0+1} a_{n_1+1} a_{n_2+1} \cdots$ where $n_0, n_1, n_2 \ldots$ are the successive integers n such that $\phi(a_0 a_1 \ldots a_n) = 1$ where

ϕ is an "admissible" place-selection rule.

What is an "admissible" place-selection rule was not definitely settled by von Mises. Alonzo Church, 1940, proposed that admissibility be exactly computability.

It is not difficult to prove that the family of infinite binary sequence satisfying the above condition has probability one for any place-selection rule. Taking the intersection over all computable place-selection rules, we see that the family of von Mises-Church random sequences has probability one.

However, von Mises-Church notion of random sequence is too large. There are probability laws which do not reduce to tests with place-selection rules and are not satisfied by all von Mises-Church random sequences. As shown by Jean Ville, [45] 1939, this is the case for the law of iterated logarithm. This very important law (due to A. I. Khintchin, 1924) expresses that with probabililty one

$$\lim_{n \to +\infty} \sup \frac{S_n^*}{\sqrt{2\log\log(n)}} = 1 \quad \text{and} \quad \lim_{n \to +\infty} \inf \frac{S_n^*}{\sqrt{2\log\log(n)}} = -1,$$

where $S_n^* = \frac{S_n - \frac{n}{2}}{\sqrt{\frac{n}{4}}}$ (cf. William Feller's book [15], p. 186, 204–205).

Q: Wow! What do these equations mean?

A: They are quite meaningful. The quantities $\frac{n}{2}$ and $\sqrt{\frac{n}{4}}$ are the expectation and standard deviation of S_n. So that, S_n^* is obtained from S_n by normalization: S_n and S_n^* are linearly related as random variables, and S_n^*'s expectation and standard deviation are 0 and 1.

Let's interpret the lim sup equation, the other one being similar (in fact, it can be obtained from the first one by symmetry).

Remember that $\lim\sup_{n \to +\infty} f_n$ is obtained as follows. Consider the sequence $v_n = \sup_{m \geq n} f_m$. The bigger is n the smaller is the set $\{m : m \geq n \}$. So that the sequence v_n decreases, and $\lim\sup_{n \to +\infty} f_n$ is its limit.

The law of iterated logarithm tells you that with probabililty one the set $\{n : S_n^* > \lambda\sqrt{2\log\log(n)}\}$ is finite in case $\lambda > 1$ and infinite in case $\lambda < 1$.

Q: OK.

A: More precisely, there are von Mises-Church random sequences which satisfy $\frac{S_n}{n} \geq \frac{1}{2}$ for all n, a property which is easily seen to contradict the law of iterated logarithm.

Q: So, von Mises' approach is definitely over.

A: No. Kolmogorov, 1963 [21], and Loveland, 1966 [30], independently considered an extension of the notion of place-selection rule.

Q: Kolmogorov once more...

A: Indeed. Kolmogorov allows place-selection rules giving subsequences proceeding in some new order, i.e., mixed subsequences. The associated notion of randomness is called Kolmogorov stochastic randomness (cf. [25] 1987). Since there are more conditions to satisfy, stochastic random sequences form a subclass of von Mises-Church random sequences. They constitute, in fact, a proper subclass ([30]).

However, it is not known whether they satisfy all classical probability laws.

8.3   Martin-Löf Random Sequences

Q: So, how to come to a successful theory of random sequences?

A: Martin-Löf found such a theory.

Q: That was not Kolmogorov? The same Martin-Löf you mentioned concerning random finite strings?

A: Yes, the same Martin-Löf, in the very same paper [33] in 1965. Kolmogorov looked for such a notion, but it was Martin-Löf, a Swedish mathematician, who came to the pertinent idea. At that time, he was a pupil of Kolmogorov and studied in Moscow. Martin-Löf made no use of Kolmogorov random finite string to get the right notion of infinite random sequence. What he did is to forget about the frequency character of computable statistical tests (in von Mises-Church notion of randomness) and look for what could be the essence of general statistical tests and probability laws. Which he did both for finite strings and for infinite sequences.

Q: Though intuitive, this concept is rather vague!

A: Indeed. And Martin-Löf's analysis of what can be a probability law is quite interesting.

To prove a probability law amounts to prove that a certain set X of sequences has probability one. To do this, one has to prove that the exception set — which is the complement $Y = \{0,1\}^{\mathbf{N}} \setminus X$ — has probability zero. Now, in order to prove that $Y \subseteq \{0,1\}^{\mathbf{N}}$ has probability zero, basic measure theory tells us that one has to include Y in open sets with arbitrarily small probability. I.e., for each $n \in \mathbf{N}$ one must find an open set $U_n \supseteq Y$ which has probability $\leq \frac{1}{2^n}$.

If things were on the real line $\mathbf{R}$ we would say that U_n is a countable union of intervals with rational endpoints.

Here, in $\{0,1\}^{\mathbf{N}}$, U_n is a countable union of sets of the form $I_u = u\{0,1\}^{\mathbf{N}}$ where u is a finite binary string and I_u is the set of infinite sequences which extend u. Well, in order to prove that Y has probability zero, for each $n \in \mathbf{N}$ one must find a family $(u_{n,m})_{m \in \mathbf{N}}$ such that $Y \subseteq \bigcup_m I_{u_{n,m}}$ and $Proba(\bigcup_m I_{u_{n,m}}) \leq \frac{1}{2^n}$ for each $n \in \mathbf{N}$.

And now Martin-Löf makes a crucial observation: mathematical probability laws which we can consider necessarily have some effective character. And this effectiveness should reflect in the proof as follows:

the doubly indexed sequence $(u_{n,m})_{n,m \in \mathbf{N}}$ is recursive.

Thus, the set $\bigcup_m I_{u_{n,m}}$ is a recursively enumerable open set and $\bigcap_n \bigcup_m I_{u_{n,m}}$ is a countable intersection of a recursively enumerable family of open sets.

Q: This observation has been checked for proofs of usual probability laws?

A: Sure. Let it be the law of large numbers, that of iterated logarithm... In fact, it's quite convincing.

Q: This open set $\bigcup_m I_{u_{n,m}}$ could not be recursive?

A: No. A recursive set in $\{0,1\}^{\mathbf{N}}$ is always a finite union of I_u's.

Q: Why?

A: What does it mean that $Z \subseteq \{0,1\}^{\mathbf{N}}$ is recursive? That there is some Turing machine such that, if you write an infinite sequence α on the input tape then after finitely many steps, the machine tells you if α is in Z or not. When it does answer, the machine has read but a finite prefix u of α, so that it gives the same answer if α is replaced by any $\beta \in I_u$. In fact, an application of König's lemma (which we shall not detail) shows that we can bound the length of such a prefix u. Whence the fact that Z is a finite union of I_u's.

Q: OK. So, we shall take as random sequences those sequences which are outside any set which is a countable intersection of a recursively enumerable family of open sets and has probability zero.

A: This would be too much. Remember, $Proba(\bigcup_m I_{u_{n,m}}) \leq \frac{1}{2^n}$. Thus, the way the probability of $\bigcup_m I_{u_{n,m}}$ tends to 0 is recursively controled.

So, here is Martin-Löf's definition:

Definition 23. A set of infinite binary sequences is constructively of probability zero if it is included in $\bigcap_n \bigcup_m I_{u_{n,m}}$ where $(m,n) \mapsto u_{n,m}$ is a partial recursive function $\mathbf{N}^2 \to \{0,1\}^*$ such that $Proba(\bigcup_m I_{u_{n,m}}) \leq \frac{1}{2^n}$ for all n.

And now comes a very surprising theorem (Martin-Löf, [33], 1966):

Theorem 24. *There is a largest set of sequences (for the inclusion ordering) which is constructively of probability zero.*

Q: Largest? Up to what?

A: Up to nothing. Really largest set: it is constructively of probability zero and contains any other set constructively of probability zero.

Q: How is it possible?

A: Via a diagonalization argument. The construction has some technicalities but we can sketch the ideas. From the well-known existence of universal r.e. sets, we get a recursive enumeration $((O_{i,j})_i)_j$ of sequences of r.e. open sets. A slight transformation allows to satisfy the inequality $Proba(O_i) \leq \frac{1}{2^i}$. Now, set $\Omega_j = \bigcup_e O_{e,e+j+1}$ (here lies the diagonalization!) Clearly, $Proba(\Omega_j) \leq \sum_e \frac{1}{2^{e+j+1}} = \frac{1}{2^j}$, so that $\bigcap_j \Omega_j$ is constructively of probability zero. Also, $\Omega_j \supseteq O_{i,j}$ for all $j \geq i$ whence $(\bigcap_j \Omega_j) \supseteq (\bigcap_j O_{i,j})$.

Q: So, Martin-Löf random sequences are exactly those lying in this largest set.

A: Yes. And all theorems in probability theory can be strengthened by replacing "with probability one" by "for all Martin-Löf random sequences".

8.4   Bottom-Up Approach to Randomness of Infinite Sequences

Q: So, now, what is the bottom-up approach?

A: This approach looks at the asymptotic algorithmic complexity of the prefixes of the infinite binary sequence $a_0 a_1 a_2 \ldots$, namely the $K(a_0 \ldots a_n)$'s.

The next theorem is the first significant result relevant to this approach. Point 2 is due to Albert Meyer and Donald Loveland, 1969 [31] p. 525. Points 3, 4 are due to Gregory Chaitin, 1976 [11]. (Cf. also [29] 2.3.4 p.124.)

Theorem 25. *The following conditions are equivalent:*

1) $a_0 a_1 a_2 \ldots$ is recursive ,
2) $K(a_0 \ldots a_n \mid n) = O(1)$,
3) $|K(a_0 \ldots a_n) - K(n)| \leq O(1)$,
4) $|K(a_0 \ldots a_n) - \log(n)| \leq O(1)$.

Q: Nice results.

Let me tell what I see. We know that $K(x) \leq |x| + O(1)$. Well, if we have the equality, $K(a_0 \ldots a_n) = n - O(1)$, i.e. if maximum complexity occurs for all prefixes, then the sequence $a_0 a_1 a_2 \ldots$ should be random! Is it indeed the case?

A: That's a very tempting idea. And Kolmogorov had also looked for such a characterization. Unfortunately, as Martin-Löf proved around 1965 (1966,

[34]), *there is no such sequence!* It is a particular case of a more general result (just set $f(n)$ =constant).

Theorem 26 (Large oscillations, [34]). *Let $f : \mathbf{N} \to \mathbf{N}$ be a recursive function such that $\Sigma_{n \in \mathbf{N}} 2^{-f(n)} = +\infty$. Then, for every binary sequence $a_0 a_1 a_2 \ldots$ there are infinitely many n's such that $K(a_0 \ldots a_n \mid n) < n - f(n)$.*

Q: So, the bottom-up approach completely fails as concerns a characterization of random sequences. Hum... But it does succeed as concerns recursive sequences, which were already fairly well characterized. Funny!

A: It's however possible to sandwich the set of Martin-Löf random sequences between two sets of probability one defined in terms of the K complexity of prefixes.

Theorem 27 ([34]). *Let $f : \mathbf{N} \to \mathbf{N}$ be recursive such that the series $\Sigma 2^{-f(n)}$ is recursively convergent. Set*

$$X = \{a_0 a_1 \ldots : K(a_0 \ldots a_n \mid n) \geq n - O(1) \text{ for infinitely many } n\text{'s}\}.$$

$$Y_f = \{a_0 a_1 \ldots : K(a_0 \ldots a_n \mid n) \geq n - f(n) \text{ for all but finitely many } n\text{'s}\}.$$

Denote ML the set of Martin-Löf random sequences. Then X and Y_f have probability one and $X \subset ML \subset Y_f$.

NB: Proper inclusions have been proved by Peter Schnorr, 1971 [37] (see also [29] 2.5.15 p.154).

Let's illustrate this theorem on an easy and spectacular corollary which uses the fact that $2^{-2 \log(n)} = \frac{1}{n^2}$ and that the series $\Sigma \frac{1}{n^2}$ is recursively convergent: *if $K(a_0 \ldots a_n \mid n) \geq n - c$ for infinitely many n's, then $K(a_0 \ldots a_n \mid n) \geq n - 2 \log(n)$ for all but finitely many n's.*

8.5 Randomness and Prefix Complexity

Q: What about considering prefix Kolmogorov complexity?

A: The idea does work with prefix Kolmogorov complexity. This has been proved by Claus Peter Schnorr (1974, unpublished, cf. [10] Remark p. 106, and [12] p. 135-137 for a proof).

Robert M. Solovay, 1975 (unpublished [42]) strengthened Schnorr's result (cf. [12] p. 137-139).

Theorem 28. *The following conditions are equivalent:*

1) $a_0 a_1 a_2 \ldots$ is Martin-Löf random,

2) $H(a_0 \ldots a_n) \geq n - O(1)$ for all n,

3) $\lim_{n \to +\infty} (H(a_0 \ldots a_n) - n) = +\infty$,

4) For any r.e. sequence $(A_i)_i$ of open subsets of $\{0,1\}^{\mathbf{N}}$ if $\Sigma_i Proba(A_i) < +\infty$ then $a_0 a_1 a_2 \ldots$ belongs to finitely many A_i's.

These equivalences stress the robustness of the notion of Martin-Löf random sequence.

8.6   Top-Down/Bottom-Up Approaches: A Sum Up

Q: I get somewhat confused with these two approaches. Could you sum up.

A: The top-down and bottom-up approaches both work and lead to the very same class of random sequences.

Kolmogorov looked at the bottom-up approach from the very beginning in 1964. But nothing was possible with the original Kolmogorov complexity, Levin-Chaitin's variant H was needed.

Q: Ten years later...

A: As for the top-down approach, it was pionneered by von Mises since 1919 and made successful by Martin-Löf in 1965. Martin-Löf had to give up von Mises frequency tests. However, Kolmogorov was much interested by these frequency tests ([21]), and he refined them in a very clever way with the purpose to recover Martin-Löf randomness, which lead him to the notion of Kolmogorov stochastic randomness. Unfortunately, up to now, we only know that

Martin-Löf random $\Rightarrow$ stochastic random $\Rightarrow$ von Mises-Church random.

The second implication is known to be strict but not the first one. Would it be an equivalence, this would give a quite vivid characterization of random sequences via much concrete tests.

8.7   Randomness with Other Probability Distributions

Q: All this is relative to the uniform probability distribution. Can it be extended to arbitrary probability distributions?

A: Not arbitrary probability distributions, but computable Borel ones: those distributions P such that the sequence of reals $(P(I_u))_{u \in \{0,1\}^*}$ (where I_u is the set of infinite sequences which extend u) is recursive, i.e. there is a recursive function $f : \{0,1\}^* \times \mathbf{N} \to \mathbf{Q}$ such that
$$|P(I_u) - f(u,n)| \leq \tfrac{1}{2^n}.$$
Martin-Löf's definition of random sequences extends trivially. As for characterizations with variants of Kolmogorov complexity, one has to replace the length of a finite string u by the quantity $-log(P(I_u))$.

8.8   Chaitin's Real Ω

Q: I read a lot of things about Chaitin's real Ω.

A: Gregory Chaitin, 1987 [13], explicited a spectacular random real and made it very popular.

Let's again use $PASCAL^{bin}$ programs which have no input (cf. 3.1). Observe that no $PASCAL$ program can be a proper prefix of another $PASCAL$ program. This is due to the "*end.*" delimiter which terminates any program. Thus, the open sets $\pi\{0,1\}^{\mathbf{N}}$, where π varies over $PASCAL^{bin}$ programs, are pairwise disjoint subsets of $\{0,1\}^{\mathbf{N}}$. Since $\pi\{0,1\}^{\mathbf{N}}$ has probability $2^{-|\pi|}$, this shows that the series

$$\Sigma\{2^{-|\pi|} \ : \ \pi \text{ is a } PASCAL^0 \text{ program}\}$$

is convergent and has sum < 1.

This leads to define a probability P on the set of $PASCAL^{bin}$ programs:

$$P(\rho) = \frac{2^{-|\rho|}}{\Sigma\{2^{-|\pi|} \ : \ \pi \text{ is a } PASCAL^0 \text{ program}\}}. \tag{17}$$

Now, Chaitin's real Ω is the probability that a $PASCAL^{bin}$ program halts:

$$\Omega = \Sigma\{2^{-|\pi|} \ : \ \pi \text{ halts } \}. \tag{18}$$

Theorem 29. *The binary expansion of Ω is Martin-Löf random.*

Q: How does one prove that Ω is random?

A: Since $\Sigma\{2^{-|\pi|} \ : \ \pi \text{ is a } PASCAL^0 \text{ program}\} < 1$, any halting $PASCAL^{bin}$ program with length n contributes for more than 2^{-n} to Ω. Thus, if you know the first k digits of Ω then you know the number of halting $PASCAL^0$ programs with length $\leq k$. From this number, by dovetailing, you can get the list of the halting $PASCAL^{bin}$ programs with length $\leq k$ (cf. §2.1,2.2). Having these programs, you can get the first string u which is not the output of such a program. Clearly, $H(u) > k$. Now, u is recursively obtained from the first k digits of Ω, so that by Proposition 8 we have $H(u) \leq H(\omega_0 \ldots \omega_k) + O(1)$. Whence $H(\omega_0 \ldots \omega_k) \geq k + O(1)$, which is condition 2 of Theorem 28 (Schnorr condition). This proves that the binary expansion of Ω is a Martin-Löf random sequence.

Q: Ω seems to depend on the programming language.

A: Sure. We can speak of the class of Chaitin Ω reals: those reals which express the halting probability of some universal prefix programming language. Cristian Calude, Peter Hertling, Bakhadyr Khoussainov, and Yongge Wang, [6] (cf. also Antonìn Kučera and Theodore Slaman, [26]) proved a very beautiful result: r is a Chaitin Ω real if and only if (the binary development of) r is Martin-Löf random and r is recursively enumerable from below (i.e., the set of rational numbers $< r$ is r.e.).

Q: I read that this real has incredible properties.

A: This real has a very simple and appealing definition. Moreover, as we just noticed, there is a simple way to get all size n halting programs from its n first digits. This leads to many consequences due to the following fact: any Σ_1^0 statement of the form $\exists \vec{x} \Phi(\vec{x})$ (where Φ is a recursive relation) is equivalent to a statement insuring that a certain program halts, and this program is about the same size as the statement. Now, deciding the truth of Σ_1^0 statements is the same as deciding that of Π_1^0 statements.

And significant Π_1^0 statements abound! Like Fermat's last theorem (which is now Wiles' theorem) or consistency statements. This is why Chaitin says Ω is the "Wisdom real".

Other properties of Ω are common to all reals which have Martin-Löf random binary expansions. For instance, transcendance and the fact that any theory can give us but finitely many digits.

Hum... About that last point, using Kleene's recursion theorem, Robert Solovay, 1999 [43], proved that there are particular Chaitin Ω reals about which a given theory cannot predict *any* single bit!

8.9 Non Recursive Invariance

Q: In some sense, Martin-Löf randomness is a part of recursion theory. Do random sequences form a Turing degree or a family of Turing degrees?

A: Oh, no! Randomness is definitely not recursively invariant. It's in fact a very fragile notion: quite insignificant modifications destroy randomness. This makes objects like Ω so special.

Let's illustrate this point on an example. Suppose you transform a random sequence $a_0 a_1 a_2 a_3 \ldots$ into $a_0 0 a_1 0 a_2 0 a_3 0 \ldots$ The sequence you obtain has the same Turing degree as the original one, but it is no more random since its digits with odd ranks are all 0. A random sequence has to be random everywhere. Hum ... for Martin-Löf random reals, I should rather say "every r.e. where".

Q: Everywhat?

A: "Every r.e. where". I mean that if f is a recursive function from $\mathbf{N}$ into $\mathbf{N}$ (in other words, a recursive enumeration of an r.e. set), then the sequence of digits with ranks $f(0), f(1), f(2), \ldots$ of a Martin-Löf random sequence has to be Martin-Löf random. In fact, you recognize here an extraction process à la von Mises for which a random sequence should give another random sequence.

Q: OK. What about many-one degrees?

A: Same. Let's represent a binary infinite sequence α by the set X_α of positions of digits 1 in α. Then,

$$n \in X_{a_0 a_1 a_2 \ldots} \Leftrightarrow 2n \in X_{a_0 0 a_1 0 a_2 0 \ldots}.$$

Also, let $\varphi(2n) = n$ and $\varphi(2n+1) = k$ where k is some fixed rank such that $a_k = 0$, then

$$n \in X_{a_0 0 a_1 0 a_2 0 ldots} \Leftrightarrow \varphi(n) \in X_{a_0 a_1 a_2 \ldots}$$

These two equivalences prove that $X_{a_0 a_1 a_2 \ldots}$ and $X_{a_0 0 a_1 0 a_2 0 \ldots}$ are many-one equivalent.

9 More Randomness

There are more things in heaven and earth, Horatio,
Than are dreamt of in your philosophy.

Hamlet, William Shakespeare

9.1 Beyond R.E.

Q: Are there other random reals than Chaitin Ω reals ?

A: Sure. Just replace in Martin-Löf's definition the recursive enumerability condition by a more complex one. For instance, you can consider Σ_2^0 sets.

Q: Wait, wait. Just a minute ago, you said that for all classical probability laws, r.e. open sets, i.e., Σ_1^0 sets, are the ones which come in when proving that the exception set to the law has probability zero. So, what could be the use of such generalizations?

A: Clearly, the more random sequences you have which satisfy classical probability laws, the more you strengthen these theorems as we said earlier. In this sense, it is better to stick to Martin-Löf's definition. But you can also want to consider random sequences as worst objects to use in some context. Depending on that context, you can be lead to ask for much complex randomness conditions.

Also, you can have some very natural objects much alike Chaitin real Ω which can be more complex.

Q: Be kind, give an example!

A: In a recent paper, [2], Verónica Becher, Chaitin, and Sergio Daicz consider the probability that a prefix universal programming language produces a finite output, though possibly running indefinitely. They prove that this probability is an Ω' Chaitin real, i.e., its binary expansion is $\emptyset'$-random. Becher and

Chaitin, [1], consider the probability for the output to represent a cofinite set of integers, relatively to some coding of sets of integers by sequences. They prove it to be an Ω'' Chaitin real. General forms of these results are considered in Becher and Grigorieff [3,4].

Such reals are as much appealing and remarkable as Chaitin's real Ω and also they are logically more complex.

9.2 Far Beyond: Solovay Random Reals in Set Theory

Q: I heard about Solovay random reals in set theory. Has it anything to do with Martin-Löf random reals?

A: Hum... These notions come from very different contexts. But well, there is a relation: proper inclusion. Every Solovay random real is Martin-Löf random. The converse being far from true. In fact, these notions of randomness are two extreme notions of randomness. Martin-Löf randomness is the weakest condition whereas Solovay randomness is really the strongest one. So big indeed that for Solovay reals you need to work in set theory, not merely in recursion theory, and even worse, you have to consider two models of set theory, say M_1 and an inner submodel M_2 with the same ordinals...

Q: You mean transfinite ordinals?

A: Yes, $0, 1, 2, 3, \ldots, \omega, \omega + 1, \omega + 2, \ldots, \omega + \omega$ (which is $\omega.2$) an so on: $\omega.3, \ldots, \omega.\omega$ (which is ω^2) $, \ldots, \omega^3, \ldots, \omega^\omega, \ldots$

In a model of set theory, you have reals and may consider Borel sets, i.e., sets obtained from rational intervals via iterated countable unions and countable intersections.

Thus, you have reals in M_1 and reals in M_2 and every M_2 real is also in M_1. You also have Borel sets defined in M_2. And to each such Borel set X_2 corresponds a Borel set X_1 in M_1 with the same definition (well, some work is necessary to get a precise meaning, but it's somewhat intuitive). One can show that $X_2 \subseteq X_1$ and that X_1, X_2 have the very same measure, which is necessarily a real in M_2. Such a Borel set X_1 in M_1 will be called a M_2-coded Borel set.

Now, a real r in M_1 is Solovay random over M_2 if it lies in no measure zero M_2-coded Borel set of M_1. Such a real r can not lie in the inner model M_2 because $\{r\}$ is a measure zero Borel set and if r were in M_2 then $\{r\}$ would be M_2-coded and r should be outside it, a contradiction.

In case M_1 is big enough relative to M_2 it can contain reals which are Solovay random over M_2. It's a rather tough subject, but you see:

— Martin-Löf random reals are reals outside all r.e. G_δ sets (i.e., intersection of an r.e. sequence of open sets) constructively of measure zero. In other words, outside a very smooth countable family of Borel sets. Such Borel sets are, in fact, coded in any inner submodel of set theory.

— Solovay random reals over a submodel of set theory are reals outside every measure zero Borel set coded in that submodel. Thus Solovay random reals can not be in the inner submodel. They may or may not exist, depending on how big is M_1 relative to M_2.

Q: What a strange theory. What about the motivations?

A: Solovay introduced random reals in set theory at the pionneering time of independence results in set theory, using the method of forcing invented by Paul J. Cohen. That was in the 60's. He used them to get a model of set theory in which every set of reals is Lebesgue measurable [41].

Q: Wow! It's getting late.

A: Hope you are not exhausted.

Q: I really enjoyed talking with you on such a topic.

Note. The best reference to the subject is Li-Vitanyi's book [29] (caution: they denote C, K what is here – and in most papers – denoted K, H).

Among other very useful references: [5], [14], [16], [38] and [44].

Gregory Chaitin's papers are available on his home page.

References

1. V. Becher and G. Chaitin. Another example of higher order randomness. *Fundamenta Informaticae*, 51(4):325–338, 2002.
2. V. Becher, G. Chaitin, and S. Daicz. A highly random number. In C.S. Calude, M.J. Dineen, and S. Sburlan, editors, *Proceedings of the Third Discrete Mathematics and Theoretical Computer Science Conference (DMTCS'01)*, pages 55–68. Springer-Verlag, 2001.
3. V. Becher and S. Grigorieff. Possibly infinite computations: random reals in $\emptyset'$. Submitted.
4. V. Becher and S. Grigorieff. Possibly infinite computations and higher order randomness. In preparation.
5. C. Calude. *Information and Randomness*. Springer, 1994.
6. C.S. Calude, P.H. Hertling, B. Khoussainov, and Y. Wang. Recursively enumerable reals and Chaitin Ω numbers. In *STACS 98 (Paris, 1998)*,

number 1373 in Lecture Notes in Computer Science, pages 596–606. Springer-Verlag, 1998.

7. G. Chaitin. On the length of programs for computing finite binary sequences. *Journal of the ACM*, 13:547–569, 1966.

8. G. Chaitin. On the length of programs for computing finite binary sequences: statistical considerations. *Journal of the ACM*, 16:145–159, 1969.

9. G. Chaitin. Computational complexity and gödel incompleteness theorem. *ACM SIGACT News*, 9:11–12, 1971.

10. G. Chaitin. A theory of program size formally identical to information theory. *Journal of the ACM*, 22:329–340, 1975.

11. G. Chaitin. Information theoretic characterizations of infinite strings. *Theoret. Comput. Sci.*, 2:45–48, 1976.

12. G. Chaitin. *Algorithmic Information Theory*. Cambridge University Press, 1987.

13. G. Chaitin. Incompleteness theorems for random reals. *Advances in Applied Math.*, pages 119–146, 1987.

14. J.P. Delahaye. *Information, complexité, hasard.* Hermès, 1999 (2d edition).

15. W. Feller. *Introduction to Probability Theory and Its Applications*, volume 1. John Wiley, 1968 (3d edition).

16. P. Gács. Lectures notes on descriptional complexity and randomness. *Boston University*, pages 1–67, 1993. http://cs-pub.bu.edu/ faculty/gacs/Home.html.

17. S. Grigorieff and J.Y. Marion. Kolmogorov complexity and nondeterminism. *Theoret. Comput. Sci.*, 271:151–180, 2002.

18. Y. Gurevich. The Logic in Computer Science Column: On Kolmogorov machines and related issues. *Bull. EATCS*, 35:71–82, 1988. http://research.microsoft.com/~gurevich/ paper 78.

19. D. Knuth. *The Art of Computer Programming. Volume 2: Semi-Numerical Algorithms.* Addison-Wesley, 1981 (2d edition).

20. A.N. Kolmogorov. *Grundbegriffe der Wahscheinlichkeitsrechnung.* Springer-Verlag, 1933. English translation 'Foundations of the Theory of Probability', Chelsea, 1956.

21. A.N. Kolmogorov. On tables of random numbers. *Sankhya, The Indian Journal of Statistics, ser. A*, 25:369–376, 1963.

22. A.N. Kolmogorov. Three approaches to the quantitative definition of information. *Problems Inform. Transmission*, 1(1):1–7, 1965.

23. A.N. Kolmogorov. Some theorems about algorithmic entropy and algorithmic information. *Uspekhi Mat. Nauk*, 23(2):201, 1968 (in Russian).

24. A.N. Kolmogorov. Combinatorial foundation of information theory and the calculus of probability. *Russian Math. Surveys*, 38(4):29–40, 1983.
25. A.N. Kolmogorov and V. Uspensky. Algorithms and randomness. *SIAM J. Theory Probab. Appl.*, 32:389–412, 1987.
26. A. Kuččera and T.A. Slaman. Randomness and recursive enumerability. *SIAM J. on Computing*, 2001. to appear.
27. L. Levin. On the notion of random sequence. *Soviet Math. Dokl.*, 14(5):1413–1416, 1973.
28. L. Levin. Random conservation inequalities; information and independence in mathematical theories. *Information and Control*, 61:15–37, 1984.
29. M. Li and P. Vitanyi. *An Introduction to Kolmogorov Complexity and Its Applications*. Springer, 1997 (2d edition).
30. D. Loveland. A new interpretation of von Mises's concept of random sequence. *Z. Math. Logik und Grundlagen Math.*, 12:279–294, 1966.
31. D. Loveland. A variant of the Kolmogorov concept of complexity. *Information and Control*, 15:510–526, 1969.
32. M. Machtey and P. Young. *An Introduction to the General Theory of Algorithms*. North-Holland, 1978.
33. P. Martin-Löf. The definition of random sequences. *Information and Control*, 9:602–619, 1966.
34. P. Martin-Löf. Complexity of oscilations in infinite binary sequences. *Z. Wahrscheinlichkeitstheorie verw. Geb.*, 19:225–230, 1971.
35. W. Paul. Kolmogorov's complexity and lower bounds. In L. Budach, editor, *Proc. 2nd Int. Conf. Fundamentals of Computation Theory*, pages 325–334. Akademie Verlag, 1979.
36. B. Russell. Mathematical logic as based on the theory of types. *Amer. J. Math.*, 30:222–262, 1908. Reprinted in 'From Frege to Gödel A source book in mathematical logic, 1879-1931', J. van Heijenoort ed., p. 150-182, 1967.
37. P. Schnorr. A unified approach to the definition of random sequences. *Math. Systems Theory*, 5:246–258, 1971.
38. A. Shen. Kolmogorov complexity and its applications. *Lecture Notes, Uppsala University, Sweden*, pages 1–23, 2000. http://www.csd.uu.se/~vorobyov/ Courses/KC/2000/all.ps.
39. A. Shen and V. Uspensky. Relations between varieties of Kolmogorov complexities. *Math. Systems Theory*, 29:271–292, 1996.
40. R.J. Solomonoff. A formal theory of inductive inference, part 1 and part 2. *Information and Control*, 7:1–22, 224–254, 1964.
41. R.M. Solovay. A model of set theory in which every set of reals is Lebesgue

measurable. *Annals of Mathematics*, 92:1–56, 1970.

42. R.M. Solovay. Draft of a paper (or a series of papers) on Chaitin's work. 1975. Unpublished manuscript, IBM Research Center, NY.

43. R.M. Solovay. A version of Ω for which ZFC can not predict a single bit. *Centre for Discrete Math and Comp. Sc., Auckland, New Zealand*, 104:1–11, 1999. http://www.cs.auckland.ac.nz/staff-cgi-bin/mjd/secondcgi.pl.

44. V.A Uspensky, A.L Semenov, and A.Kh. Shen. Can an individual sequence of zeros and ones be random? *Russian Math. Surveys*, 41(1):121–189, 1990.

45. J. Ville. *Etude critique de la notion de Collectif.* Gauthier-Villars, 1939.

46. R. von Mises. Grundlagen der Wahrscheinlichkeitsrechnung. *Mathemat. Zeitsch.*, 5:52–99, 1919.

47. R. von Mises. *Probability, Statistics and Truth.* Macmillan, 1939. Reprinted: Dover, 1981.

48. A. Zvonkin and L. Levin. The complexity of finite objects and the development of the concepts of information and randomness by means of the theory of algorithms. *Russian Math. Surveys*, 6:83–124, 1970.

HOW TO FIND A COIN: PROPOSITIONAL PROGRAM LOGICS MADE EASY

NIKOLAY V. SHILOV

A.P. Ershov Institute of Informatics Systems
Siberian Division of Russian Academy of Science
Novosibirsk, Russia
E-mail: shilov@iis.nsk.su

KWANG YI

School of Computer Science and Engineering
Seoul National University
Seoul, Korea
E-mail: kwang@ropas.snu.ac.kr

1 Introduction

In spite of the importance of propositional program logics (PPLs) to the development of reliable software and hardware, the area is not well known to non-professionals. In particular, many hacker programmers and hardware designers presume that PPLs are too pure for their poor mathematics, while many mathematical purists believe that PPLs are too poor for their pure mathematics. After 25 years of progress in PPLs research a lot of hardware and software people remain illiterate in PPLs and reluctant to apply them [26].

Maybe, a deficit of popular papers on the topic is the main reason for this ignorance. Our article is aiming to overcome this deficit and presents propositional program logics in a popular (but mathematically sound) manner. The basic ideas, definitions and properties are illustrated by puzzles and game examples. In particular, the fable of the article is a model-checking-based solution for a complicated puzzle to identify a single false coin among given ones balancing them limited times. Only some knowledge of propositional calculus and elementary set theory is assumed.

The rest of the article is organized as follows. The balancing puzzle and a related programming problem are discussed informally in Section 2. Then Section 3 introduces formalisms of finite games, Elementary Propositional Dynamic Logic (EPDL) [14] and discusses utility of this logic for reasoning about finite games. Notions of model checking and abstraction are also introduced and illustrated in Section 3. The propositional μ-Calculus (μC) [17] is defined in the section 4 as an extension of EPDL. The expressive power of μC and its utility for solving finite games are discussed in the same section. A brief survey (but with some formal details) of basic algorithmic problems for the propositional μ-Calculus (i.e., model checking, decidability, and axiomatization) is presented in Section 5. In contrast, a purely informal survey of program logic history and research is given in Section 6. Finally we give in Section 7 a high-level design (in terms of μC model checking and abstraction) of an efficient algorithm for the programming version of the coin balancing puzzle which was introduced in Section 2.

We would like to conclude this introduction with many thanks to Andrzej Murawski and Mike Barnett. Their very useful remarks and language suggestions have helped us to make propositional program logics easy.

2 How the Story Began

2.1 A Hard Puzzle

Once upon a time a program committee for a regional middle school contest in mathematics discussed problems for a forthcoming competition. The committee comprised a professor, several Ph.D. holders and a couple of Ph.D. students. All were experienced participants or organizers of mathematical contests on the regional and national level; several had international experience. A thunder-storm was unexpected, but it came. Suddenly (when a set of problems was almost complete) one of the youngest participants suggested another problem to be included. It was the following 15-coin puzzle:

A set of 15 coins consists of 14 valid coins and a false one. All valid coins have one and the same weight while the false coin has a different weight. One of the valid coins is marked but all other coins (including the false one) are unmarked. Is it possible to identify the false coin using a balance at most 3 times?

"If it is known that the false coin is heavier than the valid one then the problem is suitable for 11–13-year-old school-children" the professor said. "Sorry, but it is not known whether the false coin is heavier or lighter than the valid one," the youngster replied and added: "To the best of my knowledge it is really a hard puzzle. I did not solve it during the national contest several years ago and I still do not know a solution". "In this case it would be better not to include the puzzle into the problem list for the forthcoming contest" the professor concluded.

Problem 1 *Solve the 15-coin puzzle.*

One of the committee members was a computer scientist specializing in program logics and their applications. He agreed to exclude the puzzle from the problem list, since he could not solve it either. Nevertheless he was concerned and decided to try his luck. The day passed without real progress while the coins and balance became his nightmare... The following morning the computer scientist decided to overcome the trouble and adopted the following plan with two concurrent approaches to finding a solution:

- human-aided,

- computer-aided.

The computer-aided approach and its relation to propositional program logics is the main topic of the paper. As far as the human-oriented approach is concerned, the idea was very simple: the puzzle was offered (with a special bonus for the first solution[a]) to students and faculty of the Mathematics Department. But the first who solved the puzzle was the computer scientist's wife[b]. A week later the computer scientist got several correct (and very similar) solutions from students. Then several weeks later some faculty members solved the puzzle correctly as well...

But the human-aided approach had some unexpected implications. The University where the computer scientist is employed is situated in a cozy scientific town,[c] not in a political, industrial or financial center. Several months later a local book seller began to offer a special deal for textbooks: if a customer could find in one hour a strategy to identify a single false coin among 39 coins with aid of a marked valid coin[d] and weighing coins at most 4 times, then the customer would get his money back; if the customer could find a strategy in one day then he would get 50% of his money back.

2.2 Put It for Programming

Let us turn to the computer-aided approach and understand how the 15-coin puzzle can be be generalized for programming. The problem is not to identify a false coin but to find *a strategy* to identify this coin. From the programming viewpoint, a natural model for a strategy is a program which chooses the next step using the information available after previous steps. In this setting the following programming problem is a natural generalization and formalization of the 15 coins puzzle:

---

[a] The bonus was a photocopy of $100.
[b] So the bonus remained at home.
[c] Can you guess the name of the town and where it is?
[d] Valid coins have the same weight while the false coin has a different weight.

Write a program with 3 inputs

- a number $N \geq 0$ of coins under question,
- a number $M \geq 0$ of marked valid coins,
- a limit $K \geq 0$ of the number of weighings

which outputs either the string impossible, or another executable interactive program ALPHA (in the same language) with respect to existence of a strategy to identify a single false coin among N coins with use of additional M marked valid coins and weighing coins K times at most. Your program should output impossible iff there is no such strategy. Otherwise it should output the program ALPHA which implements a strategy in the following settings.

All $(N + M)$ coins are enumerated by consecutive numbers from 1 to $(N + M)$, all marked valid coins are enumerated by initial numbers from 1 up to M. These are called *coin numbers*.

Every interactive session with ALPHA begins with user's initial decision on the coin number of the false coin in $[(M + 1)..(N + M)]$ and whether it is lighter or heavier.

Every interactive session with ALPHA consists of a series of rounds and the number of rounds in the session can not exceed K. In each round i $(1 \leq i \leq K)$ the program ALPHA outputs two disjoint subsets of coin numbers to be placed on the left and the right pans of the balance and prompts the user with ? for a reply. The user in his/her turn replies with $<$, $=$ or $>$ in accordance with the initial decision on the number of the false coin and its weight.

Every interactive session with ALPHA finishes with the final output string false coin number is followed by the coin number of the false coin.

Since the problem is to write a program which generates another program we would like to refer to the first program as the *metaprogram* and to the problem as the *metaprogram problem* respectively. For the first time the problem was designed and offered for training university students for a regional edition of the 1999 ACM Collegiate Programming Contest [33].

Problem 2 *Solve the metaprogram problem.*

Let us illustrate the metaprogram problem by examples of inputs/outputs.

The triple 5, 1 and 2 is an example of possible input for a metaprogram. The semantics of this particular input is a request for a strategy which can

user:	2nd is heavier	3rd is lighter	4th is heavier	5th is lighter
prog:	{1,2} {3,4}	{1,2} {3,4}	{1,2} {3,4}	{1,2} {3,4}
user:	>	>	<	=
prog:	{3} {4}	{3} {4}	{3} {4}	{1} {5}
user:	=	<	<	>
prog:	2	3	4	5

Figure 1. A summary of four sessions with this program ALPHA (Fig. 2) which identifies a single false coin among five coins with aid of a special marked valid coin and weighing coins at most twice.

identify a single false coin among five coins ($N = 5$) using an additional marked valid coin ($M = 1$) and balancing coins at most twice ($K = 2$). All $6 = (N + M)$ coins are enumerated by consecutive numbers from 1 to 6, and the unique marked valid coin has the number 1. The PASCAL program ALPHA presented in Fig. 2 is a possible corresponding output of the metaprogram. A summary of four sessions with ALPHA is presented in Fig. 1.

The triple 9, 1 and 2 is another example of valid input. It asks for a strategy which can identify a single false coin among nine coins with the aid of an extra marked valid coin and balancing coins at most twice. The correct output of the metaprogram for this particular input is impossible.

3 Games with Dynamic Logic

3.1 Game Interpretation

The examples of sessions in Fig. 1 naturally lead to a game interpretation for 15-coin puzzle and metaprogram problem.

Let M and N be non-negative integer parameters and let $(N + M)$ coins be enumerated with consecutive numbers from 1 to $(N + M)$. Coins with numbers in $[1..M]$ are valid while there is a single false coin among those with numbers in $[(M + 1)..(M + N)]$. The $GAME(N,M)$ between two players *user* and *prog* consists of a series of rounds. In each round a move of *prog* is a pair of disjoint subsets (with equal cardinalities) of $[1..(M + N)]$. A possible move of *user* is either $<, =$ or $>$, but the reply should be *consistent* with all previous rounds in the following sense: some number in $[1..(M + N)]$ and the weight of the false coin meet all constraints induced on the current and previous rounds. *Prog* wins the $GAME(N,M)$ as soon as a *unique*

```pascal
program ALPHA
var R: '<','=','>';
begin
writeln(1,2); writeln(3,4); writeln('?'); readln(R);
if R='='
   then
      begin
      writeln(1); writeln(5); writeln('?'); readln(R);
      if R='='
         then writeln('false coin number is 6')
         else writeln('false coin number is 5')
      end
   else
      if R='<'
         then
            begin
            writeln(3); writeln(4); writeln('?'); readln(R);
            if R='='
               then writeln('false coin number is 2')
               else if R='<'
                       then writeln('false coin number is 4')
                       else writeln('false coin number is 3')
            end
         else
            begin
            writeln(3); writeln(4); writeln('?'); readln(R);
            if R='='
               then writeln('false coin number is 2')
               else if R='<'
                       then writeln('false coin number is 3')
                       else writeln('false coin number is 4')
            end
end.
```

Figure 2. A PASCAL program which identifies a single false coin among five coins with the aid of a special marked valid coin and balancing coins at most twice.

number in $[1..(M + N)]$ satisfies all constraints induced during the game.

Now problems 1 and 2 can be reformulated as follows.

1. Find a 3-round (at most) winning strategy for *prog* in the $GAME(14, 1)$.

2. Write a metaprogram which for any $N \geq 1$, $K \geq 0$ and $M \geq 0$ generates (if possible) a K-round (at most) winning strategy for *prog* in the $GAME(N,M)$.

The above game interpretation is still too complicated for analysis. So let us introduce and analyze another simpler game example, namely, the following Millennium Game Puzzle:

On the eve of New Year 2001 Alice and Bob play the *millennium game*. Positions in the game are dates in 2000 and 2001. An *initial position* is a random date of the year 2000. Then Alice and Bob made alternating moves: Alice, Bob, Alice, Bob, etc. Available moves are one and the same for both Alice and Bob: if a current position is a *date* then *the next calendar date* or *the same day of the next month* are possible next positions. A player wins the game iff the other player is the first to launch the year 2001. Problem: Find all initial positions where Alice has a winning strategy.

A mathematical model for the millennium game is quite obvious. It is a directed labeled graph $G_{2000/2001}$. Nodes of this graph correspond to game positions: dates of years 2000 and 2001. All dates of the year 2001 are marked by *fail* while all other dates are unmarked. Edges of the graph correspond to possible moves and are marked by *move*. We would like to consider *fail* and *move* as variables for collections of nodes and sets of edges and call them propositional and action variables respectively. The model fixes the interpretation (i.e., values) of these variables in the manner described above.

In general, a *finite game of two players* A and B is a tuple (P, M_A, M_B, F), where:

- P is a nonempty finite set of *positions*,

- $M_A, M_B \subseteq P \times P$ are *moves* of A and B,

- $F \subseteq P$ is a set of *final positions*.

A *session* (or *play*) of the game is a finite sequence of positions s_0, ..., s_n ($n > 0$) where all even pairs are moves of one player (ex., all $(s_{2i}, s_{2i+1}) \in M_A$) while all odd pairs are moves of another player (ex., all $(s_{2i+1}, s_{2i+2}) \in M_B$). A pair of consecutive moves of two players in a session comprising three consecutive positions (ex., $(s_{2i}, s_{2i+1}, s_{2(i+1)})$) is called a *round*. We say that a session $s_0, ..., s_n$ consists of $\left\lceil \frac{n+1}{2} \right\rceil$ rounds. A player *loses* a session iff after a move of the player the session enters a final position for the first time. A player *wins* a session iff the other player loses the session. A *strategy* of a player is a subset of the player's possible moves. A *winning strategy* for a player is a strategy of the player which always leads to the player's win: the player wins every session which he/she begins and in which he/she implements this strategy instead of all possible moves. The millennium game is just an example of a finite game.

Finite games of two players can easily be presented as directed labeled graphs. Nodes correspond to game positions, those which correspond to final positions are marked by $fail$, while all other nodes are unmarked. Edges of these graphs correspond to possible moves of players and are marked by $move_A$ and $move_B$ respectively. Let us denote by $G_{(P,M_A,M_B,F)}$ the labeled graph corresponding to a game (P, M_A, M_B, F). We would like to consider $fail$, $move_A$ and $move_B$ as variables for sets of nodes and sets of edges respectively.

3.2 Elementary Propositional Dynamic Logic

Let $\{true, false\}$ be boolean constants, Prp and Act be disjoint finite alphabets of *propositional* and *action* variable respectively. (In the previous subsection they are $\{fail\}$ and $\{move, move_A, move_B\}$.)

The syntax of the classical propositional logic consists of *formulae* which are constructed from propositional variables and boolean connectives $\neg$ (*negation*), $\wedge$ (*conjunction*) and $\vee$ (*disjunction*) in accordance with the standard rules:

1. all propositional variables and boolean constants are formulae;

2. if ϕ is a formula then $(\neg\phi)$ is a formula;

3. if ϕ and ψ are formulae then $(\phi \wedge \psi)$ is a formula,

4. if ϕ and ψ are formulae then $(\phi \vee \psi)$ a formula.

Elementary Propositional Dynamic Logic (EPDL)[14] has additional formula constructors, modalities, which are associated with action variables:

5. if a is an action variable and ϕ is a formula then $([a]\phi)$ is a formula[e],

6. if a is an action variable and ϕ is a formula then $(\langle a \rangle \phi)$ is a formula[f].

---

[e] which is read as "*box a ϕ*" or "*after a always ϕ*"
[f] which is read as "*diamond a ϕ*" or "*after a sometimes ϕ*"

We would like to use several standard abbreviations $\rightarrow$ and $\leftrightarrow$ with the usual meaning: if ϕ and ψ are formulae then $(\phi \rightarrow \psi)$ and $(\phi \leftrightarrow \psi)$ are abbreviations for formulae $((\neg\phi) \vee \psi)$ and $((\phi \rightarrow \psi) \wedge (\psi \rightarrow \phi))$ respectively. Then we would like to avoid extra parentheses and use the standard precedence of connectives and modalities: $\neg$, $\langle \rangle$, $[\ ]$, $\wedge$, $\vee$, $\rightarrow$, $\leftrightarrow$. We also use the *meta-symbol* $\equiv$ for *syntactical equality*.

The semantics of EPDL is defined in models, which are called *labeled transition systems* by computer scientists and *Kripke structures* by mathematicians. A model M is a pair (D_M, I_M) where the *domain* D_M is a nonempty set, while the *interpretation* I_M is a pair of special mappings (P_M, R_M). Elements of the domain D_M are called *states*. The interpretation maps propositional variables to sets of states and action variables to binary relations on states:

$$P_M : Prp \rightarrow \mathcal{P}(D_M) \ , \ R_M : Act \rightarrow \mathcal{P}(D_M \times D_M)$$

where $\mathcal{P}$ is the power-set operation. We write $I_M(p)$ and $I_M(a)$ instead of $P_M(p)$ and $R_M(a)$ frequently whenever it is implicit that p and a are propositional and action variables respectively.

Every model $M = (D_M, I_M)$ can be viewed as a directed graph with nodes and edges labeled by sets of propositional and action variables respectively. Its nodes are states of D_M and a node $s \in D_M$ is marked by a propositional variable $p \in Prp$ iff $s \in I_M(p)$. A pair of nodes $(s_1, s_2) \in D_M \times D_M$ is an edge of the graph iff $(s_1, s_2) \in I_M(a)$ for some action variable $a \in Act$; the edge (s_1, s_2) is then marked with the action variable a. Conversely, graphs with nodes and edges labeled by sets of propositional and action variables respectively can be considered as models too. Thus the graph $G_{2000/2001}$ of the millennium game is really a model for EPDL as well as the graph $G_{(P,M_A,M_B,F)}$ of a game (P, M_A, M_B, F).

For every model $M = (D_M, I_M)$ the *validity* relation $\models_M$ between states and formulae can be defined inductively with respect to the structure of formulae:

1. for every state $s \models_M$ *true* and not $s \models_M$ *false*;
   for all states s and propositional variables p: $s \models_M p$ iff $s \in I_M(p)$;

2. for any state s and formula ϕ:
   $s \models_M (\neg\phi)$ iff it is not the case that $s \models_M \phi$;

3. for any state s, formulae ϕ and ψ: $s \models_M (\phi \wedge \psi)$ iff $s \models_M \phi$ and $s \models_M \psi$;

4. for any state s, formulae ϕ and ψ: $s \models_M (\phi \vee \psi)$ iff $s \models_M \phi$ or $s \models_M \psi$;

5. for any state s, action variable a and formulae ϕ:
   $s \models_M (\langle a \rangle \phi)$ iff $(s, s') \in I_M(a)$ and $s' \models_M \phi$ for some state s' ;

6. for any state s, action variable a and formulae ϕ:
   $s \models_M ([a]\phi)$ iff $(s, s') \in I_M(a)$ implies $s' \models_M \phi$ for every state s'.

3.3 Finite Games in EPDL

First let us illustrate the above definition by several examples in the model $G_{2000/2001}$. The formula $fail$ is valid in the states where the game is lost. Then the formula $[move]fail$ is valid in the states from which all possible moves lead to a loss. Hence the formula $\neg fail \wedge [move]fail$ is valid in the states where the game is not over but all possible moves lead to a lost game. Consequently, the formula $\langle move \rangle (\neg fail \wedge [move]fail)$ is valid iff there is a move after which the game is not lost but all possible moves lead to a lost game. Finally we get: the formula

$$\neg fail \wedge \langle move \rangle (\neg fail \wedge [move]fail)$$

is valid in those states where the game is not over, there exists a move after which the game is not lost, and then all possible moves always lead to a loss in the game. So the last EPDL formula is valid in those states of $G_{2000/2001}$ (i.e. dates of years 2000 and 2001) where Alice has a 1-round winning strategy against Bob[9]. So it is natural to denote this formula by win_1. It becomes quite clear from the above arguments that the following formula

$$\neg fail \wedge \langle move \rangle (\neg fail \wedge [move](fail \vee win_1))$$

is valid in those states of $G_{2000/2001}$ where Alice has a winning strategy with at most 2 rounds. So it is natural to denote this formula by win_2. Let us define formulae win_i for all $i \geq 1$ similarly to win_1 and win_2: for every $i \geq 1$ let

$$win_{i+1} \equiv \neg fail \wedge \langle move \rangle (\neg fail \wedge [move](fail \vee win_i)).$$

Let win_0 be $false$ in addition. After the above discussion about win_1 and win_2 it becomes quite simple to prove the following by induction:

Assertion 1 *For every $i \geq 1$ the formula win_i is valid in those states of $G_{2000/2001}$ where Alice has a winning strategy against Bob with at most i rounds.*

The following proposition is just a generalization of the above assertion 1.

---

[9] Alice has all odd-numbered moves while Bob has all even-numbered moves.

191

	inputs	outputs
global	a model and a formula	all states of the model where the formula is valid
local	a model, a formula, and a state	a boolean value of the formula in the state of the model

Figure 3. Global vs. local model checking

Proposition 1 *Let* (P, M_A, M_B, F) *be a finite game of two players, a formula,* WIN_0, *be false and for every* $i \geq 1$ *let* WIN_{i+1} *be a formula*

$$\neg fail \wedge \langle move_A \rangle \big(\neg fail \wedge [move_B](fail \vee WIN_i) \big).$$

For every $i \geq 0$ *the formula* WIN_i *is valid in those states of* $G_{(P,M_A,M_B,F)}$ *where a player* A *has a winning strategy against a counterpart* B *with at most* i *rounds.*

3.4 Model Checking and Abstraction

Model checking is testing a model against a formula. The *global checking* problem consists in calculation of *the set of all states* of an input model where an input formula is valid. The *local checking* problem consists in testing the boolean value of an input formula in an input state of an input model. Thus the corresponding model checking algorithms as well as their implementations (called *model checkers*) can be characterized by their inputs and outputs as shown in Fig. 3.

We are especially interested in model checking problems for finite models, i.e., models with finite domains. For these models both model checking problems are algorithmically equivalent:

- for global checking just check locally all states and then collect states where a formula is valid,

- for local checking just check globally and check whether a state is in the validity set of a formula.

Of course, the above reduction of global checking to local checking leads to changes in time complexity: the global checking complexity is less than or equal to the local checking complexity multiplied by the number of states. We would like to concentrate on global model checking only since this complexity difference is not important for logics discussed in the paper. A more important topic is the parameters used for measuring this complexity. If

$M = (D_M, (R_M, P_M))$ is a finite model, then let d_M and r_M be the number of states in D_M and edges in R_M respectively; let m_D be the overall complexity $(d_M + r_M)$. (If the model M is implicit then we use these parameters without subscripts.) If ϕ is a formula then let f_ϕ be the size of the formula presented as a string. (If the formula ϕ is implicit then we simply write this parameter without subscript.) The following proposition is a straightforward implication of EPDL semantics.

Proposition 2 *The model checking problem for EPDL formulae in finite models is decidable with time complexity $O(m \times f)$.*

Thus the model checking complexity for EPDL in finite models is linear in both arguments: model and formula size. This upper bound seems to be pretty good and the best possible. But it is not the case due to a disproportion between the model and formula sizes which occurs frequently: models of software and hardware are very big and even huge, while logical specifications presented by formulae are comparatively small.

Let us consider the millennium game. If we would like to check in what initial dates of 2000 and 2001 Alice has a n-round winning strategy against Bob (n is a parameter) then we can model-check the EPDL formula win_n in the model $G_{2000/2001}$. This model consists of $d_{2000/2001} = 730$ positions and $r_{2000/2001} = 1415$ moves, i.e., its overall size is $m_{2000/2001} = 2145$. The size of the formula win_n is $f_n = (14 \times n - 3)$. Intuitively it seems very likely that Alice has a winning strategy against Bob iff there is a winning strategy with at most 12 rounds. But the size of the formula win_{12} is more than 12 times smaller than the size of the model $G_{2000/2001}$. In real life examples the difference between the model and formula sizes is much more serious.

There are several techniques for curbing the model size, but we would like to discuss *abstraction* only. In general, let Φ be a set of formulae, $M_1 = (I_1, D_1)$ and $M_2 = (I_2, D_2)$ be two models, and $g : D_1 \to D_2$ be a mapping. The model M_2 is called an *abstraction* [h] of the model M_1 with respect to formulae in Φ iff for any formula $\phi \in \Phi$ and any state $s \in D_1$ the following holds: $s \models_1 \phi \Leftrightarrow g(s) \models_2 \phi$.

In particular, let G_{2000} be a model where states are dates of the year 2000 extended by a special state 2001, the propositional variable $fail$ is interpreted as a singleton $\{2001\}$, and the action variable *move* is interpreted as a move from a date in 2000 to

$$\begin{cases} \text{the next calendar date, if it is still in the year 2000,} \\ \text{the same date of the next month, if it remains in 2000,} \\ \text{the special state 2001, otherwise.} \end{cases}$$

---

[h] g is called an *abstraction mapping* in this case.

Let $abs_{2001} : D_{2000/2001} \rightarrow D_{2000}$ be the following mapping

$$\lambda\ date \cdot \begin{cases} date, \text{ if } date \in \text{ year } 2000, \\ 2001, \text{ if } date \in \text{ year } 2001. \end{cases}$$

Assertion 2 G_{2000} *is an abstraction of* $G_{2000/2001}$ *with respect to EPDL formulae constructed from a single propositional variable* $fail$ *and a single action variable* $move$. *The corresponding abstraction mapping is* abs_{2001}.
The abstract model G_{2000} consists of $d_{2000} = 366$ states and $r_{2000} = 722$ moves, i.e., its overall size is $m_{2000} = 1088$. Thus it is almost twice as small as the original model $G_{2000/2001}$. But the abstract model preserves all EPDL properties of the original one. Hence it is possible to model-check EPDL formulae in the abstract model instead of the original. This model checking is twice as efficient due to smaller model size.

4 Propositional μ-Calculus

4.1 Toward Stronger Logic

We have assumed that Alice has a winning strategy against Bob in the millennium game iff there is a winning strategy with 12 rounds (at most). The only intuition behind this conjecture was: the number of months in a year is 12. But we have not proved that this 12-round hypothesis really holds. It is the first disadvantage of the conjecture.

The size of formulae $win_1, \ldots win_{12}$ is another disadvantage of the 12-round hypothesis. Really, the formula win_3 unfolds as

$$\neg f \wedge \langle m \rangle \big\{ \neg f \wedge [m] \{ f \vee \big\{ \neg f \wedge \langle m \rangle \big(\neg f \wedge [m] \big(f \vee \big(\neg f \wedge \langle m \rangle (\neg f \wedge [m] f) \big) \big) \big) \big\} \} \big\},$$

where f and m are abbreviations for $fail$ and $move$. Formula win_{12} is, approximately, 4 times larger than win_3, thus 4 lines are necessary for its presentation.

Finally, it is not clear whether in general it is possible to express the existence of winning strategies in finite games in terms of EPDL. Informally speaking, the existence of winning strategies can be expressed by an *infinite* disjunction

$$WIN_0 \vee WIN_1 \vee WIN_2 \vee WIN_3 \vee WIN_4 \vee \ldots = \bigvee_{i \geq 0} WIN_i,$$

but this expression *is not a legal* formula in EPDL. The following argument proves formally that EPDL is too weak for expressing it.

$$NEG \; : \; ... \xrightarrow{move} (-i-1) \xrightarrow{move} \underbrace{(-i) \xrightarrow{move} ...(-1) \xrightarrow{move} \overset{fail}{(0)}}_{NEG_i}$$

Figure 4. Model NEG

Let us consider all non-positive integers as a domain and interpret $fail$ to be valid on 0 only, $move$, $move_A$, and $move_B$ to be interpreted as the successor function $\lambda x.(x+1)$ on negatives. Let us denote this model by NEG (Fig. 4). Let us define an *action nesting* for EPDL formulae by induction:

1. $nest(fail) = nest(true) = nest(false) = 0$,

2. $nest(\neg\phi) = nest(\phi)$,

3. $nest(\phi \wedge \psi) = \max\{nest(\phi), nest(\psi)\}$,

4. $nest(\phi \vee \psi) = \max\{nest(\phi), nest(\psi)\}$,

5. $nest([move]\phi) = nest([move_A]\phi) = nest([move_B]\phi) = 1 + nest(\phi)$,

6. $nest(\langle move \rangle \phi) = nest(\langle move_A \rangle \phi) = nest(\langle move_B \rangle \phi) = 1 + nest(\phi)$.

In this setting, for every EPDL formula ϕ, for all $k, l > nest(\phi)$ the following can be trivially proved by induction on formula's structure:

$$(-k) \models_{NEG} \phi \; \Leftrightarrow \; (-l) \models_{NEG} \phi.$$

Thus for every formula of EPDL there exists a non-positive number prior to which the formula is a boolean constant. But the infinite disjunction $\bigvee_{i>0} WIN_i$ is valid in all even negative integers, and is invalid in 0 and all odd negative integers. Finally we can remark that no EPDL formula ϕ can distinguish the finite model NEG_i (Fig. 4) with $i > nest(\phi)$ from the infinite model NEG. But every NEG_i ($i \geq 0$) is a finite game. Thus we have proved **Assertion 3** *No EPDL formula can express the existence of winning strategies in all finite games NEG_i, where $i \geq 0$.*

So it seems reasonable to have another logic with stronger expressive power. Below we are going to describe the so-called *propositional μ-Calculus* (μC) [17] which is an extension of the EPDL. Both syntax and semantics of this logic are more complicated than those of EPDL.

4.2   μ-Calculus Syntax

Let us extend the syntax of EPDL with two new features:

7. if p is a propositional variable and ϕ is a formula then $(\mu p.\phi)$ is a formula[i],

8. if p is a propositional variable and ϕ is a formula then $(\nu p.\phi)$ is a formula[j].

Informally speaking $\mu p.\phi$ and $\nu p.\phi$ are "abbreviations" for infinite disjunction and conjunction

$$false \vee \phi_p(false) \vee \phi_p(\phi_p(false)) \vee \phi_p(\phi_p(\phi_p(false))) \vee \dots = \bigvee_{i \geq 0} \phi_p^i(false),$$

$$true \wedge \phi_p(true) \wedge \phi_p(\phi_p(true)) \wedge \phi_p(\phi_p(\phi_p(true))) \wedge \dots = \bigwedge_{i \geq 0} \phi^i(true),$$

where $\phi_p(\psi)$ is the result of substituting ψ for p in ϕ, $\phi_p^0(\psi)$ is ψ and $\phi_p^{i+1}(\psi)$ is $\phi_p(\phi_p^i(\psi))$ for every $i \geq 0$. In particular, if ϕ is a formula

$$\neg fail \wedge \langle move_A \rangle \big(\neg fail \wedge [move_B](fail \vee win) \big)$$

where win is a new propositional variable, then WIN_0 is just $\phi_{win}^0(false)$, the formula WIN_1 is equivalent to

$$\phi_{win}^1(false) \equiv \neg fail \wedge \langle move_A \rangle \big(\neg fail \wedge [move_B](fail \vee false) \big)$$

and for every $i \geq 0$ formula WIN_{i+1} is equivalent to

$$\phi_{win}^{i+1}(false) \equiv \neg fail \wedge \langle move_A \rangle \big(\neg fail \wedge [move_B](fail \vee \phi_{win}^i(false)) \big).$$

Finally, the infinite disjunction $\bigvee_{i \geq 0} WIN_i$ should be equivalent to

$$\mu\ win.\ \phi \equiv \mu\ win. \Big(\neg fail \wedge \langle move_A \rangle \big(\neg fail \wedge [move_B](fail \vee win) \big) \Big).$$

Let us denote the last formula by WIN.

The above definition of formulae is too loose. We would like to impose a context-sensitive restriction. In formulae $(\mu p.\phi)$ and $(\nu p.\phi)$ the range of μp and νp is the formula ϕ and all instances of the variable p are called *bound* in $(\mu p.\phi)$ and $(\nu p.\phi)$. An instance of a variable in a formula is called *free* iff it is not bound. In a formula $(\neg \phi)$ the range of negation is the formula ϕ. An instance of a propositional variable in a formula is called *positive/negative* iff

---

[i] which is read as "*mu p ϕ*" or "*the least fixpoint p of ϕ*"
[j] which is read as "*nu p ϕ*" or "*the greatest fixpoint p of ϕ*"

it is located in the scope of an even/odd number of negations. The context-sensitive restriction reads as follows: *No bound instance of a propositional variable can be negative.*

Thus the definition of the syntax of the μ-Calculus formulae is over. But, as usual, we would like to avoid extra parentheses and extend the standard precedence to: $\neg$, $\langle\rangle$, $[\,]$, μ, $,\nu$, $\wedge$, $\vee$, $\rightarrow$, $\leftrightarrow$.

4.3 μ-Calculus Semantics

The semantics of μ-Calculus is defined in the same models as that of EPDL in terms of sets of states in which formulae are valid. For every model $M = (D_M, I_M)$ let us denote by $M(formula)$ a set of all states of the model where the *formula* is valid. The first 6 clauses of the definition deal with EPDL features:

1. for boolean constants $M(true) = D_M$ and $M(false) = \emptyset$;
   for every propositional variable p, $M(p) = I_M(p)$;

2. for every formula ϕ, $M(\neg\phi) = D_M \setminus M(\phi)$;

3. for all formulae ϕ and ψ, $M(\phi \wedge \psi) = M(\phi) \cap M(\psi)$;

4. for all formulae ϕ and ψ, $M(\phi \vee \psi) = M(\phi) \cup M(\psi)$;

5. for any action variable a and formula ϕ, $M(\langle a\rangle\phi) = \{s \in D_M : (s, s') \in I_M(a) \text{ and } s' \in M(\phi) \text{ for some state } s' \in D_M\}$;

6. for any action variable a and formula ϕ, $M([a]\phi) = \{s \in D_M : (s, s') \in I_M(a) \text{ implies } s' \in M(\phi) \text{ for every state } s' \in D_M\}$.

As far as new features μ and ν are concerned, let us define their semantics in *finite* models only since it is the major domain for model checking applications:

7. for every formula ϕ, $M(\mu p.\ \phi) = \bigcup_{i \geq 0} M(\phi_p^i(false))$,

8. for every formula ϕ, $M(\nu p.\ \phi) = \bigcap_{i \geq 0} M(\phi_p^i(true))$.

Let us define the *validity* relation $\models'_M$ for all formulae and states in a natural way: $s \models'_M \phi$ iff $s \in M(\phi)$. Let us remark also that we can use the same notation $\models_M$ in the framework of the μ-Calculus as in the framework of EPDL since the following holds:

Proposition 3 *The μ-Calculus is a conservative extension of EPDL: $s \models'_M \phi$ iff $s \models_M \phi$, for any EPDL formula ϕ, any model M and any state s.*

In accordance with the definition of semantics in finite models, $\mu p.\ \phi(p)$ and $\nu p.\ \phi(p)$ are really "abbreviations" for the infinite disjunction $\bigvee_{i \geq 0} \phi_p^i(false)$ and conjunction $\bigwedge_{i \geq 0} \phi^i(true)$. In particular the formula WIN is really equivalent to the infinite disjunction $\bigvee_{i \geq 0} WIN_i$. Hence, this formula of the μ-Calculus expresses the existence of winning strategies in finite games of two players. In accordance with assertion 3, it is not equivalent to any formula of EPDL. These arguments prove the following

Proposition 4 *The μ-Calculus is more expressive then EPDL. The following formula $WIN \equiv \mu\ win.\Big(\neg fail \wedge \langle move_A\rangle\big(\neg fail \wedge [move_B](fail \vee win)\big)\Big)$, which expresses the existence of winning strategies in finite games, is not expressible in EPDL.*

The above formula WIN is not the only μC formula of interest. For example, let us consider another formula

$$FAIR \equiv \nu q.\big([a]q \ \wedge \ \mu r.(p \vee [a]r)\big).$$

A sub-formula $\phi \equiv \mu r.(p \vee [a]r)$ of this formula is valid in a model in the states where every infinite a-path eventually leads to p. A formula $\nu q.([a]q \wedge x)$ is valid in a model in the states where every a-path always leads to x (x is a propositional variable). Hence, $FAIR \equiv \nu q.([a]q \wedge \phi) \equiv \nu q.\big([a]q \ \wedge \ \mu r.(p \vee [a]r)\big)$ is valid in a state of a model iff every infinite a-path infinitely often visits states where p holds. An infinite sequence is said to be *fair* with respect to a property iff the property holds for an infinite amount of elements of the sequence. In these terms $FAIR$ holds in a state of a model iff every infinite a-path is fair with respect to p. For example, a *scheduler* of CPU time among several permanent resident jobs $job_1,... job_n$ is fair with respect to a concrete job_i iff it schedules this job for execution by CPU infinitely often. This fairness can be expressed by the following instance of the formula $FAIR$: $\nu q.\big([scheduler]q \ \wedge \ \mu r.(active(job_i) \vee [scheduler]r)\big)$.

4.4 Properties of μC Semantics

The semantics of formulae as well as the semantics of propositional variables are sets of states. This gives us a new opportunity to consider the semantics of μC formulae as functions which map interpretations of a propositional variables into sets where the formulae are valid in corresponding interpretations. For example, let ϕ be a μC formula with a free propositional variable x. In every model M we can consider a function

$$\lambda S.\ M_{S/x}(\phi)\ :\ \mathcal{P}(D_M) \longrightarrow \mathcal{P}(D_M),$$

where $M_{S/x}$ is a model which agrees with M everywhere except x: x is interpreted as S in $M_{S/x}$. It maps each $S \subseteq D_M$ to $M_{S/p}(\phi) \subseteq D_M$.

Let us illustrate this new approach to the μ-Calculus semantics with a game example. Let ϕ be the formula $\neg fail \wedge \langle move_A \rangle (\neg fail \wedge [move_B](fail \vee win))$. Let (P, M_A, M_B, F) be a finite game of two players and $M = G_{(P,M_A,M_B,F)}$ be the corresponding model.

Let $S_0 = \emptyset$ and let S_i ($i \geq 1$) be a set of all positions where the player A has a winning strategy against B with at most i rounds. Due to the proposition 1, $S_i = G_{(P,M_A,M_B,F)}(WIN_i)$ and $WIN_{i+1} \equiv \neg fail \wedge \langle move_A \rangle (\neg fail \wedge [move_B](fail \vee WIN_i))$ for every $i \geq 1$. It implies $M_{S_i/win}(\phi) = S_{i+1}$ for every $i \geq 0$. For every $i \geq 1$ the natural inclusion $S_i \subseteq S_{i+1}$ holds, since a i-round winning strategy is automatically a $(i+1)$-round winning strategy. Let us summarize it all as follows:

$$\text{argument } S: \quad \emptyset \subseteq S_1 \subseteq S_2 \subseteq \dots S_i \subseteq \dots$$
$$\lambda S.\big(M_{S/win}(\phi)\big): \quad \downarrow \quad \downarrow \quad \downarrow \qquad \downarrow$$
$$\text{result } M_{S/win}(\phi): S_1 \subseteq S_2 \subseteq S_3 \subseteq \dots S_{i+1} \subseteq \dots$$

As follows from the table, the mapping $\lambda S.\big(M_{S/win}(\phi)\big)$ non-decreases monotonically on $\{S_i : i \geq 0\}$.

This mapping $\lambda S.\big(M_{S/win}(\phi)\big)$ has another important *fixpoint* property: if $S = \bigcup_{i \geq 0} S_i$ then S is a *fixed point* of $M(\phi)$, i.e. $M_{S/win}(\phi) = S$. Informally speaking, the above equality is very natural: if the player A is in a position where he/she has a winning strategy, then he/she has a move prior to and after which the game is not lost, but after which every move of another player B leads to a position where the game is lost for him/her, or A has a winning strategy.

Are the above monotonicity and fixpoint accidental properties of special formulae in special models? Not at all! Monotonicity is a basic property of the μ-Calculus:

Proposition 5 *For any model M, sets of states $S' \subseteq S''$, propositional variable p and formula ϕ*

- *if p has no negative instances in ϕ then $M_{S'/p}(\phi) \subseteq M_{S''/p}(\phi)$,*

- *if p has no positive instances in ϕ then $M_{S''/p}(\phi) \subseteq M_{S'/p}(\phi)$.*

This property has very important semantical implications. In particular, it leads to a fixpoint characterization of semantics of μ and ν:

Proposition 6 *For any propositional variable p, any μC formula ϕ without negative instances of p, and any model $M = (D_M, (R_M, P_M))$, $M(\mu p.\phi)$ and*

$M(\nu p.\phi)$ are the least and the greatest fixpoints (with respect to subset inclusion $\subseteq$) of the function $(\lambda S \subseteq D_M. M_{S/p}(\phi))$: $\mathcal{P}(D_M) \longrightarrow \mathcal{P}(D_M)$, which maps each $S \subseteq D_M$ to $M_{S/p}(\phi) \subseteq D_M$.

5 Algorithmic Problems for the μ-Calculus

5.1 Model Checking

Let us return to the Millennium Game Puzzle. In this puzzle we are interested in a set of positions where a winning strategy exists, i.e., in states of the model $G_{2000/2001}$ where the formula WIN holds. It is a typical model checking problem, but this time for the μ-Calculus.

Let us first recall the parameters used for measuring model checking complexity and then formulate a statement about complexity. If $M = (D_M, (R_M, P_M))$ is a finite model then d_M and r_M are the number of states in D_M and edges in R_M, respectively; m is the overall model size, $(d_M + r_M)$. If ϕ is a formula, then f_ϕ is the formula size. In addition, let n_ϕ be μ and ν nesting depth of a formula ϕ.

We skip the subscripts with d, r, m, f, and n whenever a model and/or a formula are implicit.

In contrast to EPDL, the semantics of the μ-Calculus defined in the section 4.3 is not a model checking algorithm for the μ-Calculus in finite models, due to non-constructive semantics of μ and ν. But thanks to the monotonicity property 5, we can revise the semantics of μ and ν in finite models as follows:

7'. for every formula ϕ, $M(\mu p. \ \phi) \ = \ \bigcup_{0 \leq i \leq d_M} M(\phi_p^i(false))$,

8'. for every formula ϕ, $M(\nu p. \ \phi) \ = \ \bigcap_{0 \leq i \leq d_M} M(\phi_p^i(true))$.

in every finite model M. These arguments imply

Proposition 7 *The model checking problem for the μ-Calculus in finite models is decidable with an upper time bound $O(m \times f \times d^n)$.*

In particular, a computer-aided solution of the Millennium Game Puzzle, becomes just technical: implement the above model checking algorithm for the μ-Calculus, code the model $G_{2000/2001}$ and then "plug and play", i.e., model check the formula WIN.

The only problem is model size, but abstraction can help us again. In accordance with the revised semantics above, every μC formula ϕ in every finite model M is equivalent to some EPDL formula ψ (which just unfolds d_M times all fixpoints in ϕ). Hence, we have:

Proposition 8 *For all finite models M_1 and M_2, where M_1 is an abstraction of M_2 with respect to μC formulae (written within propositional and action* *variables Prp and Act) iff M_1 is an abstraction of M_2 with respect to EPDL formulae (written within the same propositional and action variables).* Combined with Assertion 2, this leads to another more efficient computer-aided solution of the Millennium Game Puzzle: just model-check formula WIN in the model G_{2000}.

A large model size is not the single critical factor in the upper bound of the model checking complexity in the above Proposition 7. Another critical factor is the exponent, where the power depends on the input formula. A problem how to close a complexity gap between linear model checking EPDL (Proposition 2) and exponential model checking the μ-Calculus (Proposition 7) in finite models is an important research topic. Unfortunately, the best known model checking algorithms for the μ-Calculus and finite models are exponential. For example, a time bound of the Faster Model Checking Algorithm (FMC-algorithm) [7] is roughly

$$O(m \times f) \times \left(\frac{m \times f}{a}\right)^{a-1},$$

where an alternating depth a of a formula is the maximal number of alternating nesting μ and ν with respect to the syntactical dependences. (A formal definition is out of scope of the paper due to space limitations. We would like to point out only that the alternating depth is always less then or equal to the nesting depth for every formula: $a_\phi \leq n_\phi$.)

The best known complexity class for the model checking problem for the μ-Calculus in finite models is $\mathcal{NP} \cap co\text{-}\mathcal{NP}$ [10], i.e., the problem is not more complicated then satisfiability and provability in the classical propositional logic. For this reason it seems very hard to prove an exponential lower bound for the model checking problem for the μ-Calculus in finite models. Since it is not known whether the problem is $\mathcal{NP}$-complete, it seems more realistic to try to find a polynomial model checking algorithm for the μ-Calculus in finite models. At least several expressive fragments of the μ-Calculus with polynomial model checking algorithms for finite models have been identified [10,1]. As follows from the upper bound for the FMC-algorithm, formulae with a bounded alternating nesting depth form a fragment of this kind too.

Problem 3 *(a) Describe new fragments of the μ-Calculus with a polynomial model checking in finite models. (b) Prove a polynomial upper or an exponential lower time bound for model checking the μ-Calculus in finite models.*

5.2 Decidability and Axiomatizations

Decidability is another important algorithmic problem. Its essence is to check whether a given formula of the μ-Calculus is a tautology, i.e., it is valid in *all* models. It is known that it is possible to check validity not in *all* models but in *all finite* models only due to a so-called *finite-model property* of the μ-Calculus formulae: a formula is satisfiable in a model iff it is satisfiable in a *finite* model [11]. But this reduction does not make the problem trivial! Moreover, the reduction itself is just a corollary of the decidability of the μ-Calculus with an exponential upper bound. In principle, an exponential decidability result for this logic can be proved indirectly by means of an automata-theoretic technique [29,11]. Basically, the automata-theoretic approach comprises two stages: first, a reduction of the decidability problem for a particular logic to the emptiness problem for a particular class of automata on infinite trees, and then application of a direct decision procedure for this emptiness problem. This and other impressive applications of the automata-theoretic technique have led the program logic community to the opinion [30] that the automata-theoretic approach is the unique paradigm for proving decidability for complicated propositional program logics. In spite of the theoretical importance of the automata approach, it seems to be inefficient for implementations due to an indirect, round-about character.

Problem 4 *An efficient direct decision procedure for the μ-Calculus.*

Another complicated algorithmic problem for μ-Calculus is axiomatization. In this context we would like to remark that in the original paper [17] a natural sound axiomatization for the μ-Calculus was proposed, but the completeness of the axiomatization was proved for a fragment of this logic only. The completeness problem for the μ-Calculus was open for 10 years. Finally it was solved in [30,31,32] using the theory of infinite games and theory of automata on infinite trees. Nevertheless the completeness proof is very complicated and any simplifying suggestions are welcome!

Problem 5 *A complete axiomatization of the μ-Calculus made easy.*

6   Program Logics in General

6.1   What Are "Program Logics"?

The logics we have discussed so far are the Elementary Propositional Dynamic Logic and the μ-Calculus. An experienced mathematician can remark that EPDL is just a polymodal variant of the classical and basic modal logic **K** [3] and the μ-Calculus is just a polymodal variant of the μ**K**, i.e., **K** extended by fixpoints. Actually, in terms of EPDL, **K** is a variant of EPDL with a unique action variable. Since in this case a name of this variable is not important, it is possible to omit the variable in formulae and write $\Box$ and $\Diamond$ instead of [...] and $\langle ... \rangle$ respectively. These "new" modalities are read "*box*" or "*always*" and "*diamond*" or "*sometimes*". In particular, the formulae win_i $(i \geq 0)$ for positions in the millennium game where Alice has a i-round (at most) winning strategy, are all formulae of $\mathbf{K}$ and can be rewritten in the $\Box$ and $\Diamond$ notation as $win_0 \equiv false$ and $win_{i+1} \equiv \neg fail \wedge \Diamond(\neg fail \wedge \Box(fail \vee win_i))$ for every $i \geq 1$. In this notation the following formula μ $win.$ $\Big(\neg fail \wedge \Diamond(\neg fail \wedge \Box(fail \vee win))\Big)$ of $\mu\mathbf{K}$ characterizes the set of all game positions where Alice has a winning strategy. So it is reasonable to consider EPDL as a polymodal variant the modal logic $\mathbf{K}$ and the μ-Calculus as a polymodal variant of the $\mu\mathbf{K}$. Why do people call them *program logics*? And why do we give non-mathematical names for them?

The answers are quite simple. *Program logics* are modal logics used in software and hardware verification and specification for reasoning about *programs*. In 1980s program logics comprised

- *dynamic logics* [15,18,16],

- *temporal logics* [27,9],

and their extensions by means of fixpoints. EPDL is the simplest dynamic logic; μC is a very expressive extension of EPDL by fixpoints μ and ν. Temporal logics are fragments of μC with a single action variable *next* for discrete next-time. A more recent addition to the family of program logics is the *logic of knowledge* [12]. The utility of this logic is in providing a language which formalizes notions that are used informally in reasoning about multi-agent systems when a pure dynamic/temporal approach is not very convenient. The "given names" of program logics are sometimes traditional and closely related to their mathematical names[k], sometimes they are invented with respect to intuition about application domain[l]. The situation with "given names" is quite similar to the situation with a generic name of models for program logics: some researchers prefer the mathematical name *Kripke structures* while other prefer the application-oriented name *labeled transition systems*.

6.2   Why Should We Know Program Logics?

The role of the logical approach in the development of computer hardware and software increases as systems become more complex and require more effort for their specification and verification. A logical approach to verification and specification comprises the following choices:

---

[k]Ex., *temporal* is a program logic, while *tense* is a basic one.
[l]Ex., *dynamic* is a program logic, while $\mathbf{K}$ is a basic one.

- a specification language for property presentation,

- a formal proving technique for specified properties.

Specification languages which are in use for the presentation of properties range from propositional to high-order logics while a proving technique is either model checking (a semantical approach) or deductive reasoning (a syntactical approach).

It is possible (in principle) to construct a complete first-order axiomatization for every finite model and then try to prove a desired property (semi)automatically by means of any available logical framework [2,21,8]. But this purely deductive approach is sometimes not practical for complexity reasons. Let us consider a finite model of a moderate size with approximately $100,000$ states. If it has a "clear" structure then it is reasonable to try to "capture" the model by means of a sound axiomatization and then to try to prove a desired property in a (semi)automatic style. But if a model has a "vague" structure which can be generated automatically (e.g., all possible configurations of a "small" distributed system) then it is reasonable to apply an automatic model checker to the generated system and a desired property, presented as a formula of a propositional program logic. In this case decidability and complexity issues of model checking for a particular logic arise. The problem of choosing an efficient model checking algorithm and an implementation problem follow. Efficiency issues become more important as soon as model checking is applied to huge models with, say, 10^{100} states, since with large sets representation problem arises.

We would like to give some recommendations on further reading on program logics. Some books and special chapter of handbooks can be recommended for those who are interested in the theory of program logics[m]: first [12], then [15,?,27,18,9] (in any order). There are also several books which discuss the pragmatics and applications of program logics. A comprehensive survey (from the implementation perspective) on automatic model checking techniques and applications is given in [6]. The temporal logic approach to specification and to manual deductive verification of reactive and concurrent systems is presented in [19,20].

6.3 People and Ideas in Program Logics

Program logics became a legitimate part of theoretical computer science and an essential element of information processing culture in the middle of the

---

[m]Especially for those who have not a special logical background.

1970s [15,27,18,9]. A decade later, they were adopted by the formal method community as a convenient framework for specifying and reasoning about properties of a broad class of systems which can be presented or simulated by computer programs [19,20,12,6]. Thus it is absolutely natural to pay a tribute to some people whose research were milestones in history of program logics.

Program logics as a special research domain were launched by V.R. Pratt in 1976 when he suggested *Dynamic Logic* (basically, First-Order DL) [23]. He realized that Hoare-Dijkstra *weakest pre-conditions* are modalities and incorporated weakest pre-conditions into the first-order logic as follows: for a program α and a post-condition ϕ let $([\alpha]\phi)$ be a formula which is valid in a state iff every computation of α starting in this state either diverges or terminates in another state where ϕ holds. Thus we can celebrate the 25th anniversary of program logics this year.

A decidable propositional variant of dynamic logic — the *Propositional Dynamic Logic* — was suggested by M.J. Fisher and R.E. Ladner in 1977 [13]. A couple of years later K. Segerberg developed a sound and complete axiomatization for this logic.

A. Pnueli was the first to propose the use of temporal logic for reasoning about programs[n] [22]. His approach to the specification of concurrent and reactive systems is now well developed [19] as well as a manual deductive methodology for proving special properties [20]. This approach consists in proving properties of a program from a set of axioms that describe the behavior of the individual statements and problem-oriented inductive proof principles. Since it is a deductive approach where proofs are constructed by hand, the technique is often difficult to automate and use in practice.

Part of the reason for the further success of program logics is automatic model checking of specifications expressed in propositional level temporal logics for finite state systems [6]. Branching temporal logic CTL and polynomial model checking algorithms were developed as a new mathematical background for a new verification methodology for finite state systems by E.M. Clarke and E.A. Emerson [5], J.-P. Queille and J. Sifacis [24] in the early 1980s. An improved model checking algorithm for CTL was implemented in the EMC model checker which was able to treat models with up to 100,000 states.

At the end of the 1980s model checking researchers, encouraged by polynomial complexity of model checking for CTL in finite models and the success of model checking verification experiments for systems of a moderate size, had moved to further research topics, such as model checking for more expressive

---

[n] Logics of time, tense and temporal logics had been studied before A. Pnueli by philosophers and logicians, but not computer scientists.

program logics (like the μ-calculus) in huge finite (10^{20} states and far beyond) and infinite models. Ordered Binary Decision Diagrams (OBDD) were created in 1987-92 [4] for handling huge finite models. OBDDs provide a canonical form for boolean formulas that is often more compact then conjunctive or disjunctive normal form and very efficient dynamic algorithms have been developed and implemented for manipulating them. A very popular modern model checker, SMV, was implemented by combining a CTL model checking algorithm with the symbolic representation of finite models. The most recent versions of SMV for UNIX, Linux, and Windows are available for download [34].

The propositional μ-Calculus was suggested by D. Kozen in 1983 [17] as a logic which can combine and unify propositional dynamic and temporal logics due to its expressive power. As was mentioned before, several complete axiomatization were developed by I. Walukiewicz in 1990s [30,31,32] on the basis of the theory of infinite games and the theory of automata on infinite trees.

A complete survey of program logics is outside of the scope of this paper. Only some propositional program logics were discussed, while first-order program logics were mentioned only in a brief historic survey. Due to space limitations, there is no room for more details on program logics theory, utility, and history. Nevertheless we would like to list more people, who have contributed to the theory and methodology of program logics[o]: D.Harel, J.Halpern, L.Lamport, Z.Manna, R.Parikh, J. Tiuryn, M.Vardi, etc. We would like to also remark that the most recent achievement in the theory of program logics is a sound and complete axiomatization for full branching time temporal logic CTL* by M Reynolds [25].

7 Back to the Metaprogram Problem

7.1 Concrete Model

Now we are ready to return to the metaprogram problem and solve it with aid of the propositional μ-Calculus, model checking and abstraction.. First we would like to discuss a *concrete model* GAME(N,M) ($N \geq 1$, $M \geq 0$). Positions in this parameterized game are tuples (U, L, H, V, Q) where:

- U is a set of coin numbers in $[(M + 1)..(M + N)]$ which *were not* tested against other coins;

---

[o]It is not a complete list and, of course, it represents a personal viewpoint.

- L is a set of coin numbers in $[(M+1)..(M+N)]$ which *were* tested against other coins and were *lighter* than other coins;

- H is a set of coin numbers in $[(M+1)..(M+N)]$ which *were* tested against other coins and were *heavier* than other coins;

- V is a set of coin numbers in $[1..(N+M)]$ which are known to be *valid*;

- Q is a *balancing query*, i.e., a pair of disjoint subsets of $[1..(N+M)]$ of equal cardinality.

Three constraints are natural:

1. U, L, H and V are disjoint,

2. $U \cup L \cup H \cup V = [1..(N+M)]$,

3. $U \cup L \cup H \neq \emptyset$.

In addition we can claim that

4. $U \neq \emptyset$ iff $L \cup H = \emptyset$,

5. if $Q = (S_1, S_2)$, then either $S_1 \cap V = \emptyset$ or $S_2 \cap V = \emptyset$.

Since (4) the single false coin is among untested coins iff all previous balancings gave equal weights, and since (5) it is not reasonable to add extra valid coins on both pans of a balance. A possible move of the player *prog* is a query for balancing two sets of coins, i.e., a pair of positions

$$(U, \ L, \ H, \ V, \ (\emptyset, \emptyset)$$

$$\Big|$$

$$move_{prog}$$

$$\downarrow$$

$$(U, \ L, \ H, \ V, \ (S_1, S_2)),$$

where S_1 and S_2 are disjoint subsets of $[1..(N+M)]$ with equal cardinalities. A possible move of the player *user* is a reply $<$, $=$ or $>$ for a query which causes position change

$$(U, \ L, \ H, \ V, \ (S_1, S_2))$$

$$\Big|$$

$$move_{user}$$

$$\downarrow$$

$$(U', \ L', \ H', \ V', \ (\emptyset, \emptyset)).$$

In accordance with the query and the reply: if $S_1 = U_1 \cup L_1 \cup H_1 \cup V_1$ and $S_2 = U_2 \cup L_2 \cup H_2 \cup V_2$, respectively, with $U_1, U_2 \subseteq U$, $L_1, L_2 \subseteq L$, $H_1, H_2 \subseteq H$, $V_1, V_2 \subseteq V$, then

$$U' = \begin{cases} \emptyset & \text{if the reply is } <\text{,} \\ (U \setminus (U_1 \cup U_2)) & \text{if the reply is } =\text{,} \\ \emptyset & \text{if the reply is } >\text{,} \end{cases}$$

$$L' = \begin{cases} (L_1 \cup U_1) & \text{if the reply is } <\text{,} \\ (L \setminus (L_1 \cup L_2)) & \text{if the reply is } =\text{,} \\ (L_2 \cup U_2) & \text{if the reply is } >\text{,} \end{cases}$$

$$H' = \begin{cases} (H_2 \cup U_2) & \text{if the reply is } <\text{,} \\ (H \setminus (H_1 \cup H_2)) & \text{if the reply is } =\text{,} \\ (H_1 \cup U_1) & \text{if the reply is } >\text{,} \end{cases}$$

$$V' = [1..(N + M)] \setminus (U' \cup L' \cup H').$$

A final position is a position $(U, L, H, V, (\emptyset, \emptyset))$ where $|U| + |L| + |H| = 1$.

We suppose that positions, moves of the player *prog*, and final positions are modeled in the obvious way and additional comments are not required while some auxiliary intuition on moves of the player *user* is essential. Since $U \neq \emptyset$ iff $L \cup H = \emptyset$, there are two disjoint cases: $U = \emptyset$ XOR $L \cup H = \emptyset$. Let us consider the first one only, since the second is similar. In this case $U_1 = U_2 = U' = \emptyset$. Then

$$L' = \begin{cases} L_1 & \text{if the reply is } <\text{, since in this case a false coin is} \\ & \text{either in } L_1 \text{ and is lighter or it is in } H_2 \text{ and is heavier;} \\ (L \setminus (L_1 \cup L_2)) & \text{if the reply is } =\text{, since in this case a false coin is} \\ & \text{neither in } L_1 \text{ or } L_2 \text{ nor is it in } H_1 \text{ or } H_2; \\ L_2 & \text{if the reply is } >\text{, since in this case a false coin is} \\ & \text{either in } L_2 \text{ and is lighter or it is in } H_1 \text{ and is heavier;} \end{cases}$$

$$H' = \begin{cases} H_2 & \text{if the reply is } <\text{, since in this case a false coin is} \\ & \text{either in } L_1 \text{ and is lighter or it is in } H_2 \text{ and is heavier;} \\ (H \setminus (H_1 \cup H_2)) & \text{if the reply is } =\text{, since in this case a false coin is} \\ & \text{neither in } L_1 \text{ or } L_2 \text{ nor is it in } H_1 \text{ or } H_2; \\ H_1 & \text{if the reply is } >\text{, since in this case a false coin is} \\ & \text{either in } L_2 \text{ and is lighter or it is in } H_1 \text{ and is heavier.} \end{cases}$$

The above model is quite good from the mathematical viewpoint, but too large from the viewpoint of the computer scientist, since the number of possible positions and possible moves is an exponential function of N. Actually, for all possible U, L and H the number of possible queries ranges from 1 up to

$$Q(N) \;=\; \sum_{i=0}^{i=[\frac{N}{2}]} (C_i^N \times C_i^{N-i}),$$

where all C_k^l are binomial coefficients. Since there are 2^N possible values for U and 3^N possible values for disjoint L and H, then the total amount of positions is

$$(2^N + 3^N) \;\leq\; P(N) \;\leq\; (2^N + 3^N) \times Q(N).$$

The amount of possible moves of the player *prog* is $P(N)$ too, while the amount of possible moves of the player *user* is bounded by the same number and triple $P(N)$. So the total amount of possible moves is

$$2 \times P(N) \;\leq\; M(N) \;\leq 4 \times P(N).$$

In general, the overall model size (i.e., the number of possible position and moves) of the concrete model is exponential in N. In particular, a concrete model $GAME(14,1)$ for the 15 coins puzzle is too big for explicit representation in modern personal computers.

7.2   Abstract Model

Abstraction can overcome the deficit of the power of modern computers and solve the metaprogram problem: let's consider *amounts of coins* instead of *coin numbers*. This idea is natural: when somebody is solving puzzles he/she operates in terms of amounts of coins of different kinds not in terms of their numbers! Let us present this hint in formal terms as an *abstract model game(N,M)* ($N \geq 1$, $M \geq 0$). Positions in this parameterized game are tuples (u, l, h, v, q) where:

- u is the amount of coins in $[1..N]$ which *were not* tested against other coins;

- l is the amount of coins in $[1..N]$ which *were* tested against other coins and turned out to be *lighter* than other coins;

- h is the amount of coins in $[1..N]$ which *were* tested against other coins and turned out to be *heavier* than other coins;

- v is an amount of coins in $[1..(N+M)]$ which are currently known to be *valid*;

- q is a *balancing query*, i.e. a pair of quadruples $((u_1, l_1, h_1, v_1)$, $(u_2, l_2, h_2, v_2))$ of numbers of $[1..(N + M)]$.

Five constraints are absolutely natural and are closely related to constraints 1–5 for the concrete model: $(1)u+l+h \leq N$, $(2)u+l+h+v = N+M$, $(3)u+l+h \geq 1$, $(4)u \neq 0$ iff $l+h = 0$, and $(5)v_1 = 0$ or $v_2 = 0$. Additional constraints should be imposed for queries (since we can borrow coins for weighing from available untested, lighter, heavier and valid ones): $(6)u_1 + u_2 \leq u$, $(7)l_1 + l_2 \leq l$, $(8)h_1 + h_2 \leq h$, $(9)v_1 + v_2 \leq v$, $(10)u_1 + l_1 + h_1 + v_1 = u_2 + l_2 + h_2 + v_2$. A possible move of a player *prog* is a query for balancing two sets of coins, i.e. pair of positions

$$(u, l, h, v, ((0,0,0,0), (0,0,0,0))) \xrightarrow{prog} (u, l, h, v, ((u_1, l_1, h_1, v_1), (u_2, l_2, h_2, v_2))).$$

A possible move of a player *user* is a reply $<, =$ or $>$ for a query which causes position change
$$(u, l, h, v, ((u_1, l_1, h_1, v_1), (u_2, l_2, h_2, v_2))) \xrightarrow{user}$$
$$(u', l', h', v', ((0,0,0,0), (0,0,0,0)))$$
in accordance with the query and a reply:

$$u' = \begin{cases} 0 \text{ if the reply is } <, \\ (u - (u_1 + u_2)) \text{ if the reply is } =, \\ 0 \text{ if the reply is } >, \end{cases}$$

$$l' = \begin{cases} (l_1 + u_1) \text{ if the reply is } <, \\ (l - (l_1 + l_2)) \text{ if the reply is } =, \\ (l_2 + u_2) \text{ if the reply is } >, \end{cases}$$

$$h' = \begin{cases} (h_2 + u_2) \text{ if the reply is } <, \\ (h - (h_1 + h_2)) \text{ if the reply is } =, \\ (h_1 + u_1) \text{ if the reply is } >, \end{cases}$$

$$v' = ((N + M) - (u' + l' + h')).$$

The final position is a position $(u, u, h, v, ((0,0,0,0), (0,0,0,0)))$ where $u + l + h = 1$. Thus the game and the corresponding abstract model are complete. The overall model size (i.e., the number of possible positions and moves) of the abstract model is polynomial in N and is less than $\frac{(N+1)^6}{6}$.

In order to utilize abstraction, let us consider both models $GAME(N, M)$ and $game(N, M)$ ($N \geq 1$, $M \geq 0$) and define a *counting* mapping $count$: $D_{GAME(N,M)} \rightarrow D_{game(N,M)}$ as follows:

$$count : (U, L, H, V, (S_1, S_2)) \mapsto (|U|, |L|, |H|, q),$$

where q is

$$((|S_1 \cap U|, |S_1 \cap L|, |S_1 \cap H|, |S_1 \cap V|), (|S_2 \cap U|, |S_2 \cap L|, |S_2 \cap H|, |S_2 \cap V|)).$$

This counting mapping can be component-wise extended on pairs of positions.

Assertion 4 *For all $N \geq 1$ and $M \geq 0$ the counting mapping is a homomorphism of a labeled graph $GAME(N, M)$ onto another labeled graph $game(N, M)$ with the following property for every position (U, L, H, Q) in the $GAME(N, M)$:*

1. *count maps all moves of a player which begins in the position onto moves of the same player in the $game(N, M)$ which begins in $count(U, L, H, Q)$;*

2. *count maps all moves of a player which finishes in the position onto moves of the same player in the $game(N, M)$ which finishes in $count(U, L, H, Q)$.*

The following assertion is an immediate consequence of the above one.

Assertion 5 *For all $N \geq 1$ and $M \geq 0$ the $game(N, M)$ is an abstraction of the $GAME(N, M)$ with respect to formulae of EPDL written with use of the unique propositional variable $fail$ and two action variables $move_A$ and $move_B$.*

Finally, we are ready to present a high-level model-checking-based design for the metaprogram:

1. (a) input numbers N and M of coins under question and of valid coins, the bound K for the number of balancing;

   (b) to model check formulae WIN^i_{win} for all $i \in [0..K]$ in the abstract model $game(N, M)$;

   (c) if WIN^K_{win} valid in an *initial* position $(N, 0, 0, M, ((0, 0, 0, 0), (0, 0, 0, 0)))$ then go to 2 else output `impossible` and halt;

2. output a program, which model checks formulae $\neg fail \wedge [move_B](fail \vee WIN^i_{win}(false))$ for $i \in [0..(K-1)]$ in the abstract model $game(N, M)$ and has K interactive rounds with its user as follows: for every i from K to 1 it outputs to the user a move from a *current position* to an *intermediate position* in the concrete model $GAME(N, M)$ such that

$$count(intermediate\ position) \models_{game(N,M)}$$
$$\models_{game(N,M)} \neg fail \wedge [move_B](fail \vee WIN^{i-1}_{win}(false));$$

then it inputs the user's reply $<$, $=$ or $>$ and defines a *next position* for count(*intermediate position*) in accordance with the reply in the abstract model $game(N, M)$; finally the program reconstructs a next position $count^-(next\ position)$ in the concrete model $GAME(N, M)$.

The correctness of the final high-level design follows from Proposition 5. Implement, plug and play!

Acknowledgments

This work is supported by Creative Research Initiatives of the Korean Ministry of Science and Technology.

References

1. Berezine S.A., Shilov N.V. An Approach to Effective Model-Checking of Real-Time Finite-State mMchines in Mu-Calculus. *Lecture Notes in Computer Science*, 813 (1994), 47–55.
2. Boyer R.S., Moor J.S. *A Computational Logic*. Academic Press, 1979.
3. Bull R.A., Segerberg K. Basic Modal Logic. *Handbook of Philosophical Logic*, v.II, Reidel Publishing Company, 1984 (1-st ed.), Kluwer Academic Publishers, 1994 (2-nd ed.), 1–88.
4. Burch J.R., Clarke E.M., McMillan K.L., Dill D.L., Hwang L.J. Symbolic Model Checking: 10^{20} states and beyond. *Information and Computation*, 98, 2 (1992), 142–170.
5. Clarke E.M., Emerson E.A. Design and Synthesis of synchronization skeletons using Branching Time Temporal Logic. *Lecture Notes in Computer Science*, 131, 1982, 52–71.
6. Clarke E.M., Grumberg O., Peled D. Model Checking. MIT Press, 1999.
7. Cleaveland R., Klain M., Steffen B. Faster Model-Checking for Mu-Calculus. *Lecture Notes in Computer Science*, 663, 1993, 410–422.
8. Crow J., Owre S., Rushby J., Shankar N., Srivas M. *A tutorial introduction to PVS*. http://www.csl.sri.com/sri-csl-fm.html
9. Emerson E.A. Temporal and Modal Logic. *Handbook of Theoretical Computer Science*, v.B, Elsevier and The MIT Press, 1990, 995–1072.
10. Emerson E.A., Jutla C.S., Sistla A.P. On model-checking for fragments of Mu-Calculus. *Lecture Notes in Computer Science*, 697, 1993, 385–396.
11. Emerson E.A., Jutla C.S. The Complexity of Tree Automata and Logics of Programs. *SIAM J. Comput.*, 29, 1 (1999), 132–158.
12. Fagin R., Halpern J.Y., Moses Y., Vardi M.Y. *Reasoning about Knowledge*. MIT Press, 1995.

212

13. Fisher M.J., Ladner R.E. Propositional Dynamic Logic of Regular Programs. *J. Comput. System Sci.*, 18, 2 (1979), 194–211.
14. Harel D. *First-Order Dynamic Logic.* Lecture Notes in Computer Science, 68, 1979.
15. Harel D. Dynamic Logic. *Handbook of Philosophical Logic*, v.II, Reidel Publishing Company, 1984 (1-st ed.), Kluwer Academic Publishers, 1994 (2-nd ed.), 497–604.
16. Harel D., Kozen D., Tiuryn J. *Dynamic Logic.* MIT press, 2000.
17. Kozen D. Results on the Propositional Mu-Calculus. *Theoretical Computer Science*, 27, 3 (1983), 333–354.
18. Kozen D., Tiuryn J. Logics of Programs. *Handbook of Theoretical Computer Science*, v.B, Elsevier and The MIT Press, 1990, 789–840.
19. Manna Z., Pnueli A. The Temporal Logic of Reactive and Concurrent Systems. Springer-Verlag, 1991.
20. Manna Z., Pnueli A. Temporal Verification of Reactive Systems: Safety. Springer-Verlag, 1995.
21. Paulson L.S. *Logic and Computation: Interactive Proof with Cambridge LCF.* Cambridge University Press, 1987.
22. Pnueli A. Temporal Logic of Programs. *Theoretical Computer Science*, 13, 1 (1981), 45–60.
23. Pratt V.R. Semantical Considerations on Floyd-Hoare Logic. *Proc. 17th IEEE Symposium on Foundations of Computer Science*, 1976, 109–121.
24. Queille J.-P., Sifakis J. Specification and Verification of Concurrent Systems in CESAR. *Lecture Notes in Computer Science*, 137, 1982, 337–351
25. Reynolds M. An Axiomatization of Full Computation Tree Logic. To appear in *Journal of Symbolic Logic*, 2001 (a draft is available at URL http://www.it.murdoch.edu.au/~mark/research/online).
26. Schlipf T., Buechner T., Fritz R., Helms M., Koehl J. Formal Verification Made Easy. *IBM Journal of Research & Development*, 41, 4/5 (1997).
27. Stirling C. Modal and Temporal Logics. *Handbook of Logic in Computer Science*, v.2, Clarendon Press, 1992, 477–563.
28. Streett R.S. Emerson E.A. An Automata Theoretic Decision Procedure for the Propositional Mu-Calculus. *Information and Computation*, 81, 3 (1989), 249–264.
29. Vardi M.Y. Reasoning About the Past with Two-Way Automata. *Lecture Notes in Computer Science*, 1443, 1998, 628–641.
30. Walukiewicz I. *A Complete Deduction System for the μ-Calculus.* Doctoral Thesis, Warsaw, 1993.
31. Walukiewicz I. On Completeness of the μ-Calculus. IEEE Computer Society Press, *Proc. of 8th Ann. IEEE Symposium on Logic in Computer*

Science, 1993, 136–146.

32. Walukiewicz I. Completeness of Kozen's Axiomatization of the Propositional μ-Calculus. *Inform. and Comp.*, 157, 3 (2000), 142–182.

33. *ACM International Collegiate Programming Contest.*
http://acm.baylor.edu/acmicpc/default.htm

34. *Model Checking Code Available.*
http://www.cs.cmu.edu/~modelcheck/code.html

ALGORITHMS VS. MACHINES

ANDREAS BLASS

Mathematics, University of Michigan
Ann Arbor, MI 48109-1109, USA

YURI GUREVICH

Microsoft Research
One Microsoft Way
Redmond, WA 98052, USA
E-mail: gurevich@microsoft.com

Yiannis Moschovakis argues that some recursive algorithms, and in particular the mergesort algorithm, cannot be adequately described in terms of state machines. His claim contradicts the ASM thesis according to which every algorithm can be adequately represented as an abstract state machine. Here we show how to represent the mergesort algorithm, on its natural level of abstraction, as a distributed abstract state machine. The same can be achieved by more modest means: a standard ASM with submachines. However, there are recursive algorithms easily representable as distributed ASMs that do not lend themselves to a natural submachine representation.

1 Prelude

Quisani: I have a question about the ASM thesis, the claim that every algorithm can be expressed, on its natural level of abstraction, by an abstract state machine (ASM). Do you still believe this thesis?

Authors: Yes. In fact, there has been some recent progress [3], extending the proof from the sequential algorithms covered in [5] to parallel algorithms. To be precise, we deal with parallel algorithms that operate in sequential time and have bounded sequentiality within each step.

Q: Wait a minute; I'm confused. You go beyond the sequential case yet still assume sequential time?

A: Right. "Sequential time" means only that the algorithm proceeds in a sequence of discrete steps. "Sequential" means in addition that only a bounded amount of work is done in each step. So a sequential algorithm obeys all the postulates in [5], not just the sequential time postulate. (We think "small-step algorithm" may be a better name than "sequential algorithm," but the latter terminology is prevalent in the literature.)

215

Q: So the parallel algorithms in [3] have discrete steps but can do an unbounded amount of work in each step.

A: Right, provided the work is done in parallel; we don't allow (except in one section of the paper) unbounded sequentiality within a step.

Q: I came across a provocative article "What is an algorithm?" by Yiannis Moschovakis [9], casting doubt on the ASM thesis. The article begins, "When algorithms are defined rigorously in Computer Science literature (which only happens rarely), they are generally identified with *abstract machines.*" Then Moschovakis argues that "this does not square with our intuitions about algorithms," and he speaks about the problem of defining algorithms correctly. "This problem of *defining algorithms* is mathematically challenging, as it appears that our intuitive notion is quite intricate and its correct, mathematical modeling may be quite abstract—much as a 'measurable function on a probability space' is far removed from the naive (but complex) conception of a 'random variable'.

In addition, a rigorous notion of algorithm would free many results in complexity theory from their dependence on specific (machine) models of computation, and it might simplify their proofs." He proposes "a plausible solution" according to which "algorithms are *recursive definitions* while machines model [are] *implementations,* a special kind of algorithms."

A: It's not clear *a priori* that the problem of rigorous definition of *algorithm* is solvable; does this intricate intuitive notion lend itself to mathematical definition? Is there one mathematical model for all algorithms? Like Moschovakis, we hope that the answer is positive; in fact this was one motivation for the ASM project. From the beginning, this project was oriented toward real-world computer systems. Nowadays, our group at Microsoft Research works on practical (and executable!) specification of large, complicated, highly interactive, and highly distributed systems related to Microsoft's .NET initiative. In this context, an approach via recursive equations looks quite impractical, but an approach via machine models is working well.

Q: Moschovakis seems to be interested more in a general definition of algorithms for theoretical purposes (like complexity theory) than in practical applicability. Though he doesn't say so in his paper, he would probably think that your practical work forces you to think of implementations more than of algorithms. He is quite willing to identify implementations with machines, but he says that algorithms are something more general.

What it boils down to is that you say that an algorithm is a machine and Moschovakis says it is not.

A: A reasonable conclusion would be that different meanings are being attached to "algorithm" or "machine" or both.

Q: Or, as President Clinton suggested, to "is."

A: The semantics of "is" is in general not so simple but there seems to be no disagreement about it here; let's stick to "algorithm" and "machine." In fact, it seems that Moschovakis uses both of these words differently than we do.

2 Sequential Machines

Q: In the case of "machine," it should be easy to figure out what's going on. Moschovakis explicitly defines what he calls "an *abstract* (or *sequential*) *machine*" with inputs in a set X and outputs in a set Y. It consists of

- a set S of states,
- an initial state $s_0 \in S$,
- a transition function $\sigma : X \times S \to S$,
- a set $T \subseteq S$ of terminal states, and
- an output function $o : X \times T \to Y$.

Apart from the presence of terminal states and an output function, this looks very similar to the sequential time postulate in [5]. And as for the output, Moschovakis adds in a footnote that "Gurevich, in effect, 'identifies' the output with the computation [the sequence of states] ..., so he can model algorithms which 'run forever'."

A: That footnote seems to be a misunderstanding. The sequential time postulate of [5] asserts that every sequential algorithm has states, initial states and a transition function. The postulate says nothing about the output. But in [5], states are not just points in the state space as in the case of abstract machines. They have internal structure which may include an output. See for example the ASMs used in [1]. In [3] we define a more general notion of "sequential ASM with output" that allows output not only at the end of the computation but at any step. In any case, the output is not identified with the state or the sequence of states.

Q: I haven't seen [3] yet, but I remember [1]. The sort of ASMs used there, with "output" and "halt" as dynamic functions, seem to fall into the category of the machines described by Moschovakis. In fact I see only two differences between his machines and sequential time algorithms, like sequential time ASMs. Both differences relate to the way inputs are handled, and both are apparently inessential.

First, ASMs have many possible initial states, one for each possible input, while Moschovakis's machines have just one initial state s_0. But Moschovakis's transition function σ is defined on pairs $\langle input, state \rangle$, so it can take $\langle input, s_0 \rangle$ to the state that, from the ASM viewpoint, would be the initial state for that input.

Second, Moschovakis's transition function acts, as I just said, on pairs $\langle input, state \rangle$, not just on states. But this difference can be eliminated by redefining "state" to include the input. In fact, if the transition function really uses the input, then you'd insist that the input be remembered as part of the state; I've heard you say often that the state must include everything relevant to the future progress of the computation.

A: Right. There seems to be no essential difference between Moschovakis's description of abstract machines and the sequential time postulate, if the latter is adjusted to demand (rather than merely permit) terminal states and output.

Q: In fact, an earlier paper [8] of Moschovakis, referred to in [9], gives a description of "iterators" that is even closer to the sequential time postulate.

So you and Moschovakis agree about what a *machine* is, and we should look instead at the concepts of *algorithm*.

A: Not so fast! Moschovakis's notion of abstract machine (or iterator) is very similar to the sequential time postulate, but not all machines satisfy that postulate. Specifically, distributed ASMs [6] and other distributed algorithms may not run in sequential time. In computations of such algorithms, one has an initial state, but what happens next may depend on which one of many agents acts first. So there will not in general be a uniquely determined second state. The whole idea of a computation as a single, linear sequence of states is tied to the notion of sequential time.

So it is not surprising that Moschovakis finds abstract machines inadequate to model general algorithms. It could mean simply that not all algorithms are sequential time algorithms.

Q: It would be nice if this fully explained why Moschovakis regards machines as inadequate.

3 Mergesort Equations

Q: Moschovakis uses the example of the mergesort algorithm to show how interesting results can be established just on the basis of a recursive definition without descending to the level of an implementation. He shows that merge-sort needs only $O(n \log n)$ comparisons to sort a string of length n. Since he emphasizes this specific example let's look at it and try to understand what's going on.

A: OK. How does Moschovakis define mergesort?

Q: Not surprisingly, he defines it by recursion. It is the function *sort* defined, along with another function *merge*, by the equations:

$$\text{sort}(u) = \begin{cases} u, & \text{if } |u| \leq 1, \\ \text{merge}(\text{sort}(h_1(u)), \text{sort}(h_2(u))), & \text{otherwise,} \end{cases} \quad (1)$$

$$\text{merge}(v, w) = \begin{cases} w, & \text{if } v = \varnothing, \\ v, & \text{else, if } w = \varnothing, \\ \langle v_0 \rangle * \text{merge}(\text{tail}(v), w), & \text{else, if } v_0 \leq w_0, \\ \langle w_0 \rangle * \text{merge}(v, \text{tail}(w)), & \text{otherwise.} \end{cases} \quad (2)$$

Here u, v, w range over strings on a fixed alphabet, $|u|$ is the length of u, $\leq$ is a linear ordering of the alphabet, $h_1(u)$ and $h_2(u)$ are the first and second halves of the string u "appropriately adjusted when $|u|$ is odd", $\varnothing$ is the empty string, $\text{tail}(v)$ is the string obtained from v by deleting its first letter v_0, and $*$ is the concatenation operation on strings.

An abstract machine (in Moschovakis's sense) may implement mergesort but any such implementation will be too specific. It may sort $h_1(u)$ first, or sort $h_2(u)$ first, or interleave the two computations. Whatever it does, it is too specific. In your favorite phrase, there is no abstract machine that implements the mergesort algorithm on its natural abstraction level. I wonder if there is any state-based way to capture the mergesort algorithm on its natural abstraction level.

A: Wait a minute. Equations (1) and (2) give a specification, not an algorithm. As you said, they define the functions sort and merge. But unless some further information is given or assumed, we could "implement" this definition of sort by using quicksort and checking that the result satisfies (1).

Q: You're right. I presume that the intention, in calling these equations an algorithm, is that, given a string u of length greater than 1, you should sort it by splitting it into the two halves $h_1(u)$ and $h_2(u)$, sorting these, and merging the results.

A: With that presumption and an analogous one for computing merge, you have described an algorithm. It can be modeled faithfully by a recursive ASM in the sense of [7][a]. Recursive ASMs are state-transition systems but need not satisfy the sequential time postulate.

If we model equation (1) by a recursive ASM, temporarily regarding merge as a given function, we get a distributed algorithm that sorts strings in the way you described, namely to sort both halves and then merge the results. It allows runs in which $h_1(u)$ is sorted first, other runs in which $h_2(u)$ is sorted first, and others in which these two operations are performed in parallel, or by interleaving subcomputations for the substrings $h_i(h_j(u))$ and for smaller substrings.

If we don't regard merge as a given function but include its computation in our recursive ASM, then more implementations become available, for example interleaving parts of one sorting operation with parts of another merging operation.

Q: Runs like these correspond to the various implementation options mentioned by Moschovakis in [9]. So I'll be asking you to explain recursive ASMs and their runs.

4 Implementations of Recursive Equations

Q: But first, I wonder whether we (and Moschovakis) shouldn't consider a broader class of implementations.

A: What sorts of implementations do you have in mind?

Q: Well, these recursive equations are to be interpreted as defining the least fixed-point of an operator on partial functions, as explained in [9, Sections 2 and 4]. And the natural way to compute least fixed-points is the iterative

---

[a]After the first version of this paper appeared in the Bulletin of the European Association for Theoretical Computer Science, Egon Börger and Tommaso Bolognesi showed in [2] that the mergesort algorithm, as well as numerous other recursive algorithms, can be adequately described by special recursive ASMs that became popular with the development of various ASM tools, namely traditional (non-distributed) ASMs equipped with submachines. Below we describe vassal agents. Submachines are vassal agents of a particular and elegant type. In general, however, the more general recursive ASMs in the sense of [7] are needed. For instance, the recursive ASM of the Example 3.1 in [7] does not lend itself to a natural submachine description.

process described, for example, in [8, Section 6.7]. In the mergesort example, this amounts to first sorting all strings of length 1, then sorting all strings of length 2, then those of lengths 3 and 4, and so on until you've sorted the given string u. At each step, sort strings by applying equation (1) to previously sorted shorter strings. (I'm using merge as a given function, but a similar description would apply if it were computed recursively along with sort.)

In the case of mergesort, this bottom-up process is inefficient, because it sorts a lot of strings not relevant to the given instance u. But for other algorithms, it may make good sense, and it may be more efficient than the top-down process. For example, to compute the Fibonacci numbers, defined recursively by

$$F(n) = \begin{cases} 1, & \text{if } n = 1 \text{ or } n = 2, \\ F(n-1) + F(n-2), & \text{otherwise,} \end{cases}$$

the bottom-up approach works well but a (naive) top-down approach recomputes the same values $F(k)$ absurdly often.

But apart from questions of efficiency, it seems reasonable to regard the bottom-up process as an implementation. How does this look from the point of view of recursive ASMs?

A: One can use nondeterministic recursive ASMs to include more of mergesort's implementations, but there is no reason to believe that every declarative specification can be faithfully captured by an algorithm. Fairness, for example, is a legitimate ingredient for specifications but is not algorithmic.

As for the bottom-up implementation of mergesort, didn't you say that Moschovakis proves that mergesort needs only $O(n \log n)$ comparisons to sort a string of length n? The bottom-up implementation you described would use many more comparisons, since it sorts a lot of irrelevant strings.

Q: We'd better look more closely at Moschovakis's definition of "needs only q comparisons." He gives a precise mathematical definition of this concept, along the following lines. Take the recursive equations (1) and (2) and replace every mention of the order relation $x \leq y$ by $c(x, y)$ where c is a parameter representing a partial binary relation on the alphabet. This means that $c(x, y)$ can be true or false or undefined. We're interested in c's that are subrelations of $\leq$ in the sense that if $c(x, y)$ is true (resp. false) then $x \leq y$ (resp. $x \not\leq y$), i.e., c is obtained from $\leq$ by making it undefined at certain arguments. Since c is only a part of $\leq$ (and since the recursion equations define an operator monotone[b] in c), the functions sort_c and merge_c defined using c are subfunctions of sort and merge. Now what Moschovakis proves is that, for every string u of length n there exists a subrelation c of $\leq$ such that $\text{sort}_c(u)$ is defined (and thus equal to $\text{sort}(u)$) and such that c is defined on only $O(n \log n)$ pairs. Intuitively, this means that the value of $\text{sort}(u)$ is computed, via the recursive equations, using only those comparisons that are given by c, and thus using at most $O(n \log n)$ comparisons.

A: This looks like a perfectly reasonable definition of information usage by recursive computations. We especially like it because it seems to match what we'd get using recursive ASMs.

It means, however, that either this sort of resource bound for an algorithm might fail to carry over to its implementations or else your bottom-up implementation of mergesort isn't really an implementation. For the bound on the number of comparisons is, as we saw, violated by the bottom-up implementation.

Q: Moschovakis intends that the comparison count, once established for the general mergesort algorithm, applies automatically to all its implementations. Specifically, for algorithms like mergesort[c] a mathematical definition of "implementation" is given in [8]. In [9], Moschovakis briefly describes this notion of "implementation" and says that "it behaves well with respect to resource use, e.g., it justifies extending to all implementations of the mergesort the comparison counts established for the algorithm."

A: So it seems that the bottom-up "implementation" that you suggested would not qualify as an implementation according to the definition in [8]. Maybe we should compare it with the definition to see just what goes wrong[d].

Q: That may get a bit complicated, but I tried to improve my understanding of the definition of "implementation" by checking it in the case of the factorial function on the natural numbers. I used the obvious recursive definition

$$n! = \begin{cases} 1, & \text{if } n = 0, \\ n \cdot (n-1)!, & \text{otherwise.} \end{cases}$$

---

[b]To be precise, the clause "if $v_0 \leq w_0$", the only occurrence of $\leq$ in (1) and (2), becomes "if $c(v_0, w_0)$" and is to be understood as follows. If $c(v_0, w_0)$ is true then this case applies; if $c(v_0, w_0)$ is false then move on to the next case; and if $c(v_0, w_0)$ is undefined then the result of this merge_c is undefined. Monotonicity means that if we change any c to be defined at more arguments, without changing the true or false values it already has, then sort_c and merge_c only become more defined if they change at all.
[c]"Like mergesort" here means that the range of outputs of the algorithm is an ordinary set, as opposed to a general complete poset, which is allowed in [9].
[d]The material from here to the end of this section can be safely skipped.

The first implementation I tried was a top-down computation given by the program

```
step
   read n
   var p = 1        // introduce a variable p, initially 1
   var x = n        // introduce a variable x, initially n
step until x = 0
   p := p · x
   x := x − 1
step
   Result := p.
```

A: Both the recursive equation and the program look OK. Does the program implement the recursion by Moschovakis's definition of "implement"?

Q: Yes. With a couple of pages of work, I was able to verify the definition.

Next, I tried a bottom-up approach. Rather than write out a program, I'll describe this as an abstract machine in Moschovakis's sense. The states are the initial state s_0 and all pairs $\langle n, s \rangle$ where $n \in \mathbb{N}$ and s is a partial function from $\mathbb{N}$ to itself. The transition function for input m sends s_0 to $\langle m, \varnothing \rangle$ and sends $\langle n, s \rangle$ to $\langle n, s' \rangle$ where

$$s'(k) = \begin{cases} 1, & \text{if } k = 0, \\ k \cdot s(k-1), & \text{otherwise.} \end{cases}$$

Terminal states are the pairs $\langle n, s \rangle$ with n in the domain of s, and the output function sends $\langle m, \langle n, s \rangle \rangle$ (where m is the input and $\langle n, s \rangle$ a terminal state) to $s(n)$.

A: We agree that this computes the factorial function in a bottom-up manner. The successive states of the computation have, in their second components, longer and longer initial segments of the factorial function. But the machine looks awkward. The first component of a state $\langle n, s \rangle$ just keeps track of the input, which plays no role during the main computation. And the output is given by a function of input and state, so you don't need to remember the input as part of the state in order to produce the output.

Q: True, but in Moschovakis's definition the input is not available when you determine whether a state is terminal. The definition of "terminal" in my machine is the only place where I need that the state remembers the input.

A: We don't think Moschovakis would mind an amendment to his definition, making the input available when deciding whether a state is terminal.

Q: I agree, but I was trying to understand exactly his definitions. So I refrained from amending anything.

I worked out what Moschovakis's definition would require in order to call this abstract machine an implementation of the factorial. As far as I can see, the requirement is not satisfied.

A: You say "as far as I can see." Does that mean there's no easy way to decide whether a machine implements an algorithm?

Q: No, the definition of "implements" requires the existence of two functions. One maps inputs to inputs and seems to be just a matter of reformatting the input. In the present situation, where both the algorithm and the machine take as input the number whose factorial is to be computed, this function would be the identity. The other function, though, is more complicated. Its domain consists, in our example, of partial functions from $\mathbb{N}$ to $\mathbb{N}$, and its range consists of partial functions from states to numbers, subject to some requirements.

A: That sounds pretty complicated. Maybe we should look closely at the definition and try to understand it better.

Q: We probably should, but it might be more efficient if I first try to understand examples better and then discuss it with you. Besides, time is limited and I still want to hear about recursive ASMs and their runs.

A: OK. Anyway, it makes sense that a bottom-up computation of the factorial doesn't count as an implementation for Moschovakis. We already saw that a bottom-up computation of mergesort had better not count as an implementation because it violates the resource bound.

5 A Recursive ASM for Mergesort

A: Now about recursive ASMs, let's begin with the simplest case, which is treated in [7, Section 2], and which suffices to handle mergesort.

The key idea is that recursive computations are to be viewed as a special case of distributed computation.

Q: So in the case of mergesort, there would be one agent for the function sort and another for merge.

A: No, there would in general be many agents for each function. The idea is that to call a function means to create a new "vassal" agent whose job is to execute that function call. The agent who calls the function — we call it the "lord" of the vassal[e] — passes the appropriate arguments for the function to the vassal, and when the vassal's work is complete it passes the computed value of the function back to the lord.

Notice that the information often stored in a stack, telling who reports to whom, is here stored locally. Each vassal just remembers who its lord is.

Q: Why don't you use a stack? Standard implementations of recursion do.

A: Stack implementations work as long as recursive calls occur sequentially, one at a time. But sometimes it is useful and natural to make many recursive calls in parallel. Our stack-free approach makes this work well.

In [7], a convenient notation was developed for recursive ASMs. Rather than repeating details here, we'll just exhibit the recursive ASM that expresses the mergesort algorithm (see Figure 1). Most of the program will be self-explanatory, and we'll be happy to answer your questions about the rest. (To avoid clutter, we omitted lots of end-markers like endif that the notation of [7] requires. Just assume that the beginning of every line closes all open blocks that started with the same or greater indentation, except that else and elseif don't close the open if-block that began with the same indentation. Equivalently, just use common sense.)

Q: Let me make sure I'm reading this program correctly. The two blocks labeled rec tell how to compute the functions sort and merge, so they are the programs for two sorts of vassals. The lines preceding the first rec are the main program, which just starts the recursive computation and puts the final result into Output. Whenever any agent executes a rule involving Sort, a vassal is created to carry out the sorting, and similarly for Merge. The dynamic, nullary symbol Result in a vassal's program gets the value to be passed to the lord; the lord uses this result as the value of the term for which he created the vassal.

A: Right. We also used the convention that each agent starts with Mode equal to Initial and finishes when Mode becomes equal to Final.

Q: But something's wrong with dynamic symbols like Mode and Result that are shared by all the agents. Updates by one agent will interfere with other agents' computations.

---

[e]In [7] the terminology was "master" and "slave" but recently we have used "lord" and "vassal." We also changed the Return of [7] to Result, since a noun is more appropriate.

```
if Mode=Initial then
   Output := Sort(Input), Mode := Final

rec Sort(u)
   if Mode=Initial then
      if |u| ≤ 1 then
         Result := u, Mode := Final
      else
         v := Sort(h₁(u))
         w := Sort(h₂(u))
         Mode := Halfway
   elseif Mode=Halfway then
      Result := Merge(v,w), Mode := Final

rec Merge(v,w)
   if Mode=Initial then
      if v = ∅ then Result := w
      elseif w = ∅ then Result := v
      elseif v₀ ≤ w₀ then Result := ⟨v₀⟩ * Merge(tail(v),w)
      else Result := ⟨w₀⟩ * Merge(v,tail(w))
      Mode := Final
```

Figure 1. Mergesort

A: Those locations are not really shared. Each agent has his own copy of these memory locations. In the official notation of [7], there is a nullary Mode used by the main program (the first two lines in our example) and a unary function, say Mode'(Me) such that each agent a uses Mode'(a) where we have written simply Mode in the program. But the primes[f] and the Me's required by this official notation are so cumbersome that a convention was adopted in [7] whereby they can be omitted. The general convention is that any dynamic function occurring in the program of a vassal is understood as implicitly having an extra argument Me (and a prime if needed to distinguish it from a symbol in the main program).

---

[f] We could avoid the primes by having an initial agent that executes the main program; then Mode would be a unary function everywhere.

Q: With that convention, the program looks good to me. Let me check how the information flow works when we sort a string u. For simplicity, I'll assume (as Moschovakis does in [8,9] when he checks details) that the length of u is a power of 2, say $n = 2^m$. The main program creates a sort-agent, whose result will be the final output, and it passes the input u to this agent. This agent, executing the program in the block rec $\text{Sort}(u)$ and being in Initial mode, creates two vassals, each sorting half of u, i.e., a string of length 2^{m-1}. Then these create vassals who sort strings of length 2^{m-2}, and so on. If I cleverly start numbering levels of this tree of vassals at 0, then there are 2^k sort-agents at level k, each sorting a string of length 2^{m-k}. That continues until at level m there are 2^m agents sorting strings of length 1. They don't need further vassals, as a string of length 1 is already sorted. So these agents pass their (sorted) strings to their (immediate) lords. Each of these lords can now assign values to its v and w and, having completed the "Mode = Initial" part of its program, goes into Mode = Halfway. It therefore creates a merge-vassal. In general, each sort-agent in the tree (except for leaves) will get a sorted string from each of its two vassals, assign values to v and w, go into Mode = Halfway, and create a merge-vassal to merge those two strings.

Merge-agents form chains rather than trees, since each one (unless it is at the bottom of its chain) extracts one element from one of its two sequences and passes the rest to a single vassal to merge. When it gets the vassal's result, it prepends the extracted element and passes the result to its lord. At the bottom of each chain is a merge-agent one of whose two input sequences is empty, and this agent just returns the other input sequence to its lord.

A: Right. Now it's fairly easy to estimate the number of comparisons made during this computation.

Each merge-agent with nonempty input sequences makes exactly one comparison, to decide which sequence's head is earlier, and a sort-agent makes no comparisons. So the problem is to estimate the number of merge-agents with nonempty inputs. A sort-agent at level $k < m$ creates a merge-agent whose job is to merge two sequences of length 2^{m-k-1}. Each time a merge-agent creates a vassal, the total length of the sequences to be merged by the vassal is 1 less than the total length for the lord. So the chain of merge-agents descending from a sort-agent at level k consists of at most 2^{m-k} agents, all but the last of which make a comparison. So from one sort-agent at level k we get fewer than 2^{m-k} comparisons; from all 2^k sort-agents at level k, we get fewer than 2^m comparisons; and so altogether, since there are m levels to consider, there are fewer than $2^m \cdot m$ comparisons. Since $|u| = n = 2^m$, this bound is $n \cdot \log n$.

Q: So we get the same estimate as Moschovakis. In fact, the "big O" in his estimate is unnecessary.

A: That's because of the simplifying assumption that n is a power of 2; for general n, there will be a small constant factor in the estimate, and so the "big O" is needed after all.

Q: Of course. I forgot that Moschovakis also gets $n \cdot \log n$ without a big O when n is a power of 2.

You claimed that the recursive ASM in Figure 1 faithfully models the algorithm described by Equations (1) and (2)

A: Don't forget that the equations alone just define the functions. To describe an algorithm, they must be supplemented with an understanding that the sort function is to be computed by splitting the input, sorting the halves, and merging the results — as the equations suggest but do not demand.

Q: Right. The agreement between the estimate of comparisons that I made here and Moschovakis's bound lends some support to your claim. In fact, I see some additional support in the proofs of these estimates. Admittedly, your computation doesn't look exactly like the one Moschovakis gives, but they match up pretty closely. Moschovakis's proof works with statements of the form "we can compute sort(u) (or merge(v, w)) with at most so many comparisons," and it seems that these statements correspond to statements of the form "the agent responsible for sorting u (or for merging v and w) in the recursive ASM has among its subordinates (i.e., vassals, vassals of vassals, etc.) at most so many merge-agents with nonempty inputs."

A: Good. Perhaps one could also count, as evidence for our claim, that the program in Figure 1 looks very similar to Equations (1) and (2). Of course the syntactic details are different[g], but the updates (except for Mode) in the figure match what would be computed in evaluating the right sides of the equations.

6 Recursive ASMs as Distributed ASMs

Q: Right. But you also claimed that the runs of this recursive algorithm include the various implementations mentioned by Moschovakis, like sorting the left half first, or sorting the right half first, or interleaving the computations. So what, exactly, are the runs of a distributed algorithm?

---

[g]The notation of [7] can be improved to match the recursive equations more closely; such an improvement is incorporated in the ASM-based specification language AsmL [4]

A: That's a long story, written out in detail in [7, Subsection 2.2] and [6, Section 6]; the former converts recursive ASMs to distributed ASMs, and the latter defines runs of distributed ASMs. Rather than repeating the details here, let us just explain the essential ideas, with reference to the mergesort algorithm in Figure 1.

Converting a recursive ASM to a distributed ASM amounts to making explicit the creation of vassals, the waiting for the vassals' return values, and the use of these return values to continue the computation.

Q: This sequentialization will involve more modes, right?

A: Exactly. In [7] there was, in addition to the Mode involved in the recursive ASM, an additional RecMode in the distributed algorithm, whose purpose is to keep track of where in the "creating vassals, waiting for values, using the values" process an agent is.

Q: I suppose this RecMode is really a private RecMode(Me), and that it has three possible values, corresponding to creating, waiting, and using.

A: You're right about Me, but in fact we need only two values for RecMode, since we can conveniently combine the waiting and using parts.

To make sure the idea is clear, let's describe what a sort-agent does in the non-trivial case where its input has length > 1. It starts with Mode = Initial and RecMode = Create[h] In this situation, it creates vassal sort-agents for the two halves of its input, and it goes into RecMode = Wait. (By "creates" we mean that it imports two elements from the reserve and makes them vassals with the appropriate inputs.)

Q: How does it know to create the sort-agents corresponding to the lines $v := \mathrm{Sort}(h_1(u))$ and $w := \mathrm{Sort}(h_2(u))$ in the rec Sort block of Figure 1? Why doesn't it also create a merge-agent corresponding to the last line of the block?

A: Because it's in Initial mode, only the former lines are enabled, i.e., the guards governing them are true. The distributed program is arranged so that vassal agents are created only for the computations needed in enabled updates.

Q: This could get messy if an update involves nesting of recursively defined functions.

---

[h] In [7] the values of RecMode were CreatingSlaveAgents and WaitingThenExecuting. We shorten them here.

A: In [7], the mess was avoided by a convention forbidding such nesting. That's why Figure 1 has the updates involving Sort separate from those involving Merge, rather than having a single line

Result := Merge(Sort($h_1(u)$),Sort($h_2(u)$)).

Q: Moschovakis uses a similar disentangling of nested functions, though for a different reason, for example when he converts an abstract machine (or the corresponding tail recursion) to a recursor in [9, Section 4].

It seems clear that nesting of recursively defined functions can always be eliminated in this way.

A: Right. And if we didn't eliminate it in our recursive ASMs then the elimination would have to be incorporated into the conversion of recursive to distributed ASMs[i].

Let's get back to our sort-agent, which was last seen in Mode = Initial and RecMode = Wait. In this RecMode, the agent does nothing until its vassals are all in Mode = Final. Then it takes the vassals' Result values and puts them in place of the terms that had caused the creation of the vassals. Here this means that the vassals' Result values replace the terms Sort($h_i(u)$). Now our sort-agent can execute the rest of its instructions. It assigns these values to v and w and enters Mode = Halfway. Having completed its Wait work, it also returns to RecMode = Create.

Since it's now in mode Halfway, the enabled update in its instructions is Result := Merge(v, w). So it creates a merge-agent with inputs v and w and enters RecMode = Wait.

Here it does nothing until its merge-vassal returns a value. Then, following its instructions, it assigns this value to Result and enters Mode = Final (and RecMode = Create).

Q: And here it does nothing, because there's nothing to do in Final mode.

A: Right. Final mode terminates the computation. Should we also look at what a merge-agent does in the distributed computation?

Q: No, it's pretty clear in view of your explanation for sort-agents. Let's move on to the notion of runs.

---

[i]This would be the right approach, not artificially restricting recursive ASMs.

7 Runs of Distributed ASMs

A: OK. There are actually two kinds of runs defined in [6, Section 6]. The simpler kind, sequential runs, are adequate to describe implementations of the sort you quoted Moschovakis as mentioning, so let's concentrate on these sequential runs first. Later, if we have time, we can look at the more general partially ordered runs.

A *pure sequential run* of a distributed ASM is a sequence of states S_n, in which the first state S_0 is an initial state of the ASM and each subsequent state S_{n+1} is obtained from its predecessor S_n by executing a move of an agent in S_n.

Q: That raises several questions. First, by "executing a move of an agent" do you mean performing the updates specified by that agent's program?

A: Yes. Recall that the agent's whole program describes a single computational step.

Q: Is the run a finite sequence or an infinite one?

A: It could be either. Of course for algorithms like mergesort, where a final answer is expected, the runs of interest would be the finite ones that end by giving Output a value (other than its original value of undef).

Q: Why is the word "pure" in the definition? What would an impure run be?

A: "Pure" means that all state changes come from the ASM, not from the environment. An impure run would allow intervention by the environment, for example a user typing input. Since we won't deal with impure runs here, we'll sometimes omit "pure."

Q: So a pure sequential run of a distributed ASM amounts to an arbitrary interleaving of the moves of the agents.

A: Right, but keep in mind that agents can be created and destroyed. So the possible moves from state S_n to state S_{n+1} depend on which elements of (the base set of) S_n are agents and which programs they have been assigned.

Q: OK. So for your mergesort ASM, there would be runs in which $h_1(u)$ is always sorted before $h_2(u)$, others in which they are sorted in the opposite order, and still others where the two sorting operations are interleaved, for example by having the merge-agents subordinate to these two sortings interleave their moves.

A: This is what we meant when we said that the runs of the mergesort ASM include implementations of the sort you quoted from Moschovakis.

Q: Do they include *all* implementations in Moschovakis's sense?

A: Answering that would require looking in detail at Moschovakis's definition of "implementation," a task that you suggested postponing.

Q: OK. That gives me some more motivation for understanding that notion of implementation.

Meanwhile, since pure sequential runs cover the obvious implementations, what's left for the more general partially ordered runs that you mentioned?

A: The idea here is that the relative order of some moves can be left unspecified. More precisely, a *pure partially ordered run*, or for short just a *run*, of a distributed ASM consists of

- a partially ordered set $(M, \leq)$ of (abstract) *moves*,

- a function A assigning to each move x an element $A(x)$ of the base set of the ASM's states (intuitively, $A(x)$ is the agent who makes move x), and

- a function σ assigning to each finite initial segment X of M a state $\sigma(X)$ of the ASM.

(An initial segment is just a downward-closed set.) These data are subject to the following requirements.

- For each $x \in M$, the set of predecessors $\{y \in M : y \leq x\}$ is finite.

- For each a, the subset $\{x \in M : A(x) = a\}$ of M is linearly ordered (by the ordering $\leq$ of M).

- $\sigma(\varnothing)$ is an initial state.

- If X is a finite initial segment of M, if x is a maximal element in X, and if $Y = X - \{x\}$, then $A(x)$ is an agent in the state $\sigma(Y)$, and $\sigma(X)$ is obtained from $\sigma(Y)$ by executing a move of this agent.

Q: That sounds pretty complicated. Can you give an intuitive explanation?

A: We can try. An element $x \in M$ represents a move made by an agent $A(x)$. (Part of the last requirement guarantees that when this move is made, $A(x)$ will be an agent rather than just some arbitrary element of the state.) The order relation $\leq$ on M refers to the relative timing of moves. $y < x$ means that move y must be completed before move x begins.

Q: When you say "must be," you leave open the possibility that y might be completed before x begins even if they are incomparable in M.

A: Right. Nothing is required about the relative timing of incomparable elements of M.

This is why the set $\{x \in M : A(x) = a\}$ of moves made by a single agent is required to be linearly ordered. Moves of a single agent occur in a definite order.

If X is a finite initial segment of M, then $\sigma(X)$ represents the state after the moves in X (and no others) have been made. So it certainly makes sense to require $\sigma(\varnothing)$ to be initial; it is in fact the starting state of the run.

The point of the final, complicated condition in the definition of run is that $\sigma(X)$ should be the state you reach by performing the moves in X in any order consistent with $\leq$. In particular, any maximal element x of X could be the last move in X. Just before that move, the state would be $\sigma(Y)$ where $Y = X - \{x\}$. So we require that, in this state, $A(x)$ is an agent, a move of which will lead to the state $\sigma(X)$.

Q: Now the definition makes more sense. What's the connection between sequential and partially ordered runs?

A: In the first place, every sequential run can be regarded as a partially ordered run in which the ordering $\leq$ of M happens to be a linear ordering. It's easy to check that, for linear $\leq$, the definition of partially ordered run essentially reduces to that of sequential run.

Secondly, if we have a partially ordered run and we increase the order relation, say from $\leq$ to $\leq'$ where $y \leq x$ always implies $y \leq' x$, then every initial segment with respect to $\leq'$ is also an initial segment with respect to $\leq$. So we can get a new run, using the same M and A, using $\leq'$ as the order, and restricting σ to the set of $\leq'$-initial segments — provided $\{y \in M : y \leq' x\}$ is finite as required in the definition.

In particular, $\leq'$ could be any linear extension of $\leq$ with finite initial segments. So, by linearizing the order, we can convert any partially ordered run to a sequential run.

Q: The linearization amounts to taking incomparable pairs, moves for which no relative timing was specified, in the partially ordered run, and arbitrarily imposing a relative order on them.

A: Right. Of course the "arbitrarily" is constrained by the demand that the result be an order. For example, if $y < z$ were both incomparable with x, then you couldn't put x before y and after z.

Q: Of course; I didn't intend "arbitrarily" to include absurdities, but I recognize the need to make intentions precise.

234

8 Algorithms

Q: Let me return to another issue that we barely mentioned earlier. You said that Moschovakis uses both the words *algorithm* and *machine* differently than you do. So far, we've discussed machines; the main difference seems to be that Mochovakis's machines operate in sequential time, while you allow for distributed computation. I'd be interested in hearing about the difference in meanings of "algorithm."

A: To localize the disagreement, let's first mention two points of agreement. First, there are some things that are obviously algorithms by anyone's definition — Turing machines, sequential-time ASMs, and the like. Even abstract machines in Moschovakis's sense are algorithms as long as the functions used by the machine (e.g., transition function and output function) are regarded as given.

Second, at the other extreme are specifications that would not be regarded as algorithms under anyone's definition, since they give no indication of how to compute anything. For example, the function sort could be specified by saying that sort(u) is the sequence with the same terms as u (with the same multiplicities) but in nondecreasing order. This can be regarded as a specification but it is too general to describe an algorithm. In fact, it is easy to give a declarative specification for uncomputable things, even though all the ingredients of the specification are computable. An example is the problem of deciding whether a given multi-variable polynomial with integer coefficients has an integer root.

Between the two extremes, there is a whole spectrum of things that give more or less information about how something is to be computed. The issue is how detailed this information has to be in order to count as an algorithm. Apparently, Moschovakis is more lenient here than we are, as far as recursion is concerned. He allows as algorithms some things that we would call only declarative specifications, and he would probably use the word "implementation" for the things that we call algorithms.

To be specific, let's look first at mergesort. Moschovakis says that the system of equations (1) and (2), or a recursor embodying these equations, defines an algorithm. We say that more information is needed before you have an algorithm. As already noted, the algorithm had better say that sort(u) is to be computed by the split-and-merge technique suggested by the equations, not by just any method that can be proved to satisfy the equations.

But there is more. The bottom-up approach you mentioned, where you sort all shorter strings before proceeding to any longer ones, is not among the approaches that Moschovakis's mergesort embodies, since it violates the bound on comparisons. Yet it certainly sorts strings by the split-and-merge technique suggested by the equations. Indeed, as you said, it's the algorithm implicit in the usual construction of least fixed points of monotone operators (like recursors).

Q: Isn't there another construction of a least fixed point, as the intersection of all sets closed under the operator?

A: Yes, and this leads to an even worse interpretation of the recursion equations — worse in the sense of computational feasibility.

It seems likely to us that, by the time one adds to recursion equations (or to a recursor) all the "fine print" needed to exclude unintended approaches to the computation (like the bottom-up approach or this intersection idea) that nevertheless flow from the equations in some sense, one has something that we'd call an algorithm. But we'd say that the algorithm is given not just by the recursor but by the combination of the recursor and the fine print. And we'd expect, in accordance with the ASM thesis, that this combination could be modeled by an ASM, in general a distributed one, as was the case for mergesort.

Acknowledgments

The work of the first author was partially supported by NSF grant DMS–0070723 and by a grant from Microsoft Research. This paper was written during a visit to Microsoft Research.

References

1. A. Blass, Y. Gurevich, and S. Shelah, Choiceless polynomial time, *Ann. Pure Appl. Logic* 100 (1999) 141–187; addendum 112 (2001) 117.
2. E. Börger and T. Bolognesi, Remarks on turbo ASMs for functional equations and recursive schemes, *Springer Lecture Notes in Computer Science* 2589, 218–228.
3. A. Blass and Y. Gurevich, Abstract state machines capture parallel algorithms, *ACM Trans. Computational Logic*, to appear.
4. Foundations of Software Engineering Group, Microsoft Research, AsmL Web Page, http://research.microsoft.com/foundations/#AsmL.
5. Y. Gurevich, Sequential abstract state machines capture sequential algorithms, *ACM Trans. Computational Logic* 1 (2000) 77–111.

6. Y. Gurevich, Evolving algebras 1993: Lipari guide, in *Specification and Validation Methods* (ed. E. Börger), Oxford Univ. Press (1995) 9–36.

7. Y. Gurevich and M. Spielmann, Recursive abstract state machines, *J. of Universal Computer Science* 3 (1997) 233–246.

8. Y.N. Moschovakis, On founding the theory of algorithms, in *Truth in Mathematics* (ed. H.G. Dales and G. Oliveri), Clarendon Press, Oxford (1998) 71–104.

9. Y.N. Moschovakis, What is an algorithm? in *Mathematics Unlimited* (ed. B. Engquist and W. Schmid), Springer-Verlag (2001) 919–936.

PAIRWISE TESTING

ANDREAS BLASS
Mathematics, University of Michigan
Ann Arbor, MI 48109-1109, USA

YURI GUREVICH
Microsoft Research
One Microsoft Way
Redmond, WA 98052, USA
E-mail: gurevich@microsoft.com

We discuss the following problem, which arises in software testing. Given some independent parameters (of a program to be tested), each having a certain finite set of possible values, we intend to test the program by running it several times. For each test, we give the parameters some (intelligently chosen) values. We want to ensure that for each pair of distinct parameters, every pair of possible values is used in at least one of the tests. And we want to do this with as few tests as possible.

1 Introduction

Quisani: I suppose that, with Andreas visiting Microsoft for an extended period, you've been working together on logic and abstract state machines.

Authors: Actually, we've recently been looking into software testing and related combinatorial problems.

Q: Is that connected with your work on abstract state machines?

A: Indirectly. It is related to what our group, the Foundation of Software Engineering group at Microsoft Research, is doing. The group has developed AsmL, a specification language based on abstract state machines. To make AsmL specifications more useful, the group is working on automated derivation of test suites from AsmL specifications. This work generated considerable interest among Microsoft test architects and test engineers.

Q: What combinatorial problems arise in testing?

A: The problem we've looked into is how to generate a test suite (a set of tests) that is *pairwise adequate* in the following sense. Suppose a program involves c parameters, each with a certain number of possible values; say the ith parameter has n_i possible values. A *test* is determined by giving a value for each parameter. We want to find a test suite such that, for each pair of distinct parameters, say the ith and j^{th}, and for each pair of possible values of these parameters, say x and y, there is a test in our suite where the ith parameter has value x and the jth has value y. The objective is to accomplish this with as few tests as possible.

Q: I guess you assume that, for any two parameters, every pair of possible values is relevant.

A: Indeed we do. Moreover, we assume[a] that every assignment of values to the parameters is legal and so can be tested.

Q: Since this is for computer purposes, not for pure mathematics, I assume all the n_i are finite.

A: Of course.

Q: But won't some of them be awfully large? The parameters could, for example, represent floating-point numbers.

A: Yes, but in that case one reduces the number of values by taking into account the program to be tested. The program usually suggests a splitting of the range of a floating-point parameter into a few sub-ranges, within each of which the program acts similarly. Then for testing purposes one uses just one representative (or a small number of representatives) from each sub-range. In the applications that our group has encountered, c and all the n_i were no larger than 50. And often some of the parameters were Boolean ones, so some of the n_i were only 2.

Q: Were you able to make good progress?

A: We did but can't claim much credit. When we began looking at these matters we were told that [8] had the essential information. That paper cites [3,4] where related ideas are used. We looked at the methods proposed in these papers and felt that certain combinatorial ideas could be profitably applied, giving test suites that have few tests and are easy to find. We developed three such ideas, which we call the "affine," "recursive," and "Boolean" ideas. We realized that some classical combinatorial issues, like Latin squares and projective geometry, are relevant. In the meantime, we traced references back to earlier sources and we also found one recent relevant paper. The affine idea, it turns out, goes back at least to [2] in pure combinatorics, and recently Williams [13] had applied it and the recursive idea to testing. The Boolean

---

[a]The purpose of this assumption is to simplify our exposition, not to limit the applicability of pairwise testing. It may, for example, be useful to test illegal situations, to see what error messages occur.

idea uses well-known combinatorial results from [5,6,7,12]; their relevance to testing is described in the introduction of [11].

Q: I'd like to hear more about it, and I hope that the record of our discussion may benefit others as well. It is useful to have in one place all those seemingly unrelated facts scattered in the literature as well as your own insight.

A: All right. Let's begin by looking at the methods proposed in the papers we first looked at, [3,4,8].

2 Incremental Constructions

Q: Before that, just to make sure I understand the problem, let me check that some things that look obvious to me are really correct.

If you increase the number of parameters (leaving the n_i for the old parameters unchanged), or if you increase some n_i's then the number of tests you need will increase or, at best, stay the same. Also, the number of tests you need is at least the product of the two largest n_i's. If you're so lucky as to have only two parameters ($c = 2$), then this product is exactly the number of tests you need.

A: Right; all these things are indeed obvious. In fact, the product of the two largest n_i's is exactly the number of tests you need even if there are three parameters. But that's not quite so obvious; it will become clear in a while.

Everyone seems to agree that a convenient way to represent a test suite is as a matrix. There is one row for each test, and there is one column for each parameter. The entry in any particular row and column is the value of the column's parameter in the row's test. Pairwise adequacy of the test suite means that the columns are pairwise independent, i.e., for every two columns and every choice of a possible entry in each of them, there is a row where the chosen entries occur in those two columns. (The idea behind the terminology "independent" is that, if you know an entry in one column, that gives you no information about the entry in the same row and another column. To avoid confusion, we stress that we do not ask for probabilistic independence of two columns, where each pair of values would occur in the same number of rows. The simpler sort of independence that we use is sometimes called *qualitative independence*, a terminology that goes back to [9]. We'll omit "qualitative" because we won't need any other sort of independence.)

We'll use the notation r for the number of rows in our matrices (to go with c for the number of columns); thus r represents the number of tests in a suite, and it is what we want to minimize (for fixed c and n_i's).

Let's use the word *requirement* for a set of two ordered pairs, which we write in the form $\{i \mapsto x, j \mapsto y\}$ where i and j are distinct columns (representing parameters) and x and y are possible values of those parameters. We'll say that a matrix *satisfies* this requirement if it has a row in which the entries in columns i and j are x and y, respectively. So we seek matrices that satisfy all the requirements.

With this terminology, we can describe the two methods that we were aware of when we began our work. They both involve building a matrix gradually, trying to satisfy the requirements as efficiently as possible.

2.1 The AETG Method

A: One method, presented in [3,4], builds the matrix one row at a time. It keeps track of the requirements that remain to be satisfied, and it chooses each new row by a combination of randomization and greed, with a view to satisfying many of the as yet unsatisfied requirements. In more detail, the algorithm creates a new row as follows, as long as any requirements remain unsatisfied. Choose a column i and a value x for the corresponding parameter such that $i \mapsto x$ occurs in the largest number of unsatisfied requirements. Fill in x as the value in the new row and column i. Then fill in the remaining places in the new row in a random order, choosing the value for each entry in turn so as to maximize the number of previously unsatisfied requirements that become satisfied. Of course, the result here depends on the random ordering. So the authors suggest in [4] that each row be computed some number of times (they suggest 50), with different random orders, and that the best result be used (where "best" means satisfying the most previously unsatisfied requirements).

2.2 The Lei-Tai Method

A: Another method, presented in [8], involves building up the number of parameters gradually, so that at a typical stage in the process one has a test suite for the first c' parameters, where $c' < c$, and one wants to enlarge it to a test suite for the first $c' + 1$ parameters. The method starts with the first two parameters, where, as you observed, it's trivial to find an optimal test matrix. The general step, from c' to $c' + 1$, involves adding to the matrix a new column (for the new parameter) and, unless we're very lucky, adding some new rows to make this column independent of the previous ones. The step proceeds in two parts, a "horizontal" part, filling in the part of the new column that involves existing rows, and a "vertical" part, adding new rows.

The authors of [8] observe that, once the horizontal part is completed, there is no choice about the number of new rows to be added in the vertical part. Here are the details. For each value v of the new parameter and for each old column i, let $D(v,i)$, the *deficit* of value v with respect to column i, be the number of unsatisfied requirements of the form $\{i \mapsto x, c' + 1 \mapsto v\}$. At the end of the horizontal part of the step, satisfying such requirements will demand $D(v,i)$ new rows with v in the new column. A single new row can handle requirements from any or all of the old columns i, so the vertical part needs to add

$$D(v) = \max_{i \leq c'} D(v,i)$$

new rows with v in the last column, for a total of

$$\sum_v D(v) = \sum_v \max_i D(v,i)$$

new rows at this step. We'll refer to $D(v)$ as the *(total) deficit* of the value v.

Q: So the real work in this method is in the horizontal part of each step.

A: Essentially. There is some freedom in the vertical part, even though the number of new rows is fixed. For example, which pairs of requirements, involving the same v and different i's, should be satisfied by the same row? And if $D(v,i) < D(v)$ for certain v and i, then there will be some places in column i where any value could be entered. These sorts of freedom might be used to make future steps work better, but this issue is not addressed in [8]. So, indeed, the work is done in the horizontal part.

In fact, two approaches to the horizontal part are proposed in [8]. One approach tries all possible ways to fill in the horizontal part and chooses one to minimize the number of new rows in the vertical part.

Q: Wait a minute. Aren't there usually a huge number of ways to fill in the horizontal part? Will this computation terminate in reasonable time?

A: You're right, and this problem is recognized in [8]. The authors point out that the work can be reduced somewhat, since permuting the values of the new parameter has no effect. Nevertheless, this approach is feasible only for very small cases. That's why a second approach is offered.

The second approach to the horizontal part amounts to the following greedy algorithm. Fill in the entries in the new column one by one, choosing each value so as to maximize the number of previously unsatisfied requirements that become satisfied.

242

Q: For the first entry to be filled in, any one of the new values will satisfy c' new requirements, so it doesn't matter what value is used for this entry.

A: Right. In fact, for the first few entries in the new column, the greedy strategy can fill in distinct values of the new parameter, as each will satisfy the maximum possible number c' of previously unsatisfied requirements. Things become non-trivial only in rows that remain after each possible value has been used once.

Q: Are the entries in the new column and old rows filled in a random order?

A: The algorithm in [8] just fills them in top-to-bottom order. But one could randomize, try it several times, and take the best of the results.

2.3   A Variation on the Lei-Tai Heuristics

A: There is another way to improve the algorithm. As it stands, the horizontal part is greedily maximizing the number of requirements that get satisfied. But that goal isn't really what's wanted. Suppose a value v has, at the end of the horizontal part, just two unsatisfied requirements and they involve the same column i. Then v will have to be the new-column entry in two new rows, with different elements in column i to satisfy the two requirements. Suppose, on the other hand, that v has, at the end of the horizontal part, more than two unsatisfied requirements, but all referring to different columns. Then these requirements can be satisfied with just one new row having v in the last column. So we are better off in the second scenario, even though the number of unsatisfied requirements is greater. To put it another way, algorithm seeks to minimize

$$\sum_v \sum_i D(v,i),$$

but the number of new rows needed in the vertical part is, as we saw,

$$\sum_v \max_i D(v,i).$$

So we should try to minimize that instead.

We therefore considered modifying the horizontal part of the Lei-Tai algorithm from [8] to greedily reduce this sum of maxima. At each row, put into the new column a value whose $D(v)$ is thereby reduced.[b]

---

[b]If there is no such value, then you may want to choose a value v so as to reduce as much as possible the number of i's for which $D(v,i) = D(v)$; the point of that reduction is that it improves our chances of reducing $D(v)$ later.

We experimented on some specific values of c and the n_i's, and we found that this modification needs to be refined in order to produce real benefits. The modification is useful in the late stages of the horizontal part, but it seems counterproductive in the early stages. We tried several versions of the algorithm, greedily reducing various weighted combinations of the sum of all the $D(v,i)$'s (as in the Lei-Tai algorithm) and the sum over v of the maximum over i of $D(v,i)$ (as in our proposed modification). The weight factors depended on the row number, giving the Lei-Tai version more weight for the early rows and giving our modification more weight for the later rows. In our experiments, the best results occurred when the ratio of the two weights was proportional to the cube of the row number. But the number of experiments we did was too limited to support any general claims.

Q: Is this modification of the Lei-Tai algorithm one of the ideas anticipated in [2,11], and [13]?

A: No. The ideas they anticipated are what we call the affine idea,[c] the Boolean idea, and the recursive idea.

3   The Affine Idea

Q: What are those ideas?

A: Let's start with the affine idea in a special case. Let p be a prime number. Then there is a matrix with p^2 rows, p columns, entries in $\{0, 1, \ldots, p-1\}$, and all columns independent.

Q: So this would correspond to p parameters, each with p values. One of my trivial observations was that we'll need p^2 rows even for just two p-valued parameters, so you're saying it costs no more rows to handle p such parameters than to handle just two.

A: Right. In fact, the method extends to handle $p + 1$ such parameters, but let's look at p of them first.

The idea is to work with affine functions over the prime field $\mathbb{Z}/p$ of p elements. Imagine the p^2 rows of our matrix as being labeled with the ordered pairs (a, b) of elements from $\mathbb{Z}/p$ and imagine the p columns as labeled by the elements of $\mathbb{Z}/p$. Then the entry in row (a, b) and column i is $ai + b$, where addition and multiplication are done modulo p, i.e., done in the field $\mathbb{Z}/p$.

---

[c]The anticipation covers the affine idea over fields, not the most general case described below.

$0i + 0$	0	0	0
$0i + 1$	1	1	1
$0i + 2$	2	2	2
$1i + 0$	0	1	2
$1i + 1$	1	2	0
$1i + 2$	2	0	1
$2i + 0$	0	2	1
$2i + 1$	1	0	2
$2i + 2$	2	1	0

Figure 1. Affine Matrix for $p = 3$

Q: So the row labels (a, b) are viewed as designating the p^2 affine functions of one variable over $\mathbb{Z}/p$.

A: Right; that's why we call this construction the affine idea. Figure 1 shows the matrix for $p = 3$. The actual matrix is the part to the right of the vertical line; the column to the left just shows the row labels.

Q: You don't show the column labels?

A: They're the entries in the row $1i + 0$, so it didn't seem worthwhile to repeat them across the top of the figure.

Q: OK. In this example it's easy to see that the columns are pairwise independent.

A: It's easy to see it in general. Indeed, to satisfy the requirement $\{i \mapsto x, j \mapsto y\}$, we need a row (a, b) such that

$$ai + b = x,$$
$$aj + b = y.$$

The determinant of this linear system of equations for a, b is $\begin{vmatrix} i & 1 \\ j & 1 \end{vmatrix} = i - j \neq 0$. As $\mathbb{Z}/p$ is a field, the required a and b exist.

Q: This establishes your claim about p parameters with p values being handled in p^2 tests. You also claimed that this can be improved to handle one more parameter; how do you do that?

A: Add another column, whose entry in row (a, b) is a. See Figure 2. To see that this column is independent of the previous ones, we need to solve for a, b

$0i + 0$	0	0	0	0
$0i + 1$	1	1	1	0
$0i + 2$	2	2	2	0
$1i + 0$	0	1	2	1
$1i + 1$	1	2	0	1
$1i + 2$	2	0	1	1
$2i + 0$	0	2	1	2
$2i + 1$	1	0	2	2
$2i + 2$	2	1	0	2

Figure 2. Extended Affine Matrix for $p = 3$

equations of the form

$$ai + b = x,$$
$$a = y,$$

and this is trivial. (It does not need that p is prime.)

Q: The obvious question now is whether yet another column can be added, maintaining pairwise independence, without adding more rows.

A: The answer is negative; $p + 1$ is the best you can do. Let's postpone the proof for a while and continue discussing the affine method.

Q: OK. The method looks pretty good if

- the two largest n_i are equal,

- their common value n is prime, and

- $c \leq n + 1$.

Then you get n^2 rows, and we know there's no possibility of doing better. But what if those conditions aren't all satisfied?

A: If the two largest n_i's are not equal but not very different, the affine method may still be reasonably good if the largest n_i is prime and c is at most 1 larger. If the largest n_i is significantly larger than all the others, then a reasonable approach is to first solve the problem without the largest n_i (hence with c reduced by 1) and then to restore the omitted n_i by (the variant described above of) the method of Lei and Tai.

Q: What if the two largest n_i's are equal, say to n, and $c \leq n + 1$, but n isn't prime?

A: A natural approach is to use the affine method with p being the first prime $\geq n$.

Q: How much bigger than n is that p likely to be? I remember reading somewhere that there's always a prime between n and $2n$, but if p is near $2n$ then the number of rows you get, p^2, is unpleasantly large compared to the n^2 that one might hope for.

A: The situation isn't quite that bad. In the first place, the prime number theorem says that the density of primes near n is close to $1/\ln n$, so usually one needs to look only logarithmically[d] past n to find a prime.

Q: That's "usually"; what about the worst case?

A: For that, one needs an expert on the distribution of primes, so we asked Hugh Montgomery of the University of Michigan. He provided most of the following asymptotic information.

There is a constant $\theta < 1$ such that, for all sufficiently large n, there is a prime between n and $n + n^\theta$. The best (smallest) θ currently known is 0.525 (see [1]), but it is conjectured that every positive θ will work. On the other hand, there are, for any K, infinitely many n with no prime between n and $n + K \log n$. There is no consensus (let alone a theorem) about, say, $n + K(\log n)^2$.

So for large n, there is relatively little penalty for going to the next prime: $n^2 + O(n^{1.525})$ tests in the worst case and $n^2 + O(n \log n)$ on average, compared to an optimum n^2 (when the two largest n_i are both n).

In practice, the values of n that arise are not so large. In fact, they are small enough so that a simple lookup table can give the least prime $p \geq n$. For $n \leq 100$ we always have $p \leq n + 7$ (and $p \leq n + 5$ except when $n = 90$ or 91). In addition, the following variants of the affine idea may help.

The affine idea works over any finite field, whether or not it has the form $\mathbb{Z}/p$. Every power q of any prime p is the number of elements of a finite field. For any such q, the affine idea produces a matrix with q^2 rows, $q+1$ columns, q different entries, and all columns independent.

Consider, for example, the 4-element field. It has characteristic 2, i.e., $x + x = 0$ for all x in this field. The four elements are 0, 1, g, and $g + 1$ where $g^2 + g + 1 = 0$. The two equations $x + x = 0$ and $g^2 + g + 1 = 0$ (together with the field axioms) determine the arithmetic of this field and thus let us write down a 16 by 5 matrix (Figure 3) with 4 entries and with all columns independent.

---

[d] We use ln for the natural logarithm, base e, and log for the logarithm with base 2.

$0i+0$	0	0	0	0	0
$0i+1$	1	1	1	1	0
$0i+g$	g	g	g	g	0
$0i+g+1$	$g+1$	$g+1$	$g+1$	$g+1$	0
$1i+0$	0	1	g	$g+1$	1
$1i+1$	1	0	$g+1$	g	1
$1i+g$	g	$g+1$	0	1	1
$1i+g+1$	$g+1$	g	1	0	1
$gi+0$	0	g	$g+1$	1	g
$gi+1$	1	$g+1$	g	0	g
$gi+g$	g	0	1	$g+1$	g
$gi+g+1$	$g+1$	1	0	g	g
$(g+1)i+0$	0	$g+1$	1	g	$g+1$
$(g+1)i+1$	1	g	0	$g+1$	$g+1$
$(g+1)i+g$	g	1	$g+1$	0	$g+1$
$(g+1)i+g+1$	$g+1$	0	g	1	$g+1$

Figure 3. Extended Affine Matrix over 4-Element Field

Q: So in effect a prime power is as good as a prime.

A: Right, provided you don't mind doing arithmetic in general finite fields.

There is another variant of the affine method that uses rings of the form $\mathbb{Z}/q$ for non-prime values of q.

Q: Those rings aren't fields, so your proof that the columns are independent won't work.

A: Right; in fact the columns won't all be independent, but some of them will be. Specifically, if we let i range from 0 to $p-1$ where p is the smallest prime divisor of q, then the columns labeled i will be pairwise independent. Indeed, proceeding as in the field case, we find that when i and j are in this range and distinct then the equations we must solve for a and b have a determinant $i-j$, which is non-zero and smaller than p in absolute value. Thus, this determinant is relatively prime to q and therefore invertible in $\mathbb{Z}/q$. Therefore, the required a and b exist (and are unique).

Q: So you get a matrix with q^2 rows, q entries per column, pairwise independent columns, but only p columns, rather than the q columns you could get using a field.

A: Right. You can get one more column as before; its entry in row (a,b) is a.

Q: Could you get more columns by using as your column labels not simply 0 through $p - 1$ but some cleverly chosen set of more than p elements of $\mathbb{Z}/q$?

A: No. No matter how clever you are, any set of more than p elements will have two members that are congruent modulo p. Then the two corresponding columns will not be independent.

Q: So $p + 1$ is the best you can hope for with the affine method over $\mathbb{Z}/q$. That looks considerably worse than what you get by using finite fields.

A: This method is useful if the required number c of columns happens to be small compared to the largest n_i. Even if the given c is large, the recursive idea (to be explained in a moment) sometimes leads to sub-problems with small c.

4 The Recursive Idea

A: Let n be the largest n_i, and suppose that c is significantly larger than n. The affine idea requires us to use a prime power q that is at least $c - 1$ (or, in the ring version, a number whose smallest prime divisor is at least $c - 1$, which is even worse). So we get a matrix with $q^2 \geq (c - 1)^2$ rows. Every column of the matrix has q distinct entries, far more than we need, but the affine method can't take advantage of this to reduce the number of rows.

The affine method can, nevertheless, make a contribution even in the case of large c. One approach is to begin by considering only some subset of the parameters, small enough so that the affine method provides a good matrix, and then to extend this matrix by the Lei-Tai method, perhaps modified as discussed above, to incorporate the rest of the parameters.

Q: So you'd use a matrix built using the affine idea instead of the two-column matrix that Lei and Tai use as the starting point for their construction.

A: Right. We experimented a bit with this method on one of the examples given by Lei and Tai, 20 parameters with 10 values each. We used the affine method with $p = 11$. The results were somewhat better, but not dramatically better, than the Lei-Tai method.

4.1 Multiple Layers

A: There is another, more systematic way to use the affine method with large c. We call it the recursive idea. Choose $q \geq n$ as before but $q < c$. Let w be the number of columns we can handle with this q, namely $q + 1$ if q is a

0	0	0	0	0	0	0	0	0	0	0	0
1	1	1	0	1	1	1	0	1	1	1	0
2	2	2	0	2	2	2	0	2	2	2	0
0	1	2	1	0	1	2	1	0	1	2	1
1	2	0	1	1	2	0	1	1	2	0	1
2	0	1	1	2	0	1	1	2	0	1	1
0	2	1	2	0	2	1	2	0	2	1	2
1	0	2	2	1	0	2	2	1	0	2	2
2	1	0	2	2	1	0	2	2	1	0	2

Figure 4. Partial Matrix for 12 Three-Valued Variables

prime power (and we use the field of size q) or $p + 1$ where p is the smallest prime divisor of q (if we use $\mathbb{Z}/q$). Form the $q^2 \times w$ matrix given by the affine method, and repeat it horizontally to fill the required c columns. Columns i and j are independent except when i and j are congruent modulo w. Figure 4 shows an example where $n = 3$ and $c = 12$. (The vertical lines in the figure are just to make the copies of the original, 4-column matrix easier to see.)

Now we need to add more rows to make the columns within each congruence class modulo w pairwise independent. There are w congruence classes, each of size c/w (rounded to an integer). For each congruence class, we handle the columns in that class separately, by adding copies of the original $q^2 \times w$ matrix below the matrix already constructed. In our example, the first congruence class is handled as shown in Figure 5.

We'll refer to the newly added rows as the second layer of the matrix (and the original rows as the first layer).

Q: The first three rows in the second layer of Figure 5 don't contribute to the independence of these columns. They just duplicate earlier rows.

A: That's right, so we can omit these three rows. Notice, though, that if we had $c \geq 13$ and thus had four columns in some equivalence class, then only the first row of the second layer would be redundant. The second and third rows would not be constant, so they actually contribute to the independence.

In our example, omitting the three redundant rows and handling the other congruence classes similarly, we get Figure 6.

That finishes the job in this example, but in general two columns would still be identical if their positions differed by a multiple of w^2. So if c were greater than w^2 then we'd need a third layer to handle these congruence classes. In general, we get a matrix with $\lceil \log_w c \rceil = \lceil \log c / \log w \rceil$ layers of

250

```
0  0  0  0  0  0  0  0  0  0  0  0
1  1  1  0  1  1  1  0  1  1  1  0
2  2  2  0  2  2  2  0  2  2  2  0
0  1  2  1  0  1  2  1  0  1  2  1
1  2  0  1  1  2  0  1  1  2  0  1
2  0  1  1  2  0  1  1  2  0  1  1
0  2  1  2  0  2  1  2  0  2  1  2
1  0  2  2  1  0  2  2  1  0  2  2
2  1  0  2  2  1  0  2  2  1  0  2
0        0        0
1        1        1
2        2        2
0        1        2
1        2        0
2        0        1
0        2        1
1        0        2
2        1        0
```

Figure 5. More of the Matrix for $c = 12$ and $n = 3$

$q^2 - 1$ rows each, except that the first layer has q^2 rows. (The $q^2 - 1$ comes from the fact that the first, all-zeros row would be the same in every layer, so it can be omitted from all layers but one.)

Q: It seems the extra column added to the affine method, the column not given by affine functions, is causing trouble here by allowing only the first row of each layer to be omitted.

A: That's true. If we used the original, "pure," affine method, then each layer but the first would have only $q^2 - q$ rows, because all the affine functions of the form $0i + b$ would give redundant rows. On the other hand, w would be decreased by 1, so there is a danger that we might need an additional layer. So there is a trade-off, whose value often depends on the effect of rounding the ratio of logarithms to an integer.

One can improve on this pure affine method as follows. In the first layer, use the affine method with the extra column. Any two columns that are not yet independent are in fact identical. So in subsequent layers we don't need any constant rows. So in all layers but the first we can use the pure affine method minus its first q rows.

0	0	0	0	0	0	0	0	0	0	0	0
1	1	1	0	1	1	1	0	1	1	1	0
2	2	2	0	2	2	2	0	2	2	2	0
0	1	2	1	0	1	2	1	0	1	2	1
1	2	0	1	1	2	0	1	1	2	0	1
2	0	1	1	2	0	1	1	2	0	1	1
0	2	1	2	0	2	1	2	0	2	1	2
1	0	2	2	1	0	2	2	1	0	2	2
2	1	0	2	2	1	0	2	2	1	0	2
0	0	0	0	1	1	1	1	2	2	2	2
1	1	1	1	2	2	2	2	0	0	0	0
2	2	2	2	0	0	0	0	1	1	1	1
0	0	0	0	2	2	2	2	1	1	1	1
1	1	1	1	0	0	0	0	2	2	2	2
2	2	2	2	1	1	1	1	0	0	0	0

Figure 6. The Whole Matrix for $c = 12$ and $n = 3$

Q: How is this better than the pure affine method? They both use q^2 rows in the first layer and $q^2 - q$ rows in each subsequent layer.

A: Yes, but the improvement uses a larger w in the top layer, so the congruence classes to be treated in subsequent layers are a little smaller. As a result, we may get by with one fewer layer.

There is another variation that is occasionally useful. We can choose q independently for the different layers. This may be particularly useful at the last layer, where the congruence classes remaining to be treated may be smaller than n and we can therefore use a q that is not a prime power and still have w large enough.

Q: You mentioned that the affine and recursive ideas are already in the literature.

A: Yes, Bose [2] uses the affine idea (over fields, not over general $\mathbb{Z}/q$) to construct what amount to test matrices, though he uses the terminology of Latin squares. (When he wrote his paper, software testing and even computers were far in the future.) Williams [13] applies Bose's construction along with the recursive idea to the problem of testing.

4.2 An Explicit Formula

A: It seems useful to observe — and it doesn't seem to be in the literature — that the matrices given by the pure affine idea for a prime p plus the recursive idea admit a rather simple, explicit description. Number the rows and columns starting at 0. The entry in row z and column i is z if $0 \le z < p$ and

$$\left(a \left\lfloor \frac{i}{p^l} \right\rfloor + b \right) \bmod p, \text{ if } z = p + l(p^2 - p) + (a-1)p + b,$$

with $1 \le a < p$, $0 \le b < p$, and $0 \le l$.

Q: I'm not sure that's really "rather simple". I understand "z if $0 \le z < p$", which just means that the first p rows are constant. But please explain the non-trivial part of the formula.

A: OK, let's look at the formula piece by piece, starting with the part $z = p + l(p^2 - p) + (a-1)p + b$. This is just a compact way of saying that row z is in layer l, where we start numbering layers at 0, and within layer l it is row number $(a-1)p + b$. Remember that, when we use the pure affine method, each layer but the first has $p^2 - p$ rows, so $p + l(p^2 - p)$ is the number of rows in layers strictly preceding layer l. (For uniformity of terminology here, we regard the first p rows, the constant ones, as strictly preceding layer 0.) So, as we start numbering rows at 0, layer l begins at row $p + l(p^2 - p)$ and continues to row $p + (l+1)(p^2 - p) - 1$, inclusive. This is precisely the range of $p + l(p^2 - p) + (a-1)p + b$ as a ranges from 1 to $p-1$ and b ranges from 0 to $p-1$.

Now within layer l, increasing z corresponds to lexicographically increasing the pair (a, b). This is because b ranges only from 0 to $p-1$, so any increase of a, even by only 1, increases $(a-1)p + b$ by at least p and thus outweighs any decrease in b. So as z increases through layer l, the pair (a, b) runs through all the relevant coefficients for affine functions $ax + b$ over $\mathbb{Z}/p$, in lexicographic order. (Remember that $a = 0$ is omitted since it would produce constant rows, duplicating rows we already had earlier.)

It remains to see how these affine functions are used. Let's look first at the easiest case, layer 0. Here we should have, in the first p columns, the matrix given by the affine method, and in subsequent columns simply repetitions of this matrix. So in the first p columns, where $0 \le i < p$, we should have entries $ai + b$, calculated in $\mathbb{Z}/p$, i.e., calculated modulo p. These entries and the repetitions in later columns, with period p, are given by $a(i \bmod p) + b$ calculated modulo p, which simplifies to $ai + b \bmod p$. (It's a simplification of the mathematical description, reducing modulo p only once, at the end. For computation, it may be better to reduce as you go rather than waiting until the end.) And this simplified formula is exactly the one we had above, when $l = 0$, since then $\lfloor i/p^l \rfloor = i$.

In the next layer, where $l = 1$, we take care of the pairs of columns that have not already achieved independence, namely those whose numbers are congruent modulo p. And we take care of them by putting more copies of the same affine matrix, but with columns labeled differently. Thus, the first p columns ($0 \le i < p$) are each the first in their respective congruence classes, so their entries in layer 1 are like the entries of the first column, $i = 0$, in layer 0. Similarly, the next p columns ($p \le i < 2p$) get, in layer 1, the entries that the next single column, $i = 1$, had in layer 0. Continuing in this way, we see that columns from pj to $(p+1)j - 1$ inclusive get, in layer 1, the entries that column j had in layer 0. In other words, the layer 1 entries in column i are the layer 0 entries in column $j = \lfloor i/p \rfloor$, namely

$$\left(a \left\lfloor \frac{i}{p} \right\rfloor + b \right) \bmod p.$$

Q: OK. I see how, when you continue recursively, you'll get higher powers of p in the denominator, because in layer l you're concerned with pairs of columns whose numbers i are congruent modulo p^l. Now that I see what's going on, the formula does look simple.

5 The Boolean Idea

Q: What is the third idea you mentioned, the Boolean idea?

A: As the name might suggest, it applies in the special case where all the parameters are Boolean, i.e., all $n_i = 2$. Then a solution of the testing problem, an $r \times c$ Boolean matrix, can be viewed as a family (indexed by the columns, i.e., by the parameters) of subsets of an r-element set, say $\{1, 2, \ldots, r\}$. The set indexed by i consists of those m such that the entry in row m, column i is **true** (or 1).

Independence of the rows is equivalent to the following requirements on these sets:

- No one is a subset of another.

- No two are disjoint.

- No two cover the whole set $\{1, 2, \ldots, r\}$.

Indeed, the first of these three requirements says that the pairs of values $(1,0)$ and $(0,1)$ occur in each pair of columns, the second requirement says that $(1,1)$ occurs, and the last requirement says that $(0,0)$ occurs.

An equivalent way of expressing these requirements is:

- No two of the sets are complementary.

- The sets and their complements form an antichain (i.e., none is included in another).

So we are looking for antichains, closed under complementation, in the Boolean algebra of subsets of $\{1, 2, \ldots, r\}$. Then our test matrix is formed by choosing, in this antichain, one member of each complementary pair and using (the characteristic functions of) the chosen sets as the columns of our matrix.

How big can a complement-closed antichain of subsets of $\{1, 2, \ldots, r\}$ be? Half of that will be the largest c that can be handled with r rows in the Boolean situation.

If r is even, Sperner's theorem [12] says that the largest possible antichain of subsets of an r-set consists of the subsets of size $r/2$. Since this antichain is closed under complementation, we find that the largest c that can be handled with r rows is

$$c = \frac{1}{2} \binom{r}{r/2} = \binom{r-1}{r/2}.$$

If r is odd, Sperner's theorem says that the largest antichains have size $\binom{r}{(r-1)/2}$, but these are not closed under complementation.

You can construct a complement-closed antichain by fixing one element in the r-set, say 1, and taking all of the $(r-1)/2$-element subsets that contain 1 and all of the $(r+1)/2$-element subsets that don't contain 1.

It turns out (as a consequence of the Erdős-Ko-Rado theorem [5]) that these are the largest complement-closed antichains. So the largest c that can be handled with r rows is

$$c = \binom{r-1}{(r-3)/2}.$$

Q: What is this Erdős-Ko-Rado theorem?

A: The theorem asserts that, for any r and any $k \le r/2$, if $\mathcal{F}$ is a family of k-element subsets of an r-set and if every two elements of $\mathcal{F}$ intersect, then the cardinality $|\mathcal{F}|$ is at most $\binom{r-1}{k-1}$.

Q: So it's not directly about complement-closed antichains. How does it imply a bound on the size of those?

A: Well, suppose $\mathcal{A}$ is a complement-closed antichain of subsets of an r-set where r is odd. Let $\mathcal{B}$ consist of those elements of $\mathcal{A}$ whose cardinality is smaller than $r/2$. Notice that the elements of $\mathcal{A}$ that are not in $\mathcal{B}$, namely those of size greater than $r/2$, are exactly the complements of the sets in $\mathcal{B}$. Notice also that every two sets in $\mathcal{B}$ intersect, for if X were disjoint from Y then X would be a subset of the complement of Y, contradicting the fact that $\mathcal{A}$ is an antichain.

Q: So if all the sets in $\mathcal{B}$ had the same size $k < r/2$, then the Erdős-Ko-Rado theorem would imply that

$$|\mathcal{B}| \leq \binom{r-1}{k-1} \leq \binom{r-1}{(r-3)/2},$$

which agrees with your claim. But I don't see why all the sets in $\mathcal{B}$ should have the same size.

A: They won't in general, but we can modify $\mathcal{B}$, without decreasing its cardinality, and without losing its crucial properties that it is an antichain and that every two members meet, yet so that after the modification all its members have size $(r-1)/2$.

Q: How do you do that? If it works, it clearly finishes the proof.

A: We'll need the following well known fact.

Lemma 1 *If $k < r/2$ then there is a one-to-one function that assigns to each k-element subset of an r-set a $(k+1)$-element superset of it.*

Q: I haven't seen this lemma before, but I think I see how it will finish your proof. Apply the lemma to the smallest elements in $\mathcal{B}$, and replace each of these smallest elements of $\mathcal{B}$ by its image, a set larger by 1. This clearly preserves the property that all pairs of sets from $\mathcal{B}$ meet, as we've replaced certain sets by supersets. It also preserves the antichain property, equally trivially. And it doesn't decrease the size of $\mathcal{B}$ because the newly added sets were not there before, as $\mathcal{B}$ was an antichain.

So, as long as the minimum size of sets in $\mathcal{B}$ is smaller than $(r-1)/2$, we can increase it. Repeating this process, we end up with all sets in $\mathcal{B}$ having size $(r-1)/2$, so the Erdős-Ko-Rado theorem applies.

But how do you prove the lemma?

A: It's an application of the matching theorem. By that theorem, it suffices to show that, if we take any collection $\mathcal{X}$ of k-element subsets of our r-set and if we define

$$\mathcal{Y} = \{Y : |Y| = k + 1 \text{ and } \exists X \in \mathcal{X} \, X \subset Y\},$$

then $|\mathcal{X}| \leq |\mathcal{Y}|$. And this is easy if we just count in two ways the number P of pairs (X, Y) with $X \in \mathcal{X}$, $Y \in \mathcal{Y}$ and $X \subset Y$.

On the one hand, each $X \in \mathcal{X}$ occurs in exactly $r - k$ such pairs, for any element of the complement of X can be added to form a Y. So $P = (r-k)|\mathcal{X}|$. On the other hand, any $Y \in \mathcal{Y}$ occurs in at most $k + 1$ such pairs, as each possible X is obtained by removing one of the $k + 1$ elements of Y. So $P \leq (k + 1)|\mathcal{Y}|$. Therefore

$$(r - k)|\mathcal{X}| \leq (k + 1)|\mathcal{Y}|.$$

As $k < r/2$, we have $r - k \geq k + 1$, and it follows that $|\mathcal{X}| \leq |\mathcal{Y}|$.

Q: So for Boolean parameters, you know exactly how many pairwise independent columns can be obtained from a given number of rows. How does this compare with what the affine and recursive ideas give you?

A: Using Stirling's approximation for the factorials involved in the binomial coefficients, we find that, for large r,

$$c \sim 2^{r-1} \sqrt{\frac{2}{\pi r}}.$$

Inverting this, to express r in terms of c, we get

$$r = \log c + O(\log \log c).$$

The constant in the $O(\dots)$ is small; any constant $> 1/2$ will do.

For comparison, the affine and recursive ideas give, for the Boolean case, asymptotically $2 \log c$.

We also note that one of the examples given in [8] for comparison with [3,4] involved only Boolean parameters, 100 of them. For this example, the method of [8] gives a matrix with 15 rows, and the method of [3,4] gave a matrix of 12 rows.[e] The Boolean method needs only 10 rows for this example. Furthermore, the matrix is very easy to write down. The first row can be taken to be all 0's. Then in each column fill in exactly five 1's and four 0's in the remaining spaces. Do this in such a way that all the columns are different; for example, go through the 5-element subsets of a 9-element set in lexicographic order. (There are 126 such sets, so we could in fact handle an additional 26 columns without needing any more rows.)

---

[e]These numbers are taken from [8]. Note that the methods involve non-determinism or randomization. It appears that numerous repetitions are needed to get results this good.

Q: Do the authors of these testing papers know about the Boolean method?

A: Some of them certainly do. The fact that 100 Boolean parameters can be handled with 10 tests is stated in both [3] and [4], and the latter refers to [11] where the general result is stated. But the context in which this 10 occurs in [3,4] is a comparison of methods for getting independence with methods that get probabilistic independence. It is not suggested that the Boolean method should be used in practice or combined with other known methods.

It may be worth emphasizing that the matrices given by the Boolean method are very easy to construct. Essentially, one just has to lexicographically (or in some other convenient order) generate subsets of a fixed size in a fixed set.

Q: So the case of 2-valued variables works as nicely as one could hope. The exact optimum is known and an optimal matrix is easy to produce. Might there be similar good news for 3-valued variables?

A: Sloane briefly discusses the case of 3-valued variables in the introduction of [11]. Unfortunately the situation is nowhere near as nice as in the 2-valued case.

As we saw above, the optimal r for c 3-valued parameters is 9 for $c = 2, 3, 4$. The optimal r for $c = 5$ is 11. Beyond that, Sloane gives a table of the best known r's for c up to 12, he gives references for some explicit constructions, and he cites an asymptotic result that the optimal r satisfies $r = \frac{3}{2} \log c(1 + o(1))$.

It seems to be a difficult combinatorial problem to say more about the case of 3-valued variables. If you're interested, you should probably look up the work cited in [11].

6 Random Attempts

Q: What would happen if, instead of applying these combinatorial or algebraic methods, you just tried to build a test matrix at random?

A: That's an interesting question. It would be a shame if all this work didn't produce something better than randomness.

Consider the case of c parameters, each with the same number n of possible values. Let's fill in the entries of an $r \times c$ matrix at random, with n possible values for the entries. The questions to consider are:

- What is the probability of getting all the columns independent?

- How big must r be so that this probability is non-zero (so r rows suffice for c columns when all $n_i = n$)?

- How big must r be so that this probability is large (so that we can generate an appropriate matrix at random)?

If r is as in the second question, then we have a probabilistic proof of the existence of an $r \times c$ test matrix for n-valued parameters. If r is as in the third question, then we have a good chance of finding such a test matrix by randomization.

In fact, there's a better way to use randomization. As soon as r is big enough to make the probability p of success not too tiny, we can choose a moderate-sized k and build k/p random $r \times c$ matrices. We'll have a good chance that at least one of them will have pairwise independent columns. The "good chance" depends on k, but $k = 20$ will surely do for practical purposes; so we just need r big enough so that $20/p$ is a feasible number of attempts.

Notice, by the way, that the actual testing, with the necessary repetitions, may involve more computation time than producing the test matrix. So it may be worthwhile to expend considerable computational effort on getting the test matrix to have few rows.

Now let's estimate the probabilities. The probability that a particular requirement $\{i \mapsto x, j \mapsto y\}$ (meaning entries x, y in columns i, j) is satisfied by a particular row is $1/n^2$. So the probability that it is *not* satisfied by *any* row is, since the rows are independent in the probabilistic sense,

$$\left(1 - \frac{1}{n^2}\right)^r.$$

So the expected number of unsatisfied requirements is

$$\left(1 - \frac{1}{n^2}\right)^r \frac{c(c-1)}{2} n^2.$$

This is an upper bound for the probability that some requirement is unsatisfied. So when this expectation is < 1 then there exists an $r \times c$ matrix with entries from an n-element set and with all pairs of columns independent.

For the expectation to be < 1, we need approximately

$$r > 2n^2 \ln c + n^2(2 \ln n - \ln 2).$$

Note that this involves a term proportional to $n^2 \log n$, which our methods didn't need. Also, the other main term is

$$2n^2 \ln c = 2n^2 \frac{\log c}{\log e} = \frac{n^2 \log c}{\log \sqrt{e}}.$$

Since $\sqrt{e} < 2$, this term is larger than $n^2 \log c$, whereas the affine and recursive ideas together give asymptotically $n^2 \log c / \log w$.

Q: So randomization is not the best option.

A: Probably not. Notice, though, that we computed an r for which the expected number of unsatisfied requirements is < 1. Since this expectation is an upper bound for the probability that some requirement is unsatisfied, the r we found certainly has weaker property that there is a non-zero probability of satisfying all requirements. But it is imaginable that a smaller r might have this weaker property, which is what we really want.

Finally, to answer the third of our questions above, if we increase r to $2n^2 \ln c + n^2 (2 \ln n - \ln 2) + An^2$ then the probability of not getting all columns independent decreases to less than e^{-A}. So by choosing a moderate sized A, we have a good chance of getting a solution to the testing problem by just filling in the matrix at random.

In fact, if n isn't too big, we could choose $A = 1/n^2$, i.e., we could add just one more row to the number r computed above. The probability of not getting pairwise independent columns would be at most e^{-1/n^2}. By repeating the random experiment $O(n^2)$ times, we'd have a good chance of finding a matrix with pairwise independent columns.

7 Projective Planes

Q: You promised to explain why there can't be a $q^2 \times (q + 2)$ matrix with q entries and independent columns. In other words, why can't the matrix given by the affine method, which you already extended by one more column, be extended by even more columns without adding rows?

A: The reason for that is best explained in terms of projective planes of order q.

Q: Remind me what a projective plane is.

A: A projective plane consists of a set P of points, a set L of lines, and an incidence relation between them (the relation being expressed by saying that a point lies on a line or that a line goes through a point), subject to three axioms:

• Every two distinct points lie on a unique common line.

• Every two distinct lines go through a unique common point.

- There exist four points of which no three lie on a common line.

A projective plane has order q if there are $q + 1$ points on every line. It is a theorem that all lines have the same number of points; also, every point of a projective plane of order q lies on exactly $q + 1$ lines.

Q: What does this have to do with test matrices?

A: It turns out that a $q^2 \times (q + 1)$ matrix with q entries and pairwise independent columns is essentially the same thing as a projective plane of order q. (We're assuming $q \geq 2$. The matrix for $q = 1$ is trivial and what should be a projective plane of order 1 is (intentionally) excluded by the third axiom for projective planes.)

Q: What does "essentially the same thing" mean?

A: Probably the best way to explain it is to prove it, but for a formal definition you could say that there are two constructions, one converting the matrices in question into projective planes, and one in the reverse direction, such that both composite constructions are the identity up to isomorphism.

Q: That's pretty abstract, and you say that the proof will make it clearer, so please show me the proof.

A: OK. First, suppose we have a matrix of the specified sort. Notice that, in accordance with one of your observations near the beginning of our discussion, in every two distinct columns, every pair of entries will appear together in exactly one row.

Q: Right. Independence requires each pair to appear together, and there are just barely enough rows for that, so no pair can appear together twice.

A: In particular, each of the q entries appears exactly q times in every column.

Now define a projective plane as follows. The points are the $(q+1)q$ pairs (i, x) where i labels a column and x is an entry, plus one special point called $*$. The lines and the incidence relation are defined as follows. First, there is a line for each column; the line for column i is incident with the q points (i, x) and with $*$. Second, there is a line for each row; the line for row m is incident with those points (i, x) such that the entry in row m and column i is x.

Every two distinct points lie on a unique common line. Indeed, if the points are (i, x) and (j, y) with $i \neq j$, then the independence of columns i and j gives a row whose line contains these points, and we saw above that there is only one such row. Furthermore, no column gives a line containing both, as $i \neq j$. If, on the other hand, the points are (i, x) and (i, y), then column i

gives the required line and it is clearly unique. Finally, if the points are (i, x) and $*$, then again column i gives the unique line through both.

Every two distinct lines lie on a unique common point. It suffices to prove existence, as uniqueness is equivalent to the uniqueness proved in the preceding paragraph. (Both say that you can't have two distinct lines going through two distinct points.) If the two lines come from columns, then $*$ is a common point. If one line comes from column i and the other from row m, then the common point is (i, x) where x is the entry in row m column i. The non-trivial case is that both of the lines come from rows, say rows m and m'. What we must prove is that there is a column in which these two rows have the same entry.

To this end, we count in two ways the number of pairs $(i, \{s, t\})$ where i is a column, s and t are distinct rows, and these two rows have the same entry in column i. For the first count, we use the fact that each entry occurs exactly q times in each column. So a particular column and a particular entry will contribute $q(q-1)/2$ pairs to our count. As there are $q+1$ columns and q entries, the total count is

$$(q+1) \cdot q \cdot \frac{q(q-1)}{2} = \frac{q^2(q^2-1)}{2}.$$

The second way of counting the pairs is as follows. There are q^2 rows, so there are exactly $q^2(q^2-1)/2$ possible second components $\{s, t\}$ for one of our pairs. Each such $\{s, t\}$ contributes either one pair $(i, \{s, t\})$ or none, depending on whether there is a column i with equal entries in rows s and t. (We saw already that there can't be two such columns.) The only way for the second count to match the first is for *every* possible $\{s, t\}$ to have an appropriate i and so to contribute a pair. This completes the proof of the second axiom of projective planes.

Q: You can skip the third axiom; I already see how it follows immediately from what you've proved and $q \geq 2$.

A: OK. Now we can answer your question about why you couldn't have a matrix like those considered here but with $q+2$ columns.

Suppose you had such a matrix. Pick arbitrarily one column, call it column i, and let s and t be two rows in which column i has the same entry. (Remember that each column has each entry q times and $q \geq 2$.) Now imagine the matrix without column i. That determines a projective plane. In particular (by the hardest part of the proof just completed), there is a column j where rows s and t have the same entry; and $j \neq i$ since we're looking at the matrix without column i. But now look at another submatrix, obtained by restoring column i and deleting some column other than i and j. This has two columns, i and j, in which rows s and t have equal entries, contrary to what we proved above.

Q: That answers my original question, but now I'm curious about something else. You produced a projective plane from a matrix, but you also claimed to be able to go in the other direction. How does that work?

A: We need to use the well-known fact that a projective plane of order q has exactly $q^2 + q + 1$ points and the same number of lines. Also, as mentioned earlier, each line has $q + 1$ points on it and each point has $q + 1$ lines through it. If you grant these facts, then the construction is easy.

Given a projective plane of order q, choose arbitrarily one of its points and call it $*$. On each of the $q + 1$ lines through $*$, arbitrarily label the q points other than $*$ by labels $1, 2, \ldots, q$. Now build a $q^2 \times (q + 1)$ matrix as follows. The $q + 1$ columns are labeled by the $q + 1$ lines l through $*$. The q^2 rows are labeled by the remaining q^2 lines. The entry in row m and column l is the label of the intersection point of lines l and m. To see that the columns are pairwise independent, consider any two distinct columns, say labeled by lines l and l', and any pair of labels x and x' in $\{1, 2, \ldots, q\}$. Let p be the point on l that was labeled x, and let p' be the point on l' that was labeled x'. Then the line m through p and p' does not go through $*$. (Proof: $*$ is the unique intersection point of l and l'. In particular p' is not on l. But p' is on m so $m \neq l$. Since l is the unique line through p and $*$ and since p is on m, it follows that $*$ is not on m.) So m determines a row of our matrix, and this row clearly has entries x and x' in columns l and l', respectively.

Q: So instead of using the affine method, starting with a field, we could get equally good results starting with any projective plane. So maybe we're not limited to prime powers for q.

A: Maybe. It's an open problem whether there are any finite projective planes whose orders are not prime powers. The first two non-prime-powers, 6 and 10, are known not to be orders of projective planes, but the question is open for 12.

Q: So it might be that the only finite projective planes are those arising from finite fields.

A: No. It is known that there are finite projective planes not isomorphic to those given by fields. But all those examples have prime power order. So, in going from the construction using fields to general projective planes, you get new examples, but not (yet) new orders of examples. By the way, the smallest

263

	0	1	2
0	0	2	1
1	2	1	0
2	1	0	2

Figure 7. A Latin Square

order for which there are non-isomorphic projective planes is 9, and there are exactly 4 isomorphism classes for this order.

8   Latin Squares

Q: You also promised to explain why the product of the two largest n_i's is an adequate number of rows not only in the obvious case where $c = 2$ but also for $c = 3$. And, while we're on that subject, what happens when $c = 4$?

A: The situation for $c = 3$ is probably easiest to see with an alternative way of describing the test matrices. Let's assume, to simplify the notation, that $n_1 \geq n_2 \geq n_3$. So we're looking for a matrix with $n_1 n_2$ rows. If the desired matrix exists, then each pair of values for the first two parameters occurs in exactly one row, so we can label the rows by these pairs of values. To visualize this, imagine an n_1 by n_2 array,[f] the rows (resp. columns) being labeled by the values of the first (resp. second) parameter. So each location in this array corresponds to a row of the original matrix. The third column of the matrix can then be represented by copying its entry from any row of the matrix into the corresponding location of the array. For example, the 3-column matrix in Figure 1 gives rise to the array in Figure 7.

The independence of the third column from each of the others is reflected in the fact that every value for the third parameter occurs in every row and in every column. When $n_1 = n_2 = n_3$ as in this example, such an array is called a *Latin square*.

Now you can see why $n_1 \cdot n_2$ rows in the matrix suffice when $c = 3$. We can fill in the array by putting the n_3 possible entries into the first n_3 spaces in the first row (there's enough room as $n_3 \leq n_2$) and then repeating this pattern in the subsequent rows, cyclically shifting it by one space from each row to the next. Then the remaining spaces in the table can be filled in arbitrarily, and the result will have the required properties. It's obvious that every one

---

[f] To avoid confusion, we'll consistently use "array" for this representation and "matrix" for the representation used in the preceding sections.

	0	1	2
0	0/0	2/1	1/2
1	2/2	1/0	0/1
2	1/1	0/2	2/0

Figure 8. A Graeco-Latin Square

of the entries appears in every row. That it also appears in every column is because $n_1 \geq n_2$ so there are enough rows for the cyclic shifts to go all the way around.

Q: So what about four parameters? Is the product of the two largest n_i's always a sufficient number of rows to handle four columns?

A: No, not even in the case that all the n_i have the same value n. The first counterexample is $n = 6$.

Notice that, if the matrix has four columns, then we can represent the third column by an array as above and the fourth column by a second such array. Each of the two arrays has, as above, the property that every value of the relevant parameter occurs in every row and in every column. Furthermore, for every pair of values of the third and fourth parameters, there must be a location occupied by those two values in the two arrays. One often superimposes the two arrays, which makes this last condition easier to check. For example, the matrix of Figure 2 gives the array (or superposed pair of arrays) of Figure 8.

When, as in this example, $n_1 = n_2 = n_3 = n_4$, we have two superposed Latin squares with the additional condition that every possible pair of entries occurs (and occurs exactly once, because there isn't enough room for more occurrences). This additional condition is often called *orthogonality*, and a pair of orthogonal Latin squares is often called a *Graeco-Latin square*. (Apparently the values of one parameter were traditionally represented by Greek letters and the values of the other by Latin letters.)

In general, to say that n^2 rows suffice for a matrix with c columns, n entries in every column, and all columns independent is the same as to say that there are $c - 2$ pairwise orthogonal Latin squares of order n.

The question about always getting a fourth column, in the special case where all the n_i are equal, thus comes down to whether Graeco-Latin squares of all orders exist.

Q: So when n is a prime power, then there are, by what we saw earlier, $n - 1$ pairwise orthogonal Latin squares of order n, and there do not exist n of them.

A: Right. The first case not settled by the affine idea (or equivalently by projective planes) is $n = 6$.

That there do not exist two orthogonal Latin squares of order 6 is a fairly classical combinatorial result, confirming the first nontrivial case of a conjecture of Euler. (Euler conjectured that there do not exist two orthogonal Latin squares of order n whenever $n \equiv 2 \pmod 4$. The first two cases, $n = 2$ and 6, are correct, but all other cases are wrong.)

Acknowledgments

The first author was partially supported by NSF grant DMS–0070723 and by a grant from Microsoft Research. This paper was written during a visit to Microsoft Research.

References

1. R.C. Baker, G. Harman, and J. Pintz, The difference between consecutive primes. II, *Proc. London Math. Soc. (3)* 83 (2001) 532–562.
2. R.C. Bose, On the application of the properties of the Galois fields to the construction of hyper Graeco-Latin squares, *Sankhya* 3 (1938) 323–338.
3. D.M. Cohen, S.R. Dalal, J. Parelius, and G.C. Patton, The combinatorial design approach to automatic test generation, *IEEE Software*, September 1996 83–87.
4. D.M. Cohen, S.R. Dalal, M.L. Fredman, and G.C. Patton, The AETG system: An approach to testing based on combinatorial design, *IEEE Trans. on Software Engineering* 23 (1997) 437–444.
5. P. Erdős, C. Ko, and R. Rado, Intersection theorems for systems of finite sets, *Quart. J. Math. Oxford Ser. (2)* 12 (1961) 313–320.
6. G.O.H. Katona, Two applications (for search theory and truth functions) of Sperner type theorems, in *Collection of Articles Dedicated to the Memory of Alfréd Rényi, II. Period. Math. Hungar.* 3 (1973), 19–26.
7. D.J. Kleitman and J. Spencer, Families of k-independent sets, *Discrete Math.* 6 (1973) 255–262.
8. Y. Lei and K.-C. Tai, A test generation strategy for pairwise testing, *Proc. 3rd IEEE High-Assurance Systems Engineering Symposium*, November 1998.
9. E. Marczewski, Indépendance d'ensembles et prolongement de mesures (résultats et problèmes), *Colloquium Math.* 1 (1948) 122–132.
10. A. Rényi, *Foundations of Probability*, Holden-Day, 1970.
11. N.J.A. Sloane, Covering arrays and intersecting codes, *J. Combinatorial*

Designs 1 (1993) 51–63.

12. E. Sperner, Ein Satz über Untermengen einer endlichen Menge, *Math. Z.* 27 (1928) 544–548.

13. A.W. Williams, Determination of test configurations for pair-wise interaction coverage, *Proc. 13th International Conf. on Testing of Communicating Systems*, August, 2000.

NEWMAN'S LEMMA – A CASE STUDY IN PROOF AUTOMATION AND GEOMETRIC LOGIC

MARC BEZEM

Department of Computer Science, Bergen University
Postboks 7800, N-5020 Bergen, Norway
E-mail: bezem@ii.uib.no

THIERRY COQUAND

Department of Computer Science
Chalmers University of Technology and Gothenburg University
SE-412 96 Göteborg, Sweden
E-mail: coquand@cs.chalmers.se

Newman's Lemma states that a graph is confluent if it is locally confluent and has no infinite paths. Newman's Lemma requires essentially higher-order logic. We show that the induction step in Huet's inductive proof of Newman's Lemma is completely first-order and can be automated easily with the help of a resolution theorem prover. The resolution proof uses classical logic. For the automation of a constructive proof we consider Newman's Lemma in geometric logic and sketch an algorithm leading to a constructive proof. We formalize the proof procedure and prove its completeness for geometric logic by a direct topological argument.

1 Introduction

A directed graph G is called *confluent* if any two diverging paths having the same start node can be extended to paths leading to the same end node. Directed graphs are ubiquitous, but often go by different names:

- abstract rewriting systems (underlying functional languages, etc.),
- labelled transition systems (underpinning operational semantics),
- Kripke frames (the basis of the semantics of modal logic).

In the respective cases, confluence is a key notion for:

- uniqueness of normal forms (independence of the evaluation strategy),
- certain forms of determinism (in operational semantics),
- quantifier shifts (in dynamic logic).

The graph G is called *locally confluent* if any two different *steps* (paths of length one) departing from the same node can be extended into paths leading to the same end node. As we will see in the next section, local confluence is strictly weaker than confluence. Newman's Lemma [12] (NL hereafter) states

267

268

that local confluence implies confluence provided there are no infinite paths. We have automated the combinatorial core of Huet's [6] proof of NL using the resolution theorem prover Otter [13]. Otter is not the fastest theorem prover anymore, but is by far the best documented, see [15,16]. We discuss the various sensitivities regarding the precise formulation in relation to the theorem proving procedure in Section 3. Geometric logic is introduced in Section 4, its proof theory in Sections 5 and 6, and the semantics and the completeness results in Section 7.

2 Local Confluence Is Weaker Than Confluence

Consider the following directed graph attributed by Hindley to Kleene.

Obviously, we have local confluence here since there are no diverging steps from a nor d, and diverging steps from b and c can be extended to paths ending in a and d, respectively, by using the cycle. However, the graph is not confluent, since the diverging paths $b \to c \to d$ and $b \to a$ cannot be extended to join. Attempts to deny this fact by applying a tiling analysis lead to the diagram below, where the cycle has been unwound into an infinite path. Here the dotted lines from a to a and from d to d represent paths of length zero for the sole purpose of keeping things orthogonal.

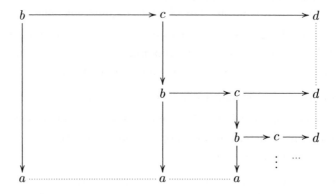

3 Proving Newman's Lemma

NL provides an interesting test case for several reasons. First, it consists of a mix of first-order and higher-order aspects. The higher-order aspects are the transitive closure and the finiteness of the paths. This makes the identification of the first-order combinatorial core of the proof non-trivial. Second, the proof of NL is not completely trivial, as experienced by everybody seeing it for the first time. In particular the automation of the constructive proof seems to provide a challenge to many theorem proving systems. For a precise analysis we have to introduce some notions from rewriting theory.

Definition 3.1 Let $\to$ be a binary relation on a set S and let $\twoheadrightarrow$ be the reflexive–transitive closure of $\to$. In other words, we consider a directed graph $(S, \to)$ with path relation $\twoheadrightarrow$.

1. We say that $x \in S$ is *confluent* if, for all $x_1, x_2 \in S$, $x \twoheadrightarrow x_1$ and $x \twoheadrightarrow x_2$ implies that $x_1 \twoheadrightarrow y$ and $x_2 \twoheadrightarrow y$ for some $y \in S$. Such a y is called a *common reduct* of x_1 and x_2. We say that $\to$ is *confluent* if every $x \in S$ is confluent.

2. We say that $x \in S$ is *locally confluent* if, for all x_1, x_2, $x \to x_1$ and $x \to x_2$ implies that $x_1 \twoheadrightarrow y$ and $x_2 \twoheadrightarrow y$ for some $y \in S$. Note $x \to x_i$ here and $x \twoheadrightarrow x_i$ above. We say that $\to$ is *locally confluent* if every $x \in S$ is locally confluent.

3. We say that $\to$ is *terminating* if there is no infinite sequence $x_0 \to x_1 \to x_2 \to \cdots$ in S.

One of the classical proofs of NL is by contradiction. Let $\to$ be locally confluent and terminating. Assume there is an x which is not confluent, that is, there exist $x_1, x_2 \in S$ such that $x \twoheadrightarrow x_1$ and $x \twoheadrightarrow x_2$ and x_1 and x_2 have no common reduct. Since $\to$ is terminating, we may assume without loss of generality that x is an $\to$-maximal[a] non-confluent element. If not, there would be a non-confluent x' with $x \to x'$, and if that x' is not $\to$-maximal, then there would be a non-confluent x'' with $x' \to x''$ and so on, leading to a sequence contradicting the termination of $\to$. (This part is difficult to explain, it actually uses the Axiom of Dependent Choice, DC.) Hence we have that every $y \in S$ with $x \to y$ is confluent. From the fact that x_1 and x_2 have no common reduct, it follows that we do not have $x = x_1$ or $x = x_2$, so there

---

[a] If the transitive closure of $\to$ is viewed as a *greater than* ordering, then it would be natural to speak of $\to$-*minimal* instead.

must exist intermediate points i_1, i_2 such that $x \to i_1 \twoheadrightarrow x_1$ and $x \to i_2 \twoheadrightarrow x_2$. To x and these intermediate points we can apply local confluence to obtain a common reduct of the intermediate points. By the maximality of x we can then complete the diagram below. This is a contradiction and hence NL has been proved.

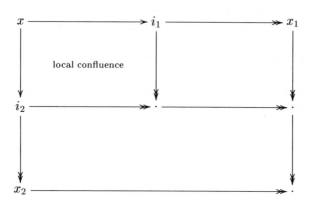

The formalization of the above argument requires higher-order logic (to express transitive closure), DC and (most naturally) three-sorted first-order logic: one sort for the set S, one for the natural numbers and one for infinite sequences of elements of S. There exist many alternative proofs of NL, for example, based on the multiset extension of $\to$. All those proofs are a bit complicated by the fact that the absence of infinite paths has to be turned into an inductive argument, which again requires DC.

An important improvement, essentially due to Huet, is obtained by taking a constructive reformulation of NL as point of departure. In this formulation the infinite sequences such as used in the definition of termination and in DC are avoided by using an inductively defined predicate called accessibility (which can be traced back to Gentzen [4] 'erreichbar').

Definition 3.2 Let $\to$ be a binary relation on a set S. The unary predicate $Acc_\to$ is inductively defined by the closure property $(*)$ if $Acc_\to(y)$ for all $y \in S$ such that $x \to y$, then $Acc_\to(x)$. By $Acc_\to(S)$ we express that $Acc_\to(x)$ for all $x \in S$.

In other words, all $\to$-maximal elements are accessible, as well as all elements whose successors are all $\to$-maximal, and so on. The inductive definition stipulates $Acc_\to$ to be the *smallest* unary predicate closed under $(*)$. For this to be well-defined, one easily checks that the intersection of an arbitrary set of unary predicates which are closed under ($*$) is itself closed under ($*$). Furthermore, any infinite sequence $x_0 \to x_1 \to x_2 \to \cdots$ consists of elements that are not accessible. The reason is that they can be left out without violating the closure property ($*$). On the other hand, if there exists a non-accessible $x_0 \in S$, then there must be a non-accessible $x_1 \in S$ with $x_0 \to x_1$, and hence a non-accessible $x_2 \in S$ with $x_1 \to x_2$, and so on. Thus one proves using DC that $\to$ is terminating if and only if all elements of S are accessible, that is, if $Acc_\to(S)$.

The point is now that we avoid the above equivalence proof by adopting $Acc_\to(S)$ straightaway as the 'positive' formulation of the absence of infinite paths. The advantages of using $Acc_\to(S)$ instead of the traditional formulation of termination are three-fold.

- DC is not needed anymore in the proof of NL.

- The sorts for the natural numbers and for infinite sequences are not needed.

- We can reason by induction[b] on $Acc_\to(x)$, the induction step being first-order.

These reasons motivate the following reformulation of NL.

Lemma 3.3 *If $Acc_\to(S)$, then confluence of $\to$ follows from local confluence.*

We could have added a fourth advantage to the three advantages above, namely that the proof of NL in the formulation with the accessibility predicate can be done constructively, as shown in the next paragraph. The constructive proof is not more complicated than the classical one, it is actually shorter, but the relevant point here is that we do not know a theorem prover that is able to generate the constructive proof. Instead we had to use a resolution theorem prover, which first clausifies the negation of the statement and then searches for a resolution refutation of the resulting clauses. The automation of a constructive proof will be explored later, in the sections on geometric logic.

We will sketch the constructive argument. By induction one proves that every accessible $x \in S$ is confluent. By $Acc_\to(S)$ we then obtain confluence. The induction step we have to prove is that confluence is preserved under the closure property ($*$) in the inductive definition of $Acc_\to$. In other words,

---

[b]Induction is a very practical method. You can, for example, also cook by (magnetic) induction.

we have to prove that x is confluent if the induction hypothesis (IH) holds, that is, if every $y \in S$ such that $x \to y$ is confluent. Assume IH and let $x_1, x_2 \in S$ such that $x \twoheadrightarrow x_1$ and $x \twoheadrightarrow x_2$. If $x = x_1$ or $x = x_2$ then x_2 or x_1 is a common reduct of x_1, x_2. Otherwise, actually appealing to the inductive definition of the reflexive–transitive closure, there exist intermediate points as in the classical proof above. Now a common reduct can be obtained in exactly the same way as in the classical proof, with IH replacing the $\twoheadrightarrow$-maximality of x. This proves the induction step.

The above proof of the induction step is completely first-order and can be cast in the form of a refutation problem, namely the inconsistency of the conjunction below. Note that $=, \to, \twoheadrightarrow$ are uninterpreted binary relations here, with (local) confluence shorthand and $\to \cdot \twoheadrightarrow$ the composition of (first) $\to$ and (last) $\twoheadrightarrow$.

$$\bigwedge \begin{cases} 1. & = \text{ is reflexive and symmetric} \\ 2. & \twoheadrightarrow \text{ includes} = \text{and} \to \text{and is transitive} \\ 3. & \twoheadrightarrow \text{ is included in the union of} = \text{and} \to \cdot \twoheadrightarrow \\ 4. & \to \text{ is locally confluent} \\ 5. & \text{there exists a non-confluent } x \text{ such that all } y \leftarrow x \text{ are confluent} \end{cases}$$

Some remarks on the conjuncts 1–3 and 5 above are in order here.

1. Transitivity of $=$ is not needed, which was obvious from the human proof.

2. Taking $\twoheadrightarrow$ to include $=$ is a convenient way of stating that $\twoheadrightarrow$ is reflexive. One can then conclude $a \twoheadrightarrow b$ from $a = b$ without any appeal to congruence axioms. Otter didn't use the fact that $\twoheadrightarrow$ includes $\to$. This came, admittedly, as a surprise, although it also follows from a close analysis of the human proof. It implies that NL can be strengthened to a (diamond) result for any reflexive–transitive relation satisfying conjunct 3. This strengthening is in itself not very interesting, but results in a surprising speed-up of the proof search by a factor 5.

3. It is well-known that transitive closure is not first-order definable. The conjunction of 2 and 3 is weaker than the reflexive–transitive closure. However, one can prove by induction on $Acc_{\to}(x)$ that conjunct 3 implies that $\twoheadrightarrow$ is a subset of the reflexive–transitive closure of $\to$. So in the presence of $Acc_{\to}(S)$ the conjunction of 2 and 3 exactly axiomatizes the reflexive–transitive closure. The observation that transitive closure is first-order definable for terminating relations may be of use in other applications as well.

5. This is the negation of the induction step.

Otter found a refutation within some 15 minutes (on a Sun Ultra 10), with a combination of positive hyperresolution and unit-resulting resolution. The Otter input and output files match www.ii.uib.no/ bezem/NL/NL1.* The refutation found by Otter is quite close to a human proof, see the diagram chase below. The arrows are labelled by numbers indicating the clause representing that arrow. A negative number means that the clause refutes the arrow. An ill-understood phenomenon is why it took so long after clause 477 to infer 24727 by transitivity from 45 and 70. Otter can produce many other refutations of the same set of clauses, but all seem to be inessential variations of the same diagram chase, due to the many symmetries.

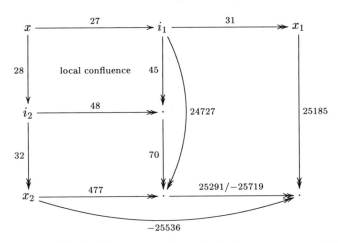

An obvious difficulty for the proof search is the symmetry of the formulation of NL. For example, by applying local confluence, any step $x \to y$ gives rise to useless common reducts of y and y. It is well-known that it is possible to distinguish between 'horizontal' and 'vertical' steps in the formulation of both confluence and local confluence. This leads to an asymmetrical version of Newman's Lemma (NLa), which can be proved by the same proof with all the steps properly labelled as either 'horizontal' or 'vertical'. NL can easily be recovered from NLa by removing the distinction. The asymmetrical analogues of confluence and local confluence are known in the literature as commutativity and weak commutativity, respectively.

Definition 3.4 Let $\to_h$ and $\to_v$ be binary relations on a set S, with reflexive–transitive closures $\twoheadrightarrow_h$ and $\twoheadrightarrow_v$, respectively.

1. We say that x is *commutative* if, for all $x_1, x_2 \in S$, $x \twoheadrightarrow_h x_1$ and $x \twoheadrightarrow_v x_2$

implies that $x_1 \twoheadrightarrow_v y$ and $x_2 \twoheadrightarrow_h y$ for some $y \in S$. We say that $\to_h$ and $\to_v$ *commute* if every $x \in S$ is commutative.

2. We say that x is *weakly commutative* if, for all $x_1, x_2 \in S$, $x \to_h x_1$ and $x \to_v x_2$ implies that $x_1 \twoheadrightarrow_v y$ and $x_2 \twoheadrightarrow_h y$ for some $y \in S$. We say that $\to_h$ and $\to_v$ *commute weakly* if every $x \in S$ is weakly commutative.

The precise statement of NLa is that $\to_h$ and $\to_v$ commute if they commute weakly, provided $Acc_{\to_{hv}}(S)$. Here $\to_{hv}$ is the union of $\to_h$ and $\to_v$. A glance at the diagram below tells us that we need the induction hypothesis both for i_1 with $x \to_h i_1$ and for i_2 with $x \to_v i_2$.

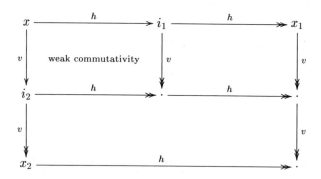

The proof of NLa follows the pattern of the proof of NL, but is based on the inconsistency of the following conjunction:

$$\bigwedge \begin{cases} = \text{ is reflexive and symmetric} \\ \twoheadrightarrow_h \text{ and } \twoheadrightarrow_v \text{ include } = \text{ and are transitive} \\ \twoheadrightarrow_h \text{ is included in the union of } = \text{ and } \to_h \cdot \twoheadrightarrow_h \\ \twoheadrightarrow_v \text{ is included in the union of } = \text{ and } \to_v \cdot \twoheadrightarrow_v \\ \to_h \text{ and } \to_v \text{ are weakly commutative} \\ \text{there exists a non-commutative } x \text{ such that all } y \leftarrow_{hv} x \text{ are commutative} \end{cases}$$

Proof search in the asymmetrical case is two orders of magnitude faster than in the symmetrical case: less than a second. The relevant Otter files match `bezem/NL/NLa.*`

4 Geometric Logic

An example of geometric logic is the formalization of projective geometry[c] by Skolem [14] (1920). There are two sorts: lines $l, m, \ldots$ and points $P, B, \ldots$ The atomic relations are (with Skolem's notation): equality of lines (lm), equality of points (PQ) and coincidence (Pl), expressing that a point P is on a line l. The theory is then (all axioms are implicitly universally closed):

(PP), $(PQ) \to (QP)$, $(PQ) \wedge (QR) \to (PR)$ (equality axioms for points)

(ll), $(lm) \to (ml)$, $(lm) \wedge (mn) \to (ln)$ (equality axioms for lines)

$(PQ) \wedge (Ql) \to (Pl)$, $(Pl) \wedge (lm) \to (Pm)$ (congruence axioms)

$(Pl) \wedge (Ql) \wedge (Pm) \wedge (Qm) \to (PQ) \vee (lm)$ (projective uniqueness axiom)

$(\exists l)((Pl) \wedge (Ql))$, $(\exists P)((Pl) \wedge (Pm))$ (projective axioms of incidence)

Geometric logic abstracts from the above example. A *geometric theory* is a set of geometric formulae. For simplicity we suppose that we have only predicate symbols and no function symbols. Terms are either variables $x, y, z, \ldots$, or parameters $a_0, a_1, \ldots$ Atomic formulae $A, A', \ldots$ are of the form $P t_1 \ldots t_n$, with $t_1, \ldots, t_n$ terms and P a predicate symbol of arity n. A *geometric formula* is a formula of the form $C \to D$ where C and D are given by the following grammar:

$$C ::= 1 \mid C \wedge A \qquad D ::= 0 \mid D \vee E \qquad E ::= (\exists \vec{x})C$$

Here 0 and 1 represent the empty disjunction and conjunction, respectively. A *closed* formula contains no free variables, only parameters and bound variables. A closed atom is also called a *fact*, denoted by $F, F' \ldots$ To sum up, we use A, C, D, E, F as stems of syntactical variables for atoms, conjunctions, disjunctions, existential formulae and facts, respectively.

We may write D for $1 \to D$, A for $1 \wedge A$ and so on, economizing on empty conjunctions, disjunctions, existential quantifications and brackets as much as possible. As an example, we prefer to write (and read) (ll) instead of $1 \to (0 \vee (\exists)(ll))$.

Note that Skolem's theory above is actually two-sorted. It would be possible to consider as well *multisorted* geometric logic. This is not strictly necessary, since the usual reduction to one sort, using unary predicates *Line*

---

[c]However, the qualifier 'geometric' does not come from this example, but refers to the origin of geometric logic in algebraic geometry [2].

and *Point* and relativizing the quantifiers, results in a one-sorted geometric theory.

In [3], the notion of geometric theory is extended by function symbols and equations on these symbols. A typical axiom is the theory of fields, with function symbols for additions and products, with the usual equational axioms for rings and the geometric axiom

$$x = 0 \vee (\exists y)(x \cdot y = 1)$$

The first-order formulation of Newman's Lemma can naturally be expressed in geometric form. The language has three binary predicates: E (for equality), R and S (approximating the reflexive–transitive closure of R), and one parameter a_0. As in Section 3, we formalise the induction step in the proof that accessibility implies confluence. However, whereas resolution logic (or rather the existing implementations) forces us to negate the conclusion and use a refutation procedure, geometric logic makes it possible to formulate the conclusion positively.

The theory NLg is the following collection of geometric formulae:

(1) $E\,x\,x$

(2) $E\,x\,y \to E\,y\,x$

(3) $E\,x\,y \wedge E\,y\,z \to E\,x\,z$

(4) $E\,x\,y \to S\,x\,y$

(5) $R\,x\,y \to S\,x\,y$

(6) $S\,x\,y \wedge S\,y\,z \to S\,x\,z$

(7) $S\,x\,y \to E\,x\,y \vee (\exists z)(R\,x\,z \wedge S\,z\,y)$ (S included in the union of E and $R \cdot S$)

(8) $R\,x\,y \wedge R\,x\,z \to (\exists u)(S\,y\,u \wedge S\,z\,u)$ (local confluence)

(9) $R\,a_0\,x \wedge S\,x\,y \wedge S\,x\,z \to (\exists u)(S\,y\,u \wedge S\,z\,u)$ (induction hypothesis)

The formulae (1)–(8) correspond with the conjuncts 1–4 on page 272 and (9) with the part of conjunct 5 expressing that $R\,a_0\,x$ implies confluence of x. The conclusion that a_0 is confluent can here be stated in a positive way:

(10) $S\,a_0\,x \wedge S\,a_0\,y \to (\exists z)(S\,x\,z \wedge S\,y\,z)$

The reader can now check that the geometric formula (10) is a first-order consequence of the theory NLg. Otter proves this much in the same way as in Section 3, the relevant files match `bezem/NL/NLg.*`

5 Proof Procedure for Geometric Theories

The following proof procedure can be seen as a specialization of the proof of the completeness theorem as presented for instance in [8]. We present it informally first, and make it precise in the next section. We divide a geometric theory in two parts: one part collects the axioms $C \to D$ with D essentially one single atom; the remaining part collects the axioms where D is 0, a proper disjunction or an existential formula. Let us call the first part the (definite) *Horn* [5] part and the second the *disjunctive* part[d]. For the theory NLg, the axioms (1)–(6) form the Horn part. Proving conclusion (10) starts with instantiating (10) with two new parameters, say a_1 and a_2, and adding the facts $S\,a_0\,a_1$, $S\,a_0\,a_2$. The proof obligation is then

$$(\exists x)(S\ a_1\ x \wedge S\ a_2\ x)$$

At each step in the proof procedure, only a finite number of parameters are alive (as in [8]). We then collect all facts that we can derive using the Horn part of the theory. In the example of the theory NL, only a_0, a_1, a_2 are alive at first and from the facts $S\,a_0\,a_1$, $S\,a_0\,a_2$ we can only derive

$$S\,a_0\,a_0,\ E\,a_0\,a_0,\ S\,a_1\,a_1,\ E\,a_1\,a_1,\ S\,a_2\,a_2,\ E\,a_2\,a_2$$

Next, we look for the possible disjunctions and existential statements that we can derive from these facts. In the example of the theory NL, we can only derive from (7)

$$E\,a_0\,a_1 \vee (\exists z)(R\,a_0\,z \wedge S\,z\,a_1) \qquad E\,a_0\,a_2 \vee (\exists z)(R\,a_0\,z \wedge S\,z\,a_2)$$

We branch then on all such disjunctions and statements[e]. For instance, in the case above we get four branches. Abbreviate $E\,a_0\,a_1$ by F_1 and $E\,a_0\,a_2$ by F_2. Instantiating the two existential statements with new parameters, say a_3 and a_4, respectively, results in four facts

$$R\,a_0\,a_3,\ S\,a_3\,a_1,\ R\,a_0\,a_4,\ S\,a_4\,a_2$$

which we abbreviate by F_3, F_3', F_4, F_4', respectively. In one branch we add the facts F_1, F_2, in the second F_1, F_4, F_4', in the third F_3, F_3', F_2 and in the fourth branch we add F_3, F_3', F_4, F_4'. In all branches we then close under the Horn part of NLg and continue.

---

[d]Such a separation of the theory appears both in [14] and [3]. In [14] this is used to prove that Desargues' Theorem is independent of the theory of projective geometry presented above.

[e]An optimisation is to first delete all such statements that hold already in the finite model defined by the facts we have so far.

In this way, we build a finitely branching search tree, to each node of which is associated a finite set of facts which is closed under the Horn part of the theory. For the present search tree, the formula

$$(\exists x)(S \ a_1 \ x \wedge S \ a_2 \ x)$$

will eventually be true on every branch in the finite model defined by the associated collection of facts. This completes the proof that (10) is a a geometric consequence of the theory NLg. Note that no Skolem functions play a role here, in contrast to the resolution method. Skolem functions make the domain infinite, which is not necessary in this case.

A similar proof procedure is used in [3] to analyse theories such as algebraically closed fields or real closed fields. A system similar in spirit, but without existential quantification and hence requiring skolemization, is the satisfiability checker and model generator SATCHMO [9]. SATCHMO has a very concise Prolog implementation which has inspired us to develop an experimental implementation of the proof procedure for geometric theories described above. A Prolog interpretation infers (10) from (1)–(9) in miliseconds. The file can be found at `bezem/NL/NLg.pro`.

6 Proof System for Geometric Theories

The relevance of geometric logic for computation has been stressed already (see for instance [2]). The previous section shows that it might have some interest for automatic proof search as well. The goal of this section is to give a precise definition of the proof procedure, and to state some remarkable theorems, that show in particular that, for this fragment, intuitionistic and classical derivability coincide. We present a possible short proof of these theorems in the next section.

Definition 6.1 Let T be a geometric theory, X a finite collection of facts and D a closed geometric disjunction. As usual, we write $X, F_1, \ldots, F_m$ for $X \cup \{F_1, \ldots, F_m\}$. We define inductively $X \vdash_T D$, which expresses that D is a geometric consequence in T of the facts in X. Here and below we simply write $\vdash$ instead of $\vdash_T$ since T is clear from the context.

- (base case) $X \vdash D$ if there is a disjunct $(\exists \vec{x})C$ of D and a closed instance C_0 of C all whose conjuncts are in X, and

- (induction step) $X \vdash D$ if there is a close instance $C_0 \to D_0$ of an axiom of T such that all conjuncts of C_0 are in X and for every disjunct

$$(\exists \vec{x})(A_1 \wedge \ldots \wedge A_m)$$

of D_0 we have

$$X, A_1[\vec{x} := \vec{a}], \ldots, A_m[\vec{x} := \vec{a}] \vdash D$$

where $\vec{a}$ consists of new parameters not occurring in $X \vdash D$, nor in D_0.

As a simple example, since the understanding of the induction step above may be hampered by the many abbreviations in geometric formulae, we infer $A \vdash D$ for arbitrary D from the geometric theory $A \to B, B \to 0$. Using the induction step with axiom $A \to B$, $A \vdash D$ follows from $A, B \vdash D$ since A is the only conjunct of $1 \wedge A$ and B is the only disjunct of $0 \vee (\exists)B$ and there is nothing to instantiate. Again using the induction step, but now with axiom $B \to 0$, since B occurs in A, B and 0 is the empty disjunction, $A, B \vdash D$ follows without any further proof obligation.

A more interesting example can be obtained by formalising the proof procedure described in the previous section along the lines of the above inductive definition.

Theorem 6.2 *If D is a consequence of X using higher-order intuitionistic logic[f], then $X \vdash D$. Here and below $X \vdash D$ is as in Definition 6.1.*

The next result is also known as Barr's Theorem [1,2,11].

Theorem 6.3 *If D is a consequence of X using higher-order classical logic, then $X \vdash D$.*

One reading of this theorem is that higher-order logic and geometric logic give the same consequence relation on geometric formulae.

Classically, given Gödel's completeness theorem for first-order logic, one possible formulation of this theorem is

Theorem 6.4 *If D holds in all models of X, then $X \vdash D$.*

A proof along the lines of [8] is direct. However, this would not be constructively valid, in contrast to the formulation of Theorem 6.3 and to the proof we present in the next section. The reference [11] presents a formulation of classical first-order sequent calculus with admissible cut-rules, in which derivations of geometric formulae are automatically geometric.

---

[f] By higher-order we mean that we allow function and relation variables, and quantification over those variables.

7   Topological Model

In order to prove Theorem 6.2, we build a special topological model of the theory T. The *domain* M of this model is the set $\{a_0, a_1, \ldots\}$ of all parameters. The truth values will form a *complete Heyting algebra* (or *frame*) H [7]. The model is defined by choosing an interpretation $\llbracket F \rrbracket \in H$ of each fact. Each closed conjunction $C = F_1 \wedge \cdots \wedge F_m$ is then interpreted as usual by a finite meet

$$\llbracket C \rrbracket = \llbracket F_1 \rrbracket \wedge \cdots \wedge \llbracket F_m \rrbracket$$

each closed existential formula $E = (\exists \vec{x})C$ by an infinite join

$$\llbracket E \rrbracket = \bigvee_{\vec{a} \subseteq M} \llbracket C[\vec{x} := \vec{a}] \rrbracket$$

and finally each closed disjunction $D = E_1 \vee \cdots \vee E_n$ by a finite join

$$\llbracket D \rrbracket = \llbracket E_1 \rrbracket \vee \cdots \vee \llbracket E_n \rrbracket$$

The Heyting algebra H and the interpretation $\llbracket \_ \rrbracket$ will be built in such a way that we have $F_1, \ldots, F_m \vdash D$ iff

$$\llbracket F_1 \rrbracket \wedge \cdots \wedge \llbracket F_m \rrbracket \leq \llbracket D \rrbracket$$

in H. Given that higher-order intuitionistic logic can be interpreted in a topological model, see [7], Theorem 6.2 will follow at once.

Following [7], we can define H by generators and relations. We take as generators the facts themselves, so that each closed conjunction C can be seen as an element $C \in H$, and for the relations we take

$$\llbracket C_0 \rrbracket \leq \llbracket D_0 \rrbracket$$

for each closed instance $C_0 \to D_0$ of an axiom $C \to D$ in the theory T.

The completeness of this model w.r.t. geometric rules of inference follows from the remark (cf. [10], page 86, for a similar remark used to give a constructive proof of Gödel's completeness theorem):

Lemma 7.1 *If we have*

$$X, F_1(a_{k+1}, \ldots, a_{k+n}), \ldots, F_m(a_{k+1}, \ldots, a_{k+n}) \vdash D$$

where $a_k, \ldots, a_{k+n}$ *do not appear in* X *and* D, *then we have for all* $u_1, \ldots, u_n \in M$

$$X, F_1(u_1, \ldots, u_n), \ldots, F_m(u_1, \ldots, u_n) \vdash D$$

A slight variation on the well-known negative translation gives a proof of Barr's Theorem 6.3. Given X and D, we consider the element $G = (\wedge_{F \in X}[\![F]\!]) \to [\![D]\!] \in H$ and we transform the frame H into a complete Boolean algebra H_0, by taking H_0 to be the frame defined by the nucleus [7] $j(p) = (p \to G) \to G$ on H. This model is now a model of all facts in X, and the fact that D holds in this model is equivalent to $G = 1 \in H$ which is equivalent, by completeness, to $X \vdash D$ as desired.

A more sophisticated argument, which uses the notion of *site* instead of complete Heyting algebra, can be given. This argument would reflect the fact that in the proof procedure we consider only a finite number of parameters at each step.

Acknowledgments

The authors are indebted to Andreas Blass, Wilfried Buchholz, Dimitri Hendriks, Gérard Huet and Tobias Nipkow for valuable comments. The second author would like to thank Jan von Plato for his explanation of Skolem's presentation of projective geometry.

References

1. M. Barr, Toposes without points, *Journal of Pure and Applied Algebra* **5**:265–280, 1974.
2. A. Blass, Topoi and computation, *Bulletin of the EATCS* **36**:57–65, October 1998.
3. M. Coste, H. Lombardi, and M.F. Roy, Dynamical methods in algebra: effective Nullstellensätze, *Annals of Pure and Applied Logic* **111**(3):203–256, 2001.
4. G. Gentzen, Die Widerspruchsfreiheit der reinen Zahlentheorie, *Mathematische Annalen* **112**:493–565, 1936.
5. A. Horn, On sentences which are true of direct unions of algebras, *Journal of Symbolic Logic* **16**(1):14–21, 1951.
6. G. Huet, Confluent reductions: Abstract properties and applications to term rewriting systems, *Journal of the ACM* **27**(4):797–821, 1980.
7. P. Johnstone, *Stone Spaces*, Cambridge Studies in Advanced Mathematics **3**, Cambridge University Press, 1982.
8. S.C. Kleene, *Mathematical Logic*, John Wiley & Sons, Inc., New York-London-Sydney, 1967.
9. R. Manthey and F. Bry, SATCHMO: a theorem prover implemented in Prolog. In E. Lusk and R. Overbeek, editors, *Proceedings of the 9-th*

Conference on Automated Deduction, Lecture Notes in Computer Science **310**:415–434, Springer-Verlag, 1988.

10. P. Martin-Löf, *Notes on Constructive Mathematics,* Almqvist & Wiksell, Stockholm, 1970.

11. S. Negri, Contraction-free sequent calculi for geometric theories, with an application to Barr's Theorem, to appear in *Archive for Mathematical Logic.*

12. M.H.A. Newman, On theories with a combinatorial definition of 'equivalence', *Annals of Mathematics* **43**(2):223–243, 1942.

13. Otter, www-unix.mcs.anl.gov/AR/otter/

14. T. Skolem, *Selected Works in Logic,* edited by J.E. Fenstad, Universitetsforlaget, Oslo, 1970.

15. L. Wos, *The Automation of Reasoning: an Experimenter's Notebook with Otter Tutorial,* Academic Press, 1996.

16. L. Wos and G. Pieper, *A Fascinating Country in the World of Computing: Your Guide to Automated Reasoning,* World Scientific, 2000.

ALGORITHMS: A QUEST FOR ABSOLUTE DEFINITIONS

ANDREAS BLASS
Mathematics, University of Michigan
Ann Arbor, MI 48109-1109, USA

YURI GUREVICH
Microsoft Research
One Microsoft Way
Redmond, WA 98052, USA
E-mail: gurevich@microsoft.com

What is an algorithm? The interest in this foundational problem is not only theoretical; applications include specification, validation and verification of software and hardware systems. We describe the quest to understand and define the notion of algorithm. We start with the Church-Turing thesis and contrast Church's and Turing's approaches, and we finish with some recent investigations.

1 Introduction

In 1936, Alonzo Church published a bold conjecture that only recursive functions are computable [10]. A few months later, independently of Church, Alan Turing published a powerful speculative proof of a similar conjecture: every computable real number is computable by the Turing machine [54]. Kurt Gödel found Church's thesis "thoroughly unsatisfactory" but later was convinced by Turing's argument. Later yet he worried about a possible flaw in Turing's argument. In Section 2 we recount briefly this fascinating story, provide references where the reader can find additional details, and give remarks of our own.

By now, there is overwhelming experimental evidence in favor of the Church-Turing thesis. Furthermore, it is often assumed that the Church-Turing thesis settled the problem of what an algorithm is. That isn't so. The thesis clarifies the notion of computable function. And there is more, much more to an algorithm than the function it computes. The thesis was a great step toward understanding algorithms, but it did not solve the problem what an algorithm is.

Further progress in foundations of algorithms was achieved by Kolmogorov and his student Uspensky in the 1950s [39,40]. The Kolmogorov machine with its reconfigurable "tape" has a certain advantage over the Turing machine. The notion of pointer machine was an improvement of the notion of Kolmogorov machine. These issues are discussed in Section 3

This paper started as a write-up of the talk that the second author gave at the Kolmogorov Centennial conference in June 2003 in Moscow. The talk raised several related issues: physics and computation, polynomial time versions of the Turing thesis, recursion and algorithms. These issues are very briefly discussed in Section 4.

In 1991, the second author published the definition of sequential abstract state machines (ASMs, called evolving algebras at the time) [23]. In 2000, he published a definition of sequential algorithms derived from first principles [27]. In the same paper he proved that every sequential algorithm A is behaviorally equivalent to some sequential ASM B. In particular, B simulates A step for step. In Section 5 we outline the approach of [27].

In 1995, the second author published the definition of parallel and distributed abstract state machines [25]. The Foundations of Software Engineering group at Microsoft Research developed an industrial strength specification language AsmL that allows one to write and execute parallel and distributed abstract state machines [2]. In 2001, the present authors published a definition of parallel algorithms derived from first principles as well as a proof that every parallel algorithm is equivalent to a parallel ASM [7]. Section 6 is a quick discussion of parallel algorithms.

The problem of defining distributed algorithms from first principles is open. In Section 7 we discuss a few related issues.

Finally let us note that foundational studies go beyond satisfying our curiosity. Turing machines with their honest counting of steps enabled computational complexity theory. Kolmogorov machines and pointer machines enabled better complexity measures. Abstract state machines enable precise executable specifications of software systems though this story is only starting to unfold [1,2,9].

2 The Church-Turing Thesis

2.1 Church + Turing

The celebrated Church-Turing thesis [10,54] captured the notion of computable function. Every computable function from natural numbers to natural numbers is recursive and computable, in principle, by the Turing machine. The thesis has been richly confirmed in practice. Speaking in 1946 at the Princeton Bicentennial Conference, Gödel said this [19, article 1946]:

> Tarski has stressed in his lecture (and I think justly) the great importance of the concept of general recursiveness (or Turing's computability). It seems to me that this importance is largely due to the

fact that with this concept one has for the first time succeeded in giving an absolute definition of an interesting epistemological notion, i.e., one not depending on the formalism chosen. In all other cases treated previously, such as demonstrability or definability, one has been able to define them only relative to the given language, and for each individual language it is clear that the one thus obtained is not the one looked for. For the concept of computability, however, although it is merely a special kind of demonstrability or decidability, the situation is different. By a kind of miracle it is not necessary to distinguish orders, and the diagonal procedure does not lead outside the defined notion.

2.2 Turing – Church

It became common to speak about the Church-Turing thesis. In fact the contributions of Church and Turing are different, and the difference between them is of importance to us here. Church's thesis was a bold hypothesis about the set of computable functions. Turing analyzed what can happen during a computation and thus arrived at his thesis.

Church's Thesis The notion of an effectively calculable function from natural numbers to natural numbers should be identified with that of a recursive function.

Church had in mind total functions [10]. Later Kleene improved on Church's thesis by extending it to partial functions [32]. The fascinating history of the thesis is recounted in [14]; see also [51].

Originally Church hypothesized that every effectively calculable function from natural numbers to natural numbers is definable in his lambda calculus. Gödel didn't buy that. In 1935, Church wrote to Kleene about his conversation with Gödel [14, page 9].

In discussion [sic] with him the notion of lambda-definability, it developed that there was no good definition of effective calculability. My proposal that lambda-definability be taken as a definition of it he regarded as thoroughly unsatisfactory. I replied that if he would propose any definition of effective calculability which seemed even partially satisfactory I would undertake to prove that it was included in lambda-definability. His only idea at the time was that it might be possible, in terms of effective calculability as an undefined notion, to state a set of axioms which would embody the generally accepted properties of this notion, and to do something on this basis.

Church continued:

> Evidently it occurred to him later that Herbrand's definition of recursiveness, which has no regard to effective calculability, could be modified in the direction of effective calculability, and he made this proposal in his lectures. At that time he did specifically raise the question of the connection between recursiveness in this new sense and effective calculability, but said he did not think that the two ideas could be satisfactorily identified "except heuristically".

The lectures of Gödel mentioned by Church were given at the Institute for Advanced Study in Princeton from February through May 1934. In a February 15, 1965, letter to Martin Davis, Gödel wrote [14, page 8]:

> However, I was, at the time of these lectures [1934], not at all convinced that my concept of recursion comprises all possible recursions.

Soon after Gödel's lectures, Church and Kleene proved that the Herbrand-Gödel notion of general recursivity is equivalent to lambda definability (as far as total functions are concerned), and Church became sufficiently convinced of the correctness of his thesis to publish it. But Gödel remained unconvinced.

Indeed, why should one believe that lambda definability captures the notion of computability? The fact that lambda definability is equivalent to general recursivity, and to various other formalizations of computability that quickly followed Church's paper, proves only that Church's notion of lambda definability is very robust.

To see that a mathematical definition captures the notion of computability, one needs an analysis of the latter. This is what Turing provided to justify his thesis.

Turing's Thesis Let Σ be a finite alphabet. A partial function from strings over Σ to strings over Σ is effectively calculable if and only if it is computable by a Turing machine.

Remark 2.1 Turing designed his machine to compute real numbers but the version of the Turing machine that became popular works with strings in a fixed alphabet. Hence our formulation of Turing's thesis.

Turing analyzed a computation performed by a human computer. He made a number of simplifying without-loss-of-generality assumptions. Here are some of them. The computer writes on graph paper; furthermore, the usual graph paper can be replaced with a tape divided into squares. The computer uses only a finite number of symbols, a single symbol in a square.

"The behavior of the computer at any moment is determined by the symbols which he is observing, and his 'state of mind' at that moment". There is a bound on the number of symbols observed at any one moment. "We will also suppose that the number of states of mind which need to be taken into account is finite... If we admitted an infinity of states of mind, some of them will be 'arbitrarily close' and will be confused". He ends up with a Turing machine simulating the original computation. Essentially Turing derived his thesis from more or less obvious first principles though he didn't state those first principles carefully.

"It seems that only after Turing's formulation appeared," writes Kleene in [33, page 61], "did Gödel accept Church's thesis, which had then become the Church-Turing thesis." "Turing's arguments," he adds in [34, page 48], "eventually persuaded him."

Church's lambda calculus was destined to play an important role in programming theory. The mathematically elegant Herbrand-Gödel-Kleene notion of partial recursive functions served as a springboard for many developments in recursion theory. The Turing machine gave us honest step counting and became eventually the foundation of complexity theory.

2.3 Remarks on Turing's Analysis

Very quickly the Church-Turing thesis acquired the status of a widely shared belief. Meantime Gödel grew skeptical of at least one aspect of Turing's analysis. In a remark published after his death, Gödel writes this [19, article 1972a, page 306].

A philosophical error in Turing's work. Turing in his [54, page 250], gives an argument which is supposed to show that mental procedures cannot go beyond mechanical procedures. However, this argument is inconclusive. What Turing disregards completely is the fact that *mind, in its use, is not static, but constantly developing,* i.e. that we understand abstract terms more and more precisely as we go on using them, and that more and more abstract terms enter the sphere of our understanding. There may exist systematic methods of actualizing this development, which could form part of the procedure. Therefore, although at each stage the number and precision of the abstract terms at our disposal may be *finite,* both (and therefore, also Turing's number of *distinguishable states of mind*) may *converge toward infinity* in the course of the application of the procedure.

Gödel was extremely careful in his published work. It is not clear whether the remark in question was intended for publication as is. In any case, the question whether mental procedures can go beyond mechanical procedures is beyond the scope of this paper, which focuses on algorithms. Furthermore, as far as we can see, Turing did not intend to show that mental procedures cannot go beyond mechanical procedures. The expression "state of mind" was just a useful metaphor that could be and in fact was eliminated: "we avoid introducing the 'state of mind' by considering a more physical and definite counterpart of it" [54, page 253].

But let us consider the possibility that Gödel didn't speak about biology either, that he continued to use Turing's metaphor and worried that Turing's analysis does not apply to some algorithms. Can an algorithm learn from its own experience, become more sophisticated and thus compute a real number that is not computable by the Turing machine? Note that the learning process in question is highly unusual because it involves no interaction with the environment. (On the other hand, it is hard to stop brains from interacting with the environment.) Gödel gives two examples "illustrating the situation", both aimed at logicians.

Note that something like this indeed seems to happen in the process of forming stronger and stronger axioms of infinity in set theory. This process, however, today is far from being sufficiently understood to form a well-defined procedure. It must be admitted that the construction of a well-defined procedure which could actually be carried out (and would yield a non-recursive number-theoretic function) would require a substantial advance in our understanding of the basic concepts of mathematics. Another example illustrating the situation is the process of systematically constructing, by their distinguished sequences $\alpha_n \to \alpha$, all recursive ordinals α of the second number-class.

The logic community has not been swayed. "I think it is pie in the sky!" wrote Kleene [34, page 51]. Here is a more expansive reaction of his [34, page 50].

But, as I have said, our idea of an algorithm has been such that, in over two thousand years of examples, it has separated cases when mathematicians have agreed that a given procedure constitutes an algorithm from cases in which it does not. Thus algorithms have been procedures that mathematicians can describe completely to one another *in advance* of their application for various choices of the arguments. How could someone describe completely to me *in a finite interview* a process for finding the values of a number-theoretic function, the execution of which process for various arguments would be keyed to more than the *finite* subset of our mental states that would have developed by the end of the interview, though the total number of mental states might converge to infinity if we were immortal? Thus Gödel's remarks do not shake my belief in the Church-Turing thesis ...

If Gödel's remarks are intended to attack the Church-Turing thesis, then the attack is a long shot indeed. On the other hand, we disagree with Kleene that the notion of algorithm is that well understood. In fact the notion of algorithm is richer these days than it was in Turing's days. And there are algorithms, of modern and classical varieties, not covered directly by Turing's analysis, for example, algorithms that interact with their environments, algorithms whose inputs are abstract structures, and geometric or, more generally, non-discrete algorithms. We look briefly at the three examples just mentioned.

Interactive algorithms

This is a broad class. It includes randomized algorithms; you need the environment to provide random bits. It includes asynchronous algorithms; the environment influences action timing. It includes nondeterministic algorithms as well [27, section 9.1]. Clearly, interactive algorithms are not covered by Turing's analysis. And indeed an interactive algorithm can compute a non-recursive function. (The nondeterministic Turing machines, defined in computation theory courses, are known to compute only partial recursive functions. But a particular computation of such a machine cannot in general be simulated by a deterministic Turing machine.)

Computing with abstract structures

Consider the following algorithm P that, given a finite connected graph $G = (V, E)$ with a distinguished vertex s, computes the maximum distance of any vertex from s.

A $S := \{s\}$ and $r := 0$.

B   If $S = V$ then halt and output r.

C   If $S \neq V$ then $S := S \cup \{y : \exists x\, (x \in S \wedge E(x, y))\}$ and $r := r + 1$.

D   Go to **B**.

P is a parallel algorithm. Following Turing's analysis we have to break the assignment $S := \{y : \exists x\, (x \in S \land E(x,y))\}$ into small tasks of bounded complexity, e.g., by going systematically though every $x \in S$ and every neighbor y of x. But how will the algorithm go through all $x \in S$? The graph G is not ordered. A nondeterministic algorithm can pick an arbitrary vertex and declare it the first vertex, pick one of the remaining vertices and declare it the second vertex, etc. But a deterministic algorithm cannot do that.

Algorithms like P are not covered directly by Turing's analysis. But there is an easy patch if you don't care about resources and use parallelism. Let n be the number of vertices. In parallel, the desired algorithm orders the vertices in all $n!$ possible ways and then carries on all $n!$ computations.

Non-discrete computations

Turing dealt with discrete computations. His analysis does not apply directly, e.g., to the classical, geometrical ruler-and-compass algorithms. The particular case of ruler-and-compass algorithms can be taken care of; such algorithms do not allow you to compute a non-recursive function [36]. In general, however, it is not clear how to extend Turing's analysis to non-discrete algorithms.

3 Kolmogorov Machines and Pointer Machines

The problem of the absolute definition of algorithm was attacked again in 1953 by Andrei N. Kolmogorov; see the one-page abstract [39] of his March 17, 1953, talk at the Moscow Mathematical Society. Kolmogorov spelled out his intuitive ideas about algorithms. For brevity, we express them in our own words (rather than translate literally).

• An algorithmic process splits into steps whose complexity is bounded in advance, i.e., the bound is independent of the input and the current state of the computation.

• Each step consists of a direct and immediate transformation of the current state.

• This transformation applies only to the active part of the state and does not alter the remainder of the state.

• The size of the active part is bounded in advance.

• The process runs until either the next step is impossible or a signal says the solution has been reached.

In addition to these intuitive ideas, Kolmogorov gave a one-paragraph sketch of a new computation model. The ideas of [39] were developed in the article [40] written by Kolmogorov together with his student Vladimir A. Uspensky. The Kolmogorov machine model can be thought of as a generalization of the Turing machine model where the tape is a directed graph of bounded in-degree and bounded out-degree. The vertices of the graph correspond to Turing's squares; each vertex has a color chosen from a fixed finite palette of vertex colors; one of the vertices is the current computation center. Each edge has a color chosen from a fixed finite palette of edge colors; distinct edges from the same node have different colors. The program has this form: replace the vicinity U of a fixed radius around the central node by a new vicinity W that depends on the isomorphism type of the digraph U with the colors and the distinguished central vertex. Contrary to Turing's tape whose topology is fixed, Kolmogorov's "tape" is reconfigurable.

Remark 3.1 We took liberties in describing Kolmogorov machines. Kolmogorov and Uspensky require that the tape graph is symmetric — for every edge (x, y) there is an edge (y, x). The more liberal model is a bit easier to describe. And the symmetry requirement is inessential in the following sense: any machine of either kind can be step-for-step simulated by a machine of the other kind.

Like Turing machines, Kolmogorov machines compute functions from strings to strings; we skip the description of the input and output conventions. In the footnote to the article title, Kolmogorov and Uspensky write that they just wanted to analyze the existing definitions of the notions of computable functions and algorithms and to convince themselves that there is no hidden way to extend the notion of computable function. Indeed, Kolmogorov machines compute exactly Turing computable functions. It seems, however, that they were more ambitious. Here is a somewhat liberal translation from [40, page 16].

> To simplify the description of algorithms, we introduced some conventions that are not intrinsic to the general idea, but it seems to us that the generality of the proposed definition remains plausible in spite of the conventions. It seems plausible to us that an arbitrary algorithmic process satisfies our definition of algorithms. We would like to emphasize that we are talking not about a reduction of an arbitrary algorithm to an algorithm in the sense of our definition but that every algorithm essentially satisfies the proposed definition.

In this connection the second author formulated a Kolmogorov-Uspensky thesis [22, page 227]: "every computation, performing only one restricted local action at a time, can be viewed as (not only being simulated by, but actually being) the computation of an appropriate KU machine". Uspensky concurred [55, page 396].

Kolmogorov's approach proved to be fruitful. It led to a more realistic complexity theory. For example, given a string x, a Kolmogorov machine can build a binary tree over x and then move fast about x. Leonid Levin used a universal Kolmogorov machine to construct his algorithm for NP problems that is optimal up to a multiplicative constant [41,22]. The up-to-a-multiplicative-constant form is not believed to be achievable for the multitape Turing machine model popular in theoretical computer science. Similarly, the class of functions computable in *nearly linear* time $n(\log n)^{O(1)}$ on Kolmogorov machines remains the same if Kolmogorov machines are replaced, e.g., by various random access computers in the literature; it is not believed, however, that the usual multitape Turing machines have the same power [29].

Kolmogorov machines allow one to do reasonable computations in reasonable time. This may have provoked Kolmogorov to ask new questions. "Kolmogorov ran a complexity seminar in the 50s or early 60s," wrote Leonid Levin, a student of Kolmogorov, to us [42]. "He asked if common tasks, like integer multiplication, require necessarily as much time as used by common algorithms, in this case quadratic time. Unexpectedly, Karatsuba reduced the power to $\log_2(3)$ [31]." (Readers interested in fast integer multiplication are referred to [38].)

It is not clear to us how Kolmogorov thought of the tape graph. One hypothesis is that edges reflect physical closeness. This hypothesis collides with the fact that our physical space is finite-dimensional. As one of us remarked earlier [27, page 81], "In a finite-dimensional Euclidean space, the volume of a sphere of radius n is bounded by a polynomial of n. Accordingly, one might expect a polynomial bound on the number of vertices in any vicinity of radius n (in the graph theoretic sense) of any state of a given KU machine, but in fact such a vicinity may contain exponentially many vertices."

Another hypothesis is that edges are some kind of channels. This hypothesis too collides with the fact that our physical space is finite-dimensional.

Probably the most natural approach would be to think of informational rather than physical edges. If vertex a contains information about the whereabouts of b, draw an edge from a to b. It is reasonable to assume that the amount of information stored at every single vertex a is bounded, and so the out-degree of the tape graph is bounded. It is also reasonable to allow more and more vertices to have information about b as the computation proceeds, so that the in-degree of the tape graph is unbounded. This brings us to Schönhage machines. These can be seen as Kolmogorov machines (in the version with directed edges) except that only the out-degrees are required to be bounded. The in-degrees can depend on the input and, even for a particular input, can grow during the computation.

"In 1970 the present author introduced a new machine model (cf. [47]) now called *storage modification machine* (SMM)," writes Schönhage in [48], "and posed the intuitive thesis that this model possesses extreme flexibility and should therefore serve as a basis for an adequate notion of time complexity." In article [48], Schönhage gave "a comprehensive presentation of our present knowledge of SMMs". In particular, he proved that SMMs are "real-time equivalent" to successor RAMs (random access machines whose only arithmetical operation is $n \mapsto n + 1$). The following definitions appear in [48, page 491].

Definition 3.2 A machine M' is said to *simulate* another machine M "in real time", denoted $M \xrightarrow{r} M'$, if there is a constant c such that for every input sequence x the following holds: if x causes M to read an input symbol, or to print an output symbol, or to halt at time steps $0 = t_0 < t_1 < \cdots < t_l$, respectively, then x causes M' to act in the very same way with regard to those external actions at time steps $0 = t'_0 < t'_1 < \cdots < t'_l$ where $t'_j - t'_{j-1} \leq c(t_j - t_{j-1})$ for $1 \leq j \leq l$. For machine classes $\mathcal{M}, \mathcal{M}'$ *real time reducibility* $\mathcal{M} \xrightarrow{r} \mathcal{M}'$ is defined by the condition that for each $M \in \mathcal{M}$ there exists an $M' \in \mathcal{M}'$ such that $M \xrightarrow{r} M'$. *Real time equivalence* $\mathcal{M} \xleftrightarrow{r} \mathcal{M}'$ means $\mathcal{M} \xrightarrow{r} \mathcal{M}'$ and $\mathcal{M}' \xrightarrow{r} \mathcal{M}$. □

Dima Grigoriev proved that Turing machines cannot simulate Kolmogorov machines in real time [21].

Schönhage introduced a precise language for programming his machines and complained that the Kolmogorov-Uspensky description of Kolmogorov machines is clumsy. For our purposes here, however, it is simplest to describe Schönhage machines as generalized Kolmogorov machines where the in-degree of the tape graph may be unbounded. It is still an open problem whether Schönhage machines are real time reducible to Kolmogorov machines.

Schönhage states his thesis as follows: "$\mathcal{M} \xrightarrow{r} \text{SMM}$ holds for all *atomistic* machine models $\mathcal{M}$."

Schönhage writes that Donald E. Knuth "brought to his attention that the SMM model coincides with a special type of 'linking automata' briefly explained in volume one of his book (cf. [37, pages 462-463]) in 1968 already. Now he suggests calling them 'pointer machines' which, in fact, seems to be the adequate name for these automata." Note that Kolmogorov machines also modify their storage. But the name "pointer machine" fits Knuth-Schönhage machines better than it fits Kolmogorov machines.

A successor RAM is a nice example of a pointer machine. Its tape graph consists of natural numbers and a couple of special registers. Each special register has only one pointer, which points to a natural number that is intuitively the content of the register. Every natural number n has only a pointer to $n + 1$, a pointer to another natural number that is intuitively the content of register n, and a pointer to every special register.

The notion of pointer machine seems an improvement over the notion of Kolmogorov machine to us (and of course the notion of Kolmogorov machine was an improvement over the notion of Turing machine). And the notion of pointer machine proved to be useful in the analysis of the time complexity of algorithms. In that sense it was successful. It is less clear how much of an advance all these developments were from the point of view of absolute definitions. The pointer machine reflected the computer architecture of real computers of the time. (The modern tendency is to make computers with several CPUs, central processing units, that run asynchronously.)

Remark 3.3 In an influential 1979 article, Tarjan used the term "pointer machine" in a wider sense [53]. This wider notion of pointer machines has become better known in computer science than the older notion.

4 Related Issues

We mention a few issues touched upon in the talk that was the precursor of this paper. It is beyond the scope of this paper to develop these issues in any depth.

4.1 Physics and Computations

What kind of computations can be carried out in our physical universe? We are not talking about what functions are computable. The question is what algorithms are physically executable. We don't expect a definitive answer soon, if ever. It is important, however, to put things into perspective. Many computer science concerns are above the level of physics. It would be great if quantum physics allowed us to factor numbers fast, but this probably will not greatly influence programming language theory.

Here are some interesting references.

- Robin Gandy attempted to derive Turing's thesis from a number of "principles for mechanisms" [17]. Wilfried Sieg continues this line of research [52].

- David Deutsch [15] designed a universal quantum computer that is supposed to be able to simulate the behavior of any finite physical system. Gandy's approach is criticized in [16, pages 280–281]. Deutsch's approach and quantum computers in general are criticized in [43, Section 2].

- Charles H. Bennett and Rolf Landauer pose in [3] important problems related to the fundamental physical limits of computation.

- Marian Boykan Pour-El and Ian Richards [45] investigate the extent to which computability is preserved by fundamental constructions of analysis, such as those used in classical and quantum theories of physics.

4.2 Polynomial Time Turing's Thesis

There are several versions of the polynomial time Turing's thesis discussed in theoretical computer science. For simplicity, we restrict attention to decision problems.

To justify the interest in the class P of problems solvable in polynomial time by a Turing machine, it is often declared that a problem is feasible (= practically solvable) if and only if it is in P. Complexity theory tells us that there are P problems unsolvable in time n^{1000}. A more reasonable thesis is that a "natural problem" is feasible if and only if it is in P. At the 1991 Annual Meeting of the Association of Symbolic Logic, Steve Cook argued in favor of that thesis, and the second author argued against it. Some of the arguments can be found in [11] and [24] respectively.

A related but different version of the polynomial time Turing thesis is that a problem is in P if it can be solved in polynomial time at all, by any means. The presumed reason is that any polynomial time computation can be polynomial time simulated by a Turing machine (so that the computation time of the Turing machine is bounded by a polynomial of the computation time of the given computing device). Indeed, most "reasonable" computation models are known to be polytime equivalent to the Turing machine. "As to the objection that Turing machines predated all of these models," says Steve Cook [12], "I would reply that models based on RAMs are inspired by real computers, rather than Turing machines."

Quantum computer models can factor arbitrary integers in polynomial time [50], and it is not believed that quantum computers can be polynomial time simulated by Turing machines. For the believers in quantum computers, it is more natural to speak about probabilistic Turing machines. We quote from [4].

Just as the theory of computability has its foundations in the Church-Turing thesis, computational complexity theory rests upon a modern strengthening of this thesis, which asserts that any "reasonable" model of computation can be efficiently simulated on a probabilistic Turing Machine (an efficient simulation is one whose running time is bounded by some polynomial in the running time of the simulated machine). Here, we take reasonable to mean in principle physically realizable.

Turing's analysis does not automatically justify any of these new theses. (Nor does it justify, for example, the thesis that polynomial time interactive Turing machines capture polynomial time interactive algorithms.) Can any of the theses discussed above be derived from first principles? One can analyze Turing's original justification of his thesis and see whether all the reductions used by Turing are polynomial time reductions. But one has to worry also about algorithms not covered directly by Turing's analysis.

4.3 Recursion

According to Yiannis Moschovakis, an algorithm is a "recursor", a monotone operator over partial functions whose least fixed point includes (as one component) the function that the algorithm computes [44]. He proposes a particular language for defining recursors. A definition may use various givens: functions or recursors.

Moschovakis gives few examples and they are all small ones. The approach does not seem to scale to algorithms interacting with an unknown environment. A posteriori the approach applies to well understood classes of algorithms. Consider for example non-interactive sequential or parallel abstract state machines (ASMs) discussed below in Sections 5 and 6. Such an ASM has a program for doing a single step. There is an implicit iteration loop: repeat the step until, if ever, the computation terminates. Consider an operator that, given an initial segment of a computation, augments it by another step (unless the computation has terminated). This operator can be seen as a recursor. Of course the recursion advocates may not like such a recursor because they prefer stateless ways.

We are not aware of any way to derive from first principles the thesis that algorithms are recursors.

5 Formalization of Sequential Algorithms

Is it possible to capture (= formalize) sequential algorithms on their natural levels of abstraction? Furthermore, is there one machine model that captures all sequential algorithms on their natural levels of abstraction? According to [27], the answer to both questions is yes. We outline the approach of [27] and put forward a slight but useful generalization.

As a running example of a sequential algorithm, we use a version Euc of Euclid's algorithm that, given two natural numbers, computes their greatest common divisor d.

1. Set a = Input1, b = Input2.
2. If a = 0 then set d = b and go to 1
   else set a, b = b mod a, a respectively and go to 2.

Initially Euc waits for the user to provide natural numbers Input1 and Input2. The assignment on the last line is simultaneous. If, for instance, $a = 6$ and $b = 9$ in the current state then $a = 3$ and $b = 6$ in the next state.

5.1 Sequential Time Postulate

A sequential algorithm can be viewed as a finite or infinite state automaton.

Postulate 1 (Sequential Time) *A sequential algorithm A is associated with*

- *a nonempty set $S(A)$ whose members are called* states *of A,*

- *a nonempty[a] subset $\mathcal{I}(A)$ of $S(A)$ whose members are called* initial states *of A, and*

- *a map $\tau_A : S(A) \longrightarrow S(A)$ called the* one-step transformation *of A.*

The postulate ignores final states [27, section 3.3.2]. We are interested in runs where the steps of the algorithm are interleaved with the steps of the environment. A step of the environment consists in changing the current state of the algorithm to any other state. In particular it can change the "final" state to a non-final state. To make the one-step transformation total, assume that the algorithm performs an idle step in the "final" states. Clearly Euc is a sequential time algorithm. The environment of Euc includes the user who provides input numbers (and is expected to take note of the answers).

This sequential-time postulate allows us to define a fine notion of behavioral equivalence.

---

[a] In [27], $\mathcal{I}(A)$ and $S(A)$ were not required to be nonempty. But an algorithm without an initial state couldn't be run, so is it really an algorithm? We therefore add "nonempty" to the postulate here.

Definition 5.1 Two sequential time algorithms are behaviorally equivalent if they have the same states, the same initial states and the same one-step transformation.

The behavioral equivalence is too fine for many purposes but it is necessary for the following.

Corollary 5.2 *If algorithms A and B are behaviorally equivalent then B step-for-step simulates A in any environment.*

The step-for-step character of simulation is important. Consider a typical distributed system. The agents are sequential-time but the system is not. The system guarantees the atomicity of any single step of any agent but not of a sequence of agent's steps. Let A be the algorithm executed by one of the agents. If the simulating algorithm B makes two steps to simulate one step of A then another agent can sneak in between the two steps of B and spoil the simulation.

5.2   Small-Step Algorithms

An object that satisfies the sequential-time postulate doesn't have to be an algorithm. In addition we should require that there is a program for the one-step transformation. This requirement is hard to capture directly. It will follow from other requirements in the approach of [27].

Further, a sequential-time algorithm is not necessarily a sequential algorithm. For example, the algorithm P in subsection 2.3 is not sequential. The property that distinguishes sequential algorithms among all sequential-time algorithms is that the steps are of bounded complexity. The algorithms analyzed by Turing in [54] were sequential:

> The behavior of the computer at any moment is determined by the symbols which he is observing and his 'state of mind' at that moment. We may suppose that there is a bound B to the number of symbols or squares which the computer can observe at one moment. If he wishes to observe more, he must use successive observations. We will also suppose that the number of states of mind which need be taken into account is finite.

The algorithms analyzed by Kolmogorov in [39] are also sequential: "An algorithmic process is divided into separate steps of limited complexity."

These days there is a tendency to use the term "sequential algorithm" in the wider sense of the contrary of the notion of a distributed algorithm. That is, "sequential" often means what we have called "sequential-time". So we use the term "small-step algorithm" as a synonym for the term "sequential algorithms" in its traditional meaning.

5.3   Abstract State Postulate

How does one capture the restriction that the steps of a small-step algorithms are of bounded complexity? How does one measure the complexity of a single-step computation? Actually we prefer to think of bounded work instead of bounded complexity. The work that a small-step algorithm performs at any single step is bounded, and the bound depends only on the algorithm and does not depend on input. This complexity-to-work reformulation does not make the problem easier of course. How does one measure the work that the algorithm does during a step? The algorithm-as-a-state-automaton point of view is too simplistic to address the problem. We need to know more about what the states are. Fortunately this question can be answered.

Postulate 2 (Abstract State)   • *States of a sequential algorithm A are first-order structures.*

• *All states of A have the same vocabulary.*

• *The one-step transformation τ_A does not change the base set of any state.*

• $\mathcal{S}(A)$ *and* $\mathcal{I}(A)$ *are closed under isomorphisms. Further, any isomorphism from a state X onto a state Y is also an isomorphism from $\tau_A(X)$ onto $\tau_A(Y)$.*

The notion of first-order structure is well-known in mathematical logic [49]. We use the following conventions:

• Every vocabulary contains the following *logic symbols:* the equality sign, the nullary relation symbols `true` and `false`, and the usual Boolean connectives.

• Every vocabulary contains the nullary function symbol `undef`.

• Some vocabulary symbols may be marked *static*. The remaining symbols are marked *external* or *dynamic* or both[b]. All logic symbols are static.

• In every structure, `true` is distinct from `false` and `undef`, the equality sign has its standard meaning, and the Boolean connectives have their standard meanings on Boolean arguments.

The symbols `true` and `false` allow us to treat relation symbols as special function symbols. The symbol `undef` allows us to deal with partial functions; recall that first-order structures have only total functions. The static functions (that is the interpretations of the static function symbols) do not change during the computation. The algorithm can change only the dynamic functions. The environment can change only the external functions.

It is easy to see that higher-order structures are also first-order structures (though higher-order logics are richer than first-order logic). We refer to [27] for justification of the abstract-state postulate. Let us just note that the experience of the ASM community confirms that first-order structures suffice to describe any static mathematical situation [1].

It is often said that a state is given by the values of its variables. We take this literally. Any state of a sequential algorithm should be uniquely determined (in the space of all states of the algorithm) by the interpretations of the dynamic and external function symbols.

What is the vocabulary (of the states) of Euc? In addition to the logic symbols, it contains the nullary function symbols `0`, `a`, `b`, `d`, `Input1`, `Input2` and the binary function symbol `mod`. But what about labels 1 and 2? Euc has an implicit program counter. We have some freedom in making it explicit. One possibility is to introduce a Boolean variable, that is a nullary relational symbol, `initialize` that takes value `true` exactly in those states where Euc consumes inputs. The only dynamic symbols are `a`, `b`, `d`, `initialize`, and the only external symbols are `Input1`, `Input2`.

5.4 Bounded Exploration Postulate and the Definition of Sequential Algorithms

Let A be an algorithm of vocabulary Υ and let X be a state of A. A *location* ℓ of X is given by a dynamic function symbol f in Υ of some arity j and a j-tuple $\bar{a} = (a_1, \ldots, a_j)$ of elements of X. The *content* of ℓ is the value $f(\bar{a})$.

An *(atomic) update* of X is given by a location ℓ and an element b of X and denoted simply (ℓ, b). It is the action of replacing the current content a of ℓ with b.

By the abstract-state postulate, the one-step transformation preserves the set of locations, so the state X and the state $X' = \tau_A(X)$ have the same

---

[b]This useful classification, used in [23,25] and in ASM applications, was omitted in [27] because it wasn't necessary there. The omission allowed the following pathology in the case when there is a finite bound on the size of the states of A. The one-step transformation may change the values of `true` and `false` and modify appropriately the interpretations of the equality relation and the Boolean connectives.

locations. It follows that X' is obtained from X by executing the following set of updates:

$$\Delta(X) = \{(\ell, b) : \quad b = Content_{X'}(\ell) \neq Content_X(\ell)\}.$$

If A is Euc and X is the state where $a = 6$ and $b = 9$ then $\Delta(X) = \{(a, 3), (b, 6)\}$. If Y is a state of A where $a = b = 3$ then $\Delta(Y) = \{(a, 0)\}$.

Now we are ready to formulate the final postulate. Let X, Y be arbitrary states of the algorithm A.

Postulate 3 (Bounded Exploration) *There exists a finite set T of terms in the vocabulary of A such that $\Delta(X) = \Delta(Y)$ whenever every term $t \in T$ has the same value in X and Y.*

In the case of Euc, the term set $\{\texttt{true}, \texttt{false}, 0, a, b, d, b \bmod a, \texttt{initialize}\}$ is a bounded-exploration witness.

Definition 5.3 A *sequential algorithm* is an object A that satisfies the sequential-time, abstract-state and bounded-exploration postulates.

5.5 Sequential ASMs and the Characterization Theorem

The notion of a sequential ASM rule of a vocabulary Υ is defined by induction. In the following definition, all function symbols (including relation symbols) are in Υ and all terms are first-order terms.

Definition 5.4 If f is a j-ary dynamic function symbol and $t_0, \ldots, t_j$ are first-order terms, then the following is a rule:

$$f(t_1, \ldots, t_j) := t_0.$$

Let φ be a Boolean-valued term, that is φ has the form $f(t_1, \ldots, t_j)$ where f is a relation symbol. If P_1, P_2 are rules, then so is

if φ then P_1 else P_2.

If P_1, P_2 are rules then so is

do in-parallel
  P_1
  P_2

The semantics of rules is pretty obvious but we have to decide what happens if the constituents of the do in-parallel rule produce contradictory updates. In that case the execution is aborted. For a more formal definition, we refer the reader to [27]. Syntactically, a sequential ASM program is just a rule; but the rule determines only single steps of the program and is supposed

302

to be iterated. Every sequential ASM program P gives rise to a map $\tau_P(X) = Y$ where X, Y are first-order Υ-structures.

Definition 5.5 A sequential ASM B of vocabulary Υ is given by a sequential ASM program Π of vocabulary Υ, a nonempty set $\mathcal{S}(B)$ of Υ-structures closed under isomorphisms and under the map τ_Π, a nonempty subset $\mathcal{I}(B) \subseteq \mathcal{S}(B)$ that is closed under isomorphisms, and the map τ_B which is the restriction of τ_Π to $\mathcal{S}(B)$.

Now we are ready to formulate the theorem of this section.

Theorem 5.6 (ASM Characterization of Small-Step Algorithms)
For every sequential algorithm A there is a sequential abstract state machine B behaviorally equivalent to A. In particular, B simulates A step for step.

If A is our old friend Euc, then the program of the desired ASM B could be this.

```
if initialize then
   do in-parallel
      a := Input1
      b := Input2
      initialize := false
else
   if a = 0 then
      do in-parallel
         d := b
         initialize := true
   else
      do in-parallel
         a := b mod a
         b := a
```

We have discussed only deterministic sequential algorithms. Nondeterminism implicitly appeals to the environment to make the choices that cannot be algorithmically prescribed [27]. Once nondeterminism is available, classical ruler-and-compass constructions can be regarded as nondeterministic ASMs operating on a suitable structure of geometric objects.

A critical examination of [27] is found in [46].

6 Formalization of Parallel Algorithms

Encouraged by the success in capturing the notion of sequential algorithms in [27], we "attacked" parallel algorithms in [7]. The attack succeeded. We gave an axiomatic definition of parallel algorithms and checked that the known (to us) parallel algorithm models satisfy the axioms. We defined precisely a version of parallel abstract state machines, a variant of the notion of parallel ASMs from [25], and we checked that our parallel ASMs satisfy the definitions of parallel algorithms. And we proved the characterization theorem for parallel algorithms: every parallel algorithm is behaviorally equivalent to a parallel ASM.

The scope of this paper does not allow us to spell out the axiomatization of parallel ASMs, which is more involved than the axiomatization of sequential ASMs described in the previous section. We just explain what kind of parallelism we have in mind, say a few words about the axioms, say a few words about the parallel ASMs, and formulate the characterization theorem. The interested reader is invited to read — critically! — the paper [7]. More scrutiny of that paper is highly desired.

6.1 What Parallel Algorithms?

The term "parallel algorithm" is used for a number of different notions in the literature. We have in mind sequential-time algorithms that can exhibit unbounded parallelism but only bounded sequentiality within a single step. Bounded sequentiality means that there is an *a priori* bound on the lengths of sequences of events within any one step of the algorithm that must occur in a specified order. To distinguish this notion of parallel algorithms, we call such parallel algorithms *wide-step*. Intuitively the width is the amount of parallelism. The "step" in "wide-step" alludes to sequential time.

Remark 6.1 Wide-step algorithms are also bounded-depth where the depth is intuitively the amount of sequentiality in a single step; this gives rise to a possible alternative name *shallow-step algorithms* for wide-step algorithms. Note that the name "parallel" emphasizes the potential rather than restrictions; in the same spirit, we choose "wide-step" over "shallow-step".

Here is an example of a wide-step algorithm that, given a directed graph $G = (V, E)$, marks the well-founded part of G. Initially no vertex is marked.

1. For every vertex x do the following.
   If every vertex y with an edge to x is marked
   then mark x as well.
2. Repeat step 1 until no new vertices are marked.

6.2 A Few Words on the Axioms for Wide-Step Algorithms

Adapt the sequential-time postulate, the definition of behavioral equivalence and the abstract-state postulate to parallel algorithms simply by replacing "sequential" with "parallel". The bounded-exploration postulate, on the other hand, specifically describes sequential algorithms. The work that a parallel algorithm performs within a single step can be unbounded. We must drop the bounded-exploration postulate and assume, in its place, an axiom or axioms specifically designed for parallelism.

A key observation is that a parallel computation consists of a number of processes running (not surprisingly) in parallel. The constituent processes can be parallel as well. But if we analyze the computation far enough then we arrive at processes, which we call *proclets*, that satisfy the bounded-exploration postulate. Several postulates describe how the proclets communicate with each other and how they produce updates. And there is a postulate requiring some bound d (depending only on the algorithm) for the amount of sequentiality in the program. The length of any sequence of events that must occur in a specified order within any one step of the algorithm is at most d.

There are several computation models for wide-step algorithms in the literature. The two most known models are Boolean circuits and PRAMs [35]. (PRAM stands for "Parallel Random Access Machines".) These two models and some other models of wide-step algorithms that occurred to us or to the referees are shown to satisfy the wide-step postulates in [7].

6.3 Wide-Step Abstract State Machines

Parallel abstract state machines were defined in [25]. Various semantical issues were elaborated later in [26]. A simple version of parallel ASMs was explored in [8]; these ASMs can be called BGS ASMs. We describe, up to an isomorphism, an arbitrary state X of a BGS ASM. X is closed under finite sets (every finite set of elements of X constitutes another element of X) and is equipped with the usual set-theoretic operations. Thus X is infinite but a finite part of X contains all the essential information. The number of *atoms* of X, that is elements that are not sets, is finite, and there is a nullary function symbol Atoms interpreted as the set of all atoms. It is easy to write a BGS ASM program that simulates the example parallel algorithm above.

```
forall x ∈ Atoms
    if {y :  y ∈ Atoms :  E(y,x) ∧ ¬(M(y))} = ∅
    then M(x) := true
```

Note that x and y are mathematical variables like the variables of first-order logic. They are not programming variables and cannot be assigned values. In comparison to the case of sequential ASMs, there are two main new features in the syntax of BGS ASMs:

- set-comprehension terms $\{t(x) : x \in r : \varphi(x)\}$, and

- `forall` rules.

In [6], we introduced the notion of a background of an ASM. BGS ASMs have a set background. The specification language AsmL, mentioned in the introduction, has a rich background that includes a set background, a sequence background, a map background, etc. The background that naturally arises in the analysis of wide-step algorithms is a multiset background. That is the background used in [7].

6.4 The Wide-Step Characterization Theorem

Theorem 6.2 (ASM Characterization of Wide-Step Algorithms)
For every parallel algorithm A there is a parallel abstract state machine B behaviorally equivalent to A. In particular, B simulates A step for step.

Thus, Boolean circuits and PRAMs can be seen as special wide-step ASMs (which does not make then any less valuable). The existing quantum computer models satisfy our postulates as well [20] assuming that the environment provides random bits when needed. The corresponding wide-step ASMs need physical quantum-computer implementation for efficient execution.

7 Toward Formalization of Distributed Algorithms

Distributed abstract state machines were defined in [25]. They are extensively used by the ASM community [1] but the problem of capturing distributed algorithms is open. Here we concentrate on one aspect of this important problem: interaction between a sequential-time agent and the rest of the system as seen by the agent. One may have an impression that this aspect has been covered because all along we studied runs where steps of the algorithm are interleaved with steps made by the environment. But this interleaving mode is not general enough.

If we assume that each agent's steps are atomic, then interleaving mode seems adequate. But a more detailed analysis reveals that even in this case a slight modification is needed. See Subsection 7.1.

But in fact an agent's steps need not be atomic because agents can interact with their environments not only in the inter-step fashion but also in the intra-step fashion. It is common in the AsmL experience that, during a single step, one agent calls on other agents, receives "callbacks", calls again, etc. It is much harder to generalize the two characterization theorems to intra-step interaction.

7.1 Trivial Updates in Distributed Computation

Consider a small-step abstract state machine A. In Section 5, we restricted attention to runs where steps of A are interleaved with steps of the environment. Now turn attention to distributed computing where the agents do not necessarily take turns to compute. Assume that A is the algorithm executed by one of the agents. Recall that an update of a location ℓ of the current state of A is the action of replacing the current content a of ℓ with some content b. Call the update *trivial* if $a = b$. In Section 5 we could ignore trivial updates. But we have to take them into account now. A trivial update of ℓ matters in a distributed situation when the location ℓ is shared: typically only one agent is allowed to write into a location at any given time, and so even a trivial update by one agent would prevent other agents from writing to the same location at the same time.

Recall that $\Delta(X)$ is the set of nontrivial updates computed by the algorithm A at X during one step. Let $\Delta^+(X)$ be the set of all updates, trivial or not, computed by A at X during the one step. It seems obvious how to generalize Section 5 in order to take care of trivial updates: just strengthen the bounded-exploration postulate by replacing Δ with Δ^+. There is, however, a little problem. Nothing in the current definition of a small-step algorithm A guarantees that there is a $\Delta^+(X)$ map associated with it. ($\Delta(X)$ is definable in terms of X and $\tau_A(X)$.) That is why we started this subsection by assuming that A is an ASM. Euc also has a $\Delta^+(X)$ map: if X is the state where $a = 6$ and $b = 9$ then $\Delta^+(X) = \{(a, 3), (b, 6)\}$, and if Y is a state of A where $a = b = 3$ then $\Delta(Y) = \{(a, 0)\}$ and $\Delta^+(Y) = \{(a, 0), (b, 3)\}$.

To generalize Section 5 in order to take into account trivial updates, do the following.

- Strengthen the abstract-state postulate by assuming that there is a mapping Δ^+ associating a set of updates with every state X of the given algorithm A in such a way that the set of non-trivial updates in $\Delta^+(X)$ is exactly $\Delta(X)$.

- Strengthen the definition of behavioral equivalence of sequential algorithms by requiring that the two algorithms produce the same $\Delta^+(X)$ at every state X.

- Strengthen the bounded exploration postulate by replacing Δ with Δ^+.

It is easy to check that Theorem 5.6, the small-step characterization theorem, remains valid.

Remark 7.1 In a similar way, we refine the definition of wide-step algorithms and strengthen Theorem 6.2, the wide-step characterization theorem.

Remark 7.2 Another generalization of Section 5, to algorithms with the output command, is described in [7]. The two generalizations of Section 5 are orthogonal and can be combined. The output generalization applies to wide-step algorithms as well.

7.2 Intra-Step Interacting Algorithms

During the execution of a single step, an algorithm may call on its environment to provide various data and services. The AsmL experience showed the importance of intra-step communication between an algorithm and its environment. AsmL programs routinely call on outside components to perform various jobs.

The idea of such intra-step interaction between an algorithm and its environment is not new to the ASM literature; external functions appear already in the tutorial [23]. In simple cases, one can pretend that intra-step interaction reduces to inter-step interaction, that the environment prepares in advance the appropriate values of the external functions. In general, even if such a reduction is possible, it requires an omniscient environment and is utterly impractical.

The current authors are preparing a series of articles extending Theorems 5.6 and 6.2 to intra-step interacting algorithms. In either case, this involves:

- axiomatic definitions of intra-step interacting algorithms,

- precise definitions of intra-step interacting abstract state machines,

- the appropriate extension of the notion of behavioral equivalence,

- verification that the ASMs satisfy the definitions of algorithms,

- a proof that every intra-step interacting algorithm is behaviorally equivalent to an intra-step interacting ASM.

Acknowledgments

We thank Steve Cook, John Dawson, Martin Davis, Sol Feferman, Leonid Levin, Victor Pambuccian and Vladimir Uspensky for helping us with references. We thank John Dawson, Sol Feferman, Erich Grädel, Leonid Levin, Victor Pambuccian and Dean Rosenzweig for commenting, on very short notice (because of a tight deadline), on the draft of this paper.

308

The work of the first author was partially supported by NSF grant DMS–0070723 and by a grant from Microsoft Research.

References

1. ASM Michigan Webpage, http://www.eecs.umich.edu/gasm/, maintained by James K. Huggins.
2. The AsmL webpage, http://research.microsoft.com/foundations/AsmL/.
3. C.H. Bennett and R. Landauer, Fundamental physical limits of computation, *Scientific American* 253:1 (July 1985), 48–56.
4. E. Bernstein and U. Vazirani, Quantum complexity theory, *SIAM Journal on Computing* 26 (1997), 1411–1473.
5. A. Blass and Y. Gurevich, The linear time hierarchy theorem for abstract state machines and RAMs, *Springer Journal of Universal Computer Science* 3:4 (1997), 247–278.
6. A. Blass and Y. Gurevich, Background, reserve, and Gandy machines, *Springer Lecture Notes in Computer Science* 1862 (2000), 1–17.
7. A. Blass and Y. Gurevich, Abstract state machines capture parallel algorithms, Technical Report MSR-TR-2001-117. A journal version is scheduled to appear in *ACM Transactions on Computational Logic* 4:4, October 2003.
8. A. Blass, Y. Gurevich, and S. Shelah, Choiceless polynomial time, *Annals of Pure and Applied Logic* 100 (1999), 141–187.
9. E. Börger and R. Stärk, *Abstract State Machines*, Springer, 2003.
10. A. Church, An unsolvable problem of elementary number theory, *American Journal of Mathematics* 58 (1936), 345–363. Reprinted in [13, 88–107].
11. S.A. Cook, Computational complexity of higher type functions, *Proceedings of 1990 International Congress of Mathematicians*, Kyoto, Japan, Springer–Verlag, 1991, 55–69.
12. S.A. Cook, Private communication, 2003.
13. M. Davis, *The Undecidable*, Raven Press, 1965.
14. M. Davis, Why Gödel didn't have Church's thesis, *Information and Control* 54 (1982), 3–24.
15. D. Deutsch, Quantum theory, the Church-Turing principle and the universal quantum computer, *Proceedings of the Royal Society, A*, vol. 400 (1985), 97–117.
16. D. Deutsch, A. Ekert, and R. Lupaccini, Machines, logic and quantum physics, *The Bulletin of Symbolic Logic* 6 (2000), 265–283.

17. R. Gandy, Church's thesis and principles for mechanisms, In J. Barwise, H. J. Keisler, and K. Kunen, Eds., *The Kleene Symposium*, North-Holland, 1980, 123–148.
18. R. Gandy, The confluence of ideas in 1936, in R. Herken, Editor, *The Universal Turing Machine: A Half-Century Story*, Oxford University Press, 1988, 55–111.
19. K. Gödel, *Collected Works*, Volume II, Oxford University Press, 1990.
20. E. Grädel and A. Nowack, Quantum computing and abstract state machines, Springer *Lecture Notes in Computer Science* 2589 (2003) 309–323.
21. D. Grigoriev, Kolmogorov algorithms are stronger than Turing machines, *Journal of Soviet Mathematics* 14:5 (1980), 1445–1450.
22. Y. Gurevich, Kolmogorov machines and related issues, in G. Rozenberg and A. Salomaa, Editors, *Current Trends in Theoretical Computer Science*, World Scientific, 1993, 225–234; originally in *Bull. EATCS* 35 (1988).
23. Y. Gurevich, Evolving algebras: An attempt to discover semantics, in G. Rozenberg and A. Salomaa, Editors, *Current Trends in Theoretical Computer Science*, World Scientific, 1993, 266–292; originally in Bull. EATCS 43 (1991).
24. Y. Gurevich, Feasible functions, *London Mathematical Society Newsletter*, 206 (June 1993), 6–7.
25. Y. Gurevich, Evolving algebra 1993: Lipari guide, in E. Börger, Editor, *Specification and Validation Methods*, Oxford University Press, 1995, 9–36.
26. Y. Gurevich, May 1997 draft of the ASM guide, *Technical Report* CSE-TR-336-97, EECS Department, University of Michigan, 1997.
27. Y. Gurevich, For every sequential algorithm there is an equivalent sequential abstract state machine, *ACM Transactions on Computational Logic*, vol. 1, no. 1 2000), 77–111.
28. Y. Gurevich and J.K. Huggins, The semantics of the C programming language, *Springer Lecture Notes in Computer Science* 702 (1993), 274–308.
29. Y. Gurevich and S. Shelah, Nearly linear time, *Springer Lecture Notes in Computer Science* 363 (1989), 108–118.
30. Y. Gurevich and M. Spielmann, Recursive abstract state machines, *Springer Journal of Universal Computer Science* 3:4 (1997), 233–246.
31. A. Karatsuba and Y. Ofman, Multiplication of multidigit numbers on automata, *Soviet Physics Doklady* (English translation), 7:7 (1963), 595–596.
32. S.C. Kleene, On notation for ordinal numbers, *Journal of Symbolic Logic*

3 (1938), 150–155.

33. S.C. Kleene, Origins of recursive function theory, *Annals of the History of Computing* 3:1 (January 1981), 52–67.

34. S.C. Kleene, Turing's analysis of computability, and major applications of it, in R. Herken, Editor, *The Universal Turing Machine: A Half-Century Story*, Oxford University Press, 1988, 17–54.

35. R.M. Karp and V. Ramachandran, Parallel algorithms for shared-memory machines, in J. van Leeuwen, Editor, *Handbook of Theoretical Computer Science, Vol. A: Algorithms and Complexity*, Elsevier and MIT Press (1990), 869–941.

36. D. Kijne, *Plane Construction Field Theory*, Van Gorcum, Assen, 1956.

37. D.E. Knuth, *The Art of Computer Programming, volume 1: Fundamental Algorithms*, Addison-Wesley, Reading, MA, 1968.

38. D.E. Knuth, *The Art of Computer Programming, volume 2: Seminumerical Algorithms*, Addison-Wesley, Reading, MA, 1981.

39. A.N. Kolmogorov, On the concept of algorithm, *Uspekhi Mat. Nauk* 8:4 (1953), 175–176, Russian. An English translation is found in [56, pages 18–19].

40. A.N. Kolmogorov and V.A. Uspensky, On the definition of algorithm, *Uspekhi Mat. Nauk* 13:4 (1958), 3–28, Russian; translated into English in *AMS Translations* 29 (1963), 217–245.

41. L.A. Levin, Universal search problems, *Problemy Peredachi Informatsii*, 9:3 (1973), 265–266, Russian. The journal is translated into English under the name *Problems of Information Transmission*.

42. L.A. Levin, Private communication.

43. L.A. Levin, The tale of one-way functions, *Problemy Peredachi Informatsii*, 39:1 (2003), 92–103, Russian. The journal is translated into English under the name *Problems of Information Transmission*. The English version is available online at http://arXiv.org/abs/cs.CR/0012023.

44. Y.N. Moschovakis, What is an algorithm? in B. Engquist and W. Schmid, Editors, *Mathematics Unlimited*, Springer-Verlag (2001) 919–936.

45. M.B. Pour-El and J.I. Richards, *Computability in Analysis and Physics (Perspectives in Mathematical Logic)*, Springer-Verlag 1989.

46. W. Reisig, On Gurevich's theorem on sequential algorithms, *Acta Informatica* 39 (2003), 273–305.

47. A. Schönhage, Universelle Turing Speicherung, in J. Dörr and G. Hotz, Editors, *Automatentheorie und Formale Sprachen*, Bibliogr. Institut, Mannheim, 1970, 369–383. In German.

48. A. Schönhage, Storage modification machines, *SIAM Journal on Computing* 9 (1980), 490–508.

49. J.R. Shoenfield, *Mathematical Logic*, Addison-Wesley 1967.

50. P.W. Shor, Polynomial-time algorithms for prime factorization and discrete logarithms on a quantum computer, *SIAM Journal on Computing* 26:5 (1997), 1484–1509.

51. W. Sieg, Step by recursive step: Church's analysis of effective calculability, *Bulletin of Symbolic Logic* 3:2 (1997), 154–180.

52. W. Sieg, An abstract model for parallel computations: Gandy's thesis, *The Monist* 82:1 (1999), 150–164.

53. R.E. Tarjan, A class of algorithms which require nonlinear time to maintain disjoint sets, *Journal of Computer and System Sciences* 18 (1979), 110–127.

54. A.M. Turing, On computable numbers, with an application to the Entscheidungsproblem, *Proceedings of London Mathematical Society*, series 2, vol. 42 (1936–1937), 230–265; correction, *ibidem*, vol. 43, 544–546. Reprinted in [13, 155–222] and available online at http://www.abelard.org/turpap2/tp2-ie.asp.

55. V.A. Uspensky, 1992, Kolmogorov and mathematical logic, *Journal of Symbolic Logic* 57:2 (1992), 385–412.

56. V.A. Uspensky and A.L. Semenov, *Algorithms: Main Ideas and Applications*, Kluwer, 1993.

3
CONCURRENCY
Mogens NIELSEN

CONTENTS

Introductory Remarks
Some of My Favourite Results in Classic Process Algebra
(by L. Aceto)
Roadmap of Infinite Results (by J. Srba)
Construction and Verification of Concurrent Performance and
Reliability Models (by H. Hermanns)
Does Combining Nondeterminism and Probability Make Sense?
(by P. Panangaden)
The Algebraic Structure of Petri Nets (by V. Sassone)

Mogens Nielsen
Computer Science Department
University of Aarhus
Bldg. 540 Ny Munkegade
DK-8000 Aarhus C, Denmark
E-mail: mn@brics.dk

INTRODUCTORY REMARKS

The area of Concurrency aims at a formal understanding of the behaviour of distributed interacting systems as the basis for their description, analysis, implementation and verification.

In the following you will find five contributions from the Concurrency Column over the last three years. The five papers cover a few (but by no means all) of the major trends in Concurrency. The papers are written in a tutorial like style, summarizing major contributions and open problems, or raising questions for discussion.

The first two contributions ("Some of My Favourite Results in Classic Process Algebra" by Luca Aceto, and "Roadmap of Infinite Results" by Jiri Srba) present some major results from the area of process algebra. The next two contributions ("Construction and Verification of Concurrent Performance and Reliability Models" by Holger Hermanns, and "Does Combining Nondeterminism and Probability Make Sense?" by Prakash Panangaden) deal with the role of probability theory within Concurrency, and the final contribution ("The Algebraic Structure of Petri Nets" by Vladimiro Sassone) presents an algebraic approach to Petri nets, one of the significant models from Concurrency theory.

The papers are all presented here as updated versions of the contributions originally presented in the Concurrency Column.

The Concurrency Column first appeared in the Bulletin in June 1993. I have had the pleasure of being the editor of the Column since its beginning, and I have seen the area of Concurrency develop enormously over the ten year period. I hope that the Columns have contributed to and illustrated this development.

Editing the Concurrency chapter of this book is my final act as the editor of the Concurrency Column. However, I am sure that the Concurrency Column will be an important forum for the exchange of ideas and information from Concurrency theory also in the future, with Luca Aceto (author of the first of the contributions in the following) as the new editor.

I would like to thank all my colleagues who have contributed to the Concurrency Column over the years, and in particular the authors contributing to this chapter.

Mogens Nielsen

SOME OF MY FAVOURITE RESULTS IN CLASSIC PROCESS ALGEBRA

LUCA ACETO

Department of Computer Science
Aalborg University
9220 Aalborg Ø, Denmark
E-mail: luca@cs.auc.dk

This note is dedicated to Anna and Róbert.

"What I had done so far amounted to a mere fraction of nothing at all. It was so much dust, and the slightest wind would blow it away."
[13, Page 207]

1 Introduction and Disclaimers

I have been asked a few times what my favourite results in process algebra are, and often thought that it might be a useful exercise to reflect a little on that question, and pen down my thoughts. The spur for attempting this somewhat foolish enterprise at this point in time comes from the workshop on "Process Algebra: Open Problems and Future Directions" that I co-organize with Zoltán Ésik, Wan Fokkink and Anna Ingólfsdóttir. My co-organizers and I hope that, apart from being a celebration of over twenty years of research in process algebra, that workshop will bear witness to the continuing vitality of this field of investigation, and I believe that one of the ways to contribute to the solution of new problems and the development of new avenues for research is to mull over the results that have been achieved so far and the open problems they raise.

Whether the writing of this note means that I am "past the best before date" as an active researcher in the process algebra community I must leave to others to judge—I certainly am if Godfrey Harold Hardy was to be trusted when he wrote

"It is a melancholy experience for a professional mathematician to find himself writing about mathematics. [...] I write about mathematics because [...] I have no longer the freshness of mind, the energy, or the patience to carry on effectively with my proper job. [43, pp. 61 and 63]"

However, I hope that Gian-Carlo Rota's statement from [71] that

"Not only is it good for you to write an expository paper once in a while, but such writing is essential for the survival of mathematics."

will prove to be true for me in this case.

It goes without saying that the list of results in process algebra that I will present in what follows is very partial, is based entirely on my personal views of the moment and my tastes, and is limited by my (lack of) knowledge, energy and time. (Indeed, I can guarantee that if I were to draw a similar list in a few months' time, then that list would most likely be different.) I apologize to all the colleagues of mine whose excellent results are not mentioned here, and whose work I know less than I should. There are just so many beautiful results in our field of interest, and the variety is so large, that there is no hope to do justice to even a tiny fragment of them in a piece like this one—the interested reader is invited to browse through [21] to obtain a bird's eye view of research in process algebra. Indeed, if ever there is a message to be gleaned from this note, then it is that the process algebra research community should be proud of its non-trivial achievements.

As the readers of this note will notice, the results mentioned below are not just confined to the algebraic aspects of process theory, and reflect my very generous, and somewhat arbitrary, view of what process algebra is. I believe that algebraic ideas underlie many facets of process theory in that algebra provides *structure and reasoning techniques* that turn out to guide our thoughts even when we work with plain automata based formalisms, logics, testing approaches and so on. Moreover I see the results in process algebra proper, and process theory in general, as belonging to the same body of work regardless of whether algebraic techniques play an explicit role in them or not. That is why this survey mentions results which appear to be purely about logic and/or automata. I hope that this position won't upset any sensibilities amongst my colleagues—indeed, it is meant to bring a sense of unity to the work of what I see as a community of kindred spirits with different tastes and interests in research.

In keeping with the foolish nature of this whole enterprise, I have decided to restate some of the items that populate my "to do" list as problems in this note. Some of them are very specific, some others are very vague and most likely are just wishful thinking. I hope to be able to settle at least one of them in the rest of my career.

The presentation is based on my notes for an imaginary talk on my favourite results in classic process algebra, and is aimed at readers who are familiar with concurrency theory, and process algebra in particular. I have made no real attempt to turn it into a polished piece of scientific writing that is accessible to a wide readership. I hope that the bibliographic references will help the patient uninitiated reader find much better and thorough reviews of the results mentioned in this note.

The structure of the note is as follows. Section 2 presents results and problems related to behavioural equivalences and their relationships with modal logic. Section 3 discusses theorems on the (non-)existence of finite equational axiomatizations for behavioural equivalences over fragments of process algebras. Two results from the meta-theory of process algebras based on structural operational semantics are reviewed in Section 4. Section 5 is devoted to a taste of expressiveness results in classic process algebra. The note concludes with the mention of two theorems highlighting the connections, and the differences, between the theory of process algebra and the classic theory of automata and formal languages (Section 6).

2 Behavioural Equivalences and Logic

Let me start with a classic example of an early result proven by Hennessy and Milner in [45] that has had a monumental impact on many aspects of research in process theory, is based on a cute idea, but does not have a mind-bogglingly complex proof—once one has seen it, of course! It is the kind of result that we regularly teach our students in Aalborg in an introductory concurrency theory course, and whose proof has reached what Paul Erdős might have called the "Book Proof" stage.

Most researchers in process theory will agree that one of the fundamental notions of behavioural equivalence over labelled transition systems is (strong) bisimulation equivalence [60,66]. This notion of equivalence has many alternative characterizations. Amongst these, I want to mention here the characterization of bisimulation equivalence in terms of a modal logic that is often referred to as *Hennessy-Milner Logic*.

Result 1 (Hennessy and Milner [45]) *Two image finite processes are bisimulation equivalent if, and only if, they afford the same properties that can be expressed in Hennessy-Milner Logic.*

Variations on this result abound in the literature (see, e.g., [2,11,33,39,53,58,78]). Indeed one of the tests for the reasonableness of a behavioural equivalence is that it has a pleasing, natural modal characterization. Modal characterizations of behavioural equivalences and preorders have important uses in, e.g.,

- automatic verification of reactive systems (for instance, in providing a convenient formalism for expressing *distinguishing formulae*—see, e.g., [52,55]),

- characterizing equivalence classes of (finite) processes with respect to some notion of behavioral equivalence by means of the so-called *characteristic formulae* [49,77],

- showing finitariness and algebraicity of behavioural preorders [11],

- the characterization of the largest congruences included in completed trace equivalence that are induced by SOS formats—see, e.g., [41,42], and

- non-finite axiomatizability proofs [9].

The interpretation of Hennessy-Milner Logic that matches notions of bisimulation preorder, as developed in [58,78], has pleasing connections with intuitionistic logics.

The second result I want to mention here also makes use of Result 1 in the generation of tests from formulae in Hennessy-Milner logic to characterize bisimulation equivalence as a testing equivalence. It is one of the main results in a line of research that was quite popular in the late 1980's and early 1990's, when an effort was being made to justify, or at least clarify, the observational nature of bisimulation equivalence.

Result 2 (Abramsky [1]) *Abramsky's characterization of bisimulation equivalence as a testing equivalence.*

A notable, albeit maybe not so well known, result buried in Abramsky's paper is a theorem to the effect that adding any collection of monotonic tests to the language for tests used in the proof of Result 2 does not increase the distinguishing power of the test language. To my mind, this is possibly the closest we have come to giving a precise solution to the following

Problem 1 *Can one prove in a formal sense that bisimulation equivalence is the finest "reasonable" behavioural equivalence?*

3 Axiomatizations of Behavioural Equivalences

One of the natural outcomes of the algebraic structure of process description languages is that we can formulate general (in)equivalences between process terms that we expect to hold with respect to the chosen notion of behavioral semantics in the linear time-branching time spectrum [39] in terms of (in)equations. Several natural questions immediately arise pertaining to the (non-)existence of (finite) axiomatizations for behavioural equivalences over fragments of process description languages. I will now mention some of my favourite results in this line of research. It will come as no surprise to the readers of this note who know about my work that I am very partial to this type of contribution, and this is reflected by the role they play in this presentation.

3.1 Positive Results

The axiomatization of bisimulation equivalence over the recursion-free fragment of CCS offered in [45] employs an axiom schema, the seminal and well known *expansion theorem*. This begged the question of whether one could replace this axiom schema with a finite set of equations. Bergstra and Klop showed that this can be done by extending the language with two auxiliary operators, the *left merge* and the *communication merge*, that can be used to finitely axiomatize the parallel composition operator in bisimulation semantics.

Result 3 (Bergstra and Klop [19]) *Bergstra and Klop's axiomatization of the merge operator in terms of the auxiliary left merge and communication merge operators.*

Again, this is an example of a seminal result which is based on an ingenious idea, but whose proof is not technically very complicated once the appropriate machinery is in place. An analysis of the reasons why operators like the left merge and the communication merge are equationally well behaved in bisimulation semantics has led to general algorithms for the generation of (finite) equational axiomatizations for behavioural equivalences from their operational semantics—see, e.g., [4] and the references in [10].

Problem 2 *Can one give a finite axiomatization for the weak behavioural preorders studied in [86] over the recursion-free fragment of CCS enriched with the constant Ω (to stand for a divergent process), the left merge and the communication merge?*

To my mind, two of the most satisfying results in the theory of processes are:
Result 4 (Milner [59,61]) *Milner's axiomatizations of bisimilarity and observation congruence over the regular fragment of CCS.*

Even though one can trace the general proof strategy employed in the proofs of those results to Salomaa's axiomatization of the theory of regular expressions [72], the axioms given by Milner are so elegant, and the proofs are so crisp, that those results set high standards for the whole community. Other axiomatization results for regular processes use similar proof strategies—see [12,37,70] to list but a few. Let me remark in passing that the axiomatization first presented by Bergstra and Klop in [20] played a seminal role in the discovery of the laws for observational congruence given by Milner in [61]. Indeed, Milner himself states in *op. cit.* that his axioms were inspired by a reading of [20].

Problem 3 *Settle Milner's conjecture in [59] regarding the axiomatization of bisimulation equivalence over the language of regular expressions.*

Problem 4 *Characterize those recursive equations over the regular fragment of CCS that yield a process that can be represented by a regular expression modulo strong bisimulation equivalence. (This open question was originally raised by Milner in [59].) Some work on this problem has been done by Bosscher in [25, Chapter 3] and by De Nicola and Labella in [32].*

Problem 5 *Axiomatize all the equivalences in the linear time-branching time spectrum over regular processes. Obtain axiomatizations for these equivalences that are relative to those for iteration algebras given by Bloom and Ésik—see, e.g., [24].*

Axiomatization results for behavioural equivalences based on interleaving over fragments of process algebras that cannot describe infinite behaviours usually consist of a collection of laws that allow one to reduce terms to finite synchronization trees, and laws that axiomatize the equivalence under consideration over finite synchronization trees. This strategy is not directly applicable when the equivalence under consideration treats parallelism as a primitive notion. To my mind, the most satisfying approach in this setting is to isolate a collection of axioms that explicitly characterize the relevant properties of the parallel composition operator. (See, e.g., [26,31] for the application of an alternative, very ingenious approach to the problem.) One of the earliest examples of such a set of laws is given by

Result 5 (Hennessy [44]) *Hennessy's axiomatization of the relation of timed congruence (also known as split-2 congruence) over a recursion-free process language.*

This result was published in 1988 by the *SIAM Journal on Computing*, but was actually obtained in 1981–1982. In particular, I am quite partial to the decomposition result that underlies the completeness proof. This is an example of a result that very few researchers cared about when it was obtained (see the publication delay!), but that became fashionable and relevant at the heyday of the study of non-interleaving equivalences for process description languages. This is also an example of a result whose "proof" employs techniques that are, I believe, seminal, but whose statement turned out to be incorrect—more precisely, one of the proposed axioms is not sound (see, e.g. [3] for a general discussion of this problem, and a correct proof of Hennessy's result). To my mind, this does not diminish the importance of the contribution to the research area, and I still recall the astonishment—maybe common amongst PhD. students—I had when I read that paper the first time at the mere thought that somebody could have proven such a result.

Result 6 (Fokkink [34]) *The completeness proof for bisimulation equivalence over BPA* published by Fokkink in op. cit.*

This completeness theorem was first proven by Fokkink and Zantema in [35], but the proof presented in [34] is probably the "Book Proof" for that result. Its main interest lies in the wealth of proof techniques that it introduces, which have turned out to be useful in establishing related results—see, e.g., [7,29,30].

Problem 6 *Is bisimulation equivalence finitely based over the language obtained by adding the empty process to BPA* ?*

Problem 7 *Give an equational axiomatization of bisimulation equivalence over the language BPA^*_δ obtained by adding the constant δ to BPA* ?*

Conway showed in [28] that any equational axiomatization for the language of regular expressions must contain an infinite number of equations in two or more variables. Does the same hold for equational axiomatizations of bisimulation equivalence over the language BPA^*_δ ?

3.2 Negative Results

Christos Papadimitriou once wrote in [65, Page 2] that "negative results are *the only possible* self-contained theoretical results", and I often like to cite him to "justify" my partiality towards negative results pertaining to the non-existence of finite equational axiomatizations for behavioural equivalences over process description languages. Amongst the extant such results, I would like to mention here

Result 7 (Moller [62,63]) *Moller's proofs of non-finite axiomatizability for bisimulation equivalence over CCS and over PA without the left-merge.*

To the best of my knowledge, these were the first such results in process theory, and offered a powerful demonstration of the usefulness of proof theoretic techniques in proofs of non-finite axiomatizability for behavioural equivalences over process algebras. Indeed, most of the proofs of such negative results in process algebra I know of have used proof theoretic techniques (two exceptions are the menagerie of non-finite axiomatizability results over BPA* for all of the behavioural congruences in between ready simulation and completed traces offered in [8]—that are based on Conway's results for regular expressions [28]—, and the toy result for trace and simulation equivalence over BPA with a singleton action set [5,6]—that, despite its toy nature, has a rather non-trivial proof, if I may say so). Moller's proofs use a very neat unique decomposition result for processes. It is quite remarkable, albeit maybe not wholly unexpected, how useful decomposition results turn out to be in very different settings!

The interested reader will find further examples of non-finite axiomatizability results in, e.g., [9,22,74]. The last of these references is notable in that it deals with a language with finite-state recursive definitions.

Problem 8 *Are the left merge and communication merge operators necessary to obtain a finite axiomatization of strong bisimulation equivalence? Can one obtain a finite axiomatization by adding only one binary operator to the signature of CCS? In particular, does bisimulation equivalence admit a finite equational axiomatization over the language obtained by adding Hennessy's auxiliary operator from [44] to CCS?*[a]

Problem 9 *Give a model theoretic proof of Moller's theorem.*

Problem 10 *Can one prove that observation congruence is also not finitely based over CCS?*

Problem 11 *Can one come up with sufficient conditions of a reasonably general nature (be they syntactic or semantic) that ensure that bisimulation equivalence is finitely based?*

Problem 12 *Is it decidable whether a "finite process language" is finitely based modulo bisimulation equivalence? (This requires some sort of characterization of a process language.) See McKenzie's solution to Tarski's celebrated finite basis problem in [57].*

4 SOS Theory

Structural operational semantics [68] has played a key role in the development of the theory of process algebras. Moreover, it has been a key tool in the development of the meta-theory of process description languages by providing the technical framework for the generalization of results proven for many different specific process algebras to families of such languages—see [10] for a survey of these results.

Amongst the wealth of theorems that have been developed in this field of research, let me mention a result that was ahead of its time, and offered the blueprint for a series of developments that became very popular from the late 1980's onwards.

---

[a] As was recently pointed out to me by Jos Baeten and Rob van Glabbeek, it is certainly possible to obtain a finite axiomatization of (strong/weak/branching) bisimulation congruence by adding one ternary operator to the signature of CCS.

Result 8 (de Simone [75]) *Expressive completeness modulo FH-equivalence of Meije-SCCS with respect to the collection of operators that can be described using rules in de Simone's format.*
This result offers possibly the main example of a process algebra, viz. Meije [14], whose design was explicitly guided by a deep analysis of expressiveness considerations. Variants on de Simone's original result are reported in, e.g., [38,50,67,83]. The use of FH-bisimulation—essentially a notion of bisimulation that can be defined directly over open terms, using derived SOS rules for contexts as *formal hypotheses*—in the aforementioned result of de Simone's also offered a sound, albeit incomplete, technique for establishing the validity of equations modulo bisimulation equivalence over de Simone languages. This work was the precursor of that on contexts as action transducers developed in, e.g., [54,84]. I have the feeling that there is still life in the search for bisimulation-like proof techniques that apply to more generous formats of SOS transition rules for establishing validity of equations using "operational rules as transitions", and this leads me to formulate the following

Problem 13 *Devise variations on FH-bisimulation that apply to formats of operational rules like the tyft/tyxt format [42], and formats allowing for the use of predicates [85].*

In order to support compositional reasoning techniques, and indeed to be considered as a reasonable notion of equality, behavioural relations over process algebras ought to be preserved by the operators in the language under consideration. Establishing such congruence results for different languages and behavioural relations has been a major enterprise in process algebra research. The commonalities amongst many congruence results for bisimulation equivalence was highlighted by the following key result

Result 9 (Groote and Vaandrager [42]) *Bisimulation equivalence is preserved by operators whose operational semantics is given by rules in the tyft/tyxt format. Moreover, the largest congruence contained in completed trace equivalence with respect to that format is 2-nested simulation equivalence.*

Together with [23], this paper has generated a veritable industry of results on the meta-theory of SOS and process algebras. (See [10] for a mention of some of these achievements and pointers to the original literature.) The proof techniques used in these results were extremely ingenious, and have paved the way to many similar developments. Again, the role played by the modal characterizations of behavioural equivalences in the proof of the characterizations of the largest congruences is remarkable.

5 Expressiveness Results

One of the classic topics in the theory of computation that is taught in most Computer Science curricula is the Chomsky hierarchy of languages, and the connection between classes of languages and the simplest machines that recognize them. These results are prime examples of *expressiveness results*, and have their counterparts in process algebra. Indeed, the study of the expressiveness of process algebras has a rather long history, and its continuing role in the development of this field of research is witnessed, for instance, by a workshop that is entirely devoted to expressiveness in concurrency, and whose tenth edition took place in September 2003.

Naturally enough, all full blown process algebras are Turing complete, and results to this effect have been amongst the earliest expressiveness theorems in the field. However, as argued eloquently in, e.g., [83], there are other important, and perhaps more interesting, measures of the expressiveness of fragments of process algebras. One of them we have already met in Result 8, viz. the characterization of the collection of operators that can be denoted in a given language modulo bisimulation equivalence. Another measure of the expressiveness of a language, and the one I would like to focus on here, is the study of the collection of processes that can be described using it. Early results in this area that still stand out for the very ingenious proofs needed to establish them are:

Result 10 (Bergstra and Klop [18]) *Bergstra and Klop's theorems to the effect that, modulo strong bisimulation equivalence, there is*

1. *a process, viz. a stack or a counter over a finite data type, that is recursively definable over BPA but not over the regular fragment of CCS,*

2. *a process, viz. a bag over a finite data type with cardinality at least two, that is finitely definable over PA but not over BPA, and*

3. *a process over a binary action alphabet that is finitely definable over ACP but not over PA.*

Further undefinability results of this type may be found, for example, in [15,16,83]. A general Chomsky-like hierarchy of process languages has been first proposed by Moller in [64], and further refined by Mayr in [56].

Problem 14 *Establish many more expressiveness results that offer insight on the power of different process description languages, and of the features they are based on.*

6 Connections with Automata and Formal Language Theory

The behaviour of processes can be described by labelled transition systems, which, in some form or the other, are also one of the objects of study in the classic theory of automata and formal languages. Moreover, the usefulness of algebraic techniques has long been recognized in automata theory, a field that arguably uses much more sophisticated notions and results from algebra than our own. (See, e.g., the monograph [81] for a survey of topics in algebraic automata theory, and a taste of the algebraic results used in this line of research.) It is therefore not overly surprising that there are connections between these fields of theoretical computer science. To highlight the connections, and the differences, between automata theory and process algebra, I would like to close this note by mentioning two results pertaining to decidability of behavioural equivalences over classes of infinite state processes and to axiomatic issues related to the theory of languages.

A classic result in automata theory is the fact that language equivalence for context-free languages is undecidable (see, e.g., [48] for a textbook presentation). That bisimulation equivalence for context-free processes enjoys different decidability properties was first highlighted by

Result 11 (Baeten, Bergstra and Klop [17]) *Baeten, Bergstra and Klop's theorem to the effect that strong bisimulation equivalence is decidable for context-free processes without redundant nonterminals.*

This surprising result spurred a flurry of research activity studying the decidability properties of behavioural equivalences in the linear time-branching time spectrum over classes of infinite state processes, and mapping the territory between decidable and undecidable equivalence problems. (See the references [27,76] for excellent overviews of the wealth of results achieved in this line of study.)

Techniques from the field of process algebra have also been used with remarkable effect to improve upon, or simplify, extant results in automata and formal language theory. I limit myself to mentioning two examples of these applications here.

Hirshfeld, Jerrum and Moller have shown in [47] that strong bisimulation equivalence is decidable in polynomial time over normed BPA. Since strong bisimulation equivalence coincides with language equivalence over deterministic processes, this result dramatically improves upon the doubly exponential upper bound for the equivalence problem for deterministic context-free grammars established by Korenjak and Hopcroft in [51].

A mixture of techniques developed in concurrency and language theory have been employed by Stirling in [79], where he offered a simplification of

Sénizergues' remarkable proof from [73] of the decidability of the equivalence problem for deterministic pushdown automata. (Sénizergues was awarded the 2002 Gödel prize for this achievement.) In subsequent work presented in [80], Stirling established a primitive recursive upper bound for this problem.

Problem 15 *Is weak bisimulation equivalence decidable over BPA and BPP?*

Problem 16 *Is strong bisimulation equivalence decidable over the language PA? Hirshfeld and Jerrum have shown in [46] that the answer is positive for normed PA.*

Given the role that axiomatic results have played in this note, it is perhaps fitting for me to bring it to a close by mentioning

Result 12 (Tschantz [82]) *Tschantz's axiomatization of the theory of languages over concatenation and shuffle.*

Where is the theory of processes there, you may ask? Well, to prove this result Steven Tschantz (a pure mathematician at Vanderbilt University) essentially rediscovered the concept of pomset [69]—a model of concurrency based on partial orders whose algebraic aspects have been investigated by Gischer in [36]—, and his proof can be phrased in terms of what some of us would call ST-trace equivalence [40].

Techniques from classic formal language theory have been used in process theory—see, e.g., the Conway type arguments in [8,36] to name but two examples. I expect that more interaction between the two fields would lead to a useful synergy.

Problem 17 *Can process algebraic techniques be brought to bear on scheduling problems, and cost optimality problems? These are currently tackled purely using automata, and that's great, but in formal language theory regular expressions with multiplicities over semirings play a role, they allow one to define measures of non-determinism in automata etc. Can we contribute?*

The mention of this last result brings me back to the first research meeting I ever attended, viz. the workshop on Concurrency and Compositionality organized in 1988 in Königswinter by van Glabbeek, Goltz and Olderog. It is there that I heard Pratt ask the question that led to Result 12, and met, for the first time, many of the players that have shaped the field of process algebra. I hope that, by writing this note, I have not done a disservice to their work and to the field.

Acknowledgments

I thank all of my co-authors and colleagues who have taught me the little I know about this fascinating field of research. Jos Baeten, Wan Fokkink and Jiří Srba offered incisive comments on previous drafts of this paper. *The opinions expressed in this note, and any infelicity herein, are solely my responsibility.*

References

1. S. Abramsky, Observation equivalence as a testing equivalence, *Theoretical Comput. Sci.*, 53 (1987), 225–241.
2. S. Abramsky, A domain equation for bisimulation, *Information and Computation*, 92 (1991), 161–218.
3. L. Aceto, On "Axiomatising Finite Concurrent Processes", *SIAM J. Comput.*, 23 (1994), 852–863.
4. L. Aceto, B. Bloom, and F. Vaandrager, Turning SOS rules into equations, *Information and Computation*, 111 (1994), 1–52.
5. L. Aceto, Z. Ésik, and A. Ingólfsdóttir, On the two-variable fragment of the equational theory of the max-sum algebra of the natural numbers, in *Proceedings of the 17th International Symposium on Theoretical Aspects of Computer Science*, STACS 2000 (Lille), H. Reichel and S. Tison, eds., vol. 1770 of Lecture Notes in Computer Science, Springer-Verlag, Feb. 2000, pp. 267–278.
6. L. Aceto, Z. Ésik, and A. Ingólfsdóttir, The max-plus algebra of the natural numbers has no finite equational basis, *Theoretical Comput. Sci.*, 293 (2003), 169–188.
7. L. Aceto and W. Fokkink, An equational axiomatization for multi-exit iteration, *Information and Computation*, 137 (1997), 121–158.
8. L. Aceto, W. Fokkink, and A. Ingólfsdóttir, A menagerie of non-finitely based process semantics over BPA*—from ready simulation to completed traces, *Mathematical Structures in Computer Science*, 8 (1998), 193–230.
9. L. Aceto, W. Fokkink, R. van Glabbeek, and A. Ingólfsdóttir, Nested semantics over finite trees are equationally hard, *Technical Report RS–03–27*, BRICS, Department of Computer Science, Aalborg University, August 2003.
10. L. Aceto, W. Fokkink, and C. Verhoef, Structural operational semantics, in *Handbook of Process Algebra*, North-Holland, 2001, pp. 197–292.
11. L. Aceto and M. Hennessy, Termination, deadlock and divergence, *J. Assoc. Comput. Mach.*, 39 (1992), 147–187.
12. L. Aceto and A. Jeffrey, A complete axiomatization of timed bisimulation for a class of timed regular behaviours, *Theoretical Comput. Sci.*, 152 (1995), 251–268.
13. P. Auster, *The New York Trilogy—The Locked Room*, Faber and Faber, 1988.

14. D. Austry and G. Boudol, Algèbre de processus et synchronisations, *Theoretical Comput. Sci.*, 30 (1984), 91–131.

15. J. Baeten and J. Bergstra, Global renaming operators in concrete process algebra, *Information and Computation*, 78 (1988), 205–245.

16. J.C. Baeten, J. Bergstra, and J.W. Klop, On the consistency of Koomen's fair abstraction rule, *Theoretical Comput. Sci.*, 51 (1987), 129–176.

17. J.C. Baeten, J. Bergstra, and J.W. Klop, Decidability of bisimulation equivalence for processes generating context-free languages, *J. Assoc. Comput. Mach.*, 40 (1993), 653–682.

18. J. Bergstra and J.W. Klop, The algebra of recursively defined processes and the algebra of regular processes, in *Proceedings 11th ICALP, Antwerpen*, J. Paredaens, ed., vol. 172 of Lecture Notes in Computer Science, Springer-Verlag, 1984, 82–95.

19. J. Bergstra and J.W. Klop, Process algebra for synchronous communication, *Information and Computation*, 60 (1984), 109–137.

20. J. Bergstra and J.W. Klop, A complete inference system for regular processes with silent moves, in *Proceedings Logic Colloquium 1986*, F. Drake and J. Truss, eds., Hull, 1988, North-Holland, 21–81.

21. J. Bergstra, A. Ponse, and S. Smolka, eds., *Handbook of Process Algebra*, North-Holland, 2001.

22. S. Blom, W. Fokkink, and S. Nain, On the axiomatizability of ready traces, ready simulation and failure traces, in *Proceedings 30th Colloquium on Automata, Languages and Programming—ICALP'03*, Eindhoven, Lecture Notes in Computer Science, Springer-Verlag, 2003. To appear.

23. B. Bloom, S. Istrail, and A. Meyer, Bisimulation can't be traced, *J. Assoc. Comput. Mach.*, 42 (1995), 232–268.

24. S. L. Bloom and Z. Ésik, *Iteration Theories: The Equational Logic of Iterative Processes*, EATCS Monographs on Theoretical Computer Science (W. Brauer, G. Rozenberg and A. Salomaa eds.), Springer-Verlag, 1993.

25. D.J.B. Bosscher, *Grammars Modulo Bisimulation*, PhD thesis, CWI, Amsterdam, 1997.

26. G. Boudol and I. Castellani, Concurrency and atomicity, *Theoretical Comput. Sci.*, 59 (1988), 25–84.

27. O. Burkart, D. Caucal, F. Moller, and B. Steffen, Verification on infinite structures, in *Handbook of Process Algebra*, North-Holland, Amsterdam, 2001, 545–623.

28. J.H. Conway, *Regular Algebra and Finite Machines*, Mathematics Series (R. Brown and J. De Wet eds.), Chapman and Hall, London, United Kingdom, 1971.

29. F. Corradini, R. De Nicola, and A. Labella, A finite axiomatization of nondeterministic regular expressions, *Theor. Inform. Appl.*, 33 (1999), 447–465.

30. F. Corradini, R. De Nicola, and A. Labella, An equational axiomatization of bisimulation over regular expressions, *J. Logic Comput.*, 12 (2002), 301–320. Fixed points in computer science, 2000 (Paris).

31. P. Darondeau and P. Degano, *Causal trees*, Publication Interne No. 442, IRISA, Rennes Cedex, France, 1988. An extended abstract appeared in: Proceedings ICALP 89, Stresa (G. Ausiello, M. Dezani-Ciancaglini & S. Ronchi Della Rocca), LNCS 372, Springer-Verlag, pp. 234–248.

32. R. De Nicola and A. Labella, Nondeterministic regular expressions as solutions of equational systems. *Proceedings of FICS* 2000 (Paris), 2000.

33. R. De Nicola and F.W. Vaandrager, Three logics for branching bisimulation, *J. Assoc. Comput. Mach.*, 32 (1995), 458–487.

34. W. Fokkink, On the completeness of the equations for the Kleene star in bisimulation, in *Algebraic Methodology and Software Technology: 5th International Conference*, AMAST '96, Munich, Germany, M. Wirsing and M. Nivat, eds., vol. 1101 of Lecture Notes in Computer Science, Springer-Verlag, July 1996, 180–194.

35. W. Fokkink and H. Zantema, Basic process algebra with iteration: Completeness of its equational axioms, *Computer Journal*, 37 (1994), 259–267.

36. J.L. Gischer, The equational theory of pomsets, *Theoretical Comput. Sci.*, 61 (1988), 199–224.

37. R. van Glabbeek, A complete axiomatization for branching bisimulation congruence of finite-state behaviours, in *Mathematical Foundations of Computer Science* 1993, Gdansk, Poland, A. Borzyszkowski and S. Sokołowski, eds., vol. 711 of Lecture Notes in Computer Science, Springer-Verlag, 1993, 473–484.

38. R. van Glabbeek, On the expressiveness of ACP, in *Proceedings 1st Workshop on the Algebra of Communicating Processes*, Utrecht, The Netherlands, A. Ponse, C. Verhoef, and B. van Vlijmen, eds., Workshops in Computing, Springer-Verlag, 1995, 188–217.

39. R. van Glabbeek, The linear time–branching time spectrum. I. The semantics of concrete, sequential processes, in *Handbook of Process Algebra*, North-Holland, Amsterdam, 2001, 3–99.

40. R. van Glabbeek and F. Vaandrager, Petri net models for algebraic theories of concurrency, in *Proceedings PARLE conference*, Eindhoven, Vol. II (Parallel Languages), J. d. Bakker, A. Nijman, and P. Treleaven, eds., vol. 259 of Lecture Notes in Computer Science, Springer-Verlag, 1987, 224–242.

332

41. J.F. Groote, Transition system specifications with negative premises, *Theoretical Comput. Sci.*, 118 (1993), 263–299.
42. J.F. Groote and F.W. Vaandrager, Structured operational semantics and bisimulation as a congruence, *Information and Computation*, 100 (1992), 202–260.
43. G.H. Hardy, *A Mathematician's Apology*, Canto, Cambridge University Press, Cambridge, 1992. With a foreword by C.P. Snow, Reprint of the 1967 edition.
44. M. Hennessy, Axiomatising finite concurrent processes, *SIAM J. Comput.*, 17 (1988), 997–1017.
45. M. Hennessy and R. Milner, Algebraic laws for nondeterminism and concurrency, *J. Assoc. Comput. Mach.*, 32 (1985), 137–161.
46. Y. Hirshfeld and M. Jerrum, Bisimulation equivalence is decidable for normed process algebra (extended abstract), in *Automata, Languages and Programming* (Prague, 1999), vol. 1644 of Lecture Notes in Comput. Sci., Springer, Berlin, 1999, 412–421.
47. Y. Hirshfeld, M. Jerrum, and F. Moller, A polynomial algorithm for deciding bisimilarity of normed context-free processes, *Theoretical Comput. Sci.*, 158 (1996), 143–159.
48. J. Hopcroft and J. Ullman, *Introduction to Automata Theory, Languages and Computation*, Addison-Wesley, 1979.
49. A. Ingólfsdóttir, J.C. Godskesen, and M. Zeeberg, *Fra Hennessy-Milner logik til CCS-processer*, Master's thesis, Department of Computer Science, Aalborg University, 1987. In Danish.
50. A. Jeffrey, *CSP is completely expressive*, Computer Science Technical Report 92:02, School of Cognitive and Computing Sciences, University of Sussex, 1992.
51. A.J. Korenjak and J.E. Hopcroft, Simple deterministic languages, in *Conference Record of Seventh Annual Symposium on Switching and Automata Theory*, Berkeley, California, 26–28 October 1966, IEEE, 1966, 36–46.
52. H. Korver, Computing distinguishing formulas for branching bisimulation, in *Proceedings of the Third Workshop on Computer Aided Verification*, Aalborg, Denmark, July 1991, K. Larsen and A. Skou, eds., vol. 575 of Lecture Notes in Computer Science, Springer-Verlag, 1992, 13–23.
53. K.G. Larsen and A. Skou, Bisimulation through probabilistic testing, *Information and Computation*, 94 (1991), 1–28.
54. K.G. Larsen and L. Xinxin, Compositionality through an operational semantics of contexts, *Journal of Logic and Computation*, 1 (1991), 761–795.
55. T. Margaria and B. Steffen, Distinguishing formulas for free, in *Proc.*

EDAC-EUROASIC'93: IEEE European Design Automation Conference, Paris (France), IEEE Computer Society Press, February 1993.

56. R. Mayr, Process rewrite systems, *Information and Computation*, 156 (2000), 264–286.

57. R. McKenzie, Tarski's finite basis problem is undecidable, *Internat. J. Algebra Comput.*, 6 (1996), 49–104.

58. R. Milner, A modal characterisation of observable machine behaviour, in *CAAP '81: Trees in Algebra and Programming, 6th Colloquium*, E. Astesiano and C. Böhm, eds., vol. 112 of Lecture Notes in Computer Science, Springer-Verlag, 1981, 25–34.

59. R. Milner, A complete inference system for a class of regular behaviours, *J. Comput. System Sci.*, 28 (1984), 439–466.

60. R. Milner, *Communication and Concurrency*, Prentice-Hall International, Englewood Cliffs, 1989.

61. R. Milner, A complete axiomatisation for observational congruence of finite-state behaviors, *Information and Computation*, 81 (1989), 227–247.

62. F. Moller, The importance of the left merge operator in process algebras, in *Proceedings 17th ICALP*, Warwick, M. Paterson, ed., vol. 443 of Lecture Notes in Computer Science, Springer-Verlag, July 1990, 752–764.

63. F. Moller, The nonexistence of finite axiomatisations for CCS congruences, in *Proceedings 5th Annual Symposium on Logic in Computer Science*, Philadelphia, USA, IEEE Computer Society Press, 1990, 142–153.

64. F. Moller, Infinite results, in *Proceedings of CONCUR '96, Concurrency Theory, 7th International Conference*, Pisa, Italy, August 26–29, 1996, U. Montanari and V. Sassone, eds., vol. 1119 of Lecture Notes in Computer Science, Springer-Verlag, 1996, 195–216.

65. C.H. Papadimitriou, Database metatheory: Asking the big queries, in *Proceedings of the Fourteenth ACM SIGACT-SIGMOD-SIGART Symposium on Principles of Database Systems*, May 22-25, 1995, San Jose, California, ACM Press, 1995, 1–10.

66. D. Park, Concurrency and automata on infinite sequences, in *5th GI Conference*, Karlsruhe, Germany, P. Deussen, ed., vol. 104 of Lecture Notes in Computer Science, Springer-Verlag, 1981, 167–183.

67. J. Parrow, The expressive power of parallelism, *Future Generation Computer Systems*, 6 (1990), 271–285.

68. G. Plotkin, *A structural approach to operational semantics*, Report DAIMI FN-19, Computer Science Department, Aarhus University, 1981.

69. V. Pratt, Modeling concurrency with partial orders, *International Journal of Parallel Programming*, 15 (1986), 33–71.

70. A.M. Rabinovich, A complete axiomatisation for trace congruence of fi-

nite state behaviors, in *Mathematical Foundations of Programming Semantics, 9th International Conference*, New Orleans, LA, USA, April 7-10, 1993, Proceedings, S.D. Brookes, M.G. Main, A. Melton, M.W. Mislove, and D.A. Schmidt, eds., vol. 802 of Lecture Notes in Computer Science, Springer-Verlag, 1994, 530–543.

71. G.-C. Rota, Ten rules for the survival of a mathematics department, in *Indiscrete Thoughts*, F. Palombi, ed., Birkhäuser Boston, Inc., Boston, MA, 1996. With forewords by Reuben Hersh and Robert Sokolowski. A version of this article is available from http://www.rota.org/hotair/rules.html.

72. A. Salomaa, Two complete axiom systems for the algebra of regular events, *J. Assoc. Comput. Mach.*, 13 (1966), 158–169.

73. G. Sénizergues, $L(A) = L(B)$? decidability results from complete formal systems, *Theoretical Comput. Sci.*, 251 (2001), 1–166.

74. P. Sewell, Nonaxiomatisability of equivalences over finite state processes, *Annals of Pure and Applied Logic*, 90 (1997), 163–191.

75. R. d. Simone, Higher-level synchronising devices in MEIJE–SCCS, *Theoretical Comput. Sci.*, 37 (1985), pp. 245–267.

76. J. Srba, *Roadmap of infinite results*, December 2002. Available from http://www.brics.dk/~srba/roadmap/roadmap.pdf.

77. B. Steffen and A. Ingólfsdóttir, Characteristic formulae for processes with divergence, *Information and Computation*, 110 (1994), 149–163.

78. C. Stirling, Modal logics for communicating systems, *Theoretical Comput. Sci.*, 49 (1987), 311–347.

79. C. Stirling, Decidability of DPDA equivalence, *Theoretical Comput. Sci.*, 255 (2001), 1–31.

80. C. Stirling, Deciding DPDA equivalence is primitive recursive, in *Proceedings of the 29th International Colloquium on Automata, Languages and Programming*, ICALP 2002, Malaga, Spain, July 8-13, 2002, P. Widmayer, F. T. Ruiz, R. Morales, M. Hennessy, S. Eidenbenz, and R. Conejo, eds., vol. 2380 of Lecture Notes in Computer Science, Springer-Verlag, 2002, 821–832.

81. H. Straubing, *Finite Automata, Formal Logic, and Circuit Complexity*, vol. 11 of Progress in Theoretical Computer Science, Birkäuser, 1994.

82. S.T. Tschantz, Languages under concatenation and shuffling, *Mathematical Structures in Computer Science*, 4 (1994), 505–511.

83. F. Vaandrager,Expressiveness results for process algebras, in *Proceedings REX Workshop on Semantics: Foundations and Applications*, Beekbergen, The Netherlands, June 1992, J. de Bakker, W. d. Roever, and G. Rozenberg, eds., vol. 666 of Lecture Notes in Computer Science,

Springer-Verlag, 1993, 609–638.

84. F. Vaandrager and N. Lynch, Action transducers and timed automata, in *Proceedings CONCUR* 92, Stony Brook, NY, USA, W.R. Cleaveland, ed., vol. 630 of Lecture Notes in Computer Science, Springer-Verlag, 1992, 436–455.

85. C. Verhoef, A congruence theorem for structured operational semantics with predicates and negative premises, *Nordic Journal of Computing*, 2 (1995), 274–302.

86. D. Walker, Bisimulation and divergence, *Information and Computation*, 85 (1990), 202–241.

ROADMAP OF INFINITE RESULTS

JIŘÍ SRBA

Basic Research in Computer Science - BRICS
Centre of the Danish National Research Foundation
Department of Computer Science, Aalborg University
Fr. Bajersvej 7B, 9220 Aalborg East, Denmark
E-mail: `srba@brics.dk`

This paper provides a comprehensive summary of equivalence checking results for infinite-state systems. References to the relevant papers will be updated continuously according to the development in the area. The most recent version of this document is available from the web-page `http://www.brics.dk/~srba/roadmap`.

1 Introduction

The growing interest in verification of infinite-state systems during the last decade led to the situation where many new results and novel approaches were invented. The first attempt to map the fundamental techniques and results for the equivalence checking problems was done by Moller in his overview paper "Infinite Results" [1], followed by the paper "More Infinite Results" [2] by Burkart and Esparza focusing on the model checking problems.

A large survey of equivalence and model checking techniques "Verification on Infinite Structures" appeared in the handbook of process algebra [3] due to Burkart, Caucal, Moller and Steffen. Yet another overview paper "Equivalence-Checking with Infinite-State Systems: Techniques and Results" [4] by Kučera and Jančar contains some recent techniques for simulation and bisimulation checking.

Although these comprehensive survey papers provide a valuable overview of proof techniques, the state-of-the-art advances so rapidly that many papers contain outdated information even before they are published.

The main objective of the presented work is to offer a complete overview of known decidability and complexity results for equivalence checking in the most studied classes of infinite-state systems. The most recent version of this document is available from the web-page `http://www.brics.dk/~srba/roadmap` and we

would like to encourage you

to send notifications about improvements of the results presented in this paper to the author. Any such improvement will be promptly incorporated into this document and the updated version will appear at the URL mentioned above.

We hope that the overview we provide will stimulate further research on fundamental equivalence checking problems for infinite-state systems and it will eventually lead towards a definitive closing of all the gaps in the mosaic of infinite results.

2 Basic Definitions

In this section we introduce the classes of infinite-state processes by means of process rewrite systems (PRS). Process rewrite systems are an elegant and universal approach defined by Mayr [5] and they contain many of the formalisms studied in the context of equivalence checking.

Let $Const$ be a set of *process constants*. The classes of process expressions called 1 (process constants plus the empty process), $\mathcal{P}$ (parallel process expressions), $\mathcal{S}$ (sequential process expressions), and $\mathcal{G}$ (general process expressions) are defined by the following abstract syntax:

$$1: \quad E ::= \epsilon \mid X$$

$$\mathcal{P}: \quad E ::= \epsilon \mid X \mid E\|E$$

$$\mathcal{S}: \quad E ::= \epsilon \mid X \mid E.E$$

$$\mathcal{G}: \quad E ::= \epsilon \mid X \mid E\|E \mid E.E$$

where 'ϵ' is the *empty process*, X ranges over $Const$, the operator '.' stands for a sequential composition and '$\|$' stands for a parallel composition. Obviously, $1 \subset \mathcal{S}$, $1 \subset \mathcal{P}$, $\mathcal{S} \subset \mathcal{G}$ and $\mathcal{P} \subset \mathcal{G}$. The classes $\mathcal{S}$ and $\mathcal{P}$ are incomparable and $\mathcal{S} \cap \mathcal{P} = 1$.

We do not distinguish between process expressions related by a *structural congruence*, which is the smallest congruence over process expressions such that the following laws hold:

- '.' is associative,

- '$\|$' is associative and commutative, and

- 'ϵ' is a unit for '.' and '$\|$'.

Let $\alpha, \beta \in \{1, \mathcal{S}, \mathcal{P}, \mathcal{G}\}$ such that $\alpha \subseteq \beta$ and let Act be a set of *actions*. An (α, β)-PRS [5] is a finite set

$$\Delta \subseteq (\alpha \smallsetminus \{\epsilon\}) \times Act \times \beta$$

of *rewrite rules*, written $E \xrightarrow{a} F$ for $(E, a, F) \in \Delta$.

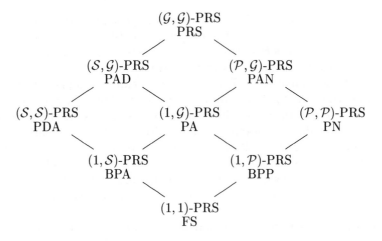

Figure 1. Hierarchy of process rewrite systems

An (α, β)-PRS determines a labelled transition system where *states* are process expressions from the class β (modulo the structural congruence), $\mathcal{A}ct$ is the set of *labels*, and the *transition relation* is the least relation satisfying the following SOS rules (recall that '$\|$' is commutative):

$$\frac{(E \xrightarrow{a} E') \in \Delta}{E \xrightarrow{a} E'} \qquad \frac{E \xrightarrow{a} E'}{E.F \xrightarrow{a} E'.F} \qquad \frac{E \xrightarrow{a} E'}{E\|F \xrightarrow{a} E'\|F}$$

Many classes of infinite-state systems studied so far — e.g., basic process algebra (BPA), basic parallel processes (BPP), pushdown automata (PDA), Petri nets (PN) and process algebra (PA) — are contained in the hierarchy of process rewrite systems presented in Figure 1. This hierarchy is strict w.r.t. strong bisimilarity and we refer the reader to [5] for further discussions. It is worth mentioning that even the class $(\mathcal{G}, \mathcal{G})$-PRS is not Turing powerful since e.g., the reachability problem remains decidable [5].

An (α, β)-*process* is a pair (P, Δ) where Δ is an (α, β)-PRS and $P \in \beta$ is a process expression.

An (α, β)-process (P, Δ) is *normed* iff for all $E \in \beta$ such that $P \longrightarrow^* E$ it is the case that $E \longrightarrow^* \epsilon$. In other words, from every reachable state in (P, Δ) there is a computation ending in the empty process 'ϵ'.

In some papers, the definition of normedness requires only the fact that from every reachable state there is a terminating computation, not necessarily ending in the empty process. However, e.g., for BPA, in order to achieve a reasonable notion of normedness, it is also assumed that every process constant used in the system can perform a transition, i.e., it has at least one rewrite rule associated to it. This alternative definition implies the notion of normedness introduced above. Moreover, the definition we gave becomes more interesting even for the models like PDA, PN, PAD, PAN and PRS where our notion of normedness guarantees deadlock freedom (here the empty process is not understood as a deadlock). This means that e.g. in the case of PDA the stack can always be emptied, and in the case of PN all tokens in places can be removed. Considering simply the possibility of termination without reaching the empty process usually does not restrict the power of the models sufficiently.

We will now introduce the notion of strong and weak bisimilarity [6,7]. A binary relation R over process expressions is a *strong bisimulation* iff whenever $(E, F) \in R$ then for each $a \in \mathcal{A}ct$:

- if $E \xrightarrow{a} E'$, then $F \xrightarrow{a} F'$ for some F' such that $(E', F') \in R$,

- if $F \xrightarrow{a} F'$, then $E \xrightarrow{a} E'$ for some E' such that $(E', F') \in R$.

Processes (P_1, Δ) and (P_2, Δ) are *strongly bisimilar*, written $(P_1, \Delta) \sim (P_2, \Delta)$ iff there is a strong bisimulation R such that $(P_1, P_2) \in R$. Given two processes (P_1, Δ_1) and (P_2, Δ_2) with disjoint sets of process constants contained in Δ_1 and Δ_2, we write $(P_1, \Delta_1) \sim (P_2, \Delta_2)$ iff $(P_1, \Delta_1 \cup \Delta_2) \sim (P_2, \Delta_1 \cup \Delta_2)$.

Assume that $\mathcal{A}ct$ contains a distinguished silent action τ. A *weak transition relation* is defined as follows: $\xRightarrow{a} \overset{\text{def}}{=} (\xrightarrow{\tau})^* \circ \xrightarrow{a} \circ (\xrightarrow{\tau})^*$ if $a \in \mathcal{A}ct \smallsetminus \{\tau\}$, and $\xRightarrow{a} \overset{\text{def}}{=} (\xrightarrow{\tau})^*$ if $a = \tau$.

A binary relation R over process expressions is a *weak bisimulation* iff whenever $(E, F) \in R$ then for each $a \in \mathcal{A}ct$:

- if $E \xrightarrow{a} E'$, then $F \xRightarrow{a} F'$ for some F' such that $(E', F') \in R$,

- if $F \xrightarrow{a} F'$, then $E \xRightarrow{a} E'$ for some E' such that $(E', F') \in R$.

Processes (P_1, Δ) and (P_2, Δ) are *weakly bisimilar*, written $(P_1, \Delta) \approx (P_2, \Delta)$ iff there is a weak bisimulation R such that $(P_1, P_2) \in R$. Given two processes (P_1, Δ_1) and (P_2, Δ_2) with disjoint sets of process constants contained in Δ_1 and Δ_2, we write $(P_1, \Delta_1) \approx (P_2, \Delta_2)$ iff $(P_1, \Delta_1 \cup \Delta_2) \approx (P_2, \Delta_1 \cup \Delta_2)$.

3 Studied Problems

In this section we define the basic decidability problems studied in the area of equivalence checking of infinite-state systems.

Strong/Weak Bisimilarity ($\sim$/$\approx$)
The problem is to decide whether a pair of processes from a given class of systems is strongly/weakly bisimilar. Bisimilarity was originally introduced by Park [7] and Milner [6] and it is perhaps the most studied behavioural equivalence because of many pleasant properties it enjoys.

Strong/Weak Bisimilarity with Finite-State Systems ($\sim$ FS/$\approx$ FS)
The problem is to decide whether a process from a given class of systems is strongly/weakly bisimilar to a given finite-state process. Questions of this nature are interesting because they enable to relate a complex behaviour of infinite-state systems with their finite-state specifications. Moreover, recent development showed that many of these problems become computationally feasible and in some instances they are solvable even in polynomial time.

Strong/Weak Regularity ($\sim$ reg/$\approx$ reg)
The problem is to decide whether for a process from a given class of systems there exists a finite-state process such that the two processes are strongly/weakly bisimilar. The interest in regularity checking is based on the fact that for bisimilarity checking of finite-state processes we already have efficient polynomial time algorithms [8,9]. A positive answer to the regularity question for a given pair E and F of infinite-state processes, together with the possibility of algorithmic construction of bisimilar finite-state processes provides an immediate answer to bisimilarity checking between E and F.

Remark 1 *In the hierarchy of process rewrite systems there is a very close and obvious relationship between strong regularity checking of normed processes and the boundedness problem: a normed process is strongly regular if and only if it has only finitely many (on the syntactical level) reachable states. This property, however, does not hold for weak regularity.*

4 Summary of Known Results

This section gives a summary of currently known decidability and complexity results for the systems in the PRS-hierarchy. We consider both unnormed and normed systems and for each decision problem we provide the best complexity bounds achieved so far. Each box in the tables below contains the information whether the considered problem is decidable or not, and in the positive case we present the best known upper bound in the upper part of the box and lower bound in the lower part.

4.1 BPA (Basic Process Algebra)

	BPA	normed BPA
~	∈ 2-EXPTIME [10] PSPACE-hard [11]	∈ P [12] P-hard [13]
≈	? EXPTIME-hard [14]	? EXPTIME-hard [14]
~ FS	∈ P [15] P-hard [13]	∈ P [12] P-hard [13]
≈ FS	∈ P [15] P-hard [13]	∈ P [15] P-hard [13]
~ reg	∈ 2-EXPTIME [16,10] PSPACE-hard [11]	∈ NL [17] NL-hard [11]
≈ reg	? EXPTIME-hard [14]	? NP-hard [18,19]

4.2 BPP (Basic Parallel Processes)

	BPP	normed BPP
~	∈ PSPACE [20] PSPACE-hard [21]	∈ P [22] P-hard [13]
≈	?, R. 2 PSPACE-hard [18]	?, R. 2 PSPACE-hard [18]
~ FS	∈ PSPACE [23] P-hard [13]	∈ P [22] P-hard [13]
≈ FS	∈ PSPACE [23] P-hard [13]	∈ P [15] P-hard [13]
~ reg	decidable [24] PSPACE-hard [21]	∈ NL [17] NL-hard [21]
≈ reg	? PSPACE-hard [18]	? PSPACE-hard [18]

Remark 2 *At INFINITY'02 Jančar conjectured [25] that the method later published in [20] might be used to show decidability of weak bisimilarity for BPP.*

4.3   PDA (Pushdown Automata)

	PDA	normed PDA
~	decidable [26], R. 3 EXPTIME-hard [27]	decidable [28] EXPTIME-hard [27]
≈	undecidable [29]	undecidable [29]
~ FS	∈ PSPACE [27] PSPACE-hard [30]	∈ PSPACE [27] PSPACE-hard [30], R. 4
≈ FS	∈ PSPACE [27] PSPACE-hard [30]	∈ PSPACE [27] PSPACE-hard [30], R. 5
~ reg	? EXPTIME-hard [27,11], R. 6	∈ P [31], R. 7 NL-hard [11]
≈ reg	? EXPTIME-hard [27,11], R. 6	? EXPTIME-hard [27,11], R. 5,6

Remark 3 *Additional useful references concerning deterministic PDA are [32], [33] and [34].*

Remark 4 *The reduction from [30] (Theorem 8) uses unnormed processes but can be modified to work also for the normed case. An important observation is that the stack size of the PDA from Theorem 8 is bounded by the number of variables in the instance of quantified boolean formula from which the reduction is done.*

Remark 5 *Lemma 3 in [29] gives a polynomial time reduction from weak bisimilarity between two pushdown processes (and between a pushdown process and a finite-state process) to the normed instance of the problem. The reduction moreover preserves the property of being weakly regular.*

Remark 6 *In [27] a polynomial time reduction from the acceptance problem of alternating linear-bounded automata to strong bisimilarity of normed PDA is provided. Even though there are infinitely many reachable configurations in the constructed PDAs, one can observe that only a fixed part from the top of the stack is relevant for the construction. Hence it is possible to ensure that the PDAs are strongly regular and Theorem 2 from [11] can be applied.*

Remark 7 *Strong regularity of normed PDA is equivalent to the boundedness problem (Remark 1). Boundedness (even for unnormed PDA) is decidable in polynomial time using the fact that the set of all reachable configurations of a pushdown process is a regular language L [35] and a finite automaton A recognizing L can be constructed in polynomial time (see e.g. [31]). The check whether A generates a finite language can also be done in polynomial time.*

4.4 PA (Process Algebra)

	PA	normed PA
~	? PSPACE-hard [21]	2-NEXPTIME [36] P-hard [13]
≈	undecidable [37]	? EXPTIME-hard [14]
~ FS	decidable [38] P-hard [13]	2-NEXPTIME [36] P-hard [13]
≈ FS	decidable [23] P-hard [13]	decidable [23] P-hard [13]
~ reg	? PSPACE-hard [21]	∈ NL [39] NL-hard [21]
≈ reg	? EXPTIME-hard [14]	? PSPACE-hard [18]

4.5 PN (Petri Nets)

	PN	normed PN
~	undecidable [40]	undecidable [40], R. 8
≈	undecidable [40]	undecidable [40], R. 8
~ FS	decidable [41] EXPSPACE-hard [42], R. 9	decidable [41] P-hard [13]
≈ FS	undecidable [24]	? EXPSPACE-hard [42], R. 9
~ reg	decidable [24] EXPSPACE-hard [42], R. 10	∈ EXPSPACE [43], R. 1 EXPSPACE-hard [42], R. 10
≈ reg	undecidable [24]	? EXPSPACE-hard [42], R. 10

Remark 8 *The technique for proving undecidability of strong bisimilarity for Petri nets from [40] can be slightly modified to ensure that the constructed nets are normed. Essentially, it is enough to add extra transitions which enable to remove all tokens from places. Moreover, whenever such an extra transition is fired the two nets are forced to become bisimilar.*

Remark 9 *The problem whether a given place p of a PN can ever become marked is EXPSPACE-hard (follows from Lipton's construction [42], for a more accessible proof see e.g. [44]). We can now easily see that this problem is reducible in polynomial time to strong nonbisimilarity between PN and FS. All transitions in a given Petri net N are assigned the same label 'a' and we add one more place q (initially marked) and an extra transition labelled by 'a' which takes a token from the place q and returns it back. Moreover we add another transition labelled by 'b' which can be fired whenever there is a token in the place p. Let P be a finite-state process defined by $P \xrightarrow{a} P$. The following property is immediate: the place p can become marked iff N is not strongly bisimilar to P. This reduction works also for normed PN and weak bisimilarity: we take our modified net N and for each its place we add one extra transition labelled by 'τ' such that the transition takes a token from the place and removes it. To the finite-state process P we add the rewrite rule $P \xrightarrow{\tau} \epsilon$. The net N is now normed and moreover it is weakly bisimilar to P iff the place p can never become marked.*

Remark 10 *Regularity of normed PN is equivalent to the boundedness problem (Remark 1). Boundedness of PN is decidable in EXPSPACE, more precisely in space $2^{cn \log n}$ for some constant c [43]. Moreover, the boundedness problem of normed PN is EXPSPACE-hard because it can be easily seen to be polynomially equivalent to the boundedness problem of general (unnormed) PN and this problem is EXPSPACE-hard [42] (see also [44]).*

4.6 PAD

	PAD	normed PAD
~	? EXPTIME-hard [27]	? EXPTIME-hard [27]
≈	undecidable [29]	undecidable [29]
~ FS	decidable [38] PSPACE-hard [30]	decidable [38] PSPACE-hard [30], R. 4
≈ FS	decidable [23] PSPACE-hard [30]	decidable [23] PSPACE-hard [30], R. 5
~ reg	? EXPTIME-hard [27,11], R. 6	decidable [45], R. 1 NL-hard [11]
≈ reg	? EXPTIME-hard [27,11], R. 6	? EXPTIME-hard [27,11], R. 5,6

4.7 PAN

	PAN	normed PAN
~	undecidable [40]	undecidable [40], R. 8
≈	undecidable [40]	undecidable [40], R. 8
~ FS	? EXPSPACE-hard [42], R. 9	decidable [45], R. 1 P-hard [13]
≈ FS	undecidable [24]	? EXPSPACE-hard [42], R. 9
~ reg	? EXPSPACE-hard [42], R. 10	decidable [45], R. 1 EXPSPACE-hard [42], R. 10
≈ reg	undecidable [24]	? EXPSPACE-hard [42], R. 10

4.8 PRS (Process Rewrite Systems)

	PRS	normed PRS
~	undecidable [40]	undecidable [40], R. 8
≈	undecidable [40]	undecidable [40], R. 8
~ FS	? EXPSPACE-hard [42], R. 9	decidable [45], R. 1 PSPACE-hard [30], R. 4
≈ FS	undecidable [24]	? EXPSPACE-hard [42], R. 9
~ reg	? EXPSPACE-hard [42], R. 10	decidable [45], R. 1 EXPSPACE-hard [42], R. 10
≈ reg	undecidable [24]	? EXPSPACE-hard [42], R. 10

Acknowledgments

Work supported in part by the GACR, grant No. 201/03/1161.

I would like to thank Ivana Černá, Petr Jančar, Antonín Kučera, Mogens Nielsen and Paulo Borges Oliva for reading a draft of this paper. My special thanks go to Richard Mayr for his help, suggestions and numerous comments.

References

1. F. Moller. Infinite results. In *Proceedings of the 7th International Conference on Concurrency Theory (CONCUR'96)*, volume 1119 of *LNCS*, pages 195–216. Springer-Verlag, 1996.
2. O. Burkart and J. Esparza. More infinite results. *Bulletin of the European Association for Theoretical Computer Science*, 62:138–159, June 1997. Columns: Concurrency.
3. O. Burkart, D. Caucal, F. Moller, and B. Steffen. Verification on infinite structures. In J. Bergstra, A. Ponse, and S. Smolka, editors, *Handbook of Process Algebra*, chapter 9, pages 545–623. Elsevier Science, 2001.
4. A. Kučera and P. Jančar. Equivalence-checking with infinite-state systems: Techniques and results. In *Proceedings of the 29th Annual Conference on Current Trends in Theory and Practice of Informatics (SOFSEM'02)*, volume 2540 of *LNCS*, pages 41–73. Springer-Verlag, 2002.
5. R. Mayr. Process rewrite systems. *Information and Computation*, 156(1):264–286, 2000.
6. R. Milner. A calculus of communicating systems. *LNCS*, 92, 1980.
7. D.M.R. Park. Concurrency and automata on infinite sequences. In *Proceedings of the 5th GI Conference*, volume 104 of *LNCS*, pages 167–183. Springer-Verlag, 1981.
8. P.C. Kanellakis and S.A. Smolka. CCS expressions, finite state processes, and three problems of equivalence. *Information and Computation*, 86(1):43–68, 1990.
9. R. Paige and R. Tarjan. Three partition refinement algorithms. *SIAM Journal of Computing*, 16(6):973–989, 1987.
10. O. Burkart, D. Caucal, and B. Steffen. An elementary decision procedure for arbitrary context-free processes. In *Proceedings of the 20th International Symposium on Mathematical Foundations of Computer Science (MFCS'95)*, volume 969 of *LNCS*, pages 423–433. Springer-Verlag, 1995.
11. J. Srba. Strong bisimilarity and regularity of basic process algebra is PSPACE-hard. In *Proceedings of the 29th International Colloquium on Automata, Languages and Programming (ICALP'02)*, volume 2380 of *LNCS*, pages 716–727. Springer-Verlag, 2002.
12. Y. Hirshfeld, M. Jerrum, and F. Moller. A polynomial algorithm for deciding bisimilarity of normed context-free processes. *Theoretical Computer Science*, 158(1–2):143–159, 1996.
13. J. Balcazar, J. Gabarro, and M. Santha. Deciding bisimilarity is P-

complete. *Formal Aspects of Computing*, 4(6A):638–648, 1992.

14. R. Mayr. Weak bisimilarity and regularity of BPA is EXPTIME-hard. In *Proccedings of the 10th International Workshop on Expressiveness in Concurrency (EXPRESS'03)*, pages 160–143, 2003. To appear in ENTCS.

15. A. Kučera and R. Mayr. Weak bisimilarity between finite-state systems and BPA or normed BPP is decidable in polynomial time. *Theoretical Computer Science*, 270:667–700, 2002.

16. O. Burkart, D. Caucal, and B. Steffen. Bisimulation collapse and the process taxonomy. In *Proceedings of the 7th International Conference on Concurrency Theory (CONCUR'96)*, volume 1119 of *LNCS*, pages 247–262. Springer-Verlag, 1996.

17. A. Kučera. Regularity is decidable for normed BPA and normed BPP processes in polynomial time. In *Proceedings of the 23th Annual Conference on Current Trends in Theory and Practice of Informatics (SOFSEM'96)*, volume 1175 of *LNCS*, pages 377–384. Springer-Verlag, 1996.

18. J. Srba. Complexity of weak bisimilarity and regularity for BPA and BPP. *Mathematical Structures in Computer Science*, 13:567–587, 2003.

19. J. Stříbrná. Hardness results for weak bisimilarity of simple process algebras. In *Proceedings of the MFCS'98 Workshop on Concurrency*, volume 18 of *Electronic Notes in Theoretical Computer Science*. Springer-Verlag, 1998.

20. P. Jančar. Strong bisimilarity on basic parallel processes is PSPACE-complete. In *Proceedings of the 18th Annual IEEE Symposium on Logic in Computer Science (LICS'03)*, pages 218–227. IEEE Computer Society Press, 2003.

21. J. Srba. Strong bisimilarity and regularity of basic parallel processes is PSPACE-hard. In *Proceedings of the 19th International Symposium on Theoretical Aspects of Computer Science (STACS'02)*, volume 2285 of *LNCS*, pages 535–546. Springer-Verlag, 2002.

22. Y. Hirshfeld, M. Jerrum, and F. Moller. A polynomial-time algorithm for deciding bisimulation equivalence of normed basic parallel processes. *Mathematical Structures in Computer Science*, 6(3):251–259, 1996.

23. P. Jančar, A. Kučera, and R. Mayr. Deciding bisimulation-like equivalences with finite-state processes. *Theoretical Computer Science*, 258(1–2):409–433, 2001.

24. P. Jančar and J. Esparza. Deciding finiteness of Petri nets up to bisimulation. In *Proceedings of 23rd International Colloquium on Automata, Languages, and Programming (ICALP'96)*, volume 1099 of *LNCS*, pages 478–489. Springer-Verlag, 1996.

25. P. Jančar. New results for bisimilarity on basic parallel processes. In *Proceedings of the 4th International Workshop on Verification of Infinite-State Systems (INFINITY'02)*, page 153. Technical report, Faculty of Informatics, Masaryk University Brno, FIMU-RS-2002-04, 2002. Short presentation.

26. G. Sénizergues. Decidability of bisimulation equivalence for equational graphs of finite out-degree. In *Proceedings of the 39th Annual Symposium on Foundations of Computer Science(FOCS'98)*, pages 120–129. IEEE Computer Society, 1998.

27. A. Kučera and R. Mayr. On the complexity of semantic equivalences for pushdown automata and BPA. In *Proceedings of the 27th International Symposium on Mathematical Foundations of Computer Science (MFCS'02)*, volume 2420 of *LNCS*, pages 433–445. Springer-Verlag, 2002.

28. C. Stirling. Decidability of bisimulation equivalence for normed pushdown processes. *Theoretical Computer Science*, 195(2):113–131, 1998.

29. J. Srba. Undecidability of weak bisimilarity for pushdown processes. In *Proceedings of the 13th International Conference on Concurrency Theory (CONCUR'02)*, volume 2421 of *LNCS*, pages 579–593. Springer-Verlag, 2002.

30. R. Mayr. On the complexity of bisimulation problems for pushdown automata. In *Proceedings of IFIP International Conference on Theoretical Computer Science (IFIP TCS'00)*, volume 1872 of *LNCS*. Springer-Verlag, 2000.

31. J. Esparza, D. Hansel, P. Rossmanith, and S. Schwoon. Efficient algorithms for model checking pushdown systems. In *Proceedings of the 12th International Conference on Computer Aided Verification (CAV'00)*, volume 1855 of *LNCS*, pages 232–247. Springer-Verlag, 2000.

32. G. Sénizergues. $L(A) = L(B)$? decidability results from complete formal systems. *Theoretical Computer Science*, 251(1–2):1–166, 2001.

33. G. Sénizergues. $L(A) = L(B)$? a simplified decidability proof. *Theoretical Computer Science*, 281(1–2):555–608, 2002.

34. C. Stirling. Decidability of DPDA equivalence. *Theoretical Computer Science*, 255(1–2):1–31, 2001.

35. J.R. Büchi. Regular canonical systems. *Arch. Math. Logik u. Grundlagenforschung*, 6:91–111, 1964.

36. Y. Hirshfeld and M. Jerrum. Bisimulation equivalence is decidable for normed process algebra. In *Proceedings of 26th International Colloquium on Automata, Languages and Programming (ICALP'99)*, volume 1644 of *LNCS*, pages 412–421. Springer-Verlag, 1999.

37. J. Srba. Undecidability of weak bisimilarity for PA-processes. In *Pro-

ceedings of the 6th International Conference on Developments in Laguage Theory (DLT'02), volume 2450 of *LNCS*, pages 197–208. Springer-Verlag, 2003.

38. P. Jančar and A. Kučera. Bisimilarity of processes with finite-state systems. In *Proceedings of the 2nd International Workshop on Verification of Infinite State Systems (INFINITY'97)*, volume 9 of *Electronic Notes in Theoretical Computer Science*, 1997.

39. A. Kučera. Regularity is decidable for normed PA processes in polynomial time. In *Proceedings of the 16th International Conference on Foundations of Software Technology and Theoretical Computer Science (FSTTCS'96)*, volume 1180 of *LNCS*, pages 111–122. Springer-Verlag, 1996.

40. P. Jančar. Undecidability of bisimilarity for Petri nets and some related problems. *Theoretical Computer Science*, 148(2):281–301, 1995.

41. P. Jančar and F. Moller. Checking regular properties of Petri nets. In *Proceedings of the 6th International Conference on Concurrency Theory (CONCUR'95)*, volume 962 of *LNCS*, pages 348–362. Springer-Verlag, 1995.

42. R. Lipton. The reachability problem requires exponential space. Technical Report 62, Department of Computer Science, Yale University, 1976.

43. C. Rackoff. The covering and boundedness problems for vector addition systems. *Theoretical Computer Science*, 6(2):223–231, 1978.

44. J. Esparza. Decidability and complexity of Petri net problems – an introduction. In *Lectures on Petri Nets I: Basic Models*, volume 1491 of *LNCS*, pages 374–428. Springer-Verlag, 1998.

45. R. Mayr and M. Rusinowitch. Reachability is decidable for ground AC rewrite systems. In *Proceedings of 3rd International Workshop on Verification of Infinite State Systems (INFINITY'98)*, volume TUM-I9825 of *Technical Report, Technishe Universität München*, pages 53–64, 1998.

CONSTRUCTION AND VERIFICATION OF CONCURRENT PERFORMANCE AND RELIABILITY MODELS

HOLGER HERMANNS

Saarland University, Department of Computer Science
P.O. Box 151150, 66041 Saarbrücken, Germany
and
University of Twente, Department of Computer Science,
P.O. Box 217, 7500 AE Enschede, The Netherlands
E-mail: hermanns@cs.uni-sb.de

Over the last two decades formal methods have been extended towards performance and reliability evaluation. This paper tries to provide a rather intuitive explanation of the basic concepts and features in this area. Instead of striving for mathematical rigour, the intention is to give an illustrative introduction to the basics of stochastic models, to stochastic modelling using process algebra, and to model checking as a technique to analyse stochastic models.

1   Introduction

Modern industrial systems, such as communication networks, transport systems, or manufacturing systems, are more and more operating in a stochastic context: communication lines can break, buffers can overflow, a lorry with material for a just-in-time production line might get stuck in a traffic jam. Each of these phenomena is stochastic by nature, its absence or presence can only be predicted up to some probability. Since these stochastic phenomena have impact on the system under consideration, it is nowadays commonly agreed that the systems themselves exhibit stochastic behaviour. As a consequence, performance and reliability studies of industrial systems have to take into account that rigid assessments ("It is impossible that the system fails") only hold under unrealistic assumptions.

The construction and analysis of models suited for performance and reliability studies of real-world phenomena is a difficult task. To a large extent this problem is attacked using human intelligence and experience. Due to increasing size and complexity of systems, this tendency seems even growing: performance as well as reliability modelling becomes a task dedicated to specialists, in particular for systems exhibiting a high degree of irregularity. Traditional performance models such as queueing networks lack hierarchical composition and abstraction means, significantly hampering the modelling of systems that are developed nowadays. Some notable results and concepts have been developed [8,38,39,40], but they remain isolated from the system design cycle, due to the lack of a well-founded theory of hierarchy, composition and abstraction.

On the other hand, for describing the plain functional behaviour of systems various specification formalisms have been developed that are strongly focussed on modelling systems in a compositional, hierarchical manner. A prominent example of such specification formalisms is *process algebra* [17]. Developed on a strong mathematical basis, process algebra has emerged as an important framework to achieve compositionality. Process algebra provides a formal apparatus for reasoning about structure and behaviour of systems in a compositional way.

During the last decade, *stochastic process algebra* has emerged as a promising way to carry out compositional performance and reliability modelling, mostly on the basis of continuous time Markov chains (CTMCs). Following the same philosophy as ordinary process algebra, the stochastic behaviour of a system is described as the composition of the stochastic behaviours of its components.

To analyse properties of formally specified models *model checking* is a very successful technique to establish the correctness of the model, relative to a given set of temporal logic properties the model is supposed to satisfy [12,11]. Using efficient encoding techniques, model checking has been applied to industrial size designs involving more than 10^{30} states.

It appears valuable to apply efficient model checking techniques also to performance and reliability properties of industrial systems. Since performance and reliability models are stochastic in nature, the properties of interest are stochastic as well, and have to be described in an appropriate extension of a temporal logic. The model checking algorithm then involves the calculation (or approximation) of probabilities of certain properties to hold.

This paper tries to provide a rather intuitive explanation of the basic concepts and features of stochastic models, of stochastic modelling using process algebra, and of model checking as a technique to analyse stochastic models. For the sake of being illustrative the paper tends to treat various fine points much more simplistic than the advanced reader probably desires.

The paper is organised as follows. Section 2 introduces the basic concepts of stochastic models. Section 3 exemplifies the use of process algebra for modelling stochastic phenomena by means of a real-world example, and Section 4 describes the model checking approach to analyse stochastic models. Section 5 concludes the paper. This paper is a revised version of an invited contribution to the 5th International ERCIM Workshop on Formal Methods for Industrial Critical Systems (FMICS 2000) [25], first published in [26].

2 Stochastic Models

A stochastic model is basically a means to describe the evolution of a real-world phenomenon as time[a] passes, with a particular emphasis on phenomena with stochastic timing characteristics. In other words, repeated observations of the same phenomenon can have varying timing characteristics, but their variation exhibits a specific kind of randomness.

Figure 1. At the door of a gambler

As an example, consider a gambler that throws a die every minute. Observing the gambler, one might wish to study a phenomenon, such as the time it takes to throw a ⚅. Starting the observation at some arbitrary minute, one counts the minutes till the die shows a ⚅. Obviously, repeated observations will usually lead to different results, at least if gambling with a fair die. Nevertheless, the variation among these observations exhibits a specific kind of randomness: The time needed to throw a ⚅ is known to follow the so-called geometric probability distribution.

Probability distribution. A probability distribution is a function that assigns a probability (a real value between 0 and 1) to each element of some given set. For instance, the geometric probability distribution P assigns probabilities to natural numbers. For the gambler, these numbers enumerate the minutes he is already gambling (remind that he throws the die once per minute).

---

[a]It is a bit narrow minded to consider the time domain as the only possible domain of variability. Spatial Markov processes, for instance, are used to describe the evolution of a phenomenon as its position in some appropriate space changes, as opposed to the time.

For some t, $P(t)$ is the probability to see the first ⚅ after t minutes, and is given by:

$$P(t) \;=\; \Pr\{\text{see a ⚅ within first } t \text{ minutes}\} \;=\; 1-\left(\frac{5}{6}\right)^t, \qquad t \in \{0,1,2,\ldots\},$$

or complementary,

$$1 - P(t) \;=\; \Pr\{\text{still no ⚅ after } t \text{ minutes}\} \;=\; \left(\frac{5}{6}\right)^t, \qquad t \in \{0,1,2,\ldots\}.$$

For instance, the probability of not having seen a ⚅ after $t = 2$ minutes, i.e., after throwing the die twice, equals $25/36$.

To make the example a bit more interesting, assume that the gambler is throwing the die somewhere outside his office. Before leaving his office he has put a note on the door, as depicted in Figure 1. In fact, his intention is to return to his office as soon as the die shows a ⚅. Now let us assume that someone arrives at his door, finding the door closed. How long will he have to wait for the gambler? Probably just a minute, but probably (more likely) more than a minute, probably (unlikely) more than ten minutes. Since this experiment is governed by the above geometric distribution, the probability of having to wait more than a minute is $5/6$, the probability of waiting more than ten minutes is $(5/6)^{10}$. Figure 2 depicts these probabilities for the first 15 minutes.

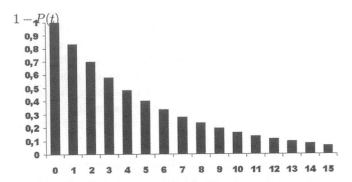

Figure 2. A geometric probability distribution[b]: Will the gambler still be absent at time t?

---

[b]The reader familiar with the standard pictorial representation might be surprised that the plot in Figure 2 (and Figure 5) tends to zero for $t \to \infty$, instead of tending towards 1. What is depicted is not the probability distribution $P(t)$ (nor its probability density), but its complement $1 - P(t)$. This is done for didactic reasons.

Markov chain. Having explained the gambler's behaviour, we are now in the position to specify a stochastic model of his behaviour. It is depicted in Figure 3. As many other (formal or semi-formal) models, the model is a graph, consisting of states and transitions. There are two states in this model. One state represents the absence of the gambler, one represents his presence in the office. The model contains three transitions representing possible events that might induce a change of state. One transition indicates that every minute the absent gambler has a 1-out-of-6 chance to return to his office. Another transition indicates that with probability 5/6 the absent gambler will miss the ⊞, and hence has to stay absent for at least another minute. In case he is back in his office, the third transition indicates that he stays there (ad infinitum). The small arrow on top of the left state indicates the initial state. i.e. the state occupied at time zero.

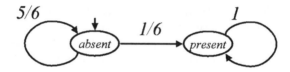

Figure 3. A discrete-time Markov chain describing the gambler's behaviour

The stochastic model of the gambler's behaviour is a very simple one. It is a Markov chain, named after A.A. Markov who studied models of this kind in the beginning of the last century [36]. More specific, it is a discrete-time Markov chain (DTMC), since state changes are only possible at discrete points in time: The gambler can return to his office precisely every minute only. DTMCs restrict the possible time points for state changes to a discrete subset of dense real time. As in our example, these time points are often (but not necessarily) equidistant.

Markov chain analysis. For a given stochastic model, such as a Markov chain, there is usually a variety of interesting properties that one might want to study. Two substantially different classes of properties can be distinguished. *Transient analysis* investigates the evolution of the model up to a given point in time. On the contrary, *steady-state analysis* focusses on the long-run average behaviour. It requires that on the long-run initial start-up effects (the transient phase) do not have a measurable impact.

A trivial steady-state property for the gambler is that with probability zero he will be absent on the long-run. As an example for a transient property, we have already indicated that the probability of still being absent after 10 minutes is $(5/6)^{10}$. A variant of steady-state analysis gives us that on average it takes the gambler six minutes to throw a ⊞. So, the sign on the office door is essentially right, the gambler will be back in six minutes, on average. (This can also be directly derived from the fact that the expected (or average) value of a geometric distribution is $1/p$ where $p = 1/6$ is the chance of a successful event.)

Analysis techniques. In practice, three fundamentally different techniques are used to analyse stochastic models. They differ with respect to accuracy, applicability and computational requirements. Here, we only give a concise subjective summary on differences and similarities, and refer to Jain's textbook [35] for a more elaborate discussion.

Simulation. The stochastic model is mimicked by a simulator throwing dice and producing statistics of simulated time spent in states. The fraction of simulated time spent in a particular state is used as an estimate for the state probability. This technique is generally applicable, in particular it is suitable also for non-Markov stochastic models. However, it should be noticed that good accuracy tends to require long simulation runs, and hence limits applicability in practise: To increase the accuracy of the simulation by a factor of n, one needs to increase the length of the simulation runs (and hence the run-time of the simulation) by a factor of n^2.

Numerical solution. The transient or steady-state behaviour of a stochastic model is obtained by an exact or approximate numerical algorithm where model parameters are instantiated with numerical values. This approach gives accurate results in general, up to numerical precision. Typically the solution time increases logarithmically with an increase in accuracy. On the other hand, its applicability is restricted to finite Markov chains (with a few exceptions, see e.g. [21,34]). Furthermore the number of states of the model is a limiting factor, because of computational and especially storage requirements. A very readable textbook on numerical solution methods is [43].

Analytical solution. The transient or steady state property of interest is expressed as a closed formula over the parameters of the model. This is the most simple, accurate and elegant technique. However, analytical solutions are available only for highly restricted classes of stochastic models.

Absence of memory. Markov chains are widely used as stochastic models of real-world phenomena. This is mainly because they possess a distinguishing feature that simplifies both modelling and analysis. They obey the so called *memory-less property*: The future evolution of a Markov chain model is independent of the past, it only depends on the state currently occupied. This property is best explained in terms of the absent gambler. The probability that the gambler returns to his office after one minute from now is $1/6$, independent of the fact that someone might be waiting for him in front of his door for ten minutes (or years) already. This is a direct consequence of the fact that a fair die has no memory; the die does not change if it has not shown a ⊡ for ages. This should not be mixed with the fact that the probability of actually having to wait for ten minutes is low, $(5/6)^{10}$. Under the assumption that this unlikely case becomes reality, it still needs another six minutes waiting time on average, as the sign on the door indicates.

Discrete vs. continuous time. Discrete-time Markov chains are convenient to describe the stochastic evolution of sequential systems. In each state, the outgoing transitions define how the probability mass will be spread at the next time instant. Since DTMCs evolve in a discrete time domain, the flow of probability is not continuous, instead it possesses jumps, and remains unchanged in the time interval between two relevant time points, such as between $t = 2$ and $t = 3$. This is relatively convenient for sequential systems. But it is not convenient in a concurrent probabilistic setting, for both theoretical as well as pragmatic reasons.[c]

As an example, imagine that the gambler's office door is checked by some customer. In case he finds the door closed he probabilistically decides to check again after either 24 or 48 seconds. Note that the basic time unit of this DTMC is 24 seconds. For instance, one might want to study the probability that the customer finds an open door after 72 seconds.

Without specifying the model in all detail, we are already in the position to understand the problem: In order to develop a concurrent probabilistic model of both gambler and customer, we have to relate events that may happen at every 24 seconds to events that happen may every 60 seconds. One solution is to change the basic time unit of both models to 12 seconds, the greatest common divisor of their basic time units. In other words, the gambler's model is blown up to record in 4 additional states that while being absent, four times 12 seconds pass till he may throw the die in the last twelve

---

[c]DTMCs are appropriate for some types of concurrent systems possessing globally synchronising clocks, such as ATM-switches or certain manufacturing systems.

358

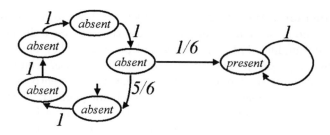

Figure 4. A discrete-time Markov chain describing the gambler's behaviour if observed every 12 seconds

seconds of the minute (cf. Figure 4).[d] After a similar change in the customer's sub-model, one can combine both models (by essentially taking the cross-product of states and the products of transition probabilities). To determine the concurrent stochastic behaviour at the next point in time (i.e. after 12 seconds) one synchronously updates the respective states in the two sub-models, because state changes now occur exactly at the same time. The probability for such a joined transition is given by the product of the transition probabilities in the sub-models.

This strategy has two practical limitations, at least. First, it tends to induce a tremendous blow-up of the size of the model, caused by the number of auxiliary states needed in general. Second, it fails if there is no greatest common divisor, for instance if the customer shows up every π seconds, or if time points are not equidistant. As a consequence, virtually all stochastic models of concurrent systems are developed in a continuous time domain, including models of modern computer systems (even though each component of such a system can be considered as working in discrete time, changing state according to fixed frequency clock ticks).

Continuous-time Markov chains. Continuous-time Markov chains (CTMCs) are Markov chains interpreted over continuous time, in contrast to DTMCs. They are widely used to model the stochastic behaviour of concurrent real-world phenomena, due to their mathematical simplicity, paired with modelling convenience.

How does the continuous-time variant of the gambler look like? In a continuous time setting, the absent gambler is able to return to his office at

---

[d]Note that this change encodes some kind of memory in an otherwise memory-less model: A sequence of states is used to keep track of the time already spent in the original state.

arbitrary time points. Still we may assume that he has a 1-out-of-6 chance to return within the first minute, and so on. Under these assumptions, we get the following probability distribution:

$$\Pr\{\text{still no } \boxdot \text{ after } t \text{ minutes}\} \;=\; (5/6)^t, \qquad t \in \mathbb{R}^+.$$

What is this? It perfectly resembles the geometric distribution appearing in the discrete time case, but it is different. The difference is that the domain of this function is the non-negative real line, instead of the natural numbers. In other words, the above function assigns a probability to all time points one may think of, instead of only to each minute. Hence, there is now a non-zero probability of returning within the first second already, namely $1 - (5/6)^{1/60}$. Instead of being a geometric distribution, this function belongs to the class of so-called (negative) exponential probability distributions, because $(5/6)^t$ can be rewritten to $e^{-\lambda t}$, with $\lambda = \ln 6 - \ln 5 \approx 0.18232$. The value λ is a parameter of the distribution, usually called 'rate'. For $t < 15$, the probabilities determined by this exponential probability distribution are depicted (by the dark plot) in Figure 5. The expected value of an exponential distribution (i.e., the average duration) is $1/\lambda$, the reciprocal value of the rate. So, the (continuously gambling) gambler returns after 5.48 minutes on average, not after six minutes.[e]

A continuous-time Markov chain model of this absent gambler is depicted in Figure 6. It consists of two states, and one transition. The transition represents that the gambler can return to his office with rate λ. The gambler stays absent as long as needed to throw a $\boxdot$. According to the value of λ the probability mass flows from state to state as time passes, that is, a fraction of $1 - e^\lambda = 1/6$ of the probability mass flows from the left state to the right state per minute.[f]

Though the above example shows one of the simplest CTMCs one can think of, it exhibits all relevant ingredients: states and transitions, the latter labelled with rates of exponential distributions. It is worth to note that – in correspondence to geometric distributions – exponential distributions are memory-less: The future evolution of a CTMC model is independent of the

---

[e]Remark that since the probability mass is flowing continuously, a sixth of the mass leaks prior to the first minute tick. Hence, to some extent the probability mass flows earlier than in the discrete-time case, where a sixth of the probability mass jumps a bit later, at each minute tick. As a consequence, the average time needed for the continuously gambling gambler is slightly smaller than 6 minutes. To obtain an average duration of 6 minutes, one has to adjust λ to $1/6$.

[f]Since the gambler continuously tries to return to his office, there is no need to record by an explicit (looping) transition that he might fail for some (continuous) time. For CTMCs, this fact is implicit, while in the DTMC scenario it is not.

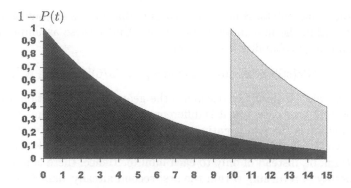

Figure 5. A negative exponential probability distribution with $\lambda = \ln 6 - \ln 5$: Will the gambler still be absent at time t?

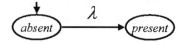

Figure 6. A continuous-time Markov chain describing the gambler's behaviour

past, it only depends on the state currently occupied. In terms of the gambler, the probability that the absent gambler returns to his office within the next minute is 1/6, independent of the fact he might have been absent for ages already.

Figure 5 allows us to illustrate the memory-less property in a pictorial way [1]. Consider the case that the gambler is still gambling after minute 10. We obtain the probability that he will still be gambling at time $10 + t$ by stretching the tail of the distribution (from time 10 to ∞) upwards in such a way that it reaches probability 1 for minute 10, i.e. $t = 0$. As a matter of fact, this stretching returns precisely the original distribution, as indicated by the light-grey plot in Figure 5, except that it is shifted by 10 minutes. The same graphical illustration holds for the geometric distribution, but for no other discrete or continuous distribution, because the exponential (resp. geometric) distribution is the only memory-less continuous (resp. discrete) distribution.

From a pragmatic point of view, the memory-less property is rather convenient. It simplifies analysis, but it also simplifies modelling. In particular, it fits well to concurrent stochastic phenomena: If two sub-models, both described in terms of CTMCs, are to be considered concurrently, one can simply interleave their evolution: If one sub-model changes from one state to another, the other sub-model is not affected. The fact that the latter has been staying in some state for some time (the time it took the former sub-model to change state) does not need to be recorded somehow, because it does not alter the future behaviour of the latter sub-model, due to the memory-less property.

Anyway, it should be clearly stated that absence of memory is an assumption that is by far not always justified when modelling real-world phenomena.[g] On the other hand, exponential distributions are the most appropriate guesses if only expected values are known. This is because among all distributions with a given expected value, the exponential distribution maximises entropy [22,41]. Actually, in performance engineering practise one hardly has measurement data at hand that allows one to determine more than an expected value.

3 Formal Specification of Continuous-Time Markov Chains

In this section we illustrate the use of formal methods to model a specific aspect of a real-world example as a CTMC. Several formal notations exist that map on CTMCs, among them stochastic Petri nets and stochastic process algebra. Here we restrict ourselves to illustrate the use of process algebra; an introduction to the Petri net based approach can be found for instance in [1]. As opposed to standard Petri nets, process algebra allows one to compose models out of smaller sub-models, by means of general composition operators such as parallel composition and choice [17], and also more specific constructs, such as exception handling [20]. We will make use of these operators to model a simplified view on the performance and reliability of the Hubble space telescope.

The Hubble space telescope. The Hubble space telescope (HST) [42] is an orbiting astronomical observatory operating from the near-infrared into the ultraviolet (cf. Figure 7). Launched in 1990 and scheduled to operate through 2010, the HST carries a variety of instruments producing imaging, spectrographic, astrometric, and photometric data.

The HST was first conceived in the 1940's. It was designed and built in

---

[g]It is possible to incorporate a notion of memory into the model, similar to what we have used to realise synchronisation of DTMCs (cf. footnote d). In this way, general non-exponential probability distributions (so-called phase-type distributions) can be represented. The price to pay for this is usually a blow up of the model.

362

Figure 7. The Hubble space telescope [42].

the 1970's and 1980's, aiming at a life span of 15 years with on-orbit servicing taking place on 3 year intervals. The HST programme is a cooperation of the National Aeronautics and Space Administration (NASA) and the European Space Agency (ESA).[h]

Since the telescope has been launched in April 1990, three servicing missions were carried out: in December 1993, in February 1997, and in December 1999. During the last mission the stabilising unit of the HST was repaired. This was necessary, since severe problems with the reliability of the gyroscopes contained therein had forced the HST to turn into a sleep mode.

The gyroscopes are part of HST pointing system. They provide a frame of reference to determine where it is pointing and how that pointing changes as the telescope moves across the sky. They report any small movements of the spacecraft to the HST pointing and control system. The computers

[h] Originally, the HST was designed to be returned to earth via the space shuttle every 5 years with on-orbit servicing every 2.5 years as well. This concept was later dropped as it was felt there was a too great risk of contamination and structural load to make the concept sound.

then command the spinning reaction wheels to keep the spacecraft stable or moving at the desired rate in order to avoid that the telescope pointing device staggers. This is of particular importance to avoid that pictures taken by the telescope are blurred. The gyroscopes work by comparing the HST motion relative to the axes of the spinning masses inside the gyroscopes.

The HST has a total of six gyroscopes, grouped into three fine guidance sensors. They are arranged in such a way that any three gyroscopes can keep the HST operating with full accuracy. Two fine guidance sensors had been replaced already during the first servicing mission in 1993. Till the end of the second servicing mission in 1997, all six gyroscopes were working normally, but then one after the other failed. Starting from January 1999 the HST had been operating with only 3 functional gyroscopes. As a consequence of a fourth gyroscope failure on November 13, 1999, HST turned itself into a sleep mode and the science program was suspended. Without operational gyroscope the telescope would have run the risk to crash. In December 1999, a space shuttle mission was sent to the HST to replace (among others) the complete stabilising unit. This mission was successful.

In order to judge whether the problems of the HST could have been expected beforehand, one might want to study the reliability of the stabilising unit by means of an abstract stochastic model. Here we construct a simple Markov chain model of the gyroscopes, and of their controller. The model is a toy example, developed to give a flavour of Markov chain modelling with process algebra. The model is developed in the algebra of interactive Markov chains (IMC) [24], an orthogonal extension of both CTMCs and basic process algebra.

Basic processes. Each gyroscope might FAIL after an exponentially distributed amount of time (it is known that exponential distributions fit relatively well to failures of technical equipment). The failure rate λ is the same for all gyroscopes. A GYRO specification is as follows:

$$\text{GYRO} = (\lambda). \text{ FAIL. STOP}$$

This specification corresponds to a graphical representation depicted in Figure 8. Apart from a transition labelled λ representing the delay prior to failure, there is a second kind of transition, indicated by a dotted arrow labelled FAIL. In abstract terms, this transition represents the potential of interaction, i.e. of synchronising with a partner transition (labelled with the same name) in a different sub-model. The potential of interaction between sub-models is one of the well-known features offered by a process algebraic approach [7,37].

Parallel composition. Six of these gyroscopes coexist independently in the

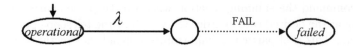

Figure 8. A simple interactive Markov chain describing the gyroscope's behaviour

stabilising unit, together with a controller that keeps track of the status of each gyroscope, by means of synchronisation on FAIL. This is realised using the operator |[FAIL]| for synchronisation, and ||| to denote independent parallelism (among the gyroscopes):

STABILISER = CONTROLLER
|[FAIL]|
(GYRO|||GYRO|||GYRO|||GYRO|||GYRO|||GYRO)

The controller counts the number of failures, and mechanically turns the telescope into sleep mode in case four gyroscopes have failed. To turn into sleep mode requires some time. For the moment we just assume an exponential distribution with rate μ. We will explain shortly how to deal with other distributions. After turning on the sleep mode, the controller notifies the base station by means of a SLEEP signal. In the meantime, further gyroscope failures might occur. If the last gyroscope fails, a CRASH is assumed to be inevitable. The graphical representation of the controller is depicted in Figure 9.

CONTROLLER = FAIL. FAIL. FAIL. FAIL.
((μ). SLEEP. STOP ||| FAIL. FAIL. CRASH. STOP))

To complete the picture, we consider the stabilising unit of the HST in the context of the base station. The base station listens to the SLEEP notification and reacts accordingly: launch a space shuttle mission to repair – and then restart – the telescope.

BASE = SLEEP. PREPARE. LAUNCH. REPAIR. RESTART. BASE

Exception handling. The complete specification consists of the STABILISER and the BASE station synchronising on SLEEP. Two events may alter the functioning of the system. If a CRASH occurs, the whole system

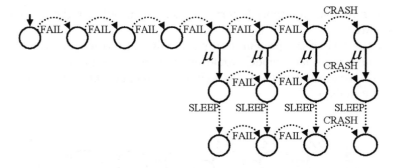

Figure 9. An interactive Markov chain describing the controller

is extinguished, but if the shuttle mission manages to repair the stabilising unit in time, the whole system will be restarted anew.[i]

HST = *try*   { STABILISER |[SLEEP]| BASE }
      catch RESTART { HST }
      catch   CRASH { STOP }

Time constraints. Of course, preparing the shuttle mission takes time, and one might wish to incorporate the expected (random) delay in the model. To do so, we can use a constraint-oriented style, as advocated in [44]. This style allows one to add constraints on the timing of certain sequences of interactions, such as between PREPARE and LAUNCH by means of a dedicated operator, defined in [29]. For instance,

on PREPARE   *delay* LAUNCH   *by* (ν). STOP
in HST

adds an exponentially distributed delay with rate ν between PREPARE and LAUNCH. Semantically speaking, this will have the same effect as specifying BASE = SLEEP. PREPARE. (ν). LAUNCH. REPAIR. RESTART. BASE, but it is much more modular and flexible, in particular because it can be used to impose very general time constraints, instead of only exponentially distributed ones, see [29]. In short, one can insert an arbitrary (phase-type distributed) delay between PREPARE and LAUNCH, by replacing (ν). STOP in the above

---

[i]The semantics of this exception handling is defined in [15].

expression by some appropriate term (in fact, an encoding of the distribution as a CTMC).

For the sake of the presentation we do not add further time constraints, even though a realistic model would at least impose some nontrivial delay between LAUNCH and REPAIR, (as well as a non-exponential delay to set up the SLEEP mode.)

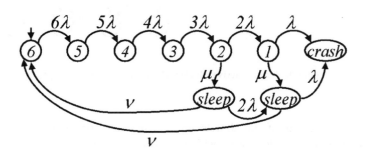

Figure 10. A continuous-time Markov chain corresponding to the stochastic behaviour of the telescope

Extracting the Markov chain. The complete HST specification gives rise to a stochastic model, a CTMC depicted in Figure 10. It is obtained from the specification by applying the formal semantics of the process algebra, and compressing the model by means of an appropriate weak bisimulation afterwards.[j] The states are labelled from left to right with the number of gyroscopes that are currently operational, except if the system is *sleep*ing, or *crash*ed.

Remark that in this CTMC the failure rate λ appears weighted with different multiplying factors. The intuitive reason is that if six gyroscopes are operational, the time to the first failure is six times smaller than if only one gyroscope is left. This increased failure rate for multiple identical components is correctly derived by the formal approach outlined above. The entire approach, as well as the necessary transformation and compression algorithms are implemented in the CADP toolbox [18,28], a widespread tool set originally designed for verifying the functional correctness of LOTOS specifications [19].

---

[j] As explained in [24], constructing the Markov chain requires to internalise all possible interactions beforehand. This is necessary but may not be sufficient to extract a CTMC, since interactive Markov chains are strictly more expressive than CTMCs (because of the absence on non-determinism in CTMCs).

4 Performance and Reliability Via Model Checking

In this section we illustrate the use of model checking to analyse performance and reliability properties of CTMC models. We discuss the main ingredients of this approach, and apply model checking to the simple Hubble space telescope example of Section 3.

Temporal logic. The model checking approach relies on the use of temporal logic for specifying properties one is interested in. For this purpose temporal logic provides means to specify undesired (or – dually – desired) evolutions. Typical specifications of properties are 'something undesired never happens' or 'eventually a desired state is reached'. A temporal logic specification is usually considered in the context of a given model (provided by some process algebraic specification, for instance). The mechanic verification whether a model satisfies a temporal logic specification is called *model checking*. It is worth to mention that basic temporal logic does not allow one to reason about delays and time points (although the name might suggest the converse). It is 'temporal' in the sense that it allows one to refer to the ordering of events as the model evolves in time.

Temporal logics for Markov chains. In the context of Markov chain models, the temporal logic approach turns into a probabilistic temporal one. It is not sufficient to decide whether 'eventually a desired state is reached'. Instead the probability of eventually reaching a desired state is much more interesting. For the gambler example in Figure 3 the standard interpretation of 'eventually the gambler will be present' would return false, because it is in principle possible to stay absent ad infinitum. However, this evolution is extremely unlikely, it has probability zero. So, a quantitative interpretation of temporal logic is needed, quantifying the likelihood of satisfying a given property. This allows one to specify properties such as 'a desired state is eventually reached with at least probability 0.95'.

Moreover, since the evolution of a Markov chain model in time is measurable (in the true sense of the word), it is possible to reason about time instances within the temporal logic. Timed properties such as 'with at most probability 0.2 the gambler will still be absent after 10 minutes' are possible.

Continuous stochastic logic. The continuous stochastic logic (CSL), first proposed in [2] and further refined in [4] provides means to reason about continuous-time Markov chain models. It is a branching time logic based on CTL [10] with dedicated means to specify time intervals, and to quantify probability. As explained in Section 2, there are two substantially different classes of properties of a CTMC: transient and steady-state properties. Therefore, CSL provides two complementary means to quantify the probability mass: a steady-state operator $\mathcal{S}$, to quantify the long-run likelihood, and a transient probability operator $\mathcal{P}$.

For instance, a steady-state property $\mathcal{S}_{\leq p}(\Phi)$ is true if the long-run likelihood of property Φ is at most p.[k] Φ can be a basic property (usually called atomic proposition) valid (or invalid) in some state. It can also be an arbitrary nested property of the logic. The transient probability operator is used to quantify the likelihood of evolving in a specified way, from a given state and a given time point on. For example $\mathcal{P}_{\leq p}(X\,\Phi)$ is true in a state if the probability of moving (in one step) to a state where Φ holds is at most p. Apart from $X\,\Phi$, there can be various other arguments for the operator $\mathcal{P}$, such as

- $\Diamond\,\Phi$ quantifies the probability for evolving in such a way that eventually a Φ-state is reached.

- $\Diamond^{[0,t]}\,\Phi$ characterises the amount of probability for reaching a Φ-state within t time units.

- $\Phi_1\,\mathcal{U}\,\Phi_2$ characterises the amount of probability for evolving only along Φ_1-states until a Φ_2-state is reached.

- $\Phi_1\,\mathcal{U}^{[t_1,t_2]}\,\Phi_2$ quantifies the probability for evolving only along Φ_1-states until a Φ_2-state is reached, under the additional constraint that Φ_1 holds at least up to time t_1, and Φ_2 holds at time t_2 the latest.

Model checking CSL. Model checking a CTMC with respect to a given CSL property involves various algorithms. Since the details are not of vital importance for a proper understanding of the approach – at least relative to the logical means to specify properties – we only give a concise overview of the ingredients.

As in other model checking strategies, a couple of graph algorithms are used. In addition, algorithms to quantify the probability mass of satisfying the above criteria are needed. In principle, these probabilities could be derived using simulation, numerical solution, or sometimes via analytical solutions. Since numerical solution of CTMCs is well-studied and generally applicable, it seems wise to use numerical solution methods to model check CSL properties [4]. In this way, model checking involves matrix-vector multiplications

---

[k]Instead of '$\leq$' one may use arbitrary comparison operators, or specify intervals of probabilities instead.

(for X), solutions of linear systems of equations (for $\Diamond$, $\mathcal{U}$ and for $\mathcal{S}$), and solutions of systems of Volterra integral equations (for $\mathcal{U}^{[\cdots]}$). Linear systems of equations can be solved iteratively by standard numerical methods [43]. Systems of integral equations can be solved either by piecewise integration after discretisation, or they can be reduced to standard transient analysis [4]. A model checker for CSL, ETMCC, is available [31]. We shall make use of ETMCC (Version 1.4) to investigate properties of the Hubble space telescope.

Properties of the telescope model. CSL provides a rich framework to study performance and reliability properties of the HST. Here we consider a few illustrative cases. In order to allow the calculation of numerical values, we first need to fix the model parameters λ, μ, and ν of the CTMC in Figure 10. Assuming a basic time unit of one year, we set $\lambda = 0.1$, i.e., we assume that each gyroscope has an average lifetime of 10 years. (Recall that $1/\lambda$ gives the average duration of an exponential distribution with rate λ.) To turn on the sleep mode may require a hundredth of a year (a bit more than three days and a half) on average, hence we set $\mu = 100$. Further assuming that preparing the repair mission will take about two months, we set $\nu = 6$. Unless otherwise stated we consider the validity of CSL properties in the initial state, i.e. the state labelled *6* in Figure 10. The state labels appearing in this figure serve as atomic state propositions for the logic.

First, let us look into long-run averages. An interesting property, often called *availability*, is the probability that the system will be available – i.e. neither *crash*ed nor *sleep*ing – on the long-run average. In CSL we assure an availability higher than p by specifying

$$\mathcal{S}_{>p}(\neg\,(\,sleep \vee crash)\,).$$

None of the states of the HST satisfies this property (whatever the value of p may be). This should not be surprising, because the telescope is not constructed for the long run. In fact, the availability of the telescope is zero, because on the long run, the modelled telescope will crash, all the probability mass will eventually be accumulated in the *crash*-state (cf. Figure 10).[l]

While checking standard availability does not make much sense for the HST, the *instantaneous availability* is of interest. Instantaneous availability is a typical transient property, it is the probability that the system is operational at a given time point t. This time point could for instance be given by the

---

[l]Generally speaking, steady-state properties provide very useful insight in the model, in particular for the widespread class of models where the probability mass can flow forever without gradually leaking into some sink (so to speak), or where more than one sink exists. Each of these sinks may in general consist of a set of mutually reachable states.

need to observe a rare astronomic event. Assuming that an interesting comet passes the telescope in five years, we specify

$$\mathcal{P}_{\geq 0.95}(\Diamond^{[5,5]} \neg \, (sleep \vee crash))$$

in order to assure that with at least probability 0.95 the telescope is neither *sleep*ing nor *crash*ed then. (Note that the time interval $[t, t]$ denotes just a single time point.) We compute a probability of more than 0.98 of satisfying this property, hence it is satisfied.

In the same vain, we may wonder about the probability to obtain blurred data at that time from the telescope, because less than three gyroscopes are operational, but sleep mode is not yet turned on. This is a very unlikely situation, and one might accept at most a probability of 10^{-6}. One way of characterising the relevant states is to isolate those (non-*sleep*) state that (with positive probability) can turn on the *sleep* mode in the next step. This gives us

$$\mathcal{P}_{\leq 10^{-6}}(\Diamond^{[5,5]} \, (\neg \, sleep \wedge \mathcal{P}_{>0}(X \, sleep)) \,),$$

a property that is not satisfied, because the probability of being in the specified states after 5 years is about 10^{-5}.

Another quantity of interest is the *time until first sleep*, i.e. the time span before the (fully operational) telescope has to be put into *sleep* mode for the first time. In reality, this happened within 2.7 years: All gyroscopes were operational at the end of the second servicing mission in early 1997, and the *sleep* mode was turned on in November 1999. We require a less than 10 % chance of such a first sleep within 2.7 years by specifying the property

$$\mathcal{P}_{<0.1}(\, \neg sleep \, \mathcal{U}^{[0,2.7]} \, sleep).$$

It turns out that this property is valid; ETMCC computes that the probability of a first sleep within 2.7 years amounts to about 0.03. A related question is whether it was likely not to witness any gyroscope failure within the four years between the first (1993) and the second servicing mission (1997). We answer this question by checking whether the probability to leave state *6* within 4 years is between, say, 0.3 and 0.7. (Notice that leaving state *6* corresponds to a gyroscope failure).

$$\mathcal{P}_{[0.3,0,7]}(\Diamond^{[0,4]} \neg \, 6)$$

In fact, this property is invalid, because the probability of a gyroscope failure within 4 years is approximately 0.9, thus exceeding the upper bound 0.7.

As a last example property, be reminded that the HST is planned to stay on orbit through 2010. Hence, it seems worth to study whether a *crash* before reaching the year 2010 can hardly be expected. To do so, we check a property saying that there is at most a 1% chance that the system will *crash* within the next 10 years (given that the system was reset to state *6* in late 1999):

$$\mathcal{P}_{<0.01}(\lozenge^{[0,10]} \; crash).$$

This property is satisfied, the probability of crashing within 10 years is calculated by ETMCC to be 0.00036. Remind that the model is a toy example, and that its timing parameters are not claimed to reflect reality.

5 Concluding Remarks

In this paper, we have tried to give an illustrative introduction to the basics of stochastic models, to stochastic modelling using process algebra, and to model checking as a technique to analyse stochastic models.

A few questions have not been addressed to a satisfactory extent. In particular we have skipped the discussion how to label states of a CTMC generated from a process algebra in such a way that these labels can be used in temporal logic property specifications. One solution to this problem is to move from a state-based logic towards a transition-based formalism [30]. As a further direction of research, we have extended CSL to so-called Markov reward models, where states are parametrised with costs. This extension allows one to specify a broad set of performability properties [3], as well as properties of energy-aware designs [23].

Another important issue for industrial strength formal analysis is the availability of tool support. Currently, prototypical tool support is available for both the stochastic modelling and the analysis phase: A couple of prototypes exist that allow a process algebraic modelling of CTMCs [5,9,27]. So far, models of about 10^7 states have been modelled and analysed compositionally [29]. A prototypical model checker for Markov chains, ETMCC, is available [31], it has been used to check the above CSL properties of the Hubble space telescope. More effort is nevertheless needed to enhance modelling and analysis convenience. In addition, it is favourable to link stochastic features to existing modelling and analysis tools that provide an open and extensible architecture. Lately, we have incorporated the described stochastic modelling and analysis features into the CADP toolbox [18,28]. CADP is a widespread tool set for the design and verification of complex systems [19], originally designed for verifying the functional correctness of LOTOS specifications.

Markov chain models have been the clear focus of this paper. Their memory-less property considerably simplifies both modelling and analysis, but the property also implies that some real-world phenomena can only roughly be approximated with Markov chains. Hence, there is a need to extend the framework sketched in this paper beyond Markov models. As one particular example, the work of D'Argenio et al. [14,16,15] develops a process algebra to specify non-Markov performance and reliability models in an elegant way. So, the benefits of a process algebraic formalism extend to performance and reliability modelling in general. Anyhow, the analysis of such models needs further investigations. First results in this direction, however, indicate that numerical solution methods are impractical in general [32]. We are currently developing an open analysis environment for such specifications [6], linking to CADP for functional verification and numerical analysis, to UPPAAL [33] for real-time model checking and to MÖBIUS [13] for discrete event simulation or numerical analysis.

Pedro R. D'Argenio, Boudewijn Haverkort and Joost-Pieter Katoen have provided very valuable comments on an earlier version of this paper.

References

1. M. Ajmone Marsan, G. Balbo, G. Conte, S. Donatelli, and G. Franceschinis. *Modelling with Generalized Stochastic Petri Nets*. Wiley, 1995.
2. A. Aziz, K. Sanwal, V. Singhal, and R. Brayton. Verifying continuous time Markov chains. In *Computer Aided Verification (CAV 96)*, LNCS 1102:269–276, Springer, 1996.
3. C. Baier, B.R. Haverkort, H. Hermanns, and J.-P. Katoen. On the logical characterisation of performability properties. In *International Colloquium on Automata, Languages, and Programming (ICALP 2000)*, LNCS 1853:780-792, 2000.
4. C. Baier, B.R. Haverkort, H. Hermanns, and J.-P. Katoen. Model checking algorithms for continuous time Markov chains. *IEEE Transactions on Software Engineering*, 29(6):524-541, 2003.
5. M. Bernardo, W.R. Cleaveland, S.T. Sims, and W.J. Stewart. TwoTowers: A tool integrating functional and performance analysis of concurrent systems. In *Proc. of IFIP Joint Int. Conf. on Formal Description Techniques and Protocol Specification, Testing and Verification*, pp. 457-467. North Holland, 1998.
6. H. Bohnenkamp, H. Hermanns, J.-P. Katoen, and R. Klaren. The MoDeST modelling tool and its implementation. In *Computer Performance Evaluation: Modeling Techniques and Tools*. LNCS 2794:116-133,

Springer, 2003.
7. T. Bolognesi and E. Brinksma. Introduction to the ISO specification language LOTOS. *Computer Networks and ISDN Systems* 14:25-59, 1987.
8. K.M. Chandy, U. Herzog, and L. Woo. Parametric analysis of queuing models. *IBM Journal of Research and Development* 19(1):36–42, 1975.
9. G. Clark, S. Gilmore, J. Hillston, and N. Thomas. Experiences with the PEPA performance modelling tools. *IEE Proceedings–Software* 146(1):11-19, February 1999.
10. E.M. Clarke, E.A. Emerson, and A.P. Sistla. Automatic verification of finite-state concurrent systems using temporal logic specifications. *ACM Tr. on Progr. Lang. and Sys.* 8(2):244-263, 1986.
11. E.M. Clarke, O. Grumberg and D. Peled. *Model Checking.* MIT Press, 1999.
12. E.M. Clarke and R.P. Kurshan. Computer-aided verification. *IEEE Spectrum*, 33(6):61–67, 1996.
13. D. Daly, D.D. Deavours, J.M. Doyle, P.G. Webster, and W.H. Sanders. Möbius: An extensible tool for performance and dependability modeling. In *Computer Performance Evaluation*, LNCS 1786:332–336, 2000.
14. P.R. D'Argenio. *Algebras and Automata for Timed and Stochastic Systems.* PhD-Thesis, University of Twente, November 1999.
15. P.R. D'Argenio, H. Hermanns, J.-P. Katoen, and R. Klaren. MoDeST – A modelling and description language for stochastic timed systems. In *Process Algebra and Probabilistic Methods, Performance Modelling and Verification.* LNCS 2165:87-104, Springer, 2001.
16. P.R. D'Argenio, J.-P. Katoen, and E. Brinksma. Specification and analysis of soft real-time systems: Quantity and quality. In *Proc. of the 20th IEEE Real-Time Systems Symposium*, pp. 104-114, IEEE CS Press, 1999.
17. W.J. Fokkink. *Introduction to Process Algebra.* Texts in Theoretical Computer Science, Springer, 2000.
18. H. Garavel and H. Hermanns. On combining functional verification and performance evaluation using CADP. In *FME 2002: Formal Methods - Getting IT Right.* LNCS 2391:410-429, Springer, 2002.
19. H. Garavel, F. Lang, and R. Mateescu. An overview of CADP 2001. *EASST Newsletter*, 4:13–24, 2002.
20. H. Garavel and M. Sighireanu. On the introduction of exceptions in E-LOTOS. In R. Gotzhein and J. Bredereke, editors, *Formal Description Techniques IX*, pp. 469-484, Chapman and Hall, 1996.
21. B. Haverkort. SPN2MGM: Tool support for matrix-geometric stochastic Petri nets. In *Proc. of IEEE International Computer Performance and Dependability Symposium*, pp. 219–228. IEEE CS Press, 1996.

22. B. Haverkort. Private communication. 2000.
23. B. Haverkort, L. Cloth, H. Hermanns, J.-P. Katoen, and C. Baier. Model checking performability properties. In *The International Conference on Dependable Systems and Networks, DSN 2002*, pp. 103–112. IEEE CS Press, 2002.
24. H. Hermanns. *Interactive Markov Chains and the Quest for Quantified Quality*. LNCS 2428, Springer, 2002.
25. H. Hermanns. Performance and reliability model checking and model construction. In *Proc. 5th International ERCIM Workshop on Formal Methods for Industrial Critical Systems (FMICS 2000)*, GMD Report, 91:11–28, 2000.
26. H. Hermanns. Construction and verification of performance and reliability models. *Bulletin of the EATCS*, 74:135-154, 2001.
27. H. Hermanns, U. Herzog, U. Klehmet, V. Mertsiotakis, and M. Siegle. Compositional performance modelling with the TIPPTOOL. *Performance Evaluation* 39(1-4):5–35, 2000.
28. H. Hermanns and C. Joubert. A set of performance and dependability components for CADP. In *9th International Conference on Tools and Algorithms for the Construction and Analysis of Systems*. LNCS 2619:425-430, Springer, 2003.
29. H. Hermanns and J.-P. Katoen. Automated compositional Markov chain generation for a plain-old telephony system. *Science of Computer Programming* 36(1):97–127, 2000.
30. H. Hermanns, J.-P. Katoen, J. Meyer-Kayser, and M. Siegle. Towards model checking stochastic process algebra, 2000. In *2nd Int. Conference on Integrated Formal Methods (IFM 2000)*, LNCS 1945:420-439, Springer, 2000.
31. H. Hermanns, J.-P. Katoen, J. Meyer-Kayser, and M. Siegle. A tool for model-checking Markov chains. *Int. Journal on Software Tools for Technology Transfer*, 4(2):153–172, 2003.
32. G.G. Infante-Lopez, H. Hermanns, and J.-P. Katoen. Beyond memoryless distributions: Model checking semi-Markov chains. In *Process Algebra and Probabilistic Methods, Performance Modelling and Verification*.LNCS 2165:57-70, Springer, 2001.
33. K.G. Larsen, P. Pettersson, and W. Yi. UPPAAL in a nutshell. *Int. J. of Software Tools for Technology Transfer*, 1(1/2):134–152, 1997.
34. C. Lindemann and R. German. Modeling discrete event systems with state-dependent deterministic service times. *Discrete Event Dynamic Systems: Theory and Applications* 3:249–270, July 1993.
35. R. Jain. *The Art of Computer Systems Performance Analysis*. J. Wiley,

New York, 1991.

36. A.A. Markov. Extension of the limit theorems of probability theory to a sum of variables connected in a chain. 1907. In *The Notes of the Imperial Academy of Sciences of St. Petersburg, VIII Series, Pysio–Mathematical College*, XXII(9), 1907. reprinted in Appendix B of R. Howard. *Dynamic Probabilistic Systems*, volume 1: Markov Chains. John Wiley and Sons, 1971.

37. E.-R. Olderog and C.A.R. Hoare. Specification oriented semantics for communicating processes. *Acta Informatica* 23:9–66, 1986.

38. B. Plateau and K. Atif. Stochastic automata network for modeling parallel systems. *IEEE Transactions on Software Engineering*, 17(10), 1991.

39. W.H. Sanders, *Construction and Solution of Performability Models based on Stochastic Activity Networks*, Ph.D. thesis, University of Michigan, 1988.

40. H.A. Simon and A. Ando. Aggregation of variables in dynamic systems. *Econometrica* 29:111-138, 1961.

41. A. N. Shiryaev. *Probability*. Graduate texts in Mathematics. Springer, 1989.

42. Space Telescope Science Institute Home Page. http://www.stsci.edu/

43. W.J. Stewart. *Introduction to the Numerical Solution of Markov Chains*. Princeton Univ. Press, 1994.

44. C.A. Vissers, G. Scollo, M. van Sinderen, and E. Brinksma. Specification styles in distributed systems design and verification. *Theoretical Computer Science*, 89(1):179–206, 1991.

DOES COMBINING NONDETERMINISM AND PROBABILITY MAKE SENSE?

PRAKASH PANANGADEN

School of Computer Science
McGill University, Canada
E-mail: prakash@cs.mcgill.ca

1 Introduction

Yes! Before I get lost in the thread of the argument let me state my position clearly. I do, however, think that we need to think about what we are doing.

Probability theory appears in many places in computer science. In algorithmics randomness appears as a computational resource, in the related field of combinatorics, probability theory appears in many areas – many of them pioneered by Erdos – and in complexity theory probability adds to the rich landscape of complexity classes. These, however, are not the areas that I want to address in this note. I am interested in probability theory as it is used in concurrency theory (probabilistic process algebra) and in performance evaluation. I wish I knew more about AI for there are many interesting things to say about probabilistic reasoning in AI. Fortunately there is an outstanding book "Probabilistic Reasoning in Intelligent Systems" by Judea Pearl [2]. I am most familiar with the situation in concurrency theory so I will concentrate on that; I hope very much that experts in AI or performance evaluation are stimulated to add their own comments.

Both probability and nondeterminism are invoked to deal with uncertainty. Crudely speaking, probability is an attempt to quantify likelihood, while with nondeterminism one tries to keep track of "all possibilities" on an equal footing. In both cases elaborate mathematical formalisms have been developed. Measure theory and probability theory are too vast to even enumerate the topics here. In the case of nondeterminism one has a variety of process algebras and – on the semantical side – there is a rich theory of powersets and powerdomains.

With nondeterminism we can keep track of what "must" happen, what "may" happen and various combinations in between. In a probabilistic analysis we can report all kinds of things like averages, variances and expectation values, all of which serve to give quantitative estimates. In this setting, what are we to make of the proliferation of formalisms that combine the two? Clearly taking an "average" is nonsensical in this case and while many calculations can be done their meaning deserves scrutiny.

In order to address these questions, it is helpful to examine the so-called Bayesian viewpoint. For one thing it highlights an acrimonious debate – which is well worth following – within the professional statistics community. For another it focuses attention in what I believe is the key issue: "what is the origin of the uncertainty?" A curious fact that I have observed is that most concurrency theorists that I have asked will tell me that they reject the Bayesian viewpoint but many of the formalisms that they use only make sense from this viewpoint.

2 Statistics vs Probabilistic Models

To begin with we should ask, "what is the difference between probability theory and statistics?" The answer can be summarized in one word: "observations." In probability theory one has a model of a real-world situation and one calculates certain probabilities and expectation values. There is very little disagreement about how these calculations should be done[a]. In statistics, on the other hand, one has data – the results of observations – and one tries to validate or refine the model based on this data.

There is a duality here. In probability one starts from the model and tries to predict what will be observed, in statistics one starts from observations and tries to understand the model. In fact statistics is sometimes called "inverse probability" for just this reason.

3 Bayesian Inference

Now in understanding the differences between Bayesians and their opponents – usually called "frequentists" – it is important to keep the distinction between statistical analysis of data and probabilistic analysis of a model in mind. Bayesians and frequentists both believe that probability is a measure of uncertainty but Bayesians believe that one can use the formalism of probability to quantify uncertainty of any kind. Frequentists believe that randomness arises in certain situations where one cannot keep track of all the data (motions of gas molecules, birth and death phenomena in a population etc.) but that you cannot treat everything as if it were a random variable. They interpret probability as follows. If you say that some quantity, say θ, is less than 1 with probability $\frac{1}{2}$ what you mean is that if you had an "ensemble of identically

---

[a]There are a few who believe that probability measures should be finitely additive rather than σ-additive but we ignore such fine points.

prepared systems" and you measured θ in each one you would get a value less than one, half the time. The underlying assumption is that there is some random process determining the value of θ.

In order to highlight the difference let us consider an example. Suppose that we wish to study whether a coin is fair. We start out saying that the probability of "heads" is $0 < p < 1$ but otherwise we know nothing about it. The classical probability dogma asserts that one can apply probabilistic analysis to random variables. Thus it would not make sense to say that the probability that p is $\frac{1}{2}$ is $\frac{1}{3}$. The reason that this makes no sense – classically – is that there is no random process choosing the value of p. However, in the Bayesian viewpoint probability is used to quantify any kind of uncertainty so such a statement makes perfect sense. It is clear that in daily life even a simple statement like "the chance of rain tomorrow is 30%" can only be read in a Bayesian sense – there is no "ensemble of identical systems" to consider here.

Bayes' theorem states that

$$Pr(H|O) = \frac{Pr(O|H) * Pr(H)}{Pr(O)},$$

where H represents a hypothesis, O represents an observation and the bar notation stands for conditional probability. Now if we write this as

$$Pr(A|B) = \frac{Pr(B|A) * Pr(A)}{Pr(B)},$$

we get a trivial "theorem" – the proof is immediate from the definition. What makes this theorem interesting is how it is used in statistical inference.

What do we mean by H? Imagine that there is a model of some random process, say the disintegration of a certain kind of nucleus. This is assumed to be a Poisson process with a certain parameter value λ. How does one deal with the fact that one is uncertain about the distribution? *The Bayesian viewpoint is to treat it as another random variable.* This is where the two viewpoints disagree sharply. According to the frequentists there is a random process choosing the times at which the nuclei disintegrate, but there is no random process choosing values of λ. According to the Bayesian viewpoint treating the number of disintegrations as a random variable reflects *our* uncertainty as to when the disintegrations occur, treating λ as a random variable corresponds to quantifying our uncertainty about this parameter value. Thus the Bayesian ascribes a more subjective interpretation to the probability values while the frequentist argues that there is some "inherent randomness" which can be treated as a random variable while other things cannot be treated as if they were random variables merely because they are unknown. Thus what makes Bayes' theorem interesting is not its actual statement but, rather, the interpretation and use of it.

How do Bayesians use Bayes' theorem? They would treat $Pr(H)$ as describing their *à priori* knowledge about the distribution of possible values. This is called the *prior*, of which more later. Then they would make observations. They would calculate $Pr(O|H)$ from the model. More precisely, given an assumption about the parameter values one could calculate what observations one would expect. Similarly, one can calculate the denominator from the model. For example, we could get it from

$$Pr(O) = Pr(O|H) \cdot Pr(H) + Pr(O|H^c) \cdot Pr(H^c).$$

The continuous analogue of Bayes' theorem is

$$f(\theta|x) = \frac{\ell(x|\theta)g(\theta)}{m(x) = \int \ell(x|\theta)g(\theta)d\theta},$$

where θ represents the parameter value that one is trying to get a better understanding of from experiment and x is the variable that one is measuring. The function $g(\theta)$ represents one's prior for θ and $m(x)$ is the marginal distribution for x. The point is that the observed quantity x and the parameter θ are *both treated as random variables on the same footing*.

Looking at all this from the point of view of pure probability theory it is hard to appreciate the difference. What one does in probability theory is exclusively to calculate $Pr(O|H)$. One has a model and one calculates what one expects to see. The difference between the viewpoints is hard to tell at this point.

The difference emerges as one refines one's prior on the basis of observations. Bayesians start with prior distributions based on whatever knowledge (or ignorance) they might possess and – using Bayes' theorem – they construct new priors as data comes in. The uncertainty that they feel about the model will continue to be expressed as a probability distribution over the possible parameter values. Thus a probabilistic situation is described by a probability model and a prior.

There is another important point. How would a frequentist describe uncertainty about the result of experiment? She would calculate the probability of seeing what was actually seen given the parameter values. If the probability is high she will say that she has high confidence in the parameters. She will definitely not assign a probability distribution to the possible parameter values. However, this in convoluted. The observations really were seen. What sense is there in asking what the probability is of seeing these observations?

The Bayesian will report $Pr(H|O)$, i.e., he takes as given that the actual observations were seen.

4 Infinite Regress and the Prior

There are two pressing questions: "where does the prior come from?" and "won't there be infinite regress in model descriptions." These are indeed subtle issues.

Imagine that there is some distribution assumed for some parameter value. This distribution may contain parameters about which one is uncertain again. Then there may be another distribution describing one's belief about these parameters. This can clearly go on forever. What is done in practice is to cut off this process at some stage. There is – as far as I understand – no general result that guarantees that the effects of these higher-order distributions become less and less important. However this is known for certain classes of distributions and widely assumed in general.

Where does the prior come from? This is often the point of attack on Bayesian theory. The prior is attacked as being subjective. I personally feel that this is not any reason to reject the entire subject. The point is that in the absence of any information one needs to choose an "uninformative" prior (often assumed to be flat). Subsequently the prior that one uses is refined as data comes in and it may become sharply peaked if the data warrants it. However the choice of prior can influence the refinement process. For example, if one starts with a strong prejudice against something then it takes much more data to convince one that the prejudice is mistaken. *This is exactly how we reason even when performing scientific experiments.* The Bayesian viewpoint says that probability theory is about how makes inferences under uncertainty. It is not about some mystical absolute randomness; any randomness is a reflection of our ignorance. Most important of all, the Bayesian does not appeal to some hypothetical "ensemble" of identical systems.

It might seem as if the use of priors lays the Bayesians open to the charge of being overly subjective. However, we all use priors. Here is a very nice example due to L.J. Savage [3]. The discussion is taken from "Statistical Decision Theory" by J.O. Berger [1]. Consider the following three statistical experiments:

- A lady who adds milk to her tea, claims to be able to tell whether the tea or the milk was poured first. In all of ten trials she turns out to be correct.

- A music expert claims to be able to distinguish a page of Haydn score

382

from a page of Mozart score. In each of ten trials he is right every time.

- A drunken friend claims that she can predict the outcome of a coin toss. In each of ten trials she is right every time.

In this case the quantity θ is the probability of the person determining the answer correctly. According to a classical analysis, the hypothesis $\theta = 0.5$ (i.e., the person is guessing) would be rejected with a confidence level of 2^{-10}. However our reactions to these statistically identical situations are very different. In the second situation we would have no reason to doubt the expert. In case three a strong *prior* disbelief in ESP would lead us to reject the data and demand more testing. In case one it is hard to formulate an opinion, it depends on what one believes is plausible. Our differing reactions are based on the use of prior information (or belief).

5 Does It Make a Difference to Concurrency Theorists?

What we are doing in concurrency theory is mainly model building, we are rarely analyzing data and refining our models. We build the models and we describe what happens. This is a reasonable activity and it makes sense. However, it behooves us to consider how we use our reasoning tools. Perhaps the semantics of our probabilistic frameworks should not be purely about predicting the results of hypothetical experiments but should describe how we revise our models in the face of observations. This is especially true as we make more contact with practitioners and engineers. There are now probabilistic model-checking tools which are beginning to be used in practice. It is time to think about what we mean by formulas that assert that the probability of such and such formula holding is between 0.3 and 0.5. Does it mean that such a probability is itself a random variable? with "uniformly distributed" probability of lying between 0.3 and 0.5? If so, perhaps we can report distributions other than flat ones. I think that it does make sense to consider such combinations.

The most important (in some sense, the only) reason to introduce non-determinism is to deal with *abstraction*. Abstraction is, of course, our most potent method for dealing with complexity. We imagine large systems being composed of smaller – well-understood – subsystems and we *compose* them together to obtain the original system. An essential part of the composition is *hiding* the interactions between the constituent subsystems. This inevitably introduces nondeterminism. To summarize; we introduce nondeterminism to express uncertainty in concurrency theory.

From a strict Bayesian viewpoint this does not make sense. They would say that any uncertainty should correspond to some distribution, perhaps even a flat one. The point is that they are talking about a situation where they get to work with real data and refine their models of real systems on the basis of their observations. We build paper (or computer) models and make predictions before the system that we are modelling has ever been built. Thus, nondeterminism *is* appropriate for concurrency theorists. However, I feel very strongly that nondeterminism makes very little sense for people doing performance analysis of actual physical systems. They are working with data and trying to refine the models based on data. They are doing statistics.

From the Bayesian viewpoint the use of probability intervals is reasonable. What one is saying is that a certain probability is a parameter of the theory and is being assumed to be flat. However it raises the idea that rather than just say that the probability lies in an interval one can imagine a richer logic where some probability is asserted to be distributed according to some distribution function. This may impact some of the logics that are currently used for concurrent stochastic processes, like pCTL*.

6 Conclusions

It would be very instructive to understand how others – AI people or economists or game theorists, for example – deal with the combination of nondeterminism and uncertainty. In my view nondeterminism certainly has a place in modelling. It corresponds to *under specification* or *abstraction*. It seems reasonable to provide designs with certain implementation decisions left unspecified. It is reasonable to calculate *bounds* on probabilities and averages before one goes ahead with implementation.

One classical source of abstraction in concurrency is the scheduler. One assumes that the behaviour of the scheduler is unknown even in a probabilistic sense. I think that this makes sense when one is discussing a paper design. However, it does not make sense when one is talking about an actual system. If one has a real live concurrent system that is being analyzed partly on the basis of experimental data, then nondeterminism has no place. Rather the scheduler should be described in terms of some unknown parameters. As the data comes, one can discover properties of these parameters.

Since I first wrote this note a number of interesting issues have come to my attention. Most interesting perhaps is the debate about quantum probability and bayesianism. Google is as good a guide as any to various online debates and resources on bayesianism.

References

1. J.O. Berger. *Statistical Decision Theory.* Springer-Verlag, 1980.
2. J. Pearl. *Probabilistic Reasoning in Intelligent Systems.* Morgan-Kaufmann, 1988.
3. J.L. Savage. The subjective basis of statistical practice. Technical report, Department of Statistics, University of Michigan, 1961.

THE ALGEBRAIC STRUCTURE OF PETRI NETS*

VLADIMIRO SASSONE

Department of Informatics
University of Sussex, UK
E-mail: vs@susx.ac.uk

This survey retraces, collects, and summarises the contributions of the author —
both individually and in collaboration with others — on the theme of algebraic,
compositional approaches to the semantics of Petri nets.

1 Introduction

An extremely successful line of research in the *semantics of concurrency*,
rooted in the very ideas of denotational semantics, is the one following the
algebraic approach. It focuses on *structural* and *compositional* aspects of systems and behaviours, and the leading idea is to describe them by means of
a few basic building blocks and a small number of *combinators* [39,62,38,64].
The appeal of this is that it tends to devise neat algebraic structures that
capture the *essential* nature of the class of systems considered.

In this paper, we first survey a line of research — detailed in [58,24,59],
[86,87,16] — aimed at recasting Petri net *processes* in the light of ideas from
process algebras and *categorical algebra*. In particular, we shall focus on Petri
net *concatenable processes* [24,86], on *strongly* concatenable processes [87,16],
and on their representation in terms of *symmetric monoidal categories*.

Petri nets were introduced in the 1960's by Carl Adam Petri in [74] (see
also the references [75,80,85,72,83]). They are a widely used model for concurrency, attractive from the theoretical point of view because of its simplicity and its intrinsically concurrent and distributed nature, and very successful in applications such as system modeling, analysis, and design (see,
e.g., [81,82,46,99] and browse through the several available computer-aided
design, analysis, and verification tools based on Petri nets [77]).

Actually, 'Petri net' is a rather generic term: in fact, Petri's original
idea can be constrained and generalised in many sensible ways, giving rise
to several net-based models widely studied in the literature. These range
from the essential *elementary* [84] and *place/transition nets* [26] to the sophisticated *predicate/transition* [88] and *coloured nets* [47,48,49], including
stochastic Petri nets [2] used in simulation and performance evaluation.

---

*A previous version has appeared in *The Bulletin of the EATCS no 70*, June 2000.

Here we shall be concerned exclusively with place/transition (PT) nets — though it would be interesting to explore to what extent these ideas and techniques can be lifted to classes of high-level nets. The reason why PT nets form an important class is that they formalise a very basic model of distributed systems, in which (instances of) places (i.e., tokens) can be understood as available resources, and transitions as concurrent activities that require exclusive use of some of these resources and that, after completion, release new resources (tokens in places) to the environment. Another suggestive possible interpretation is to look at places as 'mailboxes' and at tokens as messages, portraying a view of place/transition nets as a distributed model of concurrency with a form of asynchronous message passing. We shall study PT nets under the banner '*Petri nets are monoids*', initiated by [58]. Our first aim will be to axiomatise the (noninterleaving) computations of a net, i.e., its processes, and their structure. We seek an *algebra* to represent them; an algebra where processes can be seen as terms built up from their atomic components and whose algebraic laws can be used to compute with and reason on and them.

The mathematical structures we shall use to this purpose are the symmetric monoidal categories. *Monoidal categories* date back to [7] (see [55] for an easy thorough introduction and [28] for advanced topics). Essentially, a monoidal category is an algebraic theory of so-called 'arrows', or 'morphisms', and of two operations on them, a (partial) *sequential* composition $\_;\_$, and a *parallel* composition $\otimes$, the tensor product. But let us proceed orderly. A *category* is a graph equipped with a self-looping edge id_u for each node u, and with an associative binary operation $\_;\_$ of composition of adjacent edges. Nodes and edges here are called *objects* and *arrows*, and id_u is the *identity* arrow at object u, and behaves as a unit under composition. A *functor* is a mapping between categories that behaves homomorphically with respect to $\_;\_$ and id, i.e., it maps identities to identities. Adding a tensor product to a category amounts to adding to the graph an operation of parallel composition of objects and arrows that behaves well with respect to $\_;\_$. In this paper we shall be concerned only with a particular kind of monoidal categories, namely the 'strict' ones.

A *strict monoidal category* is a structure $(C, \otimes, e)$, where C is a category, e is an object of C, called the *unit* object, $\otimes: C \times C \to C$ is a functor that, as an operation of objects and arrows, is associative and admits e and id_e as, respectively, the unit object and arrow. A monoidal category is *symmetric* if, informally, the tensor product is *commutative* up to a chosen family of isomorphisms $c_{u,v}: u \otimes v \xrightarrow{\sim} v \otimes u$, for all objects $u, v \in C$. The collection of the arrows $c_{u,v}$ must be subject to a *naturality* condition [55] and to the all important Kelly-MacLane *coherence* axioms [54,51], and is called the *symmetry* of C.

Another relevant application of Petri nets is their use as a semantic basis to interpret concurrent languages, a task that calls for a compositional, '*process algebra-like*' description of nets. And in fact, the literature is rich of examples of process algebras and concurrent programming languages interpreted over the domain of nets, as, e.g., [71,34,23,20], and also of real net-based process algebras, such as [36,10,63]. In particular, [34] uses Petri nets to model an algebra of processes and to infer several noninterleaving behavioural equivalences on it, while [23] interprets CCS (cf. [62]) on nets — taking up a line of research initiated by [94], where event structures (cf. [96]) were used — based on an operation of decomposition of processes into sequential agents. The decomposition approach is also followed by [71], while the semantics for the π-calculus (cf. [64]) presented in [20] is based on nets with inhibitory arcs (see, e.g., [22,45]), a powerful extension of PT nets. A related line of research, as already mentioned, takes inspiration from the work on process algebras and set out to design and study net algebras. One of the most prominent approaches among these is the Petri Box calculus [10], centered around operations of asynchronous communication and synchronisation, while [36] builds on operations of parallel and non-deterministic composition. In a different context, but with a similar vein, [63] introduces the notion of named Petri nets and provides a representation for them as an action calculus.

We proceed in our survey by focusing on the algebra of nets developed in [68]. That approach is entirely based on a notion of *interface* for Petri nets that specifies what parts of the net are *public*, i.e., accessible to the environment, and what parts are *private*. Also, it partitions public net components in '*input*' places and '*output*' transitions, and dictates the discipline by which nets are composed via a minimal set of combinators forming a rudimentary calculus of nets. The most important of these is a form of asynchronous communication — message passing — by means of which a net may, via its output transitions, send messages to another net, by delivering tokens to the second net's input places. Net composition is centred on an interesting form of *recursion* consisting of *feeding back* outputs to inputs, yielding a bridge to structures of recent common interest in category theory and in computer science: the *traced monoidal categories* [50].

PETRI NETS IN THE SMALL

Among the semantics proposed for Petri nets, a role of paramount importance is played by the various notions of *process*, e.g. [76,35,9], whose merit is to provide a faithful account of computations involving many different transitions and of the *causal connections* between the events occurring in computations. This is, in fact, the essence of the *noninterleaving* approach to the semantics of concurrency, where computations are decorated with additional information describing causes and effects that ruled the occurrences of events in them. The mathematical structures arising naturally form this premises are the partially ordered multisets [79], *pomsets* for short. Thus, informally speaking, Petri net processes — whose standard version is given by the Goltz-Reisig *nonsequential processes* [35] — are net computations together with an explanation of the cause by which each transition has fired, that be represented abstractly by means of ordered sets whose elements are labelled by transitions.

Bare process models, however, fail to bring to the foreground the *algebraic structure* of the space of computations of a net. Our interest, instead, resides on abstract models that capture the mathematical essence of such spaces, possibly axiomatically, roughly in the same way as a prime algebraic domain (or, equivalently, a prime event structure [96,98]) models the computations of a net (see, e.g., [70]). The research detailed in [58,24,59,86,87] identifies such structures as *symmetric monoidal categories* — where objects are states, i.e., multisets of tokens, arrows are processes, and the tensor product and the arrow composition model, respectively, the operations of parallel and sequential composition of processes.

At a higher level of abstraction, the next important question concerns the *global structure* of the collection of such spaces, i.e., the axiomatisation '*in the large*' of net computations. In other words, the space of the spaces of computations of Petri nets. Building on [24,86], the work presented in [87] shows that the so-called *symmetric Petri categories*, a class of symmetric strict monoidal categories with free (non-commutative) monoids of objects, provide one such an axiomatisation.

In this part, we retrace and illustrate the main results achieved so far along these lines of research by the author, both in joint and individual work. The next one will look at net algebras 'in the large' from a different angle.

2 Petri Nets as Monoids

The idea of looking at nets as *algebraic structures*, e.g. [80,97], has been interpreted in [58] by viewing nets as *internal graphs* in categories of sets with structure and using monoidal categories as a suitable semantic framework for them. Precisely, a net is a graph

$$N = (pre_N, post_N : T_N \to \mu(S_N))$$

whose nodes form the free commutative monoid $\mu(S_N)$ of the *finite* multisets of S_N. Here, S_N and T_N are sets of, respectively, *places* and *transitions*, and pre_N and $post_N$ are functions assigning a *source* and a *target* multiset of places to each transition. Accordingly, a morphism of nets is graph homomorphism $\langle f_t, f_p \rangle$ whose node component respects the monoidal structure on places. This, with the obvious componentwise composition of morphisms, defines the category Petri.

Ideally, Petri net processes are simply computations carrying explicit information about cause/effect relationship between event occurrences. This is conveniently described by defining a process of N to be a map $\pi \colon \Theta \to N$, where Θ defines the process 'skeleton' and π 'labels' Θ with places and transitions of N in a way compatible with its structure.

Definition 2.1 *A process net is a finite, acyclic net* Θ *such that for all* $t \in T_\Theta$, $pre_\Theta(t)$ *and* $post_\Theta(t)$ *are sets (as opposed to multisets), and for all* $t_0 \neq t_1 \in T_\Theta$,

$$pre_\Theta(t_0) \cap pre_\Theta(t_1) = \varnothing \qquad and \qquad post_\Theta(t_0) \cap post_\Theta(t_1) = \varnothing.$$

A process of $N \in$ Petri *is (up to isomorphism) a net morphism* $\pi \colon \Theta \to N$, *where* Θ *is a process net and* π *maps places to places (as opposed to multisets of places).*

Inspired by the work in process algebras, we would like to concatenate a process $\pi_1 \colon \Theta_1 \to N$ with source u to a process $\pi_0 \colon \Theta_0 \to N$ with target u by *gluing* appropriately the *terminal* places of Θ_0 and the *initial* places of Θ_1. However, the simple minded attempt fails immediately: due to the ambiguity introduced by multiple instances of places, two processes of N can be composed sequentially in many ways, each of which gives a possibly different process of N. In other words, process concatenation has to do with merging *tokens in the process places*, that is instances of places, rather than merging *places*.

3   Concatenable Processes

It follows from the precedent argument that any attempt to recast the processes of N as an algebra that includes sequential composition must disambiguate each token in a process. This is exactly the idea of *concatenable processes* [24]: they are simply processes where, when needed, instances of places (tokens) are distinguished by appropriate decorations, e.g., by ordering the initial and terminal places that carry the same label.

Definition 3.1 *A concatenable process of* N *is a triple*

$$(\pi \colon \Theta \to N, \{<_a\}_{a \in S_N}, \{\ll_a\}_{a \in S_N}),$$

390

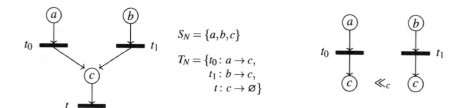

$S_N = \{a, b, c\}$

$T_N = \{t_0 : a \to c,$
$\qquad t_1 : b \to c,$
$\qquad t : c \to \varnothing\}$

Figure 1. A net N and one of its two concatenable processes $CP : a + b \to 2c$

where π is a process, and $<_a$ and $\ll_a$ are linear orderings of, respectively, the initial and terminal places of Θ contained in $\pi_p^{-1}(a)$ (cf. Figure 1).

This immediately yields an operation of concatenation: the ambiguity about multiple tokens is resolved using the additional information given by the orderings (cf. Figure 2).

Definition 3.2 Let $CP_0 : u \to v$ and $CP_1 : v \to w$ be concatenable processes of N, and let $\pi_0 : \Theta_0 \to N$ and $\pi_1 : \Theta_1 \to N$ be their underlying processes. The sequential composition, or concatenation, $CP_0 ; CP_1 : u \to w$ is obtained by gluing together π_0 and π_1, identifying injectively each terminal place of Θ_0 with an initial place of Θ_1 in the unique way compatible with the orderings $\ll_a$ on Θ_0 and $<_a$ on Θ_1 for all $a \in S_N$.

The existence of concatenation leads easily to the definition of the category of concatenable processes of N. It turns out this is a *symmetric strict monoidal category* [55] under the tensor product given by the following operation of parallel composition of processes: for $CP_0 : u_0 \to v_0$ and $CP_1 : u_1 \to v_1$, $CP_0 \otimes CP_1 : u_0 + u_1 \to v_0 + v_1$ is obtained by putting π_0 and π_1 disjointly side by side and by making the places of Θ_0 precede the places of Θ_1 (cf. Figure 2; consult [24] for further examples).

The main result of [24] is an axiomatisation of such a category, stated here in the improved enunciation proved in [86]. Its relevance is that it describes net behaviours as *algebras* in terms of *universal* constructions.

Theorem 3.1 For any net N, there exists a one-to-one correspondence — preserving source, target, sequential and parallel composition (tensor product) of processes (arrows) — between the concatenable processes of N and the arrows of the category $\mathcal{P}(N)$ obtained from the free symmetric strict monoidal category $\mathcal{F}(N)$ on N by imposing the axioms

$c_{a,b} = id_{a \otimes b}$,   if a and b are different places of N,

$s ; t ; s' = t$,   if t is a transition of N and s, s' are symmetries of $\mathcal{F}(N)$,

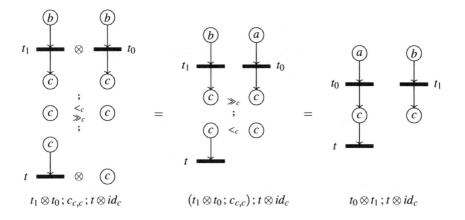

$$t_1 \otimes t_0\,;c_{c,c}\,;t \otimes id_c \qquad\qquad (t_1 \otimes t_0\,;c_{c,c})\,;t \otimes id_c \qquad\qquad t_0 \otimes t_1\,;t \otimes id_c$$

Figure 2. A net N and its concatenable process $\pi = t_0 \otimes t_1\,;t \otimes id_c$

where c, id, $\otimes$, and $_-;_-$ are, respectively, the symmetry isomorphism, the identities, the tensor product, and the composition of $\mathcal{F}(N)$.

This also yields an equational theory for net processes as, in explicit terms, $\mathcal{P}(N)$ is the category whose arrows are generated by the rules

$$\frac{u \in \mu(S_N)}{id_u\colon u \to u \text{ in } \mathcal{P}(N)} \qquad \frac{a \text{ and } b \text{ in } S_N}{c_{a,b}\colon a + b \to b + a \text{ in } \mathcal{P}(N)} \qquad \frac{t\colon u \to v \text{ in } T_N}{t\colon u \to v \text{ in } \mathcal{P}(N)}$$

$$\frac{\alpha\colon u \to v \text{ and } \beta\colon u' \to v' \text{ in } \mathcal{P}(N)}{\alpha \otimes \beta\colon u + u' \to v + v' \text{ in } \mathcal{P}(N)} \qquad \frac{\alpha\colon u \to v \text{ and } \beta\colon v \to w \text{ in } \mathcal{P}(N)}{\alpha;\beta\colon u \to w \text{ in } \mathcal{P}(N)}$$

modulo the axioms expressing that it is a strict monoidal category with composition $_-;_-$, tensor $_- \otimes _-$, and symmetry isomorphism c and the two axioms quoted above.

Example 3.1 *Figure 2 shows a concatenable process π for the net N of Figure 1 that corresponds to the arrow $t_0 \otimes t_1\,;t \otimes id_c$ of $\mathcal{P}(N)$. To exemplify the algebra of processes of N, π is expressed as parallel $(_- \otimes _-)$ and sequential $(_-;_-)$ composition of simpler processes. Such operations are matched precisely by operations and axioms of $\mathcal{P}(N)$, and this is the essence of the theorem above.*

The symmetries of $\mathcal{P}(N)$ and the related axiom on the symmetry isomorphism c play in this correspondence a role absolutely fundamental: they account for the families of orderings $\{<_a\}_{a \in S_N}$ and $\{\ll_a\}_{a \in S_N}$, which are the key to concatenable processes, guaranteeing a correct treatment of sequen-

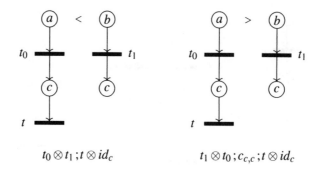

Figure 3. Two strongly concatenable processes corresponding to π of Figure 2

tial composition. In other words, they are an algebraic representation of the 'threads of causality' in process concatenation. On the other hand, the axiom is actually a problematic one: because of its negative premise, viz. $a \neq b$, it invalidates the freeness of $\mathcal{F}(N)$ on Petri. Much worse, it makes $\mathcal{P}(\_)$ act not functorially on Petri. A detailed study of this issue is undertaken in [87], where a functorial and universal construction for net computations is presented, based on a refinement of the notion of concatenable processes that is the topic of next section.

4 Strongly Concatenable Processes

Strongly concatenable processes are a slight refinement of concatenable processes introduced in [87] to yield a functorial algebraic description of net computations. The refinement, which consists of decorating initial and terminal places of processes more strongly than in concatenable processes, e.g., by ordering all of them (cf. Figure 3), is shown to be — in a very precise mathematical sense — the slightest refinement that may achieve this. As for their predecessors, strongly concatenable processes admit an axiomatisation in terms of a universal algebraic construction based on symmetric monoidal categories.

Theorem 4.1 The strongly concatenable processes of a net N are the arrows of $\mathcal{Q}(N)$, obtained from the symmetric strict monoidal category freely generated from the places of N and, for each transition t of N, an arrow $t_{u,v}: u \to v$ for each pair of linearisations (as strings) u and v of the source and target (multisets) of t, by quotienting modulo the axiom

(Φ) $s; t_{u',v} = t_{u,v'}; s'$,   for $s: u \to u'$ and $s': v' \to v$ symmetries.

The key point here is to associate to N a category whose objects form a free *non-commutative* monoid (*viz.* S_N^* as opposed to $\mu(S_N)$), i.e., to deal with *strings* as explicit *representatives* of multisets. As a consequence, each transition of N has many corresponding arrows in $\mathcal{Q}(N)$, all however 'related' to each other by the *naturality* condition (Φ), which is the second relevant feature of $\mathcal{Q}(\_)$, actually the one that keeps the computational interpretation of the category $\mathcal{Q}(N)$ (strongly concatenable processes) so surprisingly close to that of $\mathcal{P}(N)$ (concatenable processes).

Concerning functoriality, $\mathcal{Q}(\_)$ extends to a *coreflection* functor from the category of Petri nets to a category of symmetric monoidal categories. Here, as in [61], we proceed using *2-categories*, an high-level approach that has the advantage of hiding some of the gory details.

Definition 4.1 *A symmetric Petri category is a symmetric strict monoidal category* C *whose monoid of objects is* S^*, *the free monoid on* S, *for some set* S.

Symmetric Petri categories allow us to capture the essence of the arrows generating $\mathcal{Q}(N)$, i.e., the instances of the transitions of N. These have in fact two very special properties that characterise them completely: (1) they are decomposable as tensors only trivially, and as compositions only by means of symmetries, and (2) they satisfy axiom (Φ). We then use such properties, expressed in abstract categorical terms, to define the notion of *transition* in a general symmetric Petri category.

Definition 4.2 *Let* C *be a symmetric Petri category and* S^* *its monoid of objects. An arrow* τ *in* C *is primitive if (denoting by* ϵ *the empty word in* S^**)*

- τ *is not a symmetry;*

- $\tau = \alpha\,;\beta$ *implies* α *is a symmetry and* β *is primitive, or vice versa;*

- $\tau = \alpha \otimes \beta$ *implies* $\alpha = id_\epsilon$ *and* β *is primitive, or vice versa.*

A transition $\tau\colon \bar{u} \to \bar{v}$ *of* C, *for* $\bar{u}, \bar{v} \in \mu(S)$, *is a family* $\{\tau_{u,v}\colon u \to v$ *in* C$\}$ *of primitive arrows indexed by those pairs of strings* u *and* v *with underlying multisets* $\bar{u}$ *and* $\bar{v}$, *respectively, and such that* $s\,;\tau_{u',v} = \tau_{u,v'}\,;s'$, *for* $s\colon u \to u'$ *and* $s'\colon v' \to v$ *symmetries of* C.

The definition above — that can also be formalised stating that transitions are natural transformations between appropriate functors — captures the essence of $\mathcal{Q}(N)$: the transitions in $\mathcal{Q}(N)$ are *all* and *only* the families $\{t_{u,v} \mid t\colon \bar{u} \to \bar{v} \in T_N\}$. This leads us to the following characterisation the *category* (of the categories) *of net computations*. The 2-categorical notions used in the theorem below are natural extensions of the corresponding (1-)categorical concepts; the interested reader will find the detailed definitions in [52].

Theorem 4.2 *Let* SPetriCat *be the 2-category whose objects are the symmetric Petri categories, whose arrows are the symmetric strict monoidal functors that respect transitions, and with a 2-cell $F \Rightarrow G$ if there exists a monoidal natural isomorphism between F and G whose components are all symmetries.*

Then, $\mathcal{Q}(\_)$: Petri $\rightarrow$ SPetriCat *is a pseudo 2-functor (considering the category* Petri *of Petri nets as a trivial 2-category) that admits a pseudo right adjoint* $\mathcal{N}(\_)$ *forming with* $\mathcal{Q}(\_)$ *a pseudo coreflection.*

5 Pre-Nets

Although strongly concatenable processes settle the token ambiguity problem of §2, they yield a construction that is functorial only up to isomorphism, thus needing a complex quotient operation [87] or, equivalently, the 2-categorical treatment outlined above.

In [15,16] we proposed an alternative construction centred on the notion of pre-net. *Pre-nets* are nets whose states are *strings* of tokens (as opposed to *multisets*). Such states can be seen as totally ordered markings, a more concrete representation of multisets. The idea is that each transition of a pre-net must specify the precise order in which the required resources are fetched and the results are produced, as if it were an elementary strongly concatenable process.

Definition 5.1 *A pre-net is a tuple* $R = (\zeta_0, \zeta_1 : T_R \rightarrow S_R^*)$*, where* S_R *is a set of places,* T_R *is a set of transitions, and* ζ_0 *and* ζ_1 *are functions assigning, respectively, source and target to each transition.*

A pre-net can be thought of as an implementation of a net, where an abstract data structure, the multiset, is refined into a more concrete implementation data structure, the string, and where each transition $t: \bar{u} \rightarrow \bar{v}$ is simulated by *one* linear implementation $t_{u,v}: u \rightarrow v$ arbitrarily fixed for some linearisations u and v of $\bar{u}$ and $\bar{v}$. For each PT we can arbitrarily choose a pre-net representation. This corresponds to fix a total order for the pre- and post-set of each transition, and differs from the approach recalled in §4 where, in order to avoid a choice, *all* the possible linearisations of the pre- and post-sets are considered in the alternative presentation of the net. We shall see that, in order to capture the standard process semantics of nets, choosing one representative for each transition suffices. In particular, although abandoning multisets might appear at first unnatural, this approach enjoys some good properties. Here we limit ourselves to the following two.

- All pre-net implementations of the same net share the same semantic model, i.e., the semantics is independent of the choice of linearisations;

- The semantic model for the implemented net given by the construction $\mathcal{Q}(\_)$ can be recovered from any pre-net implementation.

We shall use PreNet to indicate the category of pre-nets with the obvious notion of morphisms, i.e., a graph morphism whose node component is a monoid homomorphism. Let $\mu_R: S_R^* \to \mu(S_R)$ denote the function that maps u to $\bar{u}$, the multiset consisting of the symbols in u. Then, the map $\mathcal{A}$, from pre-nets to PT nets, sending the pre-net $R = (\zeta_0, \zeta_1: T_R \to S_R^*)$ to the net $\mathcal{A}(R) = (\mu_R \circ \zeta_0, \mu_R \circ \zeta_1: T_R \to \mu(S_R))$ extends to a functor from PreNet to Petri.

The functor $\mathcal{A}(\_): \text{PreNet} \to \text{Petri}$ is neither full, nor faithful. However, if we consider the category Net whose objects are either PT nets or pre-nets and whose morphisms are graph morphisms with monoid homomorphism as node components, then Petri is the quotient of Net modulo commutativity of the monoidal structure of nodes. This establishes a strong relationship, between PT nets and pre-nets, expressible via a coreflection between Petri and Net, which supports and further motivates our approach.

The natural algebraic models for representing concurrent computations on pre-nets live in the category SSMC of symmetric strict monoidal categories. More precisely, we are only interested in the full subcategory consisting of categories whose monoid of objects is freely generated. We denote it by FSSMC. The obvious forgetful functor from the category FSSMC to the category PreNet admits a left adjoint $\mathcal{Z}$. The category $\mathcal{Z}(R)$ has as objects the strings of S_R^*, and as arrows those generated by the rules below, modulo the axioms of monoidal categories (associativity, functoriality, identities, unit), including the coherence axioms that make of c the symmetry natural isomorphism.

$$\frac{w \in S_R^*}{id_w: w \to w \in \mathcal{Z}(R)} \qquad \frac{a \text{ and } b \text{ in } S_R^*}{c_{a,b}: ab \to ba \in \mathcal{Z}(R)} \qquad \frac{t: u \to v \text{ in } T_R}{t: u \to v \in \mathcal{Z}(R)}$$

$$\frac{\alpha: u \to v \text{ and } \beta: u' \to v' \in \mathcal{Z}(R)}{\alpha \otimes \beta: uu' \to vv' \in \mathcal{Z}(R)} \qquad \frac{\alpha: u \to v \text{ and } \beta: v \to v' \in \mathcal{Z}(R)}{\alpha; \beta: u \to v' \in \mathcal{Z}(R)}$$

The above construction bears strong similarities to the work on coherence by MacLane and Kelly, and even more closely to Pfender's construction of the free S-monoidal category [78]. In computer science, similar constructions are given by Hotz's X-categories [44], and by Benson [8], with grammars as the primary area of application.

As anticipated, corresponding to the two features of our approach, we have the following results. The first states that pre-nets representing isomorphic

PT nets yield the same algebraic net semantics. The second relates $\mathcal{Q}$, $\mathcal{Z}$, and $\mathcal{A}$, and contains the entire essence of the pre-net approach: *any pre-net representation of the net $\mathcal{A}(R)$ is as good as R.*

Theorem 5.1 *Let $R, R' \in$ PreNet. If $\mathcal{A}(R) \simeq \mathcal{A}(R')$, then $\mathcal{Z}(R) \simeq \mathcal{Z}(R')$.*

Theorem 5.2 *For R a pre-net, the category $\mathcal{Z}(R)$ quotiented out by the axiom $t = s_0 ; t ; s_1$, for each transition $t \colon u \to v$ and symmetries $s_0 \colon u \to u$ and $s_1 \colon v \to v$ is equivalent to the category $\mathcal{Q}(\mathcal{A}(R))$ of strongly concatenable processes.*

6 Related Work

An alternative important line of research on Petri nets semantics is the so-called *unfolding* approach, initiated by Nielsen et al. in [67] and further developed by Winskel in [96,98], according to which the *'dynamic'* structure of nets is 'unrolled', 'unfolded' to the *'static'* structure of event structures or, equivalently, of so-called occurrence nets. Its main merit is to assign to each net a single object that represents its entire behaviour and explains in a uniform, appealing way the interplay between non-determinism and concurrency. This fact can be justified formally by considering that the unfolding is a special (co)limit construction that gives rise to a coreflection between the categories of (safe) Petri nets and prime event structures. An alternative unfolding construction is described in [69], while Engelfriet in [32] consider a wider class of nets. Meseguer et al. [60] extend the construction of [67] to the entire category of place/transition nets and, in [59], study the relationships between unfolding and process semantics.

Other semantic investigations have capitalized directly on the *algebraic structure* of Petri nets, noticed by Reisig [80], by Winkowski [92,93], and later exploited by Winskel to identify a sensible notion of *morphism* between nets [95,97] and open the way to categorical treatments. Among the algebraic/categorical approaches, a relevant place is occupied by those drawing on the analogy between nets and proofs in *liner logic*, first noticed by Asperti [3]. Among these, we mention [13,14,31]. A really excellent survey is given by Martí-Oliet and Meseguer in [57]. Other relevant approaches are by Mukund [66], which provides an account of net behaviours in terms of (step) transition systems, and by Hoogers et al. in [42], that uses (generalised) trace theory (cf. [56,27]) to the same purpose, and in [43], where a notion of net unfolding is explained in terms of a notion of local event structure.

More recently, Ehrig and Padberg [30,73], inspired by the 'Petri nets as monoid' approach, give a uniform algebraic presentation of several classes of nets based on the idea of a parameterized abstract Petri net. Desel et al. [25] attain results on the representation of net processes similar to those presented here using partial algebras, in a fashion not unlike the early work of Winkowski [92,93].

The 'Petri nets as monoids' paradigm has been applied successfully to the semantics of several extensions of place/transition nets. Among these, two recent interesting results concern *zero-safe* and *contextual nets*. Zero-safe nets, introduced by Bruni and Montanari [17,18], extend Petri nets with a simple mechanism to model transactions, i.e., two or more transitions that must always occur without any other transition occurring in between. Contextual nets [22,65,45] (see also [21,91,6,5]) are nets with 'read-arcs' used to 'read' without consuming, so allowing multiple, non-exclusive, concurrent uses of the same resource (token) and, therefore, the modeling of shared resources. Bruni and Sassone in [19] extend the categorical process semantics approach surveyed here satisfactorily to contextual nets, building on previous work by Gadducci and Montanari [33].

PETRI NETS IN THE LARGE

The previous sections have mainly focused our attention *'in the small'*, at level of single nets, whereas Petri nets are often used *'in the large'*, for instance as a semantic basis to interpret concurrent languages, which calls for the study of *algebras of nets* 'in the large' and, possibly, for their abstract characterisations. Among several existing approaches, we recall the fundamental ideas underlying the work presented in [68], focusing on *finite* nets whose transitions are *labelled* by (possibly silent) actions. We shall use a *countable* set Act of *visible* actions $\alpha_1, \alpha_2, \alpha_3, \ldots$, and a distinguished *silent* action τ.

Definition 6.1 *A labelled Petri net is a Petri net N together with an initial state $s_N \in \mu(S_N)$, and a labelling function $\lambda_N: T_N \to Act \cup \{\tau\}$.*

7 An Algebra of Nets

Similarly to [10,63], everything is based on a notion of *interface* for Petri nets. These are ordered selections of places, the 'input', and transitions, the 'output', that specify what parts of N are *public*, i.e., accessible from the environment, and what parts are *private* to the net. The private places and transitions cannot be accessed and, therefore, cannot be used directly for connecting nets to each other.

Definition 7.1 *A net with interface is a structure $p_1, \ldots, p_n; t_1, \ldots, t_m \triangleright N$, where N is a finite labelled net, and $p_1, \ldots, p_n \in S_N$, $t_1, \ldots, t_m \in T_N$ are all distinct, and $\lambda_N(t_i) \neq \tau$.*

Drawing on the experience of developments in concurrency theory, a minimal yet expressive, set of combinators should certainly include operations allowing (forms of) *interaction/communication, parallel composition, recursion,* and — to facilitate the description of modular systems — operations such as *relabelling* and *hiding.* However, in order to avoid a chaotic 'structural' calculus where everything is permitted, it is obvious that some restrictions on the allowed connections of places and transitions must be imposed. The input/output partition of interfaces readily suggest a reasonable discipline of interaction: connections between nets should go from outputs to inputs, involving *only* public components. This formalises the well-motivated and solid intuition that the only allowed interactions are achieved by *sending* and *receiving* along interfaces, thought of as communication channels, the input interfaces providing 'buffers' in which the tokens arriving from the environment are gathered, the output interfaces sending tokens out to the environment. In other words, interfaces provide the notions of 'private' and 'public' channels for nets, and their input/output partition suggests a discipline for net cooperation.

Definition 7.2 *The set* **CM** *of combinators of nets with interface consists of the combinators defined by the following rules.*

$$\triangleright \quad \frac{\vec{p}_0; \vec{t}_0 \triangleright N_0 \quad and \quad \vec{p}_1; \vec{t}_1 \triangleright N_1 \quad disjoint}{par(\vec{p}_0; \vec{t}_0 \triangleright N_0, \vec{p}_1; \vec{t}_1 \triangleright N_1) = \vec{p}_0, \vec{p}_1; \vec{t}_0, \vec{t}_1 \triangleright N_0 \| N_1}$$

where $N_0 \| N_1$ *is the (componentwise) union of* N_0 *and* N_1;

$$\triangleright \quad \frac{1 \le i \le |\vec{p}| \quad and \quad 1 \le j \le |\vec{t}|}{add(i, j, \vec{p}; \vec{t} \triangleright N) = \vec{p}; \vec{t} \triangleright N \langle p_i \leftarrow t_j \rangle}$$

where $N \langle p \leftarrow t \rangle$ *is the net* N *augmented with an arc from* t *to* p;

$\triangleright$ $rel(\phi, \vec{p}; \vec{t} \triangleright N) = \vec{p}; \vec{t} \triangleright N[\phi]$,

where $\phi: Act \to Act \cup \{\tau\}$ *is a 'relabelling' function, and* $N[\phi]$ *is obtained from* N *by relabelling via* ϕ *the transitions that carry non-τ actions;*

$$\triangleright \quad \frac{\max(P) \le |\vec{p}| \quad and \quad \max(T) \le |\vec{t}|}{hide(P, T, \vec{p}; \vec{t} \triangleright N) = \vec{p} \backslash P; \vec{t} \backslash T \triangleright N}$$

where P *and* T *are finite sets of positive natural numbers* $(\max(\varnothing) = 0)$, *and* $\vec{x} \backslash X$ *is the string obtained from* $\vec{x}$ *by removing* x_i, *for all* $i \in X$;

$$\triangleright \quad \frac{1 \le i \le |\vec{p}|}{mark(i, \vec{p}; \vec{t} \triangleright N) = \vec{p}; \vec{t} \triangleright N \bullet p_i}$$

where $N \bullet p$ *is the net* N *augmented with a token in* p.

Observe that, since the $par(\_, \_)$ combinator is defined explicitly only for disjoint nets, a 'renaming' is generally needed before applying it to its arguments. This implies that no 'fusion' of nets is allowed by **CM**. Combinator $add(i, j, \_)$ adds an arc from the ith place to the jth transitions of the interface. It provides both a form of recursion and, used in connection with $par(\_, \_)$, a form of 'asynchronous message passing' which feeds the inputs of a net with the outputs of another one.

8 Congruences and Contexts for Labelled Petri Nets

The semantic equivalence of concurrent systems can be described in terms of several kinds of models, e.g., languages, traces, pomsets, event structures, etc., which reflect different assumptions about how behaviour is to be observed. Each of these notions of 'observation' gives rise to standard equivalences: a *linear* equivalence, a *bisimulation* and possibly, fixed a set of operators, their congruence closures. A thorough study of sixteen such behavioural equivalences for nets with interfaces is exposed in [68]. Here we treat a single, yet typical, case: the step bisimulation.

Definition 8.1 *A step bisimulation of N_0 and N_1 is a relation $\mathcal{R} \subseteq \mu(S_{N_0}) \times \mu(S_{N_1})$ such that $s_{N_0} \mathcal{R} s_{N_1}$, and whenever $s \mathcal{R} \bar{s}$, then (1) for each step (fireable multiset of transitions) $s[X\rangle s'$ of N_0, there exists a sequence of steps $\bar{s}[Y_1 \cdots Y_n\rangle \bar{s}'$ of N_1 resulting in the same multiset of non-τ labels as X, and with $s' \mathcal{R} \bar{s}'$; (2) vice versa swapping the roles of N_0 and N_1.*
Nets $\vec{p}_0; \vec{t}_0 \triangleright N_0$ and $\vec{p}_1; \vec{t}_1 \triangleright N_1$ are step bisimilar, written $\vec{p}_0; \vec{t}_0 \triangleright N_0 \leftrightarrow \vec{p}_1; \vec{t}_1 \triangleright N_1$, if there exists a step bisimulation of N_0 and N_1.

For engineering reasons, related to feasibility of correctness *verification* for complex systems, for mathematical reasons, related to the simplicity of *equational reasoning*, and for conceptual reasons, related to common intuitions about system equivalence, it is important to consider equivalences which are *congruences* for a chosen set of system constructors. This guarantees that systems can be replaced by equivalent ones in any context. Since it easy to see that $\leftrightarrow$ is not a congruence for $add(i, j, \_)$, we are led to $\leftrightarrow^c$, the largest congruence contained in it, viz. $\vec{p}_0; \vec{t}_0 \triangleright N_0 \leftrightarrow^c \vec{p}_1; \vec{t}_1 \triangleright N_1$ if and only if, for each **CM**-context $\mathcal{C}$, either *both* nets are incompatible with it, or $\mathcal{C}[\vec{p}_0; \vec{t}_0 \triangleright N_0] \leftrightarrow \mathcal{C}[\vec{p}_1; \vec{t}_1 \triangleright N_1]$.

This universal quantification over *all* contexts has however obvious drawbacks. The main result of [68] is to show that it can actually be dispensed with by identifying a minimal set of context which is *universal* for it. More precisely, for each pair N_0 and N_1 of nets with interface there exists a readily-identified context $\mathcal{C}$ such that N_0 and N_1 are $\leftrightarrow$-congruent if and only if $\mathcal{C}$

does not $\leftrightarrow$-distinguish them. Here follow some of the details.

Recalling that Act is equipped with an enumeration $\alpha_1, \alpha_2, \ldots$, let ψ be the relabelling function $\alpha_i \mapsto \alpha_{3i}$, $i \in \omega$.

Definition 8.2 *Let* $\varnothing; t \triangleright U$ *and* $p; \varnothing \triangleright U'$ *be the nets with interface shown below.*

Let $C_{i,j}$ *and* $U_{i,j}$, $i, j \in \omega$, *be the contexts defined below (with self-explanatory shorthands)*

$$C_{i,j} = par\Big(par_{k=1}^i\big(\varnothing; t \triangleright U[\alpha_{3k-2}/\alpha]\big), par_{k=1}^j\big(p; \varnothing \triangleright U'[\alpha_{3k-1}/\alpha]\big)\Big),$$

$$U_{i,j} = add_{k=1}^j\Big(k, i+k, add_{k=1}^i\big(j+k, k, par(C_{i,j}, rel(\psi, \_))\big)\Big).$$

Figure 4 presents $U_{i,j}[\vec{p}; \vec{t} \triangleright N]$ for a $\vec{p}; \vec{t} \triangleright N$ with $|\vec{p}| = i$ and $|\vec{t}| = j$. The interface of $U_{i,j}[\vec{p}; \vec{t} \triangleright N]$ is shown by naming and numbering the places and transitions which belong to it. The information in parentheses concern the orderings in $\vec{p}; \vec{t}$. Concerning the labels, we use ι_k for α_{3k-2}, $k = 1, \ldots, i$, o_k for α_{3k-1}, $k = 1, \ldots, j$, and $\alpha_{k_1}, \ldots \alpha_{k_j}$ for the labels of $\vec{t}$ in N. The dashed arrows are those inserted by add.

The contexts $U_{i,j}$ are conceptually very simple. They provide a copy of $\varnothing; t \triangleright U$ for each place in $\vec{p}$, and a copy of $p; \varnothing \triangleright U'$ for each transition in $\vec{t}$. The cascade of $add(i, j, \_)$ connects together the transition-place pairs so created. The role of the collection of $\varnothing; t \triangleright U$ is to test the 'reactivity' of the 'input' sites of $\vec{p}; \vec{t} \triangleright N$ by sending in any number of tokens, at any relative speed and independently for each place in $\vec{p}$. The collection of $p; \varnothing \triangleright U'$ tests the 'output'-behaviour by recording the firings of the transitions in $\vec{t}$.

In order for these contexts to form universal collections, it is necessary to distinguish in the behaviour of $U_{i,j}[\vec{p}; \vec{t} \triangleright N]$ the actions stemming from $U_{i,j}$ from those stemming from N. This is achieved by the $rel(\psi, \_)$ combinator: since the actions of N are uniformly 'remapped' to $3k$-numbered actions, we are free to use differently numbered actions in the contexts. The soundness of this technique relies on the fact that ψ is injective and, therefore, no equivalences are enforced by the ψ-relabelling. We thus conclude as follows.

Theorem 8.1 *For* $\vec{p}_0; \vec{t}_0 \triangleright N_0$ *and* $\vec{p}_1; \vec{t}_1 \triangleright N_1$ *nets with interface,*

$$\vec{p}_0; \vec{t}_0 \triangleright N_0 \leftrightarrow^c \vec{p}_1; \vec{t}_1 \triangleright N_1 \iff |\vec{p}_0| = |\vec{p}_1| = i,\ |\vec{t}_0| = |\vec{t}_1| = j,\ and$$

$$U_{i,j}[\vec{p}_0; \vec{t}_0 \triangleright N_0] \leftrightarrow U_{i,j}[\vec{p}_1; \vec{t}_1 \triangleright N_1].$$

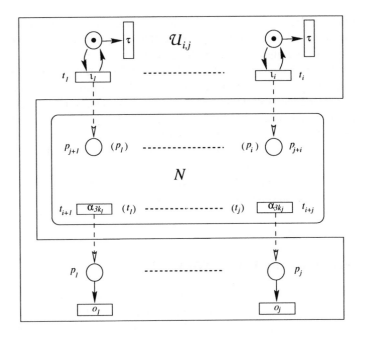

Figure 4.

9 Related Work

The work outlined in the second part of this survey relates to several Petri net calculi proposed in the literature. Among these, we mention Gorrieri and Montanari's SCONE [36], defined around operations of prefixing, parallel, and non-deterministic composition, and used to give semantics to a fragment of CCS. Differently from most other calculi, SCONE is not based on an explicit notion of interface by means of which nets are composed. It aims at describing behavioural more than structural composition, and is essentially a big net whose markings represent concurrent processes behaviours, in the same sense as CCS can be seen as a big transition system whose states represent processes.

The Petri Box calculus [10], by Best et al., has received much attention in the literature. It is inspired by CCS and motivated by the need to simplify the task of giving compositional denotational semantics to concurrent programming languages. The calculus has a very rich collection of operations, including sequential, non-deterministic, and asynchronous parallel composition with explicit multiple synchronisation based on a notion of interface constituted by designated entry and exit places. The Box calculus has been used to describe distributed algorithms, to give semantics to concurrent programming languages [11], and has been embedded in the PEP computer-aided tool [37].

A highly elegant calculus is Milner's calculus of named nets [63], arisen in the context of control structures and, as such, inspired by name passing calculi, as the π-calculus. It focuses on very few basic 'controls' by means of which places, tokens, and transitions can be glued together to form any finite net. A notable difference with the work surveyed here is that Milner's calculus is definitely more structure-oriented. The controls are in fact suggested by structural considerations rather than by behavioural intuitions such as asynchronous message passing underlying **CM**. The dynamics of named nets is demanded to an elegant reduction relation, and the question of behavioural congruences is open.

10 Conclusions and Future Work

Algebraic structures based on a central operation of *iteration*, or *feedback* — inspired by flowcharts and program schemata — have appeared rather early in computer science, see, e.g., [29,4,89,90,63] and [12], that offers for a thorough exposition of so-called '*iteration theory*' and more references. The advent of *traced monoidal categories* [50], i.e., monoidal categories equipped with a *feedback* operation completely analogous to the one considered in **CM** has recently revived interest in using such abstract structures in semantics of computation, as e.g., in [1,53,40,41]. Obviously, the calculus of [68] fits nets into this framework very nicely, although some of the details still need to be clarified. In particular, it may still lack some important operations, most notably synchronisation.

Finally, as already mentioned, it would be interesting to know how well and how uniformly can the 'Petri nets as monoids' approach be lifted to high level nets.

Acknowledgments

I would like to thank the colleagues who have been part of developing the material behind this survey. In particular, I acknowledge close collaboration with R. Bruni, J. Meseguer, U. Montanari, M. Nielsen, and L. Priese on many parts of this work.

References

1. S. Abramsky (1996), Retracing Some Paths in Process Algebra, in *Proceedings of CONCUR 96*, U. Montanari and V. Sassone (Eds.), *Lecture Notes in Computer Science* **1119**, 1–17, Springer-Verlag.

2. S. Ajmone Marsan, A. Bobbio, and S. Donatelli (1998), Petri Nets in Performance Analysis: An introduction, in *Advances in Petri Nets, Lectures on Petri Nets I: Basic Models*, W. Reisig and G. Rozenberg (Eds.), *Lecture Notes in Computer Science* **1491**, 122–173, Springer-Verlag.

3. A. Asperti, G. Ferrari, and R. Gorrieri (1990), Implicative Formulae in the "Proofs as Computations" Analogy, in *Proceedings of POPL 91*, 59–71, ACM Press.

4. E.S. Bainbridge (1976), Feedback and Generalized Logic. *Information and Control* **31**, 75–96.

5. P. Baldan (2000), *Modelling Concurrent Computations: From Contextual Petri Nets to Graph Grammars*. Ph.D. thesis, TD-1/00, Dipartimento di Informatica, Università di Pisa.

6. P. Baldan, A. Corradini, and U. Montanari (1998), An Event Structure Semantics for P/T Contextual Nets: Asymmetric Event Structures, in *Proceedings FoSSaCS'98*, M. Nivat (Ed.), *Lecture Notes in Computer Science* **1378**, 63–80, Springer-Verlag.

7. J. énabou (1963), Categories with Multiplication. *Comptes Rendus Académie Science Paris* **256**, 1887–1890.

8. D.B. Benson (1975), The Basic Algebraic Structures in Categories of Derivations. *Information and Control* **28**, 1–29.

9. E. Best and R. Devillers (1987), Sequential and Concurrent Behaviour in Petri Net Theory. *Theoretical Computer Science* **55**, 87–136.

10. E. Best, R. Devillers, and J. Hall (1992), The Petri Box Calculus: a New Causal Algebra with Multilabel Communication, in *Advances in Petri Nets 92*, G. Rozenberg (Ed.), *Lecture Notes in Computer Science* **609**, 21–69, Springer-Verlag.

11. E. Best, R. Devillers, and M. Koutny (1998), Petri Nets, Process Algebras, and Concurrent Programming Languages, in *Advances in Petri Nets, Lectures on Petri Nets II: Applications*, W. Reisig and G. Rozenberg (Eds.), *Lecture Notes in Computer Science* **1492**, 1–84, Springer-Verlag.

12. S.L. Bloom and Z. Ésik (1991), *Iteration Theories: the Equational Logic of Iterative Processes*. EATCS Monographs on Theoretical Computer Science **30**, Springer-Verlag.

13. C. Brown and D. Gurr (1992), Temporal Logic and Categories of Petri Nets, in *Proceedings of ICALP 93*, A. Lingas *et al.* (Eds.), *Lecture Notes in Computer Science* **700**, 570–581, Springer-Verlag.

14. C. Brown, D. Gurr, and V. de Paiva (1991), *A Linear Specification Language for Petri Nets*. Technical Report DAIMI PB-363, Computer Science Dept., University of Aarhus.

15. R. Bruni, J. Meseguer, U. Montanari, and V. Sassone (1999), Functorial Semantics for Petri Nets under the Individual Token Philosophy, in *Proceedings of CTCS 99*, M. Hofmann, G. Rosolini, and D. Pavlovic (Eds.), *Electronic Notes in Theoretical Computer Science* **29**, Elsevier.

16. R. Bruni, J. Meseguer, U. Montanari, and V. Sassone (2000), Functorial Models for Petri nets. *Information and Computation*, to appear.

17. R. Bruni and U. Montanari (2000), Zero-Safe Nets: Comparing the Collective and Individual Token Approaches. *Information and Computation* **156**, 46–89.

18. R. Bruni and U. Montanari (2000), Executing Transactions in Zero-safe Nets, in *Proceedings of ICATPN 2000*, D. Simpson and M. Nielsen (Eds.), *Lecture Notes in Computer Science* **1825**, 83–102, Springer-Verlag.

19. R. Bruni and V. Sassone (2000), Algebraic Models for Contextual Nets, in *Proceedings of ICALP 2000*, U. Montanari *et al.* (Eds.), *Lecture Notes in Computer Science* **1853**, 175–186, Springer-Verlag.

20. N. Busi and R. Gorrieri (1995), A Petri Net Semantics for the Pi-Calculus, in *Proceedings of CONCUR 95*, I. Lee and S. Smolka (Eds.), *Lecture Notes in Computer Science* **962**, 145–159, Springer-Verlag.

21. N. Busi and M. Pinna (1996), Non Sequential Semantics for Contextual P/T Nets, in *Proceedings of ICATPN 96*, J. Billington and W. Reisig (Eds.), *Lecture Notes in Computure Science* **1091**, 113–132, Springer-Verlag. Springer-Verlag.

22. S. Christensen and N.D. Hansen (1993), Coloured Petri Nets Extended with Place Capacities, Test Arcs and Inhibitor Arcs, in *Proceedings of ICATPN 93*, S. Ajmone Marsan (Ed.), *Lecture Notes in Computer Science* **691**, 186–205, Springer-Verlag.

23. P. Degano, R. De Nicola, and U. Montanari (1988), A Distributed Operational Semantics for CCS based on Condition/Event Systems. *Acta Informatica* **26**, 59–91.

24. P. Degano, J. Meseguer, and U. Montanari (1996), Axiomatizing the Algebra of Net Computations and Processes. *Acta Informatica* **33**, 641–667.

25. J. Desel, G. Juhás, and R. Lorenz (2000), Process Semantics of Petri Nets over Partial Algebra, in *Proceedings of ICATPN 2000*, D. Simpson and

M. Nielsen (Eds.), *Lecture Notes in Computer Science* **1825**, 146–165, Springer-Verlag.

26. J. Desel and W. Reisig (1998), Place/Transition Petri Nets, in *Advances in Petri Nets, Lectures on Petri Nets I: Basic Models*, W. Reisig and G. Rozenberg (Eds.), *Lecture Notes in Computer Science* **1491**, 122–173, Springer-Verlag.

27. V. Diekert and G. Rozenberg (Eds.) (1995), *The Book of Traces*, World Scientific.

28. S. Eilenberg, and G.M. Kelly (1966), Closed Categories, in *Proceedings of the Conference on Categorical Algebra*, S. Eilenberg *et. al.* (Eds.), 421–562, Springer-Verlag.

29. C. Elgot (1975), Monadic Computation and Iterative Algebraic Theories, in *Logic Colloquium '73*, H.E. Rose and J.C. Shepherdson (Eds.), 175–230, North-Holland.

30. H. Ehrig and J. Padberg (1997), A Uniform Approach to Petri Nets, in *Proceedings of FCT 97*, C. Freksa *et al.* (Eds.), *Lecture Notes in Computer Science* **1337**, 219–231, Springer-Verlag.

31. U. Engberg and G. Winskel (1993), Completeness Results for Linear Logic on Petri Nets, in *Proceedings of MFCS 93*, A. Borzyszkowski and S. Sokołowski (Eds.), *Lecture Notes in Computer Science* **711**, 442–452, Springer-Verlag.

32. J. Engelfriet (1991), Branching Processes of Petri Nets. *Acta Informatica* **28**, 575–591.

33. F. Gadducci and U. Montanari (1998), Axioms for contextual net processes, *Proceedings of ICALP 98*, K. Larsen *et al.* (Eds.), *Lecture Notes in Computer Science* **1443**, 296–308, Springer-Verlag.

34. R.J. van Glabbeek and F. Vaandrager (1987), Petri Net Models for Algebraic Theories of Concurrency, in *Proceedings of PARLE 87*, J.W. de Bakker *et al.* (Eds.), *Lecture Notes in Computer Science* **259**, 224–242, Springer-Verlag.

35. U. Goltz and W. Reisig (1983), The Non-Sequential Behaviour of Petri Nets. *Information and Computation* **57**, 125–147.

36. R. Gorrieri and U. Montanari (1990), Scone: A Simple Calculus of Nets, in *Proceedings of CONCUR 90*, J.C.M. Baeten and J.W. Klop (Eds.), *Lecture Notes in Computer Science* **458**, 2–31, Springer-Verlag.

37. B. Grahlmann (1998), The State of PEP, in *Proceedings of AMAST 98*, A.M. Haeberer (Ed.), *Lecture Notes in Computer Science* **1548**, 522–526, Springer-Verlag.

38. M. Hennessy (1988), *Algebraic Theory of Processes*. MIT Press.

39. C.A.R. Hoare (1985), *Communicating Sequential Processes.* Prentice Hall.
40. M. Hasegawa (1997), Recursion from Cyclic Sharing: Traced Monoidal Categories, in *Proceedings of TLCA 97*, Ph. de Groote and J.R. Hindley (Eds.), *Lecture Notes in Computer Science* **1210**, 196–213, Springer-Verlag.
41. T.T. Hildebrandt, P. Panangaden, and G. Winskel (1998), Relational Semantics of Non-Deterministic Dataflow, in *Proceedings of CONCUR 98*, D. Sangiorgi and R. de Simone (Eds.), *Lecture Notes in Computer Science* **1466**, 613–628, Springer-Verlag.
42. P.W. Hoogers, H.C.M. Kleijn, and P.S. Thiagarajan (1992), A Trace Semantics for Petri Nets, in *Proceedings of ICALP 92*, W. Kuich (Ed.), *Lecture Notes in Computer Science* **623**, 595–604, Springer-Verlag.
43. P.W. Hoogers, H.C.M. Kleijn, and P.S. Thiagarajan (1993), Local Event Structures and Petri Nets, in *Proceedings of CONCUR 93*, E. Best (Ed.), *Lecture Notes in Computer Science* **715**, 462–476, Springer-Verlag.
44. G. Hotz (1965), Eine Algebraisierung des Syntheseproblemen von Schaltkreisen, I and II. *Journal of Information Processing and Cybernetics, EIK* **1**, 185–206, 209–231.
45. R. Janicki and M. Koutny (1995), Semantics of Inhibitor Nets. *Information and Computation* **123**, 1–16.
46. K. Jensen (1998), An Introduction to the Practical Uses of Coloured Petri Nets, in *Advances in Petri Nets, Lectures on Petri Nets II: Applications*, W. Reisig and G. Rozenberg (Eds.), *Lecture Notes in Computer Science* **1492**, 237–292, Springer-Verlag.
47. K. Jensen (1992), *Coloured Petri Nets – Basic Concepts, Analysis Methods and Practical Use, Vol. 1: Basic Concepts.* EATCS Monographs in Theoretical Computer Science, Springer-Verlag.
48. K. Jensen (1994), *Coloured Petri Nets – Basic Concepts, Analysis Methods and Practical Use, Vol. 2: Analysis Methods.* EATCS Monographs in Theoretical Computer Science, Springer-Verlag.
49. K. Jensen (1997), *Coloured Petri Nets – Basic Concepts, Analysis Methods and Practical Use, Vol. 3: Practical Use.* EATCS Monographs in Theoretical Computer Science — Berlin: Springer-Verlag.
50. A. Joyal, R. Street, and D. Verity (1996), Traced Monoidal Categories. *Mathematical Proceedings of the Cambridge Philosophical Society* **119**, 447–468, Cambridge University Press.
51. G.M. Kelly (1964), On MacLane's Conditions for Coherence of Natural Associativities, Commutativities, etc. *Journal of Algebra*, **1**, 397–402.

52. G.M. Kelly, and R. Street (1974), Review of the Elements of 2-Categories, in *Category Seminar Sidney, Lecture Notes in Mathematics* **420**, 75–103, Springer-Verlag.

53. P. Katis, N. Sabadini, and R. Walters (1997), Bicategories of Processes. *Journal of Pure and Applied Algebra* **115**, 141–178.

54. S. MacLane (1963), Natural Associativity and Commutativity. *Rice University Studies* **49**, 28–46, Rice University Press.

55. S. MacLane (1971), *Categories for the Working Mathematician*. Springer-Verlag.

56. A. Mazurkiewicz (1987), Trace Theory, in *Petri Nets, Applications and Relationship to other Models of Concurrency*, W. Brauer *et al.* (Eds.), *Lecture Notes in Computer Science* **255**, 279–324, Springer-Verlag.

57. N. Martí-Oliet and J. Meseguer (1991), From Petri Nets to Linear Logic through Categories: A Survey. *International Journal of Foundations of Computer Science* **2**, 297–399.

58. J. Meseguer and U. Montanari (1990), Petri Nets are Monoids. *Information and Computation* **88**, 105–155.

59. J. Meseguer, U. Montanari, and V. Sassone (1996), Process versus Unfolding Semantics for Place/Transition Petri Nets. *Theoretical Computer Science* **153**, 171–210.

60. J. Meseguer, U. Montanari, and V. Sassone (1997), On the Semantics of Place/Transition Petri Nets. *Mathematical Structures in Computer Science* **7**, 359–397.

61. J. Meseguer, U. Montanari, and V. Sassone (1997), Representation Theorems for Petri Nets, in *Foundations of Computer Science*, C. Freksa *et al.* (Eds.), *Lecture Notes in Computer Science* **1337**, 239–249, Springer-Verlag.

62. R. Milner (1989), *Communication and Concurrency*. Prentice-Hall.

63. R. Milner (1993), Action Calculi or Syntactic Action Structures, in *Proceedings of MFCS 93*, A. Borzyszkowski and S. Sokołowski (Eds.), *Lecture Notes in Computer Science* **711**, 105–121, Springer-Verlag.

64. R. Milner (1999), *Communicating and Mobile Systems: the π-Calculus*. Cambridge University Press.

65. U. Montanari and F. Rossi (1995), Contextual Nets. *Acta Informatica* **32**, 545–596.

66. M. Mukund (1992), Petri Nets and Step Transition Systems. *International Journal of Foundations of Computer Science* **3**, 443–478.

67. M. Nielsen, G. Plotkin, and G. Winskel (1981), Petri Nets, Event Structures and Domains, Part 1. *Theoretical Computer Science* **13**, 85–108.

68. M. Nielsen, L. Priese, and V. Sassone (1995), Characterizing Behavioural Congruences for Petri Nets, in *Proceedings of CONCUR 95*, I. Lee and S. Smolka (Eds.), *Lecture Notes in Computer Science* **962**, 175–189, Springer-Verlag.

69. M. Nielsen, G. Rozenberg, and P.S. Thiagarajan (1995), Transition Systems, Event Structures and Unfoldings. *Information and Computation* **118**, 191–207, Academic Press.

70. M. Nielsen and V. Sassone (1998), Petri Nets and Other Models of Concurrency, in *Advances in Petri Nets, Lectures on Petri Nets I: Basic Models*, W. Reisig and G. Rozenberg (Eds.), *Lecture Notes in Computer Science* **1491**, 587–642, Springer-Verlag.

71. E.R. Olderog (1987), A Petri Net Semantics for CCSP, in *Advances in Petri Nets 86*, G. Rozenberg (Ed.), *Lecture Notes in Computer Science* **266**, 196–223, Springer-Verlag.

72. E.R. Olderog (1991), *Nets, Terms and Formulas*. Cambridge Tracts in Theoretical Computer Science, Cambridge University Press.

73. J. Padberg (1999), Abstract Petri nets as a Uniform Approach to High-Level Petri Nets, in *Proceedings of WADT 98*, C. Freksa *et al.* (Eds.), *Lecture Notes in Computer Science* **1589**, 241–260, Springer-Verlag.

74. C.A. Petri (1962), *Kommunikation mit Automaten*. Ph.D. thesis, Institut für Instrumentelle Mathematik, Bonn.

75. C.A. Petri (1973), Concepts of Net Theory, in *Proceedings of MFCS 73*, 137–146, Mathematics Institute of the Slovak Academy of Science.

76. C.A. Petri (1977), *Non-Sequential Processes*. Interner Bericht ISF–77–5, Gesellschaft für Mathematik und Datenverarbeitung, Bonn.

77. *Petri Net Tools on the Web*, web page. http://www.daimi.au.dk/~petrinet/tools/, DAIMI, University of Aarhus.

78. M. Pfender (1974), *Universal Algebra in S-Monoidal Categories*, Algebra-Berichte 20, Department of Mathematics, University of Munich.

79. V. Pratt (1986), Modelling Concurrency with Partial Orders. *International Journal of Parallel Programming* **15**, 33–71.

80. W. Reisig (1985), *Petri Nets (an Introduction)*. EATCS Monographs on Theoretical Computer Science **4**, Springer-Verlag.

81. W. Reisig (1991), *System Design Using Petri Nets*. Springer-Verlag.

82. W. Reisig (1998), *Elements of Distributed Algorithms: Modeling and Analysis with Petri Nets*. EATCS Monographs on Theoretical Computer Science, Springer-Verlag.

83. W. Reisig and G. Rozenberg (1998), Informal Introduction to Petri Nets, in *Advances in Petri Nets, Lectures on Petri Nets I: Basic Models*, W. Reisig and G. Rozenberg (Eds.), *Lecture Notes in Computer Science*

1491, 1–11, Springer-Verlag.

84. G. Rozenberg and J. Engelfriet (1998), Elementary Net Systems, in *Advances in Petri Nets, Lectures on Petri Nets I: Basic Models*, W. Reisig and G. Rozenberg (Eds.), *Lecture Notes in Computer Science* **1491**, 12–121, Springer-Verlag.

85. G. Rozenberg and P.S. Thiagarajan (1986), Petri Nets: Basic Notions, Structure, Behaviour, in *Current Trends in Concurrency*, J. de Bakker *et al.* (Eds.), *Lecture Notes in Computer Science* **224**, 585–668, Springer-Verlag.

86. V. Sassone (1996), An Axiomatization of the Algebra of Petri Net Concatenable Processes. *Theoretical Computer Science* **170**, 277–296.

87. V. Sassone (1998), An Axiomatization of the Category of Petri Net Computations. *Mathematical Structures in Computer Science* **8**, 117–151.

88. E. Smith (1998), Principles of High-Level Net Theory, in *Advances in Petri Nets, Lectures on Petri Nets I: Basic Models*, W. Reisig and G. Rozenberg (Eds.), *Lecture Notes in Computer Science* **1491**, 174–210, Springer-Verlag.

89. G. Ştefănescu (1987), On Flowchart Theories: Part I. The Deterministic Case. *Journal of Computer and System Sciences* **35**, 163–191.

90. G. Ştefănescu (1987), On Flowchart Theories: Part II. The Nondeterministic Case. *Theoretical Computer Science* **52**, 307–340.

91. W. Vogler (1997), Partial order semantics and read arcs, in *Proceedings of MFCS'97*, P. Degano *et al.* (Eds.), *Lecture Notes in Computer Science* **1295**, 508–517, Springer-Verlag.

92. J. Winkowski (1980), Behaviours of Concurrent Systems. *Theoretical Computer Science* **12**, 39–60.

93. J. Winkowski (1982), An Algebraic Description of System Behaviours. *Theoretical Computer Science* **21**, 315–340, Elsevier.

94. G. Winskel (1982), Event Structure Semantics for CCS and related languages, in *Proceedings of ICALP 82*, M. Nielsen and E.M. Schmidt (Eds.), *Lecture Notes in Computer Science* **140**, 561–576, Springer-Verlag.

95. G. Winskel (1984), A New Definition of Morphism on Petri Nets, in *Proceedings of STACS 84*, M. Fontet and K. Mehlhorn (Eds.), *Lecture Notes in Computer Science* **166**, 140–150, Springer-Verlag.

96. G. Winskel (1986), Event Structures, in *Advances in Petri Nets 86*, W. Brauer *et al.* (Eds.), *Lecture Notes in Computer Science* **255**, 325–392, Springer-Verlag.

97. G. Winskel (1987), Petri Nets, Algebras, Morphisms and Compositionality. *Information and Computation* **72**, 197–238, Academic Press.

98. G. Winskel (1988), An Introduction to Event Structures, in *Linear time,*

branching time, and partial order in logics and models for concurrency, J.W. de Bakker *et al.* (Eds.), *Lecture Notes in Computer Science* **354**, 365–397, Springer-Verlag.

99. A. Yakolev and A. Koelmans (1998), Petri Nets and Digital Hardware Design, in *Advances in Petri Nets, Lectures on Petri Nets II: Applications,* W. Reisig and G. Rozenberg (Eds.), *Lecture Notes in Computer Science* **1492**, 154–236, Springer-Verlag.

4
FORMAL LANGUAGE THEORY

Arto SALOMAA

CONTENTS

Introductory Remarks
Combinatorics on Words — A Tutorial
    (by J. Berstel and J. Karhumäki)
Two Problems on Commutation of Languages
    (by J. Karhumäki and I. Petre)
Counting (Scattered) Subwords (by A. Salomaa)
Post Correspondence Problem – Recent Results
    (by V. Halava and T. Harju)
The DF0L Language Equivalence Problem (by J. Honkala)
An Overview of Conjunctive Grammars (by A. Okhotin)
State Complexity of Finite and Infinite Regular
    Languages (by S. Yu)
GSMs and Contexts (by C. Martín-Vide and A. Mateescu)
The Depth of Functional Compositions (by A. Salomaa)
Language Generating by Means of Membrane Systems
    (by C. Martín-Vide and Gh. Păun)
Membrane Computing: New Results, New Problems
    (by C. Martín-Vide, A. Păun, and Gh. Păun)

Arto Salomaa
Turku Centre for Computer Science
Lemminkäisenkatu 14A, 20520 Turku, Finland
E-mail: asalomaa@it.utu.fi

411

INTRODUCTORY REMARKS

The theory of formal languages and automata, as well as combinatorics on words, are the oldest and most fundamental in the field of theoretical computer science. Indeed, research in some problem areas is already close to one hundred years old. The origins of the theory, as we know it today, come from different parts of human knowledge, ranging from logic and mathematics to linguistics, biology and genetics. Apart from offering beautiful mathematical problems, the theory is remarkably versatile in modeling various phenomena in many fields of study. This has been the key to its applicability.

The articles in this chapter give glimpses over the current language theory. Each article can be studied alone and can also be used as supplementary reading material for related courses in theoretical computer science. In most cases very little, if any, previous knowledge is required on the part of the reader. Without any attempt of being complete, the articles in this chapter depict typical ongoing work. While some of them present modern views on classical mathematical and logical problems, others deal with very recent topics, notably the currently very active and important field of membrane computing.

The article by Berstel and Karhumäki constitutes a tutorial, unique of its kind, about combinatorics on words. The subsequent articles by Karhumäki, Petre and Salomaa deal with special issues in combinatorics on words: commutation and number of subwords. New results on classical decision problems are presented by Halava, Harju and Honkala. Various aspects on automata and grammars, both classical and recent modifications, are contained in the work of Okhotin, Yu, Martín-Vide, Mateescu and Salomaa. The final contributions by Gh. Păun, A. Păun and Martín-Vide form a compact yet comprehensive package about results and open problems in membrane computing.

Arto Salomaa

COMBINATORICS ON WORDS – A TUTORIAL

JEAN BERSTEL

Institut Gaspard-Monge
Université de Marne-la-Vallée
77454 Marne-la-Vallée Cedex 2, France
E-mail: jean.berstel@univ-mlv.fr

JUHANI KARHUMÄKI

Turku Centre for Computer Science
and
Department of Mathematics, University of Turku
20014 Turku, Finland
E-mail: karhumak@cs.utu.fi

1 Introduction

During the last two decades research on combinatorial problems of words, i.e., on *Combinatorics on Words*, has grown enormously. Although there has been important contributions on words starting from the very beginning of last century, they were scattered and typically needed as tools to achieve some other goals in mathematics. A notable exception is combinatorial group theory, which studies combinatorial problems on words as representing group elements, see [121] and [123]. Now, and particularly after the appearance of Lothaire's book – Combinatorics on Words – in 1983 the topic has become a challenging research topic of its own. In the latest classification of Mathematical Reviews combinatorics on words constitutes its own section under the chapter discrete mathematics related to computer science. Although the applications of words are, by no means, only in computer science the classification catches the basic of the nature of combinatorics on words.

Recent developments of the field culminated in Lothaire's second book – Algebraic Combinatorics on Words – which appeared in 2002. Its more than 500 pages witness the vital stage of the topic. The new book repeats basically nothing from the first one, and actually most of the results were discovered during the last twenty years. A biannual conference – referred to as WORDS – devoted entirely to combinatorics on words has also been created. The fourth event will be in Turku in 2003.

A word is a sequence of symbols, finite of infinite, taken from a finite alphabet. A natural environment of a finite word is a free monoid. Consequently, words can be seen as a discrete combinatorial objects or discrete algebraic objects in a noncommutative structure. These two facts – discreteness and noncommutativity – are the two fundamental features of words. At the same time they explain why many problems are so difficult.

Words are central objects of automata theory, and in fact in any standard model of computing. Even when computing on numbers computers operate on words, i.e., representations of numbers as words. Consequently, on one hand, it is natural to study algorithmic properties of words. On the other hand, the undecidability of problems is most easily stated in terms of words – the Post Correspondence Problem being a splendid example. Both these elements of words – algorithmic aspects and undecidability – are visible, often implicitly, throughout our presentation.

The goal of the tutorial is to discuss – without aiming to be exhaustive – several typical problems on words, as well as to try to point out several applications. With a few exceptions the proofs are not presented here, however, in some cases we use examples to illustrate the basic ideas. Open problems form an important part of our presentation.

The contents of this tutorial is as follows. At the end of this introductory section we discuss briefly the history of combinatorics on words, and fix some basic terminology. Then in Section 2 we consider connections to other fields of mathematics and computer science. Section 3 is devoted to the most fundamental notion of words, namely to periodicity. Dimension properties of words constitute Section 4, while Section 5 concentrates one of the most studied and most characteristic feature of words, namely unavoidable regularities. Words, indeed, are very suitable objects to formulate such fundamental properties. In Section 6 complexity issues of infinite words are studied from different points of view. An interesting phenomenon is that what is considered to be complicated in a classical sense, e.g., algebraically, need not be so from the point of view of words. Finally, in Section 7 we discuss about some extensions of the theory to finite sets of words, and in Section 8 collect a list of important open problems, many of those being apparently very difficult. As we said everywhere above algorithmic and decidability issues are present.

We conclude by some bibliographic remarks. Combinatorics on words has now become a rich area, with many connections to algorithms, to number theory, to symbolic dynamics, and to applications in biology and text processing. Several books have appeared quite recently, or will appear in the next months, that emphasize these connections. What have to be mentioned are the book of Allouche and Shallit [5], where the emphasis is on relation to automata theory, and the book by Pytheas-Fogg [147] which is a *nom de plume* for the Marseille group. Quite recently the book by Crochemore and Rytter [52] appeared as a follow-up book to [51]. A detailed introduction into algorithms on words is given in the book [49]. Algorithms on words are also described, from a more biological point of view, in Gusfield's book [78]. Finally, we should point to algebraic applications of combinatorics on words, as they appear in the book of de Luca and Varricchio [64].

1.1 History

The history of combinatorics on words goes back to the beginning of the last century, when A. Thue started to work on repetition-free words. He proved, among other things, the existence of an infinite square-free word over a ternary alphabet. Interestingly, it seems that Thue had no outside motivation for his research on words. He published his results in two long papers [165] and [166], but unfortunately in a less known Norwegian journal, so that his results became known only much later, cf. [13]. Actually many of those were reproved several times.

The notion of word is, of course, so natural that it can be found even in several older mathematical works. Even Gauss considered a problem which was nothing but a problem on combinatorics on words, cf. [74] and [106], and in 1850s Prouhet [146] introduced the most famous infinite word redefined by Thue. However, Thue was clearly the first to study systematically problems on words, and moreover as problems of their own.

After Thue during the first half of the previous century there were only a few isolated works on words, such as those of [8], [132], [133] and [134]. In these works, as it has been very typical for the whole field, properties of words were not that much the research topic of itself rather than tools for solving problems in other areas.

It took till the second half of the last century when the theory of words arose. This happened more or less simultaneously in France and Russia. In France it grew up from research of M.P. Schützenberger on theory of codes, see [161]. The Russian school, in turn, developed from the seminal work of P.S. Novikov and S. Adian on Burnside Problem for groups, see [1]. Especially, in Russia results on words, not to speak about the theory, were not so explicit, although their studies culminated rather soon to remarkable results, such as Makanin's algorithm for satisfiability of word equations, see [124]. In France, the theory of words became an independent topic of its own rather soon, very much due to the stimulating paper [114] from 1967. Other stimulating early works were (hand written) book [113] and [89].

Once the foundations of the theory were laid down it developed rapidly. One influencial paper should be mentioned here, from year 1979. In [10] repetition-free words were studied very extensively, and an important notion of an avoidable pattern, as well as many open problems, were formulated. The $D0L$ systems, and particularly the $D0L$ problem [53], was an important source of many questions on combinatorics on words, including the Ehrenfeucht Compactness Property, see [95].

In fifteen years or so, in 1983 the active research on words culminated to the first book of the topic, namely Lothaire's book Combinatorics on Words. The starting point of Lothaire's book was a mimeographed text of lectures given by M.P. Schützenberger at the University of Paris in 1966 and written down by J.F. Perrot. It had an enormous influence on the further development of the field. Results of this impact, including several jewels of theory, can be seen from Lothaire's second book – Algebraic Combinatorics on Words – which appeared last year.

1.2   Notions and notations

We conclude this Introduction by fixing the terminology and a few notions needed in this presentation. For more detailed definitions we refer to [120] or [39].

We denote by A a finite set of symbols referred to as an *alphabet*. Sequences, finite or infinite, of letters from A are called *words*. The empty sequence is called the *empty word* and is denoted by 1 or ε. The set of all finite words, in symbols A^*, is the *free monoid* generated by A under the operation of *product* or *concatenation* of words: $u \cdot v = uv$. The *free semigroup* generated by A, in symbols A^+, is $A^* \setminus \{1\}$. The set of one-way *infinite* words over A is denoted by A^w. Formally, such words are mappings from $\mathbf{N}$ into A.

For two words u and v we say that u is a *prefix* (resp. a *suffix* or a *factor*) of u if there exist a word x (or words x and y) such that $v = ux$ (resp., $v = xu$ or $v = xuy$). In the case of prefix we write $u = vx^{-1}$. Note that the mapping $(v, x) \mapsto vx^{-1}$ can be viewed as a partial mapping from $A^* \times A^*$ into A^*. These notions extend straightforwardly to subsets, i.e., to *languages*, of A^*. A very crucial notion in combinatorics on words is that of a *morphism* from the free monoid A^* into itself (or into another free monoid B^*), that is to say a mapping $h : A^* \to A^*$ satisfying $h(uv) = h(u)h(v)$ for all words u and v. Examples of important morphisms are

$$\mu : \begin{array}{l} a \mapsto ab \\ b \mapsto ba \end{array} \quad \text{and} \quad \varphi : \begin{array}{l} a \mapsto ab \\ b \mapsto a \end{array}.$$

The former, discovered by Thue, is so-called *Thue-Morse*, sometimes referred to *Prouhet-Thue-Morse*, *morphism*. It plays an important role in the study of repetition-free words. The other morphism is called *Fibonacci morphism.* These morphisms has a property that they map a to a word starting with a as a prefix. This implies that the limits

$$t = \lim_{i \to \infty} \mu^i(a) \quad \text{and} \quad f = \lim_{i \to \infty} \varphi^i(a)$$

exist. We say that f and t are obtained by *iterating morphisms* μ and φ at the word a. Clearly, f and t are the unique fixed-points of these morphisms. They are called *Thue-Morse* and *Fibonacci words*, respectively. We have, for example,

$$f = abaababaabaab\dots$$

It is easy to see that alternatively

$$f = \lim_{i \to \infty} f_i$$

where

$$f_0 = a, \quad f_1 = ab \quad \text{and} \quad f_{n+1} = f_n f_{n-1} \quad \text{for} \quad n \ge 1.$$

These formulas explain the name Fibonacci morphism.

In order to state some properties of these words, let us say that a word w is *k-free* if it does not contain as a factor any word of the form u^k. This notion extends, cf. [39], in a natural way to nonnegative rational numbers, and also to real numbers ζ, when the requirement is that w does not contain a factor of the form u^k with $k \in \mathbf{Q}$ and $k > \zeta$. If $w = xu^{k'}y$, with $k' \ge k$ and $u \ne 1$, we say that w contains a *repetition of order k*. By a k^+-free word we mean a word which is k'-free for any $k' > k$ (but not necessarily k-free).

What Thue proved was that the Thue-Morse word is 2^+-free, i.e. does not contain repetitions of higher order than 2. Indeed, it – like any binary word of length at least four – contains a repetition of order 2. For the Fibonacci word the repetitions which are avoided in it are exactly those being of order $> \varphi^2 + 1$ when φ is the number of the golden ratio, i.e. $\varphi = \frac{\sqrt{5}+1}{2}$. In other words, the Fibonacci word is $(\varphi^2 + 1)^+$-free, cf. [128]. This is just one of the many special properties of the Fibonacci word. In fact, it is almost a universal counterexample for conjectures or an example showing an optimality, an exception being a problem in [30].

2 Connections

In this section we point out some connections of combinatorics on words and other areas of mathematics and computing. Such connections are quite broad and has been fruitful in both directions. In fact, many important properties of words has been discovered when looking for tools to solve other completely different problems. More concretely, we discuss here three different connections, one to matrices, one to algebra and one to algorithms. These reflects, we hope, different aspects of such connections. Other connections to combinatorial group theory, to algebraic combinatorics, and to general combinatorics are sketched or described in [123] and [121]. More specifically, let us just mention Lie Algebras, see [152], words as codings of combinatorial structures, and words as codings of permutations.

For the beginning, however, let us consider another typical and interesting relation between words and some classical mathematical notions. *Hilbert's space filling curve* has played an important role describing an intuitive anomaly in topology. From the point of view of topology it can be seen as quite a complicated object. However, from the point of view of words it is nothing but an infinite word over a four element alphabet which, moreover, is easy to define: it is a morphic image under a length preserving morphism, i.e., a coding, of the fixed-point of an iterated morphism.

2.1   To matrices

As the first connection we consider that of words and matrices, more precisely, that of multiplicative semigroups of matrices. Let us denote by $M_{n \times n}(S)$ the family of $n \times n$ matrices with entries in the semigroups S. It has been known since 1920s that free monoids can be embedded into the multiplicative semigroup of 2×2 matrices over $\mathbf{N}$, i.e. into $M_{2 \times 2}(\mathbf{N})$. For $A = \{a, b\}$ such an embedding is given, for instance, by the mapping

$$(1) \qquad a \mapsto \begin{pmatrix} 1 & 1 \\ 0 & 1 \end{pmatrix} \quad \text{and} \quad b \mapsto \begin{pmatrix} 1 & 0 \\ 1 & 1 \end{pmatrix}.$$

In fact, this mapping is an isomorphism between $\{a, b\}^*$ and $SL_2(\mathbf{N})$, the set of matrices in $M_{2 \times 2}(\mathbf{N})$ having a determinant equal to 1. Arbitrary, even countable, free semigroups can be embedded in $M_{2 \times 2}(\mathbf{N})$ by employing an embedding from $\{a_i | i \in \mathbf{N}\}^*$ into A^* given by

$$a_i \mapsto ab^i \quad \text{for} \quad i \geq 0.$$

The above ideas become even more usable when we associate above with a morphism $h : A^* \to A^*$. In order to simplify the notation we set $A = \{1, 2\}$ and define the mapping

$$1 \mapsto \begin{pmatrix} k^{|h(1)|} & 0 \\ \nu(h(1)) & 1 \end{pmatrix} \quad \text{and} \quad 2 \mapsto \begin{pmatrix} k^{|h(2)|} & 0 \\ \nu(h(2)) & 1 \end{pmatrix},$$

where the vertical bars are used to denote the length of a word and ν : $A^+ \rightarrow \mathbf{N}$ maps a word into the number it represents in base $k > 3$. It is straightforward to see that this mapping too is an embedding, that is to say, for any word $u = a_1 \cdots a_n$, we have

$$u = a_1 \cdots a_n \mapsto \begin{pmatrix} k^{|h(u)|} & 0 \\ \nu(h(u)) & 1 \end{pmatrix}.$$

Consequently, questions asking something about images of a morphism of A^* can be transformed into questions about matrices. More concretely; this allows to transfer the undecidability of the Post Correspondence Problem into undecidability results on matrices. Paterson [141] was among the first to use this idea when showing (i) in the following theorem, for the other parts we refer to [82], where also further references can be found.

Theorem 2.1 *The following questions are undecidable:*

(i) Does a given finitely generated multiplicative subsemigroup of $M_{3\times 3}(\mathbf{Z})$ contain the zero matrix?

(ii) Does a given finitely generated multiplicative subsemigroup of $M_{3\times 3}(\mathbf{Z})$ contain a matrix having the zero in the right upper corner?

(iii) Is a given finitely generated multiplicative subsemigroup of $M_{3\times 3}(\mathbf{N})$ free?

Part (iii) is undecidable even for upper triangular matrices.

All of the above problems are open in dimension $n = 2$. Another interesting open problem is the question of part (i) for the identity matrix. The embedding methods used in Problems (i)-(iii) does not seem to work here, see [32]. In the dimension $n = 2$ this problem is decidable, see [41].

Embeddings like (1) are important not only to conclude the above undecidability results, but also to obtain results for words from those of matrices. The Ehrenfeucht Compactness Property, discussed in Section 4, is a splendid example of that.

2.2 To algebra

The second connection we consider is that to algebra. We want to give a concrete example rather than recalling that words are, after all, elements of free monoids or that representations of groups are relations on words. This example, due to [136], is an application of repetition-free words to solve *Burnside Problems for semigroups*. The problem asks whether the assumptions (i): the semigroup S is finitely generated; and (ii): each element of S is of a finite

422

order, i.e. generates a finite cyclic subsemigroup, imply that the semigroup S itself is finite.

Theorem 2.2 *The Burnside Problem for semigroups has a negative answer.*

The answer is achieved as follows, cf. [119]. Let A be a three letter alphabet. Then by a result of Thue, there exists a square-free word over A, and consequently the set of finite square-free words is infinite. Now, adjoin to the free semigroup A^+ the zero element, and define a congruence $\approx$ on $A^+ \cup \{0\}$: each square-free word forms an equivalence class of its own, and the rest belongs to the class containing 0. Then the quotient semigroup

$$S = A^+ \cup \{0\}/ \approx$$

is well defined and has the required properties. For finitely generated groups the Burnside Problem is much more complicated, cf. [1].

2.3 To algorithmics

Finally, we discuss about connections to algorithmics. We consider very natural algorithmic problem, and point out how a certain property of words can be used to obtain an efficient solution to the problem. We ask

Question. How can we decide efficiently whether a given word is primitive?

The problem has a brute force quadratic solution: divide the input into two parts and check whether the right part is a power of the left part. But how to get a faster solution? The answer comes from the property of primitive words: a word w is nonprimitive if and only if it is a factor of $^\bullet ww^\bullet$, i.e., w occurs properly as a factor in ww. For the definition of the operator $^\bullet$ see the next section. So the problem is reduced to a simple instance of the *string matching problem*, and hence doable in linear time, see e.g., [51].

Despite of the simplicity of the above example it is very illustrative: it shows how the correctness of an algorithm is finally based on a combinatorial property of words. This seems to be a common rule in efficient string algorithms. Or even more strongly, whenever a fundamental property of words is revealed, it has applications in improving algorithms on words, cf. e.g., [129].

String matching and pattern matching are only two – although important – aspects of algorithmics on words, see [51], [49] for expositions, and [78]. Other algorithmic problems we do not consider here are: systematic generation of words (e.g., Dyck words), ranking, unranking, and random generation of words, see e.g., [160], [18] and [73]. All of these are used in order to code combinatorial structures.

Another important topic on algorithmic combinatorics on words, which is neither considered in our tutorial, is the *satisfiability problem* for word equations, i.e. the decision question whether a given word equation with constants possesses a solution. The classical paper of Makanin [124] answers this question affirmatively. However, his algorithm is one of the most complicated algorithms ever presented, see Chapter 12 in [120] for a detailed exposition. Rather recently W. Plandowski showed, by his completely new algorithm, that the problem is actually in *PSPACE*, cf. [144]

3 Periodicity

In this section we consider one of the most fundamental notions of words, namely periodicity. We discuss three different topics, all of those being very fundamental.

3.1 Fine and Wilf's theorem

One of the oldest results in combinatorics on words concerns commutation of words. It is the following well-known statement. Typically this result, in one form or another, has been proved when needed, see e.g., [122].

Theorem 3.1 *Let x and y be nonempty words. The following properties are equivalent:*

(i) $xy = yx$,

(ii) *the infinite words x^ω and y^ω are equal,*

(iii) *there exists a word z such that $x, y \in z^+$,*

(iv) *$\{x, y\}$ is not a code, i.e. satisfies a nontrivial relation.*

There is another rather old result, due to Fine and Wilf, strongly related to this theorem. It uses the notion of a period. Let $w = a_1 \cdots a_n$ be a word, with $a_1, \ldots, a_n$ letters. An integer p is a *period* of w, if $1 \leq p \leq n$ and $a_i = a_{p+i}$ for $i = 1, \ldots, n - p$. Thus $a_1 \cdots a_{n-p} = a_{p+1} \cdots a_n$, and the word $w' = a_1 \cdots a_{n-p}$ is both a prefix and a suffix of w. Provided $p < n$, the word w' is called a *border* of w. Conversely, if z is a border of w, then the integer $n - |z|$ is a period of w.

Clearly, an integer p, for $1 \leq p \leq n$, is a period of w if and only if w is a prefix of the infinite word x^ω, where $x = a_1 \cdots a_p$.

A word of length n always has at least the period n. If w has two periods p and q, then w also has the period $p + q$ provided $p + q \leq n$. The set $\Pi(w)$ of all periods of a word w has been described in [77] (see also Chapter 8 of [120]). The shortest integer in $\Pi(w)$ is frequently called *the period* of w.

Theorem 3.2 (Fine and Wilf's Theorem) *Let w be a word of length n. If w has two periods p and q and $n \geq p + q - \gcd(p,q)$, then also $\gcd(p,q)$ is a period of w.*

For the proof of Fine and Wilf's theorem, we consider a variation of Theorem 3.1. Given a word $w = a_1 \cdots a_n$, where $a_1, \ldots, a_n$ are letters, we set $w^\bullet = a_1 \cdots a_{n-1}$. In particular, $a^\bullet = \varepsilon$ for a letter a, and $\varepsilon^\bullet$ is undefined.

Lemma 3.1 *Let x and y be nonempty words. If $xy^\bullet = yx^\bullet$, then $xy = yx$.*

Proof. By induction on $|xy|$. If $|xy| = 2$, and more generally, if $|x| = |y|$, one gets $x = y$. Otherwise, one may assume $|x| > |y|$. Then y is a proper prefix of x, and $x = yz$ for some nonempty word z. It follows that $zy^\bullet = yz^\bullet$. By induction, $zy = yz$, and consequently $xy = yx$. □

We now prove Fine and Wilf's theorem. First, we show that p and q may be assumed to be relatively prime. Indeed, assume $d = \gcd(p,q) > 1$, set $w = a_0 \cdots a_{n-1}$ and define d words $w^{[i]} = a_i a_{i+d} \cdots a_{i+n_i d}$, where $n_i = \lfloor (n - i - 1)/d \rfloor$, for $i = 0, \ldots, d - 1$. These words have periods p/d and q/d and length at least n/d. By the conclusion, each $w^{[i]}$ is a power of some letter. Thus w is the power of some word of length d, that is w has period d.

Suppose now that p and q are relatively prime. Let x and y be the prefixes of w of length p and q, respectively. Then w is a common prefix of x^ω and y^ω. Moreover, setting $w = xw'$, the word w' is a prefix of w, so w' is a prefix of y^ω and thus w is a prefix of xy^ω. Symmetrically, w is a prefix of yx^ω. Since the length of w is at least $p + q - 1$, one gets $xy^\bullet = yx^\bullet$. By Lemma 3.1, one gets $xy = yx$. Thus x and y are in some z^+. But since $\gcd(p,q) = 1$, this implies that z is a letter. This completes the proof. □

Fine and Wilf's original paper [72] contains three theorems. The first one is basically Theorem 3.2. It states indeed that if two infinite words u and v have periods p and q respectively, and they share a common prefix of length $p + q - \gcd(p,q)$, then they are equal. The two other theorems are in the same vein, but concern real continuous periodic functions.

The proof of Theorem 3.2 in Fine and Wilf's original paper [72] is quite different and deserves a short description. Any letter of the alphabet is considered as a number. Any infinite word $a_0 a_1 a_2 \cdots a_n \cdots$ corresponds to a formal series $a_0 + a_1 t + a_2 t^2 + \cdots + a_n t^n + \cdots$. Thus, the infinite periodic word x^ω, with $x = a_1 \cdots a_p$, corresponds to the formal series $F(t) = P(t)/(1 - t^p)$, with $P(t) = a_1 + \cdots + a_p t^{p-1}$, and similarly y^ω, with $y = b_1 \cdots b_q$, corresponds to $G(t) = Q(t)/(1 - t^q)$, with $Q(t) = b_1 + \cdots + b_q t^{q-1}$. Now, a computation with rational fractions shows that

$$H(t) = F(t) - G(t) = \frac{1 - t^{\gcd(p,q)}}{(1 - t^p)(1 - t^q)} R(t) \,,$$

where $R(t)$ is a polynomial of degree at most $p + q - \gcd(p, q) - 1$. By assumption, $R(t) = 0$, and consequently $F = G$ and $x^\omega = y^\omega$.

Several other proofs of the theorem are known. Some are by induction on the length of the period (e.g., Chapter 8 of [120] and [49]). There are also proofs that argue directly on congruential properties of the indices [39]. Extension to more than two periods are given in [35], [92] and [167]. Further related results are shown in [36], [14] and [131].

The bound in Fine and Wilf's theorem is sharp. A concrete example is the word *abaababaaba*. It has periods 5 and 8 and length $11 = 8 + 5 - 2$, and is not a power of a single letter. In fact, *all* words of length $p + q - 2$, with periods p and q, for coprimes p, q, are known. They are all binary, and, more precisely, prefixes of infinite standard Sturmian words; see Chapter 2 of [120] for a description and references.

3.2 Critical factorization theorem

The Critical Factorization Theorem stated below gives a relation between the global period of a word, and a notion of local period called local repetition, associated to a factorization of the word. As it will appear, global periods are always longer than local periods, but the remarkable fact is that for any word, there is always a factorization whose local period is equal to the global period. Such a factorization is called critical.

In order to formalize the above we say that two words x and y are *prefix comparable* (resp. *suffix comparable*) if one of the words is a prefix (resp. a suffix) of the other. Further, given a word w and a factorization $w = uv$ into nonempty words, a *repetition* at (u, v) is a nonempty word z such that z and u are suffix comparable, and z and v are prefix comparable. The (*local*) *period* of the factorization (u, v) is the length of the shortest repetition at (u, v). It is easy to see that any local period of a word is shorter that the period. A factorization (u, v) is *critical* if its period is equal to the period of w.

Consider for example the word $w = abaab$ which has the period 3. The factorization $(a, baab)$ has the repetition ba, so its period is 2. The factorization (aba, ab) has period 1. The factorizations (ab, aab) and $(abaa, b)$ both have period 3, and these are the critical factorizations of the word w. The following theorem shows that critical factorizations are unavoidable.

Theorem 3.3 (Critical Factorization Theorem.) *Every word of length at least 2 has a critical factorization.*

The first statements and proofs of the theorem are given in [37] and [68]. A proof of the critical factorization theorem in its present form, and a discussion, is given in Chapter 8 of [120]. A short proof is in [50]. Recent results related to this topic appear in [85].

We sketch now an interesting application of the Critical Factorization Theorem. Consider a finite set $X \subset A^+$ of nonempty words. Given a word $w \in A^+$, a sequence of nonempty words

$$(s, x_1, \ldots, x_m, p)$$

is an *X-interpretation* of w if $w = p x_1 \cdots x_m p$, and p is a prefix of a word in X, s is a suffix of a word in X, and $x_1, \ldots, x_m \in X$. Two X-interpretations $(s, x_1, \ldots, x_m, p)$ and $(s', x'_1, \ldots, x'_{m'}, p')$ of a word w are *disjoint* if $s x_1 \cdots x_i \neq s' x'_1 \cdots x'_{i'}$ for $i = 1, \ldots, m$, $i' = 1, \ldots, m'$.

As an example, consider the set $X = \{a^3, b, aba, a^2 ba^2\}$. The word $a^4 ba^4 ba^4 b$ has the X-interpretation $(a, a^3, b, a^3, aba, a^3, b)$. The sequence $(a^3, aba, a^3, b, a^3, ab)$ is another X-interpretation of the word $a^4 ba^4 ba^4 b$, and this interpretation is disjoint from the previous one.

Theorem 3.4 *Let X be a finite set of nonempty words, and let p be the maximum of the periods of the words in X. Every word w with the period strictly greater than p has at most $\mathrm{Card}(X)$ disjoint X-interpretations.*

As another example consider the set $X = \{a^p\}$, consisting of a single word which has period 1. Clearly, every word w that admits an X-interpretation is a power of a and so also has period 1. The number of its disjoint X-interpretations is bounded by p, and not by $\mathrm{Card}(X)$.

Proof. (Sketch) Assume that a word w has $m > n$ disjoint X-interpretations, where $n = \mathrm{Card}(X)$. Consider any factorization $w = uv$. There exist m distinct pairs (y, z) of words such that $yz \in X$, u and y are suffix comparable, and v and z are prefix comparable. Since $m > n$, there are at least two pairs (y_1, z_1) and (y_2, z_2) such that $y_1 z_1 = y_2 z_2$. Set $x = y_1 z_1 = y_2 z_2$. Assume $|y_1| > |y_2|$. Next y_1 and y_2 are prefix comparable, or z_1 and z_2 are suffix comparable. Except for some special cases, which we do not consider in this sketch, the number $d = |y_1| - |y_2| = |z_2| - |z_1|$ is a period of x. This implies that there is a repetition of length d at (u, v). Thus the local period at (u, v) is at most p.

Thus, all local periods are smaller than p. However, by the Critical Factorization Theorem, at least one local period is strictly greater than p. This yields a contradiction. $\qquad\square$

A detailed proof is given in [119]. An application to the order of the subgroups of the syntactic monoid of the set X^* was given in [162]. There is a renewal of research on this topic now, see [142].

In [126] examples were given showing that the bound for the number of disjoint X-interpretations is optimal in Theorem 3.4. For example, the set $\{a^i b a^i \mid i = 1, \ldots, n-1\} \cup \{ba^n b\}$ is such a set.

3.3 Characterizations for ultimately periodic words

We conclude this section with a third fundamental periodicity result of words derived in [129], see also [130]. It characterizes one-way infinite ultimately periodic words in terms of local periodicity. Intuitively, it tells how much *local regularity*, i.e., periodicity, is needed to guarantee the *global regularity*, i.e., ultimate periodicity. Such results are the most basic goals in mathematics.

In order to continue let us fix a few notions. Let $\rho \geq 1$ be a real and $p \geq 1$ a natural number. We say that a finite word is ρ-*legal* if it contains as a suffix a repetition of order ρ (or equivalently – by definition – of order larger than or equal to ρ), and that it is (ρ, p)-*legal* if it contains as a suffix a repetition of order ρ of a word of length at most p. Similarly, an infinite word w is ρ-legal or (ρ, p)-legal if it so for all of its long enough prefixes. Note that (ρ, ∞)-legality can be interpreted as simply ρ-legality.

We describe the usefulness of these notions in the following two examples, which are illustrations of subsequent theorems.

Example 1. We claim that the Fibonacci word

$$f = \lim_{i \to \infty} f_i = abaababaabaab \cdots$$

where $f_0 = a$, $f_1 = ab$ and $f_{n+1} = f_n f_{n-1}$ for $n \geq 1$, is $(2, 5)$-legal, as first observed by J. Shallit, personal communication.

It is straightforward to see that f can be decomposed uniquely into blocks of ab and aba, such that ab does not occur twice and aba three times in a row. Consequently, suffixes of prefixes of f ending at one of the blocks are of the forms:

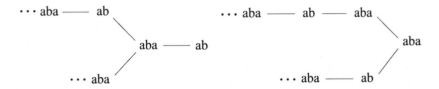

Now consider the suffixes ending at the rightmost ab in the left graph, i.e. ending either at a or b there. In the former case there is a suffix aa, a

428

square. In the latter case there is necessarily either square *aabaab* or square *abaababaab*, i.e., also a square of a word of length at most five. The similar argumentation applies for the right graph.

Note that the word *f* is not ultimately periodic, see Section 6.3.   □

Example 2. In this example we point out a striking difference of (2, 5)-legal and $(2 + \varepsilon, 5)$-legal infinite words for any $\varepsilon > 0$. Let us search for (2, 5)-legal infinite words containing a factor $(abaab)^2$. Now, we try to extend a suffix ending to the above mentioned factor exhaustively symbol by symbol preserving the (2, 5)-legality, and not reporting the extensions leading only to ultimately periodic words. We obtain the graph:

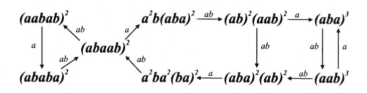

Here the labels tell the extensions, and the nodes correspond the suffixes obtained at particular moments. In the suffixes a short square is always shown (proving the legality) together with a sufficient amount of other letters needed in further steps. In some nodes some continues are not shown – in these cases only ultimately periodic words would be (2, 5)-legal; for instance from $(abaab)^2$ by *b* we would obtain a (2, 5)-legal word, which, however, could be continued only by *b*s preserving the legality.

It follows from the construction that all words spelled from this graph are (2, 5)-legal. In particular, there exist nondenumerably many such infinite words, since the graph contains intersecting loops, labeled by noncommuting words. One can also show that actually this graph gives all (2, 5)-legal nonultimately periodic words. We did the exhaustive search for a particular square, the other squares do not give any other nonultimately periodic (2, 5)-legal infinite words.

Now, an interesting observation is that if instead of the (2, 5)-legality the $(2 + \varepsilon, 5)$-legality is considered, then the node $(aba)^2(ab)^2$ is no longer legal. Indeed, independently of *x* the word *xabaabaabab* does not contain at the end a repetition of order strictly larger than 2 of a word of length at most 5. Consequently, intersecting loops are lost, meaning that any $(2 + \varepsilon, 5)$-legal infinite word is necessarily ultimately periodic.

Constructing graphs similar to the above one for (2, 4)-legal words one can conclude that all (2, 4)-legal words are ultimately periodic.   □

Above examples are special cases of much deeper results. If in Example 1 cubes instead of squares were asked our approach would not work. Indeed, all 3-legal infinite words are ultimately periodic, or even much strongly ρ-legal infinite words are necessarily ultimately periodic if and only if $\rho \geq \varphi^2 = \varphi + 1 = 2.6\ldots$ where φ is the number of golden ratio $\frac{1+\sqrt{5}}{2}$. This is a remarkable theorem, conjectured by J. Shallit in 1994, and proved in [129] by F. Mignosi, A. Restivo and S. Salemi in 1995:

Theorem 3.5   *(i) Each φ^2-legal word is periodic.*

(ii) The Fibonacci word is $(\varphi^2 - \varepsilon)$-legal for any $\varepsilon > 0$.

Example 2 considers a similar phenomena is a simple setting yielding the following result, cf. [98]. As outlined in the example the optimality is with respect to both of the parameters.

Theorem 3.6   *(i) Each $(2, 4)$-legal infinite word is ultimately periodic.*

(ii) For any $\varepsilon > 0$, each $(2+\varepsilon, 5)$-legal infinite word is ultimately periodic.

(iii) There exists nondenumerably many $(2, 5)$-legal infinite words, including the Fibonacci word.

In [117] the similar optimal value of ρ is found for any finite length n of the period. For example, and interestingly, the optimal ρ for $n = 5, 6, \ldots, 11$ is the same, namely 2, while for $n = 12$ it is $2\frac{1}{12}$. Further, after some anomaly in small values of n, the behaviour of such optimal ρs is regular, but amazing: there exists just one jump in between two values of consecutive Fibonacci numbers, except that every sixth jump is missing. Also suprisingly, it is not exactly the Fibonacci word, but very related one, which determines these jumps.

We conclude this section with a few remarks. First the above results are beautiful examples, not only in combinatorics on words, but in a much broader perspective, where a local regularity implies the global one, and, in fact, in an optimal way. In other words, they can be seen as results strictly separating a *predictable*, i.e., ultimately periodic, behaviour from a *chaotic* one, i.e., allowing nondenumerably choices. This is more discussed in [98].

As the second final comment we state another similar result, the proof of which is related to the Critical Factorization Theorem. Consider an infinite word $w = a_1 a_2 \cdots$ with $a_i \in A$. We say that w contains a square *centered at position i* if there exists a $t \in [1, i]$ such that $a_{i-t+1} \cdots a_i$ is a prefix of $a_{i+1} a_{i+2} \cdots$. Then we have:

Theorem 3.7 *An infinite word $w = a_1 a_2 \cdots$ is ultimately periodic if and only if, for any large enough i, there exists a square centered at position i.*

For a proof of this and related results we refer to Chapter 8 in [120], where also the optimality of the result is shown: no smaller amount than a square, i.e., of order 2, of centered repetition guarantees the ultimate periodicity.

4 Dimension Properties

In this section we consider properties of words which can be called *dimension properties*. We approach this by considering a finite set X as a solution of a constant-free equation. Natural questions to be asked are, what can be said about X if it satisfies a nontrivial equation, or several "different" equations? And how many different equations it can satisfy?

Here an *equation* over the variables $\Xi = \{z_1, \ldots, z_n\}$ is just a pair (u, v), usually written as $u = v$, of words of Ξ, and $X = (x_1, \ldots, x_n) \subseteq (A^*)^n$ is a *solution* if x_is substituted for z_is makes the equation to be an equality in A^*. More formally, a solution of the equation $u = v$ is a morphism $\varphi : \Xi \to A^*$ such that $\varphi(u) = \varphi(v)$. Actually, for simplicity, we sometimes overlook the fact that X must be ordered, and consider it only as a set.

We say that two systems of equations are *equivalent* if they have exactly the same solutions, and a system S is *independent* if it is not equivalent to any of its proper subsystems. We use the independency to formalize the notion that "equations are different". Note also that we have defined only constant free equations.

We start with the following simple example

Example 3. As an extension of the well known fact that two words satisfy a nontrivial relation if and only if they are powers of a common word, cf. Section 3, we consider the set $X = \{x, y, z\} \subseteq A^+$ of three nonempty words satisfying the equations

$$(1) \qquad x\alpha = y\beta \quad \text{and} \quad x\gamma = z\delta$$

with α, β, γ and δ in X^*. If two of the words are powers of a common word so is the third, by above. Consequently, assume that $x = yt$ for a nonempty word t. Now, substituting $x = yt$ to the equations in (1) we obtain two relations on words t, y, $z \in A^+$. More specifically, the first equation comes into the form

$$u\alpha' = t\beta' \quad \text{with} \quad u \in \{y, z\} \quad \text{and} \quad \alpha', \beta' \in \{t, y, z\}^*,$$

and the second equation comes into the form

$$t\gamma' = z\delta' \quad \text{with} \quad \gamma', \delta' \in \{t, y, z\}^*.$$

Since $|tyz| < |xyz|$ induction applies showing that t, x and y are powers of a common word, and so are x, y and z. For the case $y = xt$ with $t \neq 1$, the reasoning is the same. Therefore, we have proved that nonempty words satisfying the pair (1) is necessarily *cyclic*, i.e., a subset of w^+ for some word w. □

4.1 Defect theorems

We continue by recalling so-called *defect theorem*: if a set of n words satisfies a nontrivial relation, then these words can be expressed as products of at most $n - 1$ words. In other words, we can say that a nontrivial equation implies a *defect effect* of its solutions. Consequently, the defect theorem states a dimension type property for words.

Actually, there does not exist just one, but rather several, defect theorems witnessing the above defect effect. Namely, the set of $n - 1$ words might be defined in different ways. In order to formalize those we recall that a submonoid M of A^* is called *right unitary* if its minimal generating set is a prefix code, cf. [15]. Then we define the *free hull* and the *prefix hull* of a finite set $X \subseteq A^+$ as

$$F(X) = \bigcap_{\substack{M \text{ is a free monoid} \\ X \subseteq M}} M,$$

and

$$P(X) = \bigcap_{\substack{M \text{ is right unitary} \\ X \subseteq M}} M,$$

respectively. By the basic properties of these semigroups, $F(X)$ is free and $P(X)$ is right unitary. Hence, by definition, they are the smallest such semigroups containing X (and hence also X^*). The cardinalities of the minimal generating sets of $F(X)$ and $P(X)$ are called the *free rank* and the *prefix rank* of X, and those are denoted by $f(X)$ and $p(X)$, respectively. Before formulating several versions of the defect theorem we still define the *combinatorial rank* of X, in symbols $r(X)$, as the minimal cardinality of a set F such that $X \subseteq F^*$. Note that contrary to the above minimal generating sets F need not be unique. Now the defect theorem can be formulated, cf. e.g., [16], [119] or [39]:

Theorem 4.1 *For any finite $X \subseteq A^+$ we have*

$$c(X) \leq p(X) \leq f(X) \leq \text{card}(X),$$

and moreover the last inequality is proper if X satisfies a nontrivial equation.

The methods to compute these different ranks are discussed in [39]. Also the following example showing that all of these inequalities can be simultaneously proper is from [39].

Example 4. Consider the set $X = \{aa, \ aaba, \ bac, \ cbb, \ bbaa, \ baa\}$. It satisfies a nontrivial relation:

$$aa. \ bac. \ bbaa = aaba. \ cbb. \ aa$$

so that $f(X)$ should be < 6. By the well known method, see [16], one can compute that $X(f) = \{aa, \ ba, \ c, \ bb, \ baa\}$. But $(X(f))^+$ is not right unitary, so that, by methods in [39], one computes $X(p) = \{a, \ ba, \ c, \ bb\}$. Hence the cardinality of $X(p)$ is strictly smaller than that of $X(f)$. Finally, $X(p)$ is of combinatorial rank 3, yielding the following sequence of inequalities

$$3 = c(X) < p(X) < f(X) < \text{card}(X) = 6.$$

$\square$

The above shows that the notion of the defect effect is quite involved. In order to further emphasize this we recall that even sets generating isomorphic subsemigroups of A^+ might have nonisomorphic free hulls, cf. [81].

Example 4, and even more Example 3, might suggest that several different equations satisfied by X imply a *cumulative* defect effect for X. For example, two equalities would imply that $r(X)$ is at most $\text{card}(X) - 2$. This indeed was the case in Example 3. However, words do not possess such a strong dimension property:

Example 5. The pair

$$xzy = yzx \quad \text{and} \quad xzzy = yzzx$$

has a solution $x = y = a$ and $z = b$ of (any) rank 2, and still the equations are independent. For example, $x = abba$, $y = a$ and $z = b$ is a solution of the latter but not of the former. $\square$

We do not know whether there exist independent systems of equations with three unknowns, containing more than two equations and having a non-cyclic solution.

The above indicates that it is very difficult to impose a cumulative defect effect, and indeed there are very few results in that direction. Chapter 6 in [120] gives one example showing that if X is a code, but not ω-code neither to the right nor to the left, then the rank of X is at most $\text{card}(X) - 2$. Here being not an ω-code means that some one-way infinite word can be decomposed in two different ways by X. Another complicated but still very special case is obtained in [100].

In the following lines, however, we show a simple but in many cases useful cumulative defect effect. In order to state it we need some terminology. We associate a finite set $X \subseteq A^+$ with a graph G_X as follows: the nodes of G_X are the elements of X, and there exists an edge between two nodes x and y if and only if

$$xX^+ \cap yX^+ \neq \emptyset.$$

G_X is called the *dependency graph* of X. Then the number of connected components of G_X, in symbols $c(G_X)$, gives an upper bound for the rank of X, cf. [81]:

Theorem 4.2 *Let $X \subseteq A^+$ be finite. Then we have*

$$c(X) \leq p(X) \leq c(G_X).$$

In particular, and this is typically the power of Theorem 4.2, if $c(G_X)$ is connected, then X is cyclic. Note that Example 3 is a simple special case of this result. Unlike in the usual defect theorems here it is crucial that all words of X are nonempty.

Defect theorems hold when X is not a code. A natural question is, can this assumption be weakened, for example, requiring only that X is not an ω-code, i.e., finite relations are replaced one-way infinite relations or even two-way infinite relations.

For one-way infinite relations the answer is easy: all results we stated, in particular Theorems 4.1 and 4.2, hold for one-way infinite relations as well. Even the proofs are basically the same. For two-way infinite words the situation is completely different. Strictly speaking no defect theorem holds, as shown by the set $X = \{ab, \ ba\}$ and two factorizations depicted as:

$$\cdots \ \overset{\frown}{ab}\overset{\frown}{ab}\overset{\frown}{ab}\overset{\frown}{ab}\overset{\frown}{ab} \ \cdots$$

However, one can prove the following defect theorem for two-way infinite words. In order to state it we need a few notions. Let $X \subseteq A^+$ be a finite set and w a two-way infinite word. Any decomposition of w into consecutive blocks of elements of X is an X-*factorization* of w, and two X-factorizations of w are *disjoint* if they do not match at any point of w. Finally, w is nonperiodic if it is not a two-way infinite repetition of a single word. We have, see [101]:

Theorem 4.3 *Let* $X \subseteq A^+$ *be finite. If there exists a nonperiodic two-way infinite word with two disjoint X-factorizations, then*

$$c(X) < \mathrm{card}(X).$$

An interesting point here is that, unlike in all other known cases, the defect effect is witnessed only by the combinatorial rank, for a counterexample see [126].

We conclude our discussion on defect effect by returning to Example 4. It shows that different notions of a rank of a finite set do not coincide, and this is unavoidable. Fortunately, however, the *rank* of an equation can be defined in the unique way. Let us define the rank of an equation as the maximal rank of its solutions. In theory, that would lead – in our considerations – to three different notions of the rank of an equation, namely the free rank, the prefix rank and the combinatorial rank. However, we have, see [39]:

Theorem 4.4 *Let* $u = v$ *be a constant-free equation over variables* Ξ *and* A *an alphabet such that* $\mathrm{card}(A) \geq \mathrm{card}(\Xi)$. *The following numbers coincide*

(i) the maximal of free ranks of solutions of $u = v$ in A^*,

(ii) the maximal of prefix ranks of solutions of $u = v$ in A^*,

(iii) the maximal of combinatorial ranks of solutions of $u = v$ in A^*.

The number specified in Theorem 4.4 is called the *rank* of an equation $u = v$.

4.2 Ehrenfeucht Compactness Property

In above we saw that words have certain dimension type properties, in fact even a rich theory in that direction. However, the dimension properties of words are rather weak. A natural question arises: How weak are they? Or more concretely, how large independent systems of equations can exist? These questions are partially answered in the following Ehrenfeucht Compactness Property:

Theorem 4.5 *Each system S of equations with a finite number of variables Ξ over free monoid A^* is equivalent to some of its finite subsets S_0.*

This compactness claim, conjectured by A. Ehrenfeucht – after studying the $D0L$ sequence equivalence problem, cf. [95] – was proved simultaneously in [2] and [76]. The proof is a marvelous example of the usefulness of the embedding (1) in Section 2.1. That allows to conclude the result of Theorem 4.5 from Hilbert's Basis Theorem for polynomials over commuting variables.

Interestingly, no bound for the cardinality of S_0, e.g. in the number of variables, is known. That leads to the following fundamental problem. Does there exist any such bound? Or would the bound 2^n, where n is the number of unknowns, be enough? The best known lower bounds for the maximal size of independent systems of equations are $\Theta(\text{card}(\Xi)^3)$ and $\Theta(\text{card}(\Xi)^4)$ in free semigroups and in free monoids, respectively, see [104]. It is interesting to note that there exist monoids, where Ehrenfeucht Compactness Property holds, but no bound for the maximal size of independent systems exists. An example of this is the variety of finitely generated commutative monoids, see again [104]. On the other hand, the property does not hold for all finitely generated monoids, see e.g. [83] and [82].

5 Unavoidable Regularities

In this section we consider several properties of words related to repetitions. It appears that some repetitions, or more generally some other regularities, are unavoidable, others are avoidable. For instance, it is easily checked that every binary word of length 4 contains a square. So squares are unavoidable over two letters. One may ask whether there exist arbitrarily long cube-free words over two letters. The answer is positive. Thus cubes are avoidable over two letters.

5.1 Power-free words

The *Thue-Morse* word defined earlier is cube-free. As we already mentioned in Section 1.2, the Thue-Morse word is even 2^+-free. This means that it is *overlap-free*, that is it does not contain any factor of the form $axaxa$, where a is a letter and x is a word.

As another example, we consider the infinite word z defined below, and we prove that it is cube-free. We choose to consider this infinite word rather than the Thue-Morse word because the proof is quite simple, although the argument of the proof is rather the same as for the Thue-Morse word. The cube-freeness of z is optimal in the sense that there are repetitions in z that are cubes up to one letter. One may say that z is 3^--free.

Consider the morphism

$$\zeta : \begin{array}{l} a \mapsto aba \\ b \mapsto abb \end{array}$$

Starting with a, it generates the infinite word

$$z = \zeta^\omega(a) = abaabbabaabaabbabbabaabbabaabaabbabaabaabbabbabaabbabb\cdots$$

Inspection shows that there are many factors of the form $uuu^{\bullet}$, that is cubes up to a final letter. For example, aab, bba, $abaabaabb$, $abbabbaba$ are almost cubes, and in fact all words $\zeta^n(aab)$ and $\zeta^n(bba)$ for $n \geq 1$ are almost cube factors of the infinite word z.

Fact 5.1 *The infinite word z is cube-free.*

Proof. We prove that ζ is a *cube-free* morphism in the sense that it preserves cube-free words: if w is cube-free, then $\zeta(w)$ is cube-free. This suffices to show that z is cube-free.

Assume the contrary, and consider a finite cube-free word w of minimal length n such that $\zeta(w)$ contains a cube uuu. The word $\zeta(w)$ has length $3n$, and it is a product of n blocks, each being either aba or abb.

Observe first that $|u|$ must be a multiple of 3. Indeed, the initial letter of u appears in w at three positions i, $j = i + |u|$, $k = i + 2|u|$ for some i, and if $|u| \not\equiv 0 \mod 3$, then i, j, k take all possible values (mod 3). This means that the initial letter of u must appear in the images $\zeta(a) = aba$ and $\zeta(b) = abb$ at the first, the second and the third letter. However, b does not appear as an initial letter, and a does not appear as a middle letter. This proves the claim.

Next, observe that ζ is one-to-one. Indeed, the argument can be retrieved from the image of a letter because it is just the last letter of the image. This means that if $\zeta(w) = xuuuy$ for some x, y, we may assume that $|x| \equiv 0 \mod 3$. We may even assume that x is the empty word because w was chosen to be minimal. But then, there is a unique word v such that $u = \zeta(v)$ and w starts with v^3. $\square$

As already mentioned earlier, the arguments in the proof are rather typical. Even the construction is typical: iterating a morphism f is a general tool for the construction of infinite words with predictable properties. Next, the property to be proved by induction (or by contradiction) uses the fact that one can infer a property for a word w from a property of the image $f(w)$ (in the previous example, of $\zeta(w)$). This step may be involved, because the morphism f may not always have such a simple form as the morphism ζ. In the present case, we proved that ζ is a *cube-free* morphisms, that is a morphisms that preserves cube-free words. Another, rather old, example is given e.g., in [79]. It is the morphism

$$a \mapsto abc$$
$$b \mapsto ac$$
$$c \mapsto b$$

This morphism does not preserve square-free words, because the image of aba is $abcacabc$. However, iterating the morphism yields an infinite square-free word.

The question whether a morphism is k-free, that is whether it preserves k-free words, is not yet completely solved. The simplest, but not the easiest case is that of square-free morphisms. The final answer to this case was given in [48]. For a nonerasing morphism h on A, set

$$M(h) = \max_{a \in A} |h(a)|, \ m(h) = \min_{a \in A} |h(a)|.$$

Then the following holds:

Theorem 5.2 *Let $h : A^* \to B^*$ be a nonerasing morphism. If h preserves square-free words of length $K(h) = \max (3, 1 + \lceil (M(h) - 3)/m(h) \rceil)$, then h is square-free.*

As a special case, any *uniform* morphism h, i.e. such that the images of all letters have the same length, is square-free as soon as it preserves square-free words of length 3. In the ternary case, one has the following theorem [48]:

Theorem 5.3 *A ternary endomorphism h is square-free if h preserves square-free words of length 5.*

No general result is known for cube-free morphisms. In the case of binary morphisms, one has the following bound [94]:

Theorem 5.4 *A binary morphism h is cube-free if h preserves cube-free words of length 10.*

This bound was improved to the length 7 in [112]. In the same direction, we mention the following striking result concerning *power-free* morphisms, i.e. k-frees morphisms for all k [111].

Theorem 5.5 *A morphism h is power-free if h preserves square-free words and if the words $h(a^2)$ for a a letter, are cube-free.*

Deciding whether a given morphism is k-free, for a fixed $k \geq 3$, or even cube-free, is a difficult open problem.

Abelian repetitions, i.e. repetitions of commutatively equal blocks, constitute another type of interesting repetitions of words. Of course, every repetition of words is also Abelian repetitions, but not vice versa. It was shown in [70] that Abelian squares can be avoided in infinite words if the alphabet contains 25 letters. In [145] the result was improved to five letter alphabets, and finally the four letter case – known as an Erdös Problem – was solved in a complicated paper in [107]. The required infinite word is obtained by iterating a uniform morphism, where the images of letters are of length 85! This amazing result has been completed by Carpi [24] who shows that the number of Abelian square-free words over 4 letters of given length grows exponentially. He also proves that there are "many" Abelian square-free morphisms, i.e., morphisms that map Abelian square-free words on Abelian square-free words. He shows that the monoid of Abelian square-free morphisms is not finitely generated. Similarly in [91] it was shown that Abelian fifth powers can be avoided in a binary alphabet, and later [60] filled the gaps: Abelian fourth powers can be avoided in a binary alphabet and cubes in a ternary alphabet. Moreover, all these results are optimal, for instance all binary words avoiding Abelian cubes are finite, in fact, of length at most 7.

Most, if not all, known repetition-free words are defined by iterating a morphism, or as a morphic image of such. However, this approach can capture only very few repetition-free words, as witnessed by the following result proved in [19]. In order to formulate it we denote by $\rho - F_k(n)$ the number of ρ-free words of length n over a k-letter alphabet.

Theorem 5.6 (i) *The number of cubefree words of length n over a binary alphabet is exponential, i.e., there exist constants $A, B > 0$ and $\alpha, \beta > 1$ such that*

$$A\alpha^n \leq 2 - F_3(n) \leq B\beta^n$$

(ii) *There exist nondenumerably many squarefree infinite words over a ternary alphabet.*

Both parts of the above theorem holds also for squarefree words over a ternary alphabet, see again [19]. On the other hand, for 2^+-free binary words the situation is different:

Theorem 5.7 (i) *The number of 2^+-free words of length n over a binary alphabet is polynomial, i.e., there exist constants $A, B > 0$ and $\alpha, \beta > 1$ such that*

$$An^\alpha \leq 2^+ - F_2(n) \leq Bn^\beta$$

(ii) *There exist nondenumerably many 2^+-free infinite words over a binary alphabet.*

Part (i) above is shown in [151], while part (ii) is an exercise in [119]. The values of the parameters α and β in Theorem 5.7 (ii) are studied in [110] and [116], see also [29] and [22].

Very recently in [105] Theorems 5.6 and 5.7 were extended to determine the exact borderline between polynomial and exponential growth in numbers of binary ρ-free words of length n:

Theorem 5.8 *The cardinality of $2_1/3 - F_2(n)$ is polynomial while that of $2_1/3^+ - F_2(n)$ is exponential.*

Amazingly the Thue-Morse morphism plays a central role in the proof of Theorem 5.8.

Recently, it has been shown [148] that the only binary 7/3-power-free word that can be obtained by iterating a morphism is the Thue-Morse word. Moreover, the Thue-Morse morphism is the basically the only 7/3-power-free morphism: if h is a binary morphism, and if $h(01101001)$ is 7/3-power-free, then h is a power of the Thue-Morse morphism (up to inverting of 0 and 1)

5.2 Test sets and test words

A convenient framework is to define test sets for morphisms. A finite set $T \subset A^*$ is a *test set* for overlap-free (resp. square-free, cube-free) morphisms if every morphism $f : A^* \to B^*$ is overlap-free (resp. square-free, cube-free) as soon as $f(w)$ is overlap-free (resp. square-free, cube-free) for all $w \in T$. Theorem 5.4 can be rephrased as follows: the set of binary cube-free words of length 10 is a test set for binary cube-free morphisms. Test sets for overlap-free morphisms are characterized in [155]. Test sets for k-free morphisms with $k \geq 3$ are studied in [159]. It has been shown that no test sets exist for the set of square-free morphisms over a 4-letter alphabet.

Another interesting notion is that of test word. A word $w \in A^*$ is a *test word* for overlap-free (resp. square-free, cube-free) morphisms if every morphism $f : A^* \to B^*$ is overlap-free (resp. square-free, cube-free) as soon as the word $f(w)$ is overlap-free (resp. square-free, cube-free). Thus w is a test word if $\{w\}$ is a test set. It has been shown [17] that *abbabaab* is a test word for overlap-free morphisms. We refer to [155] and [159] for a detailed study of test words in various cases.

Overlap-free morphisms were already characterized by Thue [166]. The following is Satz 16 of his 1912 paper; the morphism μ was given in the introduction.

Theorem 5.9 *Let h be an overlap-free binary endomorphism. Then there is an integer n such that $h = \mu^n$ or $h = \pi \circ \mu^n$, where π is the endomorphism that exchanges the two letters of the alphabet.*

Clearly, this means that the monoid of binary overlap-free endomorphisms is finitely generated. The same does not hold for larger alphabets, neither for overlap-free morphisms, nor for k-power free morphisms: all these monoids of endomorphisms are not finitely generated [154]. Many other monoids of endomorphisms are not finitely generated, such as the monoid of primitive morphisms (that is, preserving primitive words) or of Lyndon morphisms (that is, preserving Lyndon words), see [153].

5.3 Repetition threshold

More general repetitions can be considered as well. Thue himself called a word on n letters *irreducible* if two distinct occurrences of a nonempty factor are always separated by at least $n-2$ letters. Thus, irreducible means overlap-free if $n = 2$, and square-free if $n = 3$. A more general concept, first considered

440

by F. Dejean [59], is to require that the length of the word y separating two occurrences of x is bounded from below by the length of x times some factor. This is precisely what we called earlier a repetition: a word xyx, where x is nonempty, is a repetition of order k, where $k = |xyx|/|xy|$.

We have seen that every binary word of length 4 contains a square, and that there exist infinite binary overlap-free words (such as the Thue-Morse word): these words are 2^+-free.

A similar property holds for ternary words: every ternary word of length 39 contains a repetition of order $7/4$, and there exists [59] an infinite ternary word that has no repetition of order $> 7/4$. More precisely, we have:

Theorem 5.10 *The word generated by the endomorphism*

$$a \mapsto abcacbcabcbacbcacba$$
$$b \mapsto bcabacabcacbacabacb$$
$$c \mapsto cabcbabcabacbabcbac$$

has no repetitions of order $> 7/4$. So it is $(\frac{7}{4})^+$-free.

Call *repetition threshold* the smallest number $s(k)$ such that there exists an infinite word over k letters that has only repetitions of order less than or equal to $s(k)$. We know that $s(2) = 2$, $s(3) = 7/4$. It is conjectured in [59] that $s(4) = 7/5$ and $s(k) = k/(k-1)$ for $k \geq 5$. We know that this conjecture is true up to 11, see [139] and [137], but the general case is still open.

5.4 Unavoidable patterns

Another topic on unavoidable regularities concerns *unavoidable patterns*. This is a generalization of the notion of square-freeness and k-power-freeness. Interestingly, this notion has a rather deep relation to universal algebra, see [9]. We consider two alphabets, the first denoted by A as usual, and the second one, by E, called the *pattern alphabet*. Given a pattern $p \in E^*$, the *pattern language* associated to p on A is the set of all words $h(p)$, where h is a non-erasing morphism from E^* to A^*. A word w is said to *avoid* the pattern p, if no factor of w is in the pattern language of p. For example, consider the pattern $p = \alpha\alpha\beta\beta\alpha$, where α and β are letters. The word $1(011)(011)(0)(0)(011)1$ does not avoid p. On the contrary, 0000100010111 avoids p. A pattern is *avoidable* on A if there exists an infinite word on A that avoids p, otherwise it is unavoidable. A pattern is k-avoidable if it is avoidable on a k letter alphabet.

For instance, since there exist infinite square-free words over three letters, the pattern $\alpha\alpha$ is 3-avoidable. Also, the Thue-Morse infinite word avoids the patterns $\alpha\alpha\alpha$ and $\alpha\beta\alpha\beta\alpha$, the latter one corresponding to overlaps.

Clearly, the pattern $\alpha\beta\alpha$ is unavoidable. More generally, define the *Zimin words* Z_n as follows. Let α_n, for $n \geq 0$, be distinct letters in E. Set $Z_0 = \varepsilon$ and $Z_{n+1} = Z_n \alpha_n Z_n$ for $n \geq 1$.

Fact 5.11 *The Zimin words Z_n are all unavoidable.*

In some sense, these words are all the unavoidable words. Indeed, say that a pattern p *divides* a pattern p' if p', viewed as an ordinary word, has a factor in the pattern language of p.

Theorem 5.12 *A pattern p is unavoidable if and only if it divides some Zimin word.*

There exists an algorithm to decide whether a pattern is avoidable. This has been given independently in almost the same terms by [10] and [169]. Let us just sketch the construction.

Let $p \in E^*$ be a pattern, and let P the set of variables occurring in p. The *adjacency graph* of p is the bipartite graph $G(p)$ with two copies of P as vertices, denoted P^L and P^R, and with an edge between λ^L and μ^R if and only if $\lambda\mu$ is a factor of p. For example, the adjacency graph of the pattern $p = \alpha\beta\alpha\gamma\beta\alpha$ has six vertices and four edges.

A subset F of P is *free* if there is no path in $G(p)$ from a vertex λ^L to a vertex μ^R with λ, μ in F. In our example, the free sets are $\{\alpha\}$ and $\{\beta\}$. Given a pattern p and a free set F for p, we *reduce* p to q by deleting in p all occurrences of the letters of F. In our example, $p = \alpha\beta\alpha\gamma\beta\alpha$ reduces to $q = \beta\gamma\beta$ by the free set $\{\alpha\}$, and q itself reduces to γ which itself reduces to the empty word. A pattern is *reducible* if it can be reduced to the empty word in a finite number of steps. The remarkable theorem that yields the algorithm is:

Theorem 5.13 *A pattern p is avoidable if and only if it is reducible.*

As shown by the pattern $\alpha\alpha$, an avoidable pattern is not necessarily avoidable on two letters. In other terms, the same pattern may be 2-unavoidable, but k-avoidable for some larger k. The *avoidability index* $\mu(p)$ of a pattern p is the smallest integer k such that p is k-avoidable, or ∞ if p is unavoidable. Contrary to the previous theorem, there is no known algorithm to compute the avoidability index of a given pattern. Even for short patterns, the exact value of $\mu(p)$ may be unknown. For instance, it is not known whether the value of $\mu(\alpha\alpha\beta\beta\gamma\gamma)$ is 2 or 3, although there is some experimental evidence that the index is 2, see Chapter 3 in [120]. However, the proof of Theorem 5.13, if analyzed carefully, provides an upper bound on the avoidability index of a pattern.

Theorem 5.14 *Let p be a pattern on k symbols. If p is avoidable, then $\mu(p) \leq 2k + 4$.*

The above bound is probably far from being optimal. In fact, it is quite difficult to find patterns with high avoidability index. A pattern which has index 4 is

$$p = \alpha\beta\zeta_1\beta\gamma\zeta_2\gamma\alpha\zeta_3\beta\alpha\zeta_4\alpha\gamma$$

over a pattern alphabet of 7 symbols. No pattern of index 5 is known, and one may ask whether such a pattern exists. Many results on avoidable and unavoidable patterns are reported in Chapter 3 of [120], while [57] is a source of several open problems. Recent results concerning complexity of the reduction algorithm appear in [86], [87] and [88].

5.5 Shirshov's theorem

An unavoidable regularity is a property of words that can be observed on any word, provided it is sufficiently long. Several of these unavoidable regularities exist. The most famous are Ramsey's theorem, van der Waerden's theorem and Shirshov's theorem. We just state here Ramsey's and van der Waerden's theorems in the perspective of words, and then discuss Shirshov's theorem and some of its consequences.

Let A be a finite alphabet, S a set and $k \geq 2$ an integer. A map $f : A^* \to S$ is called k-*ramseyan* if there exists an integer $L(f, k)$ such that any word w of length at least $L(f, k)$ admits a factor u of the form $u = w_1 \cdots w_k$, with $w_1, \ldots, w_k$ nonempty words, such that

$$f(w_i \cdots w_j) = f(w_{i'} \cdots w_{j'})$$

for all $1 \leq i \leq j \leq k$, $1 \leq i' \leq j' \leq k$. Further f is *ramseyan* if it is k-ramseyan for some k. Ramsey's theorem, see [75], can be stated in a number of combinatorial structures. On words it can be stated as the following unavoidable regularity:

Theorem 5.15 (Ramsey's theorem) *Every map $f : A^* \to S$ into a finite set S is ramseyan.*

Given a word $w = a_1 \cdots a_n$, where $a_1, \ldots, a_n$ are letters, a *cadence* of w of order r is a sequence $0 < t_1 < \cdots < t_r \leq n$ such that $a_{t_1} = a_{t_2} = \cdots = a_{t_r}$. A cadence is *arithmetic* if the integers are in arithmetic progression, that is if $t_{i+1} - t_i = t_i - t_{i-1}$ for $1 < i < r$. Now, we can formulate the second unavoidable regularity of words:

Theorem 5.16 (van der Waerden's theorem) *Let A be an alphabet with k letters. For any positive integer n, there exists an integer $W(k, n)$ such that any word w over A of length at least $W(k, n)$ contains an arithmetic cadence of order n.*

Ramsey's and van der Waerden's theorems are rather well known. However, the evaluation of the integers $W(k,n)$, as well as the function L, is very difficult and not at all completely known, see [75]. We refer to [119] and to [63] for proofs of our above formulations and further discussions.

We now turn to Shirshov's theorem, which is much less known. It was proved by Shirshov in connection with so-called polynomial identities (see [119] for a discussion of this issue). The unavoidable regularity concerned by this result has also other far reaching applications.

Let A be a totally ordered alphabet, and let $<$ denote the *lexicographic* order on A^* induced by the order on the alphabet. Denote by S_n the symmetric group on n elements. A sequence $(u_1, u_2, \ldots, u_n)$ of nonempty words is called an *n-division* of the word $u = u_1 u_2 \cdots u_n$ if, for any nontrivial permutation σ of S_n, one has

$$u_1 u_2 \cdots u_n > u_{\sigma(1)} u_{\sigma(2)} \cdots u_{\sigma(n)}$$

Example 6. Consider the binary alphabet $A = \{a, b\}$ ordered by setting $a < b$. The word $w = ababbaba$ is 3-divided by the sequence $(ababb, ab, a)$. One can also verify that this is the only 3-division of w and that there is no 4-division. $\square$

Now we can formulate our third unavoidable regularity:

Theorem 5.17 (Shirshov's theorem) *Let A be an alphabet with k letters. For any positive integers n, k, there exists an integer $N(k, p, n)$ such that any word w over A of length at least $N(k, p, n)$ contains as a factor an n-divided word or a pth power.*

Again, the integers $N(k, p, n)$ are quite difficult to compute. It is also quite interesting that this result admits an extension to infinite words, in contrast to van der Waerden's theorem. An infinite word s is called ω-*divided* if it can be factorized into an infinite product $s = s_1 s_2 \cdots s_n \cdots$ of nonempty words such that $(s_1, \ldots, s_n)$ is an n-division for all $n > 0$. Now, by denoting by $F(s)$ the set of all (finite) factors of an infinite word s we can formulate:

Theorem 5.18 *For any infinite word t over A, there exists an infinite word s such that $F(s) \subset F(t)$ and s is ultimately periodic or s is ω-divided.*

This is, in fact, a consequence of another structural result of infinite words. In order to state this, we recall that a *Lyndon word* is a word w that is primitive and that is smaller (for the lexicographic order) than all of its conjugates, i.e., such that whenever $w = xy$ with x, y nonempty, then $xy < yx$. Then we have:

Theorem 5.19 *For any infinite word t over A, there exists an infinite word s such that $F(s) \subset F(t)$ and s is a product of an infinite sequence of non increasing Lyndon words: $s = \ell_1 \ell_2 \cdots \ell_n \cdots$, with $\ell_n \geq \ell_{n+1}$ and ℓ_n is a*

Lyndon word for all n.

As we already said Shirshov's theorem has quite interesting consequences. We consider here one of those. A semigroup S is called *periodic* if every sub-semigroup of S generated by a single element is finite. A sequence $(s_1, \ldots, s_n)$ of n elements of S is called *permutable* if there exists a nontrivial permutation σ of S_n such that $s_1 \cdots s_n = s_{\sigma(1)} \cdots s_{\sigma(n)}$. The semigroup is called *n-permutable* if any sequence of n elements of S is permutable, and S is called *permutable* if S is n-permutable for some n. A language L is called *periodic* (resp. *permutable*) if its syntactic semigroup is periodic (resp. permutable). A striking characterization of rational languages can now be stated:

Theorem 5.20 *A language L is rational if and only if it is periodic and permutable.*

The proof is based on Shirshov's theorem, see [150], [63]. Also the proofs of Theorems 5.18 and 5.19, as well as more related results can be found in [63].

5.6 Unavoidable sets of words

We conclude this section with still another notion of an unavoidability, namely the notion of *unavoidable set* of words. A set X of words over A is unavoidable if any long enough word over A has a factor in X, that is if $A^* - A^*XA^*$ is finite.

For example, the set $\{a, bb\}$ is unavoidable over $\{a, b\}$. Indeed, any word of length 2 either contains an a or contains bb. Since a superset of an unavoidable set is again unavoidable, it is natural to consider *minimal* unavoidable sets. Every minimal unavoidable set is finite. Indeed, if X is unavoidable, then let d be the maximal length of the words in the finite set $A^* - A^*XA^*$. Let Z be the set of words in X of length at most $d + 1$. Every word of length $d + 1$ has a factor in X which actually is in Z. Thus Z is unavoidable and finite.

In fact, there exists an algorithm to decide whether a finite set X of words in unavoidable, and the structure of unavoidable sets of words is rather well understood, see Chapter 1 of [120] for a general exposition and for references. A recent result concerns unavoidable sets of words of the same length, i.e., *uniform* unavoidable sets. For $k, q \geq 1$, let $c(k, q)$ be the number of conjugacy classes of words of length k on q letters. An unavoidable set of words of length k on q symbols clearly has at least $c(k, q)$ elements. It is quite remarkable that the converse holds as well, see [38]:

Theorem 5.21 *For any $k, q \geq 1$, there exists an unavoidable set of words of length k on q letters having exactly $c(k, q)$ elements.*

As an illustration assume that $k = 3$ and $q = 2$, so that $c(k, q) = 4$. Now the sets $\{aaa, aab, aba, bbb\}$ and $\{aaa, aab, bba, bbb\}$, for example, are avoidable, the former because it does not intersect all the conjugacy classes and the latter since it avoids $(ab)^\omega$. On the other hand, the set $X = \{aaa, aab, bab, bbb\}$ is unavoidable. Indeed, infinite words containing no letter a or the factor aa clearly contains a factor from X, and all the other words contain either bab or bbb.

6   Complexity

Given a set X of words over an alphabet A the complexity function of X is the function p_X defined by $p_X(n) = \mathrm{Card}(X \cap A^n)$. We are interested here in the (*subword*) *complexity* (one should say *factor* complexity!) of a finite or an infinite word u. It is the function p_u which is the complexity function for the set $F(u)$ of factors of u, thus $p_u(n) = \mathrm{Card}(F(u) \cap A^n)$ is just the number of factors of length n in u. The study of infinite words of given complexity has revealed a large set of surprising results. Moreover, there are strong relations to number theory and symbolic dynamics. Subword complexity was studied, in relation with languages generated by D0L-systems, already in [69].

6.1   Subword complexity of finite words

The subword complexity of a finite word w is simply the function p_w such that $p_w(n)$ is the number of factors of length n of w. Of course, $p_w(0) = p_w(|w|) = 1$, and $p_w(n) = 0$ for $n > |w|$. The description of the shape of the function p_w uses the parameter G_w defined as follows: G_w is the maximal length of a *repeated* factor, that is a factor that appears at least twice in w. For instance, let $w = abccacbccabaab$. The word $bcca$ is a repeated factor of maximal length, so $G_w = 4$. The shape of the function p_w is given by the following result, see [62], [26], [25] and [118]:

Theorem 6.1 *Let w be a word over at least two letters. There is an integer m_w such that the function $p_w(n)$ behaves as follows:*

(i) it is strictly increasing for $0 \le n \le m_w$,

(ii) it is constant for $m_w \le n \le G_w + 1$,

(iii) it is decreasing for $G_w + 1 \le n \le |w|$, and more precisely $p_w(n+1) = p_w(n) - 1$ for $n = G_w + 1, \ldots, |w|$.

Consider again the word $w = abccacbccabaab$. One gets $p_w(1) = 3$, $p_w(2) = 8$, $p_w(3) = 10$, $p_w(4) = 11$, and this is the maximum because $G_w = 4$. Then it decreases by 1 at each step: $p_w(5) = 10 \ldots$. In our example, the integer m_w is equal to G_w.

A precise description of the parameter m_w is missing. On the contrary, the parameter G_w is strongly related to other structural parameters of the word w. Denote by R_w the minimal number such that there is no factor x of w of length R_w that has two right extensions in w, i.e., such that xa and xb are factors of w for distinct letters a and b. Next, let K_w be the length of the shortest suffix of w which is an unrepeated factor of w. Then it can be shown, see [26], that $G_w + 1 = \max(R_w, K_w)$. The parameter G_w has the following interesting property, proved in [26]:

Theorem 6.2 *A word w is completely determined by its set of factors of length at most $G_w + 2$.*

For example, the word $w = abccacbccabaab$, of length 14, is entirely determined by its factors of length 6. Many combinatorial facts, and properties of distribution of these parameters, are given in [27] and [28].

Related to Theorem 6.2 one can ask several questions when a given word is uniquely determined by its factors or *sparse subwords*. Besides these two variants one can also ask the same when multiplicities are taken into account. This leads to four different problems, see [125] or Chapter 6 in [119]. Among those is a question, sometimes referred to as Milner's Problem, asking what is the minimal length of sparse subwords with multiplicities which defines the word uniquely.

6.2 Subword complexity of infinite words

Let us start with two examples. For the infinite word $01(10)^\omega$, the complexity function is easily computed. One gets $p(0) = 1$, $p(1) = 2$, $p(2) = 3$, $p(n) = 4$ for $n \geq 4$. More generally, it is easily seen that an ultimately periodic infinite word has a complexity function that is bounded, and therefore is ultimately constant because a complexity function is never decreasing. On the contrary, consider the infinite binary word c known as the Champernowne word:

$$c = 0110111001011101111000 \cdots$$

This is obtained by concatenating the binary expansions of all positive integers in order. Clearly, every binary word is a factor of c and thus $p_c(n) = 2^n$ for all $n \geq 0$. These examples show that both extreme behaviours are possible for complexity functions. However, there are gaps in the growth of complexity functions. The first such result was given in [135,46]:

Theorem 6.3 *Let x be an infinite word. The following are equivalent:*

(i) x is ultimately periodic,

(ii) $p_x(n) = p_x(n + 1)$ for some n,

(iii) $p_x(n) < n + k - 1$ *for some* $n \geq 1$, *where* k *is the number of letters appearing in* x,

(iv) $p_x(n)$ *is bounded.*

Proof. The implications (1) $\Rightarrow$ (4) $\Rightarrow$ (3) $\Rightarrow$ (2) are easy. For the remaining implication (2) $\Rightarrow$ (1) we observe that each factor of length n in x can be extended in exactly one manner to a factor of length $n + 1$. This means that each occurrence of a given factor of length n is always followed by the same letter in x. Consider any factor u of length n that appears twice in x, and denote by y the word that separates the two occurrences, so that uyu is a factor of x. Since the letters that follow u are determined by u, this means that in fact $uyuy$ is a factor of x, and that $(uy)^\omega$ is a suffix of x. $\square$

This result shows a "gap" for complexity functions: either a function p is ultimately constant, or $p(n) \geq n + 1$ for all n. So an infinite aperiodic word, that is a word that is not ultimately periodic, cannot have a complexity function bounded by n. It appears that aperiodic infinite words of complexity $p(n) = n + 1$ indeed exist (see also [108]). These words are called *Sturmian words*.

For another gap of complexity functions see [31].

6.3 Sturmian words

A Sturmian word x is always a binary word because $p_x(1) = 2$ and $p_x(1)$ is the number of letters appearing in x. Every factor of length n can be extended to the right into a factor of length $n + 1$. Since $p_x(n + 1) = 1 + p_x(n)$, this extension is unique for all factors up to one, and this last factor has two extensions. A factor with two extension is called *right special*. More precisely, call the *(right) degree* of a word u the number of distinct letters a such that ua is a factor of x. Then, in the binary case, a right special factor is a word u of degree 2. A Sturmian word has exactly one special factor of each length. We give an example:

Fact 6.4 *The Fibonacci word* $f = 010010100100101001010 \cdots$ *is Sturmian.*
To check this, we observe that f is the fixed-point of the morphism φ given in Section 1.3. Thus f is a product of words 0 and 01. In particular, 11 is not a factor of f and $p_f(2) = 3$. Also, the word 000 is not a factor of f since otherwise it is a factor of the image of a factor of f that must contain 11.

Next, we show that for all finite words x, neither $0x0$ nor $1x1$ is a factor of f. This is clear if x is the empty word or is a single letter. Arguing by induction, assume that both $0x0$ or $1x1$ are factors of f. Then x starts and ends with 0, so $x = 0y0$ for some word y. Since $10y01$ is a factor of f, there exists a factor z of f such that $\varphi(z) = 0y$. Moreover, $00y00 = \varphi(1z1)$ and $010y01 = \varphi(0z0)$ are factors of f, showing that $0z0$ and $1z1$ are factors, a contradiction.

We now prove that f has at most one special factor of each length. Assume that u and v are right special factors of f of the same length, and let x be the longest common suffix of u and v. Then the four words $0x0$, $0x1$, $1x0$, $1x1$ are factors of f which contradicts our previous observation.

We finally prove that f has at least one special factor of each length. For this, it suffices to prove that f is aperiodic. Recall that f is the limit of the sequence of finite Fibonacci words defined by $f_0 = a$, $f_1 = ab$, and $f_{n+2} = f_{n+1}f_n$. It is easily shown that the

$$\frac{|f_n|_a}{|f_n|} \to \frac{1}{\tau}, \qquad n \to \infty,$$

with $\tau = (1 + \sqrt{5})/2$, whereas in a ultimate periodic word, this limit is a rational number. □

We now give two other descriptions of Sturmian words, namely as balanced words and as mechanical words. Given two binary words u and v of the same length, the *balance* of u and v is the number $b(u, v) = ||u|_1 - |v|_1|$, that is the absolute value of the difference of the number of occurrences of the letter 1 in the words u and v. Since u and v have the same length, one could also have defined this number by taking the number of 0's instead of the number of 1's. As an example, for 01001 and 11001, the balance is 1. An infinite word x is *balanced* if the balance of any two factors of x of the same length is at most 1. Intuitively, a balanced word cannot have big differences in factors. In particular, a balanced word cannot contain simultaneously the factors $0u0$ and $1u1$. Moreover, it can be shown that a balanced word x has a *slope*, that is that the limit $\lim_{n\to\infty} b_n/n$ exists, where b_n is the number of 1's in the prefix of length n. As an example, the slope of the Fibonacci word is $1/\varphi^2$, where $\varphi = (1 + \sqrt{5})/2$.

Another notion strongly related to Sturmian words is of more arithmetical nature. Given two real numbers α and ρ with $0 \le \alpha \le 1$, we define two infinite words $s_{\alpha,\rho} = s_{\alpha,\rho}(0)s_{\alpha,\rho}(1)\cdots$ and $s'_{\alpha,\rho} = s'_{\alpha,\rho}(0)s'_{\alpha,\rho}(1)\cdots$ by

$$s_{\alpha,\rho}(n) = \lfloor \alpha(n+1) + \rho \rfloor - \lfloor \alpha n + \rho \rfloor$$
$$s'_{\alpha,\rho}(n) = \lceil \alpha(n+1) + \rho \rceil - \lceil \alpha n + \rho \rceil$$
for $n > 0$.

The word $s_{\alpha,\rho}$ is the *lower mechanical word* and $s'_{\alpha,\rho}$ is the *upper mechanical word* with *slope* α and *intercept* ρ. It is clear that we may assume $0 \le \rho \le 1$. If α is irrational, $s_{\alpha,\rho}$ and $s'_{\alpha,\rho}$ differ by at most one factor of length 2.

The terminology stems from the following graphical interpretation. Consider the straight line defined by the equation $y = \alpha x + \rho$. The points with integer coordinates just below this line are $P_n = (n, \lfloor \alpha n + \rho \rfloor)$. Two consecutive points P_n and P_{n+1} are joined by a straight line segment that is horizontal if $s_{\alpha,\rho}(n) = 0$ and diagonal if $s_{\alpha,\rho}(n) = 1$. The same observation holds for the points located just above the line.

A special case deserves to be considered separately, namely when $0 < \alpha < 1$ and $\rho = 0$. In this case, $s_{\alpha,0}(0) = 0$, $s'_{\alpha,0}(0) = 1$, and if α is irrational

$$s_{\alpha,0} = 0c_\alpha, \quad s'_{\alpha,0} = 1c_\alpha,$$

where the infinite word c_α is called the *characteristic* word of α.

Mechanical words can be interpreted in several other ways. One is as cutting sequences, and is as follows. Consider again a straight line $y = \beta x + \rho$, for some $\beta > 0$ not restricted to be less than 1, and ρ not restricted to be positive. Consider the intersections of this line with the lines of the grid with nonnegative integer coordinates. We get a sequence of intersection points. Writing a 0 for each vertical intersection point and a 1 for each horizontal intersection point, we obtain an infinite word $K_{\beta,\rho}$ that is called the *cutting sequence*. Then

$$K_{\beta,\rho} = s_{\beta/(1+\beta),\rho/(1+\beta)}$$

Indeed, the transformation $(x, y) \mapsto (x + y, x)$ of the plane maps the line $y = \beta x + \rho$ to $y = \beta/(1 + \beta)x + \rho/(1 + \beta)$. Thus, cutting sequences are just another formulation of mechanical words, see also [47] for a more detailed discussion.

Mechanical words can also be generated by rotations. Let $0 < \alpha < 1$. The *rotation* of angle α is the mapping $R = R_\alpha$ from $[0, 1[$ into itself defined by

$$R(z) = \{z + \alpha\}$$

Iterating R, one gets $R^n(\rho) = \{n\alpha + \rho\}$. Thus, defining a partition of $[0, 1[$ by

$$I_0 = [0, 1 - \alpha[, \quad I_1 = [1 - \alpha, 1[,$$

one gets

$$s_{\alpha,\rho}(n) = \begin{cases} 0 & \text{if } R^n(\rho) \in I_0 \\ 1 & \text{if } R^n(\rho) \in I_1 \end{cases}.$$

The three properties are related by the following theorem [135]:

Theorem 6.5 *Let s be an infinite word. The following are equivalent:*

(i) s is Sturmian;

(ii) s *is balanced and aperiodic;*

(iii) s *is mechanical with an irrational slope.*

A proof can be found in Chapter 2 of [120]. As a example, the Fibonacci word f is indeed the lower mechanical word with slope and intercept equal to $1/\varphi^2$. There is a special class of Sturmian words called *characteristic* Sturmian words. These are the words where the intercept equals the slope. Each characteristic Sturmian word s has a description as the limit of a sequence s_n of finite words, quite as the Fibonacci word f is the limit of the finite words f_n. The recurrence relation is slightly more complicated. It has the form

$$s_n = s_{n-1}^{d_n} s_{n-2} \qquad \text{for } n \geq 1$$

with $s_{-1} = 1$, $s_0 = 0$, and where $d_1, d_2, \ldots$ is a sequence of integers with $d_1 \geq 0$ and $d_n > 0$ for $n > 1$. This sequence is related to the slope α of s by the fact that $[0, 1 + d_1, d_2, \ldots]$ is the continued fraction expansion of α. In the case of the Fibonacci word, the continued fraction expansion of $1/\varphi^2$ is indeed $[0, 2, 1, 1, \ldots]$ and the d_n are all equal to 1. The sequence s_n is called the standard sequence, and every word that appears in a standard sequence is a standard word.

A beautiful theorem, proved in [47], describes those irrational numbers α for which the standard Sturmian word can be generated by iterating a morphism. We give here the description that follows from a complement given in [3].

Theorem 6.6 *Let $0 < \alpha < 1$ be an irrational number. The characteristic Sturmian word of slope α is a fixed-point of some nontrivial morphism if and only if α is a quadratic irrational number such that $1/\bar{\alpha} < 1$.*

In this theorem, $\bar{\alpha}$ denotes the *conjugate* of the number α, that is the other root of its minimal polynomial. This result shows a relation between a combinatorial property of words and an arithmetical counterpart.

Sturmian words have a tremendous amount of combinatorial or arithemetic properties. An account can be found in Chapter 2 of [120] and in [147].

A final comment: why Sturmian words are called *Sturmian*? This term was introduced by Morse and Hedlund in their work on symbolic dynamics. The term is rather unfortunate in that the mathematician Sturm (1803–1855) never worked on these sequences. The argument is as follows ([135], page 40 and 41): consider a linear homogeneous second order differential equation

$$y'' + \phi(x)y = 0$$

where ϕ is continuous and has period 1. For an arbitrary solution $u(x)$ of this equation, one considers the infinite word $a_0 \cdots a_n \cdots$ where a_n is the number of zeros of u in the interval $[n, n+1)$. According to the well-known *Sturmian separation theorem*, this infinite word is Sturmian (over a convenient alphabet). This observation motivates the choice of the terminology.

For additional bibliographic comments about the origins, see the answer to exercise 1.2.8-36 in Knuth's volume 1, as well as [164] which dates back the Fibonacci word to J. Bernoulli III and A.A. Markov, see [12] and [127].

6.4 Episturmian words

There have been several attempts to extend the notion of Sturmian words. By the definition, Sturmian words are binary, and so relaxations of the constraints on the complexity function were looked for. It appears that a very good extension is rather related to what is called *Arnoux-Rauzy*, or more generally *episturmian words*. We start with a typical word of this family called *Tribonacci* word. This word is defined, like the Fibonacci word, as the limit of a sequence of words defined by a recurrence relation:

$$t_{n+3} = t_{n+2}t_{n+1}t_n, \qquad t_0 = 0, \ t_1 = 01, \ t_2 = 0102$$

So the Tribonacci word is

$$t = 0102010010201010201\cdots$$

It is also defined as the fixed-point of the mophism

$$0 \mapsto 01$$
$$1 \mapsto 02$$
$$2 \mapsto 0$$

It is not very difficult to see that $p_t(n) = 2n + 1$ for $n \geq 0$. This means that for each n, there must be 2 additional extensions to the right of factors of length n. To do this, there are two possibilities: either there are 2 distinct right special factors, each of which has degree 2, or there is just one right special factor which has degree 3. It can be checked that the second property holds for the Tribonacci word. The right special factors are ε, 0, 10, 010, 2010,.... As in the case of the Fibonacci words, the right special factors are the reversal of the prefixes of t.

Infinite words that have exactly one right special factor of each length, and each having degree 3, where introduced by Arnoux and Rauzy in [7], and are therefore called Arnoux-Rauzy words, or AR-words for short. This terminology has been extended to words over k-letters, see e.g., [168], by requiring that for each length n, there is a unique right special factor with degree k. This definition is relaxed in [65] and [93] to allow right special factors of degree at most k. Infinite words with this property are called *episturmian* words, and AR-words are called strict episturmian [93]. Strict episturmian binary words are Sturmian, whereas episturmian binary words may be ultimately periodic, so they are the mechanical words.

6.5   Hierarchies of complexities

One of the first papers on subword (factor) complexity is [69]. In this paper, it is shown that the subword complexity of a D0L language is bounded by cn^2 (resp. $cn \log n$, cn) if the morphism that generates the languages is arbitrary (resp. growing, uniform). This result was extended in [138]:

Theorem 6.7 *The subword complexity of an infinite word generated by iterating a morphism is of one of the following types:* $\Theta(n)$, $\Theta(n \log n)$, $\Theta(n \log n \log n)$, $\Theta(n^2)$, *or* $\Theta(1)$.

Each of the complexity classes corresponds to a class of morphisms. We just give some examples. The morphism

$$a \mapsto ab$$
$$b \mapsto bc$$
$$c \mapsto c$$

generates the infinite word

$$abbcbc^2 bc^3 \cdots bc^n \cdots$$

having quadratic complexity. Consider next the morphism

$$a \mapsto abc$$
$$b \mapsto bb$$
$$c \mapsto ccc$$

It generates the infinite word

$$abcb^2 c^3 b^4 c^9 \cdots b^{2^n} c^{3^n} \cdots$$

which has complexity $\Theta(n \log n)$. Consider finally the morphism

$$a \mapsto abab$$
$$b \mapsto bb$$

Starting with a, one gets the infinite word

$$abab^3 abab^7 ababbbabab^{15} \cdots$$

which has complexity $\Theta(n \log \log n)$.

6.6   Subword complexity and transcendence

Consider the Thue-Morse word t and the Fibonacci word f written over the alphabet $\{0,1\}$:

$$t = 0110100110010110100101100110100 1 \cdots$$
$$f = 01001010010010100101 0 \cdots$$

One may consider the infinite words as binary expansions of real numbers in the interval $[0,1]$, and ask whether these numbers are algebraic or transcendental. We address this and related questions in this section.

It is well known that the expansion in an integral base $b \geq 2$ of a rational number is ultimately periodic. This means that the subword complexity of a rational number is very low. On the other hand, it has been conjectured by Borel, see [4] for a more detailed discussion, that the infinite word representing the expansion in base b of an algebraic number is "normal", which means that all words appear as factors, and that all factors of length n appear with the same frequency $1/b^n$. This conjecture is presently far from being proved, and even the following, much weaker conjecture, seems to be very difficult: let x be the expansion in base b of a real number r. If $p_x(n) < b^n$ for all n, then r is either a rational or a transcendental number, again see [4].

However, there exist several results in number theory related to the fact that algebraic numbers cannot be well approximated by rational numbers. In other terms, if a number is too well approximated, then it is either rational or transcendental. Two of these results are the famous theorem of Roth and a refinement of this, which is the theorem of Ridout, see [4] for references. It is remarkable that these results can be translated into combinatorial properties of infinite words [71]:

Theorem 6.8 *Let x be the expansion in base $b \geq 2$ of a real number $r \in [0,1]$. If there exist real numbers $\alpha > 0$ and $\varepsilon > 0$ such that the word x has infinitely many prefixes of the form $uv^{2+\varepsilon}$, with $|u| \leq \alpha|v|$, then r is either a rational or a transcendental number.*

The first condition means that x must contain arbitrarily long powers of exponent strictly greater than 2, and the second condition requires that these powers appear "not too far" from the beginning of the word. In fact, the present statement is the translation of Ridout's theorem, and when u is assumed to be the empty word, that is when it is required that x starts with infinitely many $2 + \varepsilon$ powers, this is Roth's theorem. If the infinite word x has the prefix $uv^{2+\varepsilon}$, then $x = uv^{2+\varepsilon}y$ for some infinite word y, and x is "close" to the ultimately periodic word uv^ω, so the real r is "close" to the rational number represented by uv^ω. For the complete proof of Theorem 6.8, however, some further work is needed.

Theorem 6.8 gives a powerful tool to prove that real numbers are transcendental. As the first example, we consider the number whose binary expansion is the Fibonacci word f. Recall that f is the limit of the sequence of finite words f_n defined by $f_0 = 0$, $f_1 = 01$, $f_{n+2} = f_{n+1}f_n$. It is easily checked that f starts with infinitely many $(2 + 1/\varphi^2 - \varepsilon)$-powers. Indeed, for $n \geq 4$, the infinite word f starts with $f_n f_n g_{n-2}$, where g_n is equal to f_n up to the last two letters. For instance, f starts with $(01001010)(01001010)(01010)$. Thus the number whose binary expansion is the Fibonacci word is indeed transcendental.

The Fibonacci word is a special case of a general result of [71]:

Theorem 6.9 *Let x be the expansion in base 2 of a real number $r \in [0, 1]$. If x is a Sturmian word, then r is transcendental.*

It is shown also in [71] that the same result holds for above mentioned Arnoux-Rauzy words.

We know that the Thue-Morse word is overlap-free, so it does not contain 2^+-powers. Thus Theorem 6.9 does not apply. However, the transcendence of the number represented by the Thue-Morse word has been proved directly by Mahler and Dekking, see again [4] for references.

Recently, the case of infinite words that are fixed-points of morphisms has been considered. An endomorphism h of A^* is called *primitive*, if there exists an integer m such that each word $h^m(a)$, for $a \in A$, contains at least one occurrence of every letter in A. For instance, the Fibonacci morphism is primitive. The result is the following, see [6] or already [71] for primitive morphisms:

Theorem 6.10 *If the binary expansion of a real number is the fixed-point of a non-trivial morphism that is either primitive or uniform, then this number is either rational or transcendental.*

We mention that it is decidable whether the fixed-point of a non-trivial morphism is an ultimately periodic word, see [140] and [84], or [163] for the complete characterization of the binary case. Thus, it is decidable whether the number in Theorem 6.10 is rational or transcendental.

6.7 Descriptive and computational complexity

In addition to subword complexity the classification of infinite words can be based on many other measures reflecting different aspects of complexity. Here we consider briefly two such directions, namely *descriptive* and *computational* complexities. The former one measures how complicated mechanisms are needed to generate infinite words. In general, this is not obvious to formalize, however, concrete examples can be given to illustrate it, see [54] for different such mechanisms. Computational complexity, in turn, asks how much computational resources are needed to generate a particular infinite word, say by a Turing machine, see e.g., [90]. The most frequently used method of defining an infinite word is, as we have already seen, that of iterating a morphism. More complicated methods are, for example, iterating two or more morphisms periodically, iterating a sequential transducer and so on. The famous *Kolakoski word* can be obtained by iterating two morphisms periodically, see Section 8 and [55], but it is not known whether it can be obtained as a morphic image of an infinite word obtained by iterating a morphism. By iterating sequential transducers one can define even much more complicated words as shown below.

Example 7. For a natural number n let $\text{bin}_r(n)$ denote the reverse binary representation of n. Then, clearly, a sequential transducer can compute

$$\text{bin}_r(n) \mapsto \text{bin}_r(n+1),$$

and consequently the infinite word

$$S\,\text{bin}_r(1)\#\text{bin}_r(2)\#\cdots\#\text{bin}_r(n)\cdots$$

can be generated by iterating a sequential transducer. □

Example 8. Let $\mathcal{M}$ be a Turing machine and

$$w_0,\ w_1,\ w_2,\ \ldots$$

the sequence of configurations of its computation on an input word w. Then, similarly to above, the word

$$Sw_0\#w_1\#w_2\cdots$$

can be generated by iterating a sequential transducer. Consequently, problems on such words are typically undecidable. □

Neither of the above words is, in general, definable by iterating a morphism. This follows, for example, the subword complexity considerations, cf. Theorem 6.7.

Infinite words definable by iterating a morphism are simple, not only descriptively, but also computationally. In order to formalize this we consider Turing machines as generators of infinite words: The machine has one one-way write only tape for the generation and several two-way working tapes for the computations. At the beginning all the tapes are empty, and the *space complexity* of the machine is the number of cells used in working tapes for printing the nth letter of the word. It follows from standard considerations in the complexity theory that the first complexity class after the trivial class $\mathcal{O}(1)$ is that of $\mathcal{O}(\log n)$, for details see [90]. The former one corresponds to ultimately periodic infinite words.

Now, we can state:

Theorem 6.11 *Each infinite word obtained by iterating a morphisms is of space complexity* $\mathcal{O}(\log n)$.

Of course, the class of $\mathcal{O}(\log n)$ is much larger than that of infinite words obtained by iterated morphisms. Indeed, the question whether or not all words obtained by iterating sequential transducers are in this class is equivalent to a classical open problem in complexity theory, see [67].

7 From Words to Finite Sets of Words

So far we have been interested in properties of single words, finite or infinite, and not sets of words. Even in the defect theorems, although those deal with finite sets of words, the crucial point is that those sets are considered as solutions of single (or several) word equations. Similarly, avoidable sets of words avoided a single word. A natural question is to ask whether at least some of the basic properties of words can be extended to finite sets of words. Among the most natural such question is the one asking what can be said about the commutation of (finite) sets of words. This and some related problems have been considered in several recent papers, cf. [96] for a survey.

7.1 Conway's Problem

More than 30 years ago Conway asked in his book [45] whether the maximal set commuting with a given rational set R is rational as well. Such a maximal set, which clearly exists – it is the union of all sets commuting with R – is called the *centralizer* of R, in symbols $\mathcal{C}(R)$. It is straightforward to see that the centralizer is a semigroup or a monoid depending on whether the considerations are in A^+ or A^*. Apart from some trivial observations the problems seems to be equally hard, but not known to be related, in these two cases. We concentrate on the semigroup case here.

Conway's Problem asks a very natural and simple looking question on rational languages. Surprisingly, however, the answer is not known even for finite languages, and in fact even a much simpler looking question, namely whether the centralizer of a finite X is recursive, or equivalently recursively enumerable, is unanswered. Here, the equivalence comes from the fact that the complement of the centralizer of even a recursive set, is recursively enumerable, as is rather easy to see. The following simple example from [42] reveals something of the complexity of the commutation of finite languages.

Example 9. Consider the four element set $X = \{a,\ ab,\ ba,\ bb\}$. As is straightforward to compute, it commutes with the sets

$$Y_1 = X \cup X^2 \cup \{bab,\ bbb\}$$

and

$$Y_2 = \{a,\ b\}^+\{b\},$$

the latter one being the centralizer of X (in A^+). Note that Y_2 is not only rational but also finitely generated, since $Y_2 = (X \cup \{bab,\ bbb\})^+$. □

Obviously, X^+ is always a subset of the centralizer, or more generally, any semigroup generated by a *root* of X, i.e. a set Y such that $X = Y^i$ for some $i \geq 1$, is a subset of the centralizer of X. Let us call a root of X *minimal* if it is not a proper root of any set, and denote it by $\rho_m(X)$. A minimal root of a set need not be unique, for example, even a unary set like $\{a^i \mid 0 \leq i \leq 30, i \neq 1, 8, 11, 23\}$ can possess two different (minimal) square roots, see [40]. If X possesses just one minimal root we call it the *primitive* root and denote it by $\rho(X)$. In the case of codes or nonperiodic two or three element sets the primitive root exist. We call a set *primitive* if $\rho(X) = X$.

We can state the following simple estimates for the centralizer: for any $X \subseteq A^+$, we have

$$\rho_m(X)^+ \subseteq \mathcal{C}(X) \subseteq \mathrm{Pref}(X^+) \cap \mathrm{Suf}(X^+),$$

where $\rho_m(X)$ is any minimal root of X. The left inclusion is obvious and the right one is easy to conclude. We say that $\mathcal{C}(X)$ is *trivial* if it coincides with $\rho_m(X)^+$ for some minimal root of X. Being trivial does not mean that the triviality is easy to check. Indeed, we do not know whether the question "Is $\mathcal{C}(X) = X^+$?" is decidable even for finite sets X.

An affirmative answer of Conway's Problem has been shown in a number of special cases, see e.g. [42], [103] and [143] for a general treatment. The first nontrivial result was that of [149] solving the problem for prefix sets. This together with a recent extension of the above special cases, see [KLP03], are summarized as follows:

Theorem 7.1 *(i) For each three element set X the centralizer of X is either w^+, for a primitive word w, or X^+ depending on whether X is periodic or not.*

(ii) For each prefix set X the centralizer of X is $\rho(X)^+$.

In particular, in both of these cases Conway's Problem has an affirmative answer.

458

It is a challenge to find a short proof for Part (ii) in Theorem 7.1. In what follows we give a short proof, see [102], for a special case of part (i) in Theorem 7.1, namely for the case when X is binary. This is based on so-called branching point approach. For $X \subset A^+$, we say that $w \in \text{Pref}(X^+)$ is a *branching* point if w can be extended in $\text{Pref}(X^+)$ at least by two different letters

Theorem 7.2 *Let $X = \{x, y\} \subseteq A^+$. Then the centralizer of X is either w^+, for a primitive word w, or X^+ depending on whether or not $xy = yx$.*

Proof. The case when x and y commute is a simple application of the defect theorem for two element sets.

So assume that $xy \neq yx$. Let z be the maximal common prefix of xy and yx, in symbols $z = xy \wedge yx$. Hence, as seen in Lemma 3.3, $|z| \leq |xy| - 2$. Further let us call a two element set *marked* if the first symbols of the words are different.

Claim I. For a marked Z we have $\mathcal{C}(Z) = Z^+$.

Claim I follows directly from the following three facts: First, the centralizer is a subset of $\text{Pref}(Z^+)$. Second the set Z has branching points only in Z^+. This, indeed, is true since Z is marked. Third, $\mathcal{C}(Z)$ is a semigroup, so that if $z' \in \mathcal{C}(Z) \subseteq \text{Pref}(Z^+)$ so do $z'x$ and $z'y$. Consequently, $\mathcal{C}(Z)$ can contain only branching points of Z.

Now, we are done if X is marked. If not, say $X \subseteq aA^*$ with $a \in A$, we set $X' = a^{-1}Xa$, and show

Claim II. $\mathcal{C}(X) = a\mathcal{C}(X')a^{-1}$.

In order to prove Claim II, we first write $\mathcal{C}(X) = aY$, with $y \subseteq A^*$. This is possible since $X\mathcal{C}(X) = \mathcal{C}(X)X$. Recalling that $aX' = Xa$ we can compute

$$XC(X)a = XaYa = aX'Ya$$

and

$$\mathcal{C}(X)Xa = aYXa = aYaX'.$$

Since the left hand sides are equal so are the right ones.This means that Ya commutes with X' and hence, by the maximality of the centralizer, we obtain that $Ya \subseteq \mathcal{C}(X')$. This, however, can be written in the form $\mathcal{C}(X) = aY \subseteq a\mathcal{C}(X')a^{-1}$.

Starting from the fact that $\mathcal{C}(X') = Y'a$ for some $Y' \subseteq A^+$, we conclude similarly that $aY' \subseteq \mathcal{C}(X)$ or, equivalently, that $\mathcal{C}(X') \subseteq a^{-1}\mathcal{C}(X)a$. This can be rewritten in the form $aC(X')a^{-1} \subseteq C(X)$. Hence, Claim II follows. Now, the existence of z and Claims I and II yield the theorem. $\qquad\square$

Above theorems deserve a few remarks. First, the equality of two sets in Claim II can not be done in a usual way showing that an element from the left is also on the right hand side, and vice versa. Instead sets of words has to be considered. Second, although in three element case the reduction of the proof of Theorem 7.2 does not lead to a marked instance, the branching point approach is a cornerstone in the proof of Part (i) in Theorem 7.1 as well. Third, as shown by Example 4, no similar result for the centralizer of a four element set is possible. Finally, the above results lead to a nice characterization of all sets commuting with a given set of the considered types, as seen in the next section.

7.2   Characterization of commuting sets

In order to formulate results of this section, we say that a set $X \subseteq A^+$ possesses *BTC-property* if the following implication holds:

$$\forall Y \subseteq A^+ : \text{ if } XY = YX, \text{ then there exist } I, J \subseteq \mathbf{N} \text{ and } V \subseteq A^+$$

such that

$$(1) \qquad\qquad X = \cup_{i \in I} V^i \text{ and } Y = \cup_{j \in J} V^j.$$

Note that in the case of nonperiodic two or three element sets the condition (1) reduces to

$$(2) \qquad\qquad\qquad Y = \cup_{i \in I} X^i.$$

The above property is similar to that characterizing commutation of polynomials and formal power series over noncommuting variables, cf. [11], [44] and Chapter 9 in [120].

The abbreviation BTC comes from there: Bergman type of characterization. We could also say that sets satisfying BTC are of *word type*.

We have:

Theorem 7.3 *Any two element set possesses BTC. Consequently, any set commuting with $X = \{x, y\}$, where $xy \neq yx$, is of the form $\cup_{i \in I} X^i$ for some $I \subseteq \mathbf{N}$.*

Proof. It is enough to show that, if $XY = YX$ and $w \in Y \cap X^n$, then $X^n \subseteq Y$. This, however, follows directly from the fact that X is a code: Indeed, assume that $y = x_1 \cdots x_n$, with $x_i \in X$. Then, for any $x_{x+1} \in X$, we can write

$$x_1 \cdots x_n x_{n+1} = x_1' w' \quad \text{with} \quad w' \in Y \subseteq \mathcal{C}(X) = X^+.$$

Consequently, $x_1 = x_1'$ and $w' = x_n \cdots x_{n+1} \in Y$. Repeating the argument we obtain that any word in X^n is in Y. $\qquad\square$

The similar reasoning can be used to obtain corresponding result for all three element sets. In the this case the considerations are, however, much more involved – due to the fact that such a set need not be a code.

Theorem 7.4 *(i) Any three element set possesses BTC. In particular, any set commuting with a nonperiodic three element set is a union of powers of X.*

(ii) Any prefix set possesses BTC. Consequently, any set commuting with a prefix set X is a union of powers of the primitive root of X.

We recall that Part (i) is optimal in the sense that the BTC property does not hold for four element sets – as shown again by Example 9.

As a summary of the above we can say that the commutation of languages is well understood in above special – but still very interesting – cases. Common to all of those is that the centralizer is always trivial, although to show that is not always easy. In general, tools to attack Conway's Problem seems to be completely lacking. Results of the next section might explain, at least intuitively, why the problem looks so difficult. In Section 8 several open problems on commutation are formulated.

7.3 Undecidability results for finite sets

In this section we show that some simple questions on finite sets of words are actually undecidable.

In [80] it was proved, based on Theorem 7.3:

Theorem 7.5 *It is undecidable whether a given two element set and a given context-free language commute.*

In order to formulate another undecidability result on finite sets of words we need some terminology. We call a morphism from A^* into the monoid of finite languages a *finite substitution*. Following [56] we say that two mappings f, g defined on A^* *are equivalent* on language $L \subseteq A^*$ if they map all the words of L into the same element. In the case of finite substitutions the requirement is that, for any $w \in L$, the finite languages $f(w)$ and $h(w)$ coincide. In [99] the following undecidability result was proved.

Theorem 7.6 *It is undecidable whether two given finite substitutions f and* *g are equivalent on the language ab*c, i.e., whether or not*

$$f(ab^i c) = g(ab^i c) \quad \text{for all} \quad i \geq 0.$$

Despite of being an interesting, and maybe also surprising, undecidability result as such Theorem 7.6 has also a few nice consequences. We formulate here just one of those, for the other see [99].

We say that two finite sets X and Y of words are *conjugates* if there exists a set Z such that

$$XZ = ZY.$$

Actually, the above splits into two notions, since the set Z might be required to be finite or allowed to be arbitrary. Problems on conjugacy was considered in [34]. However, the following natural question was not answered: is it decidable whether two given finite sets are conjugates? Even the case where X and Y are biprefix sets seems not to be trivial, although decidable, cf. [33]. Note that the above question can be viewed as a very special question on equations over the monoid of (finite) languages: the equation contains only one unknown and two constants. The equation

$$\{a, \ ab, \ abb, \ ba, \ babb\}Z = Z\{a, \ ba, \ bba, \ bbba\}$$

is an instance of such an equation. It happens to have a solution $Z = \{a, \ ab\}$.

The above motivates to propose a general problem. Is it decidable whether a given equation with constants has a solution in the monoid of finite languages?

Very little seem to be known about this important problem. One thing separating the finite set case from the word case is a consequence of our Theorem 7.6. In order to formulate it we need some terminology. We consider infinite systems of equations with a finite number of unknowns Ξ and constants C. We say that a system $\{u_i = v_i | i \in \mathbf{N}\}$ is *rational* if the set $\{(u_i, \ v_i) | i \in \mathbf{N}\}$ is a rational subset of $(\Xi \cup C)^2$. In other words there is a finite transducer mapping each left hand side of the equations to the corresponding right hand side. Now, the corollary is:

Theorem 7.7 *It is undecidable whether a given rational system of equations over the monoid of finite sets of words has a solution.*

Interestingly, the satisfiability problem for rational systems of word equations is decidable. Indeed, such a system is computably equivalent to one of its finite subsystems, and each finite system of equations can be encoded into a single equation. The first reduction here is an effective variant of Ehrenfeucht Compactness Property, that is Theorem 4.5, cf. [82], and the second reduction is easy, see e.g., [89]. So the satisfiability problem for rational word equations is reduced to that of a single equation, i.e. to the seminal result of Makanin.

8 Open Problems

In this final section we formulate several open problems, many of those being already discussed in previous sections. We start with two decidability questions of matrices.

Problem 1. Given a finite set of $n \times n$ matrices over integers with $n \geq 3$, is it decidable whether or not the identity matrice is obtainable as a product of these matrices?

Problem 2. Given a finite set of 2×2 matrices over natural numbers is it decidable whether the multiplicative semigroup generated by these matrices is free?

Of course, the decidability of Problem 1 may depend on the parameter n, for $n = 2$ the problem is decidable, see [41]. As an evidence of an intriguing nature of Problem 2 we recall from [32] that we do not even know whether the concrete matrices

$$A = \begin{pmatrix} 2 & 0 \\ 0 & 3 \end{pmatrix} \quad B = \begin{pmatrix} 3 & 5 \\ 0 & 5 \end{pmatrix}$$

generate a free semigroup. Accordingly the problem is open even in the case $n = 2$.

As a consequence of the critical factorization theorem we know that two-way infinite noncyclic word w cannot have $n+1$ pairwise disjoint factorizations of a set X of n words. On the other hand, Theorem 4.3 shows that if such a word w has two disjoint X-factorizations then the combinatorial rank of X is at most $\mathrm{card}(X) - 1$. This motivates the following:

Problem 3. Let X be a finite set of words, and w a two-way noncyclic infinite word. What is the relation between the number of pairwise disjoint X-factorizations of w, in symbols $df(X)$, and the combinatorial rank of X, in symbols $r_c(X)$? More concretely, is it true that $r_c(X) \leq \mathrm{card}(X) - df(X) + 1$?

A result in [100] proves the inequality of Problem 3 in a special case when X is a prefix set and $df(X) = 3$.

Two other open problems on dimension properties concern independent systems of equations.

Problem 4. Does there exist an independent system of three constant-free equations with three unknowns possessing a noncyclic solution?

Problem 5. (i) Does there exist a function $f : \mathbf{N} \to \mathbf{N}$ such that any independent system of constant-free equations with n unknowns contains at most $f(n)$ equations?
(ii) Does the requirement of part (i) hold for the function $f(n) = 2^n$?

As shown in [104] the Ehrenfeucht Compactness Property might hold in some monoids, like in Abelian monoids, without giving any bound asked in Problem 5. We recall that some lower bounds for the function $f(n)$ are also given in [104]

Next we formulate a few problems on the avoidability (for additional questions and comments, see [57], the recent survey of J. Currie [58], and the paper [156]).

Problem 6. Is it decidable whether a given morphism $h : A^* \to B^*$ is k-free for a fixed integer $k \geq 3$?

We recall that repetition threshold on an n letter alphabet is the smallest number $s(n)$ such that infinite words on n letters can contain only repetitions of order less than or equal to $s(n)$.

Problem 7. Is the repetition threshold for $n \geq 12$ equal to $n/(n-1)$?

Another crucial questions on avoidable patterns are:

Problem 8. Does there exist a pattern which is avoidable in a five-letter alphabet but unavoidable in a four-letter alphabet?

Problem 9. Is the size of the smallest alphabet where a give pattern is avoidable, i.e., its avoidability index, algorithmically computable?

In order to formulate our next problem we say that u is a *sparse subword* of a word w if it is obtained from w by deleting some occurrences of letters, i.e., there exist words $u_1, \ldots, u_t$ and $v_0, \ldots, v_t$ such that $u = u_1 \cdots u_t$ and $w = v_0 u_1 v_1 \cdots u_t v_t$. Then, for $k > 0$, k *spectrum* of a word w is the set of all sparse subwords of w with multiplicities and of length at most k. Hence, the k spectrum is a formal polynomial of degree k. For example, the 2 spectrum of the word $aabba$ is $3a+2b+3aa+4ab+2ba+bb$. In algebra these polynomials are often defined as results of Magnus Transform of a word. Now we formulate, for more see [125]:

Problem 10. What is the minimal $k = k(n)$ such that the k spectrum of a word w of length n determines w uniquely?

Superpolynomial lower bound for $k(n)$ was recently shown in [66].

One of the amazing sequences of words is that of *Kolakoski word k*. It can be defined as a self-reading sequence by the following rule: it consists of blocks of 1s and 2s each block being of length either 1 or 2, and the length of the ith block is equal to the ith element of the word. Consequently, the word k starts as

$$k = 2211212212211\ldots\, .$$

Descriptionally the Kolakoski word is quite easy: it can be defined by iterating a sequential transducer, or even by iterating periodically two morphisms, namely

$$h_1 : \begin{cases} 1 \mapsto 2, \\ 2 \mapsto 22 \end{cases} \quad \text{and} \quad h_2 : \begin{cases} 1 \mapsto 1, \\ 2 \mapsto 11 \end{cases} .$$

There is a larger literature on the Kolakoski sequence, e.g., [61], [21], [23], [20], [43] and [115].

However, very little is known about the Kolakoski word. For example, it is not known whether the numbers of 1s and 2s are asymptotically equal. Connected to this tutorial we can state:

Problem 11. Is the subword complexity of Kolakoski word at most quadratic?

Problem 12. Is Kolakoski word obtainable as a morphic image of a fixed-point of an iterated morphism?

Clearly, a negative answer to Problem 11 would give that for Problem 12, due to Theorem 6.7. It is also relatively easy to show that k is not obtainable as a fixed-point of an iterated morphism, see e.g. [55].

We conclude with open problems on finite (and rational) sets of words, in particular, on commutation of those. We formulate several variants of Conway's Problem:

Problem 13. Is the centralizer of a given rational set a) rational, b) recursive?

Problem 14. Is the centralizer of a given finite set a) finitely generated, b) rational, c) recursive?

As other problems on finite sets of words we state

Problem 15. Is it decidable whether two finite sets X and $Y \subseteq A^+$ are conjugates, i.e., there exists a set Z such that $XZ = ZY$?

Problem 16. Is it decidable whether a given equation with constants has a solution in the monoid of finite languages?

Note that Problem 15 contains actually two variants depending on whether Z is allowed to be arbitrary or finite. In Problem 16 the constants are, of course, elements of the monoid, i.e. finite languages.

Acknowledgments

Many thanks to J.-P. Allouche, J. Cassaigne, A. Lepistö, G. Richomme, P. Séébold and J. Shallit for their careful reading of parts of a preliminary version of the paper. In addition the authors are grateful to A. Lepistö for his help to complete the presentation. We are also grateful to D.E. Knuth for his advices and bibliographic comments.

The work of the second author was done while visiting Institut Gaspard-Monge Université de Marne-la-Vallée, and was supported by the Academy of Finland under the grant 44087.

References

1. S.I. Adian, *The Burnside Problem and Identities in Groups*, Springer-Verlag, 1979.
2. M.H. Albert and J. Lawrence, A proof of Ehrenfeucht's conjecture, *Theoret. Comput. Sci.* 41, 121–123, 1985.
3. C. Allauzen, Une caractérisation simple des nombres de Sturm, *J. Théo. Nombres Bordeaux* 10, 237–241, 1998.
4. J.-P. Allouche, Nouveaux résultats de transcendance de réels à développement non aléatoire, *Gazette des Mathématiciens* 84, 19–34,

2000.

5. J.-P. Allouche and J. Shallit, *Automatic Sequences: Theory, Applications, Generalizations*, Cambridge University Press, 2003.

6. J.-P. Allouche and L.Q. Zamboni, Algebraic irrational binary numbers cannot be fixed points of non-trivial constant length or primitive morphisms, *J. Number Theory* 69, 119–124, 1998.

7. P. Arnoux and G. Rauzy, Représentation géométrique de suites de complexité $2n + 1$, *Bull. Soc. Math. France* 119, 199–215, 1991.

8. S.E. Aršon, Proof of the existence on n-valued infinite asymmetric sequences, *Mat. Sb.* 2(44), 769–779, 1937.

9. K. A. Baker, G. F. McNulty, and W. Taylor, Growth problems for avoidable words, *Theoret. Comput. Sci.* 69, 319–345, 1989.

10. D. R. Bean, A. Ehrenfeucht, and G. F. McNulty, Avoidable patterns in strings of symbols, *Pacific J. Math.* 85, 261–294, 1979.

11. G. Bergman, Centralizers in free associative algebras, *Transactions of the American Mathematical Society* 137, 327–344, 1969.

12. J. Bernoulli III, *Sur une novelle expèce de calcul, Recueil poue les astronomes*, vols. 1,2, Berlin, 1772.

13. J. Berstel, Axel Thue's papers on repetition in words: a translation, *Publications de Laboratoire de Combinatoire et d'Informatique Mathématique*, Université du Québec á Montréal 20, 1995.

14. J. Berstel and L. Boasson, Partial words and a theorem of Fine and Wilf, WORDS (Rouen, 1997), *Theoret. Comput. Sci.* 218, 135–141, 1999.

15. J. Berstel and D. Perrin, *Theory of Codes*, Academic Press, 1985.

16. J. Berstel, D. Perrin, J.-F. Perrot, and A. Restivo, Sur le théorème du défaut, *J. Algebra* 60, 169–180, 1979.

17. J. Berstel and P. Séébold, A characterization of overlap-free morphisms, *Discr. Appl. Math.* 46, 275–281, 1993.

18. A. Bertoni, D. Bruschi, and M. Goldwurm, Ranking and formal power series, In: *Algorithms and complexity (Rome, 1990)*, 159–171, World Sci. Publishing, Teaneck, NJ, 1990.

19. F.-J. Brandenburg, Uniformly growing k-th power-free homomorphisms, *Theoret. Comput. Sci.* 23, 69–82, 1983.

20. S. Brlek and A. Ladouceur, A note on differentiable palindromes, *Theoret. Comput. Sci.* (to appear).

21. A. Carpi, Repetitions in the Kolakovski sequence, *Bull. EATCS* 50, 194–196, 1993.

22. A. Carpi, Overlap-free words and finite automata, *Theoret. Comput. Sci.* 115, 243–260, 1993.

23. A. Carpi, On repeated factors in C^∞-words, *Inform. Process. Lett.*

52(6), 289–294, 1994.

24. A. Carpi, On the number of Abelian square-free words on four letters, *Discr. Appl. Math.* 81, 155–167, 1998.

25. A. Carpi and A. de Luca, Periodic-like words, periodicity, and boxes, *Acta Inform.* 37, 597–618, 2001.

26. A. Carpi and A. de Luca, Words and special factors, *Theoret. Comput. Sci.* 259, 145–182, 2001.

27. A. Carpi and A. de Luca, On the distribution of characteristic parameters of words, *Theoret. Inform. Appl.* 36, 67–96, 2002.

28. A. Carpi and A. de Luca, On the distribution of characteristic parameters of words II, *Theoret. Inform. Appl.* 36, 97–127, 2002.

29. J. Cassaigne, Counting overlap-free binary words, In: P. Enjalbert, A. Finkel, and K.W. Wagner (Eds.), *Proc. of STACS, LNCS* 665, 216–225, Springer-Verlag, 1993.

30. J. Cassaigne, On a conjecture of J. Shallit, In: P. Degano, R. Gorrieri, and A. Marchetti-Spaccamela (Eds.), *Automata, Languages and Programming, LNCS* 1256, 693–704, Springer-Verlag, 1997.

31. J. Cassaigne, Complexité et facteurs spéciaux, *Bull. Belg. Math. Soc.* 4, 76–88, 1997.

32. J. Cassaigne, T. Harju, and J. Karhumäki, On the undecidability of freeness of matrix semigroups, *Intern. J. Alg. & Comp.* 9, 295–305, 1999.

33. J. Cassaigne and J. Karhumäki, manuscript in preparation, 2003.

34. J. Cassaigne, J. Karhumäki, and J. Manuch, On conjugacy of languages, *Theor. Inform. Appl.* 35, 535–550, 2001.

35. M.G. Castelli, F. Mignosi, and A. Restivo, Fine and Wilf's theorem for three periods and a generalization of Sturmian words, *Theoret. Comput. Sci.* 218, 83–94, 1999.

36. S. Cautis, F. Mignosi, J. Shallit, M.-W. Wang, and S. Yasdani, Periodicity, morphisms, and matrices, *Theoret. Comput. Sci.* 295, 107–121, 2003.

37. Y. Césari and M. Vincent, Une caractérisation des mots périodiques, *C. R. Acad. Sci. Paris (Série A)* 286, 1175–1177, 1978.

38. J.-M. Champarnaud, G. Hansel, and D. Perrin, Unavoidable sets of constant length, *Inter. J. Algebra Comput.* (to appear).

39. C. Choffrut and J. Karhumäki, Combinatorics of words, In: A. Salomaa and G. Rozenberg (eds.), *Handbook of Formal Languages, Vol. 1*, 329–438. Springer-Verlag, 1997.

40. C. Choffrut and J. Karhumäki, On Fatou properties of rational languages, In: C. Martin-Vide and V. Mitrana (eds.), *Where Mathematics, Computer Science, Linguistics and Biology Meet*, Kluwer, Dordrecht 2000.

41. C. Choffrut and J. Karhumäki, Some decision problems on integer matrices, manuscript 2002.

42. C. Choffrut, J. Karhumäki, and N. Ollinger, The commutation of finite sets: a challenging problem, *Theoret. Comput. Sci.* 273, 69–79, 2002.

43. Vašek Chvátal, Notes on the Kolakoski sequence, *DIMACS technical report* 93-84, 1993.

44. P.M. Cohn, Centralisateurs dans les corps libres, In: J. Berstel (ed.), *Series Formelles*, Paris, 45–54, 1978.

45. J.H. Conway, *Regular Algebra and Finite Machines*, Chapman Hall, 1971.

46. E.M. Coven and G.A. Hedlund, Sequences with minimal block growth, *Math. Systems Theory* 7, 138–153, 1973.

47. D. Crisp, W. Moran, A. Pollington, and P. Shiue, Substitution invariant cutting sequences, *J. Théor. Nombres Bordeaux* 5, 123–137, 1993.

48. M. Crochemore, Sharp characterizations of square-free morphisms, *Theoret. Comput. Sci.* 18, 221–226, 1982.

49. M. Crochemore, C. Hancart, and T. Lecroq, *Algorithmique du texte*, Vuibert, 2001.

50. M. Crochemore and D. Perrin, Two-way string matching, *J. Assoc. Comput. Mach.* 38(3), 651–675, 1991.

51. M. Crochemore and W. Rytter, *Text algorithms*, Oxford University Press, 1994.

52. M. Crochemore and W. Rytter, *Jewels in Stringology*, World Scientific, 2002.

53. K. Culik II and I. Fris, The decidability of the equivalence problem for D0L-systems, *Information and Control* 35, 20–39, 1977.

54. K. Culik II and J. Karhumäki, Iterative devices generating infinite words, *Int. J. Found. Comput. Sci.* 5, 69–97, 1994.

55. K. Culik II, J. Karhumäki, and A. Lepistö, Alternating iteration of morphisms and Kolakovski sequence, In: G. Rozenberg and A. Salomaa (eds.), *Lindermayer Systems, Impacts on Theoretical Computer Science, Computer Graphics and Developmental Biology*, 93–106, Springer-Verlag, 1992.

56. K. Culik II and A. Salomaa, On the decidability of homomorphism equivalence for languages, *J. Comput. Syst. Sci.* 17, 163–175, 1978.

57. J.D. Currie, Open problems in pattern avoidance, *Amer. Math. Monthly* 100, 790–793, 1993.

58. J.D. Currie, Pattern avoidance: themes and variations, In: T. Harju and J. Karhumäki (eds.), *Proceedings of WORDS'03*, TUCS General Publication 27, 14–26, 2003.

59. F. Dejean, Sur un théorème de Thue, *J. Combin. Th. A* 13, 90–99, 1972.

60. F.M. Dekking, Strongly non-repetitive sequences and progression-free set, *J. Combin. Th. A* 27, 181–185, 1979.

61. F.M. Dekking, What is the long range order in the Kolakoski sequence?, In: R. V. Moody and J. Patera (eds.), *The Mathematics of Long-Range Aperiodic Order (Waterloo, ON, 1995)*, NATO Adv. Sci. Inst. Ser. C Math. Phys. Sci. 489, 115–125, Kluwer Acad. Publ., Dordrecht, 1997.

62. A. de Luca, On the combinatorics of finite words, *Theoret. Comput. Sci.* 218, 13–39, 1999.

63. A. de Luca and S. Varricchio, Regularity and finiteness conditions, In: G. Rozenberg and A. Salomaa (eds.), *Handbook of Formal Languages I*, Springer-Verlag, 737–810, 1997.

64. A. de Luca and S. Varricchio, *Finiteness and Regularity in Semigroups and Formal Languages*, Springer-Verlag, 1999.

65. X. Droubay, J. Justin, and G. Pirillo, Episturmian words and some constructions of de Luca and Rauzy, *Theoret. Comput. Sci.* 255, 539–553, 2001.

66. M. Dudik and L.J. Schulman, Reconstruction from subsequences, *J. Combin. Th. A* **103**, 337–348, 2002.

67. P. Ďuriš and J. Manuch, On the computational complexity of infinite words, *Theoret. Comput. Sci.* (to appear).

68. J.-P. Duval, Périodes et répétitions des mots du monoïde libre, *Theoret. Comput. Sci.* 9(1), 17–26, 1979.

69. A. Ehrenfeucht, K.P. Lee, and G. Rozenberg, Subword complexities of various classes of deterministic developmental languages without interaction, *Theoret. Comput. Sci.* 1, 59–75, 1975.

70. A. A. Evdokimov, Strongly asymmetric sequences generated by a finite number of symbols, *Dokl. Akad. Nauk. SSSR* 179, 1268–1271, 1968 (English transl. *Soviet. Math. Dokl.* 9, 536–539, 1968).

71. S. Ferenczi and C. Mauduit, Transcendence of numbers with a low complexity expansion, *J. Number Theory* 67, 146–161, 1997.

72. N.J. Fine and H.S. Wilf, Uniqueness theorem for periodic functions, *Proc. Amer. Math. Soc.* 16, 109–114, 1965.

73. P. Flajolet, P. Zimmerman, and B. Van Cutsem, A calculus for the random generation of labelled combinatorial structures, *Theoret. Comput. Sci.* 132, 1–35, 1994.

74. C.F. Gauss, *Werke*, Teubner, Leibzig, 1900 (pp. 272 and 282–286).

75. R.L. Graham, B.L. Rothschild, and J.H. Spencer, *Ramsay Theory*, Second Edition, John Wiley & Sons, 1990.

76. V.S. Guba, The equivalence of infinite systems of equations in free groups and semigroups to their finite subsystems, *Math. Zametki* 40, 321–324,

1986.

77. J.L. Guibas and A. Odlyzko, Periods in strings, *J. Combin. Th. A* 30, 19–42, 1981.

78. D. Gusfield, *Algorithms on Strings, Trees and Sequences*, Cambridge University Press, 1997.

79. M. Hall, Generators and relations in groups – the Burnside problem, In: T.L. Saaty (ed.), *Lectures on Modern Mathematics*, vol. 2, 42–92. Wiley, 1964.

80. T. Harju, O. Ibarra, J. Karhumäki, and A. Salomaa, Some decision problems concerning semilinearity and commutation, *J. Comput. Syst. Sci.* 65, 278–294, 2002.

81. T. Harju and J. Karhumäki, On the defect theorem and simplifiability, *Semigroups Forum* 33, 199–217, 1986.

82. T. Harju and J. Karhumäki, Morphisms, In: G. Rozenberg and A. Salomaa (eds.), *Handbook of Formal Languages*, 439–510, Springer-Verlag, 1997.

83. T. Harju, J. Karhumäki, and W. Plandowski, Compactness of systems of equations in semigroups, *Intern. J. Alg. & Comp.*, 457–470, 1997.

84. T. Harju and M. Linna, On the periodicity of morphisms in free monoids, *Theoret. Inform. Appl.* 20, 47–54, 1986.

85. T. Harju and D. Nowotka, Density of critical factorizations, *Theoret. Inform. Appl.*, 2002.

86. C.E. Heitsch, Exact distribution of deletion sizes for unavoidable strings, *Fundamenta Informaticae*, 2002.

87. C.E. Heitsch, Insufficiency of the four known necessary conditions on string avoidability, *J. Algorithms*, 2002.

88. C.E. Heitsch, Intractability of the reductive decision procedure for unavoidability testing, a special case of generalized pattern matching, *J. Algorithms*, 2002.

89. Y.I. Hmelevskii, Equations in free semigroups, *Proc. Stoklov Inst. Math.* 107, 1971 (English transl. *Amer. Math. Soc. Translations*, 1976).

90. J. Hromkovič, J. Karhumäki, and A. Lepistö, Comparing descriptional and computational complexity of infinite words, In: J. Karhumäki, H. Maurer, and G. Rozenberg (Eds.), *Results and Trends in Theoretical Computer Science, LNCS* 812, 169–182, Springer-Verlag, 1994.

91. J. Justin, Characterization of the repetitive commutative semigroups, *J. Algebra* 21, 87–90, 1972.

92. J. Justin, On a paper by Castelli, Mignosi, Restivo, *Theoret. Inform. Appl.* 34, 373–377, 2000.

93. J. Justin and G. Pirillo, Episturmian words and episturmian morphisms,

Theoret. Comput. Sci. 276, 281–313, 2002.

94. J. Karhumäki, On cube-free ω-words generated by binary morphisms, *Discr. Appl. Math.* 5, 279–297, 1983.

95. J. Karhumäki, The impact of the D0L problem, In: G. Rozenberg and A. Salomaa (eds.), *Current Trends in Theoretical Computer Science, Essays and Tutorials*, 586–594, World Scientific, 1993.

96. J. Karhumäki, Combinatorial and computational problems on finite sets of words, In: M. Margenstern and Y. Rogozhin (Eds.), *Machines, Computations, and Universality, LNCS* 2055, 69–81, Springer-Verlag, 2001.

97. J. Karhumäki, A. Latteux, and I. Petre, The commutation with codes and ternary sets of words, Proceedings of STACS'03, *LNCS* (to appear).

98. J. Karhumäki, A. Lepistö, and W. Plandowski, Locally periodic infinite words and a chaotic behaviour, *J. Comb. Theor., Ser. A* 100, 250–264, 2002.

99. J. Karhumäki and L. P. Lisovik, The equivalence problem of finite substitutions an ab^*c, with applications, In: P. Widmayer, F. Triguero, R. Morales, M. Hennessy, S. Eidenbenz, and R. Conejo (Eds.), *Automata, Languages and Programming, LNCS* 2380, 812–820, Springer-Verlag, 2002.

100. J. Karhumäki and J. Manuch, Multiple factorizations of words and defect effect, *Theoret. Comput. Sci.* 273, 81–97, 2002.

101. J. Karhumäki, J. Manuch, and W. Plandowski, A defect theorem for two-way infinite words, *Theoret. Comput. Sci.* (to appear).

102. J. Karhumäki and I. Petre, Conway's problem and the commutation of languages, *Bull. of EACTS* 74, 171–177, 2001.

103. J. Karhumäki and I. Petre, Conway's problem for three word sets, *Theoret. Comput. Sci.* 289, 705–725, 2002.

104. J. Karhumäki and W. Plandowski, On the size of independent systems of equations in semigroups, *Theoret. Comput. Sci.* 168, 105–119, 1996.

105. J. Karhumäki and J. Shallit, Polynomial versus exponential growth in repetition-free binary words, manuscript, 12pp, 2003.

106. L. Kari, S. Marcus, Gh. Păun, and A. Salomaa, In the prehistory of formal language theory: Gauss languages, *Bull. EATCS* 46, 124–139, 1992.

107. V. Keränen, Abelian squares are avoidable on 4 letters, In: W. Kuich (ed.), *Automata, Languages and Programming, LNCS* 623, 41–52, Springer-Verlag, 1992.

108. D.E. Knuth, Sequences with precisely $k + 1$ k-blocs, *Amer. Math. Monthly* **72**, 773–774 (Solution to problem E2307), 1972.

109. D.E. Knuth, *The Art of Computer Programming, Vol. I: Fundamental*

472

Algorithms, Addison-Wesley, Third Edition, 1997.

110. Y. Kobayashi, Enumeration of irreducible binary words, *Discr. Appl. Math.* 20, 221–232, 1988.

111. M. Leconte, A characterization of power-free morphisms, *Theor. Comput. Sci.* 38, 117–122, 1985.

112. M. Leconte, *Codes sans répétitions*, Thèse 3ième cycle, Univ. Paris VII, Technical Report LITP 85-56, 1985.

113. A. Lentin, *Equations dans les monoïdes libres*, Gouthiers-Villars, Paris, 1972.

114. A. Lentin and M.P. Schützenberger, A combinatorial problem in the theory of free monoids, In: R.C. Bose and T.E. Dowling (eds.), *Combinatorial Mathematics*, North Carolina Press, 112–144, 1967.

115. A. Lepistö, Repetitions in Kolakoski sequence, In: G. Rozenberg and A. Salomaa (eds.), *Developments in Language Theory*, Proceedings of DLT'93, World Scientific, 130–143, 1994.

116. A. Lepistö, *A Characterization of 2^+-free Words over a Binary Alphabet*, Master's Thesis, TUCS Technical Report **74**, University of Turku, 1996.

117. A. Lepistö, On Relations between Local and Global Periodicity, Ph.D. Thesis, University of Turku, *TUCS Dissertations* 43, 2002.

118. F. Levé and P. Séébold, Proof of a conjecture on word complexity, *Bull. Belg. Math. Soc.* 8, 277–291, 2001.

119. M. Lothaire, *Combinatorics on Words*, Encyclopedia of Mathematics 17, Addison-Wesley, 1983. Reprinted in the *Cambridge Mathematical Library*, Cambridge University Press, 1997.

120. M. Lothaire, *Algebraic Combinatorics on Words*. Encyclopedia of Mathematics 90, Cambridge University Press, 2002.

121. R.C. Lyndon and P.E. Schupp, *Combinatorial Group Theory*, Springer-Verlag, 1977.

122. R.C. Lyndon and M.P. Schützenberger, The equation $a^m = b^n c^p$ in a free group, *Michigan Math J.* 9, 289–298, 1962.

123. W. Magnus, A. Karrass and D. Solitar, *Combinatorial Group Theory*, Wiley, 1966.

124. G.S. Makanin, The problem of solvability of equations in a free semigroup, *Mat. Sb.* 103, 147–236, 1977 (English transl. in *Math. USSR Sb.* 32, 129–198).

125. J. Manuch, Characterization of a word by its subwords, *Proc. of DLT*, 210–219, World Scientific, 2000.

126. J. Manuch, *Defect Theorems and Infinite Words*, Ph.D. Thesis, University of Turku, *TUCS Dissertations* 41, 2002.

127. A.A. Markov, Sur une question de Jean Bernoulli, *Math. Ann.* **19**, 27–36,

1882.

128. F. Mignosi and G. Pirillo, Repetitions in the Fibonacci infinite word, *RAIRO Theor. Inform. Appl.* 26, 199–204, 1999.

129. F. Mignosi, A. Restivo, and S. Salemi, A periodicity theorem on words and applications, In: J. Wiedermann and P. Hajek (Eds.), *Mathematical Foundations of Computer Science 1995, LNCS* 969, 337–348, Springer-Verlag, 1995.

130. F. Mignosi, A. Restivo, and S. Salemi, Periodicity and golden ratio, *Theoret. Comput. Sci.* 204, 153–167, 1998.

131. F. Mignosi, A. Restivo, and P.V. Silva, On Fine and Wilf's theorem for bidimensional words, *Theoret. Comput. Sci.* 292, 245–262, 2003.

132. M. Morse, Reccurent geodesics on a surface of negative curvature, *Trans. Am. Math. Soc.* 22, 84–100, 1921.

133. M. Morse, A solution of the problem of infinite play in chess, *Bull. Amer. Math. Soc.* 44, 632, 1938.

134. M. Morse and G. Hedlund, Symbolic dynamics, *Amer. J. Math.* 60, 815–866, 1938.

135. M. Morse and G.A. Hedlund, Symbolic dynamics II: Sturmian trajectories. *Amer. J. Math.* 62, 1–42, 1940.

136. M. Morse and G. Hedlund, Unending chess, symbolic dynamics and a problem in semigroups, *Duke Math. J.* 11, 1–7, 1944.

137. J. Moulin-Ollagnier, Proof of Dejean's conjecture for alphabets with 5, 6, 7, 8, 9, 10 and 11 letters, *Theoret. Comput. Sci.* 95, 187–205, 1992.

138. J.-J. Pansiot, Complexité des facteurs des mots infinis engendrés par morphismes intérés, In: J. Paredaens (ed.), *Automata, Languages and Programming, LNCS* 172, 380–389, Springer-Verlag, 1984.

139. J.-J. Pansiot, A propos d'une conjecture de F. Dejean sur les répétitions dans les mots, *Discr. Appl. Math.* 7, 297–311, 1984.

140. J.-J. Pansiot, Decidability of periodicity for infinite words, *Theoret. Inform. Appl.* 20, 43–46, 1986.

141. M.S. Paterson, Unsolvability in 3 × 3-matrices, *Studies in Appl. Math.* 49, 105–107, 1970.

142. D. Perrin and G. Rindone, On renewal systems, Technical report, Institut Gaspard Monge, Université de Marne-la-Vallée, 2002.

143. I. Petre, *Commutation Problems on Set of Words and Formal Power Series*, Ph.D. Thesis, University of Turku, *TUCS Dissertations* 38, 2002.

144. W. Plandowski, Satisfiability of word equations is in PSPACE, Proc. of FOCS, 495–500, 1999.

145. P.A.B. Pleasants, Non-repetitive sequences, *Math. Proc. Cambridge Philos. Soc.* 68, 267–274, 1970.

146. E. Prouhet, Mémoire sur quelques relations entre les preissances des nombres, *C. R. Acad. Sci. Paris* 33, Cahier 31, 225, 1851.
147. N. Pytheas-Fogg, *Substitutions in Dynamics, Arithmetics and Combinatorics, Lecture Notes in Mathematics* 1794, Springer-Verlag, 2002.
148. N. Rampersad, Words avoiding 7/3-powers and the Thue-Morse morphism, manuscript, July 2003, available at http://www.arxiv.org/abs/math.CO/0307401
149. B. Ratoandramanana, Codes et motifs, *RAIRO Theor. Inform. Appl.* 23, 425–444, 1989.
150. A. Restivo and C. Reutenauer, Rational languages and the Burnside problem, *Theoret. Comput. Sci.* 40, 13–30, 1985.
151. A. Restivo and S. Salemi, Overlap-free words on two symbols, In: M. Nivat and D. Perrin (eds.), *Automata on Infinite Words, LNCS* 192, 198–206, 1984.
152. C. Reutenauer, *Free Lie Algebras*, London Mathematical Monographs New Series No. 7, Claredon Press, 1993.
153. G. Richomme, Lyndon morphisms, Technical report LaRia 2002-15, Laboratoire de Recherche en Informatique d'Amiens (Laria), Université d'Amiens, 2002.
154. G. Richomme, Some non finitely generated monoids of repetition-free endomorphisms, *Inform. Proc. Letters*, 2002.
155. G. Richomme and P. Séébold, Characterization of test-sets for overlap-free morphisms, *Discr. Appl. Math.*, 98:151–157, 1999.
156. G. Richomme and P. Séébold, Some conjectures about morphisms generation k-power-free words, *Technical Report, Laria*, Amiens 2003, also to appear in a special issue of IJFCS.
157. G. Richomme and F. Wlazinski, About cube-free morphisms, In: H. Reichel and S. Tison (eds.), *STACS '2000, LNCS* 1770, 99–109. Springer-Verlag, 2000.
158. G. Richomme and F. Wlazinski, Finite test-sets for overlap-free morphisms, In: K. Diks and W. Rytter (eds.), *Mathematical Foundations of Computer Science 2002, LNCS* 2420, 605–614. Springer-Verlag, 2002.
159. G. Richomme and F. Wlazinski, Some results on k-power-free morphisms, *Theoret. Comput. Sci.* 273, 119–142, 2002.
160. F. Ruskey, Generating t-ary trees lexicographically, *SIAM J. Comput.* 7, 424–439, 1978.
161. M.P. Schützenberger, Une théorie algébrique du codage, *Seminaire Dubreil-Pisot 1955–1956 Expose 15*, Institut H. Poincare, Paris, 1956.
162. M.P. Schützenberger, A property of finitely generated submonoids of free monoids, In: G. Pollak (ed.), *Algebraic Theory of Semigroups*, Proc.

Sixth Algebraic Conf., Szeged, 1976, 545–576. North-Holland, 1979.

163. P. Séébold, An effective solution to the $D0L$-periodicity problem in the binary case, *Bull. EACTS* 36, 137–151, 1988.

164. K.B. Stolarsky, Beatty sequences, continued fractions and certain shift operators, *Canad. Math. Bull.* 19(4), 473–482, 1976.

165. A. Thue, Über unendliche Zeichenreihen, *Norske Vid. Selsk. Skr. I. Mat. Nat. Kl., Christiana* 7, 1–22, 1906.

166. A. Thue, Über die gegenseitige Lage gleicher Teile gewisser Zeichenreihen, *Norske Vid. Selsk. Skr. I. Mat. Nat. Kl., Christiana* 10, 1–67, 1912.

167. R. Tijdeman and L. Zamboni, Fine and Wilf words for any periods, *Indag. Math.* (to appear)

168. N. Wozni and L.Q. Zamboni, Frequencies of factors in Arnoux-Rauzy sequences, *Acta Arith.* 96, 261–278, 2001.

169. A.I. Zimin, Blocking sets of terms, *Matem. Sbornik* 119, 363–375, 1982. English translation: *Math. USSR Sbornik* 47, 353–364, 1984.

TWO PROBLEMS ON COMMUTATION OF LANGUAGES

JUHANI KARHUMÄKI

Department of Mathematics, University of Turku and
Turku Centre for Computer Science
Turku 20014, Finland
E-mail: karhumak@cs.utu.fi

ION PETRE

Department of Computer Science
Åbo Akademi University
Turku 20520, Finland
E-mail: ipetre@abo.fi

We survey the known results on two old open problems on commutation of languages. The first problem, raised by Conway in 1971, is asking if the centralizer of a rational language must be rational as well – the centralizer of a language is the largest set of words commuting with that language. The second problem, proposed by Ratoandromanana in 1989, is asking for a characterization of those languages commuting with a given code – the conjecture is that the commutation with codes may be characterized as in free monoids. We present here simple proofs for the known results on these two problems.

1 Introduction

The focus of this paper is on the commutation $XY = YX$, one of the fundamental equations in any algebraic structure. While its solution is well known for free monoids, i.e., for finite words over a given alphabet, almost nothing is known for sets of words, although the problem was considered in the last few decades in various contexts, see [11], [13], [29], [37]. Two natural and apparently very difficult combinatorial problems have crystalized in the mean time: one proposed (somewhat in passing) by Conway in 1971, [11], and another one raised by Ratoandromanana in 1989 [34]. We survey in this paper all known results on these two problems, together with the most elementary proofs known in each case.

The centralizer $\mathcal{C}(L)$ of a language L is the largest set of words commuting with L, i.e., the maximal solution of the language equation $XL = LX$. As it can be readily seen, the notion of a centralizer of L is well defined for any language L; as a matter of fact, $\mathcal{C}(L)$ is the union of all languages commuting with L. A simple-looking question regarding the centralizers was raised by Conway [11] more than thirty years ago.

Conway's Problem: Is it true that for any rational language, its centralizer is rational?

Surprisingly enough, very little is known on Conway's problem. In fact, a much weaker question than Conway's is unanswered up to date: *it is not known whether or not the centralizer of a finite language is even recursively enumerable!*

Characterizing the commutation of two sets of words is a natural problem. Formally, for a given language L, the problem is to characterize all sets of words X such that $LX = XL$. While a general solution to this problem seems unlikely, the case of L being a code may be different. It has been conjectured by Ratoandromanana [34] that the commutation of an arbitrary language with a code may be characterized as in free monoids, although not even the set of codes is free:

Conjecture 1 ([34]). *For any code X and any language Y commuting with X, there is a language $R \subseteq \Sigma^+$ such that $X = R^n$ and $Y = \cup_{i \in I} R^i$, for some $n \in \mathbb{N}$, $I \subseteq \mathbb{N}$.*

Note that the commutation of two polynomials and that of two formal power series in noncommuting variables, with coefficients in a commutative field may be characterized in a similar way, as in free monoids – these results are due to Bergman and Cohn, see [2], [9], and [10]. The property conjectured above for codes is called sometimes the *BTC-property* – the acronym stands for Bergman-type of characterization for the commutation of two sets of words.

The above problems recently received some well-deserved attention and a number of different approaches have been investigated, see [4], [19], [26], [33] for some presentations. We survey in this paper all known results, presenting in each case the most simple proofs known at this point. We also present a number of open problems and discuss the perspectives as they appear today.

2 Preliminaries

We recall here several notions and results needed throughout the paper. For basic notions and results of Combinatorics on Words we refer to [6], [30], and [31]. For details on the notion of centralizer and the commutation of languages we refer to [25], [26], and [33]. For basic notions on Automata Theory we refer to [3], [17], or [36].

In this paper we denote additively the union of two sets: $L + R$ stands for $L \cup R$. Also, for a set S, we denote by 2^S the set of all its subsets.

Throughout the paper, Σ denotes a finite alphabet, Σ^* the set of all finite words over Σ, and Σ^ω the set of all (right) infinite words over Σ. We denote by 1 the empty word and by $|u|$ the length of a finite word $u \in \Sigma^*$.

We say that a word u is a *prefix* of a word v, denoted as $u \leq v$, if $v = uw$, for some $w \in \Sigma^*$. We denote $u < v$ if $u \leq v$ and $u \neq v$. We say that u and v are *prefix comparable* if either $u \leq v$, or $v \leq u$. For a word $u \in \Sigma^+$, $\mathrm{pref}_1(u)$ denotes the first letter of u. For $L \subseteq \Sigma^+$, we denote $\mathrm{pref}_1(L) = \{\mathrm{pref}_1(u) \mid u \in L\}$. The word u is a *root* of v if $v = u^n$, for some $n \in \mathbb{N}$; v is *primitive* if it has no root other than itself.

A language L of cardinality two (resp. three) is called *binary* (resp. *ternary*). L is called *periodic* if $L \subseteq u^*$, for some $u \in \Sigma^*$. For a set of words L and a subset $I \subseteq \mathbb{N}$, we denote $L^I = \cup_{i \in I} L^i$.

For a word u and a language L, we say that $v_1 \ldots v_n$ is an L-*factorization* of u if $u = v_1 \ldots v_n$ and $v_i \in L$, for all $1 \leq i \leq n$. A *relation* over L is an equality $u_1 \ldots u_m = v_1 \ldots v_n$, with $u_i, v_j \in L$, for all $1 \leq i \leq m$, $1 \leq j \leq n$; the relation is *trivial* if $m = n$ and $u_i = v_i$, for all $1 \leq i \leq m$. We say that $L \subseteq \Sigma^+$ is a *code* if any word of Σ^* has at most one L-factorization. Equivalently, L is a code if and only if all relations over L are trivial.

Let Σ be a finite alphabet, and Ξ a finite set of unknowns in a one-to-one correspondence with a set of nonempty words $X \subseteq \Sigma^*$, say $\xi_i \leftrightarrow x_i$, for some fixed enumeration of X. A (constant-free) *equation* over Σ with Ξ as the set of unknowns is a pair $(u, v) \in \Xi^\omega \times \Xi^\omega$, usually written as $u = v$. The subset X *satisfies* the equation $u = v$ if the morphism $h : \Xi^\omega \to \Sigma^\omega$, $h(\xi_i) = x_i$, for all $i \geq 0$, verifies $h(u) = h(v)$. These notions extend in a natural way to *systems of equations*.

We define the *dependence graph* of a system of equations S, as the nondirected graph G, whose vertices are the elements of Ξ, and whose edges are the pairs $(\xi_i, \xi_j) \in \Xi \times \Xi$, with ξ_i and ξ_j appearing as the first letters of the left and right handsides of some equation of S, respectively. The following basic result on combinatorics of words ([6]), known as *Graph Lemma*, is very useful and efficient in our later considerations. Note that in Graph Lemma it is crucial that *all words are nonempty*.

Lemma 1 ([6], Graph Lemma). *Let S be a system of equations and let $X \subset \Sigma^+$ be a subset satisfying it. If the dependence graph of S has p connected components, then there exists a subset F of cardinality p such that $X \subseteq F^+$.*

3 Conway's Problem

For a given language $L \subseteq \Sigma^+$, consider the set of all languages commuting with L,

$$\mathfrak{COM}(L) = \{S \subseteq \Sigma^+ \mid LS = SL\}.$$

It is easy to see that for any $L \subseteq \Sigma^+$, $\mathcal{COM}(L)$ is closed under product and union. If the commutation is considered in Σ^*, then $\{1\} \in \mathcal{COM}(L)$ for any language L and so, $(\mathcal{COM}(L), +, \cdot)$ is a subsemiring of 2^{Σ^+} with the empty set $\emptyset$ as the zero, and $\{1\}$ as the unity. The following lemma is easy to prove, see [33], and provides the basis of defining the centralizer of a language.

Lemma 2. *For any sets of words L, $\mathcal{COM}(L)$ has a unique maximal element, with respect to inclusion. Moreover, this unique maximal element of $\mathcal{COM}(L)$ is the union of all sets in $\mathcal{COM}(L)$.*

Definition 1. *For a language L, its centralizer $\mathcal{C}(L)$ is the largest set of words – with respect to inclusion – commuting with L.*

Example 1. Let $\Sigma = \{a, b\}$ be the alphabet.

(i) If $L_1 = \{a, ab\}$, then $\mathcal{C}(L_1) = L_1^+$.

(ii) If $L_2 = \{aa, ab, ba, bb\}$, then $\mathcal{C}(L_2) = \{a, b\}^+$.

(iii) If $L_3 = \{a, ab, ba, bb\}$, then $\mathcal{C}(L_3) = \{a, b\}^+ \setminus \{b\}$. Also, in this case, we have the following strict inclusions: $L_3^+ \subset \mathcal{C}(L_3) \subset \Sigma^+$.

(iv) If $L_4 = \{a^n b^n \mid n \geq 1\}$, then $\mathcal{C}(L) = L_4^+$.

Note that the notion of the centralizer of a set is usually defined in *Algebra* with respect to element-wise commutation, see, e.g., [2], [5], [9], [14], [18]. Thus, for a *group* (alternatively, for a semigroup, a ring, or a semiring) G and a subset S of G, the *centralizer* of S in G is the set $\{x \in G \mid xs = sx, \; \forall s \in S\}$. In this respect, the centralizer of a word u in Σ^* is $\rho(u)^*$, for any $u \in \Sigma^+$. Also, by this definition, the centralizer of a language L in the semiring 2^{Σ^+} is the set of all languages commuting with L, i.e., $\mathcal{COM}(L)$. We investigate in Section 4 the problem of characterizing $\mathcal{COM}(L)$ for a given L.

As a matter of fact, the term normalizer is also used in the literature, see, e.g., [9]. For a *group* G and a subset H of G, the *normalizer* of H in G is the subset $\mathcal{N}_G(H) = \{g \in G \mid gH = Hg\}$. Thus, for a subgroup H of G, $\mathcal{N}_G(H)$ is the largest subgroup of G such that H is a normal subgroup of $\mathcal{N}_G(H)$. For singletons (e.g., for an element $L \in 2^{\Sigma^+}$, or in other words, for a set of words L), the notions of centralizer and normalizer as defined above coincide. We refer for more details to [5] and [14].

The following result is clear.

Lemma 3. *For any $L \subseteq \Sigma^+$, the centralizer $\mathcal{C}(L)$ is a subsemigroup of Σ^+.*

A notion of a monoid centralizer of a set L may also be defined. Indeed, observe that for any set of words L, there is a unique maximal element of the set $\{S \subseteq \Sigma^* \mid LS = SL\}$. We call this element the *monoid centralizer* of L and we denote it as $\mathcal{C}_m(L)$. We refer to [24]-[27] for details.

Clearly, for any L, we have $\mathcal{C}(L) \cup \{1\} \subseteq \mathcal{C}_m(L)$. However, this is a strict inclusion in general. The reason for this is that $\mathcal{C}_m(L) \setminus \{1\}$ does not commute with L for all sets of words L.

Example 2. (i) For $L = \{a, ab, ba, bb\}$,

$$\mathcal{C}_m(L) = \{a, b\}^* \quad \text{and} \quad \mathcal{C}(L) = \{a, b\}^+ \setminus \{b\}.$$

Note that $\mathcal{C}_m(L) = \mathcal{C}(L) \cup \{1, b\}$.

(ii) For $\Sigma = \{a, b\}$ and $L = \Sigma^* b \Sigma^*$, $\mathcal{C}_m(L) = \Sigma^*$ and $\mathcal{C}(L) = L^+$.

It is in fact an interesting open problem whether or not for any language (or at least for any rational language), the difference between its monoid and its semigroup centralizers is always a rational set. The relevance of this question comes from Conway's Problem, formulated bellow: it is not known whether or not Conway's Problem for monoid centralizers can be reduced to the same problem for semigroup centralizers or viceversa.

We only consider in this paper the notion of semigroup centralizer.

The best known problem concerning the centralizer of a language is the question raised by Conway more than thirty years ago in [11]. His question, still unanswered today, is whether or not the centralizer of any rational language is rational.

Conway's Problem [11]: *Is the centralizer of any rational language, rational as well?*

This problem is far from being answered. In fact, it is not even known whether or not the centralizer of a rational language is always recursive or recursively enumerable. Attempts to simplify Conway's problem have been made replacing the rational language by a finite language and replacing Conway's question by "Is the centralizer recursive or even recursively enumerable?" The problem remains open even in this weaker form.

There are only a few known results in connection with the notion of centralizer of a language and Conway's problem. In the following we review all of those and aim to give the most simple proofs known at this point.

3.1   The Fixed Point Approach and the Co-RE Result

The lack of proper tools to handle the commutation of languages and the notion of maximal solution of a language equation makes Conway's problem very challenging and up to date, no clear strategy towards a solution has been found. For concrete examples, the centralizer can be computed – typically rather easily – and in most cases it coincides with X^+ or Σ^+. On the other hand, no efficient general method to compute the centralizer in general is known. As shown in [12] and [16], the centralizer can be elegantly defined as the *maximal fixed point* of a mapping, but this might lead to infinite iterations. The centralizer or in fact, its complement, can also be computed by "exhaustive search"-method as described below. Interestingly, in the following result there is no difference whether the language is finite, rational, or recursive, in any case the centralizer is in Co-RE.

Theorem 4. *([25]) For any recursive set, the complement of its centralizer is recursively enumerable.*

Proof. Let L be a recursive language and let Z be its centralizer. Our claim is that there is an algorithm such that given an input word x, the computation stops if and only if $x \notin Z$.

Since Z is the maximal set commuting with L, an element y is not in Z if and only if there is a word $u \in L$ such that either one of the following conditions is satisfied:

(i) For all $v \in L$, if $yu = vz$, for some $z \in \Sigma^*$, then $z \notin Z$.

(ii) For all $v \in L$, if $uy = zv$, for some $z \in \Sigma^*$, then $z \notin Z$.

We set $\mathcal{L}_1 = \{x\}$ and in the n-th step of the algorithm, we test the words from $\mathcal{L}_n$ for their membership to Z, in the following way: for each word $z \in \mathcal{L}_n$, we choose nondeterministically a word $u \in L$ (this is possible since L is recursive) and one of the conditions (i) or (ii) to be checked. Assuming that we chose (i), we consider the word zu, and for all the words $v \in L$, such that there is a word z' with $zu = vz'$, we add to the set $\mathcal{L}_{n+1}$ the word z'. If we chose (ii), then we are looking for words z' such that $uz = z'v$.

It is important to observe here that if none of the words in $\mathcal{L}_{n+1}$ is from Z, then the same is true also for the words of $\mathcal{L}_n$, for any $n \geq 1$. Indeed, if we had a $z \in \mathcal{L}_n \cap Z$, then for all $u \in L$ we would have $zu = v_1 y_1$, and $uz = y_2 v_2$, for some words $v_1, v_2 \in L$, and $y_1, y_2 \in Z$, which implies that some words from Z should be in $\mathcal{L}_{n+1}$ as well.

If the list $\mathcal{L}_{n+1}$ remains empty, then the algorithm stops: the initial word x is not in the centralizer of L. Otherwise we repeat the procedure with $\mathcal{L}_{n+1}$ instead of $\mathcal{L}_n$.

It is easy to conclude from the above that all the words for which there is a halting computation are from the complement of Z.

For the reverse inclusion, let x be a word from the complement of Z, and assume that our algorithm does not have any halting computation on the input x. Our claim is that there is $Z' \supseteq Z \cup \{x\}$ such that $Z'L = LZ'$. To begin with, let $Z' = Z \cup \{x\}$. If our algorithm does not halt on the input x, then for any $u \in L$, there are two words $v_1, v_2 \in L$ such that $xu = v_1 y_1$

and $ux = y_2 v_2$ and moreover, the algorithm does not halt on any of the input words y_1 and y_2. Indeed, if there is $u \in L$ such that the algorithm has halting computations for all y_1, y_2 as above, then it has a halting computation also for x: we just choose u in the first step of the algorithm. We add to Z' the words y_1 and y_2 and we continue the same reasoning with y_1 and y_2 instead of x. The language Z' obtained in this way clearly commutes with L. But Z is the maximal set commuting with L and so, $Z' \subseteq Z$. In particular, we obtain $x \in Z$, which is a contradiction. $\qquad\square$

The same result can be obtained also by defining $\mathcal{C}(L)$ as follows. Let $X_0 = \mathrm{Pref}(L^*) \cap \mathrm{Suf}(L^*)$ and

$$X_{n+1} = X_n \setminus \big((L^{-1}(LX_n \triangle X_n L) \,\cup\, (LX_n \triangle X_n L)L^{-1})\big),$$

for all $n \geq 0$, where $\triangle$ denotes the symmetric difference of two sets: $R \triangle S = (R \setminus S) \cup (S \setminus R)$. Then $\mathcal{C}(L) = \cap_{n \geq 0} X_n$. Note also that $\mathcal{C}(L)$ is the maximal fixed point of the following mapping:

$$\phi(Y) = Y \setminus (L^{-1}(LY \triangle YL) \cup (LY \triangle YL)L^{-1}).$$

We refer to [12] for more details on this "fixed point approach".

A related approach is described in [11], where the centralizer $\mathcal{C}(L)$ is defined as follows. For $X_0 = \Sigma^*$, let X_1 be the maximal subset of X_0 such that $X_1 L \subseteq LX_0$. Then let X_2 be the maximal subset of X_1 such that $LX_2 \subseteq X_1 L$, and so on. Then $\mathcal{C}(L) = \cap_{n \geq 0} X_n$. We refer to [11] for details, as well as for an interesting conjecture on the maximal solutions of systems of semilinear inequalities. Conway's Problem is a particular instance of such a system.

3.2 Periodic Sets

It is well-known that two words commute if and only if they have the same primitive root. Based on this, it is not difficult to prove, see [32], that a set of words X commutes with a word u if and only if $X \subseteq \rho(u^*)$, where $\rho(u)$ denotes the primitive root of u. Thus, for a word u, the centralizer of $\{u\}$ is $\rho(u)^*$.

If instead of a singleton, we consider a set of words, all powers of a same word, then the situation is not much different than that of a singleton, as we prove in the next result.

Recall that a set of words L is called *periodic* if there is a word u such that $L \subseteq u^+$.

Theorem 5. *Let $p \in \Sigma^+$ be a primitive word and $L \subseteq p^+$. Then $\mathcal{C}(L) = p^+$.*

Proof. Clearly, p^+ commutes with L and so, $p^+ \subseteq \mathcal{C}(L)$. Let $x \in \mathcal{C}(L)$ and $p^n \in L$, for some $n \geq 1$. Since $\mathcal{C}(L)L = L\mathcal{C}(L)$, it follows that $x(p^n)^\omega \subseteq L^\omega$, i.e., $xp^\omega = p^\omega$. Then, since p is primitive, $x = p^k$, for some $k \geq 1$. $\qquad\square$

Corollary 6. *Conway's problem has an affirmative answer for periodic sets of words.*

3.3 Binary Sets

The centralizer in the binary case turns out to be equally easy to describe as for periodic sets. Various proofs have been proposed for this result, see [8], [26], [27], but they all rely essentially on a reduction to *branching* languages.

The next result ([27]) shows that we can always reduce Conway's problem to the so-called branching sets of words. We say that a language L is *branching* if there are two words $u, v \in L$ such that u and v start with different letters. This simplification turns out to be essential in our considerations. The intuitive idea behind this result is that having a language L and a letter $a \in \Sigma$, Conway's problem has the same answer for languages aL and La. Thus, if all words in a language start with the same letter, we can "shift" the letter in the end, without essentially changing the problem. For any nonperiodic language, repeating this procedure a finite number of times will lead to a branching language. Note however that, as simple as this result may seem, proving it in details is not obvious, see [4] and [26].

Lemma 7 ([26]). *For any non-periodic language L, there is a branching language R such that $\mathcal{C}(L) = L^+$ if and only if $\mathcal{C}(R) = R^+$.*

Proof. If L is branching, then the claim is trivial. Assume that L is not branching, i.e., $L = aL'$, for some $a \in \Sigma$ and so, $aL'\mathcal{C}(aL') = \mathcal{C}(aL')aL'$. Thus, $\mathcal{C}(aL') = aX$, where $(L'a)(Xa) = (Xa)(L'a)$, i.e., $a^{-1}\mathcal{C}(aL')a \subseteq \mathcal{C}(L'a)$. The reverse inclusion can be proved similarly and so, $a^{-1}\mathcal{C}(aL')a = \mathcal{C}(L'a)$. Thus, clearly, $\mathcal{C}(aL') = (aL')^+$ if and only if $\mathcal{C}(L'a) = (L'a)^+$. We continue then the reasoning with $L'a$. Since L was not periodic, we obtain in a finite number of steps a branching binary language, proving the claim. $\qquad\square$

The centralizer of a binary language can then be described as in the next theorem.

Theorem 8 ([8]). *For any non-periodic binary language $F \subseteq \Sigma^+$, $\mathcal{C}(F) = F^+$.*

Proof. Using Lemma 7, we may assume without loss of generality that $F = \{u, v\}$ is branching. Clearly then, $F^+ \subseteq \mathcal{C}(F)$. Let $x \in \mathcal{C}(F)$. Then

$xu^\omega, xv^\omega \in F^\omega$:

$$xu^\omega = \alpha_1\alpha_2 \ldots \qquad xv^\omega = \beta_1\beta_2 \ldots$$

for some $\alpha_n, \beta_n \in F$, $n \geq 1$. Since F is branching, it follows that $\alpha_1 = \beta_1$ and $\alpha_1 \leq x$. Thus, $x = \alpha_1 x'$, for some $x' \in \Sigma^*$. Iterating the argument with x' instead of x, it follows that $x \in F^+$. $\qquad\square$

Corollary 9. *Conway's problem has an affirmative answer for binary sets of words.*

3.4 Ternary Sets

Conway's problem in the case of ternary sets of words was initially solved in [24] and [25] using very tedious considerations on maximal solutions of language equations. Also, the centralizer was only proved to be rational, although its exact form could not be described. The authors proposed as a conjecture that for any non-periodic ternary language F, $\mathcal{C}(F) = F^+$. This was indeed proved in the same paper for ternary codes using some involved combinatorial arguments. We present here a simple proof that solves the above mentioned conjecture. This results is from [21].

Theorem 10. *For any non-periodic ternary language $F \subseteq \Sigma^+$, $\mathcal{C}(F) = F^+$.*

Proof. We can assume by Lemma 7 that F is branching. Thus, let $F = \{u, u', v\}$, where $\mathrm{pref}_1(v) \notin \{\mathrm{pref}_1(u), \mathrm{pref}_1(u')\}$. We first prove two technical claims.

Claim 1. For any $1 < v' < v$, there is $\alpha \in F$ such that $v'\alpha$ is prefix incomparable with the words of F. Moreover, $v' \notin \mathcal{C}(F)$.

Proof of Claim 1. Let $v = v'v''$, $v'' \notin \{1, v\}$.

If $v \not\leq v'v$, then $\alpha = v$ satisfies the requirements of the claim. Indeed, $v'v \not\leq v$ by the assumption and $v'v$ is prefix-incomparable with u and u', as they start with different letters. In turn, if $v \leq v'v$, then $v'v'' \leq v'v'v''$, i.e., $\mathrm{pref}_1(v'') = \mathrm{pref}_1(v')$. Thus, $v'u$ is prefix incomparable with v, u, and u'. The second part of the claim then follows: if $v' \in \mathcal{C}(F)$, then $v'\alpha \in \mathcal{C}(F)F = F\mathcal{C}(F)$, a contradiction.

Claim 2. For any $1 < v' < v$, $\mathcal{C}(F) \cap v^+v' = \emptyset$.

Proof of Claim 2. If $v^n v' \in \mathcal{C}(F)$, $n \geq 1$, then $v^n v' \alpha^n \in \mathcal{C}(F)F^n = F^n\mathcal{C}(F)$, where $\alpha \in F$ is given by Claim 1. Thus, since $\mathrm{pref}_1(v) \notin \mathrm{pref}_1(F \setminus \{v\})$, it follows that $v'\alpha^n \in \mathcal{C}(F)$, contradicting Claim 1.

Assume now that there is $z \in \mathcal{C}(F) \setminus F^+$. Clearly, $F^+\mathcal{C}(F)$ commutes with F and so, $F^+\mathcal{C}(F) \subseteq \mathcal{C}(F)$. Since $\mathrm{pref}_1(v) \notin \{\mathrm{pref}_1(u), \mathrm{pref}_1(u')\}$, it follows that $v^* z \subseteq \mathcal{C}(F) \setminus F^+$. Consequently, there is a shortest nonempty word $x \in \Sigma^+$ such that $v^* x \cap (\mathcal{C}(F) \setminus F^+) \neq \emptyset$. In particular, note that $x \notin F^+$.

Let $n \geq 0$ be such that $v^n x \in \mathcal{C}(F) \setminus F^+$. Thus, $v^{n+1} x \in F\mathcal{C}(F) = \mathcal{C}(F)F$ and so, $v^{n+1} x = \alpha\beta$, with $\alpha \in \mathcal{C}(F)$ and $\beta \in F$. Thus, either $\alpha = v^i v'$, $i \leq n$, $v' \leq v$, or $\alpha = v^{n+1} x'$, $x' \leq x$. We distinguish the following four cases:

(i) $\alpha = v^i$, $i \leq n+1$, $\beta = v^{n+1-i} x$. Then either $v^{n+1-i} x = v$, or $i = n+1$ and $x \in F$, i.e., either $x = 1$, or $x \in F$, contradicting the choice of x.

(ii) $\alpha = v^i v'$, $i \leq n$, $\beta = v'' v^{n-i} x$, where $v = v'v''$ and $v', v'' \neq 1$. If $i \geq 1$, then this contradicts Claim 2, since $v^i v' \in \mathcal{C}(F)$. If $i = 0$, then $v' \in \mathcal{C}(F)$, again a contradiction by Claim 1.

(iii) $\alpha = v^{n+1} x'$, $\beta = x''$, where $x', x'' \neq 1$ and $x = x'x''$. If $v^{n+1} x' \in F^+$, then $x' \in F^+$ and so, $x \in F^+$, contradicting the choice of x. Thus, $v^{n+1} x' \in \mathcal{C}(F) \setminus F^+$. Since $|x'| < |x|$, this contradicts the choice of x as the shortest word y such that $v^* y \cap (\mathcal{C}(F) \setminus F^+) \neq \emptyset$.

(iv) $\alpha = v^{n+1} x$, $\beta = 1$, implying that $1 \in F$, a contradiction.

Thus, each case leads to a contradiction. Consequently, $\mathcal{C}(F) \setminus F^+ = \emptyset$, i.e., $\mathcal{C}(F) \subseteq F^+$. Since for all languages L, $L^+ \subseteq \mathcal{C}(L)$, it follows that $\mathcal{C}(F) = F^+$. □

Corollary 11. *Conway's problem has an affirmative answer for ternary sets of words.*

4 Commutation of Languages

Characterizing the commutation of two sets of words is in general a very difficult problem. It is well-known that two words commute if and only if they are powers of another word. Also, the commutation of two polynomials or of two formal power series with coefficients in a commutative field can be described in similar terms: two polynomials (formal power series, resp.) commute if and only if they are unions of powers of another polynomial (formal power series, resp.). However, nothing similar holds for the commutation of two arbitrary sets of words, unless one of them satisfies some special properties, e.g., it is a prefix code, or it is a periodic, a binary, or a ternary set of words. Despite the fact that the set of codes is not a free monoid, there has been a long-standing conjecture of Ratoandromanana ([34], 1989) that such a characterization holds for the commutation with a code, as well as for the commutation of two codes.

Conjecture 1 ([34]). *For any code X and any language Y commuting with X, there is a language $R \subseteq \Sigma^+$ such that $X = R^n$ and $Y = \cup_{i \in I} R^i$, for some $n \in \mathbb{N}$, $I \subseteq \mathbb{N}$.*

A major result on the conjecture was achieved by Ratoandromanana [34], in the case of prefix codes, using ingenious (and involved) techniques on codes and prefix sets. A simpler proof, using only elementary techniques is obtained in [22]. Conjecture 1, however, remained open in its general form.

Recall that a language X is said to satisfy the BTC-property if the commutation with X can be characterized as in the statement of Conjecture 1, that is, similarly as in Bergman's theorem, see [24]. Thus, Conjecture 1 proposes that all codes satisfy the BTC-property.

It is clear that Conjecture 1 does not hold in general and small counterexamples exist, as shown in Example 3 below. As a matter of fact, that counterexample is a boundary point: we show in this section that the commutation with all ternary sets (including non-codes) may be characterized as in Conjecture 1, a result from [21], whereas the property does not hold for all 4-word sets, see Example 3.

Example 3. In the following there are a few examples of sets of words that commute with each other, although they cannot be characterized as in free monoids.

(i,[8]) The sets $X = \{a, a^3, b, ab, ba, aba\}$ and $Y = X \cup \{a^2\}$ commute, but they cannot be expressed as unions of powers of a same set.

(ii,[1]) The sets

$$X = \{aa, ab, ba, bb, aaa\} \quad \text{and} \quad Y = \{a, b, aa, ab, ba, bb, aaa\}$$

commute, but they cannot be expressed in terms of another set of words.

(iii,[8]) The sets

$$X = \{a, ab, ba, bb\} \quad \text{and} \quad Y = X \cup X^2 \cup \{bab, bbb\}$$

commute but they are not unions of powers of another set. This is a minimal counterexample, in the sense that the BTC-property holds for all sets of words X with at most 3 elements.

4.1 Periodic Sets

The commutation with periodic sets can be easily characterized. The following result is a simple consequence of Theorem 5.

Theorem 12. *For any periodic language $L \subseteq p^+$, where $p \in \Sigma^+$ is a primitive word and any language $X \subseteq \Sigma^+$, $LX = XL$ if and only if $X \subseteq p^+$.*

Proof. If $LX = XL$, then $X \subseteq \mathcal{C}(L)$ and so, by Theorem 5, $X \subseteq p^+$. The other implication is trivial. □

4.2 Binary and Ternary Sets, Prefix Codes

Besides periodic sets, there are three other cases in which the language commutation has been characterized: prefix codes, binary and ternary sets. Various proofs exist for these results, see [4], [8], [12], [19], [24]-[27], [33], and [34]. We give here a uniform proof for all these results – this elegant approach was introduced in [21]. The basic idea is to connect the language commutation with a sharper version of Conway's problem and then characterize the commutation based on the results on Conway's problem, see Section 3.

We say that a language $L \subseteq \Sigma^+$ is *weakly singular* if there is a word $u \in L$ such that $uL^* \cap (L \setminus \{u\})L^* = \emptyset$. We say in this case that u is a singularity point for L.

Example 4. (i) Any code is weakly singular. Indeed, if X is a code, then for any $u \in X$, $uX^* \cap (X \setminus \{u\})X^* = \emptyset$.

(ii) Any nonperiodic binary set of words is weakly singular. Indeed, any such set is a code.

(iii) Any nonperiodic ternary set of words F is weakly singular. Indeed, if F is not a code, then there is a nontrivial relation $u_1 \alpha = u_2 \beta$ over F, where $u_1, u_2 \in F$, $\alpha, \beta \in F^*$. If $F = \{u_1, u_2, u_3\}$, then by Graph Lemma, $u_3 F^* \cap \{u_1, u_2\}F^* = \emptyset$.

(iv) The set of words $F = \{a, a^2, b, b^2\}$ is not weakly singular.

The next result establishes the connection between the language commutation and a problem on centralizers.

Theorem 13. *Let L be a weakly singular language, $i > 0$, and $X \subseteq \Sigma^+$ a language commuting with L^i. The following two properties are equivalent:*

(i) $X \subseteq L^+$;

(ii) $X = L^I$, *for some* $I \subseteq \mathbb{N}$.

Proof. Clearly, (ii) implies (i). For the reverse implication, let $u \in L$ such that $uL^* \cap (L \setminus \{u\})L^* = \emptyset$ and let $I = \{j \geq 1 \mid u^j \in X\}$. We shall prove that $X = L^I$.

Let $v \in X \subseteq L^+$ and let $s = |v|$. Then $u^{si}v \in L^{si}X = XL^{si}$. Thus, $u^{si}v = xl$, with $x \in X$ and $l \in L^{si}$.

Since $l \in L^{si}$ and $L \subseteq \Sigma^+$, it follows that $|l| \geq si \geq s = |v|$. Thus, $|x| \leq |u^{si}|$. Since $x \in L^+$ and u is a singularity point for L, it follows that

$x = u^j$, for some $j \geq 1$, $j \in I$. Then $l = u^{si-j}v$. Since $l \in L^{si}$ and u is a singularity point for L, it follows that $v \in L^j$, proving that $X \subseteq L^I$.

Reversely, consider $w \in L^j$, for some $j \in I$. Thus, $u^j \in X$. Then $u^{ij}w = u^j u^{ij-j}w \in XL^{ij} = L^{ij}X$, implying by the choice of u that $w \in X$. Consequently, $X = L^I$. □

Characterizing the commutation with prefix codes, binary and ternary sets of words can now be given as simple consequences of Theorem 13.

Theorem 14 ([8]). *For any nonperiodic binary language $F \subseteq \Sigma^+$ and any language $X \subseteq \Sigma^+$, $XF = FX$ if and only if $X = F^I$, for some $I \subseteq \mathbb{N}$.*

Proof. If $XF = FX$, then $X \subseteq \mathcal{C}(F) = F^+$. Thus, by Theorem 13, $X = F^I$, for some $I \subseteq \mathbb{N}$. The reverse implication is trivial. □

Theorem 15 ([21]). *For any nonperiodic ternary language F and any language X, $XF = FX$ if and only if $X = F^I$, for some $I \subseteq \mathbb{N}$.*

Proof. By Graph Lemma, any nonperiodic ternary set is weakly singular. The result follows by Theorem 10 and Theorem 13. □

The following result is proved in [22] using elementary (but non-trivial!) combinatorial arguments – we skip its proof here. The result was originally proved in [34] using ingenious techniques of combinatorics on words.

Theorem 16. *Let L be a prefix code, $\rho(L)$ its primitive root, and $\mathcal{C}(L)$ its centralizer. Then $\mathcal{C}(L) = \rho(L)^+$.*

Then the commutation with prefix codes follows by Theorem 13.

Theorem 17. *For any prefix code L and any language $X \subseteq \Sigma^+$, $LX = XL$ if and only if $L = \rho(X)^I$, for some $I \subseteq \mathbb{N}$.*

4.3 Decidability and Complexity Considerations

The fact that so few results are known in connection to language commutation might sound surprising, but is explained by several complexity results. We present in this section one simple undecidable question on commuting with finite sets of words and discuss the complexity of a few other decidable cases.

The intriguing nature of commutation is marvellously shown by the following result from [15].

Theorem 18 ([15]). *It is undecidable whether a given two element set of words and a given context-free language commute. The problem is decidable however for deterministic context-free languages.*

Another problem showing the surprising difficulty of problems on finite sets of words is the following undecidability result of [23].

Theorem 19 ([23]). *It is undecidable whether two finite substitutions ϕ, ψ : $\{a, b, c\}^+ \rightarrow \Sigma^+$ are equivalent on the language ab^*c, i.e., whether or not the identity $\phi(ab^n c) = \psi(ab^n c)$ of finite languages holds for all $n \geq 0$.*

The following results of [28] shed more light on the complexity of language commutation.

Theorem 20 ([28]). *(i) Let X be a finite language given by an acyclic non-deterministic finite automaton and let $Y = \Sigma$. Testing the commutation $XY = YX$ is co-NP complete.*

(ii) Let X and Y be regular languages given by nondetermisitic finite automata or regular expressions. Testing the commutation $XY = YX$ is PSPACE-complete.

(iii) Consider a context-free grammar generating a finite language L. Testing the commutation $L\Sigma = \Sigma L$ is co-NEXPTIME-complete.

5 Discussion and Open Problems

The commutation of languages has turned out to be a very challenging problem in general, and it is difficult even to conjecture a possible general characterization. The intriguing problem of Conway [11], asking whether the centralizer of a rational language is rational, also remains far from being solved. Except the "simple" cases of periodic, binary, ternary languages, and prefixes – solved here with elementary arguments –, nothing else is known on these two problems. In fact, it turns out that despite the various techniques we have developed for this problem, see [33] for a survey, the only cases where we could solve them are those when the centralizer is "trivial", i.e., $\mathcal{C}(X) = \rho(X)^*$. Even in these cases, the proofs remain non-trivial, despite considerable simplifications, cf. the proofs in this paper with those of [25], [27], [34].

As far as we can see, the difficulty of these two problems comes from two different directions:

(i) We seem to lack the proper combinatorial tools to deal with the commutation of two sets of words – only the "simple" cases of prefixes, periodic, binary, and ternary sets have been solved using combinatorial arguments. Our attempts to employ algebraic tools to solve the commutation of languages using Cohn's and Bergman's results on power series (the so-called multiplicity approach) have been unsuccessful so far – this approach is perhaps still insufficiently investigated. In general, our ability in solving language equations seems to be rather limited, see [29].

(ii) Even more limited are the tools one can use to reason about maximal solutions of a certain equation – the centralizer of a language L is the maximal solution of the equation $LX = XL$. A general theory of such maximal solutions of equations may be needed, a direction suggested already in [11]. We conclude by recalling once again these two remarkable problems, as well as some of their possibly simpler variants.

Problem 1 (Conway's Problem). Is it true that for any rational language, its centralizer is rational?

Problem 2. Is the centralizer of a rational set always: a) recursive, b) rational?

Problem 3. Is the centralizer of a finite set always: a) recursive, b) rational, c) finitely generated?

Problem 4. Does the Bergman type of characterization hold for all codes?

Regarding Problems 2a and 3a, it has been proved in [25] that the complement of the centralizer of any recursive language is always recursively enumerable. Thus, to solve Problems 2a and 3a, it is enough to prove that the centralizer of any rational language is recursively enumerable. It might be that Problem 3c is the right question to ask for finite sets.

Acknowledgments

Work supported under Grant 44087 from Academy of Finland.

References

1. Autebert, J.M., Boasson, L., Latteux, M., Motifs et bases de langages, *RAIRO Inform. Theor.*, 23(4) (1989) 379–393.
2. Bergman, G., Centralizers in free associative algebras, *Transactions of the American Mathematical Society*, 137 (1969) 327–344.
3. Berstel, J., *Transductions and Context-free Languages*, B.G. Teubner, Stuttgart, 1979.
4. Berstel, J., Karhumäki, Combinatorics on words – a tutorial, *Bull. EATCS*, 79 (2003) 178–228.
5. Bourbaki, N., *Éléments de mathématique. Algèbre.* Chapitres 1 à 3, Hermann, Paris, 1970.
6. Choffrut, C., Karhumäki, J., Combinatorics of words. In Rozenberg, G., Salomaa, A. (eds.), *Handbook of Formal Languages*, Vol. 1, Springer-Verlag, 1997, 329–438.
7. Choffrut, C., Karhumäki, J., On Fatou properties of rational languages, in Martin-Vide, C., Mitrana, V. (eds.), *Where mathematics, Computer Science, Linguistics and Biology Meet*, Kluwer, Dordrecht 2000.
8. Choffrut, C., Karhumäki, J., Ollinger, N., The commutation of finite sets:

a challenging problem, *Theoret. Comput. Sci.*, 273 (1-2) (2002) 69–79.

9. Cohn, P.M., Factorization in noncommuting power series rings, *Proc. Cambridge Philos. Soc.*, 58 (1962) 452–464.

10. Cohn, P.M., Centralisateurs dans les corps libres, in Berstel, J. (ed.), *Séries formelles*, Paris, (1978) 45–54.

11. Conway, J.H., *Regular Algebra and Finite Machines*, Chapman Hall, 1971.

12. Culik, K. II, Karhumäki, J., Salmela, P., Fixed point approach to commutation of languages, to appear (2004).

13. Eilenberg, S., *Automata, Languages and Machines*, Academic Press, 1974.

14. *Encyclopedia of Mathematics*, Kluwer Academic Publishers, 1988.

15. Harju, T., Ibarra, O., Karhumäki, J., Salomaa, A., Decision questions concerning semilinearity, morphisms and commutation of languages, *J. Comput. System Sci.* 65 (2002) 278–294.

16. Hirvensalo, M., personal communication.

17. Hopcroft, J.E., Ullman, J.D., *Introduction to Automata Theory, Languages, and Computation*, Reading, MA, Addison-Wesley, 1979.

18. Jacobson, N., *Structure of Rings*, American Mathematical Society, 1956.

19. Karhumäki, J., Challenges of commutation: an advertisement, in *Proc. of FCT 2001*, LNCS 2138, Springer, 2001, 15–23.

20. Karhumäki, J., Some open problems on combinatorics of words and related areas, in *Proceedings of Algebraic Systems, Formal Languages and Computations*, RIMS Proceedings 1166, Research Institute for Mathematical Sciences (2000) 118–130.

21. Karhumäki, J., Latteux, M., Petre, I., The commutation with codes and ternary sets of words, preliminary version in *Proc. of STACS 2003*, LNCS 2607, Springer (2003), 74–84; final version submitted for publication.

22. Karhumäki, J., Latteux, M., Petre, I., The commutation with prefix codes, manuscript (2003).

23. Karhumäki, J., Lisovik, L., The equivalence problem for finite substitutions on ab^*c, with applications, *Int. J. Found. Comp. Sci.* 14 (2003), 699–710; preliminary version in Springer LNCS 2380, (2002), 812–820.

24. Karhumäki, J., Petre, I., On the centralizer of a finite set, in *Proc. of ICALP 2000*, LNCS 1853, Springer, 2000, 536–546.

25. Karhumäki, J., Petre, I., Conway's problem for three-word sets, *Theoret. Comput. Sci.*, 289/1 (2002) 705–725.

26. Karhumäki, J., Petre, I., Conway's problem and the commutation of languages, *Bulletin of EATCS*, 74 (2001) 171–177.

27. Karhumäki, J., Petre, I., The branching point approach to Conway's

problem, LNCS 2300, Springer, 2002, 69–76.

28. Karhumäki, J., Plandowski, W., Rytter, W., On the complexity of decidable cases of the commutation problem of languages, preliminary version in LNCS 2138, Springer, 2001, 193–203; final version to appear.

29. Leiss, E., *Language Equations*, Springer, 1998.

30. Lothaire, M., *Combinatorics on Words*, Addison-Wesley, Reading, MA., 1983.

31. Lothaire, M., *Algebraic Combinatorics on Words*, Cambridge University Press, 2002.

32. Mateescu, A., Salomaa, A., Yu, S., On the decomposition of finite languages, TUCS Technical Report 222, http://www.tucs.fi/ (1998).

33. Petre, I., *Commutation Problems on Sets of Words and Formal Power Series*, PhD Thesis, University of Turku, 2002.

34. Ratoandromanana, B., Codes et motifs, *RAIRO Inform. Theor.*, 23(4) (1989) 425-444.

35. Restivo, A., Silva, P.V., On the lattice of prefix codes, *Theoret. Comp. Sci.*, **4270** (2002), 1–28.

36. Salomaa, A., *Formal Languages*, Academic Press, New York, 1973, 1997.

37. Shyr, H.J., *Free Monoids and Languages*, Hon Min Book Company, 1991.

COUNTING (SCATTERED) SUBWORDS

ARTO SALOMAA

Turku Centre for Computer Science
Lemminkäisenkatu 14, 20520 Turku, Finland
E-mail: asalomaa@it.utu.fi

1 Numerical Information About Words

The investigation of properties of words becomes much easier whenever the properties can be expressed as numbers. The main goal of such an *arithmetization* is to reach a situation where the products are commutative. The theory of formal power series, [2], contains numerous such constructions.

The most direct numerical fact about a word w is its *length* $|w|$. The *Parikh vector*, [7,8], $\Psi(w) = (i_1, \ldots, i_k)$ indicates the number of occurrences of the letter a_j, $1 \leq j \leq k$, in w, provided w is over the alphabet $\Sigma = \{a_1, \ldots, a_k\}$. Although the Parikh vector tells more about a word than the length, it defines the word uniquely only in case of a one-letter alphabet.

To get more information about a word, one has to focus the attention to subwords and to the number of occurrences of a specific subword in the given word. In this article, u being a *subword* of w means that w, as a sequence of letters, contains u as a subsequence. More formally, there exist words $x_1, \ldots, x_k$ and $y_0, \ldots, y_k$, some of them possibly empty, such that

$$u = x_1 \ldots x_k \text{ and } w = y_0 x_1 y_1 \ldots x_k y_k.$$

We also consider *factors* u of a word w: u is a factor of w if there are words x and y such that $w = xuy$. Throughout this article, we understand subwords and factors in the way mentioned. (In classical language theory, [8], our subwords are usually called "scattered subwords", whereas our factors are called "subwords". There is quite much confusion in the terminology. Even the same author sometimes uses *subword* in the scattered sense but *subword complexity* in the connected factor sense.)

The notation used throughout the article is $|w|_u$, the number of occurrences of the word u as a subword of the word w. Let us first clarify some details. Assume that u occurs r times as a subword of w, $|w|_u = r$. Occurrences can be viewed as vectors. If $|u| = t$, each occurrence of u in w can be identified as the t-tuple $(i_1, \ldots, i_t)$ of increasing positive integers, where for $1 \leq j \leq t$, the jth letter of u is the i_jth letter of w. For instance, the 7 occurrences of $u = abb$ in $w = aababb$ are

$$(1,3,5),\ (1,3,6),\ (1,5,6),\ (2,3,5),\ (2,3,6),\ (2,5,6),\ (4,5,6).$$

Clearly, $|w|_u = 0$ if $|w| < |u|$. We also make the *convention* that, for any w and the empty word λ,

$$|w|_\lambda = 1.$$

In [9] the number $|w|_u$ is denoted as a "binomial coefficient"

$$|w|_u = \binom{w}{u}.$$

If w and u are words over a one-letter alphabet,

$$w = a^i,\ u = a^j,$$

then $|w|_u$ equals the ordinary binomial coefficient: $|w|_u = \binom{i}{j}$. Our convention concerning the empty word reduces to the fact that $\binom{i}{0} = 1$.

It is shown in [9] that the equation

$$|vb|_{ua} = |v|_{ua} + \delta_{a,b}|v|_u,\ a,b \in \Sigma,\ \text{and}\ u,v \in \Sigma^*,$$

where

$$\delta_{a,b} = \begin{cases} 1 & \text{if } a = b, \\ 0 & \text{if } a \neq b, \end{cases}$$

together with the already mentioned equations

$$|w|_\lambda = 1,\ |w|_u = 0 \text{ for } |w| < |u|$$

suffice to compute all values $|w|_u$. However, this recursive method is very nonefficient.

Assume that Σ is an alphabet containing the letters a and b. A little reflection shows that, for any word w,

$$(|w|_a) \times (|w|_b) = |w|_{ab} + |w|_{ba}.$$

This simple equation can be viewed as a general fact about occurrences of subwords. A slight variation immediately leads to difficulties. No explicit characterization is known for the relation between $(|w|_u, |w|_v)$ and $(|w|_{uv}, |w|_{vu})$, where u, v, w are arbitrary words.

A general problem is the following. *What numbers $|w|_u$ suffice to determine the word w uniquely?* For instance, a word $w \in \{a, b\}^*$ is uniquely determined by the values

$$|w|_a = |w|_b = 3,\ |w|_{ab} = 8.$$

Indeed, $w = a^2bab^2$. On the other hand, a word $w \in \{a, b\}^*$ of length 4 is not uniquely determined by the values $|w|_u$, $|u| \leq 2$. Either one of the words $abba$ and $baab$ can be chosen as w, and still the equations

$$|w|_a = |w|_b = |w|_{ab} = |w|_{ba} = 2, \quad |w|_{aa} = |w|_{bb} = 1$$

are satisfied.

In addressing the general problem mentioned above, one should specify a class of subwords u such that (hopefully) the values $|w|_u$, where u ranges over this class, determine w uniquely. Such a class could consist of all words of a given length, or of all words of at most a given length. Indeed, a notion mentioned but not much investigated in the literature, [1,3,8], is that of a *t-spectrum*. For a fixed $t \geq 1$, the t-spectrum (resp. *full t-spectrum*) of a word w tells all the values $|w|_u$, where $|u| = t$ (resp. $|u| \leq t$.) Following the notation of formal power series, [2], the full t-spectrum of a word w in Σ^* can be viewed as a polynomial in $\mathbb{N}\langle\Sigma^*\rangle$ of degree t. Similarly, the t-spectrum is a homogeneous polynomial of degree t. (It is of course understood that if a term u is missing from the polynomial, then $|w|_u = 0$.)

For instance, the polynomial $aa + bb + 2ab + 2ba$ (resp. $aa + bb + 2ab + 2ba + 2a + 2b$) is the 2-spectrum (resp. full 2-spectrum) of the word $abba$, as well as of the word $baab$.

In general, one can define the function $\xi(t)$ as the *maximal* length such that any word of length $\xi(t)$ is uniquely determined by its full t-spectrum. Thus, the function $\xi(t)$ is defined, for $t \geq 1$, by the following two conditions.

1. If w_1 and w_2 are words of length $\xi(t)$ having the same full t-spectra, then $w_1 = w_2$.

2. There are two different words of length $\xi(t) + 1$ having the same full t-spectra.

From the discussion above it can be easily concluded that $\xi(2) = 3$. The two different words

$$abbaaab, baaabba \quad (\text{resp. } ab^2a^3ba^2b^2a, ba^3bab^2a^3b)$$

have the same full 3-spectrum (resp. full 4-spectrum), and are both of length 7 (resp. 12), [3]. This shows that

$$\xi(3) \leq 6, \quad \xi(4) \leq 11.$$

The same function ξ is defined if spectra, rather than full spectra, are used in the definition. This follows because the t-spectrum determines uniquely the full t-spectrum. In other words, if we know all values $|w|_u$ with $|u| = t$, then we know all values $|w|_u$ with $|u| < t$. An interested reader can find the details of the argument in [3]. It is straightforward to infer the values $|w|_u$ with $|u| = 1$.

The following are natural problems concerning spectra.

- Determine the function $\xi(t)$, or include the values $\xi(t)$ within as tight bounds as possible.

- Characterize the homogeneous polynomials of degree t in $\mathbb{N}\langle \Sigma^* \rangle$ that are t-spectra.

As pointed out above, a characterization of t-spectra leads to a characterization of full t-spectra. Therefore, we have stated the second problem in terms of spectra rather than full spectra.

For instance, the polynomials

$$a^2+b^2+2ab+2ba, \; a^2+b^2+3ab+ba, \; a^2+b^2+ab+3ba, \; a^2+b^2+4ab, \; a^2+b^2+4ba$$

are the only 2-spectra in $\mathbb{N}\langle \{a,b\}^* \rangle$ containing the binomial $a^2 + b^2$.

The main purpose in introducing the notion of a spectrum is to find some information about a word that characterizes the word completely. Perhaps it is not a good idea to restrict the attention to subwords of the *same* length, and to take all of them. Sometimes very few words (of different lengths) determine the word uniquely. We noticed above that the equations

$$|w|_a = |w|_b = 3, \; |w|_{ab} = 8$$

determine the word w uniquely. Following the terminology of [5], the *subword history* $3a + 3b + 8ab$ is satisfied by only one word over the alphabet $\{a, b\}$.

In general, a *subword history* is an element P of $\mathbb{N}\langle \Sigma^* \rangle$. A word w *satisfies* the subword history P if, for any term u in P, $|w|_u$ equals the coefficient of u in P.

The second problem above can now be generalized to the following form.

- Characterize the polynomials in $\mathbb{N}\langle \Sigma^* \rangle$ that are subword histories satisfied by some word.

Not much is known about the solution of this problem. Some facts are rather obvious. The coefficients of the powers a^i are not independent. In fact, one such coefficient determines all the others in a satisfiable subword history. For instance, if the coefficient of a^3 is 10, then the coefficients of a, a^2, a^4, a^5, a^6 are $5, 10, 5, 1, 0$, respectively. This follows by considering binomial coefficients.

It is also clear that the coefficient of ab (or ba) cannot exceed the product of the coefficients of a and b.

Some other phenomena are harder to explain. For instance, [5], the subword history

$$3a + 5b + 3c + 7ab + 7bc + \alpha abc$$

is satisfied for $\alpha = 2$ and $\alpha = 4$ by the words

$$bcbabccaabb, \quad \text{and} \quad bcabbccabab,$$

respectively, but not satisfiable for $\alpha = 3$.

2 The Cauchy Inequality

So far our considerations have been rather diverse. From now on we will focus the attention on a particular inequality, the *Cauchy inequality*,

$$|w|_y|w|_{xyz} \leq |w|_{xy}|w|_{yz},$$

valid for all words w, x, y, z, [5]. It can be claimed to be a fundamental property of words, because of its generality and because it reduces to equality in a great variety of cases. The choice for the name of the inequality is motivated by the resemblance to the well-known algebraic Cauchy inequality for real numbers and also by the methods used in the proof. The reader is referred to [5] for further details.

We begin with a simple example. Consider the words

$$w = a^{i_1}b^{j_1}c^{k_1}, \ x = a^{i_2}, \ y = b^{j_2}, \ z = c^{k_2}.$$

(As usual, a, b, c stand for letters.) Clearly, $|w|_y = \binom{j_1}{j_2}$. Straightforward calculations show that

$$|w|_y|w|_{xyz} = \binom{i_1}{i_2}\binom{j_1}{j_2}^2\binom{k_1}{k_2} = |w|_{xy}|w|_{yz}.$$

For instance, the setup

$$w = a^4b^4c^4, \ x = a, \ y = b, \ z = c^2$$

yields the value 384 for both sides of the equation.

In general, if

$$w = x_1y_1z_1, \ |w|_x = |x_1|_x = m, \ |w|_y = |y_1|_y = n, \ |w|_z = |z_1|_z = p,$$

then both sides of the Cauchy inequality equal mn^2p and, thus, the inequality is not proper.

Consider words over a one-letter alphabet. If the words w, x, y, z are of lengths n, i, j, k, respectively, then the inequality assumes the form

$$\binom{n}{j}\binom{n}{i+j+k} \leq \binom{n}{i+j}\binom{n}{j+k},$$

which is easily verified to be true. Here we have an equality exactly in case $i = 0$ or $k = 0$.

Assume that

$$y = a^i b^j a^k, \quad x = a^{i_1}, \quad z = a^{k_1}$$

and $w = a^{i+i_1+i'} b^{j+j'} a^{k+k_1+k'}$. Then again it is easy to verify that the inequality is not proper.

The reader might want to consider more sophisticated examples. For instance, if

$$w = a^2 b^2 a^2 b^2 a^2, \quad y = ab^2 a, \quad x = z = a,$$

then $|w|_y |w|_{xyz} = 512$, whereas $|w|_{xy} |w|_{yz} = 576$.

Below we will give two different proofs of the general result:

Theorem 1 *The inequality $|w|_{xyz} |w|_y \leq |w|_{xy} |w|_{yz}$ holds for arbitrary words w, x, y, z.*

3 A Proof Using Combinatorial Arguments

We now begin the proof of Theorem 1. The argument follows the one given in [5]. We assume that the words w, x, y, z are *fixed*. Most of our notions below depend on (some of) w, x, y, z. Since we consider them to be fixed, it is not necessary for us to indicate this dependence in the notation.

Assume that y occurs n times as a subword of w,

$$|w|_y = n.$$

We assume that $n \geq 1$ because, otherwise, there is nothing to prove. If $|y| = t$, each occurrence of y in w can be identified as the t-tuple $(i_1, \ldots, i_t)$ of increasing positive integers, where for $1 \leq j \leq t$, the jth letter of y is the i_jth letter of w. For instance, the 7 occurrences of $u = abb$ in $w = aababb$ are

$$(1, 3, 5), \ (1, 3, 6), \ (1, 5, 6), \ (2, 3, 5), \ (2, 3, 6), \ (2, 5, 6), \ (4, 5, 6).$$

We will consider linear orderings $y_1, \ldots, y_n$ of the occurrences of y in w. Some of them will be called *natural*.

Let $p_1, \ldots, p_k$, $k \geq 1$, be the integers, in increasing order of magnitude, that appear as *first* components in the occurrences of y in w. Similarly, let

$q_1, \ldots, q_l$, $l \geq 1$, be the integers, in increasing order of magnitude, that appear as the *last* components in the occurrences of y in w. In our example we have

$$k = 3, \; l = 2, \; p_1 = 1, \; p_2 = 2, \; p_3 = 4, \; q_1 = 5, \; q_2 = 6.$$

We say that an occurrence y_i of y in w is of *type*

$$(\mu, \nu), \; 1 \leq \mu \leq k, \; 1 \leq \nu \leq l,$$

if the first (resp. last) letter of y_i is the p_μth (resp. q_νth) letter of w. The set of all occurrences of y of type (μ, ν) is denoted by $T(\mu, \nu)$.

Clearly, each occurrence y_i of y belongs to exactly one set $T(\mu, \nu)$. Consequently,

$$n = \#\left(\bigcup_{\mu=1}^{k} \bigcup_{\nu=1}^{l} T(\mu, \nu) \right).$$

Observe that the number of nonempty sets $T(\mu, \nu)$ is at most kl. The number can be smaller because it may happen that there are no occurrences of a particular type.

A *natural* order of the occurrences y_i means simply the ordering of the type vectors, whereas the occurrences of the same type can be ordered arbitrarily. By definition, a linear ordering $y_i, \ldots, y_n$ of the occurrences of y in w is termed *natural* if the occurrences of different types come in the order

$$T(1,1), \ldots, T(1,l), T(2,1), \ldots, T(2,l), \ldots, T(k,1), \ldots, T(k,l).$$

We consider a *fixed natural ordering*

$$y_1, \; y_2, \; \ldots, \; y_n$$

of the occurrences of y in w. In our example, the ordering given above is natural. It remains natural if the mutual order of $(1,3,6)$ and $(1,5,6)$ (or $(2,3,6)$ and $(2,5,6)$) is changed.

So far we have considered only occurrences of y. We now start considering occurrences of x and z. We say that an occurrence x_j of x (in w) is *strictly to the left* of an occurrence y_i of y if the last letter of x_j precedes the first letter of y_i in w. Similarly, we define that an occurrence z_j of z is *strictly to the right* of an occurrence y_i of y.

Recall that we consider a fixed natural ordering $y_1, \ldots, y_n$ of the occurrences of y in w. For $1 \leq i \leq n$, let α_i (resp. β_i) be the number of occurrences of x (resp. z) strictly to the left (resp. right) of y_i. Consequently, we have

$$|w|_{xy} = \sum_{i=1}^{n} \alpha_i, \quad |w|_{yz} = \sum_{i=1}^{n} \beta_i, \quad |w|_{xyz} = \sum_{i=1}^{n} \alpha_i \beta_i.$$

On the other hand, the algebraic identity (valid for any n and real numbers α_i, β_i)

$$\sum_{i=1}^{n} \alpha_i \sum_{i=1}^{n} \beta_i = n \sum_{i=1}^{n} \alpha_i \beta_i + D,$$

where

$$D = \sum_{i,j=1, \ i<j}^{n} (\alpha_j - \alpha_i)(\beta_i - \beta_j),$$

is easy to verify. Thus, if we show that in our case $D \geq 0$, Theorem 1 immediately follows.

Let us go back to our example and choose $x = a$, $z = b$. For the natural order of the occurrences of y already given, the sequence of the α's (resp. β's) is $0, 0, 0, 1, 1, 1, 2$ (resp. $1, 0, 0, 1, 0, 0, 0$). The sum D has negative terms (resulting from $i = 2, 3$ and $j = 4$) but assumes the positive value 3.

If $|y| = 1$, then for $i < j$ we have always $\alpha_i \leq \alpha_j$ and $\beta_i \geq \beta_j$, implying that $D \geq 0$. From now on we *assume that* $|y| \geq 2$.

We next combine the types with the same μ, as well as those with the same ν. Specifically, we define the *left class*

$$L_\mu = \bigcup_{\nu=1}^{l} T(\mu, \nu), \ 1 \leq \mu \leq k,$$

and the *right class*

$$R_\nu = \bigcup_{\mu=1}^{k} T(\mu, \nu), \ 1 \leq \nu \leq l.$$

The next lemma is an immediate consequence of the following facts. The number of occurrences of x strictly to the left of a given occurrence y_i depends only on the position of the first letter of y_i. Moreover, this number increases or stays the same if the position of the first letter moves to the right. The analogous fact holds true for the number of occurrences of z strictly to the right of y_i.

Lemma 1 *Assume that $1 \leq \mu < \mu' \leq k$ and $1 \leq \nu < \nu' \leq l$. If the occurrences y_i and y_j belong to L_μ (resp. R_ν), then $\alpha_i = \alpha_j$ (resp. $\beta_i = \beta_j$). If y_i belongs to L_μ (resp. R_ν) and y_j belongs to $L_{\mu'}$ (resp. $R_{\nu'}$), then $\alpha_i \leq \alpha_j$ (resp. $\beta_i \geq \beta_j$).*

Our next lemma gives a "dual" of the Cauchy inequality, interesting also on its own right.

Lemma 2 *For all words P, Q, R, W,*

$$|PQR|_W |Q|_W \leq |PQ|_W |QR|_W.$$

Proof. We use the notation W_U for an occurrence of W as a subword of U. The idea is to map each pair (W_Q, W_{PQR}) to a pair (W_{PQ}, W_{QR}) and show that this mapping is injective.

Let (W_Q, W_{PQR}) be a given pair. We may assume that the occurrence W_{PQR} actually extends to both P- and R-parts of the word PQR because, otherwise, the given pair can be mapped either to itself or to the pair obtained by interchanging the two components. Let $|W| = r \geq 1$. As usual, we write occurrences of W as r-dimensional vectors with strictly increasing components. Assume that

$$W_{PQR} = (i_1, \ldots, i_p, i_{p+1}, \ldots, i_{p+q}, i_{p+q+1}, \ldots, i_r),$$

where $p \geq 1$, $q \geq 0$, $i_p \leq |P|$, $i_{p+1} > |P|$, $i_{p+q} \leq |PQ|$, $i_{p+q+1} > |PQ|$. Following this representation and the numbering of letters in PQR, we write W_Q in the form

$$W_Q = (j_1, \ldots, j_p, j_{p+1}, \ldots, j_{p+q}, j_{p+q+1}, \ldots, j_r),$$

where all components are greater than $|P|$ but less than or equal to $|PQ|$. Thus, for every ν, $1 \leq \nu \leq r$, the i_νth letter of PQR equals the j_νth letter of PQR.

For $1 \leq \nu \leq q$, denote

$$\gamma_{p+\nu} = \min(i_{p+\nu}, j_{p+\nu}), \quad \delta_{p+\nu} = \max(i_{p+\nu}, j_{p+\nu}).$$

We now construct the required pair (W_{PQ}, W_{QR}) by

$$W_{PQ} = (i_1, \ldots, i_p, \gamma_{p+1}, \ldots, \gamma_{p+q}, j_{p+q+1}, \ldots, j_r),$$
$$W_{QR} = (j_1, \ldots, j_p, \delta_{p+1}, \ldots, \delta_{p+q}, i_{p+q+1}, \ldots, i_r).$$

Clearly, W_{PQ} (resp. W_{QR}) is an occurrence of W in PQ (resp. QR). Moreover, by the definition of $\gamma_{p+\nu}$ and $\delta_{p+\nu}$, if one component changes in W_Q or W_{PQR}, then one component will change in W_{PQ} or W_{QR}. Thus, the association is injective, and Lemma 2 follows.

Lemma 1 can now be strengthened to the following result, which will be a central tool in our final argument.

Lemma 3 *Assume that* $1 \leq \mu < \mu' \leq k$ *and* $1 \leq \nu < \nu' \leq l$. *Then*

$$\begin{vmatrix} \#T(\mu,\nu) & \#T(\mu,\nu') \\ \#T(\mu',\nu) & \#T(\mu',\nu') \end{vmatrix} \geq 0.$$

Proof. Since $|y| \geq 2$, we may write $y = a\overline{y}b$, where a and b are letters, possibly $a = b$. Moreover, we may assume that both occurrences of a corresponding to μ, μ' precede in w the occurrences of b corresponding to ν, ν':

$$w = \dots aw_1aw_2bw_3b \dots$$

(If the first b is to the left of the second a, we have $\#T(\mu',\nu) = 0$, and the lemma follows immediately.)

We have now

$$\#T(\mu,\nu) = |w_1aw_2|_{\overline{y}}, \ \#T(\mu,\nu') = |w_1aw_2bw_3|_{\overline{y}},$$
$$\#T(\mu',\nu) = |w_2|_{\overline{y}}, \ \#T(\mu',\nu') = |w_2bw_3|_{\overline{y}}.$$

Denoting

$$w_1a = P, \ w_2 = Q, \ bw_3 = R, \ \overline{y} = W,$$

Lemma 3 now immediately follows by Lemma 2.

We are now ready for the final argument in the proof of Theorem 1. It consists of partitioning the sum D. For $1 \leq \mu < \mu' \leq k$, we first consider the sum

$$D(\mu,\mu') = \sum_{y_i \in L_\mu, \ y_j \in L_{\mu'}} (\alpha_j - \alpha_i)(\beta_i - \beta_j).$$

We obtain

$$D = \sum_{\mu,\mu'=1, \ \mu<\mu'}^{k} D(\mu,\mu').$$

Indeed, in D we may assume that i and j come from *different* sets L_μ because, otherwise, $\alpha_j - \alpha_i = 0$.

Consider a fixed sum

$$D(\mu,\mu'), \ 1 \leq \mu < \mu' \leq k.$$

All terms in it contain the nonnegative number $\overline{\alpha_{\mu'}} - \overline{\alpha_\mu}$ as a factor. We partition the sum $D(\mu,\mu')$ further by considering subsums

$$D_1(\nu,\nu') = \sum (\alpha_j - \alpha_i)(\beta_i - \beta_j), \ 1 \leq \nu < \nu' \leq l,$$

with $(y_i \in L_\mu \cap R_\nu$ and $y_j \in L_{\mu'} \cap R_{\nu'})$ or $(y_i \in L_\mu \cap R_{\nu'}$ and $y_j \in L_{\mu'} \cap R_\nu)$. We already pointed out that here $\alpha_j - \alpha_i$ is always the nonnegative number $\overline{\alpha_{\mu'}} - \overline{\alpha_\mu}$. Among the differences $\beta_i - \beta_j$,

$$\#T(\mu,\nu) \cdot \#T(\mu',\nu')$$

are equal to the nonnegative number $\overline{\beta_\nu} - \overline{\beta_{\nu'}}$, whereas

$$\#T(\mu',\nu) \cdot \#T(\mu,\nu')$$

of them are equal to $\overline{\beta_{\nu'}} - \overline{\beta_\nu}$. Hence, by Lemma 3, $D_1(\nu,\nu') \geq 0$. This implies that all sums $D(\mu,\mu')$ are nonnegative, whence $D \geq 0$. Theorem 1 follows.

4 A Proof Using Parikh Matrices

We will now present another, entirely different, proof of Theorem 1. The proof is based on *Parikh matrices*, a generalization of Parikh vectors, [7]. Parikh matrices have turned out to be very useful in several considerations dealing with words, [4,5,6]. An extension of the original notion important for the general Cauchy inequality is due to [10].

We will not give here any survey of the theory of Parikh matrices and its various applications. Rather, the subsequent exposition is tailor-made for the proof of Theorem 1. This means that we pick up only those aspects of the theory that are relevant for the proof.

We now define the notion of a *Parikh matrix mapping*. The mapping uses upper triangular square matrices, with nonnegative integer entries, 1's on the main diagonal and 0's below it. Let us denote the set of all such matrices by $\mathcal{M}$, and the subset of all matrices of dimension $k \geq 1$ by $\mathcal{M}_k$.

Recall that, for letters a and b,

$$\delta_{a,b} = \begin{cases} 1 & \text{if } a = b, \\ 0 & \text{if } a \neq b, \end{cases}$$

We are now ready to introduce the notion of a *Parikh matrix mapping*.

Definition 1 *Let $u = b_1 \ldots b_k$ be a word, where each b_i, $1 \leq i \leq k$, is a letter of the alphabet Σ. The* Parikh *matrix mapping with respect to u, denoted Ψ_u, is the morphism:*

$$\Psi_u : \Sigma^* \to \mathcal{M}_{k+1},$$

defined, for $a \in \Sigma$, by the condition: if $\Psi_u(a) = M_u(a) = (m_{i,j})_{1 \leq i,j \leq (k+1)}$, then for each $1 \leq i \leq (k+1)$, $m_{i,i} = 1$, and for each $1 \leq i \leq k$, $m_{i,i+1} = \delta_{a,b_i}$, all other elements of the matrix $M_u(a)$ being 0. Matrices of the form $\Psi_u(w)$, $w \in \Sigma^*$, are referred to as Parikh *matrices.*

Thus, the Parikh matrix $M_u(w)$ associated to a word w is obtained by multiplying the matrices $M_u(a)$ associated to the letters a of w, in the order in which the letters appear in w. The above definition implies that if a letter a does not occur in u, then the matrix $M_u(a)$ is the identity matrix.

For instance, if $u = baca$, then

$$M_u(a) = \begin{pmatrix} 1&0&0&0&0 \\ 0&1&1&0&0 \\ 0&0&1&0&0 \\ 0&0&0&1&1 \\ 0&0&0&0&1 \end{pmatrix}.$$

Similarly,

$$M_u(b) = \begin{pmatrix} 1&1&0&0&0 \\ 0&1&0&0&0 \\ 0&0&1&0&0 \\ 0&0&0&1&0 \\ 0&0&0&0&1 \end{pmatrix}, \; M_u(c) = \begin{pmatrix} 1&0&0&0&0 \\ 0&1&0&0&0 \\ 0&0&1&1&0 \\ 0&0&0&1&0 \\ 0&0&0&0&1 \end{pmatrix}.$$

In the original definition of a Parikh matrix, [4], the word u was chosen to be $u = a_1 \ldots a_k$, for the alphabet $\Sigma = \{a_1, \ldots, a_k\}$. The extension to a general u is due to [10]. If we follow the original definition and consider the word

$$w_k = a_1(a_2 a_1 a_2)(a_3 a_2 a_3)(a_4 a_3 a_4) \ldots (a_k a_{k-1} a_k),$$

the entries of the Parikh matrix constitute the Fibonacci sequence. For $k = 6$ we get the matrix

$$M_{a_1 \ldots a_6}(w_6) = \begin{pmatrix} 1&2&5&13&34&89&144 \\ 0&1&3&8&21&55&89 \\ 0&0&1&3&8&21&34 \\ 0&0&0&1&3&8&13 \\ 0&0&0&0&1&3&5 \\ 0&0&0&0&0&1&2 \\ 0&0&0&0&0&0&1 \end{pmatrix}.$$

This example already gives a hint to the following lemma. For $u = b_1 \ldots b_k$ and $1 \leq j \leq k$, we denote $U_j = b_1 \ldots b_j$. We fix a word w, and denote by $m_{i,j}$ the (i,j)th entry of the matrix $M_u(w)$, $1 \leq i, j \leq k+1$.

Lemma 4 *For every j, $1 \leq j \leq k$, we have $m_{1,1+j} = |w|_{U_j}$.*

Proof. Clearly the assertion holds if w is a letter. Assume, inductively, that it holds for a word w'. Denote by $m'_{i,j}$ the entries of the matrix $M_u(w')$. Consider a word

$$w = w'a, \quad a \in \Sigma.$$

Then $M_u(w) = M_u(w')M_u(a)$. Consider now an arbitrary j, $1 \le j \le k$, and the entry $m_{1,1+j}$ in the matrix $M_u(w)$. We separate two cases.

Case 1. a is not the letter in the jth position in u. Then clearly $|w|_{U_j} = |w'|_{U_j}$. By the definition of $M_u(a)$ and by the rule of matrix multiplication, $m_{1,1+j} = m'_{1,1+j}$. By the inductive hypothesis $|w'|_{U_j} = m'_{1,1+j}$, the claim

$$m_{1,1+j} = |w|_{U_j}$$

now follows.

Case 2. a is the jth letter in u. Thus, $U_j = U_{j-1}a$. Now

$$|w|_{U_j} = |w'|_{U_j} + |w'|_{U_{j-1}}.$$

By the inductive hypothesis,

$$|w'|_{U_j} = m'_{1,1+j}, \quad |w'|_{U_{j-1}} = m'_{1,j},$$

and by the rule of matrix multiplication,

$$m_{1,1+j} = m'_{1,1+j} + m'_{1,j}.$$

Consequently, the claim follows also in this case, which proves the lemma.

Going back to our example $u = baca$, we infer that, for any word w,

$$M_u(w) = \begin{pmatrix} 1 & |w|_b & |w|_{ba} & |w|_{bac} & |w|_{baca} \\ 0 & 1 & |w|_a & |w|_{ac} & |w|_{aca} \\ 0 & 0 & 1 & |w|_c & |w|_{ca} \\ 0 & 0 & 0 & 1 & |w|_a \\ 0 & 0 & 0 & 0 & 1 \end{pmatrix}.$$

For $w = a^3c^3bac^2ac$ we get

$$M_u(w) = \begin{pmatrix} 1 & 1 & 2 & 4 & 2 \\ 0 & 1 & 5 & 22 & 26 \\ 0 & 0 & 1 & 6 & 8 \\ 0 & 0 & 0 & 1 & 5 \\ 0 & 0 & 0 & 0 & 1 \end{pmatrix}.$$

For $1 \le i \le j \le k$, denote $U_{i,j} = b_i \ldots b_j$. As before, denote the entries of the matrix $M_u(w)$ by $m_{i,j}$. Lemma 4 is easily extended to the following form. (A very direct way to prove this is to ignore the prefix of length $i - 1$ from u.)

Lemma 5 *For all i and j, we have $m_{i,1+j} = |w|_{U_{i,j}}$.*

Lemma 6 *The value of any 2-dimensional minor of the matrix $M_u(w)$ is a nonnegative integer.*

Proof. The assertion holds if w is a letter. In this case there is no minor, where the upper right and lower left entries are both nonzero. Consequently, 0 and 1 are the only possible values for the minor.

Assume inductively that the assertion holds for the word w', and consider the word $w = w'a$, where a is a letter. Let D be the 2-dimensional minor of $M_u(w)$ determined by the four entries

$$m_{i_\mu, j_\nu}, \ 1 \le \mu, \nu \le 2, \ 1 \le i_1 < i_2 \le k+1, \ 1 \le j_1 < j_2 \le k+1.$$

Consider the second column (corresponding to j_2) in D. Its entries are

$$\text{either } m'_{i_\mu, j_2} \text{ or } m'_{i_\mu, j_2} + m'_{i_\mu, j_2-1}, \ \mu = 1, 2,$$

depending whether a is not or is the j_2th letter in u. The same conclusion holds for the first column (corresponding to j_1) in D. This means that D is the sum of at most four determinants, each of which is either a minor of $M_u(w')$ or consists of two identical columns. The assertion now follows by the inductive hypothesis.

We are now in the position to prove Theorem 1. Consider arbitrary w, x, y, z and denote $u = xyz$. Then

$$\begin{vmatrix} |w|_{xy} & |w|_{xyz} \\ |w|_y & |w|_{yz} \end{vmatrix}$$

appears as a minor in the Parikh matrix $M_u(w)$, whence Theorem 1 follows by Lemma 6.

5 A More General Form of the Cauchy Inequality

In the preceding section the Cauchy inequality was established by considering specific 2-dimensional minors of the Parikh matrix. The considerations can be extended to concern arbitrary minors, which leads to the following result.

Theorem 2 *Let $k \geq 1$ and let w, $x_1, \ldots, x_k$ be arbitrary words. Further, let D be an arbitrary minor of the matrix*

$$\begin{pmatrix} 1 & |w|_{x_1} & |w|_{x_1 x_2} & \cdots & |w|_{x_1 \ldots x_k} \\ 0 & 1 & |w|_{x_2} & \cdots & |w|_{x_2 \ldots x_k} \\ & \vdots & & \vdots & \\ & \vdots & & \vdots & |w|_{x_k} \\ 0 & \cdots & & \cdots 0 & 1 \end{pmatrix}.$$

Then $D \geq 0$.

For instance, the subsequent inequalities are obtained by Theorem 2. A suitable combination of the inequalities gives (partial) results about the cases when the Cauchy inequality is strict.

$$|w|_{xy} \leq |w|_x |w|_y,$$

$$|w|_y |w|_{xyz} \leq |w|_{xy} |w|_{yz} \text{ (Cauchy!)},$$

$$|w|_{y_1} \cdots |w|_{y_n} |w|_{xy_1 \ldots y_n z} \leq |w|_{xy_1} |w|_{y_1 y_2} \cdots |w|_{y_n z},$$

$$|w|_x |w|_{yz} + |w|_{xy} |w|_z \leq |w|_{xyz} + |w|_x |w|_y |w|_z,$$

$$|w|_x |w|_y |w|_{zu} + |w|_x |w|_{yz} |w|_u + |w|_{xy} |w|_z |w|_u + |w|_{xyzu}$$
$$\leq |w|_x |w|_{yzu} + |w|_{xy} |w|_{zu} + |w|_{xyz} |w|_u + |w|_x |w|_y |w|_z |w|_u,$$

$$|w|_{yz} |w|_{xyzu} + |w|_{xy} |w|_z |w|_{yzu} + |w|_y |w|_{xyz} |w|_{zu}$$
$$\leq |w|_{xy} |w|_{yz} |w|_{zu} + |w|_y |w|_z |w|_{xyzu} + |w|_{xyz} |w|_{yzu}.$$

References

1. Berstel, J. and Karhumäki, J., Combinatorics on words — a tutorial. *EATCS Bulletin*, 79 (2003), 178–228.
2. Kuich, W. and Salomaa, A. *Semirings, Automata, Languages.* Springer-Verlag, Berlin, Heidelberg, New York, 1986.
3. Maňuch, J., Characterization of a word by its subwords. In G. Rozenberg and W. Thomas (eds.) *Developments in Language Theory*, World Scientific Publ. Co., 2000, 210–219.
4. Mateescu, A., Salomaa, A., Salomaa, K., and Yu, S., A sharpening of the Parikh mapping. *Theoret. Informatics Appl.*, 35 (2001), 551–564.
5. Mateescu, A., Salomaa, A., and Yu, S., Subword histories and Parikh matrices. *J. Comput. Syst. Sci.*, to appear.

6. Mateescu, A. and Salomaa, A., Matrix indicators for subword occurrences and ambiguity. *TUCS Technical Report* 536 (2003), submitted for publication.

7. Parikh, R.J., On context-free languages. *J. Assoc. Comput. Mach.*, 13 (1966), 570–581.

8. Rozenberg, G. and Salomaa, A. (eds.), *Handbook of Formal Languages 1–3*. Springer-Verlag, Berlin, Heidelberg, New York, 1997 .

9. Sakarovitch, J. and Simon, I., Subwords. In M. Lothaire: *Combinatorics on Words*, Addison-Wesley, Reading, Mass., 1983, 105–142.

10. Şerbănuţă, T.-F., Extending Parikh matrices. *Theoretical Computer Science*, to appear.

POST CORRESPONDENCE PROBLEM – RECENT RESULTS

VESA HALAVA,   TERO HARJU

TUCS - Turku Centre for Computer Science
and
Department of Mathematics
University of Turku
FIN-20014 Turku, Finland
E-mail: $\{vehalava, harju\}$@*utu.fi*

1 Introduction

1.1 The Post Correspondence Problem

Let B be a finite alphabet. We denote by B^* the word monoid over B, where the *empty word* ε is the identity element. Moreover, let $B^+ = B^* \setminus \{\varepsilon\}$.

In an instance of the *Post Correspondence Problem* (or *PCP*, for short), we are given a set of n pairs of words,

$$\{(u_i, v_i) \mid u_i, v_i \in B^*, \ i = 1, \ldots, n\},$$

and it is asked to determine whether there exists a nonempty sequence $i_1, \ldots, i_k$ of indices, where $i_j \in \{1, \ldots, n\}$ for $1 \leq j \leq k$, such that

$$u_{i_1} u_{i_2} \cdots u_{i_k} = v_{i_1} v_{i_2} \cdots v_{i_k}.$$

In this general form the PCP was proved to be undecidable by Post [12].

The PCP can be redefined using morphisms $h, g \colon A^* \to B^*$, where $A = \{a_1, \ldots a_n\}$ is an alphabet of n letters and $h(a_i) = u_i$ and $g(a_i) = v_i$ for each i. Now in the PCP it is required to determine whether there exists a nonempty word $w \in A^+$ such that $h(w) = g(w)$. Such a word w is called a *solution* of the *instance* (h, g) of the PCP. The *size* of an instance is the number of letters in the domain alphabet, $n = |A|$. The set of all solutions of the instance (h, g) is denoted by

$$\mathrm{E}(h, g) = \{w \in A^* \mid h(w) = g(w)\},$$

and it is called the *equality set* of (h, g). Note that $\varepsilon \in \mathrm{E}(h, g)$.

The PCP offers many interesting questions related to undecidability, but there are also more concrete computational puzzles involved. One such problem is the hardness of simple instances. Small instances of the PCP, where the size of the domain alphabet and the lengths of the images of the morphisms

are bounded by small numbers, have been studied by various authors, see the web page "PCP@Home",
http://www.informatik.uni-leipzig.de/~pcp/pcpcontest_en.html
Example 1. The following appealing instance was independently found by J. Waldmann and by R. J. Lorentz, see the above web page for this and other interesting instances.

Let $A = \{0, 1, 2\}$, $B = \{0, 1\}$, and define $h, g: A^* \to B^*$ by

$$h(0) = 0, \quad h(1) = 1, \quad h(2) = 011,$$
$$g(0) = 1, \quad g(1) = 011, \quad g(2) = 0.$$

Despite of its simple form, the length of the smallest solution to the instance (h, g) is quite large, namely 75. This example is interesting also because in it one morphism is permuted to obtain the other one, that is, $g = h\pi$, where $\pi: A \to A$ is a permutation; see Theorem 1 for a general result of permuted instances. □

1.2 On the Edge of Undecidability

The PCP is undecidable in the general case and it is one of the most important undecidable problems, since it is very useful in proving other undecidability results. For a more extensive and general treatment of undecidability, we refer to Rozenberg and Salomaa [13].

By restricting the PCP we can investigate the borderline between decidability and undecidability. In the restricted cases some further assumptions are posed on the morphisms. For example, if we assume that the size of an instance is two, i.e., the domain alphabet A is binary, then the PCP is decidable, see Ehrenfeucht, Karhumäki and Rozenberg [1] (or [5] for a somewhat shorter proof). Note also that for the size $n = 1$ the PCP is trivially decidable. On the other hand, if $n \geq 7$, then the problem is already undecidable, see [11]. The decidability status is open for the instance sizes $3 \leq n \leq 6$. Therefore with respect to the size of the domain alphabet, the border between decidability and undecidability lies somewhere between three and six.

To get a feeling of the decision problems concerning morphisms, we now show that the PCP remains undecidable for the instances (h, g), where the second morphism is a permutation of the first one.

Theorem 1. *The PCP is undecidable for instances $(h, h\pi)$, where $h: A^* \to B^*$ is a morphism and $\pi: A \to A$ is a permutation.*

Proof. Let $h, g: A^* \to B^*$ be any two morphisms, where the domain alphabet is $A = \{a_0, a_1, \ldots, a_{n+1}\}$. It is well-known (see [13]) that it is undecidable whether such an instance (h, g) has a solution of the form $w \in a_0(A \setminus \{a_0, a_{n+1}\})^* a_{n+1}$. (This is known as the *modified PCP*.)

Let $\overline{A} = \{\overline{a}_0, \overline{a}_1, \ldots, \overline{a}_{n+1}\}$ with $\overline{A} \cap A = \emptyset$, and let a, b, d be new letters. Define the desynchronizing morphisms $\mu, \eta \colon B^* \to (B \cup \{d\})^*$ by $\mu(x) = dx$ and $\eta(x) = xd$ for all $x \in B$. Now let $h' \colon (A \cup \overline{A})^* \to (B \cup \{a, b, d\})^*$ be defined by

$$h'(a_0) = a \cdot \mu h(a_0), \qquad h'(\overline{a}_0) = ad \cdot \eta g(a_0),$$
$$h'(a_i) = \mu h(a_i), \qquad h'(\overline{a}_i) = \eta g(a_i) \text{ for } i = 1, 2, \ldots, n,$$
$$h'(a_{n+1}) = \mu h(a_{n+1}) \cdot db, \quad h'(\overline{a}_{n+1}) = \eta g(a_{n+1}) \cdot b.$$

Consider the permutation π of $A \cup \overline{A}$ given by $\pi(a_i) = \overline{a}_i$ and $\pi(\overline{a}_i) = a_i$. It is straightforward to show that the instance $(h', h'\pi)$ has a solution if and only if the instance (h, g) of the modified PCP has a solution. Indeed, the solutions of the instance $(h', h'\pi)$ are necessarily in the set

$$\left(a_0(A \setminus \{a_0, a_{n+1}\})^* a_{n+1} \cup \overline{a}_0(\overline{A} \setminus \{\overline{a}_0, \overline{a}_{n+1}\})^* \overline{a}_{n+1}\right)^*,$$

because of the marker letters a and b, and because of the desynchronizing property of μ and η. Consequently, the solutions of minimal length are in $a_0(A \setminus \{a_0, a_{n+1}\})^* a_{n+1}$ or in $\overline{a}_0(\overline{A} \setminus \{\overline{a}_0, \overline{a}_{n+1}\})^* \overline{a}_{n+1}$.

Clearly, a word $\overline{w} \in \overline{a}_0(\overline{A} \setminus \{\overline{a}_0, \overline{a}_{n+1}\})^* \overline{a}_{n+1}$ is a solution to $(h', h'\pi)$ if and only if $w = \pi(\overline{w}) \in a_0(A \setminus \{a_0, a_{n+1}\})^* a_{n+1}$ is a solution, where w is obtained from $\overline{w}$ by removing the bars from the letters. In the case $w = a_0 v a_{n+1}$ with $v \in (A \setminus \{a_0, a_{n+1}\})^*$,

$$h'(w) = a \cdot \mu h(w) \cdot db,$$
$$h'\pi(w) = ad \cdot \eta g(w) \cdot b = a \cdot \mu g(w) db,$$

and therefore $h'(w) = h'\pi(w)$ if and only if $h(w) = g(w)$, since μ is injective. This proves the claim. $\qquad\square$

By Lecerf [10], the PCP is undecidable for injective instances, that is, for instances (h, g), where both h and g are injective morphisms. This result was improved to biprefix morphisms by Ruohonen [14]. We shall mainly consider in the following sections the case, where the morphisms h and g are marked. A morphism is said to be *marked* if $h(x)$ and $h(y)$ start with a different letter whenever $x, y \in A$ and $x \neq y$. If the morphisms are marked then we call the instance of the PCP *marked*. Note that every marked morphism is injective. Halava, Hirvensalo and de Wolf [7] proved that the marked PCP is decidable for all alphabet sizes. We shall consider this proof in Section 2. Complete proofs for the most of the result can be found also from [2].

1.3 The Generalized PCP

We can also modify the problem itself. Here we shall consider a particular modification called the *generalized* PCP (*GPCP*, for short). An instance of the GPCP consists of two morphisms $h, g \colon A^* \to B^*$ and four words $p_1, p_2, s_1, s_2 \in B^*$. The problem is to determine whether or not there exists a word $w \in A^*$ such that (see Figure 1)

$$p_1 h(w) s_1 = p_2 g(w) s_2.$$

The word w is again called a *solution* of the instance $((p_1, p_2), h, g, (s_1, s_2))$ of the GPCP. It is clear that in general the GPCP is undecidable, since it is a generalization of the PCP.

p_1	$h(w)$	s_1
p_2	$g(w)$	s_2

Figure 1. A solution w of an instance of the GPCP

In the *marked* GPCP we assume that the morphisms h and g are marked. The motivation for studying the marked PCP and the marked GPCP originates from [1], where Ehrenfeucht, Karhumäki and Rozenberg proved that the binary PCP is decidable. They actually proved that every instance of the binary PCP is either periodic or it can be reduced to an equivalent instance of the marked GPCP with binary alphabet and then showed by case analysis that the binary marked GPCP is decidable.

It was proved by Halava, Harju and Hirvensalo [4] that the marked GPCP is decidable in the general setting, that is, regardless of the size of the domain alphabet. Although the proof uses the same basic idea as [7], the technical parts involved in the generalization turned out be considerably harder than for the marked PCP. The ideas behind this proof are briefly considered in Section 3.

1.4 Infinite PCP

We shall also consider a modification of the PCP to the infinite solutions. Let (h, g) be an instance of the PCP, where $h, g \colon A^* \to B^*$. Let $\omega = a_1 a_2 \ldots$ be an infinite word over A where $a_i \in A$ for each index i. Two (finite) words u and v are *comparable*, denoted by $u \bowtie v$, if one is a prefix of the other. We write $h(\omega) = g(\omega)$ if the morphisms h and g *agree* on ω, that is, if $g(u) \bowtie h(u)$ for all finite prefixes u of ω. We also say that such an infinite word ω is an *infinite solution* of the instance (h, g). It was shown by Ruohonen [14] that there is no algorithm to determine whether a general instance of the PCP has an infinite solution.

Theorem 2. *It is undecidable for instances $I = (h, g)$ of the PCP whether I has an infinite solution. Indeed, the infinite PCP is undecidable for instances where the morphisms are biprefix.*

In this paper we shall consider the decidability proof of the marked infinite PCP and we also study the decidability of the binary infinite PCP.

2   Marked PCP

2.1   Blocks

Let us first fix some notations. A word $x \in A^*$ is said to be a *prefix* of a word $y \in A^*$, if there is $z \in A^*$ such that $y = xz$. This will be denoted by $x \leq y$. Recall that x and y are *comparable* if $x \leq y$ or $y \leq x$, and it is denoted by $u \bowtie v$. We shall denote the longest common prefix of words x and y by $x \wedge y$. A word $x \in A^*$ is said to be a *suffix* of $y \in A^*$, if there is $z \in A^*$ such that $y = zx$. This will be denoted by $x \preccurlyeq y$. Moreover, x is a *proper* suffix of y, if $x \neq \varepsilon$ and $x \neq y$, denoted by $x \prec y$.

Let (h, g), where $h, g \colon A^* \to B^*$, be an instance of the marked PCP. First, we try to find the solutions of the equations

$$h(x) = g(y) \quad \text{with } a \leq h(x),\ a \leq g(y), \tag{1}$$

where the images begin with a fixed letter $a \in B$. There is an obvious method to search for a solution (if a solution exists). We define a sequence $(x_i, y_i) \in A^* \times A^*$ as follows: First, look for the letters $b, c \in A$ such that $a \leq h(b)$ and $a \leq g(c)$. These letters are unique if they exist, since the morphisms are marked. Set $(x_1, y_1) = (b, c)$. If a solution of the required type exists, then necessarily $h(x_i)$ and $g(y_i)$ are comparable, i.e., there exists a word $s \in B^*$ such that $h(x_i)s = g(y_i)$ (resp. $g(y_i)s = h(x_i)$). We shall call the word s an *overflow of h* (resp., of g).

If $s = \varepsilon$, then we, of course, terminate the process. Otherwise, there is at most one letter $x' \in A$ (resp. $y' \in A$) such that s and $h(x')$ (resp. $g(y')$) are comparable, since h (resp. g) is marked. Define $x_{i+1} = x_i x'$ and $y_{i+1} = y_i$ (resp. $x_{i+1} = x_i$ and $y_{i+1} = y_i y'$). We continue constructing the sequence (x_i, y_i) until we reach one of the following three cases:

(i) There is no suitable x' or y' or $h(x_i)$ and $g(y_i)$ are not comparable.

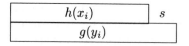

Figure 2. An overflow s of h

(ii) We have the same overflow s of h (resp. g) twice.

(iii) The overflow equals $s = \varepsilon$.

Since the morphisms are marked and there are only finitely many different possible overflows, we shall eventually end in the case (ii) if not the others. Since the construction of the sequence (x_i, y_i) is deterministic, the case (ii) implies that the overflows start to cycle and if we continue the process, we can never reach the cases (i) or (iii). Therefore in the case (ii), $h(x_i)$ and $g(y_i)$ are comparable for all $i \geq 1$, and the overflow is always nonempty. Clearly, in this case, there cannot exist any solutions to (1).

It is clear that if (1) has a solution, we have to terminate in the case (iii), say with (x_j, y_j). Then $h(x_j) = g(y_j)$ and there can be a solution of the instance (h, g) beginning with a only if x_j and y_j are comparable. Assume that this is the case. If $x_j = y_j$, then x_j is a solution. Otherwise, assume that $x_j = y_j z$ (resp. $y_j = x_j z$), where $d \leq z$ and $d \in A$. Then we can define $(x_{j+1}, y_{j+1}) = (x_j, y_j d)$ (resp. $(x_{j+1}, y_{j+1}) = (x_j d, y_j)$) and continue the construction of the sequence (x_i, y_i). If there is a solution of (h, g) beginning with the letter a, then we shall meet the case (iii) repeatedly until at some point $x_i = y_i$. The problem here is that we do not know when to stop if there is no solution.

Consider the sequence (x_i, y_i) up to the first case that terminates in one of the three cases. If the sequence terminates to (x_j, y_j) in the case (iii), then (x_j, y_j) is a minimal solution of the equation (1), and we call the pair (x_j, y_j) a *block* (*for the letter* a).

Assume that w is a solution of the instance (h, g). Then there exists a unique *block decomposition* of w,

$$w = u_1 u_2 \cdots u_k = v_1 v_2 \cdots v_k, \tag{2}$$

where (u_i, v_i) is a block (for some letter a_i) for all $i = 1, \ldots, k$. This means that each solution is a concatenation of blocks.

$h(w)$	$h(u_1)$	$h(u_2)$	$\cdots$	$h(u_k)$
$g(w)$	$g(v_1)$	$g(v_2)$	$\cdots$	$g(v_k)$

Figure 3. Block decomposition of a solution w

2.2 Successors

By using the blocks, we shall define for an instance (h, g) its *successor* (h', g') as follows. Let

$$A' = \{a \mid (u, v) \text{ is a block for } a \in A\}.$$

We define the morphisms $h', g' : (A')^* \to A^*$ by

$$h'(a) = u \quad \text{and} \quad g'(a) = v,$$

where (u, v) is a block for the letter a. Note that these new morphisms are marked, by the definition of a block, and therefore the successor (h', g') is an instance of the marked PCP. We have thus defined a new instance (h', g') of the marked PCP. We shall next prove that an instance and its successor are equivalent.

Lemma 3. *The instance $I = (h, g)$ of the marked PCP has a solution if and only if its successor $I' = (h', g')$ has a solution. Moreover, if w' is a solution of I', then $w = h'(w') = g'(w')$ is a solution of I.*

Proof. Assume first that I has a solution $w = u_1 \cdots u_k = v_1 \cdots v_k$, where (u_i, v_i) is block for a letter $a_i \in A'$, $1 \le i \le k$. By the definition of (h', g'),

$$h'(a_1 \cdots a_k) = u_1 \cdots u_k = w = v_1 \cdots v_k = g'(a_1 \cdots a_k),$$

and so $a_1 \cdots a_k$ is a solution of I'.

Assume then that $w' = a_1 \cdots a_k$ is a solution of I' and that, for $1 \le i \le k$, (u_i, v_i) is a block for a_i. Then

$$h(h'(w')) = h(u_1 \cdots u_k) = g(v_1 \cdots v_k) = g(g'(w')),$$

since $h(u_i) = g(v_i)$ for $1 \le i \le k$ by the definition of a block. This also proves the second part of the claim. $\square$

Note that, by the proof of Lemma 3, there is a one-to-one correspondence on the solutions between I and I'.

2.3 Suffix Complexity

We have defined an equivalent instance I' of the instance I of the marked PCP. Next we shall prove that I' is simpler than the original instance I, and then we recursively use the construction of a successor until we obtain an instance, where the existence of a solution can be checked. We use two measures for the hardness of an instance. The first measure is the size of the domain alphabet. It is straightforward to see that $|A'| \leq |A|$, since at most $|A|$ letters can begin an image and thus be a block letter.

In the second measure, called the *suffix complexity*, we count the nontrivial suffixes of the images $h(a)$ and $g(a)$. For this, define for each morphism h,

$$\sigma(h) = \left| \bigcup_{a \in A} \{x \mid x \prec h(a)\} \right|,$$

and let

$$\sigma(I) = \sigma(h) + \sigma(g).$$

for the instance $I = (h, g)$. The suffix complexity was used in [1], where the following lemma was shown to hold in the binary case. In the general case, the lemma was proven in [7].

Lemma 4. *Let $I = (h, g)$ be an instance of the marked PCP and $I' = (h', g')$ be its successor. Then $\sigma(I') \leq \sigma(I)$*

Proof. For each $s \in \sigma(g')$, there exists at least one block (u, v) such that $s \preccurlyeq v$, $v' = vs^{-1}$ and for some $u' \leq u$, $h(u') = g(v')z$, where $z \in \sigma(h)$. Let $p: \sigma(g') \to \sigma(h)$ be the function, for which $p(s) = z$ has the minimal length in the above. Since the morphisms are marked, the word z is unique and the function p is injective. Symmetrically, we can define an injective function from $\sigma(h')$ to $\sigma(g)$, and the claim follows from these injectivities. $\qquad\Box$

2.4 Decidability of the Marked PCP

Next lemma is obvious.

Lemma 5. *Let ℓ be a positive integer. There exist only finitely many instances $I = (h, g)$ of the marked PCP, where $h, g: A^* \to B^*$ and $\sigma(I) \leq \ell$.*

Let $I_0 = (h, g)$ be an instance of the marked PCP, where $h, g: A_0^* \to B^*$, and let $I_i = (h_i, g_i)$ be the sequence of the successors, where $I_{i+1} = I_i'$. Assume that $h_i, g_i: A_i^* \to A_{i-1}^*$ for all $i \geq 1$. Note that we may assume that $A \subseteq B$, and thus $A_i \subseteq B$ for the domain alphabets for all $i \geq 0$.

Since the alphabet size and the suffix complexity do not increase, we have, by Lemma 5, one of the following three cases:

(i) $|A_j| = 1$ for some $j \geq 0$,

(ii) $\sigma(I_j) = 0$ for some $j \neq 0$,

(iii) The sequence starts to cycle, i.e., there exist n_0 and $d \geq 1$ such that, for all $j \geq n_0$, $I_j = I_{j+d}$.

The instances of the cases (i) and (ii) can be easily checked, and therefore we only need to show that the cycling case (iii) can be decided.

Consider now the cycling case. We may assume that the cycle starts already at I_0, i.e., the sequence is of the form

$$I_0, \ldots, I_{d-1}, I_d = I_0, \ldots . \tag{3}$$

Lemma 6. *It is decidable whether a cycling instance has a solution.*

Proof. Let $I_i = (h_i, g_i)$ be the sequence in (3). By the proof of Lemma 3, for every solution x_i of I_i, there is a solution x_{i+1} of I_{i+1} such that $x_i = h_{i+1}(x_{i+1}) = g_{i+1}(x_{i+1})$. Suppose x_0 is a solution to I_0 of minimal length. Using this reduction inductively, we obtain a solution x_d of I_d such that

$$x_0 = h_1(x_1) = h_1 h_2(x_2) = \ldots = h_1 h_2 \cdots h_d(x_d)$$
$$x_0 = g_1(x_1) = g_1 g_2(x_2) = \ldots = g_1 g_2 \cdots g_d(x_d).$$

Since h_i and g_i are marked, they are not length decreasing, and hence $|x_0| \geq |x_d|$. But x_0 was chosen to be a minimal length solution of I_0, and x_d is also a solution to $I_d = I_0$, and therefore $|x_0| = |x_d|$. This implies that both g_0 and h_0 map the letters occurring in x_d to letters. However, now the first letter of x_d is already a solution of I_0, and hence $|x_0| = |x_d| = 1$. Thus I_0 has a solution if and only if I_0 has a solution in A_0, which can be trivially checked. $\square$

We shall now state the whole algorithm for deciding the marked PCP.

Decision procedure for the marked PCP

(1) Set $c = 0$, $i = 0$, $I_0 = I$.

(2) Set $i = i + 1$, and construct the successor I_i.

(3) If I_i has domain alphabet of size 1 or $\sigma(I_i) = 0$, then check whether I_i has a solution, print the result and terminate.

(4) If I_i is simpler than I_{i-1} (i.e., it has a smaller domain alphabet or $\sigma(I_i) < \sigma(I_{i-1})$), set $c = i$ and goto 2.

(5) If I_i is not simpler than I_{i-1}, then check whether $I_i = I_j$ for some $c \leq j \leq i - 1$. If there is such a j, then check whether there is a 1-letter solution, print the result and terminate; else goto 2.

Actually, Lemma 5 gives us a computable upper bound for the number of different instances (with a fixed alphabet size and suffix complexity), and therefore we could also use a counter to ensure that we enter a loop without doing any comparisons between the instances. The time complexity of the above algorithm is exponential. By using the counter, we obtain an algorithm with polynomial space complexity.

Theorem 7. *The marked PCP is decidable.*

2.5 Nearly Marked Instances

Let $k \geq 1$ be an integer. A morphism $h \colon A^* \to B^*$ is said to be k-*marked*, if for any two different letters $a, b \in A$, the longest common prefix of the images $h(a)$ and $h(b)$ has length at most $k - 1$. Hence a marked morphism is 1–marked.

The following result was proved in [7] using the undecidability of the word problem of Tzeitin's semigroup [15].

Theorem 8. *The PCP is undecidable for the 2–marked morphisms.*

Note that a 2–marked morphism need not be injective. For instance, the morphism $h(a) = a$, $h(b) = ab$, $h(c) = b$ is 2–marked, but $h(b) = ab = h(ac)$. The decidability status of the PCP is open for the *strongly* 2–marked morphisms, meaning that the morphisms are 2–marked and no image is a prefix of another image.

3 Marked Generalized PCP

In this section we consider very briefly the proof of the decidability of the marked generalized PCP from [4].

3.1 Equivalent Instance and End Blocks

Let $I = ((p_1, p_2), h, g, (s_1, s_2))$ be an instance of the marked GPCP, where $h, g \colon A^* \to B^*$ are marked morphisms and $p_i, s_i \in B^*$ for $i = 1, 2$.

We shall first simplify the instance I by removing the prefixes p_1 and p_2 from it. For this, let $\#$ be a new letter not in $A \cup B$. We extend the morphisms by defining $h(\#) = \#p_1$ and $g(\#) = \#p_2$. The original instance is equivalent to the instance $((\varepsilon, \varepsilon), h, g, (s_1, s_2))$, where $h, g \colon (A \cup \#)^* \to (B \cup \#)^*$ are marked and the solutions are from $\#A^*$. We shall denote this new instance by $(\#, h, g, (s_1, s_2))$. It is clear that if the marked GPCP is decidable for these new instances then it is decidable in the original form. Note that we cannot reduce the *end words* (s_1, s_2) in a similar fashion, because the morphisms need to be marked. However, without restriction, we can assume that $s_1 = \varepsilon$ or $s_2 = \varepsilon$, since an existence of a solution for I implies $s_1 \preccurlyeq s_2$ or $s_2 \preccurlyeq s_1$.

A solution of the marked GPCP consists of the blocks of the instance (h, g) for the marked PCP, and the (s_1, s_2)-*end blocks* (u, v), where u and v satisfy the condition $h(u)s_1 = g(v)s_2$ and there does not exists any block (r, t) such that $r \leq u$ and $t \leq v$.

Let $w \in \#A^*$ be a solution of the instance $I = (\#, h, g, (s_1, s_2))$. As in the case of the marked PCP, there is a unique *block decomposition* of w,

$$w = u_1 u_2 \ldots u_{k+1} = v_1 v_2 \ldots v_{k+1},$$

such that (u_i, v_i) is a block for each $i = 1, 2, \ldots, k$ and (u_{k+1}, v_{k+1}) is an (s_1, s_2)-end block.

$h(w)$	$h(u_1)$	$h(u_2)$	$\cdots$	$h(u_k)$	$h(u_{k+1})s_1$
$g(w)$	$g(v_1)$	$g(v_2)$	$\cdots$	$g(v_k)$	$g(v_{k+1})$

Figure 4. Block decomposition of a solution w (for $s_2 = \varepsilon$)

Note that $k = 0$ is also possible in the block decomposition of a solution. In this case the beginning block (the block for $\#$) and the end block coincide. These solutions can be considered as an end block for $\#$.

3.2 Generalized Successors

Let $I = (\#, h, g, (s_1, s_2))$ be an instance of the marked GPCP, (h', g') be the successor of (h, g) and let (u, v) be an (s_1, s_2)-end block. Then

$$I'(u, v) = (\#, h', g', (s_1', s_2'))$$

is a successor of I with respect to (u, v), where

$$(s_1', s_2') = \begin{cases} (\varepsilon, vu^{-1}), & \text{if } u \preccurlyeq v, \\ (uv^{-1}, \varepsilon), & \text{if } v \preccurlyeq u. \end{cases}$$

Note that the successor is defined only for those end blocks for which one of the suffix conditions holds.

The proof of the next lemma is a bit more difficult than the proof of Lemma 3, see [4].

Lemma 9. *The instance* $I = (\#, h, g, (s_1, s_2))$ *of the marked GPCP has a solution if and only if some successor* $I'(u, v) = (\#, h', g', (s_1', s_2'))$ *has a solution. Moreover, if* w' *is a solution of* $I'(u, v)$*, then* $w = h'(w')u = g'(w')v$ *is a solution of* I*.*

3.3 Overview of the Proof

Let $I = (\#, h, g, (s_1, s_2))$ be an instance of the marked GPCP. As for the marked PCP, we reduce I to its successors until we obtain instances, which are easy to check. The difference here is that at each reduction step there can be more than one successor, since there can be many different end blocks. We may think that the successors form a tree, where the morphisms (but not the instances) are equal for all instances at the same depth of the tree.

As in the case of the marked PCP, also here the sequence of the pairs of morphisms is eventually periodic. However, the tree of the instances (carrying the end words (s_i, s_i')) can be infinite. Indeed, although for each letter $a \in (B \cup \#)$ there exists at most one block, there might be several, even infinitely many, end blocks for a. The first important step is to prove that we can manage the infinitude of the end blocks.

It might happen that for a letter a there exists a 5-tuple (x, y, r, s, z) such that, for all $k \geq 0$, $(xr^k z, ys^k)$ (resp. $(xr^k, ys^k z)$) is an (s_1, s_2)-end block. But it can be proved that if there is such a 5-tuple (*extendible end block*), then the size of the domain alphabet will decrease, and in the next reduction step we need to consider only finitely many different successors from the end blocks $(xr^k z, ys^k)$ (resp. $(xr^k, ys^k z)$), $k \geq 0$. Moreover, if we have a new end block from an extendible end block, then the size of the alphabet decreases again. Note that there can be only finitely many extendible end blocks for a letter a.

In particular, if the morphisms cycle (as in the marked PCP), the alphabet size does not decrease, and therefore, in this case, there cannot be extendible end blocks. Since in the beginning of the cycle, there are only finitely many instances, this finiteness property holds throughout the cycle.

Since the cases for the alphabet size 1, and the cases, where the suffix complexity of the morphisms is zero, can be easily checked, we need to consider the *cycling instances*, where the morphisms enter a cycle.

The second important step in the proof is to find an upper-bound for the lengths of the new end words s in the cycle. This can be done by considering the *successor sequence of the minimal solutions*, where in every reduction step we consider the successor with respect to the end block in a solution of minimal length. It can be proven that in the successor sequence of the minimal solutions the length of the new end words can increase only up to some fixed limit. It follows that there are only finitely many possible end words to be considered, and thus in a cycle there are only finitely many instances to be checked.

Consider now the successor tree of an instance. The decision in every branch of the tree is performed as follows:

(i) If there is no end block, then the branch terminates and has no solution.

(ii) If the same instance occurs twice, then terminate the branch, since there is no solution in this branch.

(iii) If the length of an end word is more that the limit, then terminate the branch, since it is not a branch of a minimal solution.

(iv) If an end block (u, u) occurs, then determine whether the marked (not generalized) PCP has a solution beginning with the letter #.

(v) If an end block $(\#u, \#u)$ occurs, then the instance has a solution.

It can be seen that after a certain number of reductions each branch of the tree falls into one of the above cases.

Theorem 10. *The marked GPCP is decidable.*

4 Marked Infinite PCP

In this section we consider the *infinite* PCP. Let (h, g) be an instance of the PCP, where $h, g \colon A^* \to B^*$. Recall, that in the infinite PCP it is asked to determine whether or not there exists an infinite word $\omega = a_1 a_2 \cdots$ over A where $a_i \in A$ such that

$$h(\omega) = g(\omega),$$

i.e., $g(u) \bowtie h(u)$ for all finite prefixes u of ω.

We shall consider now infinite solutions of the marked PCP. We shall prove that the existence of an infinite solution is decidable for the marked PCP. Actually, our construction for the marked PCP turns out to be useful also in this occasion. For the complete proofs, see [3]. We begin with a simple lemma.

Lemma 11. *Let $I = (h, g)$ be an instance of the marked PCP and $I' = (h', g')$ be its successor. For all comparable words x and y, $h(h'(x))$ and $g(g'(y))$ are comparable.*

Proof. Assume, by symmetry, that $x \leq y$, say $y = xz$ for a word z. By the definition of block, $h(h'(x)) = g(g'(x))$, and therefore $h(h'(x)) \leq g(g'(xz))$ as required. $\square$

Assume that ω is an infinite solution of an instance $I = (h, g)$ of the marked PCP. There are three possibilities cases for ω:

(i) $\omega = w_1 w_2 \cdots$, where $w_i \in E(h, g)$ for each i,

(ii) ω has a block decomposition, but it is not as in (i),

(iii) ω does not have a block decomposition.

Note that we say that an infinite word ω has a block decomposition if

$$\omega = u_1 u_2 \cdots = v_1 v_2 \cdots ,$$

where (u_i, v_i) is a block for the letter a_i for $i \geq 1$.

First of all, the solutions of type (i) can be effectively found by Theorem 8. Note that if there exists a solution to the marked PCP, then there exists an infinite solution. Therefore we assume in the following that the instance (h, g) of the PCP has no solution and consider only infinite solutions of the other two types.

Again, the cases where the suffix complexity is zero or the domain alphabet is unary are easy.

Lemma 12. *Let I be an instance of the marked PCP. If $\sigma(I) = 0$ or the domain alphabet is unary, then the infinite solutions of I can be effectively found.*

Proof. Assume first that $\sigma(I) = 0$. It is obvious that I has an infinite solution if and only if it has a finite solution.

Assume that I is unary and let a be this single letter. Then $I = (h, g)$ has an infinite solution if and only if $h(a)^k = g(a)^\ell$ for some k and ℓ. This follows from the fact that $h(a)^t$ and $g(a)^t$ have to be comparable for all $t \geq 0$, and therefore, for some k and ℓ, $k \cdot |h(a)| = \ell \cdot |g(a)|$. If $h(a)^k = g(a)^\ell$, then $\omega = aa \cdots$ is an infinite solution of I. $\square$

Next we shall prove that a solution of the type (ii) of an instance I reduces to an infinite solution in the successor instance I'. First, we make two assumptions to the instances: $A \subseteq B$ and

$$a \leq h(a) \quad \text{for all } a \in A. \tag{4}$$

Lemma 13. *Let $I = (h, g)$ be an instance of the marked PCP. There is an infinite solution ω with a block decomposition if and only if the successor $I' = (h', g')$ has an infinite solution ω', that begins with the same letter as ω.*

Proof. Assume that there exists an infinite solution ω of the type (ii) of I. Then ω has two factorizations,

$$\omega = u_1 u_2 \cdots = v_1 v_2 \cdots , \tag{5}$$

where (u_i, v_i) is the block for the letter a_i for all i. Clearly, $h(a_1)$ and $g(a_1)$ are comparable and $h'(a_1) = u_1$ and $g'(a_1) = v_1$ are comparable. By the assumption (4) on h, they both begin with a_1. Define now $\omega' = a_1 a_2 \cdots$ By (5) it is obvious that ω' is an infinite solution of I'.

The other direction of the claim can be proved using the same idea. $\square$

By Lemma 13, for the solutions of the type (ii), instead of searching for an infinite solution of I, we can turn to the simpler instance I'. The difficulty here is that we do not know in advance, whether a possible solution of the successor is of type (ii) or (iii).

We shall first prove a simple case, where all instance of the entire successor sequence have an infinite solution of the type (ii).

Consider now the successor sequence I_i, where $I = I_0$ and $I_i = (h_i, g_i)$. Assume that n_0 and $d \geq 1$ are such that, for all $j \geq n_0$, $I_j = I_{j+d}$.

Lemma 14. *Let I_i , $i = 0, 1, \ldots$, be the successor sequence for an instance (h_0, g_0) of the marked PCP, where $h_i, g_i \colon A_i \to A_{i-1}$. There exists an infinite solution of type (ii) for all I_i if and only if there exists $b \in A_0$ such that $h_i(b) \bowtie g_i(b)$ for all $i \geq 0$.*

Proof. The first part of the claim is easy. For the second part we assume that there exists a letter b for which $h_i(b) \bowtie g_i(b)$ for all i. By Lemma 11, the words

$$x_i = h_1 \cdots h_{i-1} h_i(b) \quad \text{and} \quad y_i = g_1 \cdots g_{i-1} g_i(b)$$

are comparable and they begin with b for all i by the assumption for all i. Let $z_i = x_i \wedge y_i$, i.e., z_i is the longest common prefix of x_i and y_i. Since $z_i \leq z_{i+1}$, the word $\omega = \lim_{i \to \infty} z_i$ is an infinite solution to I_0. The claim follows inductively by setting originally $I_i = I_0$. $\square$

We have considered the two simple cases of our problem. These two are the cases where an infinite solution can be detected simply by the algorithm for the marked PCP.

We shall next prove that the infinite solutions of type (iii) can be detected.

Lemma 15. *It is decidable, whether an instance $I = (h, g)$ of the marked PCP has an infinite solution without a block decomposition.*

Proof. Let $I = I_0$ and I_i, $i = 1, 2, \ldots$, be the successor sequence of I, where $I_i = (h_i, g_i)$. Assume that ω is an infinite solution of I without a block decomposition, that is,

$$\omega = u_1 u_2 \cdots u_n \omega_1 = v_1 v_2 \cdots v_n \omega_2, \tag{6}$$

where (u_i, v_i) is the block for some letter a_i, for $1 \leq i \leq n$, and ω_1 and ω_2 are infinite words, which do not have a block as a prefix. Note that also $n = 0$ is possible.

First of all a_1 is a disappearing letter in the successor sequence (by Lemma 14). Clearly such letters can be effectively found.

On the other hand, the prefixes $u_1 \cdots u_n$ and $v_1 \cdots v_n$ in (6) can be effectively found, by a procedure similar to one defined for constructing a block. Since a_1 is disappearing, there cannot be a solution or an infinite solution with a block decomposition beginning with a_1, and hence this process ends.

Next we shall consider the words ω_1 and ω_2. It is clear that $h(\omega_1) = g(\omega_2)$, since $h(u_i) = g(v_i)$ for all $i = 1, 2, \ldots, n$. Let $b \leq h(\omega_1)$. Thus, b is a letter for which there is no block in I and, furthermore, in the process of constructing the block for b, after some step an overflow appears cyclically. Hence

$$\omega_1 = uu'u' \cdots \quad \text{and} \quad \omega_2 = vv'v'v' \cdots \tag{7}$$

for some words u, u', v and v' with $|h(u')| = |g(v')|$. There are only finitely many letters b such that there exists no blocks for b in I, and therefore all possible pairs ω_1 and ω_2 can be effectively found.

Now to decide whether this is an infinite solution, we need to check, whether $u_1 \cdots u_n \omega_1 = v_1 \cdots v_n \omega_2$, and this can be done effectively, since the words are ultimately periodic.

Since the words $u_1 \cdots u_n$ and $v_1 \cdots v_n$ are unique for a_1 and there are only finitely many possible ω_1 and ω_2, we can check all possible words $u_1 \cdots u_n \omega_1$ and $v_1 \cdots v_n \omega_2$, whether they are infinite solutions of I. $\square$

Corollary 16. *It is decidable, whether an instance of the marked PCP has an infinite solution of type (ii) or (iii).*

Proof. The claim follows by Lemma 15, since also the solutions without a block decomposition can be effectively found for the letters disappearing in successor sequence. $\square$

We have proved the following theorem.

Theorem 17. *It is decidable whether an instance of the marked PCP has an infinite solution. Indeed, it is decidable whether or not an instance of the marked PCP has an infinite solution beginning with a given letter.*

5 Binary Alphabets

5.1 Binary PCP

We shall now consider the PCP is for the binary instances. The proof uses Theorem 10 and a reduction defined in [1], where a given binary instance I was transformed to an equivalent instance of the binary marked GPCP. Note that the form of the equality set for binary instances has been recently studied in [8] and [9].

The binary PCP was shown to be decidable in [1]. There the basic idea of the proof was that each binary instance (h, g), for $h, g \colon A^* \to B^*$, is either *periodic*, i.e., $h(A^*) \subseteq u^*$ for a word $u \in B^*$, or it can be reduced to an equivalent instance of the binary generalized PCP with marked morphisms. Then it was proved in [1] that both of these two cases are decidable.

The proof of the following theorem can be found from [1].

Theorem 18. *The PCP is decidable for instances where one of the morphisms is periodic.*

Let $h \colon \{0,1\}^* \to \{0,1\}^*$ be a nonperiodic morphism. Clearly, h is then nonerasing. Let $h^{(0)} = h$. For a word w, denote by w_i the prefix of w of length i. Define a morphisms $h^{(i)}$ in a following way: for a letter $x \in A$, let j be such that $j \equiv i \pmod{|h(x)|}$ with $0 \le j < |h(x)|$, let

$$h^{(i)}(x) = (h(x)_j)^{-1}\big(h(x)h(x)_j\big).$$

In other words, the morphisms $h^{(i)}$'s are cyclic shifts of the original morphism h.

The following lemma was proved in [1].

Lemma 19. *Let $z_h = h(01) \wedge h(10)$ and denote $m = |z_h|$. Then $m \le |h(01)| - 1$, $h^{(m)}$ is a marked morphism and $h^{(m)}(w) = z_h^{-1}(h(w)z_h)$, for all $w \in \{0,1\}^*$. Moreover, for any w, if $|h(w)| \ge m$, then $z_h \le h(w)$.*

Let (h, g) be a binary instance of the PCP. Assume further that h and g are nonperiodic. Let z_h be as above, $m = |z_h|$ and $n = |z_g|$. We may assume, by symmetry, that $m \ge n$.

The following lemma is again originally from [1].

Lemma 20. *A binary instance (h, g) of the PCP has a solution if and only if the instance $((z_g^{-1}z_h, \varepsilon), h^{(m)}, g^{(n)}, (\varepsilon, z_g^{-1}z_h))$ of the generalized PCP has a solution.*

By the Theorem 17 we get the following

Theorem 21. *The binary PCP is decidable.*

5.2 Binary Infinite PCP

We shall prove that the existence of an infinite solution is decidable for the binary instances. We shall use the reduction of Lemma 20 to the marked GPCP. While considering the existence of infinite solutions, the end words s_1 and s_2 of the instances can be omitted. In fact, it is sufficient to study the infinite marked PCP.

Next example shows that the problem is not trivial. Consider the instance where h and g are defined by

	a	b
h	a	baa
g	aab	aa

The equality set $E(h,g) = \{\varepsilon\}$, but $\omega = a^2b^2a^4b^4a^8b^8\cdots$ is the unique infinite solution of the instance (that counts the powers of 2). Note that from this example it also follows that an infinite solution need not be regular, i.e., they cannot be defined by a finite automaton. Note also that if $E(h,g)$ is generated by two words - which is possible - then the instance has uncountable number of infinite solutions.

First we prove the decidability of the binary infinite PCP. We begin with a simple case of the periodic instances, i.e., instances where at least one of the morphisms is periodic.

Lemma 22. *It is decidable for periodic binary instances I of the PCP whether or not I has an infinite solution.*

Proof. Let $I = (h, g)$ be an instance of the PCP such that $h, g \colon \{0,1\}^* \to \{0,1\}^*$ where $h(\{0,1\}) \subset v^*$ for a word $v \in \{0,1\}^+$. Let $|v| = k$ and let $\nu = vv\cdots$ be the infinite word with period v. It is clear that ω is an infinite solution of the instance I if and only if $g(\omega) = \nu$, since $h(\omega) = \nu$ for all ω. Such a solution ω exists if and only if there exists a word w with $|w| = k+1$ such that $g(w)$ is a prefix of ν. $\qquad\square$

Let $I = (h, g)$ be a binary instance of the PCP with nonperiodic morphisms and let $((z_g^{-1}z_h, \varepsilon), h^{(m)}, g^{(n)}, (\varepsilon, z_g^{-1}z_h))$ be the equivalent instance of the binary marked generalized PCP provided by Lemma 20. Let $\#$ be a new *marker symbol*. We define a new instance (h', g') of the marked PCP, for $h', g' \colon \{0, 1, \#\}^* \to \{0,1\}^*$, as follows:

$$h'(\#) = \#z_g^{-1}z_h\,, \qquad h'(a) = h^{(m)}(a) \text{ for } a \in \{0,1\}\,,$$

$$g'(\#) = \#\,, \qquad g'(a) = g^{(n)}(a) \text{ for } a \in \{0,1\}\,.$$

It is obvious that the instance (h', g') is marked, but it is not binary anymore. The following lemma was proved in [6].

Lemma 23. *A binary instance (h, g) of the PCP has an infinite solution if and only if the instance (h', g') of the marked PCP has an infinite solution beginning with $\#$.*

Proof. Assume that $h(\omega) = g(\omega)$ for an infinite word $\omega = a_1 a_2 a_3 \cdots$. Let w be a prefix of ω. Then $h(w)$ and $g(w)$ are comparable. Denote $x = a_{|w|+1} a_{|w|+2} \cdots a_{|w|+m}$, where $m = |z_h|$. Then, trivially, we have

$$h(wx) = \left(z_h \left(z_h^{-1}(h(wx) z_h)\right)\right) z_h^{-1} = \left(z_h h^{(m)}(wx)\right) z_h^{-1},$$

$$g(wx) = \left(z_g \left(z_g^{-1}(g(wx) z_g)\right)\right) z_g^{-1} = \left(z_g g^{(n)}(wx)\right) z_g^{-1}$$

and therefore $\left(z_h h^{(m)}(wx)\right) z_h^{-1} \bowtie \left(z_g g^{(n)}(wx)\right) z_g^{-1}$, and so

$$\left(\#(z_g^{-1} z_h) h^{(m)}(wx)\right) z_h^{-1} \bowtie \# g^{(n)}(wx) z_g^{-1}.$$

Since $|h^{(m)}(x)| \geq |z_h|$ and $|g^{(n)}(x)| \geq |z_g|$, we obtain

$$(\# z_g^{-1} z_h) h^{(m)}(w) = h'(\#w) \bowtie \# g^{(n)}(w) = g'(\#w).$$

Therefore $\omega' = \#\omega$ is an infinite solution of (h', g').

In the other direction, we can similarly prove that if $\#\omega$ is an infinite solution of (h', g'), then ω is an infinite solution of the instance (h, g). $\square$

Now by Theorem 17 also the nonperiodic case is decidable and we obtain the following result.

Theorem 24. *It is decidable for binary instances I of the PCP whether or not I has an infinite solution.*

6 Conclusion and Future Work

We wish to mention the following open problems concerning this research:

- Is there a polynomial-time algorithm for the marked PCP? – or even for the marked GPCP?

- It follows from [14] that the strongly 5-marked PCP is undecidable. What about the decidability status of the strongly k-marked PCP for $1 < k < 5$?

- The decidability status of the PCP with elementary morphisms [13, pp. 72–77] is still open. A morphism g is *elementary* if it cannot be written as a composition $g_2 g_1$ via a smaller alphabet. Note that the marked PCP is a subcase of the PCP for elementary morphisms.

References

1. A. Ehrenfeucht, J. Karhumäki, and G. Rozenberg, The (generalized) Post correspondence problem with lists consisting of two words is decidable, *Theoret. Comput. Sci.* **21** (1982), 119–144.
2. V. Halava, *The Post Correspondence Problem for Marked Morphisms*, Ph.D. Thesis, Department of Math, Univ. of Turku. TUCS Dissertations no. 37, 2002.
3. V. Halava and T. Harju, Infinite solutions of the marked Post correspondence problem., *Formal and Natural Computing* (J. Karhumäki W. Brauer, H. Ehrig and A. Salomaa, eds.), Lecture Notes in Comput. Sci., vol. 2300, Springer-Verlag, 2002, 57–68.
4. V. Halava, T. Harju, and M. Hirvensalo, Generalized Post correspondence problem for marked morphisms, *Internat. J. Algebra Comput.* **10** (2000), no. 6, 757–772.
5. V. Halava, T. Harju, and M. Hirvensalo, Binary (generalized) Post Correspondence Problem, *Theoret. Comput. Sci.* **276** (2002), no. 1-2, 183–204.
6. V. Halava, T. Harju, and J. Karhumäki, *Decidability of the Binary Infinite Post Correspondence Problem*, Tech. Report 485, TUCS, 2002 (to appear in Discrete Appl. Math.).
7. V. Halava, M. Hirvensalo, and R. de Wolf, Marked PCP is decidable, *Theoret. Comput. Sci.* **255** (2001), no. 1-2, 193–204.
8. Š. Holub, Binary equality sets are generated by two words, *J. Algebra* **259** (2003), no. 1, 1–42.
9. S. Holub, A unique structure of two-generated binary equality languages, *Developments in Language Theory* 2002 (M. Ito and M. Toyama, eds.), Lecture Notes in Comput. Sci., vol. 2450, Springer-Verlag, 2003, 245–257.
10. Y. Lecerf, Récursive insolubilité de l'équation générale de diagonalisation de deux momomorphismes de monoïdes libres, *Computes Rendus Acad. Sci. Paris* **257** (1963), 2940–2943.
11. Y. Matiyasevich and G. Sénizergues, Decision problems for semi-Thue systems with a few rules, *Proceedings, 11th Annual IEEE Symposium on Logic in Computer Science* (New Brunswick, New Jersey), IEEE Computer Society Press, 27–30 July 1996, 523–531.
12. E. Post, A variant of a recursively unsolvable problem, *Bull. of Amer. Math. Soc.* **52** (1946), 264–268.
13. G. Rozenberg and A. Salomaa, *Cornerstones of Undecidability*, Prentice Hall, 1994.

14. K. Ruohonen, Reversible machines and Post's correspondence problem for biprefix morphisms, *Elektron. Informationsverarb. Kybernet.* (EIK) **21**, 12 (1985), 579–595.
15. G.C. Tzeitin, Associative calculus with an unsolvable equivalence problem, *Tr. Mat. Inst. Akad. Nauk* 52 (1958), 172–189 (Russian).

THE DF0L LANGUAGE EQUIVALENCE PROBLEM

JUHA HONKALA

Department of Mathematics, University of Turku
FIN-20014 Turku, Finland
E-mail: juha.honkala@utu.fi

We give a new proof of the decidability of the DF0L language equivalence problem. As a byproduct we get a new solution of the D0L language equivalence problem.

1 Introduction

The decidability of the D0L equivalence problem is one of the basic results concerning free monoid morphisms and their iterations. The simplest known solution of the D0L sequence equivalence problem relies upon Hilbert's basis theorem and other simple properties of ideals in polynomial rings (see [2,3]). The decidability of the D0L language equivalence problem follows from the decidability of the D0L sequence equivalence problem as shown by Nielsen [7].

The language equivalence problem remains decidable for D0L systems with finite axiom sets (see [4,6]). The purpose of this paper is to give a new, largely self-contained proof of this decidability result. We assume that the reader is familiar with some basic properties of D0L length sequences (see [8,9,11,12]) and word equations (see [2,5,9]).

For additional information concerning the DF0L equivalence problem the reader is referred to [4].

2 Definitions

If $w \in X^*$ is a word and $x \in X$ is a letter, the number of occurrences of the letter x in w is denoted by $|w|_x$. The *length* of w is denoted by $|w|$. If $w \in X^*$, the set $\mathrm{alph}(w)$ is defined by

$$\mathrm{alph}(w) = \{x \in X \mid |w|_x \geq 1\}.$$

We say that a word $w \in X^*$ is *full* if $\mathrm{alph}(w) = X$. A language L is *full* if we have $\mathrm{alph}(u) = \mathrm{alph}(v)$ for all $u, v \in L$.

A *D0L system* is a triple

$$G = (X, g, w),$$

where X is a finite alphabet, $g : X^* \longrightarrow X^*$ is a morphism and $w \in X^*$ is a word. A DF0L system is obtained from a D0L system by replacing the word

w by a finite set F. Hence, a *DF0L system* is a triple

$$G = (X, g, F),$$

where X is a finite alphabet, $g : X^* \longrightarrow X^*$ is a morphism and $F \subseteq X^*$ is a finite set.

The *sequence* $S(G)$ and the *language* $L(G)$ of the D0L system $G = (X, g, w)$ are defined by

$$S(G) = (g^n(w))_{n \geq 0}$$

and

$$L(G) = \{g^n(w) \mid n \geq 0\}.$$

The *language* $L(G)$ of the DF0L system $G = (X, g, F)$ is defined by

$$L(G) = \{g^n(w) \mid w \in F, \ n \geq 0\}.$$

As a tool, we use also HD0L systems. By definition, an *HD0L system* is a construct

$$H = (X, Y, g, h, w),$$

where (X, g, w) is a D0L system, Y is a finite alphabet and $h : X^* \longrightarrow Y^*$ is a morphism. The *sequence* $S(H)$ and the *language* $L(H)$ of H are defined by

$$S(H) = (hg^n(w))_{n \geq 0}$$

and

$$L(H) = \{hg^n(w) \mid n \geq 0\}.$$

If $G = (X, g, w)$ is a D0L system, then the sequence

$$(\mathrm{alph}(g^n(w)))_{n \geq 0}$$

is ultimately periodic (see [8]). Using this fact it is not difficult to see that for a DF0L system $G = (X, g, F)$ and a subset X_1 of X, the set

$$\{u \in L(G) \mid \mathrm{alph}(u) = X_1\}$$

is a DF0L language. Consequently, to prove the decidability of the DF0L language equivalence problem it suffices to consider full DF0L languages. These two observations are due to [10].

Suppose $G = (X, g, w)$ is a D0L system. G is said to be *polynomially bounded* if there is a polynomial $r(n)$ such that

$$|g^n(w)| \leq r(n)$$

for all $n \geq 0$. G is said to be *exponential* if there is a real number $\alpha > 1$ such that

$$|g^n(w)| \geq \alpha^n$$

for almost all $n \geq 0$. (We say that a property holds for almost all integers $n \geq 0$, if there is an integer n_0 such that the property holds for all $n \geq n_0$.) Every D0L system is either polynomially bounded or exponential (see [8]). It is easy to see that two D0L systems $G_i = (X, g, w_i)$, $i = 1, 2$, have the same growth type if alph(w_1) = alph(w_2). Consequently, also DF0L systems generating full languages can be divided into polynomially bounded and exponential systems.

We need two lemmas concerning D0L growth.

Lemma 1 *Let $G = (X, g, w)$ be a D0L system and assume that for every $x \in X$ there is a nonzero polynomial $p_x(n)$ such that*

$$|g^n(w)|_x = p_x(n)$$

for all $n \geq 0$. Assume that $L(G)$ is not finite. Then there is a letter $x \in X$ such that

$$p_x(n) = an + b,$$

where a and b are integers and $a \geq 1$.
Proof. See Lemma 4.1 in [11]. $\qquad\qquad\qquad\qquad\qquad\qquad\qquad\qquad\qquad$ □

Lemma 2 *Suppose $G = (X, g, w)$ is an exponential D0L system. Then there exist positive real numbers a, b, α with $\alpha > 1$, and a nonnegative integer t such thatq*

$$an^t \alpha^n \leq |g^n(w)| \leq bn^t \alpha^n$$

for almost all $n \geq 0$.
Proof. See [8,12]. $\qquad\qquad\qquad\qquad\qquad\qquad\qquad\qquad\qquad\qquad\qquad\qquad$ □

3   The HD0L Covering Problem

Let $H_i = (X_i, Y, g_i, h_i, w_i)$, $1 \leq i \leq s + 1$, be HD0L systems. Then we say that the sequences $S(H_i)$, $2 \leq i \leq s + 1$, *cover* $S(H_1)$ if

$$h_1 g_1^n(w_1) \in \{h_i g_i^n(w_i) \mid 2 \leq i \leq s + 1\}$$

for all $n \geq 0$. By the *HD0L covering problem* we understand the problem of deciding whether $S(H_i)$, $2 \leq i \leq s + 1$, cover $S(H_1)$ when the HD0L systems H_i, $1 \leq i \leq s + 1$, are given.

The HD0L covering problem is the key tool in our solution of the DF0L equivalence problem. In this section we show that methods used to solve the D0L sequence equivalence problem can be generalized to solve the HD0L covering problem (see also [5,6]). First we recall some results concerning word equations.

Let X be a fixed finite alphabet and let Z be a fixed finite set of word variables. A (*word*) *equation* is a pair $(u, v) \in Z^* \times Z^*$, also written as $u = v$. A *solution* of $u = v$ is any morphism $h : Z^* \longrightarrow X^*$ such that $h(u) = h(v)$. If E_p, $1 \leq p \leq k$, are equations, the formula

$$\bigvee_{p=1}^{k} E_p \tag{1}$$

is called an *alternative equation*. A morphism $h : Z^* \longrightarrow X^*$ is called a *solution* of (1) if h is a solution of E_p for some p, $1 \leq p \leq k$. More generally, assume that $k(n)$ is an integer for all n, $1 \leq n \leq m$, and let E_{np} be an equation for $1 \leq n \leq m$, $1 \leq p \leq k(n)$. Then a morphism $h : Z^* \longrightarrow X^*$ is called a solution of the *system of alternative equations*

$$\bigwedge_{n=1}^{m} \bigvee_{p=1}^{k(n)} E_{np}$$

if h is a solution of

$$\bigvee_{p=1}^{k(n)} E_{np}$$

whenever $1 \leq n \leq m$. Two systems of alternative equations are called *equivalent* if they have the same solutions.

Suppose now that Z has $t \geq 1$ letters. Let $\hat{Z}$ be a set of $4t$ indeterminates and let $\mathbf{Q}[\hat{Z}]$ be the polynomial ring. Hence the elements of $\mathbf{Q}[\hat{Z}]$ are polynomials having indeterminates in $\hat{Z}$ and rational coefficients. If A is an arbitrary subset of $\mathbf{Q}[\hat{Z}]$ define the set $V(A)$ by

$$V(A) = \{(c_1, \ldots, c_{4t}) \in \mathbf{Q}^{4t} \mid p(c_1, \ldots, c_{4t}) = 0 \text{ for all } p \in A\}.$$

The following lemma is well known (see, e.g., [2]).

Lemma 3 *For each equation $E = (u, v) \in Z^* \times Z^*$ we can effectively compute a finite set $P(E) \subseteq \mathbf{Q}[\hat{Z}]$ of polynomials and for each morphism $h : Z^* \longrightarrow X^*$ we can effectively compute a $4t$-tuple $TEST(h) \in \mathbf{Q}^{4t}$ such that h is a solution of E if and only if $TEST(h) \in V(P(E))$.*

For the proof of the following lemma see [2,5].

Lemma 4 *Suppose* $(P_n)_{n \geq 1}$ *is an ascending chain of finite subsets of* $\mathbf{Q}[\hat{Z}]$. *Then there exists an integer* m *such that*

$$V(P_m) = V(P_{m+1}).$$

Moreover, if the sets P_n, $n \geq 1$, *are given effectively, such an integer* m *can be computed effectively.*

Theorem 5 *The HD0L covering problem is decidable.*

Proof. Suppose $H_i = (X_i, Y, g_i, h_i, w_i)$, $1 \leq i \leq s+1$, are HD0L systems. Without restriction we assume that

$$X_i \cap X_j = \emptyset$$

whenever $1 \leq i < j \leq s+1$. Denote

$$Z = \bigcup_{i=1}^{s+1} X_i$$

and consider Z as an alphabet of word variables. If $n \geq 0$ and $2 \leq p \leq s+1$, let E_{np} be the word equation

$$g_1^n(w_1) = g_p^n(w_p).$$

Let $h : Z^* \longrightarrow Y^*$ be the common extension of the morphisms h_i, $1 \leq i \leq s+1$. Then h is a solution of E_{np} if and only if

$$h_1 g_1^n(w_1) = h_p g_p^n(w_p).$$

Consequently, for $m \geq 0$, h is a solution of

$$\bigwedge_{n=0}^{m} \bigvee_{p=2}^{s+1} E_{np}$$

if and only if

$$h_1 g_1^n(w_1) \in \{ h_p g_p^n(w_p) \mid 2 \leq p \leq s+1 \}$$

for all n, $0 \leq n \leq m$.

Next, if $n \geq 0$ and $2 \leq p \leq s+1$, let $P(E_{np}) \subseteq \mathbf{Q}[\hat{Z}]$ be as in Lemma 3. Moreover, if $m \geq 0$, define the set $P_m \subseteq \mathbf{Q}[\hat{Z}]$ by

$$P_m = \bigcup_{n=0}^{m} \prod_{p=2}^{s+1} P(E_{np}).$$

Each P_m is a finite set of polynomials which can be computed effectively. Moreover,

$$V(P_m) = \bigcap_{n=0}^{m} \bigcup_{p=2}^{s+1} V(P(E_{np}))$$

for $m \geq 0$.

Next, by Lemma 4 we can compute an integer q such that

$$V(P_q) = V(P_{q+1}).$$

To complete the proof of Theorem 5 it suffices to show that

$$h_1 g_1^n(w_1) \in \{h_i g_i^n(w_i) \mid 2 \leq i \leq s+1\} \text{ for all } n \geq 0 \tag{2}$$

if and only if

$$h_1 g_1^n(w_1) \in \{h_i g_i^n(w_i) \mid 2 \leq i \leq s+1\} \text{ for all } n \text{ such that } 0 \leq n \leq q. \tag{3}$$

Clearly, (2) implies (3). To prove that (3) implies (2) assume on the contrary that (3) holds but (2) does not. Choose the smallest m such that

$$h_1 g_1^m(w_1) \notin \{h_i g_i^m(w_i) \mid 2 \leq i \leq s+1\}.$$

Then necessarily $m > q$.

Let $g : Z^* \longrightarrow Z^*$ be the common extension of the morphisms g_i, $1 \leq i \leq s+1$, and consider the morphism $f = hg^{m-q-1}$. Because f is a solution of

$$\bigwedge_{n=0}^{q} \bigvee_{p=2}^{s+1} E_{np},$$

we have

$$\text{TEST}(f) \in \bigcap_{n=0}^{q} \bigcup_{p=2}^{s+1} V(P(E_{np})) = V(P_q),$$

where $\text{TEST}(f)$ is as in Lemma 3. Therefore

$$\text{TEST}(f) \in V(P_{q+1}) = \bigcap_{n=0}^{q+1} \bigcup_{p=2}^{s+1} V(P(E_{np})).$$

Hence there is an integer p such that $2 \leq p \leq s+1$ and

$$\text{TEST}(f) \in V(P(E_{q+1,p})).$$

In other words

$$fg_1^{q+1}(w_1) = fg_p^{q+1}(w_p)$$

or, equivalently,

$$h_1 g_1^m(w_1) = h_p g_p^m(w_p),$$

which contradicts the choice of m. This concludes the proof that (3) implies (2). □

4 The DF0L Language Equivalence Problem

In this section we use the HD0L covering problem to solve the DF0L language equivalence problem.

Theorem 6 *The DF0L language equivalence problem is decidable.*

As pointed out earlier, to prove Theorem 6 it suffices to consider DF0L systems generating full languages. Such systems can be divided into polynomially bounded and exponential systems. It is not difficult to see that two DF0L systems generating full languages and having different growth types are not language equivalent. In the following two subsections we will give a semi-algorithm for the language equivalence of two polynomially bounded (resp. exponential) DF0L systems generating full languages. This proves Theorem 6 because there is a trivial semialgorithm for the nonequivalence of two DF0L languages.

4.1 Polynomially Bounded DF0L Systems

Assume that $G_i = (X, g_i, F_i)$, $i = 1, 2$, are polynomially bounded DF0L systems such that the languages $L(G_i)$, $i = 1, 2$, are full and infinite. Without restriction we assume that $\text{alph}(u) = X$ for all $u \in L(G_1) \cup L(G_2)$.

Because G_1 is polynomially bounded, for every $x, y \in X$ there exist an integer $t(x, y) \geq 1$ and a polynomial $p_{1,x,y}(n)$ such that

$$|g_1^{nt(x,y)}(x)|_y = p_{1,x,y}(n)$$

for almost all $n \geq 0$. Let t be the product of the integers $t(x, y)$, $x, y \in X$. By replacing g_1 by g_1^t and F_1 by $\{g_1^j(w) \mid w \in F_1, 0 \leq j < t\}$ we may assume that for every $w \in F_1$ and $y \in X$ there exists a polynomial $p_{w,y}(n)$ such that

$$|g_1^n(w)|_y = p_{w,y}(n)$$

for almost all $n \geq 0$.

Similarly, we may assume that for every $v \in F_2$ and $y \in X$ there exists a polynomial $q_{v,y}(n)$ such that

$$|g_2^n(v)|_y = q_{v,y}(n)$$

for almost all $n \geq 0$.

Now, fix a word $w \in F_1$. We will give a semialgorithm for the inclusion

$$\{g_1^n(w) \mid n \geq 0\} \subseteq L(G_2).$$

This clearly gives a semialgorithm for the language equivalence of G_1 and G_2.

First, by Lemma 1 there is a letter $y \in X$ and integers a, b with $a \geq 1$ such that

$$|g_1^n(w)|_y = an + b$$

for almost all $n \geq 0$. Consider then the polynomials $q_{v,y}(n)$, $v \in F_2$. Because $\mathrm{alph}(v_1) = \mathrm{alph}(v_2)$ whenever $v_1, v_2 \in F_2$, the polynomials $q_{v,y}(n)$, $v \in F_2$, have the same degree. If this degree is not one, we have $L(G_1) \neq L(G_2)$. Therefore, assume the common degree is one and denote

$$q_{v,y}(n) = a_v n + b_v,$$

where a_v, b_v are integers and $a_v \geq 1$ for $v \in F_2$. Further, denote

$$s = \prod_{v \in F_2} a_v.$$

Now, suppose

$$\{g_1^n(w) \mid n \geq 0\} \subseteq L(G_2)$$

and fix an integer j, $0 \leq j < s$. Let

$$F_3 = \{v \in F_2 \mid a_v \text{ divides } aj + b - b_v\}$$

and denote

$$c_v = \frac{as}{a_v}, \quad d_v = \frac{aj + b - b_v}{a_v}$$

whenever $v \in F_3$. Then, for almost all $n \geq 0$, we have

$$g_1^{ns+j}(w) \in \{g_2^{c_v n + d_v}(v) \mid v \in F_3\}.$$

By Theorem 5 we obtain a semialgorithm for the inclusion

$$\{g_1^{ns+j}(w) \mid n \geq 0\} \subseteq L(G_2).$$

By repeating this step for $j = 0, 1, \ldots, s - 1$, we get a semialgorithm for the inclusion

$$\{g_1^n(w) \mid n \geq 0\} \subseteq L(G_2).$$

4.2   Exponential DF0L Systems

Assume that $G_i = (X, g_i, F_i)$, $i = 1, 2$, are exponential DF0L systems such that the languages $L(G_i)$, $i = 1, 2$, are full.

First, we claim that there is an HD0L sequence $(S_1(n))_{n \geq 0}$ such that the following conditions hold:

1. $L(G_1) = \{S_1(n) \mid n \geq 0\}$,

2. $S_1(m) \neq S_1(n)$ whenever $m \neq n$, $m, n \geq 0$,

3. there exist positive real numbers c_1, d_1, β with $\beta > 1$, and a nonnegative integer s such that
$$c_1 n^s \beta^n \leq |S_1(n)| \leq d_1 n^s \beta^n$$
for almost all $n \geq 0$.

To prove the claim, suppose first that
$$g_1^m(w_1) \neq g_1^n(w_2)$$
whenever $m, n \geq 0$, $w_1, w_2 \in F_1$ and $w_1 \neq w_2$. Then the sequence $(S_1(n))_{n \geq 0}$ is obtained simply by merging the D0L sequences $(g_1^n(w))_{n \geq 0}$ for $w \in F_1$. Condition 3 follows because the merged sequences have equal growth orders.

In the general case we first construct a DF0L system $H = (X, h, F_3)$ and a finite set F_4 such that
$$L(G_1) = L(H) \cup F_4$$
and
$$h^m(v_1) \neq h^n(v_2)$$
whenever $m, n \geq 0$, $v_1, v_2 \in F_3$ and $v_1 \neq v_2$. The existence of H follows by a straightforward induction on the cardinality of F_1. (This step is explained more fully in [1].) The existence of $(S_1(n))_{n \geq 0}$ then follows as above.

Similarly, there is an HD0L sequence $(S_2(n))_{n \geq 0}$ such that the following conditions hold:

1. $L(G_2) = \{S_2(n) \mid n \geq 0\}$,

2. $S_2(m) \neq S_2(n)$ whenever $m \neq n$, $m, n \geq 0$,

3. there exist positive real numbers c_2, d_2, γ with $\gamma > 1$, and a nonnegative integer t such that
$$c_2 n^t \gamma^n \leq |S_2(n)| \leq d_2 n^t \gamma^n$$
for almost all $n \geq 0$.

542

Suppose now that $L(G_1) = L(G_2)$. Then necessarily $\beta = \gamma$ and $s = t$. Indeed, if either $\beta = \gamma$ and $s > t$, or $\beta > \gamma$, then for a large n_1 there are at most n_1 terms in $(S_1(n))_{n \geq 0}$ of length smaller than $c_1 n_1^s \beta^{n_1}$ while the sequence $(S_2(n))_{n \geq 0}$ contains more than n_1 such terms.

Consequently, if $L(G_1) = L(G_2)$, there is a positive integer a such that

$$S_1(n) \in \{S_2(n + i) \mid -a \leq i \leq a \text{ and } n + i \geq 0\}$$

and

$$S_2(n) \in \{S_1(n + i) \mid -a \leq i \leq a \text{ and } n + i \geq 0\}$$

for all $n \geq 0$. In other words, the HD0L sequence $(S_1(n))_{n \geq 0}$ is covered by the HD0L sequences

$$(S_2(n + i))_{n \geq 0}, \quad -a \leq i \leq a,$$

and the HD0L sequence $(S_2(n))_{n \geq 0}$ is covered by the HD0L sequences

$$(S_1(n + i))_{n \geq 0}, \quad -a \leq i \leq a.$$

(Here $S_1(n + i) = S_2(n + i) = \varepsilon$ if $n + i < 0$.) By Theorem 5 this gives a semialgorithm for the language equivalence of two exponential DF0L systems generating full languages.

4.3   D0L Systems

As a special case the previous subsections give a new algorithm for the D0L language equivalence problem. In particular, the decidability of the language equivalence problem for exponential D0L systems is an almost immediate consequence of the decidability of the D0L covering problem.

References

1. J. Honkala, The equivalence problem of D0L and DF0L power series, *Fund. Inform.*, 38 (1999), 201–208.
2. J. Honkala, The D0L problem revisited, *Bull. EATCS*, 70 (2000), 142–147.
3. J. Honkala, A short solution for the HDT0L sequence equivalence problem, *Theoret. Comput. Sci.*, 244 (2000), 267–270.
4. J. Honkala, The equivalence problem for DF0L languages and power series, *J. Comput. System Sci.*, 65 (2002), 377–392.
5. J. Honkala, A note on systems of alternative word equations, *Bull. EATCS*, 78 (2002), 237–240.

6. J. Honkala, On D0L systems with finite axiom sets, *Acta Cybern.*, to appear.
7. M. Nielsen, On the decidability of some equivalence problems for D0L systems, *Inform. and Control*, 25 (1974), 166–193.
8. G. Rozenberg and A. Salomaa, *The Mathematical Theory of L Systems*, Academic Press, New York, 1980.
9. G. Rozenberg and A. Salomaa (Eds.), *Handbook of Formal Languages*, Vol. 1-3, Springer, Berlin, 1997.
10. K. Ruohonen, The decidability of the F0L-D0L equivalence problem, *Inform. Process. Lett.*, 8 (1979), 257–260.
11. K. Ruohonen, The inclusion problem for D0L languages, *Elektron. Informationsverarb. Kybernet.*, 15 (1979), 535–548.
12. A. Salomaa and M. Soittola, *Automata-Theoretic Aspects of Formal Power Series*, Springer, Berlin, 1978.

AN OVERVIEW OF CONJUNCTIVE GRAMMARS

ALEXANDER OKHOTIN

School of Computing, Queen's University
Kingston, Ontario, Canada K7L 3N6
E-mail: okhotin@cs.queensu.ca.

Conjunctive grammars were introduced in 2000 as a generalization of context-free grammars that allows the use of an explicit intersection operation in rules. Several theoretical results on their properties have been obtained since then, and a number of efficient parsing algorithms that justify the practical value of the concept have been developed. This article reviews these results and proposes numerous open problems.

1 Introduction

The generative power of context-free grammars is generally considered to be insufficient for denoting many languages that arise in practice: it has often been observed that all natural languages contain non-context-free constructs, while the non-context-freeness of programming languages was proved already in early 1960s. A review of several widely different subject areas led the authors of [5] to the noteworthy conclusion that "the world seems to be non-context-free".

This leaves the aforementioned world with the question of finding an adequate tool for denoting formal languages. As the descriptive means of context-free grammars are not sufficient but necessary for practical use, the attempts at developing new generative devices have usually been made by generalizing context-free grammars in this or that way. However, most of the time an extension that appears to be minor leads to a substantial increase in the generative power (context-sensitive and indexed grammars being good examples), which is usually accompanied by strong and very undesirable complexity hardness results. The ability to encode hard problems makes a formalism, in effect, a peculiar low-level programming language, where writing a grammar resembles coding in assembly language, while subsequent attempts to comprehend what the grammar does are no easier than reading machine code. Taking into account that even the basic decision problems often become intractable, this diminishes the practical value of such a generalization. So the question is, how to extend the context-free grammars *slightly*, so that their delicate features would not get distorted by excessive generative power?

Some of the work on *slightly extending* context-free grammars concentrated on representing languages as intersections of context-free languages: several theoretical results on finite intersections of context-free languages [9,11,30] and deterministic context-free languages [30] were obtained, and practical applicability of such intersections to computational linguistics was discussed [9]. However, despite the increased generative power of the concept and its computational feasibility, this study remained purely theoretical – probably because a tuple of context-free grammars with implicit intersection on top looks too cumbersome as a generative device for actual use.

Conjunctive grammars, introduced in 2000, use a more general and uniform approach of allowing the use of an explicit intersection operation in the body of any rules of the grammar. This increases the generative power even beyond finite intersections of context-free languages, and at the same time allows the model to remain no less convenient for practical use than ordinary context-free grammars. Moreover, many of the known parsing algorithms for context-free grammars turn out to have direct analogs for conjunctive grammars, and these analogs usually have the same computational complexity as their prototypes, which makes conjunctive grammars fit for practical use.

Let us briefly state the known results on this family of grammars. The language denoted by a conjunctive grammar is defined using derivation (which generalizes the context-free derivation), and every such derivation can be represented in the form of a tree, possibly with shared leaves [13]. The semantics of conjunctive grammars is also characterized by least solutions of systems of language equations with unrestricted concatenation, union and intersection [15], similarly to the context-free case. The family of conjunctive languages is known to be closed under union, intersection, concatenation, star [13] and inverse homomorphism [26]; it is not closed under quotient and homomorphism [13].

A subclass of conjunctive grammars called *linear conjunctive grammars*, defined by restricting the use of concatenation as in linear context-free grammars, is known to be computationally equivalent to trellis automata [3,23], and thus to one-way real-time cellular automata [6] and to a certain restricted type of Turing machines [8]. The language family they all generate is incomparable with context-free languages [29]. It contains many interesting languages, such as $\{a^n b^n c^n \mid n \geqslant 0\}$, $\{wcw \mid w \in \{a,b\}^*\}$ [13], the Dyck language [3,6], the language of all accepting computations of a given Turing machine [20], and some **P**-complete languages [8,22]. This family is closed under union, intersection, complement [6,20], inverse homomorphism [4], inverse gsm mapping [8], quotient with finite languages [20], and several subcases of concatenation (with regular languages; over disjoint alphabets; through a center marker, etc.) [8,20]; it is not closed under general concatenation [29], under ϵ-free homomorphism [4], and under quotient with regular languages [20]. The questions of implementing linear conjunctive grammars using their automaton representation are addressed in [18,21].

Many widespread context-free recognition and parsing algorithms are known to have generalizations for the case of conjunctive grammars: there exist extended versions of Cocke–Kasami–Younger [13], LL and recursive descent [14], Graham–Harrison–Ruzzo [16] and generalized LR [17] parsing algorithms, as well as an $n^2/2$-time recognition method for linear conjunctive grammars based upon trellis automata [23,18]. These generalizations, except LL, retain the complexity of their prototypes. All existing parsing algorithms for conjunctive grammars have been implemented in the parser generator [19].

In the rest of this article the mentioned results are explained in more detail, numerous open problems are listed, and some directions for future research are suggested.

2 Definition

2.1 Grammars, Formulae, Derivation

A *conjunctive grammar* is defined as a quadruple $G = (\Sigma, N, P, S)$, in which

- Σ and N are disjoint finite nonempty sets of *terminal* and *nonterminal* symbols respectively;

- P is a finite set of grammar *rules*, each formally defined as an ordered pair $(A, \{\alpha_1, \ldots, \alpha_n\})$ of a nonterminal and a finite nonempty subset of $(\Sigma \cup N)^*$, and written in the form $A \rightarrow \alpha_1 \& \ldots \& \alpha_n$;

- $S \in N$ is a nonterminal designated as the *start symbol*.

For every rule $A \rightarrow \alpha_1 \& \ldots \& \alpha_n \in P$ and for every i $(1 \leqslant i \leqslant n)$, a pair of the form (A, α_i) is called a *conjunct*; it is denoted $A \rightarrow \alpha_i$. A collection of rules for a single nonterminal is specified using the notation $A \rightarrow \alpha_{11} \& \ldots \& \alpha_{1n_1} \mid \ldots \mid \alpha_{m1} \& \ldots \& \alpha_{mn_m}$.

Similarly to the context-free case, a conjunctive grammar is called *linear conjunctive* if every rule it contains is either of the form $A \rightarrow u_1 B_1 v_1 \& \ldots \& u_n B_n v_n$ $(n \geqslant 1, u_i, v_i \in \Sigma^*, B_i \in N)$ or of the form $A \rightarrow w$ $(w \in \Sigma^*)$.

The semantics of conjunctive grammars is defined using derivation, generally in the same way as in the context-free case. The only difference is in the objects being transformed: while context-free derivation operates with strings over $\Sigma \cup N$ (i.e., formulae over concatenation), a derivation in conjunctive grammars uses formulae over concatenation and conjunction.

In order to denote such formulae as strings, special symbols, (, & and), are added (assuming that none of them is in $\Sigma \cup N$), and the work alphabet $\Sigma \cup N \cup \{(, \&,)\}$ is used. Now the set of *conjunctive formulae* corresponding to a grammar $G = (\Sigma, N, P, S)$ is defined inductively as follows:

  i. ϵ is a conjunctive formula.

  ii. Every symbol from $\Sigma \cup N$ is a formula.

  iii. If $\mathcal{A}$ and $\mathcal{B}$ are nonempty formulae, then $\mathcal{AB}$ is a formula.

  iv. If $\mathcal{A}_1, \ldots, \mathcal{A}_n$ ($n \geqslant 1$) are formulae, then $(\mathcal{A}_1 \& \ldots \& \mathcal{A}_n)$ is a formula.

Conjunctive formulae are denoted by script capital Latin letters from the beginning of the alphabet: $\mathcal{A}, \mathcal{B}, \mathcal{C}$, etc.

Given a grammar G, define the *relation* $\overset{G}{\Longrightarrow}$ *of immediate derivability* on the set of conjunctive formulae:

  i. A nonterminal can be rewritten by the body of some rule enclosed in parentheses, i.e., for all $s_1, s_2 \in (\Sigma \cup N \cup \{(, \&,)\})^*$ and for all $A \in N$, if $s_1 A s_2$ is a formula, then for all $A \to \alpha_1 \& \ldots \& \alpha_n \in P$

$$s_1 A s_2 \overset{G}{\Longrightarrow} s_1 (\alpha_1 \& \ldots \& \alpha_n) s_2. \tag{1}$$

  ii. Conjunction of several identical terminal strings enclosed in parentheses can be replaced by one such string, i.e., for all $s_1, s_2 \in (\Sigma \cup N \cup \{(, \&,)\})^*$, for all $w \in \Sigma^*$ and for all $n \geqslant 1$, if $s_1 (\underbrace{w \& \ldots \& w}_{n}) s_2$ is a formula, then

$$s_1 (\underbrace{w \& \ldots \& w}_{n}) s_2 \overset{G}{\Longrightarrow} s_1 w s_2. \tag{2}$$

It can be proved that right parts of (1) and (2) are indeed formulae, which makes the definition consistent. Let $\overset{G}{\Longrightarrow}{}^*$ be the reflexive and transitive closure of $\overset{G}{\Longrightarrow}$.

The *language generated by a formula* $\mathcal{A}$ with respect to a grammar G can now be defined as the set of all strings over Σ derivable from $\mathcal{A}$ in zero or more steps:

$$L_G(\mathcal{A}) = \{w \mid w \in \Sigma^*, \ \mathcal{A} \overset{G}{\Longrightarrow}{}^* w\}. \tag{3}$$

The *language generated by the grammar* G is the set of all strings over Σ derivable from its start symbol: $L(G) = L_G(S)$.

The following basic result on the language generated by a formula [13, Th. 1] shows that it inductively depends on the formula's structure, with the connectives corresponding to operations with languages. Let $G = (\Sigma, N, P, S)$ be a conjunctive grammar. Then for all $a \in \Sigma$, $A \in N$, $n \geqslant 1$, and formulae $\mathcal{A}, \mathcal{B}, \mathcal{A}_1, \ldots, \mathcal{A}_n$,

$$L_G(\epsilon) = \{\epsilon\}, \tag{4a}$$

$$L_G(a) = \{a\}, \tag{4b}$$

$$L_G(A) = \bigcup_{A \to \alpha_1 \& \ldots \& \alpha_m \in P} L_G((\alpha_1 \& \ldots \& \alpha_m)), \tag{4c}$$

$$L_G(\mathcal{A}\mathcal{B}) = L_G(\mathcal{A}) \cdot L_G(\mathcal{B}), \tag{4d}$$

$$L_G((\mathcal{A}_1 \& \ldots \& \mathcal{A}_n)) = \bigcap_{k=1}^{n} L_G(\mathcal{A}_k). \tag{4e}$$

Writing down the equalities (4c) for every nonterminal of a grammar and using (4a,4b,4d,4e) to interpret the connectives, one obtains a certain *system of language equations* that uses explicit union, intersection and concatenation; in these terms, the result of [13, Th. 1] basically means that for any grammar G, where $N = \{A_1, \ldots, A_n\}$, the vector of languages $(L_G(A_1), \ldots, L_G(A_n))$ is a solution of this system. Such systems of language equations were investigated in [15], where, using the same elementary fixed point theory as in the context-free case, it was shown that the mentioned solution is always the least solution of a grammar.

2.2 Examples of Grammars

Let us start with two simple examples of non-context-free languages typically mentioned in the literature – these are $\{a^n b^n c^n \mid n \geqslant 0\}$ (which represents multiple agreement) and $\{a^m b^n c^m d^n \mid m, n \geqslant 0\}$ (cross agreement). Both languages are intersections of two context-free languages, and therefore a conjunctive grammar for each of them can be constructed by using a single conjunction on top.

$S \to AB\&DC$
$A \to aA \mid \epsilon$
$B \to bBc \mid \epsilon$
$C \to cC \mid \epsilon$
$D \to aDb \mid \epsilon$

$S \to XD\&AY$	$A \to aA \mid \epsilon$
$X \to aXc \mid B$	$B \to bB \mid \epsilon$
$Y \to bYd \mid C$	$C \to cC \mid \epsilon$
	$D \to dD \mid \epsilon$

In the first example, AB and DC generate $\{a^i b^j c^k \mid j = k\}$ and $\{a^i b^j c^k \mid i = j\}$ respectively, and therefore S generates $\{a^n b^n c^n \mid n \geqslant 0\}$.

The next language $\{ba^2 ba^4 b \dots ba^{2n-2} ba^{2n} b \mid n \geqslant 0\}$ is a language with superlinear growth (the strings from this language, arranged in the lexicographical order, have length $1, 4, 9, 16, 25, \dots$), which can also be represented as an intersection of two context-free languages. However, instead of using a grammar with a single conjunction on top, which would probably require many nonterminals, let us give a more succinct one:

$$
\begin{aligned}
&S \to SAb\&Cb \mid b \\
&A \to aA \mid \epsilon \\
&C \to bCaa \mid aC \mid baa
\end{aligned}
$$

Every next string $ba^2 b \dots a^{2n} ba^{2n+2} b$ is generated out of the previous string $ba^2 b \dots a^{2n} b$ by right-concatenating twice as many a's as there are b's spread across the previous string; this behaviour is directed by the rule $S \to SAb\&Cb$, where SAb generates Sa^*b and thus adds some number of a's and then b, while the nonterminal C ensures that the number of a's added is correct. The rule $S \to b$ forms the induction basis. Another grammar for the same language is given in [20]; it contains as many as seven nonterminals, but, unlike the grammar above, it is linear conjunctive.

One of the most common examples of a non-context-free language, $\{wcw \mid w \in \{a, b\}^*\}$, forms a more interesting case, because it is provably not expressible as a finite intersection of context-free languages [30]. Let us give a linear conjunctive grammar for this language and explain how it works.

$$
\begin{aligned}
&S \to C\&D \\
&C \to aCa \mid aCb \mid bCa \mid bCb \mid c \\
&D \to aA\&aD \mid bB\&bD \mid cE \\
&A \to aAa \mid aAb \mid bAa \mid bAb \mid cEa \\
&B \to aBa \mid aBb \mid bBa \mid bBb \mid cEb \\
&E \to aE \mid bE \mid \epsilon
\end{aligned}
$$

C generates $\{xcy \mid x, y \in \{a, b\}^*, |x| = |y|\}$ and thus ensures that the string consists of two equal-length parts separated by a center marker. D takes one symbol from the left and uses A or B to compare it to the corresponding symbol at the right. At the same time, D recursively calls itself in order to process the rest of the string in the same way. Formally, A generates $\{xcvay \mid x, v, y \in \{a, b\}^*, |x| = |y|\}$, B generates $\{xcvby \mid x, v, y \in \{a, b\}^*, |x| = |y|\}$ and therefore D produces $\{uczu \mid u, z \in \{a, b\}^*\}$ (the last result may be obtained by a straightforward induction on the length of the string). Finally,

$$\{xcy \mid x, y \in \{a, b\}^*, |x| = |y|\} \cap \{uczu \mid u, z \in \{a, b\}^*\}$$
$$= \{wcw \mid w \in \{a, b\}^*\}. \tag{5}$$

Let us construct a derivation of the string $abcab$ to demonstrate that it is generated by the given grammar:

$S \Longrightarrow (C\&D) \Longrightarrow ((aCb)\&D) \Longrightarrow ((a(bCa)b)\&D) \Longrightarrow ((a(b(c)a)b)\&D) \Longrightarrow$
$((a(bca)b)\&D) \Longrightarrow ((abcab)\&D) \Longrightarrow (abcab\&D) \Longrightarrow (abcab\&(aA\&aD)) \Longrightarrow$
$(abcab\&(a(bAb)\&aD)) \Longrightarrow (abcab\&(a(b(cEa)b)\&aD)) \Longrightarrow$
$(abcab\&(a(b(c()a)b)\&aD)) \Longrightarrow (abcab\&(a(b(ca)b)\&aD)) \Longrightarrow$
$(abcab\&(a(bcab)\&aD)) \Longrightarrow (abcab\&(abcab\&aD)) \Longrightarrow$
$(abcab\&(abcab\&a(bB\&bD))) \Longrightarrow (abcab\&(abcab\&a(b(cEb)\&bD))) \Longrightarrow$
$(abcab\&(abcab\&a(b(c(aE)b)\&bD))) \Longrightarrow (abcab\&(abcab\&a(b(c(a())b)\&bD))) \Longrightarrow$
$(abcab\&(abcab\&a(b(c(a)b)\&bD))) \Longrightarrow (abcab\&(abcab\&a(b(cab)\&bD))) \Longrightarrow$
$(abcab\&(abcab\&a(bcab\&bD))) \Longrightarrow (abcab\&(abcab\&a(bcab\&bD))) \Longrightarrow$
$(abcab\&(abcab\&a(bcab\&b(cE)))) \Longrightarrow (abcab\&(abcab\&a(bcab\&b(c(aE))))) \Longrightarrow$
$(abcab\&(abcab\&a(bcab\&b(c(a(bE)))))) \Longrightarrow$
$(abcab\&(abcab\&a(bcab\&b(c(a(b())))))) \Longrightarrow$
$(abcab\&(abcab\&a(bcab\&b(c(a(b)))))) \Longrightarrow (abcab\&(abcab\&a(bcab\&b(c(ab))))) \Longrightarrow$
$(abcab\&(abcab\&a(bcab\&b(cab)))) \Longrightarrow (abcab\&(abcab\&a(bcab\&bcab))) \Longrightarrow$
$(abcab\&(abcab\&abcab)) \Longrightarrow (abcab\&abcab) \Longrightarrow abcab.$

It is important to note that the construction essentially uses the center marker, and therefore this method cannot be applied to writing a conjunctive grammar for the language $\{ww \mid w \in \{a, b\}^*\}$. The question of whether $\{ww \mid w \in \{a, b\}^*\}$ can be denoted by a conjunctive grammar remains an open problem.

Several other noteworthy languages are known to be expressible using conjunctive grammars – probably the most interesting are the languages of all accepting computations of Turing machines (a source of many undecidability results) and some **P**-complete languages [8,22]. Both can be denoted using linear conjunctive grammars, as well as all the languages mentioned earlier in this section. Generative capacity of linear conjunctive grammars will be addressed again in Section 3.3.

2.3 Derivation Trees

The theory of parsing for context-free grammars is based upon the representation of a context-free derivation in the form of a tree. It turns out that the notion of derivation tree can be extended to conjunctive grammars, where it becomes *a tree with shared leaves*.

Let $G = (\Sigma, N, P, S)$ be a conjunctive grammar and let A be a nonterminal. A certain tree with shared leaves is associated with every derivation

$A \implies \ldots \implies \mathcal{A}$ of zero or more steps, where $\mathcal{A}$ is an arbitrary formula. The leaves of such a tree are labeled with symbols from $\Sigma \cup N \cup \{\epsilon\}$, where nonepsilon leaves correspond to terminal and nonterminal symbols from $\mathcal{A}$, and a leaf can have in-degree of more than one only if it is labeled with a terminal symbol. Internal vertices of the tree are labeled with the rules used in the derivation. Outgoing arcs in each vertex are considered ordered.

A tree corresponding to a derivation is defined inductively on the length of derivation: the tree corresponding to a zero-length derivation is a single node labeled with A; for every application of a rule from P to a nonterminal, the corresponding leaf of the tree is supplied with descendants in the same way as in the context-free case (ignoring the conjunction signs); for every rewriting of $(w\& \ldots \& w)$ by w, the leaves corresponding to the substrings being merged are merged as well.

A detailed treatment of derivation trees for conjunctive grammars can be found in [16,17]. For an example of a derivation tree, consider the grammar for the language $\{wcw \mid w \in \{a, b\}^*\}$ given in Section 2.2, and the provided derivation of the string $abcab$; the tree corresponding to that derivation is given in Figure 1.

2.4 Binary Normal Form

A normal form for conjunctive grammars that naturally extends context-free Chomsky normal form was proposed in [13]. A conjunctive grammar $G = (\Sigma, N, P, S)$ is said to be in the *binary normal form*, if all rules in P are of the form

$$A \to B_1 C_1 \& \ldots \& B_m C_m, \quad \text{where } m \geqslant 1, \ A, B_i, C_i \in N, \tag{6a}$$

$$A \to a, \quad \text{where } A \in N, a \in \Sigma, \tag{6b}$$

$$S \to \epsilon, \quad \text{only if } S \text{ does not appear in the right hand side of any rule.} \tag{6c}$$

There exists an algorithm to convert a given conjunctive grammar to an equivalent grammar in the binary normal form [13]. The conversion, similarly to the context-free case, is done in three stages:

i. Removal of *epsilon conjuncts* (those of the form $A \to \epsilon$). Given a conjunctive grammar G, one can construct a grammar G' that contains no rules of the form

$$A \to \alpha_1 \& \ldots \& \alpha_{i-1} \& \epsilon \& \alpha_{i+1} \& \ldots \& \alpha_n, \tag{7}$$

such that $L(G') = L(G) \setminus \{\epsilon\}$. The standard technique of computing the set of nonterminals that derive ϵ and then reconstructing the set of rules is used.

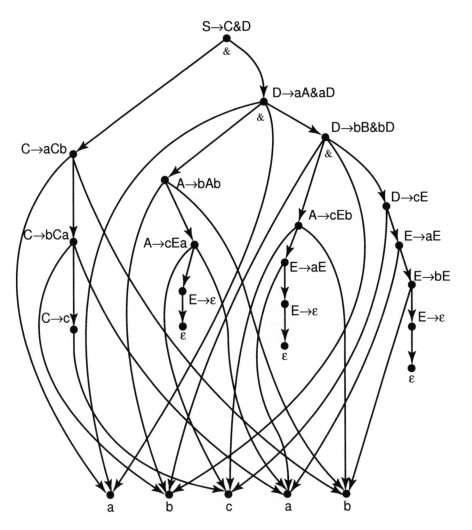

Figure 1. Sample derivation tree of $abcab \in \{wcw \mid w \in \{a, b\}^*\}$.

ii. Removal of *unit conjuncts* (those of the form $A \rightarrow B$, where $B \in N$).
Given a grammar G' without epsilon conjuncts, construct a grammar G

that contains no rules of the form

$$A \to \alpha_1 \& \ldots \& \alpha_{i-1} \& B \& \alpha_{i+1} \& \ldots \& \alpha_n \quad (B \in N), \tag{8}$$

such that $L(G) = L(G')$. As proved in [13], this can be done by finitely many instantiations of rules for B in the rules of the form (8).

iii. Finally, once every conjunct in the grammar is either of the form $A \to a$, or of the form $A \to \alpha$ ($\alpha \in (\Sigma \cup N)^*$, $|\alpha| \geqslant 2$), the conjuncts of three or more symbols long can be split in two by introducing new nonterminals, instances of terminals in conjuncts of two symbols long are moved into separate nonterminals, meaningless combinations of conjuncts like $A \to a \& b$ or $A \to a \& BC$ are removed from the grammar, and finally, if the original grammar G generated the empty string, the rules $S' \to S, S' \to \epsilon$ are added, which leaves us exactly with rules of the form (6) [13].

2.5 A Recognition Algorithm

Conjunctive grammars in the binary normal form can be parsed using an extension of the Cocke–Kasami–Younger algorithm [13]. Like in the context-free case, define a so-called *recognition matrix*, which is an upper-triangular matrix of sets of nonterminals that derive the substrings of the input string.

Let $G = (\Sigma, N, P, S)$ be a conjunctive grammar in the binary normal form. Let $w = a_1 \ldots a_n \in \Sigma^+$ ($n \geqslant 1$) be some string. Let $1 \leqslant i \leqslant j \leqslant n$. Define

$$T_{ij} = \{A \mid A \in N, \ A \stackrel{G}{\Longrightarrow}^* a_i \ldots a_j\}. \tag{9}$$

It is clear that $w \in L(G)$ if and only if $S \in T_{1n}$. In order to check the membership of S in T_{1n}, the recognition algorithm [13, Algorithm 1] computes all T_{ij} starting from $T_{11}, \ldots, T_{nn}$ and ending with T_{1n}.

Every T_{ii} ($1 \leqslant i \leqslant n$) equals $\{A \mid A \to a_i \in P\}$. It can be proved [13, Th. 5] that the task of computing every T_{ij} (for all $1 \leqslant i < j \leqslant n$) can be reduced to computing all T_{ik} ($i \leqslant k < j$) and T_{lj} ($i < l \leqslant j$) as follows:

$$T_{ij} = \{A \mid A \in N, \text{ there is a rule } A \to B_1 C_1 \& \ldots \& B_m C_m \in P, \text{ such that }$$
$$\text{for all } p \ (1 \leqslant p \leqslant m) \text{ there exists } l \ (i \leqslant l < j): B_p \in T_{i,l}, \ C_p \in T_{l+1,j}\}. \tag{10}$$

The expression (10) can be computed by first gathering the union of cartesian products $T_{i,l} \times T_{l+1,j}$ for all l (in linear time relative to the length of the input), and then constructing the set of such nonterminals A, for which there is a rule $A \to B_1 C_1 \& \ldots \& B_m C_m \in P$, such that all pairs (B_p, C_p) are in the set of pairs of nonterminals constructed above (this can be done in constant time). The recognition algorithm that implements this computation [13] therefore works in cubic time and proves that every conjunctive language is in $\textbf{DTIME}(n^3)$. But this does not give a polynomial upper bound for the complexity of the general membership problem, which is to determine whether $w \in L(G)$ for given G and w, because no polynomial upper bound for the blowup in grammar size in the course of transformation to the binary normal form is known. However, a polynomial solution for the membership problem for conjunctive grammars and its consequent $\textbf{P}$-completeness was obtained in [16] by refraining from grammar transformation.

3 Linear Conjunctive Grammars

Although linear conjunctive grammars were introduced in 2000 together with conjunctive grammars [12,13], the family they generate has been studied long before [6,3]. It is now known [23] that the following formalisms define the same family of languages: one-way real-time cellular automata [6], trellis automata [3,2,4], a certain very restricted type of Turing machines [8], linear conjunctive grammars [13,23], language equations with union, intersection and linear concatenation [15] and the recently introduced linear Boolean grammars [24]. Numerous characterizations in terms of different areas of theoretical computer science make this subclass of conjunctive grammars worth particular attention.

3.1 Linear Normal Form and a Recognition Algorithm

A linear conjunctive grammar $G = (\Sigma, N, P, S)$ is said to be in the *linear normal form*, if every rule in P is of the form

$$A \to bB_1 \& \dots \& bB_m \& C_1 c \& \dots \& C_n c \quad (m+n \geqslant 1;\ B_i, C_j \in N;\ b, c \in \Sigma),$$

$$\text{(11a)}$$

$$A \to a \quad (a \in \Sigma), \tag{11b}$$

$$S \to \epsilon, \quad \text{only if } S \text{ does not appear in the right hand side of any rule.}$$

$$\text{(11c)}$$

Every linear conjunctive grammar can be effectively transformed to an equivalent grammar in the linear normal form [13] by first removing epsilon conjuncts and unit conjuncts using the same grammar transformations as in Section 2.4 (these transformations are known to preserve linearity of a grammar), then cutting long conjuncts until all of them are of the form $A \to a$, $A \to bB$ and $A \to Cc$, and finally removing the rules with contradicting conjuncts (e.g., $A \to bB\&cC$, where $b \neq c$), which obviously cannot be used in any successful derivation.

Let T_{ij} be as in (9). Exactly like in the case of linear context-free grammars, T_{ij} $(i < j)$ is a function of $T_{i+1,j}$, $T_{i,j-1}$, a_i and a_j, and can be represented as follows:

$$T_{ij} = \{A \mid A \in N, \text{ there is a rule } A \to bB_1\& \ldots \&bB_m\&C_1c\& \ldots \&C_nc \in P,$$
$$\text{such that } b = a_i, \ c = a_j, \text{ for all } p\,(1 \leqslant p \leqslant m), \ B_p \in T_{i+1,j} \text{ and}$$
$$\text{for all } q\,(1 \leqslant q \leqslant n), \ C_q \in T_{i,j-1}\}. \tag{12}$$

The time required for computing (12) does not depend on the length of the input, and thus a recognition algorithm for linear conjunctive languages can be constructed to work in $O(n^2)$ time.

3.2 Automaton Representation

Triangular (real-time, homogeneous) trellis automata are a particular case of systolic trellis automata [3,4], in which the connections between nodes form a figure of triangular shape, as shown in Figure 2. These automata are used as acceptors of strings loaded from the bottom, and the acceptance is determined by the topmost element. In the following they will be referred to as just *trellis automata*.

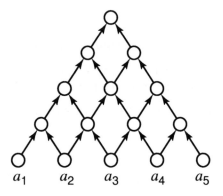

Figure 2. Computation of a trellis automaton.

In their original definition, trellis automata cannot handle the empty string, because, naturally, a triangular trellis, such as in Figure 2, cannot be of size zero. However, neither linear conjunctive grammars nor the earlier studied class of sequential machines equivalent to trellis automata [8] have problems of this kind. Aiming to enhance a weaker concept rather than decapacitate a stronger one, in makes sense to define a slightly extended version of trellis automata, straightforwardly equipping them with a means to accept or reject the empty string:

Definition 1 *A trellis automaton is a sextuple* $M = (\Sigma, Q, I, \delta, F, e)$, *where* Σ *is the input alphabet,* Q *is a finite nonempty set of states (of processing units),* $I : \Sigma \rightarrow Q$ *is a function that sets the initial states (loads values into the bottom processors),* $\delta : Q \times Q \rightarrow Q$ *is the transition function (the function computed by processors),* $F \subseteq Q$ *is the set of final states (effective in the top processor), and the bit* $e \in \{0, 1\}$ *determines whether* ϵ *is accepted or rejected.*

Given a nonempty string $a_1 \ldots a_n$ ($a_i \in \Sigma$, $n \geqslant 1$), every node of a trellis corresponds to a certain substring $a_i \ldots a_j$ ($1 \leqslant i \leqslant j \leqslant n$) of symbols on which its value depends. The value of a bottom node corresponding to one symbol of the input is $I(a_i)$; the value of a successor of two nodes is δ of the values of these ancestors. Denote the value of a node corresponding to $a_i \ldots a_j$ as $\Delta(I(a_i \ldots a_j)) \in Q$: here $I(a_i \ldots a_j)$ is a string of states (the bottom row of the trellis), while Δ denotes the result (a single state) of a triangular computation starting from a row of states. By definition, $\Delta(I(a_i)) = I(a_i)$ and $\Delta(I(a_i \ldots a_j)) = \delta(\Delta(I(a_i \ldots a_{j-1})), \Delta(I(a_{i+1} \ldots a_j)))$. Now define the language generated by M as

$$L(M) = \{w \in \Sigma^+ \mid \Delta(I(w)) \in F\} \cup \{\epsilon \mid \text{if } e = 1\}. \tag{13}$$

In [23] it was proved that a language is generated by a linear conjunctive grammar if and only if it is accepted by a trellis automaton.

The grammar-to-automaton construction methods given in [23] are based on subset construction and thus always involve exponential blowup. A more practical method is given in [18], which allows, for instance, to convert the grammar for the language $\{wcw \mid w \in \{a, b\}^*\}$ given in Section 2.2 to a 35-state automaton. On the other hand, a superpolynominal lower bound for the succinctness tradeoff between linear conjunctive grammars and trellis automata is proved in [21].

Generally, the relationship between these grammars and these automata resembles that between regular expressions and DFAs: the former are better suited for human use, while the latter are easier to implement. A survey of other formal systems computationally equivalent to these two is given in [23].

3.3 Languages Generated

As shown in Section 2.2, for some linear conjunctive languages, such as $\{wcw \mid w \in \{a, b\}^*\}$, one can construct a grammar relatively easily; in [20] the idea of construction of this grammar is extended to produce a grammar for the language of all derivations in a fixed finite string-rewriting system, and consequently for the language of all computations of any fixed Turing machine. By the results of [23,18], all such grammars can be directly converted to trellis automata, and in most cases it would be much harder to construct these automata manually.

On the other hand, some languages admit a natural and succinct representation using trellis automata, while no human-readable linear conjunctive grammar for them has been constructed so far. One such example is the known *Dyck language* of strings of matching parentheses; the general idea of constructing a one-way real-time cellular automaton for this language was given in [6], while an actual construction of a trellis automaton was independently done in [3]. Another example of this kind is the language $\{a^n b^{2^n} \mid n \geqslant 1\}$, which can be accepted by a trellis automaton that counts from 1 to 2^n in binary notation, as shown in [8].

It has recently been proved [25] that every linear conjunctive language is generated by a linear conjunctive grammar with as few as two nonterminals. On the other hand, one nonterminal is not enough even for some regular languages, e.g., ba^*b, which yields a classification of this family into one-nonterminal and two-nonterminal languages. However, it turns out that one-nonterminal grammars, which are equivalent to one-variable language equations with union, intersection and linear concatenation, can still denote some **P**-complete languages, and generally every linear conjunctive language can be represented as an intersection of a one-nonterminal linear conjunctive language with a regular language [25].

4 General Properties

Although the membership problem for conjunctive grammars is decidable in polynomial time, the rest of the commonly considered problems – e.g., emptiness, finiteness, equivalence, inclusion, regularity or context-freeness – are undecidable already for linear conjunctive grammars [13,20].

Let us discuss the position of conjunctive and linear conjunctive languages in the hierarchy of language families. Every linear context-free grammar is both context-free and linear conjunctive, while every context-free and every linear conjunctive grammar is conjunctive. Therefore, the families of context-free and linear conjunctive languages both are subsets of the family of conjunctive languages, and each of them contains all linear context-free languages.

In order to show that these inclusions are proper, let us consider a few examples of languages. The language $\{wcw \mid w \in \{a, b\}^*\}$ [13] is linear con-

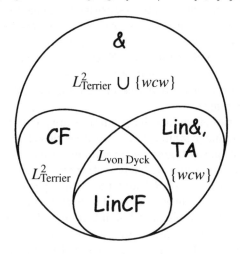

Figure 3. Relationship between families of grammars.

junctive, but not context-free. Another language $\{a^n b^n\} \cup \{a^n b(a|b)^* ab^n\}$ discovered by V. Terrier [29] is a linear context-free language by itself, but its square, although obviously context-free, is known not to be linear conjunctive [29] (the actual proof in [29] is, of course, done in terms of one-way real-time cellular automata; the equivalence result of [23] extends it to linear conjunctive grammars). This shows that these two families are incomparable subsets of the family of all conjunctive languages. There exist conjunctive languages which are neither context-free nor linear conjunctive, and $L^2_{Terrier} \cup \{wcw\}$ is an example of such a language.

As mentioned above, the family of linear context-free languages is included in the intersection of context-free and linear conjunctive languages. In order to show that this inclusion is proper, consider the Dyck language over a binary alphabet, normally defined using a context-free grammar $S \to aSb \mid SS \mid \epsilon$. It is linear conjunctive [3,6], but it is known not to be linear context-free, which proves our claim of strictness of inclusion.

The relationship between the main subsets of conjunctive languages is outlined in Figure 3. The question of what lies beyond conjunctive languages remains open. There exists a yet unpublished method [12] of converting a given conjunctive grammar to a linear bounded automaton, which implies that conjunctive languages form a subset of context-sensitive languages; another stronger method (with proof to be published) converts a certain generalization of conjunctive grammar to a deterministic linear bounded automaton [24]. Since no method of showing a context-sensitive language to be nonconjunctive has been discovered, it is still not known whether this inclusion is proper. It can only be noted that it can easily be proved to be proper under the assumption that $\mathbf{P} \neq \mathbf{PSPACE}$ [13]. Nothing is known on the relationship between conjunctive grammars and other known families of languages, such as the Boolean closure of context-free languages, and its proper subset, the co-context-free languages.

Closure properties of conjunctive grammars are partially known. It is easy to prove that the language family they generate is closed under union, intersection and concatenation (by taking two grammars with start symbols S_1 and S_2 and producing a new grammar with a new start symbol S, equipped with rules $\{S \to S_1, S \to S_2\}$, $\{S \to S_1 \& S_2\}$ and $\{S \to S_1 S_2\}$ respectively), as well as under Kleene star (using a new start symbol S with rules $\{S \to S_1 S, S \to \epsilon\}$) [13]. By a technically complicated but intuitively clear construction it was proved that they are closed under inverse homomorphism [26]. Nonclosure under homomorphism follows from the classical representability results for recursively enumerable languages [7], while nonclosure under ϵ-free homomorphism was conjectured in [22], because the opposite would imply $\mathbf{P} = \mathbf{NP}$.

Closure properties of linear conjunctive grammars have been studied much better. If a grammar representation is used, they are immediately seen to be closed under union and intersection. The first proof of their closure under complement was given in [20], which included an effective procedure for constructing a negation of a given grammar. When trellis automata are used, the closure under complement becomes self-evident, as it suffices to invert the set of accepting states, while the closure under union and intersection can be proved by a standard direct product construction [3,6]. Nonclosure under concatenation and even under square follows from [29], while the question of closure under different types of homomorphism was studied in [27] with a negative answer on unrestricted ϵ-free homomorphism. However, every inverse homomorphism preserves the class of linear conjunctive languages [4,8].

It remains an open problem whether linear conjunctive languages are closed under Kleene star; perhaps, a negative answer could be obtained using the method of [29]; probably it would make sense to try proving that $L^*_{Terrier}$ is not a linear conjunctive language.

5 Recognition and Parsing

As mentioned in the Introduction, one of the arguments for the practical value of conjunctive grammars is the existence of efficient recognition and parsing algorithms [13,14,16,17,18].

5.1 Tabular Algorithm for Arbitrary Grammars

This algorithm is based upon the general idea of the well-known context-free parsing algorithm due to Graham, Harrison and Ruzzo, which, given an input string $a_1 \ldots a_n$, constructs an upper-triangular matrix $\{t_{ij}\}_{0 \leqslant i \leqslant j \leqslant n}$ of sets of *dotted rules* of the form $A \to \alpha \cdot \beta$ (where $A \to \alpha\beta$ is a rule of the grammar), such that $A \to \alpha \cdot \beta \in t_{ij}$ if only if α derives the substring $a_{i+1} \ldots a_j$ of the input string and at the same time $S \Longrightarrow^* a_1 \ldots a_i A \gamma$ for some string γ.

The generalization of the GHR algorithm for the case of conjunctive grammars [16] creates a similar matrix $\{t_{ij}\}$ of *dotted conjuncts* of the same form $A \to \alpha \cdot \beta$, such that there exists a rule $A \to \gamma_1 \& \ldots \& \alpha\beta \& \ldots \gamma_m$. A dotted conjunct $A \to \alpha \cdot \beta$ is in t_{ij} if and only if α derives $a_{i+1} \ldots a_j$ and there exists a finite sequence of *conjuncts* $C_{t-1} \to \gamma_t C_t \delta_t$ ($0 < t \leqslant k$, where $k \geqslant 0$ is some number), such that $C_0 = S$, $C_k = A$ and there exists a factorization $a_1 \ldots a_i = u_1 \ldots u_k$, where γ_t derives u_t for every t.

The algorithm is applicable to any conjunctive grammar, works in cubic time, uses quadratic space and can construct a parse tree of the input either along with computing the matrix or after the matrix is computed [16]. If the grammar is linear, then the complexity is reduced to quadratic time and $O(n)$ space. However, in order to achieve the $O(n)$ space complexity, one has to sacrifice the possibility of parse tree construction.

5.2 Top-Down Parsing and Recursive Descent

A context-free *strong LL(k)* top-down parser attempts to construct the leftmost derivation of an input string, using k lookahead symbols to determine the rules to apply to nonterminals, and a pushdown store to hold the right parts of the sentential forms that constitute the derivation. Left parts of sentential forms are prefixes of the input string that are being compared with the input symbols and then discarded.

The conjunctive generalization of this algorithm [14] uses *tree-structured pushdown* to handle multiple branches of computation simultaneously, thus ensuring that substrings of the input string are derived from every conjunct of a rule. The precomputed parsing table used by this algorithm is a mapping from $N \times \Sigma^{\leqslant k}$ to the set of rules of the grammar, where $\Sigma^{\leqslant k}$ denotes $\{w \mid w \in \Sigma^*, \ |w| \leqslant k\}$.

In its deterministic case the algorithm is applicable to a subclass of conjunctive grammars. Although there exist grammars even for the simplest languages on which the algorithm works in exponential time and uses exponential space, its complexity is nevertheless linear for some practical cases, which include the intersection closure of context-free LL(k) languages. Similarly to context-free LL, the conjunctive LL parsing method can be implemented manually using a variation of the recursive descent technique.

5.3 LR Parsing

The Generalized LR parsing algorithm for context-free grammars, introduced by Tomita in 1986, is a polynomial-time implementation of nondeterministic LR parsing that uses a graph-structured stack to represent the contents of the nondeterministic parser's pushdown for all possible branches of computation at a single computation step.

The same idea of graph-structured pushdown turns out to be suitable for parsing conjunctive grammars. While generalized LR parsing uses graph-structured pushdown merely to simulate nondeterminism whenever it arises, the extension of this algorithm for the conjunctive case [17] additionally relies on doing several computations at once for implementing the conjunction operation. In order to reduce by a rule, it requires multiple paths corresponding to the conjuncts of the rule to be present in the graph at the same time. Instead of defining a particular way of constructing a parsing table, the algorithm was proved correct for any table that satisfies the requirements listed in [17], and an extension of context-free SLR(k) method conforming to these requirements was developed.

Although internally the algorithm is somewhat different from the context-free generalized LR, it looks very much the same from the user's side, and hence one could expect it to be as suitable for practical use as the context-free generalized LR has proved to be. The algorithm is applicable to any grammar and can be implemented to work in no more than $O(n^3)$ time. In many common cases it is even faster: for instance, it is known to work in linear time for the Boolean closure of deterministic context-free languages [17].

This completes the list of the known parsing methods for conjunctive grammars. Almost all context-free algorithms of significance have been generalized for the case if conjunctive grammars; polylogarithmic-time parallel recognition algorithms, such as Rytter's algorithm [28], form the only exception. However, it is likely that any generalization of these algorithms would have time complexity greater than polylogarithmic, as the opposite would imply $\mathbf{NC} = \mathbf{P}$ [22], which is generally believed not to be the case.

6 Open Problems

The existing results on efficient parsing for conjunctive grammars [13,14,16,17,18] are probably already sufficient for using them in the applications (especially given the parser generator [19]), and provide a certain justification of the practical value of the concept. However, the study of the theoretical properties of this language family [13,15,20,21,22,23,25,26,27] seems to be quite far from completion, with the very basic issues still unsolved.

Perhaps the most crucial thing that ought to be done in order to advance the study of conjunctive grammars is to invent a method of proving context-sensitive languages not to be expressible by conjunctive grammars. For context-free languages, one such method is given by the pumping lemma. Already for finite intersections of context-free languages an analog of pumping lemma cannot exist, since these languages do not possess bounded growth property; still the results of [11,30] cover some important cases of inexpressibility as such intersections. However, there are no results of this kind for conjunctive grammars, and no single context-sensitive language have been proved to be not conjunctive. It can be conjectured that $\{ww \mid w \in \{a,b\}^*\}$, $\{a^{2^n} \mid n \geqslant 0\}$ and all $\mathbf{NP}$-hard sets should be such languages, but no proofs of these facts have been devised so far.

A similar question for linear conjunctive grammars has been addressed and partially answered. Using a counting argument, one can prove some languages to be not linear conjunctive: e.g., the square of Terrier language [29] or the language $\{a^n b^{2^{f(n)}} \mid n \geqslant 1\}$ for any superlinear function $f : \mathbb{N} \to \mathbb{N}$. In [20], every linear conjunctive language over unary alphabet was shown to be regular.

This brings us directly to the question of whether conjunctive grammars of general form over unary alphabet can generate nonregular languages, which is an interesting number-theoretic problem in itself. Although a negative answer could be conjectured, attempts of proving it meet certain difficulties. While the proof of the similar fact for context-free grammars is already quite nontrivial and essentially relies on the pumping lemma, in the more general case of conjunctive grammars there is no pumping lemma to rely upon, and thus an entirely new proof should be found. If such a proof can be found, it would imply an entirely new proof for the context-free case, which would be interesting in itself. However, it should be noted that language equations with concatenation and complement *only* over a unary alphabet actually can denote a certain nonregular language [10], which makes the question of whether union, intersection and concatenation can denote one even more interesting and challenging.

The current state of research and bibliography on conjunctive grammars is maintained at

http://www.cs.queensu.ca/home/okhotin/conjunctive/

Since this class of grammars can potentially be used instead of context-free grammars in the language-processing tasks where the generative power of context-free grammars does not suffice, this gives a reason to continue the study of their theoretical properties – for instance, to solve open questions listed above. Another suggested direction of study is to try to invent some new formalism based upon conjunctive grammars that would be even more expressive and would still inherit the good properties of context-free grammars. The recently introduced Boolean grammars [24], which have semantics based entirely upon language equations, constitute an attempt of this kind.

Investigating all these issues and building a complete theory of conjunctive grammars and related formal systems could become a good contribution to formal language theory.

I am grateful to Michael Domaratzki and Kai Salomaa for their helpful comments on the manuscript of the earlier version of this article, published in the Bulletin of the EATCS. I wish to thank Elena Isayenkova for taking a look at the final revision.

References

1. J. Autebert, J. Berstel, and L. Boasson, Context-free languages and pushdown automata, *Handbook of Formal Languages*, Vol. 1, 111–174, Springer-Verlag, Berlin, 1997.
2. C. Choffrut and K. Culik II, On real-time cellular automata and trellis automata, *Acta Informatica*, 21 (1984), 393–407.
3. K. Culik II, J. Gruska, and A. Salomaa, Systolic trellis automata, I and II, *International Journal of Computer Mathematics*, 15 (1984) 195–212, and 16 (1984) 3–22.
4. K. Culik II, J. Gruska, and A. Salomaa, Systolic trellis automata: stability, decidability and complexity, *Information and Control*, 71 (1986) 218–230.
5. J. Dassow and Gh. Păun, *Regulated Rewriting in Formal Language Theory*, Akademie-Verlag, Berlin, and Springer-Verlag, Berlin, 1989.

6. C. Dyer, One-way bounded cellular automata, *Information and Control*, 44 (1980), 261–281.

7. S. Ginsburg, S.A. Greibach, and M. A. Harrison, One-way stack automata. *Journal of the ACM*, 14:2 (1967) 389–418.

8. O. H. Ibarra and S. M. Kim, Characterizations and computational complexity of systolic trellis automata, *Theoretical Computer Science*, 29 (1984), 123–153.

9. M. Latta and R. Wall, Intersective context-free languages, *Lenguajes Naturales y Lenguajes Formales IX*, Barcelona, 1993, 15–43.

10. E. L. Leiss, Unrestricted complementation in language equations over a one-letter alphabet, *Theoretical Computer Science*, 132 (1994), 71–93.

11. L. Y. Liu and P. Weiner, An infinite hierarchy of intersections of context-free languages. *Mathematical Systems Theory*, 7 (1973) 187–192.

12. A. Okhotin, Complexity issues in the analysis of conjunctive grammars, candidate of science (Ph.D.) thesis, Faculty of Computational Mathematics and Cybernetics, Moscow State University, 2002, in Russian; preliminary version defended as a diploma work (M.Sc. thesis) in 2001.

13. A. Okhotin, Conjunctive grammars, *Journal of Automata, Languages and Combinatorics*, 6:4 (2001), 519–535; preliminary version presented at DCAGRS 2000 workshop (London, Ontario, Canada, 27–29 July 2000).

14. A. Okhotin, Top-down parsing of conjunctive languages, *Grammars*, 5:1 (2002), 21–40.

15. A. Okhotin, Conjunctive grammars and systems of language equations, *Programming and Computer Software*, 28:5 (2002), 243–249.

16. A. Okhotin, A recognition and parsing algorithm for arbitrary conjunctive grammars, *Theoretical Computer Science*, 302 (2003), 365–399.

17. A. Okhotin, LR parsing for conjunctive grammars, *Grammars*, 5:2 (2002), 81–124.

18. A. Okhotin, Automaton representation of linear conjunctive languages, *International Journal of Foundations of Computer Science*, to appear; preliminary version in: *Implementation and Application of Automata* (Proceedings of CIAA 2002, Tours, France, July 3–5, 2002), LNCS 2608, 169–181.

19. A. Okhotin, Whale Calf, a parser generator for conjunctive grammars, *Implementation and Application of Automata* (Proceedings of CIAA 2002, Tours, France, July 3–5, 2002), LNCS 2608, 213–220; the software is available at http://www.cs.queensu.ca/home/okhotin/whalecalf/.

20. A. Okhotin, On the closure properties of linear conjunctive languages, *Theoretical Computer Science*, 299 (2003), 663–685.

21. A. Okhotin, State complexity of linear conjunctive languages, *Pre-

proceedings of DCFS 2002, London, Ontario, Canada, August 21-24, 2002, 256–270; journal version submitted.

22. A. Okhotin, The hardest linear conjunctive language, *Information Processing Letters*, 86:5 (2003), 247–253.

23. A. Okhotin, On the equivalence of linear conjunctive grammars and trellis automata, submitted; preliminary version, entitled Automaton representation of linear conjunctive languages, appeared in: *Developments in Language Theory* (Proceedings of DLT 2002, Kyoto, Japan, September 18–21, 2002), LNCS 2450, 393–404.

24. A. Okhotin, Boolean grammars, *Developments in Language Theory* (Proceedings of DLT 2003, Szeged, Hungary, July 7–11, 2003), LNCS 2710, 398–410.

25. A. Okhotin, On the number of nonterminals in linear conjunctive grammars, *Proceedings of DCFS 2003* (Budapest, Hungary, July 12–14, 2003), MTA SZTAKI, Budapest, 2003, 274–283; journal version submitted.

26. A. Okhotin, Conjunctive languages are closed under inverse homomorphism, Technical Report 2003–468, School of Computing, Queen's University, Kingston, Ontario, Canada.

27. A. Okhotin, Homomorphisms preserving trellis languages, submitted.

28. W. Rytter, On the recognition of context-free languages, *5th Symposium on Fundamentals of Computation Theory*, LNCS 208, Springer-Verlag, Berlin, 1985, 315–322.

29. V. Terrier, On real-time one-way cellular array, *Theoretical Computer Science*, 141 (1995), 331–335.

30. D. Wotschke, The Boolean closures of deterministic and nondeterministic context-free languages, In: W. Brauer (ed.), *Gesellschaft für Informatik e. V., 3. Jahrestagung 1973*, LNCS 1, 113–121.

STATE COMPLEXITY OF FINITE AND INFINITE REGULAR LANGUAGES

SHENG YU

Department of Computer Science
University of Western Ontario
London, Ontario, Canada N6A 5B7
E-mail: syu@csd.uwo.ca

1 Introduction and Recent Results

State complexity is a type of descriptional complexity for regular languages based on the deterministic finite automaton (DFA) model. The state complexity of a regular language is the number of states of the minimal DFA that accepts the language. The state complexity of a class of regular languages is the maximum among all the state complexities of the languages in the class. Clearly, state complexity is a worst-case complexity. When we speak about the state complexity of an operation on regular languages, we mean the state complexity of the resulting languages of the operation in term of the operand languages. For example, we say that the state complexity of the union of an m-state DFA language, i.e., a language accepted by an m-state complete DFA, and an n-state DFA language is mn.

The number of states of a minimal DFA that accepts a language is a natural descriptional measurement of the language. For each regular language, the minimal DFA accepting it is unique up to an isomorphism. When the size of the alphabet is known, the number of transitions of a complete DFA is totally determined by the number of states. The state complexity of an operation gives a lower bound to both the time and the space complexities of the operation.

State complexity issues in general were already considered by many researchers in the sixties and seventies [10,11,6]. However, the systematic study of the state complexity of regular language operations started much later. The first such paper was published in 1994 in [18], where the state complexities of basic operations of regular languages, i.e., catenation, Kleene star, etc., were studied. The results from [18] as well as some previously known results on the basic operations on regular languages can be summarized as follows.

Let Σ be an alphabet, L_1 and L_2 be an m-state DFA language and an n-state DFA language over Σ, respectively. A list of operations on L_1 and L_2 and their state complexities are:

- $L_1 L_2 : m2^n - 2^{n-1}$;

- $(L_2)^* : 2^{n-1} + 2^{n-2}$;

- $L_1 \cap L_2 : mn$;

- $L_1 \cup L_2 : mn$;

- $L \backslash L_2 : 2^n - 1$, where L is an arbitrary language;

- $L_2/L : n$, where L is an arbitrary language;

- $L_2^R : 2^n$.

Note that $L\backslash L_2 = \{y \mid x \in L \text{ and } xy \in L_2\}$, $L_2/L = \{x \mid y \in L \text{ and } xy \in L_2\}$, and L_2^R is the reversal of L_2. For the above results, we consider that the size of the alphabet is arbitrary (greater than or equal to 1). For most operations, the worst cases can be reached when the size of the alphabet is two. For the catenation, i.e., $L_1 L_2$, the worst cases can be reached when the size of the alphabet is at least three. The exact bound for the catenation of L_1 and L_2 over a two-letter alphabet in the worst case is still open at the moment. The state complexity of some of the above operations is much lower if we consider only languages over a unary alphabet. For languages over a unary alphabet, we have:

- $L_1 L_2 : mn$ (if $(m, n) = 1$);

- $(L_2)^* : (n-1)^2 + 1$;

- $L_1 \cap L_2 : mn$ (if $(m, n) = 1$);

- $L_1 \cup L_2 : mn$ (if $(m, n) = 1$).

By $(m, n) = 1$, we mean that $gcd(m, n) = 1$, i.e., m and n are relatively prime.

Recently, there have been quite a few papers published on state complexity issues [8,13,3,7,2,1,16].

Pighizzini and Shallit investigate the state complexity of some basic operations on unary languages in [8] and [13], respectively. Note that in [18], the state complexities for the concatenation, union, and intersection of unary languages were considered only in the cases when $(m, n) = 1$. They were open in the general cases. In [8] and [13], the general cases of those operations are studied. A unary DFA A of n states can be described by a pair (λ, μ), where $\mu \geq 0$ is the number of states on the initial "tail" and $\lambda \geq 0$ is the number of states of the "cycle", $n = \mu + \lambda$. The pair (λ, μ) is called the size of A. Let L_1 and L_2 be two unary languages accepted by DFA A_1 and A_2 of size (λ_1, μ_1) and (λ_2, μ_2), respectively. It is shown in [13] that the intersection (the union, respectively) of L_1 and L_2 is accepted by a DFA of size $(lcm(\lambda_1, \lambda_2), \max(\mu_1, \mu_2))$. It is also shown that the upper bound $(lcm(\lambda_1, \lambda_2), \max(\mu_1, \mu_2))$ is tight in general. Catenation is considered in [8]. It is shown that $L_1 L_2$ is accepted by a DFA of size (λ, μ) where $\lambda = lcm(\lambda_1, \lambda_2)$ and $\mu = \mu_1 + \mu_2 + lcm(\lambda_1, \lambda_2) - 1$, and this bound is tight in general.

In [3], Domaratzki investigates the state complexity of $\frac{1}{2}(L)$, for a regular language L, and other proportional removals, where

$$\frac{1}{2}(L) = \{x \in \Sigma^* \mid \exists y \in \Sigma^* \text{ with } |x| = |y| \text{ and } xy \in L\}.$$

Let n be the number of states of a DFA that accepts L. It is shown that the state complexity of $\frac{1}{2}(L)$ has an upper bound of $nH(n)$, where $H(n) = e^{\sqrt{n \log n}}$, and the state complexity is greater than $cH(n)$, for some constant c, for infinitely many n. For regular languages over a one-letter alphabet, say L accepted by an n-state DFA, the state complexity for $\frac{1}{2}(L)$ is n.

In [2], Câmpeanu, Salomaa, and Yu study the state complexity of the shuffle of two regular languages. It is shown that for an m-state DFA language L_1 and an n-state DFA language L_2, $2^{mn} - 1$ is an upper bound for the state complexity of the shuffle of L_1 and L_2, and this upper bound is tight in general. Note that in that paper, incomplete DFA are used. The construction uses an alphabet of size 5.

All the above mentioned results are on the worst case state complexity. In [7], Nicaud investigates average state complexity of operations on unary languages. Let A (respectively A') be an n-state (respectively n'-state) deterministic and connected unary automaton. The main results in [7] can be summarized as follows:

- The probability that A is minimal tends toward $1/2$ when n tends toward infinity.

- The average state complexity of $L(A)$ is n.

- The average state complexity of $L(A) \cap L(A')$ is $\frac{3\zeta(3)}{2\pi^2} nn'$, where ζ is the Riemann "zeta"-function.

- The average state complexity of $L(A)^*$ is bounded by a constant.

- If $n \le n' \le P(n)$, for some polynomial P, then the average state complexity of $L(A)L(A')$ is bounded by a constant (depending on P).

Examining the worst case state complexity results on the basic operations, e.g., catenation, union, intersection, and complementation, on regular languages, one would notice that all the worst cases are given by infinite languages. This observation raises a question: Are finite languages significantly different from infinite regular languages in state complexity of their operations? For example, would the state complexity of the union of two finite languages accepted by an m-state and an n-state DFA, respectively, be $O(m + n)$ instead of mn? In [1], Câmpeanu, Culik II, Salomaa, and Yu investigate the (worst case) state complexity of finite language operations.

Finite languages are, perhaps, one of the most often used but least studied classes of languages. Finite languages are exactly the languages accepted by acyclic finite automata. It has been shown that there is a linear (time) algorithm for the minimization of an acyclic DFA [9]. However, for the minimization of a general DFA, the best known algorithm has a time complexity $O(n \log n)$ by Hopcroft in 1971 [4].

In this article, we compare the state complexity results for finite and infinite regular languages. We first consider the operations on languages over a one-letter alphabet. Then we consider the general cases. In the one-letter alphabet cases, most of the operations on finite languages have a much lower state complexity than the corresponding operations on regular languages. However, in the general cases, only the catenation of two finite languages, when the first language is accepted by a DFA with a constant number of final states, has a much lower state complexity than its regular language counterpart.

2   Preliminaries

A deterministic finite automaton (DFA) is denoted by a quintuple $(Q, \Sigma, \delta, q_0, F)$ where Q is the finite set of states, Σ is the finite alphabet, $\delta : Q \times \Sigma \rightarrow Q$ is the transition function, $q_0 \in Q$ is the starting state, and $F \subseteq Q$ is the set of final states. In this paper, all the DFA are assumed to be *complete* DFA. By a complete DFA we mean that there is a transition defined for each letter of the alphabet and each state, i.e., δ is a total function. In contrast, a DFA is called an incomplete DFA if its transition function is a partial function rather than a total function.

The transition function δ is extended in the natural way to a function $\hat{\delta} : Q \times \Sigma^* \rightarrow Q$. We denote $\hat{\delta}$ simply by δ in this paper.

For any $x \in \Sigma^*$, we use $\#(x)$ to denote the length of x and $\#_a(x)$, for some $a \in \Sigma$, to denote the number of appearances of a in x. The empty word is denoted by ε.

A word $w \in \Sigma^*$ is accepted by a DFA $A = (Q, \Sigma, \delta, q_0, F)$ if $\delta(q_0, w) \in F$. The language accepted by A, denoted $L(A)$, is the set $\{w \in \Sigma^* \mid \delta(q_0, w) \in F\}$. Two DFA are said to be equivalent if they accept the same language.

A nondeterministic finite automaton (NFA) is denoted also by a quintuple $(Q, \Sigma, \eta, q_0, F)$ where $\eta \subseteq Q \times (\Sigma \cup \{\varepsilon\}) \times Q$ is a transition relation rather than a function, and Q, Σ, q_0, and F are defined similarly as in a DFA. The words and languages accepted by NFA are defined similarly to those by DFA.

For a set S, we use $\#S$ to denote the cardinality of S. For a language L, we define $L^{\leq l} = \bigcup_{i=0}^{l} L^i$.

For $L \subseteq \Sigma^*$, we define a relation $\equiv_L \subseteq \Sigma^* \times \Sigma^*$ by

$$x \equiv_L y \text{ iff } xz \in L \Leftrightarrow yz \in L \text{ for all } z \in \Sigma^*.$$

Clearly, $\equiv_L$ is an equivalence relation, which partitions Σ^* into equivalence classes. The number of equivalence classes of $\equiv_L$ is called the *index* of $\equiv_L$. The Myhill-Nerode Theorem [5] states that L is regular if and only if $\equiv_L$ has a finite index and the minimal number of states of a complete DFA that accepts L is equal to the index of $\equiv_L$.

For a rather complete background knowledge in automata theory, the reader may refer to [5,12].

The following lemma will be used in the subsequent sections. It can be proved rather easily. We omit the proof.

Lemma 1 *Let $m, n > 0$ be two arbitrary integers such that $(m, n) = 1$ (i.e., m and n are relatively prime). The largest integer that cannot be presented as $cm + dn$ for any integers $c, d \geq 0$ is $mn - (m + n)$.*

3 Finite vs. Regular Languages Over a One-letter Alphabet

As we have mentioned in the introduction, we start our comparison of the state complexity of operations between regular and finite languages over a one-letter alphabet.

We first list the basic results below and then give detailed explanations for some of the operations.

We assume that L_1 is an m-state DFA language and L_2 an n-state DFA language, $\Sigma = \{a\}$, and $m, n > 1$.

	Finite	Regular
$L_1 \cup L_2$	$\max(m,n)$	mn, for $(m,n) = 1$
$L_1 \cap L_2$	$\min(m,n)$	mn, for $(m,n) = 1$
$\Sigma^* - L_1$	m	m
$L_1 L_2$	$m + n - 1$	mn, for $(m,n) = 1$
L_1^R	m	m
L_1^*	$m^2 - 7m + 13$, for $m > 4$	$(m-1)^2 - 1$

Note that for *finite languages*, the state complexity for each of the union, intersection, and catenation operations is linear, while it is quadratic for infinite regular languages.

In the above table, all results for finite languages are relatively trivial except for L_1^*. We give an informal proof in the following. Let L_1 be accepted by an m-state DFA A_1 and A be a minimal DFA accepting L_1^*. It is clear that the length of the longest word accepted by A_1 is $m - 2$. (Note that the m states include a 'sink state'.) We consider the following three cases (1) A_1 has one final state; (2) A_1 has two final states; (3) A_1 has three or more final states. If (1), then A has $m - 1$ states. In case (2), the worst case is given by $L = \{a^{m-2}, a^{m-3}\}$, for $m > 3$. By Lemma 1, the length of the longest word that is not in L_1^* is

$$(m-2)(m-3) - (2m-5) = m^2 - 7m + 11.$$

Then A has exactly $m^2 - 7m + 13$ states. In case (3), it is easy to see that A cannot have more than $m^2 - 7m + 13$ states.

For *regular languages*, the proofs and detailed discussions can be found in [18].

For the transformation from an n-state NFA to a DFA, it is clear in the case of finite languages over a one-letter alphabet, at most n states are needed. However, in the case of an infinite regular language over a one-letter alphabet, the problem is still open.

4   Finite vs. Regular Languages Over an Arbitrary Alphabet

For the one-letter alphabet case which we have discussed in the previous section, the state complexities for most operations on finite languages are of a lower order than those for their corresponding operations on regular languages. However, this is no longer true in the case when the size of the alphabet is arbitrary. Although none of the operations on finite languages, except the complementation, can reach the exact bound for operations on regular languages, most of them have a complexity that is of the same order as the corresponding operation on regular languages.

We list the state complexity of the basic operations for both finite and regular languages over an arbitrary alphabet below. All the results for regular languages are given as exact numbers. However, we use the big "O" notation for most of the results for finite languages due to the fact that either the exact formulas we have obtained are acutely nonintuitive or we do not have an exact result, yet. More detailed explanations follow the table.

We assume that L_1 and L_2 are accepted by an m-state DFA $A_1 = (Q_1, \Sigma, \delta_1, s_1, F_1)$ and an n-state DFA $A_2 = (Q_2, \Sigma, \delta_2, s_2, F_2)$, respectively, and $m, n > 1$. We use t to denote the number of final states in A_1.

	Finite	Regular
$L_1 \cup L_2$	$O(mn)$	mn
$L_1 \cap L_2$	$O(mn)$	mn
$\Sigma^* - L_1$	m	m
$L_1 L_2$	$O(mn^{t-1} + n^t)$	$(2m - 1)2^{n-1}$
L_1^R	$O(2^{m/2})$, for $|\Sigma| = 2$	2^m
L_1^*	$2^{m-3} + 2^{m-4}$, for $m \geq 4$	$2^{m-1} + 2^{m-2}$

For *union* and *intersection* of finite languages, it was expected that their state complexities would be linear, more specifically $O(m + n)$, but it turns out that both of them are in the order of mn although neither of them can reach the exact bound mn.

It is easy to show that mn states are sufficient for both union and intersection by the following simple argument. We can construct a DFA $A = (Q, \Sigma, \delta, s, F)$ which is the cross-product of A_1 and A_2, i.e., $Q = Q_1 \times Q_2$, $\delta = \delta_1 \times \delta_2$ that is $\delta((q_1, q_2), a) = (\delta(q_1, a), \delta_2(q_2, a))$, $s = (s_1, s_2)$. For the union operation, $F = \{(q_1, q_2) \mid q_1 \in F_1 \text{ or } q_2 \in F_2\}$ and for the intersection operation, $F = \{(q_1, q_2) \mid q_1 \in F_1 \text{ and } q_2 \in F_2\}$.

Note that the pairs of the form (s_1, q_2) where $q_2 \neq s_2$ and (q_1, s_2) where $q_1 \neq s_1$ are never reached from the starting state (s_1, s_2), and therefore, are useless. So, $mn - (m + n - 2)$ states are sufficient for both the union and intersection of two finite languages accepted by an m-state and an n-state DFA, respectively. However, this is a very rough upper bound. Much tighter upper bounds for union and intersection of finite languages are given in [1], which unfortunately are in a very complicated and highly incomprehensible form. Thus, we will not quote them in this paper.

It is more interesting to show that the state complexities of those two operations are indeed of the order of mn but not lower. The following examples were originally given by Shallit [14]. Automaton-based examples are given in [1], which give better lower bounds than the examples below. We choose to present the following examples due to their clarity and intuitiveness.

For the intersection of two finite languages, consider the following example. Let $\Sigma = \{a, b\}$ and

$$L_1 = \{w \in \Sigma^* \mid \#_a(w) + \#_b(w) = 2n\},$$
$$L_2 = \{w \in \Sigma^* \mid \#_a(w) + 2\#_b(w) = 3n\}.$$

Clearly, L_1 is accepted by a DFA with $2n + 2$ states and L_2 by a DFA with $3n + 2$ states. The intersection $L = L_1 \cap L_2$ is

$$\{w \in \Sigma^* \mid \#_a(w) = \#_b(w) = n\}$$

One can prove that any DFA accepting L needs at least $(n + 1)^2 + 1$ states by the Myhill-Nerode Theorem [5].

For the union of two finite languages, the example is slightly more complicated. Let $\Sigma = \{a, b\}$ and

$$L_1 = \{w \in \Sigma^* \mid \#(w) \leq 3t \text{ and } \#_a(w) + \#_b(w) \neq 2t\},$$
$$L_2 = \{w \in \Sigma^* \mid \#_a(w) + 2\#_b(w) < 3t\}.$$

It is clear that $L_1 \cup L_2$ includes all words in Σ^* of length less than or equal to $3t$ except those words w such that $\#(w) = 2t$ and $\#_b(w) \geq t$. One can prove that any DFA accepting $L_1 \cup L_2$ needs more than t^2 states by checking the number of the equivalence classes of $\equiv_{L_1 \cup L_2}$.

We now consider the *catenation* operation. Notice that in the finite language case, if the number of final states in A_1 is a constant, then the state complexity of catenation is a polynomial in terms of m and n. In particular, if A_1 has only one final state, then the state complexity is linear, i.e., $m + n$. In contrast, for infinite regular languages, there are examples in which A_1 has only one final state but any DFA accepting the catenation of the two languages needs at least $(2m - 1)2^{n-1}$ states [18,17]. This is one of the small number of cases in which the state complexities for finite and infinite regular languages, respectively, are in different orders.

We now give the proof for the finite language case. For the general case of the catenation of regular languages, the reader may refer to [18] or [17].

A DFA $A = (Q, \Sigma, \delta, 0, F)$ with $Q = \{0, 1, \ldots, n\}$ is called an *ordered* DFA if, for any $p, q \in Q$, the condition $\delta(p, a) = q$ implies that $p \leq q$. A DFA is said to be *reduced* if each state is reached from the starting state and each state, except the sink state, can reach a final state. Without loss of generality, we assume that all the DFA in the following are reduced and ordered.

For convenience, we introduce the following notation:

$$\binom{n}{\leq i} = \sum_{j=0}^{i} \binom{n}{j}.$$

Theorem 1 *Let $A_i = (Q_i, \Sigma, \delta_i, 0, F_i)$, $i = 1, 2$, be two DFA accepting finite languages L_i, $i = 1, 2$, respectively, and $\#Q_1 = m$, $\#Q_2 = n$, $\#\Sigma = k$, and $\#F_1 = t$, for $m, n > 2$ and $k, t > 0$. Then there exists a DFA $A = (Q, \Sigma, \delta, s, F)$ such that $L(A) = L(A_1)L(A_2)$ and*

$$\#Q \leq \sum_{i=0}^{m-2} \min\left\{ k^i, \binom{n-2}{\leq i}, \binom{n-2}{\leq t-1} \right\}$$

$$+ \min\left\{ k^{m-1}, \binom{n-2}{\leq t} \right\}. \tag{*}$$

Proof. The DFA A is constructed in two steps. First, an NFA A' is constructed from A_1 and A_2 by adding an ε-transition from each final state in F_1 to the starting state 0 of A_2. Then, we construct a DFA A from the NFA A' by the standard subset construction. Again, we assume that A is reduced and ordered.

It is clear that we can view each $q \in Q$ as a pair (q_1, P_2), where $q_1 \in Q_1$ and $P_2 \subseteq Q_2$. The starting state of A is $s = (0, \emptyset)$ if $0 \notin F_1$ or $s = (0, \{0\})$ if $0 \in F_1$.

Let us consider all states $q \in Q$ such that $q = (i, P)$ for a particular state $i \in Q_1 - \{m-1\}$ and some set $P \subseteq Q_2$. Note that $m-1$ $(n-1)$ is the sink state of A_1 (A_2). Since A_1 is ordered and acyclic (except a loop at the sink state), the number of such states in Q is limited by the following three bounds: (1) k^i, (2) $\binom{n-2}{\leq i}$, and (3) $\binom{n-2}{\leq t-1}$. We explain these bounds below informally.

We have (1) as a bound since all states of the form $q = (i, P)$ are at a level $\leq i$, which have at most k^{i-1} predecessors. By saying that a state p is at level i we mean that the length of the longest path from the starting state to p is i.

We now consider (2). Notice that if $q, q' \in Q$ such that $\delta(q, a) = q'$, $q = (q_1, P_2)$ and $q' = (q'_1, P'_2)$, then $\delta_1(q_1, a) = q'_1$ and $P'_2 = \{\delta_2(p, a) \mid p \in P_2\}$ if $q'_1 \notin F_1$ and $P'_2 = \{0\} \cup \{\delta_2(p, a) \mid p \in P_2\}$ if $q'_1 \in F_1$. So, $\#P'_2 > \#P_2$ is possible only when $q'_1 \in F_1$. Therefore, for $q = (i, P)$, $\#P \leq i$ if $i \notin F_1$ and $\#P \leq i + 1$ if $i \in F_1$. In both cases, the maximum number of distinct sets P is $\binom{n-2}{\leq i}$. The number $n-2$ comes from the exclusion of the sink state $n-1$ and starting state 0 of A_2. Note that, for a fixed i, either $0 \in P$ for all $(i, P) \in Q$ or 0 is not in any set P such that $(i, P) \in Q$.

(3) is a bound since for each state $i \in Q_1 - \{m-1\}$, there are at most $t-1$ final states on the path from the starting state to i (not including i).

Therefore, except the state 0, P contains at most $t - 1$ of A_2. Whether 0 is in P is decided by whether i is a final state in A_1.

For the second term of $(*)$, it suffices to explain that for each $(m - 1, P)$, $P \subseteq Q_2$, $\#P$ is bounded by the total number of final states in F_1. $\square$

The following is a natural consequence of the above theorem.

Corollary 1 *Let $A_i = (Q_i, \Sigma, \delta_i, 0, F_i)$, $i = 1, 2$, be two DFA accepting finite languages L_i, $i = 1, 2$, respectively, $\#Q_1 = m$, $\#Q_2 = n$, and $\#F_1 = t$, where $t > 0$ is a constant. Then there exists a DFA $A = (Q, \Sigma, \delta, s, F)$ of $O(mn^{t-1} + n^t)$ states such that $L(A) = L(A_1)L(A_2)$.*

It has been shown in [1] that the bound given in Theorem 1 can be reached in the case $|\Sigma| = 2$.

On the state complexity of the *reversal* of an m-state DFA language, one may think that it should be linear (in terms of m) in the case of finite languages. In fact, it is not even polynomial for finite languages. We explain this by giving an example in the following. Note that a nontrivial proof for a tight upper bound on the state complexity of the reversal of finite languages can be found in [1].

Example 1 Let $L = \{a, b\}^n a \{a, b\}^{\leq n}$ and $m = 2n+3$, where $\{a, b\}^{\leq n}$ denotes

$$\lambda \cup \{a, b\} \cup \{a, b\}^2 \cup \cdots \cup \{a, b\}^n.$$

It is clear that L is a finite language accepted by an m-state (complete) DFA. One can prove that any DFA accepting L^R needs at least 2^n states.

For the star operation, the difference between the state complexities for finite and infinite regular languages is that the latter is 4 times of the former. Both bounds have been shown to be tight [1,18]. Here we only give two examples to demonstrate that the bounds given in the table can be reached.

Example 2 The n-state DFA A shown in Figure 1 accepts a finite language. It is shown in [1] that any DFA accepting $L(A)^*$ needs at least $2^{n-3} + 2^{n-4}$ states (assuming that n is even).

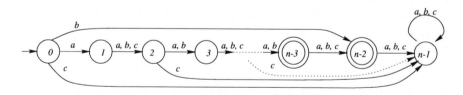

Figure 1. DFA A of n states such that $(L(A))^*$ needs $2^{n-3} + 2^{n-4}$ states

Example 3 Let L be the language accepted by the DFA shown in Figure 2. It is shown in [17] that any DFA accepting L^* requires at least $2^{n-1} + 2^{n-2}$ states.

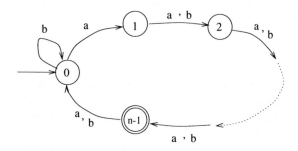

Figure 2. An n-state DFA A_n: The language $(L(A_n))^*$ requires $2^{n-1} + 2^{n-2}$ states

5 Open Problems

Many problems in this area of research are still open. We list some of them in the following.

(1) Most of the state complexity results are worst case results except that the ones in [7] by Nicaud are on the average state complexities of unary language operations. The average state complexities of general regular language operations have not been studied and they can be extremely difficult. The difficulties can be shown by the fact that "the number of non-isomorphic deterministic and connected automata with n states and say, two letters, is not even known" [7].

(2) The state complexities of other nontrivial subsets of regular languages except finite languages have not been studied. For example, it is not know whether the state complexities of the basic operations on locally testable languages are of a lower order than those for general regular languages.

(3) For the catenation of regular languages, the worst case $(2m-1)2^{n-1}$ was given by an m-state DFA language and an n-state DFA language over a three-letter alphabet. It is not known whether the worst case can be reached by the catenation of two languages over a two-letter alphabet.

(4) It is known that when an n-state NFA is transformed into an equivalent DFA, we may obtain a 2^n-state minimal DFA in the worst case. The worst case can be reached when the NFA is over an alphabet of two or more letters. What is the worst case if the NFA is over a one-letter alphabet?

References

1. C. Câmpeanu, K. Culik II, K. Salomaa, and S. Yu, State complexity of basic operations on finite languages, *Proceedings of the Fourth International Workshop on Implementing Automata*, WIA'99, Springer LNCS 2214, pp. 60–70.
2. C. Câmpeanu, K. Salomaa, and S. Yu, Tight lower bound for the state complexity of shuffle of regular languages, to appear in *Journal of Automata, Languages, and Combinatorics*.
3. M. Domaratzki, State complexity and proportional removals, *Proc. 3rd International Workshop DCAGRS*, 2001, pp. 55–66.
4. J.E. Hopcroft, An $n \log n$ algorithm for minimizing the states in a finite automaton, *The Theory of Machines and Computations (Z. Kohavi edited)*, pp. 189-196, Academic Press, New York, 1971.
5. J.E. Hopcroft and J.D. Ullman, *Introduction to Automata Theory, Languages, and Computation*, Addison Wesley (1979), Reading, Mass.
6. A.R. Meyer and M.J. Fischer. Economy of description by automata, grammars, and formal systems, FOCS 12 (1971) 188–191.
7. C. Nicaud, Average state complexity of operations on unary automata, *Mathematical Foundations of Computer Science 1999*, Springer LNCS 1672, eds. M. Kutylowski, L. Pacholki, and T. Wierzbicki, pp. 231–240.
8. G. Pighizzini, Unary language concatenation and its state complexity, *Proceedings of 5th International Conference on Implementation and Application of Automata* (CIAA 2000), Springer LNCS 2088, eds. S. Yu and A. Păun, pp. 252–262.
9. D. Revuz, Minimisation of acyclic deterministic automata in linear time, *Theoretical Computer Science* 92 (1992) 181–189.
10. A. Salomaa, *On the reducibility of events represented in automata*, Annales Academiae Scientiarum Fennicae, Series A, I. Mathematica 353, 1964.
11. A. Salomaa, *Theorems on the Representation of Events in Moore-Automata*, Turun Yliopiston Julkaisuja Annales Universitatis Turkuensis, Series A, 69, 1964.
12. A. Salomaa, *Theory of Automata*, Pergamon Press (1969), Oxford.

13. J. Shallit, State complexity and Jacobsthal's function, *Proceedings of 5th International Conference on Implementation and Application of Automata* (CIAA 2000), Springer LNCS 2088, eds. S. Yu and A. Păun, pp. 272–278.
14. J. Shallit, Private communication, Nov. 1996.
15. D. Wood and S. Yu, editors, *Automata Implementation*, — Second Intern. Workshop on Implementing Automata, WIA'97, LNCS 1436.
16. S. Yu, State complexity of regular languages, *Journal of Automata, Languages and Combinatorics*, No. 2, Vol. 6.
17. S. Yu, Chapter 2: Regular languages, *Handbook of Formal Languages*, G. Rozenberg and A. Salomaa eds., Springer, 1997.
18. S. Yu, Q. Zhuang, and K. Salomaa, The state complexity of some basic operations on regular languages, *Theoretical Computer Science* 125 (1994) 315–328.

GSMS AND CONTEXTS

CARLOS MARTÍN-VIDE

Research Group on Mathematical Linguistics
Universitat Rovira i Virgili
Pl. Imperial Tarraco 1, 43005 Tarragona, Spain
E-mail: `cmv@astor.urv.es`

ALEXANDRU MATEESCU

Faculty of Mathematics and Computer Science
University of Bucharest
Str. Academiei 14, 70109 Bucharest, Romania
E-mail: `alexmate@pcnet.ro`

1 Introduction

We introduce and investigate a special type of generalized sequential machine called *contextual generalized sequential machine* or, shortly, *contextual GSM*.

A *contextual GSM* is a *GSM* that has the features of contexts as they appear in *Marcus contextual grammars*, see [5] and [7].

We show that the contextual *GSM*s can be used to extend some well-known families of languages, like regular or context-free families of languages, to a mildly context-sensitive family of languages.

Thus, this a contribution to find new families of mildly context-sensitive of languages. Also we prove some properties of contextual *GSM*s.

The notion of a *mildly context-sensitive family of languages* is important in connection with linguistics, see [3], [4] or [1].

A mildly context-sensitive family of languages should contain the most significant languages that occur in natural languages. Languages in such a family must be semilinear languages, and, moreover they should be computationally feasible, i.e., the membership problem must be solvable in deterministic polynomial time complexity.

It is well known that the hierarchy of Chomsky does not contain such a family. Whereas the family of context-free languages has good computational properties, it does not contain some important languages that appear in the study of natural languages. The family of context-sensitive languages contains all important languages that occur in the study of natural languages, but no algorithm in deterministic polynomial time is known for the membership problem.

Definition 1.1 *By a mildly context-sensitive family of languages we mean a family $\mathcal{L}$ of languages such that the following conditions are fulfilled:*

(i) each language in $\mathcal{L}$ is semilinear,

(ii) for each language in $\mathcal{L}$ the membership problem is solvable in deterministic polynomial time, and

(iii) $\mathcal{L}$ contain the following three non-context-free languages:
- *multiple agreements:* $L_1 = \{a^i b^i c^i \mid i \geq 0\}$,
- *crossed agreements:* $L_2 = \{a^i b^j c^i d^j \mid i, j \geq 0\}$, and
- *duplication:* $L_3 = \{ww \mid w \in \{a,b\}^*\}$.

Now we recall some terminology that we will use in this paper.

If A is a set, then $\mathcal{P}(A)$ is the set of all subsets of A. Let Σ be an alphabet and let Σ^* be the set of all words over Σ with the empty word denoted by λ. The set of all nonempty words over Σ is $\Sigma^+ = \Sigma^* - \lambda$.

If $w \in \Sigma^*$, then the set of all letters occurring in w is denoted by $alph(w)$. By definition $alph(\lambda) = \emptyset$.

The families of regular, linear, context-free, context-sensitive and recursively enumerable languages are denoted by REG, LIN, CF, CS and RE.

Assume that $\Sigma = \{a_1, a_2, \ldots, a_k\}$. The *Parikh mapping* $\Psi : \Sigma^* \longrightarrow N^k$ is defined by $\Psi(w) = (|w|_{a_1}, |w|_{a_2}, \ldots, |w|_{a_k})$. If L is a language, then the *Parikh set of L* is defined by $\Psi(L) = \{\Psi(w) \mid w \in L\}$.

A *linear set* is a set $M \subseteq N^k$ such that $M = \{v_0 + \sum_{i=1}^{m} v_i x_i \mid x_i \in N\}$, for some $v_0, v_1, \ldots, v_m$ in N^k.

A *semilinear set* is a finite union of linear sets and a *semilinear set* is a language L such that $\Psi(L)$ is a semilinear set.

A *generalized sequential machine (GSM)* is a construct $M = (Q, \Sigma, \Delta, q_0, \delta, F)$, where Q is a finite set (the set of states), Σ is an alphabet (the input alphabet), Δ is an alphabet (the output alphabet) $q_0 \in Q$ is the initial state, $F \subseteq Q$ is the set of final states, and $\delta : Q \times \Sigma \longrightarrow \mathcal{P}(Q \times \Delta^*)$ is a function (the transition function).

The transition function δ defines a relation of *direct transition* on the set $\Sigma^* \times Q \times \Delta^*$, denoted $\vdash_M$ or $\vdash$ if no confusion is possible:

$$(ax, p, y) \vdash_M (x, q, yz) \text{ iff } (q, z) \in \delta(p, a),$$

where $a \in \Sigma, p, q \in Q, x \in \Sigma^*$ and $y, z \in \Delta^*$.

The transitive and reflexive closure of the relation $\vdash_M$ is denoted by $\vdash_M^*$.

A *GSM* M is used to transform a language $L \subseteq \Sigma^*$ into a language $M(L) \subseteq \Delta^*$.

The transformation is defined as follows: If $w \in \Sigma^*$, then

$$M(w) = \{w' \mid \text{there exists } q_f \in F \text{ such that } (w, q_0, \lambda) \vdash_M^* (\lambda, q_f, w')\}.$$

Now, if $L \subseteq \Sigma^*$, then the image of the language L by the GSM M, denoted $M(L)$, is:

$$M(L) = \bigcup_{w \in L} M(w).$$

A *simple Marcus contextual grammar* is an ordered system $G = (V, B, C)$, where V is *the alphabet* of G, B is a finite subset of V^*, called *the base* of G, and C is a finite subset of pairs of words over V, i.e., $C \subset V^* \times V^*$, C finite, called the set of *contexts* of G.

Let $G = (V, B, C)$ be a simple contextual grammar. The *languge generated* by G, denoted $L(G)$, is the smallest language L over V such that:

(i) $B \subseteq L$.

(ii) if $x \in L$ and $(u, v) \in C$, then $uxv \in L$.

It is easy to observe that:

$$L(G) = B \cup \{u_n \ldots u_1 x v_1 \ldots v_n \mid n \geq 1, x \in B, (u_i, v_i) \in C, 1 \leq i \leq n\}.$$

The class of all Marcus simple contextual languages is denoted by SM.

If L is a simple contextual language, then $L \in LIN$, i.e., $SM \subset LIN$. Note that, if $G = (V, B, C)$ is a simple contextual grammar, then one can define an equivalent Chomsky linear grammar $G' = (\{X\}, V, X, P)$, where X is a new symbol and the set P of productions is defined as follows:

$$P = \{X \to \alpha \mid \alpha \in B\} \cup \{X \to uXv \mid (u, v) \in C\}.$$

Note that SM is a strict subclass of LIN and, moreover, the classes SM and REG are incomparable, see [7].

A simple contextual grammar generates a language starting from a finite set of strings (the base) and iteratively adjoining to it contexts, i.e., pairs of strings from C, at the ends of the current string. In other classes of contextual grammars, such as the *internal contextual grammars*, [7], the contexts are adjoined in the middle of the current string.

2 Contextual GSMs

Assume that Δ is an alphabet. Consider all triples of words over Δ, i.e., $\mathcal{D} = \Delta^* \times \Delta^* \times \Delta^*$. On the set $\mathcal{D}$ we consider the operation $o : \mathcal{D} \times \mathcal{D} \longrightarrow \mathcal{D}$, defined by:

$$(x, y, z)o(x', y', z') = (x'x, y'y, z'z),$$

where $x, x', y, y', z'z' \in \Delta^*$.

Note that this is an associative operation with the unit element $(\lambda, \lambda, \lambda)$, i.e., $(\mathcal{D}, o, (\lambda, \lambda, \lambda))$ is a monoid.

In the sequel we write $(x, y, z)(x', y', z')$ instead of $(x, y, z)o(x', y', z')$.

Now we introduce the main definition of this paper.

Definition 2.1 *A contextual generalized sequential machine (CGSM) is a construct $CM = (Q, \Sigma, \Delta, q_0, \delta, F)$, where Q is a finite set (the set of states), Σ is an alphabet (the input alphabet), Δ is an alphabet (the output alphabet), $q_0 \in Q$ is the initial state, $F \subseteq Q$ is the set of final states, and $\delta : Q \times \Sigma \longrightarrow \mathcal{P}(Q \times \mathcal{D})$ is a function (the transition function).*

The transition function δ defines a relation of direct transition on the set $\Sigma^* \times Q \times \mathcal{D}$, denoted $\vdash_{CM}$ or $\vdash$ if no confusion is possible:

$$(ax, p, y) \vdash_{CM} (x, q, yz) \text{ iff } (q, z) \in \delta(p, a),$$

where $a \in \Sigma, p, q \in Q, x \in \Sigma^*$ and $y, z \in \mathcal{D}$.

Note that the above multiplication is performed in the monoid $\mathcal{D}$.

The transitive and reflexive closure of the relation $\vdash_{CM}$ is denoted by $\vdash_{CM}^*$.

A GSM M is used to transform a language $L \subseteq \Sigma^*$ into a language $M(L) \subseteq \mathcal{D}$. The transformation is defined as follows. If $w \in \Sigma^*$, then the t-image of w, denoted $CM_t(w)$, is:

$$CM_t(w) = \{w' \in \mathcal{D} \mid \text{ there is } q_f \in F \text{ such that } (w, q_0, \lambda) \vdash_{CM}^* (\lambda, q_f, w')\}.$$

Now, if $L \subseteq \Sigma^*$, then the t-image of the language L by the GSM CM, denoted $CM(L)$, is

$$CM_t(L) = \bigcup_{w \in L} CM_t(w).$$

From the t-image of a word $w \in \Sigma^*$ we obtain the image of w by CM, denoted $CM(w)$, as the catenation of the components of the triple $CM_t(w)$, i.e.,

$$CM(w) = \{x \in \Delta^* \mid \text{ there is } (x_1, x_2, x_3) \in CM_t(w) \text{ such that } x = x_1 x_2 x_3\}.$$

The image of the language $L \subseteq \Sigma^*$ is

$$CB(L) = \bigcup_{w \in L} CM(w).$$

Comment. Note that the t-image of a language $L \subseteq \Sigma^*$ by a contextual GSM is a subset of $\mathcal{D}$, i.e., $CM_t(L) \subseteq \mathcal{D}$, whereas the image of L by CM is a language over Δ, i.e., $CM(L) \subseteq \Delta^*$.

Remark 2.1 *In the sequel we use contextual GSMs to extend some families of languages. If $\mathcal{F}$ is a family of languages, then the extension of $\mathcal{F}$ by a contextual GSM, denoted $CGSM(\mathcal{F})$, is*

$$CGSM(\mathcal{F}) = \{L \mid \text{ there exist } L' \in \mathcal{F}$$
$$\text{and a contextual } GSM \ CM \text{ such that } L = CM(L')\}.$$

Of a special interest are the families $CGSM(REG), CGSM(LIN)$, and $CGSM(CF)$.

Remark 2.2 *Note that if $\mathcal{F}$ is a family of languages, then $CGSM(\mathcal{F})$ is an extension of $\mathcal{F}$, i.e., $\mathcal{F} \subseteq CGSM(\mathcal{F})$.*

Assume that $L \in \mathcal{F}$ and $L \subseteq \Sigma^*$. Consider the contextual GSM $CM = (Q, \Sigma, \Delta, q_0, \delta, F)$ such that $Q = \{q_0\} = F$, $\Delta = \Sigma$ and $\delta(q_0, a) = \{(q_0, (\lambda, a, \lambda)\}$, for each $a \in \Sigma$. It is easy to verify that $CM(L) = L$. Thus $\mathcal{F} \subseteq CGSM(\mathcal{F})$.

Example 2.1 *The language of multiple agreements, $L_1 = \{a^i b^i c^i \mid i \geq 0\}$, is in $CGSM(REG)$.*

Consider the contextual GSM $CM = (Q, \Sigma, \Delta, q_0, \delta, F)$, where $Q = \{q_0\} = F$, $\Sigma = \{b\}$, $\Delta = \{a, b, c\}$ and $\delta(q_0, b) = \{(q_0, (a, b, c))\}$.

Also consider the language $L = b^*$ and note that $L \in REG$. It is easy to verify that $L_1 = CM(L)$ and hence $L_1 \in CGSM(REG)$.

Example 2.2 *The language of crossed agreements, $L_2 = \{a^i b^j c^i d^j \mid i, j \geq 0\}$, is in $CGSM(REG)$.*

Consider the contextual GSM $CM = (Q, \Sigma, \Delta, q_0, \delta, F)$, where $Q = \{q_0\} = F$, $\Sigma = \{a, b\}$, $\Delta = \{a, b, c, d\}$, $\delta(q_0, a) = \{(q_0, (\lambda, a, c))\}$ and $\delta(q_0, b) = \{(q_0, (\lambda, b, d))\}$.

Also consider the language $L = a^* b^*$ and note that $L \in REG$. It is easy to prove that $L_2 = CM(L)$ and thus $L_2 \in CGSM(REG)$.

Example 2.3 *The language of duplication, $L_3 = \{ww \mid w \in \{a, b\}^*\}$, is in $CGSM(REG)$.*

Consider the contextual GSM $CM = (Q, \Sigma, \Delta, q_0, \delta, F)$, where $Q = \{q_0\} = F$, $\Sigma = \{a, b\}$, $\Delta = \{a, b\}$, $\delta(q_0, x) = \{(q_0, (\lambda, x, x))\}$ for each $x \in$.

Also consider the language $L = \Sigma^*$ and note that $L \in REG$. It is easy to prove that $L_3 = CM(L)$ and hence $L_2 \in CGSM(REG)$.

3 CGSM and Mildly CS Languages

In this section we show that the contextual GSM extension of some well-known families of languages are mildly context-sensitive families of languages.

Theorem 3.1 *If a language L is in $CGSM(CF)$, then L is a semiliniar language.*

Corollary 3.1 *Each language in the families $CGSM(LIN)$, $CGSM(REG)$, $CGSM(SM)$ is a semilinear language.*

Theorem 3.2 *The membership problem for a language in $CGSM(CF)$ is solvable in deterministic polynomial time.*

Corollary 3.2 *For each language in the families $CGSM(LIN)$, $CGSM(REG)$, $CGSM(SM)$ the membership problem is solvable in deterministic polynomial time.*

From Examples 2.1, 2.2, 2.3, Theorems 3.1, 3.2, and Corollaries 3.1, 3.2, we obtain the following result:

Theorem 3.3 *Each of the families $CGSM(CF)$, $CGSM(LIN)$, $CGSM(REG)$, and $CGSM(SM)$ is a mildly context-sensitive family of languages.*

Remark 3.1 *One can show that $CGSM(SM) \subset CGSM(LIN)$ and $CGSM(REG) \subset CGSM(LIN) \subset CGSM(CF)$ and al these inclusions are strict. Morever, $CGSM(REG)$ and $CGSM(SM)$ are incomparable families.*

Now we consider some variants of contextual GSMs.

A contextual GSM $CM = (Q, \Sigma, \Delta, q_0, \delta, F)$ is referred to as a deterministic contextual GSM, shortly $DCGSM$, iff $card(\delta(q, a)) \leq 1$, for each $q \in Q$ and $a \in \Sigma$.

If $\mathcal{F}$ is a family of languages, then the extension of $\mathcal{F}$ by a deterministic contextual GSM is denoted $DCGSM(\mathcal{F})$. As in the general case of contextual GSMs, we obtain:

Theorem 3.4 *Each of the following four families of languages, DCGSM(CF), DCGSM(LIN), DCGSM(REG) and DCGSM(SM), is a mildly context-sensitive family of languages.*

We restrict even more the notion of contextual GSM.

Remark 3.2 *Consider a contextual GSM $CM = (Q, \Sigma, \Delta, q_0, \delta, F)$. Note that a morphism from Σ^* in the monoid of triples $(\mathcal{D}, o, (\lambda, \lambda, \lambda))$ is a very special case of a deterministic contextual GSM.*

These morphisms are referred to as t-morphisms.

If $\mathcal{F}$ is a family of languages, then the extension of $\mathcal{F}$ by t-morphisms, denoted $HCGSM(\mathcal{F})$, is

$$HCGSM(\mathcal{F}) = \{L \mid \text{there exist a } t\text{-morphism } h \text{ and } L' \in \mathcal{L}$$
$$\text{such that } L = \{x_1 x_2 x_3 \mid (x_1, x_2, x_3) \in h(L')\}.$$

As in the general case of contextual GSMs we obtain:

Theorem 3.5 *Each of the following four families of languages: HCGSM(CF), HCGSM(LIN), HCGSM(REG) and HCGSM(SM) is a mildly context-sensitive family of languages.*

Comments. One can show that the 12 families of languages that occur in Theorems 3.3, 3.4, and 3.5 are distinct.

4 Conclusion

We introduced 12 mildly context-sensitive families of languages. It remains to investigate other properties of these families. Of a special interest is to study the relationships between these families of languages and families defined by contextual grammars with contexts on trajectories, introduced in [6].

References

[1] Delany, P. and Landow, G.P. (eds.), *Hypermedia and Literary Studies*, The MIT Press, Cambridge, Mass. and London, England, 1991.

[2] Ehrenfeucht, A., Rozenberg, G., and Păun, Gh., Contextual grammars and formal languages, in *Handbook of Formal Languages*, G. Rozenberg and A. Salomaa (eds.), Vol. 2, Springer, Berlin, New York, 1997, 237–294.

[3] Joshi, A.K., Vijay-Shanker, K., and Weir, D., The convergence of mildly context-sensitive grammatical formalisms, in *Foundations Issues in Natural Language Processing*, Sells, P., Shieber, S., and Wasow, T. (eds.), MIT Press, Cambridge MA, 1991.

[4] Joshi, A.K. and Schabes, Y., Tree-adjoining grammars, in *Handbook of Formal Languages*, G. Rozenberg and A. Salomaa (eds.), Vol. 3, Springer, Berlin, New York, 1997, 69–123.

[5] Marcus, S., Contextual Grammars, *Rev. Roum. Math. Pures et Appl.*, 14, 10 (1969) 1525–1534.

[6] Martin-Vide, C., Mateescu, A., and Salomaa, A., Contexts on trajectories, *International Journal of Computer Mathematics*, 73 (1999), 15–36.

[7] Păun, Gh., *Marcus Contextual Grammars*, Kluwer Academic Publishers, Dordrecht, Boston, London, 1997.

[8] Rozenberg, G. and Salomaa, A. (eds.), *Handbook of Formal Languages*, Vol. 1 - 3, Springer, Berlin, New York, 1997.

THE DEPTH OF FUNCTIONAL COMPOSITIONS

ARTO SALOMAA

Turku Centre for Computer Science
Lemminkäisenkatu 14, 20520 Turku, Finland
E-mail: `asalomaa@it.utu.fi`

1   Depth, Complete Depth and Synchronization

We return here to the subject matter of [2]. The main purpose is to see how some of the problems will change when functions of *several* variables are considered.

We will first consider functions $g(x)$ of one variable whose domain is a fixed finite set N with n elements, $n \geq 2$, and whose range is included in N. It is clear that such a setup occurs in many and very diverse situations and interpretations. Depending on the interpretation, different questions can be asked. The two interpretations we have had mostly in mind are *many-valued logic* and *finite automata*. In the former, the set N consists of n *truth values* and the functions are truth functions. In the latter, the set N consists of the *states* of a finite automaton, whereas each letter of the input alphabet induces a specific function: the next state when reading that letter.

In this section the attention is restricted to functions with *one* variable only. In many contexts, especially in many-valued logic, it is natural to consider functions of *several* variables. We will return to this in Section 2.

We make the following **convention**: n always stands for the number of elements in the basic set N. In most cases we let N simply be the set consisting of the first n natural numbers:

$$N = \{1, 2, \ldots, n\}.$$

Clearly, there are altogether n^n functions in the set N^N we are considering.

Consider a couple of examples. If we are dealing with n-valued logic, and the function g is defined by the equation

$$g(x) = n - x + 1, x = 1, 2, \ldots, n,$$

then g is the well-known *Lukasiewicz negation*. (1 is the truth value "true", n is the truth value "false", whereas the other numbers represent the intermediate truth values.) If we are dealing with a finite deterministic automaton whose state set equals N, the function g defined by the equation above could be viewed as transitions affected by a specific input letter a. Under this interpretation, the letter a interchanges the states n and 1, the states $n-1$ and 2, and so forth. Whether or not there is a *loop* affected by the letter a, that is, whether or not some state is mapped into itself, depends on the parity of n.

When we speak of "functions", without further specifications, we always mean functions in the setup defined above. Clearly, the *composition ab* of two functions a and b is again a function. We read compositions from *left to right:* first a, then b. This is in accordance of reading the input words of a finite deterministic automaton from left to right. Because of this convention, it is natural to write the argument x of a function to the left: $(x)ab = ((x)a)b$. Observe that gg equals the identity function for the Lukasiewicz negation g.

Our point of departure will be a nonempty set $\mathbf{F}$ of functions. The only assumption about the set $\mathbf{F}$ is that it is a nonempty subset of the set N^N of all functions; $\mathbf{F}$ may consist of one function or of all functions. We will consider the set $\mathbf{G}(\mathbf{F})$ of all functions *generated* by $\mathbf{F}$, that is, obtained as compositions (with arbitrarily many composition factors) of functions from $\mathbf{F}$. If a particular function f can be expressed as a composition of functions $a_i, i = 1, 2, \ldots, k$, belonging to $\mathbf{F}$,

$$f = a_1 a_2 \ldots a_k,$$

where some of the functions a_i may coincide, then the word $a_1 a_2 \ldots a_k$ is referred to as a *composition sequence* for f. (In this brief notation we assume that the set $\mathbf{F}$ is understood.) The number k is referred to as the *length* of the composition sequence. The function f is often referred to as the *target function*. Observe that our composition sequences have to be nonempty, implying that the identity function is not necessarily in $\mathbf{G}(\mathbf{F})$; it is in there exactly in case the set $\mathbf{F}$ contains at least one permutation.

Clearly, $\mathbf{G}(\mathbf{F})$ can be viewed as the *semigroup* generated by $\mathbf{F}$. However, we will prefer the more straightforward approach and will not use semigroup-theoretic terminology in the sequel.

The set $\mathbf{F}$ is termed *complete* if all of the n^n functions are in $\mathbf{G}(\mathbf{F})$. Completeness in this setup is fairly well understood, see [4,5,6]. On the other hand, fairly little is known about the length of composition sequences and about the question concerning how completeness affects the length. When do two permutations generate the whole symmetric group S_n? (At least two are needed for $n \geq 3$.) Quite much is known about this problem but very little about the lengths of the corresponding composition sequences.

Since n is finite, a specific function f can always be defined by a table. Omitting the argument values, this amounts to giving the *value sequence* of f, that is, the sequence $(1)f, (2)f, \ldots, (n)f$ of its values for the increasing values of the argument. The Lukasiewicz negation can be defined in this way by its value sequence

$$n, \ n-1, \ldots, 2, \ 1.$$

When there is no danger of confusion, we omit the commas from the value sequence. Thus, for $n = 6$, the value sequence of the Lukasiewicz negation reads 654321.

We denote by $L(\mathbf{F}, f)$ the set of all composition sequences for f, that is, the *language* over the alphabet $\mathbf{F}$ whose words, viewed as composition sequences, yield the function f. Clearly, the language $L(\mathbf{F}, f)$ can be empty (this is the case when f cannot be expressed as a composition of functions in $\mathbf{F}$) or infinite (composition sequences may contain redundant parts and be arbitrarily long). Clearly, this language is always regular.

We now come to the central notions concerning the length of composition sequences. For any language L, we denote by $\min(L)$ the length of the shortest word in L. (If L is empty, we agree that $\min(L) = \infty$.) The *depth* of a function f *with respect* to the set $\mathbf{F}$, in symbols $D(\mathbf{F}, f)$, is defined by the equation

$$D(\mathbf{F}, f) = \min(L(\mathbf{F}, f)).$$

Thus, the depth of a function with respect to a particular set can also be ∞.

The *depth of a function f* is defined by the equation

$$D(f) = \max(D(\mathbf{F}, f)),$$

where $\mathbf{F}$ ranges over all sets with the property $L(\mathbf{F}, f) \neq \emptyset$. Because, for any f, there are sets $\mathbf{F}$ with this property, we conclude that the depth of a function is always a positive integer. (The notion of depth was introduced in [2], where it was referred to as "complexity".) In general, the depth of a function cannot be bounded from above by a polynomial in n, [2,6]. Various other aspects have been presented in [7,8].

The *complete depth $D_C(f)$* of a function f is defined by the same equation $D_C(f) = \max(D(\mathbf{F}, f))$ but now $\mathbf{F}$ ranges over *complete* sets of functions. Hence, it is *a priori* clear that $L(\mathbf{F}, f) \neq \emptyset$.

It follows by the definition that every function f satisfies

$$D_C(f) \leq D(f).$$

However, lower bounds are much harder to obtain for $D_C(f)$, for the simple reason that we have much less leeway if we have to restrict the attention to complete sets $\mathbf{F}$ only.

One can show that some specific functions have intractably long composition sequences in the worst case. However, the situation is different for some other specific functions, notably *constant* functions. This is an area widely studied in the past. The area is closely linked to *synchronizable* finite automata and the so-called *Černý Conjecture*, see [2,1,3].

The depth of a constant function f_c has a cubic (in terms of n) upper bound and the lower bound $n(n-1)$:

$$D(f_c) \geq n(n-1).$$

For proofs of these and related results, see [6] or [3].

Let us still make explicit the connection to synchronizable automata.

Suppose you know the structure (graph, transition function) of a given finite deterministic automaton A, but do not know the state A is in. How can you get the situation under control? For some automata, not always, there are words, referred to as *synchronizing*, bringing the automaton always to the same state q, no matter which state you started from. Thus, you first have to feed A a synchronizing word, after which you have the situation completely under control. You can also view the graph of an automaton as a labyrinth, where you are lost. If you then follow the letters of a synchronizing word (and have the global knowledge of the graph of the automaton), you have found your way. This shows the connection with the well-known *road coloring* problem.

Clearly, a synchronizing word can be viewed as a *composition sequence for a constant*, and we are back in the setup introduced above. Indeed, consider a finite deterministic automaton, without initial and final states, as a pair $(N, \mathbf{F})$, where N is the state set of cardinality n and $\mathbf{F}$ is a set of functions mapping N into N. The set $\mathbf{F}$ determines both the input alphabet and the transition function in the natural way, and input words correspond to compositions of functions. Our convention about reading compositions from left to right is in accordance with the customary way of reading input words from left to right.

By definition, an automaton is *synchronizable* if it possesses a synchronizing word. This happens exactly in case a constant function is in $\mathbf{G(F)}$. The Černý Conjecture says that every synchronizable automaton possesses a synchronizing word of length $\leq (n-1)^2$. Results in the above setup of functional compositions can immediately be translated into this automata-theoretic terminology. One can also speak of *complete automata* in the sense that the set $\mathbf{F}$ is complete, and ask whether synchronizing words for complete automata are shorter. All examples known to us give a synchronizing word of length at most $(n-1)^2 - (n-3)$ in this case.

2   Functions of Several Variables

We now discuss the above setup in the case where the set $\mathbf{F}$ may contain functions of several variables. As before, the variables range over the same basic set N, and the function values are always included in N. Thus, for each $k \geq 1$, there are altogether n^{n^k} functions of k variables. Since practically nothing is known about the length of composition sequences in this general case, our discussion presents only some basic definitions. We mostly refer to Section 1, and only point out how the situation will change.

We use mostly the customary notation $f(x_1, \ldots, x_k)$ for a function f of k variables. The postfix notation $x_1 \ldots x_k f$ is more appropriate in some formal contexts. *Composition sequences* defined below result from "meaningful" compositions of functions. Thereby, one may identify variables in an arbitrary fashion.

For instance, consider the *Lukasiewicz implication* $f(x, y)$ (or xyf) defined by $f(x, y) = \max(1, 1 - x + y)$. Suppose our basic set $\mathbf{F}$ consists of f alone. Then each of the following functions

$$f(x, x), \ f(x, f(x, x)), \ f(f(x, y), f(x, x)), \ f(f(x, y), f(y, x)),$$
$$f(f(x, y), f(z, x)), \ f(x, f(f(x, x), y))$$

is in the set $\mathbf{G(F)}$. Clearly, the latter set contains functions of arbitrarily many variables. We leave the more detailed investigation of the functions listed above to the reader.

Each function in the set $\mathbf{F}$ has an associated natural number: the *arity* of the function. Composition sequences over $\mathbf{F}$ are defined inductively as follows. Each variable alone constitutes a composition sequence. (Variables belong to a fixed denumerable set.) Whenever $\alpha_1, \ldots, \alpha_k$ are composition sequences and f of arity k belongs to $\mathbf{F}$, then $\alpha_1 \ldots \alpha_k f$ is a composition sequence. We omit the formal definition of the function f_{cs} defined by a composition sequence cs. The definition is obvious, and f_{cs} will be a function in the variables appearing in cs.

It should now be clear how the set $\mathbf{G(F)}$ is defined in the generalized situation, where $\mathbf{F}$ (still a finite set) may contain functions of arbitrarily many variables. The set $\mathbf{G(F)}$ consists of all functions defined by a composition sequence over $\mathbf{F}$, containing at least one letter of $\mathbf{F}$. (This restriction is made because we want to avoid the automatic inclusion of the identity function in $\mathbf{G(F)}$, to have the definition fully in accordance with Section 1.)

We now come to the notion of the *depth* of a function. What is the depth of the composition $f(f(x, y), f(y, z))$? Is it the number of function letters in the composition sequence (in this case 3), or the maximum number of nested function letters (in this case 2)? Both definitions would be in accordance with the definition in Section 1. From many points of view, it is more natural to choose the latter alternative.

Thus, we will follow the inductive definition of a composition sequence over $\mathbf{F}$. A variable alone is of depth 0. If m is the greatest among the depths of k composition sequences $\alpha_1, \ldots, \alpha_k$, then the depth of the composition sequence $\alpha_1 \ldots \alpha_k f$ equals $m + 1$, provided f of arity k is in $\mathbf{F}$.

The *depth of a function* g (of arbitrarily many variables) can now be defined following exactly the definition in Section 1. We first define the depth $D(\mathbf{F}, g)$ of g with respect to a particular set $\mathbf{F}$. It equals the minimum among the depths of composition sequences over $\mathbf{F}$ defining the function g. (If g is not in $\mathbf{G}(\mathbf{F})$, the depth is infinite.) Finally, the depth $D(g)$ of g equals the maximum among the numbers $D(\mathbf{F}, g)$, where g is in $\mathbf{G}(\mathbf{F})$.

We still want to define the notion of the *complete depth* of a function with arbitrarily many variables. Before doing that, we have to make a few remarks about completeness in the setup of functions with many variables.

A set $\mathbf{F}$ of functions (over the basic set N but with arbitrarily many variables) is termed *complete* if *every function* (again over the basic set N and with arbitrarily many variables) is in $\mathbf{G}(\mathbf{F})$.

Observe the difference in regard to Section 1. If $\mathbf{F}$ contains only functions with one variable, the same holds true with respect to $\mathbf{G}(\mathbf{F})$. But if $\mathbf{F}$ contains functions with two variables, $\mathbf{G}(\mathbf{F})$ contains functions with arbitrarily many variables. In fact, it was shown by Post already in the early 20's, using a simple minimax argument, that if all functions with two variables are in $\mathbf{G}(\mathbf{F})$, then so are all functions with any number of variables.

Another difference with respect to Section 1 is that there are complete sets $\mathbf{F}$ consisting of a single function. Such functions are referred to as *Sheffer functions*, in analogy with the *Sheffer stroke* in two-valued logic. To give some examples of Sheffer functions, let us first observe that functions $f(x, y)$ with two variables are conveniently defined by a table, where the values of x (resp. y) are read from the rows (resp. columns). For instance, the Lukasiewicz implication, for $n = 6$, is defined by the table

$$
\begin{array}{|cccccc}
1 & 2 & 3 & 4 & 5 & 6 \\
1 & 1 & 2 & 3 & 4 & 5 \\
1 & 1 & 1 & 2 & 3 & 4 \\
1 & 1 & 1 & 1 & 2 & 3 \\
1 & 1 & 1 & 1 & 1 & 2 \\
1 & 1 & 1 & 1 & 1 & 1 \\
\end{array}
$$

Of course, in principle, functions with any number of variables can be defined by such a table but it is hard to visualize tables with many dimensions. (In old times, Russians were very good at this while discussing Boolean functions.)

Consider the values $n = 3, 4, 5, 6$. Each of the following functions (meaning that the positions marked by * can be filled arbitrarily) is a Sheffer function:

$$
\begin{array}{|cc|}
\hline
2 & 2 & * \\
* & 3 & 1 \\
3 & * & 1 \\
\hline
\end{array}
\qquad
\begin{array}{|cccc|}
\hline
2 & 2 & * & * \\
* & 3 & 1 & * \\
* & * & 4 & 3 \\
4 & * & * & 1 \\
\hline
\end{array}
\qquad
\begin{array}{|ccccc|}
\hline
2 & 2 & * & * & * \\
* & 3 & 1 & * & * \\
* & * & 4 & 3 & * \\
* & * & * & 5 & 4 \\
5 & * & * & * & 1 \\
\hline
\end{array}
\qquad
\begin{array}{|cccccc|}
\hline
2 & 2 & * & * & * & * \\
* & 3 & 1 & * & * & * \\
* & * & 4 & 3 & * & * \\
* & * & * & 5 & 4 & * \\
* & * & * & * & 6 & 5 \\
6 & * & * & * & * & 1 \\
\hline
\end{array}
$$

In general, for any $n \geq 3$, whenever a function $f(x,y)$ satisfies the equations

$$ fx, x) = x + 1, 1 \leq x \leq n, $$

and

$$ f1, 2) = 2, \ f(2,3) = 1, \ f(x, x+1) = x \text{ for } x \geq 3, $$

(where $n + 1 = 1$), then f is a Sheffer function. This is a very simple case, because the circular permutation $(1, 2, \ldots n)$ and transposition (12) are obtained as the composition sequences $f(x, x)$ and $f(x, f(x, x))$, respectively, whence the result in [4] becomes applicable. Observe that the two permutations mentioned generate the symmetric group S_n.

Coming back to the notion of the *complete depth*, $D_C(g)$ is defined as the maximum among the numbers $D(\mathbf{F}, g)$, where $\mathbf{F}$ now ranges over complete sets. Also now the inequality $D_C(g) \leq D(g)$ is obvious. Whether the inequality is strict and what kinds of bounds are obtainable for various functions g seem to be hard problems.

Observe also that if only functions of one variable are considered, then the depth and complete depth defined in Section 1 may be different from the depth and complete depth defined in this section, and it is not at all clear how the four notions are interrelated. The case study presented in the next section shows, for instance, that the Černý bound is not valid even for the complete depth in the generalized case.

We mention finally that composition sequences for constants can be associated with (frontier-to-root) *tree automata*: the tree resulting from such a composition sequence can be viewed as *synchronizing* similarly as in the case of finite automata.

3   A Case Study

We now consider the case $n = 3$ and the depths $D(\mathbf{F}, g)$, where $\mathbf{F}$ consists of one function only, namely, the Sheffer function $f(x, y)$ defined by the table

$$\begin{vmatrix} 2 & 2 & 1 \\ 1 & 3 & 3 \\ 1 & 2 & 1 \end{vmatrix}$$

(We have chosen a Sheffer function different from the ones presented in Section 2.) Since $\mathbf{F}$ is complete we conclude that, for any function g,

$$D_C(g) \geq D(\mathbf{F}, g).$$

We now determine the depths of all 27 functions of one variable. Each function is represented by its value sequence. Thus, 231 is the circular permutation (123) which is obtained as $f(x, x)$. Since

$$f(f(x, x), f(x, x)) = 312, \ f(x, f(x, x)) = 231, \ f(f(x, x), x) = 121,$$

we know all functions with depth 1 or 2. The following table, based on an exhaustive search, gives all functions with depth at most 3. The sources are ordered pairs: the target results by applying f to the elements of the pairs.

target	source	depth
231	123, 123	1
312	231, 231	2
121	231, 123	2
123	312, 312	3
232	121, 121	3
112	123, 312	3
122	231, 121	3
211	312, 231	3

We see, for instance, that the function with the value sequence 211 is obtained as $f(f(f(x, x), f(x, x)), f(x, x))$.

It can be shown already now that each of the constants 111, 222, and 333 must be of depth at least 5. Since the 3's in the definition of f are in the second row, the constant 222 is the necessary first component in the source of 333. The above table shows that all functions of depth at most 3 have the number 2 in their value sequence. On the other hand, since all 1's (resp. 2's) in the definition of f are in the first and third columns (resp. rows), the second (resp. first) component in the source of 111 (resp. 222) cannot have the number 2 in its value sequence and, hence, must be of depth at least 4, which shows that all constants are of depth at least 5.

Continuing the table, we obtain the functions of depths 4 and 5:

target	source	depth		target	source	depth
313	232, 232	4		331	223, 223	5
223	112, 112	4		133	322, 322	5
233	122, 122	4		332	221, 221	5
322	211, 211	4		323	212, 212	5
311	232, 231	4		321	231, 223	5
213	312, 232	4		111	231, 113	5
113	122, 312	4		131	223, 121	5
221	312, 211	4		132	121, 322	5
212	121, 211	4		222	113, 212	5

So far we have 26 functions and are still missing the constant 333. We already noticed that since the 3's in the definition of f are in the second row, the constant 222 is the necessary first component in the source of 333. (The second component must avoid the value 1; 232 is the function with the smallest depth having this property.) Consequently, 333 has the source (222,232) and is of depth 6. Thus, all constants 111, 222, and 3333 are of depth 5 or 6, whereas 4 is the Černý upper bound for the constant with the lowest depth.

The following table summarizes the depths. The functions are arranged in the "alphabetic" order of their value sequences.

function	depth		function	depth		function	depth
111	5		211	3		311	4
112	3		212	4		312	2
113	4		213	4		313	4
121	2		221	4		321	5
122	3		222	5		322	4
123	3		223	4		323	5
131	5		231	1		331	5
132	5		232	3		332	5
133	5		233	4		333	6

4 Conclusion

Completeness, both in the case of functions of one variable and in the general case, has been widely investigated in connection with *many-valued logic*. On the other hand, practically nothing is known about the *complexity* of generating various functions by complete sets (or other sets $\mathbf{F}$ such that the target function is in $\mathbf{G}(\mathbf{F})$). The recent interest in problems such as *road coloring* or

Černý Conjecture shows the significance of such complexity issues in *automata theory*. The complexity issues can be formulated in terms of the various notions of *depth* introduced above. As shown by our example in Section 3 about the depth of constants, the study of functions of several variables may shed light also in the case where all functions considered are of one variable.

References

1. J. Černý, Poznámka k homogénnym experimentom s konečnými automatmi. *Mat. fyz. čas SAV*, 14 (1964), 208–215.
2. A. Mateescu and A. Salomaa, Many-valued truth functions, Černý's conjecture and road coloring. In Gh. Păun, G. Rozenberg, and A. Salomaa (eds.), *Current Trends in Theoretical Computer Science*. World Scientific Publ. Co. (2001), 693–707.
3. J.-E. Pin, *Le problème de la synchronisation, Contribution a l'étude de la conjecture de Černý*. Thèse de 3e cycle a l'Université Pierre et Marie Curie (Paris 6), 1978.
4. A. Salomaa, A theorem concerning the composition of functions of several variables ranging over a finite set. *J. Symb. Logic*, 25 (1960), 203–208.
5. A. Salomaa, On basic groups for the set of functions over a finite domain. *Ann. Acad. Scient. Fennicae*, Ser. AI, 338 (1963).
6. A. Salomaa, Composition sequences for functions over a finite domain. To appear in *Theoretical Computer Science*.
7. A. Salomaa, Compositions over a finite domain: from completeness to synchronizable automata. In A. Salomaa, D. Wood, S. Yu (eds.), *A Half-Century of Automata Theory. Celebration and Inspiration*. World Scientific Publ. Co., 2001, 131–143.
8. A. Salomaa, Generation of constants and synchronization of finite automata. *Journal of Universal Computer Science*, 8 (2002), 332–347.

LANGUAGE GENERATING BY MEANS OF MEMBRANE SYSTEMS

CARLOS MARTíN-VIDE

Research Group on Mathematical Linguistics
Rovira i Virgili University
Pl. Imperial Tàrraco 1, 43005 Tarragona, Spain
E-mail: cmv@astor.urv.es

GHEORGHE PĂUN

Institute of Mathematics of the Romanian Academy
PO Box 1-764, 70700 Bucureşti, Romania, and
Research Group on Mathematical Linguistics
Rovira i Virgili University
Pl. Imperial Tàrraco 1, 43005 Tarragona, Spain
E-mail: george.paun@imar.ro, gp@astor.urv.es

We survey results concerning the generative power of membrane systems (P systems) with the objects described by strings which are processed by rewriting, splicing, rewriting with replication, as well as by genome specific operations such as splitting, point mutation (actually, rewriting), and crossover. The strings are sometimes organized in usual sets (languages), in other cases they form multisets (sets with multiplicities associated with their elements). In most cases, characterizations of recursively enumerable languages are obtained. Several open problems and research topics are also mentioned.

1 Introduction

P systems are distributed parallel computing models which start from the observation that the processes which take place in the complex structure of a living cell can be (and have been) interpreted as computations. The basic ingredients are a *membrane structure*, consisting of several membranes embedded in a main membrane (called the *skin*) and delimiting *regions* where multisets of certain *objects* are placed (Figure 1 illustrates these notions); the objects evolve according to given *evolution rules*, which are applied nondeterministically (the rules to be used and the objects to evolve are randomly chosen) in a maximally parallel manner (in each step, all objects which can evolve must do it). The objects can also be communicated from a region to another one. In this way, we get *transitions* from a *configuration* of the system to the next one. A sequence of transitions constitutes a *computation*; with each *halting computation* we associate a *result*, the number of objects in a

600

specified *output membrane*, or sent out of the system during the computation.

Since these computing devices have been introduced ([26]) several variants were considered. Many of them were proved to be computationally complete, able to compute all recursively enumerable sets of (vectors of) natural numbers. When membrane division is allowed, or membranes can be created from objects, NP-complete problems are shown to be solved in linear time. We refer to the web page at the address http://psystems.disco.unimib.it for details and for bibliographical information.

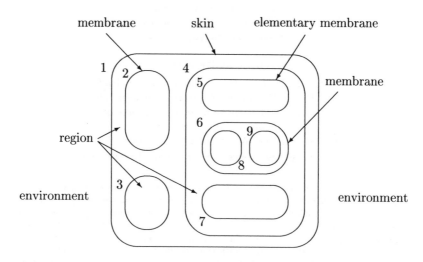

Figure 1: A membrane structure

In most of these variants, the objects are described by symbols from a given alphabet. It is also possible (this was considered already in [26]) to work with objects described by strings. The evolution rules should then be string processing rules, of any kind (rewriting, splicing, context adjoining, operations specific to DNA handling, etc.). As a result of a computation we can either consider the language of all strings computed by a system, or the number of strings produced by a system and "stored" in a specified membrane or sent out of the system during the computation. In the present paper we consider only the case of generating languages.

Morever, the strings present in the system can form either a language (a usual set), or a multiset. In the latter case we have to consider operations which can increase and decrease the number of strings (rewriting and splicing are not sufficient, as they keep the number of strings constant). Such operations are, for instance, the replication and the splitting of strings – see precise definitions in Section 4.

In all these cases, characterizations of recursively enumerable languages can be found. We here recall results of this type from [26], [24], [9], [30], [3], [18], [19], [15], [21], [14], etc. We do not enter into proof details, as the aim of our presentation is to let the reader having the flavour of the results (and to point out some questions not settled yet in this area).

2 Rewriting P Systems

We start by considering evolution rules given in the form of rewriting rules, as usual in formal language theory, but we associate with them *target* indications, telling us the region where the result of the rewriting should be placed after applying a rule.

Always we use only context-free rules, that is, the rules of our systems are of the form $(X \to v; tar)$, where $X \to v$ is a context-free rule and *tar* $\in \{here, out, in\}$, with the obvious meaning: the string produced by using this rule will go to the membrane indicated by *tar* (*here* means that the string remains in the same region, *out* indicates to send the string out of the region where the rule is applied, and *in* means to go to any directly lower membrane, nondeterministically chosen); sometimes one also uses indications of the form in_j, where j is the label of the membrane where the string should be sent).

Formally, a *rewriting P system* (with priorities, and of degree $m \geq 1$) is a construct

$$\Pi = (V, T, \mu, L_1, \ldots, L_m, (R_1, \rho_1), \ldots, (R_m, \rho_m)),$$

where V is an alphabet, $T \subseteq V$ (the terminal alphabet), μ is a membrane structure with m membranes labeled with $1, 2, \ldots, m$, $L_1, \ldots, L_m$ are finite languages over V (initial strings placed in the regions of μ), $R_1, \ldots, R_m$ are finite sets of context-free evolution rules, and $\rho_1, \ldots, \rho_m$ are partial order relations over $R_1, \ldots, R_m$. (A membrane structure is naturally represented by a string of labeled matching parentheses.)

The language generated Π is denoted by $L(\Pi)$ and it is defined as follows: we start from the initial configuration of the system and proceed iteratively, by transition steps performed by applying the rules in parallel, to all strings which can be rewritten, obeying the priority relations; when the computation halts, we collect the terminal strings sent out of the system during the computation. Note that each string is processed by one rule only, the parallelism refers here to processing simultaneously all available strings by all applicable rules.

We denote by $RP_m(Pri, i/o)$ the family of languages generated by rewriting P systems of degree at most $m \geq 1$, using priorities; when priorities are not used, we replace Pri with $nPri$.

In order to illustrate the way of working of a rewriting P system, we consider an example (which also proves that the family $RP_2(nPri, i/o)$ contains non-context-free languages):

$$\Pi = (\{A, B, a, b, c\}, \{a, b, c\}, [_1 [_2]_2]_1, \{AB\}, \emptyset, (R_1, \emptyset), (R_2, \emptyset)),$$
$$R_1 = \{(A \to aAb; in), \ (A \to ab; out), \ (B \to c; here)\},$$
$$R_2 = \{(B \to cB; out)\}.$$

It is easy to see that $L(\Pi) = \{a^n b^n c^n \mid n \geq 1\}$ (if a string $a^i A b^i c^i B$ is rewritten in membrane 1 to $a^i A b^i c^{i+1}$ and then to $a^{i+1} A b^{i+1} c^{i+1}$ and sent to the inner membrane, then it will remain here forever, the computation stops, but no string is sent out; if a string $a^{i+1} b^{i+1} c^i B$ is sent out, it is not accepted, because it is not terminal).

The following result was given independently in [9] and [24], where a result from [26] was improved (in all cases, the resulting strings are collected in an inner membrane, but the proofs can be easily changed in order to collect the strings sent out of the system).

Theorem 1 $RP_2(Pri, i/o) = RE.$

Note that the proofs from [9] and [24] deal with halting computations, but (because we use a terminal alphabet in order to select the accepted strings) we can also work with non-halting computations, just accepting the terminal strings sent out of the system at any step of the computation.

3 Splicing P Systems

The strings in a P system can also be processed by using the *splicing* operation introduced in [7] as a formal model of the DNA recombination under the influence of restriction enzymes and ligases (see a comprehensive investigation of splicing systems in [28]).

Consider an alphabet V and two symbols $\#, \$ $ not in V. A *splicing rule* over V is a string $r = u_1 \# u_2 \$ u_3 \# u_4$, where $u_1, u_2, u_3, u_4 \in V^*$. For such a rule r and for $x, y, w, z \in V^*$ we define

$$(x, y) \vdash_r (w, z) \text{ iff } x = x_1 u_1 u_2 x_2, \ y = y_1 u_3 u_4 y_2,$$
$$w = x_1 u_1 u_4 y_2, \ z = y_1 u_3 u_2 x_2,$$
$$\text{for some } x_1, x_2, y_1, y_2 \in V^*.$$

(One cuts the strings x, y in between u_1, u_2 and u_3, u_4, respectively, and one recombines the fragments obtained in this way.)

A *splicing P system* (of degree $m \geq 1$) is a construct

$$\Pi = (V, T, \mu, L_1, \ldots, L_m, R_1, \ldots, R_m),$$

where V is an alphabet, $T \subseteq V$ (the *output* alphabet), μ is a membrane structure consisting of m membranes (labeled with $1, 2, \ldots, m$), $L_i, 1 \leq i \leq m$, are languages over V associated with the regions $1, 2, \ldots, m$ of μ, $R_i, 1 \leq i \leq m$, are finite sets of *evolution rules* associated with the regions $1, 2, \ldots, m$ of μ, given in the following form: $(r; tar_1, tar_2)$, where $r = u_1 \# u_2 \$ u_3 \# u_4$ is a usual splicing rule over V and $tar_1, tar_2 \in \{here, out, in\}$.

Note that, as usual in splicing systems, when a string is present in a region of our system, it is assumed to appear in arbitrarily many copies.

A transition in Π is defined by applying the splicing rules from each region of μ, in parallel, to all possible strings from the corresponding regions, and following the target indications associated with the rules. More specifically, if x, y are strings in region i and $(r = u_1 \# u_2 \$ u_3 \# u_4; tar_1, tar_2) \in R_i$ such that we can have $(x, y) \vdash_r (w, z)$, then w and z will go to the regions indicated by tar_1, tar_2, respectively. Note that after splicing, the strings x, y are still available in region i, because we have supposed that they appear in arbitrarily many copies (an arbitrarily large number of them were spliced, arbitrarily many remain), but if a string w, z, resulting from a splicing, is sent out of region i, then no copy of it remains here (excepting the case when "old generations" of strings w, z are present; such strings continue to be present in the region).

The result of a computation consists of all strings over T which are sent out of the system at any time during the computation. We denote by $L(\Pi)$ the language of all strings of this type. Note that in this section we do not consider halting computations, but we leave the process to continue forever and we just observe it from outside and collect the terminal strings leaving the system.

We denote by $SP_m(i/o)$ the family of languages $L(\Pi)$ generated by splicing P systems as above, of degree at most m.

A proof of the following result – confirming the power of splicing – can be found in [24].

Theorem 2 $SP_2(i/o) = RE$.

4   P Systems with Genome-Like Operations

In P systems with symbol-objects we work with multisets and the result of a computation is a natural number or a vector of natural numbers; in the case of P systems with string-objects we work with sets of strings and the result of a computation is a string. We can combine the two ideas: we can work with multisets of strings and consider as the result of a computation the number of strings present in the halting configuration in a given membrane, or the language of strings sent out of the system during a computation. To this aim, we need operations with strings which can increase and decrease the number of occurrences of strings.

The following four operations were considered in [3]:

1. *Replication.* If $a \in V$ and $u_1, u_2 \in V^+$, then $r : a \to u_1 \| u_2$ is called a *replication rule*. For strings $w_1, w_2, w_3 \in V^+$ we write $w_1 \Longrightarrow_r (w_2, w_3)$ (and we say that w_1 is replicated with respect to rule r) if $w_1 = x_1 a x_2$, $w_2 = x_1 u_1 x_2$, $w_3 = x_1 u_2 x_2$, for some $x_1, x_2 \in V^*$.

2. *Splitting.* If $a \in V$ and $u_1, u_2 \in V^+$, then $r : a \to u_1 | u_2$ is called a *splitting rule*. For strings $w_1, w_2, w_3 \in V^+$ we write $w_1 \Longrightarrow_r (w_2, w_3)$ (and we say that w_1 is splitted with respect to rule r) if $w_1 = x_1 a x_2$, $w_2 = x_1 u_1$, $w_3 = u_2 x_2$, for some $x_1, x_2 \in V^*$.

3. *Mutation.* A *mutation rule* is a context-free rewriting rule, $r : a \to u$, over V. For strings $w_1, w_2 \in V^+$ we write $w_1 \Longrightarrow_r w_2$ if $w_1 = x_1 a x_2$, $w_2 = x_1 u x_2$, for some $x_1, x_2 \in V^*$.

4. *Recombination.* Consider a string $z \in V^+$ (as a *crossing-over block*) and four strings $w_1, w_2, w_3, w_4 \in V^+$. We write $(w_1, w_2) \Longrightarrow_z (w_3, w_4)$ if $w_1 = x_1 z x_2$, $w_2 = y_1 z y_2$, and $w_3 = x_1 z y_2$, $w_4 = y_1 z x_2$, for some $x_1, x_2, y_1, y_2 \in V^*$.

Note that replication and splitting increase the number of strings, mutation and recombination not; by sending strings out of the system, their number can also be decreased.

We work here only with multisets $\sigma : V^* \to \mathbf{N}$ such that only finitely many elements have a non-null multiplicity, thus we can specify σ in the form $A = \{(x_1, \sigma(x_1)), \ldots, (x_k, \sigma(s_k))\}$, where $x_i, 1 \le i \le k$, are those elements of V^* for which $\sigma(x_i) > 0$.

A *P system* (of degree $m \ge 1$) *with worm-objects* is a construct

$$\Pi = (V, \mu, A_1, \ldots, A_m, (R_1, S_1, M_1, C_1), \ldots, (R_m, S_m, M_m, C_m), i_o),$$

where:

- V is an alphabet;
- μ is a membrane structure of degree m (with the membranes labeled with $1, 2, \ldots, m$);
- $A_1, \ldots, A_m$ are multisets of finite support over V^*, associated with the regions of μ;
- for each $1 \leq i \leq m$, R_i, S_i, M_i, C_i are finite sets of replication rules, splitting rules, mutation (rewriting) rules, and crossing-over blocks, respectively, given in the following forms:

    a. replication rules: $(a \rightarrow u_1 \| u_2; tar_1, tar_2)$, for $tar_1, tar_2 \in \{here, out, in\}$;

    b. splitting rules: $(a \rightarrow u_1 | u_2; tar_1, tar_2)$, for $tar_1, tar_2 \in \{here, out, in\}$;

    c. mutation (rewriting) rules: $(a \rightarrow u; tar)$, for $tar \in \{here, out, in\}$;

    d. crossing-over blocks: $(z; tar_1, tar_2)$, for $tar_1, tar_2 \in \{here, out, in\}$;

- $i_o \in \{1, 2, \ldots, m\}$ specifies the *output membrane* of the system; it should be an elementary membrane of μ.

The $(m + 1)$-tuple $(\mu, A_1, \ldots, A_m)$ constitutes the *initial configuration* of the system. By applying the operations defined by the components $(R_i, S_i, M_i, C_i), 1 \leq i \leq m$, we can define transitions from a configuration to another one. This is done as usual in a P system, according to the following specific rules: A string which enters an operation is "consumed" by that operation, its multiplicity is decreased by one. The multiplicity of strings produced by an operation is accordingly increased. A string is processed by only one operation. For instance, we cannot apply two mutation rules, or a mutation rule and a replication one, to the same string. The strings resulting from an operation are communicated to the region specified by the target indications associated with the used rule.

The result of a halting computation consists of the strings in region i_o at the end of the computation. A non-halting computation provides no output. In [3] one considers as the result of a computation the number of strings from the output membrane, and it is proved that each recursively enumerable set of natural numbers can be computed by a P system as above; the result is improved in [18], where it is proved that the hierarchy on the number of membranes collapses, six membranes suffice.

Here we consider the language case. Initially, following [19], we consider P systems working with multisets of worm-objects, processed by rewriting and crossovering rules only, and we take as the result of a computation the language of all strings present at the end of halting computations in a specified output membrane. The work of such a system is exactly as the work of a P system with worm-objects, only the way of defining the result of a computation is different.

We denote by $RXP_m(i/o), m \geq 1$, the family of languages generated by such systems with at most m membranes, using as communication commands the indications *here, out, in*. The proof of the following result can be found in [19].

Theorem 3 $RXP_5(i/o) = RE$.

A variant is considered in [21], where one works with multisets of strings processed by means of splitting operations, point mutation rules, and *conditional concatenation*. This last operation is defined as follows.

Consider a finite set $M \subseteq V^* \times V^*$ of pairs of strings and two strings $w_1, w_2 \in V^+$. We write $(w_1, w_2) \vdash_M w_1 w_2$ if $w_1 = x_1 x_2$, $w_2 = y_1 y_2$ and $(x_2, y_1) \in M$, for some $x_1, x_2, y_1, y_2 \in V^*$. (That is, *head-tail* or *suffix-prefix* conditions are imposed on the concatenated strings.)

In the case of P systems, a target indication is added to a pair (x, y) from M, indicating the place where the result of the operation is sent.

We denote by $SCP_m(i/o)$ the family of languages generated by P systems with at most m membranes, using point mutation (rewriting), splitting, and conditional concatenation operations. The following result is proved in [21].

Theorem 4 $SCP_3(i/o) = RE$.

An interesting variant is to restrict the mutation and the splitting operations to cases where the length of the resulting string does not decrease (monotone mutation) or at most one of the resulting strings can reduce its length (monotone splitting), respectively. Thus, a *monotone* mutation rule is of the form $A \to x$ with $|x| \geq 1$, and a *monotone* splitting rule is of the form $A \to u_1 | u_2$ with $|u_1 u_2| \geq 1$. The generated families of languages are denoted by $SCMP_m(i/o)$. When target indications of the form in_j are used, where j is the label of a membrane, then we write $SCMP_m(tar)$.

We mention the following results from [21] about this restricted case (CS is the family of context-sensitive languages):

Theorem 5 $CS \subseteq SCMP_3(i/o) \subseteq SCMP_4(tar) = RE$.

Note that the equality $SCMP_4(tar) = RE$ is obtained for 4 membranes and using the strong target indication in_j; can the result be improved from these points of view?

In the above discussion we have always used multisets of strings. The case when dealing with usual languages, and with the strings processed by rewriting and replication rules was considered in [11], [1], [15]. We recall here only a result from [15] (we have denoted by $RRP_m(i/o)$ the family of languages generated by P systems with string rewriting and replicating rules, with at most m membranes):

Theorem 6 $RRP_6(i/o) = RE$.

Several results about comparing families $RRP_m(i/o)$ with $m < 6$ with the familiy of matrix languages generated without appearance checking, and with the family $ET0L$ can also be found in [15].

5 Further Researches; Discussion; Open Problems

The string-objects of a P system can evolve by any type of string processing rules, in particular, by adjoining or erasing single substrings, as in insertion-deletion grammars, or by adjoining or erasing pairs of strings, as in the case of Marcus contextual grammars. The former case was considered in [12], the latter one in [13] and [14]. We do not enter here into details, but we only mention that again characterizations of recursively enumerable languages are obtained in the case when also erasing features are provided (by the deletion of substrings or of contexts).

In the previous variants of P systems, one works sequentially at the level of each string (all strings which can be processed at a given step are processed, but only one rule is applied to a particular string). The parallel rewriting (or partially parallel: each symbol A appearing in a string is rewritten, but if several occurrences of A are present, then only one of them is rewritten) was also considered, in [10] and [22].

Other types of P systems with string-objects were considered in [5] (with leftmost, or with the rewriting controlled by the presence/absence of certain symbols), in [16], [17] (certain numbers are associated with strings, controlling their processing), in [2] (communication controlled by the presence/absence of certain symbols), etc.

As we have seen, most of the characterizations of recursively enumerable languages are obtained via systems with a reduced number of membranes. Still (with a few exceptions), one does not know whether or not these results are optimal from this point of view. A natural related *open problem* is to investigate the size and the properties of families of languages generated by systems with a number of membranes smaller than in the characterizations of RE. Which are their relations with language families in Chomsky and Lindenmayer hierarchies? Which are their closure properties?

Always when a class of P systems characterize the family RE, the hierarchy on the number of membranes collapses: start the proof from a universal type-0 grammar; as this is a fixed one (the varying parameter is the axiom), we obtain a fixed system, where we have only to change the initial contents of regions in order to generate a new language. This seems to make difficult the solution to the following *open problem*: find a class of string-objects P systems which leads to an infinite language hierarchy on the number of membranes. In view of the previous observation, we need to have a class of systems generating a strict subfamily of RE. Of course, the sought class of P systems should be defined in a non-trivial manner, not including restrictions which make "visible" the hierarchy.

The proofs of the characterizations of RE by means of P systems start from type-0 grammars (often, in normal forms, such as Kuroda or Geffert normal forms) or from matrix grammars with appearance checking (in the binary normal form). It is interesting to note that in the latter case an old problem was brought again into attention, namely concerning the number of nonterminals sufficient for generating a recursively enumerable language by a matrix grammar. In particular, the number of nonterminals used in the appearance checking manner is important, as the main proof technique used in the P systems area associates a membrane with each such a symbol; thus, in order to have a small number of membranes is necessary to have a small number of symbols used in the appearance checking manner. An old result in this respect is that from [25]: six nonterminals, all of them used in the appearance checking mode, suffice for generating all RE languages. Recently, with motivation from P systems, the result was considerably improved, [4], [6]: two nonterminals used in the appearance checking mode suffice.

Besides the generative power questions, of interest are also normal form results for P systems with string-objects. Some such results are given in [31], [32], but the topic deserves further investigations.

A related question: up to now, no systematic study was carried out on the possible influence on the generative power of P systems of the way of defining the result of a computation: internal (considering only the strings from a designated membrane) or external (considering the strings sent out of the system)? using terminal symbols or accepting all strings? considering as successful only halting computations or all computations? dealing with multisets or with usual languages? It is expected that in the extended case (when using a terminal alphabet) no difference will exist between using or not halting computations (instead of computing forever we can introduce trap-symbols). Also, it is expected that reading the result inside or outside a system does not makes a difference (maybe the number of used membranes can differ by one, as found in [29]).

Two classic ideas in language theory are to consider *hybrid* devices, that is, with rules of two or several different types (this was briefly investigated for P systems in [8]), and to consider *accepting* devices (start from a string, reduce it by means of given rules, and accept it only in the case when a specified axiom is reached). A systematic investigation of these ideas in our framework is a research topic of interest.

We conclude by expressing our conviction that membrane computing is an interesting branch of language (computation) theory, proving, for instance, the power of the compartmental computation (in this framework, of communication among cooperating "agents"), and, at a general level, proving that we still have a lot to learn from the way the alive nature "computes" (mainly, at the level of the cell).

References

1. J. Aguado, T. Bălănescu, T. Cowling, M. Gheorghe, F. Ipate, P systems with replicated rewriting and stream X-machines, in [20], 7–18.
2. P. Bottoni, A. Labella, C. Martín-Vide, Gh. Păun, Rewriting P systems with conditional communication, in *Formal and Natural Computing. Essays Dedicated to Grzegorz Rozenberg* (W. Brauer, H. Ehrig, J. Karhumäki, A. Salomaa, eds.), *Lecture Notes in Computer Science*, 2300, Springer-Verlag, Berlin, 2002, 325–353.
3. J. Castellanos, A. Rodríguez-Patón, Gh. Păun, Computing with membranes: P systems with worm-objects, *IEEE 7th. Intern. Conf. on String Processing and Information Retrieval, SPIRE 2000*, La Coruna, Spain, 64–74.
4. H. Fernau, Nonterminal complexity of programmed grammars, *Conf. on Universal Machines and Computations*, Chişinău, 2001, *LNCS*, 2055, Springer-Verlag, 2001, 202–213.
5. Cl. Ferretti, G. Mauri, Gh. Păun, Cl. Zandron, On three variants of P systems with string-objects, in [20], 63–76.
6. R. Freund, Gh. Păun, On the number of non-terminals in graph-controlled, programmed, and matrix grammars, *Conf. on Universal Machines and Computations*, Chişinău, 2001, *LNCS*, 2055, Springer-Verlag, 2001.
7. T. Head, Formal language theory and DNA: An analysis of the generative capacity of specific recombinant behaviors, *Bull. Math. Biology*, 49 (1987), 737–759.
8. S.N. Krishna, K. Lakshmanan, R. Rama, Hybrid P systems, *Romanian J. of Inf. Science and Technology*, 4, 1-2 (2001), 111–124.
9. S.N. Krishna, R. Rama, A variant of P systems with active membranes: Solving NP-complete problems, *Romanian J. of Inf. Science and Technology*, 2, 4 (1999), 357–367.

610

10. S.N. Krishna, R. Rama, A note on parallel rewriting in P systems, *Bulletin of the EATCS*, 73 (February 2001), 147–151.
11. S.N. Krishna, R. Rama, P systems with replicated rewriting, *J. Automata, Languages, and Combinatorics*, 6, 3 (2001), 345–350.
12. S.N. Krishna, R. Rama, Insertion-deletion P systems, *Proc. 7th Intern. Meeting on DNA Based Computers* (N. Jonoska, N.C. Seeman, eds.), Tampa, Florida, USA, 2001, 350–359.
13. S.N. Krishna, K. Lakshmanan, R. Rama, On the power of P systems with one-sided and erasing contextual rules, in [20], 143–156.
14. M. Madhu, K. Krithivasan, Contextual P systems, in [20], 169–180.
15. V. Manca, C. Martín-Vide, Gh. Păun, On the power of P systems with replicated rewriting, *J. Automata, Languages, and Combinatorics*, 6, 3 (2001), 359–374.
16. C. Martín-Vide, V. Mitrana, P systems with valuations, in vol. *Unconventional Models of Computation* (I. Antoniou, C.S. Calude, M.J. Dinneen, eds.), Springer-Verlag, London, 2000, 154–166.
17. C. Martín-Vide, V. Mitrana, Gh. Păun, On the power of P systems with valuations, *Computación y Sistemas*, 5, 2 (2002), 120–127.
18. C. Martín-Vide, Gh. Păun, Computing with membranes. One more collapsing hierarchy, *Bulletin of the EATCS*, 72 (October 2000), 183–187.
19. C. Martín-Vide, Gh. Păun, String-objects in P systems, *Proc. of Algebraic Systems, Formal Languages and Computations Workshop*, Kyoto, 2000, RIMS Kokyuroku, Kyoto Univ., 2000, 161–169.
20. C. Martín-Vide, Gh. Păun, eds., *Pre-Proc. of Workshop on Membrane Computing*, Curtea de Argeş, Romania, August 2001, TR 17/01 of Res. Group on Math. Ling., Rovira i Virgili Univ., Tarragona, Spain, 2001.
21. J.L. Maté, A. Rodríguez-Patón, On the power of P systems with DNA-worms, in [20], 209–220.
22. A. Păun, On rewriting P systems with partial parallelism, *Romanian J. of Inf. Science and Technology*, 4, 1-2 (2001), 203–210.
23. A. Păun, P systems with string-objects: Universality results, in [20], 229–242.
24. A. Păun, M. Păun, On the membrane computing based on splicing, in vol. *Where Mathematics, Computer Science, Linguistics, and Biology Meet* (C. Martín-Vide, V. Mitrana, ed.), Kluwer, Dordrecht, 2000, 409–422.
25. Gh. Păun, Six nonterminals are enough for generating each r.e. language by a matrix grammar, *Intern. J. Computer Math.*, 15 (1984), 23–37.
26. Gh. Păun, Computing with membranes, *Journal of Computer and System Sciences*, 61, 1 (2000), 108–143, and *Turku Center for Computer*

Science-TUCS Report No 208, 1998 (www.tucs.fi).

27. Gh. Păun, Computing with membranes. An introduction, *Bulletin of the EATCS*, 67 (1999), 139–152.

28. Gh. Păun, G. Rozenberg, A. Salomaa, *DNA Computing. New Computing Paradigms*, Springer-Verlag, Heidelberg, 1998.

29. Gh. Păun, G. Rozenberg, A. Salomaa, Membrane computing with external output, *Fundamenta Informaticae*, 41, 3 (2000), 259–266.

30. Gh. Păun, T. Yokomori, Membrane computing based on splicing, *Preliminary Proc. of Fifth Intern. Meeting on DNA Based Computers* (E. Winfree, D. Gifford, eds.), MIT, June 1999, 213–227.

31. Cl. Zandron, G. Mauri, Cl. Ferretti, Universality and normal forms on membrane systems, *Proc. Intern. Workshop Grammar Systems 2000* (R. Freund, A. Kelemenova, eds.), Bad Ischl, Austria, July 2000, 61–74.

32. Cl. Zandron, Cl. Ferretti, G. Mauri, Two normal forms for rewriting P systems, *Conf. on Universal Machines and Computations*, Chişinău, 2001, *LNCS*, 2055, Springer-Verlag, 153–164.

MEMBRANE COMPUTING: NEW RESULTS, NEW PROBLEMS

CARLOS MARTíN-VIDE

Research Group on Mathematical Linguistics
Rovira i Virgili University
Pl. Imperial Tàrraco 1, 43005 Tarragona, Spain
E-mail: cmv@astor.urv.es

ANDREI PĂUN

Department of Computer Science
College of Engineering and Science
Louisiana Tech University, Ruston
P.O. Box 10348, Louisiana, LA-71272 USA
E-mail: apaun@coes.latech.edu

GHEORGHE PĂUN

Institute of Mathematics of the Romanian Academy
PO Box 1-764, 70700 Bucureşti, Romania, and
Research Group on Mathematical Linguistics
Rovira i Virgili University
Pl. Imperial Tàrraco 1, 43005 Tarragona, Spain
E-mail: george.paun@imar.ro, gp@astor.urv.es

We briefly discuss some of the recent results in the membrane computing, mainly reported during the Workshop on Membrane Computing, Curtea de Argeş, Romania, August 19–23, 2002 (we refer below to this workshop by WMC2002). Some of these results answer problems which were open in this area, but they also suggest new open problems and research topics.

1 Introduction

Membrane computing is a rather young branch of natural computing (the systematic research started in November 1998, when the paper [18] was circulated on the web), but it is already well developed at the theoretical level. However, we do not recall here once again the basic ideas, definitions, central results of this field. A comprehensive information about membrane computing (complete bibliography, papers to be downloaded, addresses of authors, news, etc.) can be found at the web address http://psystems.disco.unimib.it. Two surveys have appeared also in the *Bulletin of the EATCS* ([17], [14]), a friendly guide-introduction is [20], while the monograph [19] covers the central notions and results in the area at the level of February-March 2002.

Thus, we assume the reader familiar with membrane computing, we refer to the above mentioned bibliographical sources for details, and we are going directly to mention some recent results and some suggestions for future research in the area derived from these results.

2 Catalysts Suffice

We start by considering one of the most surprising recent result, that from [24], stating that P systems with symbol-objects using catalysts (but no other features, such as priorities, membrane permeability control, etc) are computationally complete, they can compute all recursively enumerable sets of natural numbers.

We recall some notations from [19]. We denote by $NOP_m(\alpha, tar, pri)$ the family of sets of natural numbers which can be computed by P systems with at most $m \geq 1$ membranes, using rules of the form α, target indications of the form *here, out, in_j,* and priorities among the rules; α is one of *ncoo, cat, coo,* indicating that the rules are non-cooperating (context-free), catalytic, cooperative, respectively. If $m = 1$, then we omit the indication *tar;* also, *pri* is omitted when no priority relation is considered. If the number of membranes is not bounded, then the subscript m is replaced with $*$.

For a family FL of languages, we denote by NFL the family of length sets of languages in FL. By CF, RE we denote the families of context-free and of recursively enumerable languages, respectively.

The following results appear in [19]:

1. $NOP_*(ncoo, tar) = NOP_1(ncoo) = NCF$ (Theorem 3.3.2),
2. $NOP_1(coo) = NRE$ (Theorem 3.3.3),
3. $NOP_2(cat, tar, pri) = NRE$ (Theorem 3.4.3),

and one formulates the open problem (Q1, pages 63 and 70) of finding the size of the families $NOP_m(cat, tar)$. Moreover, the conjecture was that these families are larger than NCF but not equal to NRE. However, the main result of [24] is the following:

Theorem 1 $NOP_2(cat, tar) = NRE$.

The proof is carried out by simulating register machines by P systems with catalysts. (The result in [24] is formulated for one membrane only, but the catalysts are ignored when counting the objects in the halting configuration, which is a difference from the definitions from [19]. One further membrane is necessary in order to work with the same definition: use an additional membrane for separating the objects which are counted for the result of a computation from the catalysts.)

Of course, when having two membranes only, the membrane structure can have a unique shape (one inner membrane embedded in the skin membrane), hence the communication is done by using the weak target indications *here, out,in,* hence *tar* can be replaced with *i/o.*

The result from [24] has important implications in the study of the generative power of P systems with symbol-objects: in order to obtain the computational universality we do not need further ingredients, such as controls on rule application (priorities, permitting or forbidding conditions, rule creation, etc) or on communication (membrane permeability control, conditional communication, etc). Several results from [19], if considered in the present formulation, are direct consequences of Theorem 1 above.

The "explanation" of this result lies in the way of defining the computations in a P system: each transition means a maximally parallel use of rules, chosen in a nondeterministic manner, while a computation is successful only if it halts, a configuration is reached where no rule can be applied. Using these features, and objects and catalysts of different "colours" (primed and non-primed), one can construct a P system which simulates a register machine in such a way that only correct simulations can lead to halting computations. The reader is referred to [24] for the rather non-trivial details of the proof.

However, there is a price to be paid in order to obtain the universality with catalysts only: we need at least six catalysts. In comparison, the number of catalysts used in the proofs of universality from [19] for systems involving further features is in most cases one (see Theorems 3.4.3, 3.6.1, 3.6.4, etc.). There also are several variants of membrane systems for which the universality is obtained without using catalysts; this is the case for controls on rule application of a stronger type (Theorems 3.6.3, 3.6.5 – 3.6.8, 3.7.3, etc.). The catalysts correspond to enzymes which control the cell biochemistry, and it is known that the enzymes need a specific environment (specific reaction conditions) in order to be active, and this makes improbable the simultaneous work of several enzymes in the same compartment. These observations lead to the *open problem* – also formulated in [24] – of finding a proof of Theorem 1 with a smaller number of catalysts. Otherwise stated, in the notation of families $NOP_m(cat, \ldots)$ we also have to take into account the number of catalysts, for instance, writing $NOP_m(cat_s, \ldots)$ in the case when at most s catalysts are used, and then to look for universality results with a small s. A trade-off is expected between the number of catalysts and other features of the systems. Does such a trade-off relation exist between the number of membranes and the number of catalysts? For instance, the result from Theo-

616

rem 1 can be written in the form $NOP_2(cat_6, i/o) = NRE$. Is a result of the form $NOP_m(cat_s, i/o) = NRE$ valid, for some $m \geq 2$ and $s < 6$? If not (or, as expected, if s remains greater than 1), then we still have a motivation for introducing additional features, such as priorities, membrane thickness control, and so on (of course, motivations for having such ingredients can come from other directions: adequacy of P systems to the bio-reality, computational efficiency, length and transparency of proofs, etc.).

3 Communication Suffices

The assertion in the title of this section is not new: it is already known that P systems with symbol-objects which are never changed, but only passed through membranes, in a well-specified manner, are computationally universal. This is the case of P systems with symport/antiport rules, and of systems with carriers. Details can be found in [19] – and, of course, in the web page mentioned in the Introduction. However, several of the results from [19] were already improved, while also new types of P systems where the computations are only done by communication, by moving objects through membranes, have been introduced.

This way of computing is interesting from various points of view: it is biologically well motivated (symport and antiport are well known biological processes), it essentially involves the environment of the systems (and this is the case also in reality), it observes the conservation law (no objects is created from nothing or destroyed during a computation), it proves the power of communication.

We remind the fact that a symport rule is of the form (x, in) or (x, out), with the meaning that the objects specified by x enter, respectively, exit the membrane with which the rule is associated, while an antiport rule is of the form $(y, out; z, in)$, with the meaning that the objects specified by y exit and those specified by z enter the membrane. The family of sets of natural numbers computed by P systems with at most m membranes, using symport rules with strings x of length at most s and antiport rules with strings y, z of length at most r is denoted by $NOP_m(sym_s, anti_r)$.

The following results were mentioned in [19]:

1. $NOP_2(sym_2, anti_2) = NRE$ (Theorem 4.2.1),
2. $NOP_5(sym_2, anti_0) = NRE$ (Theorem 4.2.2),
3. $NOP_2(sym_5, anti_0) = NRE$ (Theorem 4.2.3),
4. $NOP_3(sym_4, anti_0) = NRE$ (Theorem 4.2.4),
5. $NOP_3(sym_0, anti_2) = N'RE$ (Theorem 4.2.5),

where $N'RE$ is the family of recursively enumerable sets of non-zero natural numbers.

Problem Q8 (page 140) from [19] asked whether or not these results can be improved – and the conjecture was that the answer is affirmative. The confirmation came from both [7] and [16]. The following results are given in [7]:

Theorem 2 (i) $NOP_1(sym_1, anti_2) = NRE$, (ii) $NOP_4(sym_2, anti_0) = NRE$, (iii) $NOP_2(sym_3, anti_0) = NRE$, (iv) $NOP_1(sym_0, anti_2) = N'RE$.

The proofs of all these results are based on the simulation of register machines (called counter automata, in [7]) by means of P systems with symport/antiport.

The equality $NOP_2(sym_3, anti_0) = NRE$ has been also obtained in [16], this time with the proof carried out in the "usual" way of universality proofs in membrane computing: starting from a matrix grammar with appearance checking in the Z-binary normal form.

As one can see, the results from Theorem 2 improve all results from [19] about P systems with symport/antiport rules – but still one does not know whether these new results are optimal. Thus, question Q8 from [19] is still open, with respect to the new combinations of the number of membranes, size of symport rules, and size of antiport rules as specified by Theorem 2.

Recently, a surprising related result was obtained in [2]: systems with minimal symport/antiport rules are universal. In [2] one uses 9 membranes. We recall here the result in the improved form from [10]:

Theorem 3 $NOP_6(sym_1, anti_1) = NRE$.

Of course, the optimality of this result is *open*.

4 Errata-Remark About the Z-Normal Form

We have mentioned that the proof from [16] is based on the so-called Z-normal form for matrix grammars with appearance checking. This normal form was given in [12] and it is also used in many proofs from [19].

However, the formulation of this normal form has a flaw. Let us first recall this formulation as it appears in [19] (page 35):

A matrix grammar with appearance checking $G = (N, T, S, M, F)$ is said to be in the *Z-binary normal form* if $N = N_1 \cup N_2 \cup \{S, Z, \#\}$, with these three sets mutually disjoint, and the matrices in M are in one of the following forms:

1. $(S \to XA)$, with $X \in N_1, A \in N_2$,

618

2. $(X \to Y, A \to x)$, with $X, Y \in N_1, A \in N_2, x \in (N_2 \cup T)^*, |x| \leq 2$,
3. $(X \to Y, A \to \#)$, with $X \in N_1, Y \in N_1 \cup \{Z\}, A \in N_2$,
4. $(Z \to \lambda)$.

Moreover, there is only one matrix of type 1, F consists exactly of all rules $A \to \#$ appearing in matrices of type 3, and if a sentential form generated by G contains the object Z, *then it is of the form Zw, for some $w \in T^*$ (that is, the appearance of Z makes sure that, except for Z, all objects are terminal)*; $\#$ is a trap-object, and the (unique) matrix of type 4 is used only once, in the last step of a derivation. (The emphasized words are those containing the bug.)

For this formulation, the assertion that for each recursively enumerable language L there is a matrix grammar with appearance checking in the Z-normal form which generates L is not true. In fact, the proof from [12] gives a slightly different normal form: the symbol Z appears only in strings of the form Zw, where w *is either a terminal string, or it contains occurrences of the trap-symbol $\#$.* Therefore, the appearance of Z makes sure that, except for Z, the sentential form is either terminal, or it will never lead to a terminal string, because of the presence of the trap-symbol.

Fortunately, all proofs from [19] (and the papers cited in [19]) which are based on the Z-normal form remain valid: in all these proofs one constructs a P system which simulates the initial matrix grammar in the Z-normal form; all these systems contain the object $\#$ and rules of the form $\# \to \#$ $((\#, in), (\#, out)$, in the symport case, etc.). This means that in the case when Z appears together with a terminal string, the computation in the associated P system halts, while if Z appears together with a string which contains occurrences of $\#$, then the computation will never halt. In short, Z signals correctly the end of successful computations.

5 Back to Computing by Communication

The results from Theorem 2 have some direct implications about the results concerning the recently considered mode of defining the output of a computation, by recording the traces of certain objects through the membranes of a P system, [9]. We refer to [7] for details, and we pass to mentioning one new class of P systems with the computation based on communication only. It has been introduced in [24] under the name of *communicating P systems*, and uses rules of the following three forms:

$a \to a_t$,

$$ab \to a_{t_1} b_{t_2},$$
$$ab \to a_{t_1} b_{t_2} c_{come},$$

where a, b, c are objects, t, t_1, t_2 are target indications of the forms *here, out,* in_j (j is the label of a membrane). These rules are associated with membranes, with the restriction that rules of the third type can only be associated with the skin membrane (by means of rules of this form we can bring new objects into the system, from the environment; this is indicated by the target command *come*).

Note that, for instance, rules of the form $ab \to a_{in} b_{out}$ do not correspond to symport or antiport rules: the objects a, b are from the same region, but after the use of the rule, they go into different regions, adjacent to the starting region.

In [24] it is proved that systems with rules as above are computationally universal, but the proof does not provide a bound on the number of membranes. The result has been improved in [16] to the following form ($NOP_m(com)$ is the family of sets of numbers computed by P systems with rules as above, using at most m membranes):

Theorem 4 $NOP_2(com) = NRE$.

The proof from [24] starts from register machines, the one from [16] starts from matrix grammars with appearance checking in the Z-binary normal form. By combining the two techniques, it seems that the result can be improved to systems with only one membrane – this is a remark of R. Freund, made during WMC2002.

A further variant of P systems using rules which are either communication rules or transformation rules was proposed in [3]. For instance, the communication rules are of the form $xx'[_i y'y \to xy'[_i x'y$, with the meaning that the objects specified by x' enter membrane i and the objects specified by y' exits, at the same time, membrane i; the multisets x and y should be present outside and inside membrane i, respectively. Note that such rules also involve the membranes of the system, and that they are rather general, they can encode both symport and antiport rules. Consequently, no further rules are necessary in order to achieve the computational universality, in particular, no object transforming rules (providing that the environment is supposed to contain sufficient copies of the needed objects.

6 P Automata

The problem of considering classes of P systems which do not generate/compute sets of numbers, but *accept* sets of numbers, in the sense of accepting grammars or of automata, was formulated several times in the membrane computing literature. A first answer was provided recently in [6], in the form of a class of P systems – called P automata – which work by communication only, "absorbing" multisets of objects from the environment and pushing them down in the membranes of the system. That is, the communication is performed in a one-way manner, top-down. A computation is controlled by the contents of the regions of the membrane structure, and it is successful when it reaches a configuration where each region contains a multiset which is considered *terminal*; the result of a successful computation consists of a string associated with the sequence of multisets which enter the system during the computation.

The form of the rules used in [6] is $x : y \to in$, having the same meaning as the conditional symport rule $(y, in)|_x$: if the multiset of objects x is present in region with which the rule is associated, then the objects specified by y enter this region, coming from the immediately upper region (the environment, in the case of the skin membrane).

Note that the communication is done in a one-way manner, which is rather restrictive, but the rules are applied in a permitting context mode, depending on the contents of the region where we are going to bring objects from the upper region. The multisets of objects present in each region are called *states*; final states are provided in advance, defining the end of a computation (a computation ends when all regions contain a final state). This way of defining the successful computations is new (it also correspond to the definition of successful computations by checking the presence of certain objects in certain "acknowledging" membranes, as in [8]).

Somewhat surprising, the devices defined in [6] are shown to be computationally universal: P automata with seven membranes characterize the recursively enumerable languages, modulo a certain way to "translate" a sequence of multisets into a string (the corresponding mapping is called an l-projection in [6]). The proof is again based on the characterization of recursively enumerable languages by means of counter automata.

Of course, seven looks "too large", so a natural *open problem*[a] is to improve the result from [6]. Several related research topics can be formulated (some of them are already stated in [6]): consider two-way communication, consider rules of a restricted form (what about non-conditional rules, maybe using two-way communication), consider usual symport/antiport rules, etc. We forecast significant continuations of this idea of P automata (accepting P

---

[a]This has been already done in the paper "On three classes of automata-like P systems", *Proc. DLT 2003*, Szeged, Hungary, 2003, by R. Freund, C. Martín-Vide, A. Obtulowicz, Gh. Păun: two membranes suffice.

systems), due to its interest from the point of view of parsing, decidability, etc.

7 Other Recent Developments

We now briefly mention some other recent interesting ideas and (preliminary) results, all of them suggesting appealing directions of research. We consider these subjects in the ordering of the corresponding papers in the bibliography which ends this note.

The paper [1] proposes some applications of P systems in linguistics, specifically, to pragmatics, phonetic evolution, and dialogue. To this aim, the so-called *linguistic P systems* are introduced, where a series of new operations with membranes (and their contents) are considered, such as absorption, invasion, and cloning, while the rules can change the region, can be active or sleeping, etc. The model proposed in [1] remains to be investigated from a theoretical point of view, and further considered from the point of view of application in linguistics and related areas.

Another unexpected link with linguistics is proposed in [4]: the so-called structured contextual grammars, introduced in [13], generate strings which also contain parentheses associated with the rules used during the derivation; a string of parentheses contained in a unique external parenthesis describes a membrane structure; the strings introduced by each contextual rule can be naturally considered as symport rules associated with the membranes. In this way (with some technical details which we omit here), a structured contextual grammar can be used for generating an infinite family of P systems. These systems are "syntactically similar", they grow in a way corresponding to the derivation in the "pattern grammar", and can be considered as snapshots of a computing device which evolves during solving a given problem (derivation steps in the contextual grammar can be intercalated with transitions in the generated P systems).

Up to now, the P systems were mainly considered as computing models, where 'computing' is understood in the Turing sense, as an algorithmic connection between an input and an output (in particular, the input can be a decision problem, and the output can be the answer, yes or no, to the problem). Relationships between membrane computing and distributed computing, e.g., in computer networks, were investigated in [23]. A recent approach to this question, of the possible usefulness of membrane systems as models of distributed computing, can be found in [5]. The purpose is to prove that "P systems can become a primary model for distributed computing, particularly for message-passing algorithms". Algorithms are presented for several communication tasks, such as skin membrane broadcast, generalized broadcast, convergecast, leader election, fault toterant consensus, etc. Message complexity and time complexity are evaluated for the membrane algorithms corresponding to these problems.

Two recent papers, [11] and [15], answer an important open problem of membrane computing area: to consider probabilistic systems, able to take into consideration the probabilistic nature of biochemical reactions. Actually, in [15] two classes of P systems are introduced: stochastic systems, and randomized systems (the latter being used to implement randomized algorithms).

Especially interesting are the second type of systems, because they allow to implement algorithms which solve computationally hard problems, with a low error probability, in polynomial time, making use of a subexponential number of membranes. (This should be compared with the P algorithms based on membrane division, which solve hard problems in polynomial time by using an exponential number of membranes.) The paper presents a family of randomized P systems which are used for implementing the Miller-Rabin randomized algorithms for primality testing.

A reduction of the $P \neq NP$ conjecture to the existence of an **NP**-complete problem which cannot be solved in polynomial time by a deterministic "decision P system" constructed in polynomial time is discussed in [22] (roughly speaking, a *decision P system* is a system which accepts/rejects an input multiset if it stops by sending out the special object *yes/no*). We do not enter into details, and refer the reader to [22].

References

1. G. Bel Enguix, Preliminaries about some possible applications of P systems in linguistics, in [21], 81–96.
2. F. Bernardini, M. Gheorghe, On the power of minimal symport/antiport, *Pre-proc. WMC 2003, Report 28/03*, Rovira i Virgili Univ., Tarragona, 2003, 72–83.
3. F. Bernardini, V. Manca, P systems with boundary rules, in [21], 97–102.
4. R. Ceterchi, C. Martin-Vide, Generating P systems with contextual grammars, in [21], 119–144.
5. G. Ciobanu, R. Desai, A. Kumar, Membrane systems and distributed computing, in [21], 145–162.
6. E. Csuhaj-Varju, G. Vaszil, P automata, in [21], 177–192.
7. P. Frisco, H.J. Hoogeboom, Simulating counter automata by P systems with symport/antiport, in [21], 237–248.
8. P. Frisco, S. Ji, Info-energy P systems, *Proc. Eight Intern. Meeting*

on DNA Based Computers, Sapporo 2002 (M. Hagiya, A. Ohuchi, eds.), 161–170.

9. M. Ionescu, C. Martín-Vide, Gh. Păun, P systems with symport/antiport rules: The traces of objects, in [21], 283–296.

10. L. Kari, C. Martín-Vide, A. Păun, On the universality of P systems with minimal symport/antiport rules, submitted, 2003.

11. M. Madhu, Probabilistic P systems, submitted, 2002.

12. C. Martín-Vide, A. Păun, Gh. Păun, G. Rozenberg, Membrane systems with coupled transport: Universality and normal forms, *Fundamenta Informaticae*, 49, 1-3 (2002), 1–15.

13. C. Martín-Vide, Gh. Păun, Structured contextual grammars, *Grammars*, 1, 1 (1998), 33–35.

14. C. Martín-Vide, Gh. Păun, Language generating by means of membrane systems, *Bulletin of the EATCS*, 75 (Oct. 2001), 199–218.

15. A. Obtulowicz, Probabilistic P systems, in [21], 331–332 (extended abstract; the complete paper was circulated during the workshop).

16. A. Păun, Membrane systems with symport/antiport: universality results, in [21], 333–344.

17. Gh. Păun, Computing with membranes; An introduction, *Bulletin of the EATCS*, 68 (Febr. 1999), 139–152.

18. Gh. Păun, Computing with membranes, *Journal of Computer and System Sciences*, 61, 1 (2000), 108–143, and *Turku Center for Computer Science-TUCS Report* No 208, 1998 (www.tucs.fi).

19. Gh. Păun, *Membrane Computing. An Introduction*, Springer-Verlag, Berlin, 2002.

20. Gh. Păun, G. Rozenberg, A guide to membrane computing, *Theoretical Computer Sci.*, 2002.

21. Gh. Păun, C. Zandron, eds., *Pre-proceedings of Workshop on Membrane Computing*, Curtea de Argeş, August 19-23, 2002 (Publication No. 1 of MolCoNet Project – IST-2001-32008).

22. M.J. Perez-Jimenez, A. Romero-Jimenez, F. Sancho-Caparrini, Decision P systems and the $P \neq NP$ conjecture, in [21], 345–354.

23. I. Petre, L. Petre, Mobile ambients and P systems, *J. Univ. Computer Science*, 5, 9 (1999), 588–598.

24. P. Sosik, P systems versus register machines: two universality proofs, in [21], 371–382.

ABOUT THE EDITORS

Gheorghe Păun has graduated from the Faculty of Mathematics, University of Bucharest, in 1974 and received his Ph.D. in Mathematics (specialization: Computer Science) from the same university in 1977. He held a research position at the University of Bucharest, and from 1990 he is at the Institute of Mathematics of the Romanian Academy, where he is currently a senior researcher. From 2001 he is also a research professor at Rovira i Virgili University, Tarragona, Spain. He visited numerous universities in Europe, Asia, and North America, with frequent and/or longer stays in Turku (Finland), Leiden (The Netherlands), Magdeburg (Germany, including the Alexander von Humboldt Fellowship in 1992-93), Tarragona (Spain), London, Ontario (Canada), Rome (Italy), Tokyo (Japan), Warsaw (Poland), and Vienna (Austria).

His main research areas are formal language theory and its applications, computational linguistics, DNA computing, and membrane computing (a research area initiated by him, belonging to natural computing). He has published over 400 research papers (collaborating with many researchers worldwide), has lectured at over 100 universities, and gave numerous invited talks at recognized international conferences. He has published eleven books in mathematics and computer science, has edited over twenty five collective volumes, and also published many popular science books and books on recreational mathematics (games).

He is on the editorial boards of fifteen international journals in mathematics, computer science, and linguistics, and was/is involved in the program/steering/organizing commitees for many recognized conferences and workshops.

In 1997 he was elected a member of the Romanian Academy.

Grzegorz Rozenberg received his Master and Engineer degree in electronics and computer science in 1965 from the Technical University of Warsaw, Poland. In 1968 he obtained Ph.D. in mathematics at the Polish Academy of Sciences, Warsaw. Since then he has held full time positions at the Polish Academy of Sciences (assistant professor), Utrecht University, The Netherlands (assistant professor), State University of New York at Buffalo, U.S.A. (associate professor), and University of Antwerp, Belgium (professor). Since 1979 he has been a professor at the Department of Computer Science at Leiden University and an adjoint professor at the University of Colorado at Boulder, U.S.A. He is the director of the Leiden Center for Natural Computing (LCNC).

Prof. Rozenberg was the President of the European Association for Theoretical Computer Science (EATCS) for the period 1985–1994, and his current functions include the chairmanship of the Steering Committee for International Conferences on Theory and Applications of Petri Nets, the chairmanship of the Steering Committee for the DNA Computing meetings, the chairmanship of the Steering Committee for the Developments in Formal Language Theory meetings, and the chairmanship of the European Educational Forum. He is also the director of the European Molecular Computing Consortium.

He has published about 400 papers, written 6 books, and is a (co-)editor of over 60 books. For 22 years he was the editor of the *Bulletin of the EATCS*. He is the editor-in-chief of the international journal *Natural Computing* (Kluwer), the editor-in-chief of *Theoretical Computer Science, Series C*, journal (Elsevier), the editor-in-chief of the series Advances in Petri Nets (Springer-Verlag), the managing editor of the Natural Computing Series (Springer-Verlag), and an editor-in-chief of the Monographs and Texts in Theoretical Computer Science (Springer-Verlag). He is a co-editor of the *Handbook of Formal Languages* – 3 volumes (Springer-Verlag), and the managing editor of the *Handbook of Graph Grammars and Computing by Graph Transformation* – 3 volumes (World Scientific). He has given more than 100 invited talks, with many invited talks at reputed international conferences. He has been a member of the program committees for practically all major conferences on theoretical computer science in Europe.

Prof. Rozenberg is involved in a number of externally funded research projects on both national and international levels. His current research interests are: (1) DNA computing, (2) the theory of concurrent systems, (3) the theory of graph transformations, (4) formal language and automata theory, (5) mathematical structures useful in computer science – in particular the theory of 2-structures, and (5) computer supported collaborative work (CSCW).

He is a Foreign Member of the Finnish Academy of Sciences and Letters, a member of Academia Europaea, a doctor honoris causa of the University of Turku, Finland, and a doctor honoris causa of the Technical University of Berlin, Germany. In 2003 he has received the prestigious EATCS Achievements Award.

Arto Salomaa received his Ph.D. in 1960 and was the professor of mathematics at the University of Turku 1966–98, as well as an academy professor at the Academy of Finland several periods since 1975. Currently he works at the Turku Centre for Computer Science. Prof. Salomaa was visiting professor of computer science in London, Canada 1966–68; Aarhus, Denmark 1973–75; and Waterloo, Canada 1981–82, and has made shorter visits to 150 universities in Europe, North America, and Asia.

Prof. Salomaa was EATCS President 1979–85 and is currently an editor-in-chief of EATCS Monograph and Text Series published by Springer-Verlag, as well as an editor, managing editor or honorary editor of twelve international journals of mathematics and computer science. He has authored 400 scientific publications in major journals, as well as twelve books, some of which have appeared also in Chinese, French, German, Japanese, Romanian, Russian, and Vietnamese translations.

Prof. Salomaa has supervised 25 Ph.D. students and holds the degree of doctor honoris causa at seven universities, two in Finland and five abroad. He has been an invited speaker at numerous conferences in computer science and mathematics, and a program committee member or chairman for major computer science conferences, including STOC, ICALP, MFCS, FCT, DLT. He has been the member of Academia Europaea since 1992, Academy of Sciences of Finland since 1970, Swedish Academy of Sciences of Finland since 1980, and Hungarian Academy of Sciences since 1998. He has received three major yearly prizes in Finland, including the Prize of Nokia Foundation. He became one of the twelve Fellows of the Academy of Finland in 2001. His research interests are in formal languages, automata theory, cryptography, formal power series, complexity theory, and mathematical logic.